INSTITUTIONS OF AMERICAN DEMOCRACY

THE JUDICIAL BRANCH

INSTITUTIONS OF AMERICAN DEMOCRACY SERIES

A joint project of The Annenberg Foundation Trust at Sunnylands and The Annenberg Public Policy Center of the University of Pennsylvania

The Public Schools. Edited by Susan Fuhrman and Marvin Lazerson.

The Press. Edited by Geneva Overholser and Kathleen Hall Jamieson.

The Legislative Branch. Edited by Paul J. Quirk and Sarah A. Binder.

The Executive Branch. Edited by Joel D. Aberbach and Mark A. Peterson.

The Judicial Branch. Edited by Kermit Hall and Kevin T. McGuire.

INSTITUTIONS OF AMERICAN DEMOCRACY

THE JUDICIAL BRANCH

Kermit L. Hall
Kevin T. McGuire

EDITORS

THE ANNENBERG FOUNDATION TRUST AT SUNNYLANDS

OXFORD
UNIVERSITY PRESS

OXFORD
UNIVERSITY PRESS

Oxford University Press, Inc., publishes works that further
Oxford University's objective of excellence
in research, scholarship, and education.

Oxford New York
Auckland Cape Town Dar es Salaam Hong Kong Karachi
Kuala Lumpur Madrid Melbourne Mexico City Nairobi
New Delhi Shanghai Taipei Toronto

With offices in
Argentina Austria Brazil Chile Czech Republic France Greece
Guatemala Hungary Italy Japan Poland Portugal Singapore
South Korea Switzerland Thailand Turkey Ukraine Vietnam

Published by Oxford University Press, Inc.
198 Madison Avenue, New York, New York, 10016
http://www.oup.com/us

Library of Congress Cataloging-in-Publication Data

The judicial branch / Kermit L. Hall, Kevin T. McGuire, editors.
p. cm — (Institutions of American democracy series)
Includes bibliographical references and index.
ISBN-13: 978-0-19-517172-3 (alk. paper)
ISBN-10: 0-19-517172-1 (alk. paper)
1. Courts—United States. 2. Judicial power—United States. 3. Judges—United States.
4. Democracy—United States. I. Hall, Kermit. II. McGuire, Kevin T. III. Series.
KF8700.J83 2005
347.73—dc22 2005017853

Book design by Joan Greenfield
Copyedited by Jonathan G. Aretakis

Printed in the United States of America on acid-free paper

CONTENTS

DIRECTORY OF CONTRIBUTORS

Kermit L. Hall (Editor)

President and Professor of History, University at Albany, State University of New York

Dr. Hall is a renowned historian and legal scholar. He has written and edited books including *The Magic Mirror: Law in American History* and *The Oxford Companion to the Supreme Court of the United States.* He was appointed by President Clinton to serve on the President John F. Kennedy Assassination Records Review Board. For his contributions, Dr. Hall has received such awards as the James Madison Award from the American Library Association and has been a fellow of the American Bar Foundation.

Kevin T. McGuire (Editor)

Associate Professor, Department of Political Science, University of North Carolina at Chapel Hill

Dr. McGuire is an expert on judicial politics and constitutional law. His books include *Understanding the U.S. Supreme Court* and *The Supreme Court Bar*, and his articles have appeared in leading journals of political science. He is coeditor of the University of Virginia Press's series on Constitutionalism and Democracy. Dr. McGuire is a former Fulbright scholar at Trinity College, Dublin.

Lawrence Baum

Professor, Political Science, Ohio State University

Dr. Baum's teaching and research interests focus on courts in the United States. Subjects of his research include explanation of judges' choices as decision makers, voters' decisions in state judicial elections, and the creation and roles of specialized courts. He is author of *The Supreme Court, American Courts, and The Puzzle of Judicial Behavior.*

Paul R. Brace

Clarence L. Carter Chair in Legal Studies, Department of Political Science, Rice University

Dr. Brace's research interests include judicial politics and processes, the Presidency, public opinion, legislative and state politics. His research on these topics has appeared in all of the leading journals in political science. Dr. Brace has also authored a book on state politics, coauthored a book on the presidency, and has coedited books on the presidency and state politics.

Richard A. Brisbin, Jr.

Associate Professor, Political Science, West Virginia University

Dr. Brisbin is the author of *A Strike Like No Other Strike: Law and Resistance During the Pittston Coal Strike of 1989–1990* (2002), *Justice Antonin Scalia and the Conservative Revival* (1997), coauthor of *West Virginia Politics and Government* (1996), and past editor of the *Law and Politics Book Review*. He has published numerous articles in journals, including the *American Political Science Review*, *American Journal of Political Science*, and *Political Science Quarterly*. West Virginia University named him as a Benedum Distinguished Scholar, its highest research award, and he received the Franklin L. Burdette Pi Sigma Alpha Award of the American Political Science Association for best paper presented at the Association's 1996 meeting.

Gregory A. Caldeira

Distinguished University Professor and University Chaired Professor of Political Science, Ohio State University

Professor Caldeira pursues research and teaching in the fields of judicial processes in the United States and Europe, organized interests, and American political institutions. His publications have been supported by grants from the National Science Foundation and have appeared in numerous scholarly journals. He is former editor of the *American Journal of Political Science* and has served on the executive councils of the American Political Science Association and the Midwest Political Science Association. His current research includes studies of the legitimacy of national courts and the impact of *Bush v. Gore* on public opinion.

Sue Davis

Professor, Department of Political Science and International Relations, University of Delaware

Dr. Davis has published widely in areas such as the Constitution and the American judicial system. Her most recent book is *Elizabeth Cady Stanton: Women's Rights and the American Political Traditions* (forthcoming). Dr. Davis is the 2004 section chair of the Law and Courts Section of the American Political Science Association.

Charles R. Epp

Associate Professor of Public Administration, University of Kansas

Dr. Epp's book, *The Rights Revolution: Lawyers, Activists, and Supreme Courts in Comparative Perspective,* received the American Political Science Association's Edward S. Corwin and C. Herman Pritchett awards. He has published articles in the *American Political Science Review, Law & Social Inquiry*, and *Law & Society Review*. His current research projects examine the incidence of racial profiling by the police and the impact of legal liability on local government policy reform.

Mark Graber

Professor of Government, University of Maryland;
Professor of Law, University of Maryland School of Law

Dr. Graber is the author of *Transforming Free Speech* and *Rethinking Abortion*, as well as many essays on constitutional politics, law, development and theory. He is presently completing *Dred Scott and the Problem of Constitutional Evil* (forthcoming), and beginning work on a project about civil liberties being expanded during war.

Joel B. Grossman

Professor of Political Science, Johns Hopkins University

Joel B. Grossman is Professor of Political Science at Johns Hopkins University and an adjunct member of the faculty at the University of Maryland School of Law. Before coming to Hopkins he was Professor of Political Science and Law at the University of Wisconsin-Madison. He teaches American Constitutional Law, Constitutional Theory, Comparative Constitutional Law, and related subjects. He is the author of numerous books and articles, and has served as editor of *Law & Society Review*, as chair of the Wisconsin Judicial Commission, and as chair of the political science departments at both Wisconsin and Johns Hopkins. He has received the 2005 Lifetime Achievement Award of the Law and Courts Section of the American Political Science Association.

Melinda Gann Hall

Professor of Political Science, Michigan State University

Dr. Hall's research has appeared in the *American Political Science Review*, *American Journal of Political Science*, *Journal of Politics*, and many other scholarly journals, edited volumes, and law reviews. She has received both the American Judicature Society Award and the McGraw-Hill Award from the Law and Courts Section of the American Political Science Association for her research on judicial elections. She is serving or has served on numerous editorial boards, and on a variety of committees and executive councils of political science professional associations. She also is co-principal investigator of the State Supreme Court Database Project, a multiuser database project sponsored by the National Science Foundation.

Donald P. Kommers

Joseph and Elizabeth Robbie Professor of Political Science, University of Notre Dame;
Member of the Law Faculty, University of Notre Dame

Dr. Kommers' books include *The Constitutional Jurisprudence of the Federal Republic of Germany* and the forthcoming *Black, Red, and Gold: Germany's Constitutional Odyssey*. He was editor of *The Review of Politics* for eleven years and for seven years the director of the Notre Dame Law School's International Human Rights Center. In 1998, Dr. Kommers received an honorary doctor of laws degree from Germany's Heidelberg University.

Lynn Mather

Professor of Law and Political Science, University at Buffalo Law School, The State University of New York;
Director of the Baldy Center for Law & Social Policy, University at Buffalo Law School, The State University of New York

Prior to joining the Buffalo Law faculty, Dr. Mather was the Nelson A. Rockefeller Professor of Government at Dartmouth College where she was awarded the Dartmouth

College Distinguished Teaching Award. Her research has focused on courts and public policy, litigation against tobacco companies, legal professionalism, lawyers and divorce mediation, and plea bargaining. She has authored or coauthored books including *Divorce Lawyers at Work: Varieties of Professionalism in Practice*, which received the C. Herman Pritchett Award from the American Political Science Association for the best book in the field of law and courts. She served as President of the Law and Society Association, an international scholarly association.

William E. Nelson

Edward Weinfeld Professor of Law, New York University

After obtaining a J.D. from New York University and a Ph.D. in American history from Harvard University, Dr. Nelson served as law clerk to Justice White in the October 1970 term. He is the author of, among many books and articles, *Americanization of the Common Law: The Impact of Legal Change on Massachusetts Society, 1760–1830*; *The Fourteenth Amendment: From Political Principle to Judicial Doctrine*; and *The Legalist Reformation: Law, Politics, and Ideology in New York, 1920–1980.*

Doris Marie Provine

Director, School of Justice & Social Inquiry, Arizona State University

Dr. Provine's teaching and research focus on courts and the politics of rights in domestic and international contexts. Her publications include *Case Selection in the United States Supreme Court* and *Judging Credentials: Non-lawyer Judges and the Politics of Professionalism.*

Douglas S. Reed

Associate Professor of Government, Georgetown University

Dr. Reed is the author of *On Equal Terms: The Constitutional Politics of Educational Opportunity*. He is currently writing a study of the local politics of federal education reform and the implementation of No Child Left Behind. He was recently named a Carnegie Scholar by the Carnegie Corporation of New York for his work on the politics of education and has held an Advanced Studies Fellowship from Brown University.

Gerald N. Rosenberg

Associate Professor of Political Science, University of Chicago;
Lecturer in Law, University of Chicago

Dr. Rosenberg served as the Jack N. Pritzker Distinguished Visiting Professor of Law at Northwestern University and as a Fulbright Professor at the Law School of Xiamen University in China. He also has been a visiting fellow in the Law Program at the Australian National University in Canberra. He is a member of the Washington, D.C. bar and his work has appeared in *Law & Social Inquiry, NOMOS, Supreme Court Review*, the *Journal of Supreme Court History*, the *University of Chicago Law Review*, the *University of Virginia Law Review* and other law reviews and journals. Dr. Rosenberg is the author of *The Hollow Hope: Can Courts Bring About Social Change?*

Cass R. Sunstein

Karl N. Llewellyn Distinguished Service Professor of Jurisprudence, Law School and Department of Political Science, University of Chicago

Mr. Sunstein has been involved in constitution-making and law reform activities in nations including Ukraine, Poland, China, South Africa, and Russia. A member of the American Academy of Arts and Sciences, Mr. Sunstein has been Samuel Rubin Visiting Professor of Law at Columbia, vice-chair of the ABA Committee on Separation of Powers and Governmental Organizations, and chair of the Administrative Law Section of the Association of American Law Schools. His publications include *Legal Reasoning and Political Conflict* (1996), *Republic.com* (2001), *Why Societies Need Dissent* (2003), and *The Second Bill of Rights* (2004).

Keith E. Whittington

Professor of Politics, Princeton University

Dr. Whittington is the author of *Constitutional Construction: Divided Powers and Constitutional Meaning; Constitutional Interpretation: Textual Meaning, Original Intent,* and *Judicial Review*; and coeditor of *Congress and the Constitution.* He has published widely on American constitutional theory and development, the presidency, judicial politics, and federalism.

David A. Yalof

Associate Professor of Political Science, University of Connecticut, Storrs

Dr. Yalof's *Pursuit of Justices: Presidential Politics and the Selection of Supreme Court Nominees* won the 2000 Richard E. Neustadt Award as the best book on the presidency from the American Political Science Association. He is coauthor of *The First Amendment and The Media in the Court of Public Opinion.* His articles have appeared in *Political Research Quarterly, Judicature,* and *Constitutional Commentary.* Dr. Yalof is currently completing a book-length project on the politics of investigating executive branch officials in the absence of an independent counsel.

GENERAL INTRODUCTION: THE JUDICIAL BRANCH AS AN INSTITUTION OF AMERICAN CONSTITUTIONAL DEMOCRACY

Jaroslav Pelikan

IT MUST SEEM OBVIOUS ON THE FACE OF IT THAT ANY SET OF reference books claiming to cover the "Institutions of American Democracy" must, as the Constitution itself does in Article III, pay more or less detailed attention to the judiciary. But when pressed beyond the obvious, such an inclusion of the judicial branch inevitably raises certain definitional difficulties. To invoke the formulas of the Gettysburgian definition, "of the people, by the people, for the people," the judicial branch of government at all levels may legitimately claim to be "democratic" on the grounds that it functions "*for* the people," whose "equal protection" (in the language of the Fourteenth Amendment) is indispensable to authentic democracy. But there cannot be a similar claim that as an institution the judiciary is an institution of American constitutional democracy because it is "*by* the people"; for, as Gerald N. Rosenberg specifies in his definition, "on its most basic level democracy requires that adult citizens determine, at least indirectly, what the government does." As Paul Brace and Melinda Gann Hall explain in their chapter, "the special case of electing judges" has repeatedly been advocated as a means of democratizing the judiciary and making it more directly accountable, thus "by the people." Yet the axiom quoted by Sue Davis, "the more direct democracy becomes, the more threatening it is," raises basic questions; in practice, therefore, this system has repeatedly met with what Kermit Hall describes as "enormous skepticism," especially from professionals and elites, and even its most fervent advocates would scarcely be willing to advance the argument that an elected judiciary at state and local levels is somehow more authentically "an institution of American constitutional democracy" than is the appointed judiciary at the Federal level, whose historic role has often been in fact to make state and local justice more constitutional and therefore more "democratic." There is, consequently, sufficient conflicting evidence, both constitutional and historical, to warrant the somewhat startling question of Richard A. Brisbin, Jr.: "Is it an unresponsive aristocracy or an essential component of modem American democracy?" In his discussion of "American Courts and Democracy" in a comparative international context, therefore, Donald P. Kommers advances a more subtle and more sophisticated definition than the well-known one of Abraham Lincoln: "For present purposes, democracy may be defined as a political order that combines popular government with a system of entrenched rights enforceable by independent courts of law—in short a constitutional democracy." Under such a definition, the judiciary is, as it should be, seen as indispensable to constitutional democracy, But when Alexander Hamilton in *Federalist* 78 declared,

> Whosoever attentively considers the different departments of power must perceive, that in a government in which they are separated from each, the judiciary, from the nature of its functions, will always be *the least dangerous* to the political rights of the constitution, because it will be least in a capacity to annoy or injure them,[1]

he created a formula that would take on a life and history of its own. Not only did it provide the title for one of the most provocative and durable monographs about the judiciary ever written, by my late friend and Yale colleague Alexander M. Bickel;[2] but the phrase itself has been repeated so often, also in the chapters of this present volume such as those by William E. Nelson and Doris Marie Provine, as to run the danger of becoming a truism. The first required characteristic of a *truism* is, of course, that it be *true*. The beginning of the first chapter of this volume appropriately comments on "the brevity of Article III," which contains "less than 500 words." Although it goes on to explain this historically on the basis of the timetable of the Constitutional Convention and of "the pressures under which the framers of the Constitution were operating," it is clear that the subsequent history of the judiciary has expanded its role far beyond this "brevity." It has been the Supreme Court of the United States that has decided, in *Brown v. Board of Education*, how, and with whom, American children would go to school—and even, in *Bush v. Gore*, who would be the President of the United States. Those who felt aggrieved by one or another of these and similar decisions must have found it increasingly difficult to see the judiciary as "the least dangerous" branch of the Federal government, no matter what the "brevity" of Article III.

It has been true of each of the three branches of government that the historical development of more than two centuries has altered and redefined the original constitutional provisions establishing it. Yet a comparison of how this change has happened in each of the three branches discloses a striking parallel between the judicial and the executive branches, not shared in quite the same way by the legislative branch. For just as the historical chapters in our volume on the executive branch suggest a radical scheme of historical periodization by which the entire time of one and one-half centuries from the adoption and ratification of the Constitution until the presidency of Franklin D. Roosevelt becomes one era, whereas the decades since the New Deal become another (or even *the* other) era, so, in Mark A. Graber's sweeping but fundamentally accurate formula here,

> The judiciary was a bystander in the democratic revolutions that took place in the United States from ratification until the New Deal. Suffrage was expanded to all white males, nominally to persons of color, and to women without any judicial help. Speech was protected, when protected, when American legislators and executives adhered to a libertarian tradition that developed outside the courtroom. Justices often proved more willing to declare unconstitutional legislative efforts to expand the franchise as to protect political processes from legislative regulation.

For reasons that Charles R. Epp spells out in his chapter, the courts have a more limited capacity to innovate than do the other two branches. It is noteworthy that the *Dred Scott* decision of 1857 is not only, as Cass R. Sunstein aptly describes it, "almost certainly the most vilified Supreme Court decision in American history," but, except perhaps for *Marbury v. Madison* of 1803, the decision from the nineteenth century that is cited most often in the nonspecialist literature, for the very reason that it proved to be such a spectacular failure.

Conversely, *Brown v. Board of Education* of 1954, while also "vilified" by extremists especially in its immediate aftermath, is likewise cited, also in the nonspecialist literature, as a model of how the judiciary does—and should—function as an "institution of American constitutional democracy," also because of the pivotal legal and constitutional position of public education as described in the chapter by Douglas S. Reed. As part of the history of the Supreme Court, it represented the repudiation of *Plessy v. Ferguson* of 1896, and therefore the acknowledgment that a decision of the Supreme Court, though "the law of the land," could be wrong and subject to correction in the light of further debate and development. The educational formula of *Plessy*, "separate but equal," was in fact a contradiction in terms, the unanimous decision of the Warren Court argued in *Brown*: there was an unavoidable inferiority implied in the very practice of separate education. And to back this up, the Court cited not only constitutional and legal scholarship but, in Footnote Eleven, the results of empirical study by social scientists. Though it has been painfully slow in its practical application in the elementary schools of the nation, *Brown* has properly come to be seen as landmark, turning point, and linchpin, not only socially but also constitutionally. In the summary of his introductory historical chapter on "Historical Foundations of the American Judiciary," therefore, William E. Nelson can say:

> *Brown v. Board of Education* changed everything. . . When *Brown v. Board of Education* overruled this settled practice [separate but equal, as sanctioned by *Plessy v. Ferguson*] and moved constitutional law in a new direction of racial equality, the Court was acting in a fashion in which it had never acted before. *Brown* did not resolve a constitutional ambiguity or defer to the political branches and take constitutional law in some new direction demanded by the people. Instead, it made a policy judgment that Jim Crow was so profoundly unjust that it had to be ended, whatever the will of the people. With *Brown*, the rule of law ceased to be what it had been throughout the nineteenth century—a baseline that courts administered until the people changed it.

"With that," Nelson concludes, "the aspiration . . . for the judiciary rather than the people ultimately to rule . . . assumed center stage in American constitutional thought."

Thus *Dred Scott* and *Brown* have become, both in their historic effect and especially in their symbolic significance—to invoke Thomas Kuhn's overworked concept[3]—the two diametrically opposite "paradigms" of the judiciary as an institution of American constitutional democracy, and of the relation of the judiciary to the problems of society and to the dynamics of the political process. Two still unresolved issues may serve as illustrations of this. One is what Chief Justice Warren Burger himself acknowledged to be "the somewhat tortured history of the Court's obscenity decisions"; the outcome of that history, at least for the time being, was the conclusion that "it is neither realistic nor constitutionally sound to read the First Amendment as requiring that the people of Maine or Mississippi accept public depictions of conduct found tolerable in Las Vegas, or New York City."[4] The other is the far graver question of the death penalty.[5] David A. Yalof's chapter shows the ambiguity of its development by contrasting the moratorium on executions as "both arbitrary and capricious" instituted by the Supreme Court in *Furman v. Georgia* (1972) with the decision of only four years later in *Gregg v. Georgia* (1976), which "reintroduced the death penalty as a legitimate means of punishment, on the condition that legislatures create statutory standards to guide sentencing bodies." It is impossible to suppose that the death penalty will not continue to demand judicial examination, regardless of the different "paths to the bench" that have been charted by Joel B. Grossman. The elusive norm of "contemporary community standards" is unavoidably a part of how these questions are to be decided, as the Eighth Amendment to the Constitution itself indicates when it forbids the inflicting of "cruel and *unusual* punishments," which introduces an empirical criterion, almost a statistical one. It is significant that in his careful examination here of *Roe v. Wade* as a legal decision and as an issue in the morality of public policy, Cass R. Sunstein notes that while "defenders of the decision have argued that it should be seen as a kind of *Brown* for women, in the form of a ruling that forbids states from adopting a practice that turns certain people into second-class citizens," those who question it "contend that it is more like *Dred Scott*: an unsuccessful and morally abhorrent effort to use the due process clause to settle large-scale moral issues." Once more *Dred Scott* and *Brown* take on an importance even greater than their historic one, as tests of the relation between the realities of the political scene and the ultimate responsibility of the judiciary "to protect and defend" the Constitution, but also to interpret it.

For the identification of the judiciary as "an institution of American constitutional democracy," while as valid as the chapters of this volume brilliantly show it to be, it is also fraught with the danger to which, in an atmosphere, as described by Lynn Mather, that sometimes seems to be dominated by a sports mentality, scorekeepers and the media far too easily succumb: to read the actions of the courts as no more than a continuum with the rest of the political process, to classify judges by the labels prevalent in that process, and thus to ignore the distinctiveness that the doctrine of balance of powers necessarily implies. Just as journalists and other Vatican-watchers, even within the Roman Catholic Church, seem to find it almost irresistible to classify and evaluate various Popes as "conservative" or "liberal," and to read their decisions as though the Pope were making it up as he goes along, rather than being himself subject to the authority of Scripture and Tradition, a similar tendency to impose labels and categories on judges—"liberal" and "conservative," or even "activist" and "neoconservative" (aka "neocon")—serves to oversimplify what courts and judges do and to lead to the supposition that a perceived personal "stance" can be used reliably to predict how a judge will rule officially on this or that question. The history both of the Papacy and of the judiciary can provide examples aplenty of where personal predilection has yielded to higher authority. Robert Dahl has used his astute analytic judgment as a political scientist to locate the judiciary within the policy-making function of a democratic society.[6] But he has also gone on to warn against such oversimplifications and what they can do to distort both the perception and ultimately the reality of the judiciary as a unique instrument of American constitutional democracy.

The balance is a difficult one to maintain, as the authors of the chapters in this volume have repeatedly discovered, especially because the volume is part of an entire set on *political* institutions. Therefore Keith E. Whittington insists that interpretation is ultimately not something that can be left to the individual states. And to counter the impression among the lay public, often reinforced by the analyses of various political and journalistic elites, that justices are like traffic cops with a generalized authority to roam around issuing tickets at will or that they have the power to wade into any judicial or interpretive thicket as their own personal convictions and prejudices may dictate, Mark A. Graber warns flatly:

"Justices may not correct any practice they think undemocratic. American courts resolve legal disputes by interpreting authoritative legal texts, the highest of which is the Constitution of the United States." The Constitution is an "authoritative legal text" that can be notoriously difficult and even ambiguous to "interpret"; but that does not obviate, but only complicates, the obligation to "resolve legal disputes" by interpreting it. In the case of the Constitution as in the case of the most important other "authoritative text" in the American tradition, the Bible, there has been wide fluctuation in the use of grammar and history to "construe" the text, in the strictness with which the results of such "construing" were applied, and in the authority assigned to previous "authoritative" interpretations, on the principle of *stare decisis;* and the comparison of these two histories may sometimes be useful in illuminating the methods of each.[7] But in both histories, this fluctuation has not included—or, at any rate, has not been permitted to include for very long—a free-floating method that pretends to be interpreting the text by actually ignoring it. The authors of these chapters, who have located the decisions of the judiciary in the total political context with great sensitivity and skill, have also provided the countervailing force to maintain that difficult and delicate balance. Two issues out of many may suffice to illustrate this.

One of these is federalism as a dimension of the judiciary. Paul Brace and Melinda Gann Hall are quite conscious that their chapter on this complex subject is quite "distinct," but that is ultimately because the American system—and behind it, the American Constitution—is distinct. The most flagrant example in the Constitution of how federalism can be seen as inhibiting the functioning of genuine democracy, as several chapters in our volume on the executive branch show, is the system of electing the president and the vice president by means of the electoral college. The outcome of that system has repeatedly been a discrepancy between the popular vote and the vote in the electoral college, and an outcry, at any rate by the losing side in a particular election, that the system itself is obsolete and needs to be corrected. But to an extent that is often overlooked or obscured in the public debates, the reality of the several states fundamentally defines the decisions of the federal judiciary; even *Roe v. Wade,* after all, was directed in the first instance at state legislatures. It is seen to be clear in the language of the Constitution that from public education to marriage and divorce, the responsibility and therefore also the authority of the state governments must be primary, just as, conversely, the area of international relations and foreign policy, from negotiating treaties to making war, is the prerogative of the federal government, as Richard A. Brisbin, Jr. explains in his chapter.

Another example of how "interpreting authoritative legal texts, the highest of which is the Constitution of the United States" can reintroduce earlier Constitutional norms that may have become obscure is what James W. Ely, Jr. entitles the "renewed concern for property rights." Walter Lippman, the twentieth-century American political philosopher and journalist, admonished: "Private property was the original source of freedom. It is still its main bulwark,"[8] That admonition echoed the language of the Fifth Amendment, in which the more familiar phrase, "life, liberty, and the pursuit of happiness" from the Declaration of Independence, was replaced with (or actually restored to) "life, liberty *or property*." And the Fifth Amendment continues: "Nor shall private property be taken for public use, without just compensation." The possible conflicts between that constitutional provision and the social legislation of the twentieth century have come back into both scholarly and judicial attention.[9] Reflecting that constitutional change, Chief Justice William H. Rehnquist observed in 1994: "We see no reason why the Takings Clause of the Fifth Amendment, as much a part of the Bill of Rights as the First Amendment or the Fourth Amendment, should be relegated to the status of a poor relation."[10]

If, then, the "institutions of American constitutional democracy" are distinctive above all by their being constitutional, the question of where the judiciary fits into the scheme, with which this introduction began, comes full circle: both the executive branch and the legislative branch, as well as the press and the public schools, qualify as such institutions because of their relation, direct (in the case of the two branches and the press) or indirect (in the case of the schools), to the Constitution. But it is the special mission of the judicial branch to interpret the Constitution and the laws in a way, according to the definition proposed by Donald Kommers, "that combines popular government with a system of entrenched rights enforceable by independent courts of law—in short a constitutional democracy." Amid all the possible scenarios envisioned by Lawrence Baum for the future, this would be unimaginable without the judiciary.

Notes

1. *The Federalist* 78, ed. Jacob E. Cooke (Middletown, Conn.: Wesleyan University Press, 1961), 522; italics added.
2. Alexander M. Bickel, *The Least Dangerous Branch: The Supreme Court at the Bar of Politics* (Indianapolis: Bobbs, Merrill, 1962).
3. Thomas S. Kuhn, *The Structure of Scientific Revolutions* (2d ed.; Chicago: University of Chicago Press, 1970).
4. *Miller v. California*, 413 U.S. 20, 32 (1973).
5. Hugo Adam Bedau, ed., *The Death Penalty in America* (New York: Oxford University Press, 1982).
6. Robert A. Dahl, "Decision-Making in a Democracy," in Kermit Hall, ed., *The Supreme Court in American Society: Equal Justice Under Law* (New York: Garland Publishing, 2001), 117–133.
7. Jaroslav Pelikan, *Interpreting the Bible and the Constitution.* A John W. Kluge Center Book of the Library of Congress (New Haven, Conn.: Yale University Press, 2004). The research and writing of this book were being carried on while I was participat-

ing in the discussions of the Sunnylands Commission on the Judiciary, and it is much the better for that contribution.

8. Walter Lippman, *The Method of Freedom* (New York: Macmillan Company, 1934), 101.
9. Richard A. Epstein, *Takings: Private Property and the Power of Eminent Domain* (Cambridge, Mass.: Harvard University Press, 1985).
10. *Dolan v. City of Tigard*, 512 U.S. 374, 392 (1994).

INTRODUCTION

Kermit L. Hall and Kevin T. McGuire

IN *FEDERALIST* 78, ALEXANDER HAMILTON INSISTED THAT the courts would be the "least dangerous branch" because they would have "no influence over either the sword or the purse." In Hamilton's view, the courts possessed only the capacity to render judgments. Crafting public policy and putting it into effect was entrusted to the legislative and executive branches. Whatever authority the courts possessed would be derived from the independent reason of the law. But was Hamilton right, not only for his own time but for contemporary America? After all, no sooner had the Constitution gone into effect than battle lines were drawn, when Chief Justice John Marshall asserted in *Marbury v. Madison* (1803) that the Supreme Court had the power to invalidate legislation that it judged to be contrary to the Constitution. Two hundred years later, the federal courts continue to find themselves enmeshed in similarly salient policy issues. Federal lower-court judges, for example, are regularly involved in the administration of public schools and prisons. For its part, the U.S. Supreme Court has become actively engaged in, among other things, the regulation of abortion, the development of police procedures, the congressional oversight of the federal bureaucracy, and even the determination of the 2000 presidential election.

Moreover, Hamilton was referring only to the courts of what was then a new and untested national government. At the time of the founding, the states were the principal sources of public policymaking, and their courts were seen as leading expositors of the law. Yet, even those who championed the power of states in the late eighteenth century could not have foreseen the role that state judiciaries would come to play in American life. Modern state courts resolve literally millions of disputes each year. With agendas covering such varied subjects as crime, domestic relations, employment, environmental regulation, housing, personal injury, and product liability, state courts are at the center of resolving almost every conceivable public and private dispute.

American courts, both federal and state, do not simply "announce" the law; as much as any other set of institutions, they make policy. For good or ill, the line that Hamilton so neatly drew between will and judgment has blurred, both in theory and practice. As a result, argues legal historian William E. Nelson, Americans both legal and lay now "observe with frequency that all law, whether promulgated by a court or a legislature, [is] an essentially mutable and transitory product of sovereign command."

The judiciary, then, has emerged over the past two centuries as considerably more involved with establishing and implementing public policy than Hamilton had anticipated. To be sure, the judiciary has had to respect popular sovereignty; at the same time, however, it has also fallen heir, by default, to guardianship of the fundamental law. In the end, the third and supposedly least dangerous branch of government has emerged with a dual role, one that requires judges and justices, federal and state, to be *of* the world of politics without being directly *in* that world. Is this seemingly bifurcated role appropriate to the maintenance and continued functioning of American democracy? This volume provides a variety of perspectives on this vital question.

Outline of the Volume

As the political scientist Robert G. McCloskey has noted, the "propensity to hold contradictory ideas simultaneously is and has been one of the most significant qualities of the American political mind at all stages of national history." It is this insight that helps us understand the rise of judicial power and, perhaps even more importantly, the extraordinary role that judges have come to play in the American pageant of democracy. The essays in this volume address the implications of this duality in the past, present, and the future; in the states and the federal government; and in comparison to other developed nations. In essence, the essays ask whether American democracy has been, is now, and will continue to depend on the judiciary for its vitality.

We begin by examining the historical role of courts—and the leading personalities who have guided them—in the development of the democratic ideal in America. To that end, William E. Nelson outlines the earliest understanding of courts in America, a view which held courts to be largely subservient to the popular will. The Constitution of 1787, by supplanting the idea of simple majority will with notions of a fundamental rule of law, provided the context in which judges could establish themselves as constitutional custodians; they began to enforce the legal limits on unrestrained majoritarianism that the Framers sought to impose. As respect for this judicial function took root and as legal education became institutionalized, courts came to be seen as instruments of American democracy, responsible for guaranteeing the underlying principles of the Constitution.

Cass Sunstein probes this changing role for the judiciary through the lens of the U.S. Supreme Court. By tracing some of the major turning points in the Court's history, Sunstein outlines how the justices have, over time, charted paths that have expanded the democratic nature of the Constitution. As he argues, the Court has been at its best when it has helped to define and extend the participatory character of the Constitution.

Where these two essays focus on the changing role of the federal courts, Kermit L. Hall's essay traces the rise of state judiciaries and their relevance to a democratic polity. In particular, he examines the American practice of electing judges, the means by which most judges in the United States either gain or retain their offices. Recognizing the inherent contradiction in permitting judges in a democratic system to overrule the majority, states have explored ways in which to make their courts more democratically accountable, especially as courts assume more prominent roles as policymakers. Hall's essay highlights some of the features and consequences of judicial elections by comparing the American system to the methods by which judges are chosen in Europe and Asia. Although Americans clearly prefer to elect their judges, courts at the state level, he notes, operate without the same kind of independence and influence enjoyed by their unelected brethren on the federal bench.

In the second general section of the volume, a set of contributors analyzes how courts operate within a larger political system that divides authority both within the national government and between the national and state governments. What consequences do the separation of powers and federalism have for the role of judges in American democracy? One answer to this question is offered by Richard A. Brisbin, Jr. In his chapter, Brisbin surveys the history of this doctrine in the U.S. Supreme Court and finds that its interpretation of the separation of powers has been quite varied. In a good many instances, the Court has been willing to validate claims of expanded power made by the elected branches, often for the sake of political expediency. When the justices have sought to rein in the excesses of the Congress and the president, it has typically occurred when those branches have been politically disadvantaged and when the Court senses that it can challenge the other branches without fearing fallout. By Brisbin's lights, the Court has limited the potentially tyrannical ambitions of elected officials, but only when circumstances have been propitious for doing so.

Although he approaches the question from a somewhat different perspective, Keith E. Whittington comes to a similar conclusion. Whittington discusses some of the problems, both theoretical and practical, associated with having the courts serve as final arbiters of the Constitution. After considering the various formal and informal limits that exist on judicial power, he concludes that the courts have more often been followers, rather than leaders, in pronouncing the constitutional limits on elected officials. Importantly, he notes that what appear as judicial decisions that safeguard the rights of political minorities are often little more than judges bringing occasionally anomalous policymakers back in line with the political mainstream.

To address the importance of federalism for the nation's courts, Joel B. Grossman assesses the democratic implications of judicial selection at both the state and national level. Comparing the growth of different selection methods within the states to the appearance of the "new politics" of selecting members of the U.S. Supreme Court, Grossman describes how the increasing visibility of courts as policymakers has made judicial selection—especially the selection of members of the Supreme Court—highly fractious affairs that divide both the public and their representatives.

Judicial federalism is even more central to the chapter authored by Paul Brace and Melinda Gann Hall. These scholars offer both historical and empirical assessments of the democratic influence of state courts. These scholars underscore the stabilizing the effect that these courts have had by resolving disputes within a democratic system. With data on the dockets and behavior of the fifty state supreme courts, they demonstrate that a good many of these tribunals show a remarkable tendency to confront the counter-majoritarian difficulty head-on, resolving many of the same tensions faced by their federal counterparts. From their perspective, state courts have been and continue to be equally essential to the maintenance of American democracy.

Of course, the American model represents only one example of how court systems operate within the democratic context. Many of these issues can be profitably framed through a comparative analysis of the ways in which other nations, operating from different historical experiences and governmental frameworks, have constructed their judicial power. To that end, Donald P. Kommers offers an evaluation of the democratic character of American courts by juxtaposing the American approach to the selection and decision making of judges in Canada, Germany, and South Africa. In particular, he emphasizes that the struggle to resolve the conflict between democracy and judicial review is by no means unique to the United States. Moreover, he notes that the American courts seem to have served as a kind of exemplar, in that many of their traditions and policies have been emulated elsewhere around the world.

In the third section of the volume, the contributors address how American courts relate to various popular constituencies. What place do courts occupy in the public mind? In her essay on court and public culture, Lynn Mather offers one answer by illustrating how Americans' understanding of their courts is conditioned not only by their direct experiences with courts but also by both real and fictional portrayals of the judicial system by the media. These media representations, so often atypical of the reality of American courts, create substantial misperceptions for various segments of society. At the same time, she notes that these images frequently foment healthy debate by providing the necessary impetus for citizens to think critically about the functioning of the courts.

What Americans think about their judicial system and why is surveyed in Gregory A. Caldeira and Kevin T. McGuire's chapter. Examining the evidence on the public's knowledge and evaluation of their courts, these authors conclude that public support for the judiciary is vital to its legitimacy and the acceptance of its policies. For that reason, they argue, courts tend to be quite democratic in character through their attentiveness to public opinion when making decisions. Likewise, these authors also conclude that, like elected officials, courts can play an instructive role—as well as a divisive role—the public's evaluation of many of the salient issues that arise at the intersection of law and politics.

Moving beyond a discussion of how citizens think about courts, Gerald N. Rosenberg assesses their actual interactions with courts. These interactions are far from trivial; he notes that an extraordinarily large numbers of Americans are, in one way or another, involved in litigation every year. An ideal democratic system, he maintains, would facilitate the ready and equitable resolution of these conflicts in a way consistent with the dictates of the law. In practice, however, both the civil and criminal courts often feature delay, perceptions of bias, and inconsistent results. Rosenberg's chapter seeks to put these findings into perspective and to consider how well American courts help maintain democratic ideals, despite these complications.

One potential consequence of the pervasiveness of courts is that American judges may be expounding too much law. Doris Marie Provine assesses this possibility in her chapter on the judicial activism. She explains that whether individuals perceive courts to be running amok has a good deal to do with their predispositions toward the winners and losers in courts. Her essay examines why many have concluded that the American courts have supplanted popular decision makers and the subsequent efforts to curb the capacities of judges.

A fourth set of essays examines how American courts have defined democratic processes, concepts, and relationships between government and the individual. In the first of these, Charles R. Epp traces the rise of the civil rights movement in the United States and uses it to illustrate how, through its decisions, the U.S. Supreme Court helped to establish the democratic condition of equality under the law. Although the civil right movement was aimed primarily at advancing the interesting of African Americans, it had the ancillary effect of promoting gender equality, as well. Through its decisions, Epp argues, the Court helped to lay the groundwork for some of the most basic guarantees of equality in the American system.

In a similar vein, Sue Davis focuses on the rise of popular initiatives at the state level and how some of these voter initiatives have sought to limit the political rights of various groups within society, such as illegal aliens and gays and lesbians. Although the initiatives she examines were opportunities for citizens to engage in direct democracy, the judicial invalidation of these measures, she argues, both reinforced the norms of equality and opened the door to a more deliberative (and thus more democratic) assessment of the rights of political minorities.

To what extent have American courts helped shape our notions of democratic government? Mark A. Graber's chapter takes on this question and demonstrates that the U.S. Supreme Court has had a major hand in developing the sense that United States is indeed a democracy, as opposed to a republic. Graber notes that, for much of the nation's history, the role of popular opinion in policymaking was viewed as largely ancillary, its effects filtered through elected representatives. In the late 1930s, however, the justices on the Court began to reshape the collective American consciousness by promoting values, such as freedom of speech and freedom of the press, that are considered crucial elements of a democratic government.

No less significant to the democratic ideal are the procedures that government extends to the criminally accused. As David Yalof argues in his essay, the rights of defendants are essential to guarantee that a democracy maintains a commitment to fundamental law, rather than the fleeting passions and prejudices of a majority. He describes how, under Chief Justice Earl Warren, the Supreme Court instituted a host of specific procedural safeguards that, despite numerous critics, have been difficult for both elected officials and judges to undo, even in light of the challenges posed by the threat of terrorism. Whatever their problems and however unpopular they may be, says Yalof, these procedural safeguards serve as tangible evidence of a judicial commitment to an essentially democratic ideal.

The last two essays in this section examine the linkages between individual rights and democracy. In his chapter, Douglas S. Reed examines the extent to which courts have emphasized education as an indispensable condition for democracy, even though the Constitution provides no educational guarantee. At both the state and federal levels, judges have regularly involved themselves in evaluating what kinds of educational opportunities are offered, how, and to whom. The focal point for courts in these cases, he argues, has been ensuring an informed citizenry that is able to participate fully and equally in the political process.

The other related essay focuses on the question of property rights. In this chapter, James W. Ely, Jr., explains the historical importance of private property in England, the American colonies, and the United States. Ironically, even though such rights have generally been seen as essential in a free society, courts have not been unstinting in their support. As he explains, property has been a source of conflict in the United States as often as it has been a source democratic stability.

The final section of the volume contains a single essay authored by Lawrence Baum. In this integrative chapter, Baum examines a broader set of issues concerning the future role of courts under the American democratic system. Among other things, he recognizes that courts may evolve into increasingly more specialized institutions, even as alternatives to courts develop to help resolve disputes. Because courts also evolve and adapt in response to real-world problems, Baum cautions, it will be difficult to know what the shape of the judiciary will be in the future. One issue that the courts will continue to face, however, is the amount and manner of popular control exercised over judges. Judicial independence and democratic values will therefor have to be continually rebalanced.

Taken together, these essays offer a provocative and insightful look into courts as institutions of democracy. Although none of the contributions to volume offers ready answers to the important questions raised throughout the book, each one offers a unique perspective for analyzing how courts can maintain a fidelity to the law while operating within the context of a political system.

Acknowledgments

This book benefited from the contributions of two groups. First, the National Advisory Board of the Institutions of Democracy Project, chaired by Dr. Jaroslav Pelikan, Yale University, and its members: Judge Arlin Adams, Nancy Kassebaum Baker, David Boren, John Brademas, David Gergen, Lee Hamilton, Ellen Condliffe Lagemann, Judge John T. Noonan, Jr., Leon Panetta, and George Shultz. The National Advisory Board offered encouragement and recommendations about the scope and direction of the project at its inception.

A second group, the National Commission About the Future of the American Judiciary, participated actively in the development of the book, meeting twice for two-day-long sessions to review draft outlines and offer substantive critiques of the chapters. The robust discussion generated among the Advisory Board members, the authors, and editors contributed significantly to the book's final shape. We extend special thanks to its members: Chief Justice Shirley Abrahamson, Wisconsin Supreme Court, Judge Rosemary Barkett, U.S. Court of Appeals for the 11th Circuit, Judge Judith M. Billings, Utah Court of Appeals, Joan Biskupic, journalist for *USA Today*, Mabel McKinney Browning, American Bar Association, Professor Paul D. Carrington, Duke University, Professor Walter Dellinger, Duke University, Professor Sanford V. Levinson, University of Texas School of Law, Maeva Marcus, Supreme Court Historical Society, Chief Justice Thomas J. Moyer, The Supreme Court of Ohio, The Honorable Tom Phillips, Texas Court of Appeals, David Richert, American Judicature Society, Professor Jeffrey Rosen, The George Washington University Law School, Stuart Taylor, Jr., journalist for *Newsweek* and *National Journal*, Professor John Vile, Middle Tennessee State University.

The editors and authors also acknowledge the remarkable support provided by Timothy DeWerff, Joe Clements, and Anne Savarese of Oxford University Press in bringing this project to press on time. And they offer special thanks to Jaroslav Pelikan for his active engagement with the project, for sharing his extraordinary gifts of learning, and for his remarkable sense of humor.

INSTITUTIONS OF AMERICAN DEMOCRACY

THE JUDICIAL BRANCH

SECTION I

CONSTITUTIONAL MOMENTS, JUDICIAL LEADERSHIP, AND THE EVOLUTION OF DEMOCRACY

1

THE HISTORICAL FOUNDATIONS OF THE AMERICAN JUDICIARY

William E. Nelson

THE FEDERAL CONSTITUTION OF 1787 AND STATE CONstitutions written both before and after its adoption did not create the American judicial system that exists today. The judiciary's foundations lie elsewhere—in the common law of England stretching as far back as the Middle Ages and in the societal needs that arose when the polity created by independence and the new federal and state constitutions superseded older eighteenth-century forms of governance. Even on subjects other than the judiciary, most of today's constitutional law and practice stems not from constitutional texts themselves but from pre-constitutional precedents or post-constitutional developments.

A few familiar examples from federal constitutional law will illustrate. The Constitution's prohibition on bills of attainder and its adoption of impeachment as the sole device for congressional removal of officials can only be understood against the background of earlier English history. Another example is the scope of the Commerce Clause, which was understood to give Congress much narrower authority to regulate economic affairs in 1787–1788 than it does today. Members of the first Congress and of George Washington's administration disagreed, for example, over whether Congress had power to establish a national bank or even to build lighthouses to aid seaborne traffic. In contrast, even after recent Supreme Court cases that have cut back on the breadth of the commerce power, no one doubts the authority of Congress to build an interstate highway system or of the Federal Reserve Board to regulate even purely intrastate banking transactions.

In a similar fashion, the Constitution of 1787 says nothing about presidential term limits. Nonetheless, when President George Washington refused to run for a third term, he established an important constitutional practice. For nearly a century and a half, no president sought a third term, and when President Franklin D. Roosevelt successfully did so in 1940, many viewed his reelection as a violation of the Constitution. They then proceeded to write their understanding of constitutional law into text with the adoption of the Twenty-second Amendment.

Racial segregation offers a final illustration. Few scholars believe that the men who drafted and ratified the Fourteenth Amendment had definitively resolved the issue of whether their language would outlaw *de jure* segregation. Nor does anyone seriously deny that *Brown v. Board of Education* (1954) created novel constitutional law when it ruled that the Fourteenth Amendment outlaws separate but equal facilities mandated by state law.[1]

Similarly, the Constitution of 1787 speaks only in minimal fashion of the national judiciary. Article III, which is the portion of the Constitution dealing with courts, itself is very sparse, containing less than five hundred words. Section 1 merely creates the Supreme Court, authorizes Congress to create lower courts, and gives federal judges life tenure. Section 2 provides for jury trial in criminal cases and specifies the jurisdiction of federal courts: in essence, it authorizes federal courts to hear cases arising under federal law and cases involving citizens from more than one state and remits most other cases to state courts. Article III's final section defines and limits the applicability of the crime of treason.

The pressures under which the framers of the Constitution were operating explain the brevity of Article III. It is important to realize that after the framers had drafted Articles I and II, dealing with the legislative and executive branches, they wished to finish their job quickly and get their document ratified. They were tired, they wanted to get home before winter, and above all, they needed to let the public know what they had been doing. They had readily agreed about some matters, such as the necessity of a Supreme Court and of granting life tenure to judges, and they incorporated their agreements into Article III. But other issues, especially whether lower federal courts should exist and how extensive they should be, were controversial, and the framers consciously left the controversial issues for resolution by Congress and the courts in the future.

Thus, it is necessary to understand the constitutional foundations of the federal courts as a product of development over time. The original Constitution for the most part did not create foundational law, but only the most basic of institutions. Thereafter, Congress and the courts had to work out the law under which the federal judiciary continues to function today.

State constitutions were no different. Provisions dealing with state judiciaries are more terse than provisions dealing with the other branches of state government. Moreover, they tend to deal mainly with matters of housekeeping and to ignore larger issues about the role of courts in the polity. None of the original thirteen state constitutions, for example, made any mention of judicial review—

the power of state courts to hold acts of their state legislatures unconstitutional. Mention of judicial review remains rare even today.

Of course, like Article III of the federal Constitution, state constitutional provisions on the judiciary are not entirely irrelevant. Some of the housekeeping rules they establish are important, such as the rule in most states that judges hold office for fixed terms or until a stated retirement age, whereas federal judges hold office for life, unless they resign, retire, or are impeached. But the key point bears repetition: the federal and state constitutions do not specify the role of the judiciary in the overall polity, do not explicate precisely what it is that courts and judges do, and do not untangle the relationship between the countermajoritarian judicial branch of government and the more democratic executive and legislative branches. To understand these matters it is necessary to turn to history—especially the history of the eighteenth century and the early decades of the nineteenth.

American Courts in the Eighteenth Century

Before the United States became independent in 1776, judges and their agents were the only officers of central government whom most people ever met. There were no police forces, no army, and no bureaucracy in the form of an Internal Revenue Service, a Social Security Administration, or a Motor Vehicle Bureau. Judges monopolized all of government's coercive powers. And in most eighteenth-century colonial communities, the judges were outsiders who received their commissions from the crown and held office at royal pleasure. High-court judges appeared in local communities only occasionally, perhaps once or twice a year, as they rode circuit around the colony to hear all significant cases and appeals from minor ones.

Judges were only one part of the court system, however. Juries were the other part. Since judges in most colonies had little, if any, equitable jurisdiction, they almost always sat with juries, which brought the democratic power of local communities into the courtroom. Although only white men who held property could serve on juries, property ownership was widespread, and jury duty, onerous and to be avoided. As a result, a broad cross-section of white men, not simply a privileged elite, actually represented their local communities by performing jury duty.

Eighteenth-century juries were significantly more powerful than juries are today because juries, in reaching their verdicts, determined not only the facts of a case but the applicable law as well. It was every juror's right and duty to find verdicts "according to his own best Understanding, Judgment and Conscience, tho in Direct opposition to the Direction of the Court"[2] on the law. The jury system was valued precisely because it introduced into the judiciary "a mixture of popular power"; as a result, "the subject . . . [was] guarded in the execution of the laws,"[3] and "no Man . . . [could] be condemned of Life, or Limb, or Property or Reputation, without the Concurrence of the Voice of the People."[4] It bears emphasis that juries in most cases cooperated with judges and followed the guidance they received from the bench; moreover, jurors understood that, on the rare occasions when they rejected judicially announced law, they were applying the preexisting law of their community, not formulating new law. Nonetheless, the lawfinding power of juries ultimately meant that judges were little more than keepers of a set of procedures for bringing disputes before local community representatives who could resolve them by whatever lights they saw fit.

This system of local, democratic control of law was able to function largely because the communities from which juries were drawn shared a broad consensus about the law that governed them. The realities of mid-eighteenth-century American politics kept large, divisive issues out of the local politics and out of the courtroom. The presence of French power in Canada and the Mississippi Valley, for example, prevented Americans from addressing the issues of national expansion and economic growth that ultimately would lead to civil war in the nineteenth century. British imperial policy, by its preference for an establishment of religion and its insistence on toleration of all Protestant denominations, also kept many potentially divisive religious issues under wraps. Finally, the crown's control of monetary policy and its tenacious protection of British mercantile interests limited the politicization of debtor-creditor law.

Two Visions of Democracy

The Declaration of Independence, the enactment of state constitutions, and the adoption of the federal Constitution of 1787 did not put an end to the democratic power of juries over law. But these events put issues of religion, national expansion, economic growth, and creditors' rights on the public agenda and thereby gave rise to new forms of politics. The new politics, in turn, led indirectly to new understandings about the role of the courts in a democratic American polity.

Unrestrained Majoritarian Populism

On the one hand, the coming of independence and the enactment of state constitutions strengthened popular forces of the sort that colonial juries had reflected. Independence removed royally appointed officials from American politics and made every officer of government directly or indirectly responsible to the electorate. Independence also put an end to the imperial constraints that had kept a wide range of divisive issues out of local politics. Finally, the remaking of their governments taught Americans that the people not only could find preexisting law, but also could change law to make their lives and their society better.

As a result of independence and state constitutions, the people and their representatives became fully empowered to make whatever law they wanted to make.

These new views of democratic lawmaking power were in tension with older views of popular power administered by juries. The 1792 South Carolina case of *Administrators of Moore v. Cherry*[5] will illustrate. The plaintiff in *Moore* had been a Loyalist during the Revolutionary War from whom a slave had been taken by a Patriot scouting party and then sold to the defendant. After the war, the plaintiff brought suit to recover the slave. Ignoring the court's instructions that the plaintiff, by virtue of a statute passed by the state legislature, was entitled to recover his slave, a jury found for the defendant; after a new trial had been granted, a second jury did the same. On appeal, the court granted yet a third trial, with one judge declaring, "God forbid . . . that the verdict of two juries should make the law" since "[l]egislators as well as judges would both then be useless"; and society "would be governed by such rules as private opinion would occasionally dictate."

This tension between juries and legislatures, however, was of minimal importance. There were only two significant differences between the two institutions. First, juries operated locally, whereas legislatures operated state-wide. Second, jury lawmaking required unanimity, whereas legislative lawmaking required only a majority vote. Both institutions, however, shared something more basic—in both, representatives of middling people possessed plenary power to determine the law, and they could use their power to resolve divisive issues of social policy.

In the aftermath of independence the people used their power with frequency and in fashions that impinged on the interests of their fellow citizens. In particular, middling people tried to protect themselves and their neighbors from the collection of debts they found difficult to pay. The Rhode Island legislature, for example, made inflated paper money legal tender for payment of debts—a policy that hurt not only Rhode Island creditors, but creditors in Connecticut, Massachusetts, and even New York as well. Many states placed impediments in the path of British creditors as well as British subjects seeking to recover land they owned in America. These impediments violated the 1783 treaty granting American independence, and the British government responded by refusing to evacuate forts in the Northwest Territory which the treaty had granted to America. As a result, Americans who wished to settle in the Northwest Territory were unable to do so.

Democracy with the Rule of Law

These excesses of democracy troubled James Madison and some of the other men who gathered in Philadelphia in the summer of 1787 to write a national constitution. They were not opposed to democracy as such; indeed, those who became known as Federalists during the debates over ratification of the

Constitution articulated more clearly than anyone why the people possessed ultimate power to create government and hence to make law. But Madison and his allies had a different vision of democracy. The Federalists wanted a government of divided powers and checks and balances that would force popular majorities to proceed slowly and to think hard about making law that would help some groups in the community at the expense of other groups. They incorporated devices into the Constitution, such as federalism, separation of powers, a bicameral legislature, an electoral college, and indirect election of senators by state legislatures, designed to keep transient majorities under control.

In particular, as Alexander Hamilton explained in *Federalist* No. 78, the Federalists envisioned a judiciary that would keep Congress and the president "within the limits assigned to their authority." Such a strong judiciary, however, frightened Antifederalists. One of the main concerns of those opposing ratification of the Constitution was that middling people out in localities would cower before national judges bent on depriving them of their liberty. Hamilton's response to this concern, in the famous words of *Federalist* No. 78, was that the judiciary would be the "least dangerous" branch of government because it did not control "either the sword or the purse"—it possessed "neither FORCE nor WILL, but merely judgment." Ultimately, as would become clear fifteen years later, the Federalists were prepared to allow courts only to delay, but not to obstruct a determined majority of the people.

Beneath the surface of the 1787–1788 debates over ratification of the Constitution there thus lay two competing visions of democracy. Antifederalists tended to believe that local and statewide institutions should possess power to declare the will of controlling popular majorities to be law, even if that meant overriding rights claimed by minorities. They were majoritarian democrats. Federalists, in contrast, argued that legal rights preexisted popular will. While they conceded the ultimate power of the people to change law prospectively in whatever fashion the people wished, their new Constitution strove to place obstacles in the path of change—obstacles that would become increasingly difficult to surmount as opposition to change grew more dogged. They believed in deliberative democracy.

The Politics of the 1790s

When the new federal government came into being, it did not work as its Federalist proponents had planned. Within a few years, following the 1795 signing of Jay's Treaty with Great Britain, forerunners of national political parties came into existence, and the new federal government became a vehicle for national majoritarian politics. Americans who thought that John Jay had paid too high a price when he agreed in his treaty to have the federal government pay debts still owed to British creditors ultimately formed themselves into a party that called itself Republican, under the leadership of Thomas Jefferson and James Madison. Those whose fear of the excesses of the French Revolution led them to support Jay's effort at rapprochement with Britain formed a new Federalist party, under the leadership of Alexander Hamilton and then John Adams.

Underlying these partisan divisions was the same ideological split that had emerged during the ratification debates about the meaning of democracy in the American polity. As the Federalists saw it, Jeffersonian Republicans were majoritarian populists who threatened, like the French revolutionaries had done, to use legislation to destroy existing institutions and thereby undermine the social order. The Jeffersonians were, in fact, striving to build popular majorities in states such as Massachusetts and Virginia to end one important traditional institution—government-supported religious establishments inherited from the colonial period—and many Federalists did fear that social chaos would follow if religious institutions lost power.

If the Federalists worried that Republican majorities would subvert law and the social order, the Republicans were equally convinced that, if allowed to retain power, the Federalists would subvert democratic self-government. Republican fears peaked during the administration of John Adams, when the Federalist-controlled Congress imposed a direct tax, voted to establish a standing army and navy, and adopted the Alien and Sedition Acts, pursuant to which some Jeffersonian editors were sent to jail for criticizing government policies.

The decisive battle between the two parties was fought in the presidential election of 1800, when Thomas Jefferson defeated John Adams in the latter's effort for reelection. The power of democratic majorities to make law was thereby firmly established, with Jefferson as president and his party in firm control of both houses of Congress. Federalists fled back to the few states, mainly in New England, where they retained electoral power, and to the judiciary, where in the coming decades they developed their deliberative alternative to the Jeffersonian vision of majoritarian democracy—an alternative that sought to protect ultimate principles of legal right while simultaneously recognizing the ultimate power of the people to make law.

Instituting the Rule of Law

Federalists had begun elaborating their conception of the judiciary as a counterweight to majoritarian democracy as early as 1798. In that year, Alexander Hamilton had persuaded the soon to be Speaker of the House of Representatives, Theodore Sedgwick, that a congressional committee should study reform and expansion of the federal judiciary. John Marshall, a freshman representative whom John Adams would appoint as chief justice of the United States three months after Adams had lost his reelection bid, became the most articulate member of that committee. In the same year, Hamilton persuaded

John Jay, the governor of New York, to appoint a Hamilton protégé, James Kent, to New York's Supreme Court.

During the next few years, the Hamiltonian Federalists developed a four-part program. First, they attempted to organize judges into cohesive courts capable of developing a published body of case law by which to decide future cases. Second, they planned to deprive juries of power to determine law and to confer that authority exclusively on judges. Third, they cultivated a conception of law as a science that could be grasped only by men who had received a professional legal education. Fourth, they sought to give the judiciary a broad power of judicial review—a jurisdiction, that is, to invalidate legislation with which courts disagreed on policy grounds.

The Establishment of Precedent

James Kent elaborated the first part of the Federalist program more clearly than anyone else. At the time of his appointment in 1798, New York lacked a coherent body of case law. The judges of the state's highest court rode circuit throughout the state, as they had during the colonial era, and typically passed on legal issues from the bench as they arose, without any opportunity for careful research or for formulation of a collective judgment. As Kent's biographer wrote, the decisions of the court were not the product of a mature consideration.

> It was evident that they were not the fruit of that careful and laborious investigation which is essential to the proper discharge of the judicial functions; and the authority they might otherwise have claimed was greatly impaired by those frequent differences in opinion that are the necessary result of imperfect examination and study. It was seldom that the opinions of the judges, even in the most important cases, were reduced to writing, and as no reports were then published, and no records preserved of the grounds on which their decisions were placed, the cases were numerous in which they had no rules to direct, no precedents to govern them.[6]

As Kent himself wrote, "there were no reports or State precedents." Judges who were riding circuit together delivered their opinions orally, often disagreeing with each other. "We had no law of our own, and nobody knew what it [i.e., the law] was."[7] Under the circumstances, it is not surprising that juries felt no compunction in ignoring what little guidance they received on law from the court.

Kent set out to give his state a coherent body of jurisprudence. He decided

> that he would examine for himself every case not decided on the hearing; and in such examination would not confine himself to the cases and authorities cited on the argument, but would embrace in his researches

> all the law justly applicable to the questions to be determined; and that in each case he would embody the result of his examination in a written opinion. Accordingly, at the second term that followed his appointment, in his first meeting for consultation with his brethren, and to their great astonishment, he produced a written opinion in every case that had been reserved for decision; and as these opinions were carefully prepared, were clear in style, forcible in reasoning, and well sustained by reference to authorities, his brethren . . . were in no condition to controvert and oppose them.[8]

With his introduction of "a thorough examination of cases and written opinions," Kent "acquired preponderating influence" on the court. As he wrote about one typical early case, he "presented and read my written opinion . . ., and they all gave up to me, and so I read it in court as it stands."[9]

Kent's turn to legal research and to the preparation of written opinions was, as he wrote, "the commencement of a new plan"—"the first stone in the subsequently erected temple of our jurisprudence."[10] Kent understood that in a legal system governed by precedent preparation of a written opinion reflecting thought and research would give a judicial author a comparative advantage over those of his brethren who had not prepared their positions with equal care. He also understood that it was important to get his opinions published, and accordingly he obtained the services of his friend, William Johnson, who began publishing and selling *Johnson's Reports* commercially. Within a decade, Kent's concern that New York precedent did not exist and hence that nobody knew the law was alleviated.

Under Federalist guidance, other northeastern states quickly followed New York's lead. Theodore Sedgwick, it will be recalled, had been Speaker of the House of Representatives during the Adams administration, when a committee had been formed to consider reform and expansion of the federal judiciary. Sedgwick undoubtedly participated in discussions with the Federalist members of that committee. Following the Jeffersonian triumph in 1800, Sedgwick retired from national politics and turned his attention to his own state, Massachusetts. Probably agreeing with Fisher Ames that the Federalists might "need the state tribunals as sanctuaries when Jacobinism comes to rob and slay,"[11] he obtained an appointment to the Massachusetts Supreme Judicial Court.

Once on the court, Sedgwick emulated Kent's plan. First, he sought a change in the court's practice of having all its judges ride circuit together and resolve questions of law at the session at which they arose. He proposed that judges ride circuit individually to preside over trials and then assemble together at special law terms, where a library would be available and the court would have time to study the issues presented. The legislature approved Sedgwick's plan in 1804–1805. The first volume of published *Massachusetts Reports* also appeared at the same time. The two developments quickly gave birth to a body of decisional law for the Commonwealth.

The Federalist plan for seizing control of the law from the lay public and placing it in the hands of legal professionals was carried out from state to state in the early years of the nineteenth century. Another leading Federalist was Jeremiah Smith, whom President John Adams had appointed under the Judiciary Act of 1801 as a federal circuit judge for New Hampshire. But, when the Jeffersonians repealed the legislation that had created Smith's judgeship and it became clear that Smith would never serve on the federal bench, he instead became chief justice of New Hampshire. His first step in professionalizing the law of his own state was to have issues of law resolved by the full court meeting in law terms. Although there were attempts to undo Smith's work both in the legislature and among his successors on the bench, the attempts were largely unsuccessful, and by 1810, the trend in New Hampshire was toward greater judicial control of the law.

The Federalists, of course, did not dominate politics in every state, and where they did not, Jeffersonians determined the course of judicial reform. In Kentucky, for example, where radical Jeffersonians who believed in democratic localism controlled the state legislature, the opposite of the Federalist platform was enacted: the judiciary was decentralized and deprofessionalized. Each county was given a circuit court, consisting of one legally trained circuit judge and two lay assistants who could and often did outvote him, and the circuit judges were given little opportunity to communicate with each other so as to maintain legal uniformity throughout the state. This system remained in place for fifteen years following its adoption in 1801. Similarly in Ohio, radical Jeffersonians in 1809 defeated a proposal to reduce the number of judges on the state's Supreme Court so as to make it better able to settle definitively the state's common law. Nonetheless by the 1820s, when regular publication of Supreme Court opinions began, the Ohio court had developed into an institution comparable to the highest courts of Massachusetts and New York.

A radical Jeffersonian majority in the state legislature also stymied Federalist efforts in Pennsylvania. The radicals found the legal profession a subject of concern. As they declared:

> [T]he loose principles of persons of that profession; their practice of defending right and wrong indifferently, for reward; their open enmity to the principles of free government, because free government is irreconcilable to the abuses upon which they thrive; the tyranny which they display in the courts; and in too many cases the too obvious understanding and collusion which prevails among the members of the *bench*, the *bar*, and the *officers* of the court, demand the most serious interference of the legislature, and the jealousy of the people.[12]

In 1805, however, a coalition of moderate Jeffersonians and Federalists won the governorship and control of the Pennsylvania legislature. In 1806, the coalition enacted legislation increasing the number of trial courts, limiting the original jurisdiction of the state's supreme court, and requiring it to hear appeals on issues of law annually in Pittsburgh and twice a year in Philadelphia. Judicial decisions already were being published, and a Federalist, William Tilghman, was appointed chief justice of the state's highest court. Tilghman remained chief justice for the next twenty-one years, over the course of which he consolidated the various changes instituted after the 1805 election.

The picture of change is somewhat more hazy in Virginia. It appears that between 1787 and 1809, county courts, which were a carryover from the colonial era and which continued to be staffed by lay judges, were gradually superceded by district and later superior courts, the judges of which were professional lawyers. Legislation also established a Supreme Court of Appeals, which could impose state-wide solutions to the legal issues that professional judges confronted on circuit. Developments in Virginia thus seem parallel to those in the North, but considerable archival research is needed to know for sure.

Similar research is required to know even vaguely what occurred in many other states. Nonetheless, it is clear that in the first decade of the nineteenth century Federalists, with the support of the business community and with help, in states like Pennsylvania, from moderate Jeffersonians, began to put the program of judicial reform elaborated most explicitly by James Kent into place in every major coastal state north of the Mason-Dixon line. Issues of law were reserved for state appellate courts, which began to resolve those issues with a single voice and with published opinions. Law was coming to be seen as a profession and judges as leaders of the profession, who should be drawn from among those possessing the highest professional attainments.

Comparable developments occurred at the federal level. When Congress first established federal courts in 1789, it had followed the model of most states and provided that Supreme Court justices would ride circuit around the new nation and sit with local district judges on the principal federal trial courts, which were called circuit courts. Assigning Supreme Court justices to circuit riding and allowing them to decide questions of law on circuit made federal courts in the 1790s much like other eighteenth-century courts. It deprived the justices of the benefit of an unprejudiced consultation among themselves that might have led to a single opinion that would have committed the Court to a permanent, reasoned view of the law. Instead, "in more than one Instance . . . Questions in the Circuit Court decided by one Set of Judges in the *affirmative*, ha[d] afterwards . . . been decided by others in the *negative*,"[13] which, in turn, "tend[ed] to render the law unsettled and uncertain, and thereby to create apprehension and diffidence in the public mind."[14]

Thus, the judicial reform committee on which John Marshall and other leading Federalists sat in 1799 had sought to separate the justices of the Supreme Court from the judges of the circuit courts. It achieved that end when it proposed and Congress adopted the Judiciary Act of 1801, which created new circuit courts on which Supreme Court justices did not sit. The 1801 act never took effect, however, because the new Congress elected with Thomas Jefferson in 1800 promptly enacted the Judiciary Act of 1802, which repealed the 1801 act. With the repeal, Chief Justice Marshall could do nothing to keep himself and his fellow justices from riding circuit. But he could and did take other steps to put into place the Federalist program of creating permanent, well reasoned, and centralized law.

He took a first step in the spring of 1802, after Congress had repealed the Judiciary Act of 1801 and restored the older circuit-riding duties of the justices. The justices then had to decide whether to obey Congress's command to ride circuit—"a subject," in Marshall's words, "not to be lightly resolved on."[15] "The burthen of deciding so momentous a question . . . would be very great on all the Judges assembled: but an individual Judge . . . must sink under it."[16] Marshall accordingly proposed that the justices communicate with each other by letter, act collectively if they could reach agreement on whether or not to resume circuit duties, and meet in Washington if they could not.

With the immediate crisis resolved after 1803, Marshall instituted more permanent practices to insure the Court's collegiality and cooperation. He arranged, for example, to have all the justices board and dine together during session in the same hotel or inn. There they engaged constantly in the discussion of pending matters in order to come to a consensus; as Marshall wrote in turning down a dinner invitation, he could "not absent myself from our daily consultation without interrupting the course of the business."[17] Marshall also abolished seriatim opinions by Supreme Court justices and instituted the practice of having the Court formulate a single opinion in private and then issue it as the opinion of all. Until 1812, Marshall, as chief justice, or whatever justice was presiding in his absence, almost invariably announced the opinion of the Court, whether or not he had written it.

The chief justice also discouraged dissents because he appreciated how "the habit of delivering dissenting opinions . . . weaken[ed] the authority of the Court, and [was] of no public benefit."[18] When William Johnson, the first Jeffersonian appointed to the Court delivered his first dissent, "during the rest of the session I heard nothing but lectures on the indecency of judges cutting at each other, and the loss of reputation which the Virginia appellate court had sustained by pursuing such a course, etc. At length I found I must either submit . . . or become a cypher in our consultations as to effect no good at all. I therefore bent to the current."[19]

Thus, even when the majority of the Court sometimes disagreed with a point made in a Marshall opinion, it suppressed its disagreement. Marshall, in turn, wrote and delivered opinions with which he did not fully agree, and he almost never dissented—only eight times, and just once in a constitutional case, during his thirty-four years on the bench. Marshall, as well as anyone, knew that, in order to give law the intellectual respectability and political power he wanted it to have, judges had to work together to formulate rules on which all could place their imprimatur. In the course of the first decade of the nineteenth century, in the federal courts as well as the states, judges developed the practice of doing so.

The Judicial Seizure of Lawfinding Power

It was not enough, however, simply to transform the judiciary into a cohesive, professional entity that could proclaim law in a well-reasoned, coherent fashion. It also was necessary to deprive juries of the power they had inherited from the eighteenth century to reject judge-made law and thereby treat it as something less than a uniform norm binding all.

The earliest efforts to tame juries occurred in politically charged prosecutions against pro-Jeffersonian newspaper editors under the Sedition Act of 1798. By this act, the Federalists who controlled Congress sought to silence the raucous political criticism of the Adams administration occurring at a time when the United States was threatened with war with France and perhaps even foreign invasion. Accordingly, the 1798 act made criticism of the government a federal crime.

Of course, the Jeffersonian Republican opposition claimed that the Sedition Act was an unconstitutional violation of the First Amendment's clause protecting freedom of the press. Jefferson and his main coworker, James Madison, pursued their argument of unconstitutionality in the Kentucky and Virginia Resolutions of 1798, in the presidential election of 1800, and in other political forums. Meanwhile, Jeffersonian editors who were indicted under the act raised the claim of unconstitutionality as a legal defense to the government's prosecutions.

Federalist judges who tried the proceedings were concerned that juries might accept defendants' arguments. If they did, the Jeffersonian editors would be acquitted and raucous political debate legitimated. Thus, the Federalist judges began to abandon eighteenth-century understandings about jury power and to instruct juries that legal issues about the constitutionality of the Sedition Act were solely for the courts.

The first to speak, although somewhat confusingly, was Supreme Court Justice William Paterson while riding circuit in Vermont in October 1798. In a case arising out of an indictment against a Republican congressman and newspaper editor, Matthew Lyon, Justice Paterson directed the jury that it must treat the Sedition Act as constitutional, unless and until it was "declared null and void by a tribunal competent for the purpose"[20]—namely, a court. Although the jury in this criminal case, by virtue of its capacity to return a general verdict of not guilty, had power to ignore Paterson's instruction, the justice did not so inform the jury. He certainly did not tell the jury, as Chief Justice Jay had instructed jurors merely six years earlier in *Georgia v. Brailsford*,[21] that they had a right to ignore his charge. On the other hand, Paterson was not yet ready to restrict jury power in all cases: only a few days before his charge in the *Lyon* case, he had told a different jury in a land confiscation case that both "courts and juries were the proper bodies to decide on the constitutionality of laws."[22]

Justice Samuel Chase took a more consistent position restricting juries while riding circuit in 1800 and trying two highly publicized criminal cases. He began when, in late April, he told a grand jury in Pennsylvania that "the Judges of the Supreme, and District Courts are bound by their *Oath of Office*, to regulate Decisions *agreeably to the Constitution*. The Judicial power, therefore, are the only *proper* and *competent* authority to decide whether any Law made by Congress; or any of the State Legislatures is contrary to or in Violation of the *federal* Constitution."[23]

He applied this view several days later during the treason trial of John Fries, who had led an armed mob in a protest against payment of a federal tax on windows.

Fries had been tried and convicted for treason at the previous term of court, but the conviction had been set aside for procedural reasons and a new trial ordered. At the first trial, counsel had argued the law to the jury, maintaining that mere resistance to the collection of taxes did not amount to levying war against the United States and thus did not constitute treason. At the retrial, however, it soon became clear that Justice Chase did not plan to permit counsel to make that argument again.

As the proceedings opened, Chase handed out three copies of a written opinion—one to defense counsel, one to the prosecutor, and one to the jury—containing his analysis of the law of treason. Although Chase said he was "*willing* and *desirous to hear*" counsel's argument on the law, which could be presented "either with the Jury or any other Way," he also indicated that "he would not permit improper or irrelevant authorities" to be offered. He declared that he had adopted his opinion "on great Consideration it having been settled by the Judges who still continued in that opinion"[24] and that he believed it his duty "to guard the jury against erroneous impressions regarding the law of the land."[25]

A month later, at the seditious libel prosecution of James T. Callender in the circuit court in Richmond, Virginia,[26] Justice Chase again interrupted counsel and delivered a prepared opinion. When counsel for the defense rose to urge the jury that the Sedition Act was unconstitutional, Chase twice interrupted him and finally ordered him to take his seat. Chase then delivered his opinion, which he called "the result of mature reflection,"[27] upholding the act's constitutionality as a matter of law, denying the right of the jury to consider the issue, and refusing to allow counsel to argue it.

Chase began his opinion by admitting that the jury had "a right . . . to determine what the law is in the case before them." But this meant only that the jury should "compare the statute with the facts proved, and then . . . decide whether the acts done are prohibited by the law. . . . This power," according to Chase, "the jury necessarily possesses, in order to enable them to decide on the guilt or innocence of the person accused."[28]

The power to fit the facts within the law was "a very different thing," however, from the power "to determine that the statute produced is no law." And Chase could "not conceive"—could "not possibly believe"—that Congress "intended" by the sedition act "to grant a right to a petit jury to declare a statute void." Indeed, he found the claim for jury power "entirely novel" and "very absurd and dangerous, in direct opposition to, and a breach of the constitution." He explained, in language reminiscent of the holding of the judges in *Moore v. Cherry*:

> If this power be once admitted, petit jurors will be superior to the national legislature, and its laws will be subject to their control. . . . The evident consequences of this right in juries will be, that a law of congress will be in operation in one state and not in another. A law to impose taxes will be obeyed in one state, and not in another, unless force be employed to compel submission. . . . It appears to me that the right now claimed has a direct tendency to dissolve the union of the United States.

In contrast, "the decisions in the district or circuit courts of the United States w[ould] be uniform, or they w[ould] become so by the revision and correction of the supreme court."[29] There is no question that Chase's preparation and delivery of written opinions as soon as the issue of jury lawfinding power arose was novel, and Jeffersonian Republicans, who were livid at the practice, later impeached Chase for engaging in it. Chase, however, was not alone in taking this new approach.

Theodore Sedgwick, the former Speaker of the House of Representatives who became a justice of the Massachusetts Supreme Judicial Court, also campaigned to put an end to the power of juries to determine law. But, unlike Justice Chase, Sedgwick's reasons were not overtly political; rather, his objective was to facilitate business and promote economic growth. As he argued, "In all instances where trial by jury has been practiced, and a separation of the law from the fact has taken place, there has been expedition, certainty, system and their consequences, general approbation. Where this has not been the case, neither expedition, certainty nor system have prevailed."[30]

An emerging class of New England entrepreneurs, who needed to plan their investment strategies, agreed. Businesses were disturbed at having their rights and liabilities determined by "the fluctuating estimates of juries,"[31] whose "utterly indefinite and uncertain behavior" provided investors with "no rule for their future conduct."[32] Counsel accordingly argued "that juries ought by the court to be restrained and kept within the proper and established rules,"[33] and by the end of the first decade of the nineteenth century, the verdicts of Massachusetts juries were being set aside routinely when they were contrary to law or to the evidence.

Other states followed along. In New Hampshire, for example, Jeremiah Smith ended the practice of having two or more judges deliver often conflicting instructions and thereby leave juries free to reach verdicts without proper legal guidance in response to "local prejudice, popular clamor, and party spirit."[34] Aided by statutes passed in 1804 and 1808, he was then able to assert the court's power to set aside jury verdicts that were contrary to law or evidence. A more important state was New York, where James Kent's plan was to deprive the jury of its power to find law and restrict it only to the facts. No clear evidence exists of how this plan was accomplished, but by 1804, at the latest, the civil jury had been tamed, as courts were routinely granting new trials in civil cases where the jury had ignored the court's instructions. In the same year, the Supreme Court also heard an appeal in *People v. Croswell*,[35] a seditious libel case in which the trial court had instructed the jury that it had no power to determine the law and the jury had returned a verdict of guilty. Although the Supreme Court affirmed the verdict, the legislature responded with a statute authorizing juries to find law in criminal libel cases in the future.

Similarly, in 1806 in Pennsylvania, Chief Justice William Tilghman upheld the power of the court to grant a new trial when the jury had decided against law and the weight of the evidence; even counsel arguing in favor of upholding the verdict recognized the need to tame juries by conceding that, "[w]hen juries assume upon themselves to decide against the known law, they become as dangerous as any set of tyrants, and all certainty and security in the administration of justice are banished from society, unless the judges interpose their summary powers."[36] A radical 1811 anti-lawyer tract in Virginia, proposing "that jury trials be restored to a place of eminence,"[37] also suggests that Virginia had reduced the power of juries during the preceding decade.

Assuming that Chief Justice Marshall's work on circuit was typical, federal courts also were depriving juries of their lawfinding power. Four cases that Marshall heard while riding circuit during the time span from December 1802 to December 1803 show that he was prepared to set aside verdicts when juries in civil cases misapplied the law or considered inappropriate evidence.[38] Soon after, in a January 1805 letter to Justice Samuel Chase, Marshall simply took for granted the propriety of granting a "new trial" for "a jury finding a verdict against the law of the case,"[39] and in a published 1811 opinion, *Letcher & Arnold v. Woodson*, he explicitly stated that if "a jury . . . find a verdict against law," the court had power to "set it aside and award a new trial."[40]

Despite these developments, the right of juries to find law was by no means completely destroyed by 1810. Proponents of popular democracy kept it alive in criminal cases through most of the nineteenth century, and in states like Kentucky, where radical Jeffersonian Republicans held sway, they preserved jury power for a while in civil cases as well. But the trend toward today's practice, where judges instruct juries on the law and do their best to insure that juries follow their instructions, had clearly begun.

The Emergence of Professional Legal Education

A third development at the outset of the nineteenth century, and one that would have immense importance in the distant future, was the emergence of the nation's first law school. Sometime after the Revolutionary War, Tapping Reeve, who later became a Federalist judge on the Connecticut Supreme Court, began taking young men into his law office as apprentices. Studying law in the office of an established attorney was the typical manner in which youths prepared for the bar in the eighteenth century; with his earliest students, Reeve was doing nothing unusual. But during the 1790s, as Reeve took on increasing numbers of students, his office became increasingly less of a vehicle for serving clients and more of an entity for training lawyers. Litchfield, that is, became the nation's first law school, and in the next decade it progressed from a local into a national institution designed to train future leaders of the profession not only for New England but for the nation as a whole.

Reeve, and his associate, James Gould, used their school "to forward a Federalist conception of the proper role of law in society and the proper organization of society more generally." In particular, they understood that the "laws of a given society [were] not the arbitrary determinations . . . of people, but an expression of a 'permanent, uniform and universal' code."[41] Their vision was part and parcel of the larger Federalist vision, shared by men like James Kent and Theodore Sedgwick, of seizing law from juries and recasting it into a technical body of precedent accessible only to lawyers and judges who had received the education necessary to understand and manipulate it. Along with other Federalists, Reeve and Gould thus sought to transform law from a community enterprise of ordinary men into a rigorous intellectual discipline for trained professionals.

Their law school also served an important social function. Down the street from a finishing school for young women, the Litchfield Law School became a marriage market, to which elite families sent their sons to meet the elite young women of the finishing school. National networks of power grew out of Litchfield, as its graduates went back home and became members of Congress, state officials, and especially judges.

The Litchfield Law School thrived into the 1820s, and, when it declined, Supreme Court Justice Joseph Story became the first Dane Professor of Law at

Harvard and began creating, essentially on the model of Litchfield, what would become the paradigm for American legal education today. Yet Litchfield's influence should not be overestimated, at least in its own time. There were other mid-nineteenth-century law schools, like Transylvania in Kentucky and New York University in New York, with a more democratic spirit and curriculum. Moreover, most nineteenth-century lawyers, like Abraham Lincoln, did not attend law school at all but prepared for the bar by reading law in an established attorney's office. For many decades, law remained a career open to anyone willing to do a little reading. While professional elites took control of legal education, of the federal courts, and of appellate courts, especially in the coastal states of New England and the mid-Atlantic, a more populist reality of justice remained in place in trial courts, especially in the South and the West.

Judicial Review of the Constitutionality of Legislation

At this point, a summary might be useful. After the American Revolution gave forces of populist, majoritarian democracy control of state governments, some political leaders grew concerned that majorities were trampling on the fundamental rights of minorities. These leaders played a major role in the adoption of the Constitution of 1787, which can be understood as a device for placing checks and balances in the path of majoritarian, democratic change even while conceding the ultimate power of the people to govern themselves as they will. But the Constitution's checks and balances failed, as new forms of organization invigorated majoritarian democracy even at the level of national politics. The election of 1800 demonstrated that a majority party could place its man in the presidency and gain sufficient control of Congress to enact any legislative program it wished.

At that point, antidemocratic reactionaries turned to the judiciary. If they could not control the making of law, they could try to control its interpretation and application. They could deprive juries, the democratic element in the judicial process, of their power to find and apply law and compel those juries to obey the instructions they received from the judges. They could turn law itself into a body of knowledge accessible only to professional elites trained in law schools to which only the wealthy could afford to send their sons. They could strive to insure that only leading members of the professional elite ascended the bench.

Although they did not succeed entirely, the forces opposed to populist, majoritarian democracy enjoyed remarkable success during the first decades of the nineteenth century in transforming law from a community enterprise of ordinary men into a rigorous intellectual discipline for trained professionals only. But one further obstacle blocked their path to removing the people from power—namely, the capacity of majorities to make law through legislation. Here too, High Federalists had an answer. Their answer was a stringent form of judicial review giving judges power to hold legislation unconstitutional whenever the judges disagreed with the legislature's policies.

In an effort to impose this broad vision of judicial review, the Federalist bar brought a test case, *Stuart v. Laird*.[42] It challenged the constitutionality of the Judiciary Act of 1802, by which the Jeffersonian Congress had repealed the Federalists' Judiciary Act of 1801. In *Stuart* and its companion case of *Marbury v. Madison*,[43] the High Federalists lost.

The Judiciary Act of 1801 was a key element in the reactionaries' plan to use the courts to obstruct democratic majoritarianism. It increased federal jurisdiction, created new federal judgeships that were filled by reliable Federalist lawyers, separated the Supreme Court from the lower courts in an effort to make the High Court into a cohesive appellate body capable of establishing a sound body of national law, and took preliminary steps to rein in juries. But, as soon as the Congress elected with Jefferson in 1800 met, it adopted the Judiciary Act of 1802, which repealed the 1801 act and transferred all cases pending in courts established by the 1801 act back to the courts that had existed under the 1789 Judiciary Act. *Stuart v. Laird* came to the Supreme Court when one of its parties claimed that the transfer of his case was void because the 1802 act was unconstitutional.

The Supreme Court, in a brief opinion by Justice William Paterson, rejected the claim. Paterson's specific reasons for upholding the 1802 act are not important. What really explains the decision in *Stuart* is the analysis of judicial review which Chief Justice John Marshall had announced six days earlier in *Marbury v. Madison*.

Marbury is a complicated and elusive, but centrally important case. It arose out of another act of Congress passed in conjunction with the 1801 Judiciary Act—an act creating courts for the District of Columbia. President Adams had packed these courts, like other new courts, with Federalists. Unfortunately, Secretary of State John Marshall had failed to deliver the commission of William Marbury, one of the new Justices of the Peace for the District, before the end of President Adams's term, and James Madison, the new Secretary of State, refused to make the uncompleted delivery. When Marbury brought a suit in the Supreme Court for an order directing Madison to deliver his commission, the case of *Marbury v. Madison* began.

Marbury v. Madison, along with *Stuart v. Laird*, threatened to create a direct confrontation between the Federalist judiciary left over from the Adams administration and the new Congress elected with Jefferson. But the Supreme Court, under the leadership of its new Chief Justice, John Marshall, wanted no confrontation. Although Marshall was prepared, as he wrote, to "disregard" the pressures of partisan politics when they were "put in competition with . . . his duty" to uphold the law,[44] he and his fellow Federalist justices, with the possible exception of Justice Samuel Chase, were not elitist antidemocrats, and they appreciated fully "[t]he consequences of refusing to carry . . . into effect" a law enacted by a determined popular majority.[45]

Marshall and the other justices, in short, rejected the High Federalist position, which the Court would only adopt a century and a half later in efforts to enforce *Brown v. Board of Education*. *Marbury* did not declare the Supreme Court to be the ultimate arbiter of the nation's constitutional policy choices, with power to bind coordinate branches of government to its judgments and thereby invalidate popularly supported choices with which it disagreed. *Marbury v. Madison* and *Stuart v. Laird* were narrower decisions that strove to harmonize majoritarian democracy and legal principle, not to make one either superior or subordinate to the other.

Chief Justice Marshall attained this goal in *Marbury* and *Stuart* by demarcating the domain of politics, where issues are resolved by the legislative and executive branches in response to the democratic will of the majority of the people, from the domain of law, where impartial judges resolve issues by recourse to established rules. Marshall used this distinction between law and politics to explain why the Supreme Court, even in the exercise of the power of judicial review, would not become a superlegislature that would invalidate policies adopted by Congress or the president. As *Marbury* declared, "political" matters "respecting the nation, not individual rights" were governed by the political branches, whose decisions were "never . . . examinable by the courts," but "only politically examinable."

Marbury, however, also announced that the Court would protect legal rights. Thus, the case held that President Adams's signature on William Marbury's commission completed Marbury's appointment to the office of justice of the peace and conferred on him "a vested legal right" to his commission—a right analogous to a right to land or other property. Marshall also ruled that in cases involving "the rights of individuals," every officer of government was "amenable to the laws for his conduct; and [could not] at his discretion sport away . . . vested rights . . .," and that a person such as Marbury who possessed a vested right was entitled to a remedy. In Marshall's own words, "[t]he very essence of civil liberty certainly consists in the right of every individual to claim the protection of the laws, whenever he receives an injury."

But was Marbury entitled to the specific remedy for which he had sued—a writ of mandamus issued by the Supreme Court of the United States in a suit commenced before it? The Judiciary Act of 1789 empowered the Court to grant writs of mandamus, but the judiciary article of the Constitution created a problem, in that it limited the original jurisdiction of the Supreme Court to designated classes of cases, of which mandamus was not one. In order for the Court to issue the writ, it thus would have to reach one of two conclusions: either that Congress could grant original jurisdiction to the Supreme Court in cases in which the Constitution denied it, or that an action for mandamus in the Supreme Court was not an original proceeding but rather an appeal from the official against whom the writ was being sought.

It is significant that Marbury's lawyer did not press the argument that granting mandamus would constitute an exercise of original jurisdiction by the Court. Instead, he argued mainly that the Court would exercise its appellate jurisdiction by issuing mandamus on Marbury's behalf. According to the thrust of his argument, which was based on an accurate reading of *Federalist* No. 81, "the word 'appellate' [was] not to be taken in its technical sense, . . . but in its broadest sense, in which it denotes nothing more than the power of one tribunal" to have "by reason of its supremacy . . . the superintendence of . . . inferior tribunals and officers, whether judicial or ministerial." In 1803, when the concept of appeal had not yet assumed its modern meaning, this argument was plausible, and a court eager to grant Marbury relief could easily have accepted it.

However, accepting the argument would have contradicted Marshall's distinction between law and politics. By authorizing the Court to "revis[e] and correct the proceedings in a cause already instituted" in the executive branch, counsel's argument threatened to bring before the Court all the issues—of law, of fact, and of politics—that the executive branch had previously considered and to present to the Court political questions of executive motive. To dodge this threat and to insure that the Court serve as the purely legal institution he envisioned, Marshall had to consider a mandamus against officials, as distinguished from a mandamus against lower court judges, as an original action in which the court granting the writ could confine the action's scope to properly legal rather than political matters. Thus, he rejected the claim that mandamus was a direct appeal from the executive to the Supreme Court.

That brought Chief Justice Marshall to the issue of whether Congress could grant the Supreme Court jurisdiction which the Constitution denied it. His answer was that Congress could not violate the Constitution and that the section of the 1789 Judiciary Act giving original jurisdiction in cases of mandamus was therefore unconstitutional.

This recourse to judicial review may strike many readers at the outset of the twenty-first century as even more political than granting the writ to Marbury would have been. But it was not. In 1803, the Marshall Court's assumption of the power of judicial review was hardly unprecedented; judicial review already had been widely accepted by most state courts. Moreover, Marshall did not rationalize judicial review as courts do today. He did not invoke the language of natural rights, rely on precedent or other prior judicial authority, or turn to principles that either were made by or required interpretation by judges. That is, judicial review as Marshall understood it did not place judicially administered policy values in conflict with the democratic will of the people.

Above all, the Marshall Court recognized that it could not overturn policies on which the political branches insisted. In *Marbury*, it saw that issuing a writ of mandamus directing Secretary of State Madison to put Marbury in office would have forced a confrontation between the Court and the Jefferson administration; Madison undoubtedly would have refused to obey the Court's order, and Congress might even have impeached Chief Justice Marshall and removed him from office. Six days later in *Stuart v. Laird*, the Court similarly saw that invalidating the 1802 Judiciary Act would have embroiled it in a political contest with Congress and the president that it might not have survived. If the Court was to withdraw from politics, as Marshall had said in *Marbury* it would, prudence dictated that it must capitulate to legislative judgments upon such politically controversial issues as William Marbury's appointment to the bench and the constitutionality of the 1802 Judiciary Act.

The Marshall Court's decision of *Stuart* and *Marbury* completely undercut the agenda of Jefferson's reactionary, antidemocratic Federalist opponents. Instead, the two cases revived a more nuanced democratic conservatism in which the older Federalists of 1787–1788 had believed. Unlike Jeffersonian populists, conservative democrats like John Marshall understood that law, professionally understood and interpreted, preexisted popular will. But, unlike reactionary antidemocratic Federalists, Marshall also understood that legislatures could make political judgments and hence change law by majority vote. While judges could invalidate legislation that trampled thoughtlessly on what all Americans knew to be fundamental rights, like the right to property, judicial review, as Marshall proclaimed it, could at most slow a determined majority down. The reason was that all issues ultimately could be politicized; *Stuart v. Laird* showed that, if Congress was sufficiently determined to do what the majority of the people wanted, the Supreme Court would not stand in its way.

Marbury and *Stuart* were not unique in the limited role they envisioned for judicial review. For more than five decades after *Marbury*, every federal statute challenged in the courts ultimately was upheld, while nearly every politically significant state statute passed muster in the state courts. Two cases, one in the lower federal courts, and one in the state courts, will illustrate.

United States v. The William[46] was a federal case in which John Davis, a district judge named to the bench by John Adams, upheld the constitutionality of the Jefferson administration's Embargo Act of 1807. The act reflected a major foreign policy initiative by President Jefferson, who hoped by keeping American vessels off the high seas to prevent their capture by British or French warships or privateers and thus to avoid incidents that could result in war with either power. The embargo, however, seriously damaged New England shipping interests and induced New England merchants to avoid its impact by turning to smuggling. The case of *The William* arose when federal officials seized and condemned a ship carrying allegedly smuggled goods.

Without citing either *Marbury v. Madison* or *Stuart v. Laird*, the district court arrived at a similar result. Distinguishing between legal discretion and political discretion, Judge Davis wrote:

> Legal discretion has not the means of ascertaining the grounds, on which political discretion may have proceeded. . . . [H]ow shall legal discretion determine, that political discretion, surveying the vast concerns committed to its trust, and the movements of conflicting nations, has not perceived such necessity to exist? Considerations of this nature have induced a doubt of the competency, or constitutional authority of the court, to decide an act invalid in a case of this description.

Accordingly, the court held the 1807 embargo constitutional.

In addition to drawing a line between law and politics, *The William* followed *Marbury* and *Stuart* in another respect. In *Marbury* and *Stuart*, as has been shown, Chief Justice Marshall, a Federalist, declined to adopt the position advocated by his party and thereby avoided conflict with Jeffersonian Republicans, who were advancing a political agenda they deemed important. Similarly, in *The William*, Judge Davis, another Federalist, rejected an argument about the unconstitutionality of the 1807 embargo that Massachusetts Federalists were advancing and thereby avoided a political battle with the Jefferson administration and its congressional backers. To have done otherwise would have belied claims that the courts should remain out of politics.

The state-court case that similarly avoided political decision making was *Adams v. Howe*.[47] This case, which addressed divisive issues of religious taxation and hence religious establishment in Massachusetts, reflected both *Marbury*'s and *The William*'s distinction between law and politics, although the *Adams* case cited neither precedent.

The *Adams* case required the highest court of Massachusetts to interpret the state's constitution of 1780, which had directed the legislature to make provision for the public worship of God in every town in the commonwealth. During the early 1780s the Massachusetts courts had worked out a compromise interpretation of its meaning, under which all religious groups had functioned for a quarter century. Congregationalists, who in the 1780s had constituted the majority of the population, had received control of parish institutions and dissenters had been required to pay taxes levied by the parish. But, pursuant to the 1785 case of *Murray v. First Parish in Gloucester*,[48] dissenters who were organized in congregations, whether incorporated or not, could direct that their taxes be paid to any full-time clergyman they employed. Although dissenters were required to pay taxes, they thus were placed nearly on a par with Congregationalists since their taxes, like the taxes of Congregationalists, could be used only to support their own sect.

Then, in 1810, Chief Justice Theophilus Parsons, who had been counsel for the Congregationalist parish in the *Murray* case, decided *Barnes v. First Parish in Falmouth*.[49] *Barnes*, in a strikingly partisan fashion, adopted the position for which Parsons had contended in *Murray*—namely, that dissenters' taxes could be paid over to their dissenting minister only if the congregation to which they belonged was incorporated. Since nearly all dissenting congregations were not incorporated, the *Barnes* decision had the effect of directing virtually all tax money into the hands of Congregational churches and thereby upsetting the stable consensus that had endured for nearly three decades. But rather than strengthening the establishment the *Barnes* decision provoked its downfall, for it politicized establishment law, induced dissenters to turn to politics, and, following their victory in the 1811 elections, enabled them to obtain legislative action.

Although the religious establishment in Massachusetts officially endured until 1833, the Religious Freedom Act of 1811 in practice destroyed it. The act, in which the legislature sought to clarify the provisions of the constitution on which the courts had been basing their decisions since the 1780s, overruled nearly all of those decisions and constituted a complete victory for the dissenters. And, in *Adams v. Howe*, the Supreme Judicial Court in an opinion by a new chief justice, Isaac Parker, sustained its constitutionality.

As already noted, the scope of the religious establishment had become the principal question in Massachusetts politics in 1810–1811, as the Jeffersonians campaigned against the *Barnes* decision to win both the governorship and a majority in the legislature for the first time in history. Three decades of settled law had been overruled by *Barnes*, and no court could hope to revive it. Meanwhile, the electorate had pushed matters in a new direction. Anyone looking to Chief Justice Marshall's distinction in *Marbury* between law, defined as fixed, widely accepted, impartial principles, and politics, defined as the process by which the electorate makes policy choices, knew that the issue in *Adams* was a political one that no court could decide.

Of course, the central fact in *Adams v. Howe*, as in *Marbury v. Madison* and *United States v. The William*, was that the judiciary lacked power to confront the people and to overturn a considered judgment that the people had made through the electoral process. After the people had rejected the Court's attempt in *Barnes* to turn the clock back, the Court had no choice but to follow the people into the future.

Adams v. Howe thus replicated in microcosm at the state level what had occurred in *Marbury v. Madison* at the federal. First the Massachusetts court in the *Barnes* case had allowed itself to be drawn into politics and had thereby undermined the law, just as the federal judiciary had done with its activism in the sedition prosecutions of the late 1790s. The court then recognized that it had to limit itself to deciding only questions of law and to leave issues of policy choice to the people. Emulating the Supreme Court of the United States, the Massachusetts court adopted the common method of early nineteenth-century judges and accepted the policy choice of the political process. With the law bequeathed by *Murray v. First Parish in Gloucester* obliterated by the Court's own decision in *Barnes v. First Parish in Falmouth*, the judges had no choice but to acknowledge that the issue of religious taxation had become a political one for which accepted legal standards no longer existed.

Of course, in a federal system that soon after 1800 had more than twenty states, the judicial review, even of the modest sort proclaimed by Marshall in *Marbury v. Madison* and adopted by lower courts in *United States v. The William* and *Adams v. Howe*, did not emerge uniformly. In Ohio, for example, the state Supreme Court's announcement of its power of judicial review in *Rutherford v. M'Faddon*[50] produced an unsuccessful effort to remove the offending judges through the impeachment process—an effort followed by legislation that reorganized the courts and replaced the offending judges with new ones. Likewise in Kentucky, an unpopular decision invalidating a state law led the legislature to abolish the offending court and replace it with a new one; when the old court refused to stop sitting, Kentucky for several years found itself with two competing high courts. New Hampshire also had rival appellate courts functioning for several years, while in Georgia, where the state's judges had met in a conference and declared debtor relief legislation unconstitutional, the legislature directed the judges to cease holding conferences. Meanwhile, as late as 1825 in the case of *Eakin v. Raub*,[51] John Bannister Gibson, a leading judge on the Pennsylvania Supreme Court, had dissented from the practice of judicial review.

Nonetheless, by the early nineteenth century the direction of development was clear. Judicial review, at least in the restrained form announced in *Marbury v. Madison*, was becoming an accepted practice of American constitutionalism.

The Rule of Law and the Two Visions of Democracy

While new concepts of judicial review, of the power of judges rather than juries to make law, and of the professionalization of law and legal education were slowly gaining acceptance, older ideas from the era of the American Revolution—ideas about the power of democratic majorities to make anything they want into law—persisted. Indeed, the idea of democracy as simple majority rule continues to persist today.

But an alternative idea of democracy also arose in the early nineteenth century. The alternative was grounded in the rule of law—in the assumption that, as a starting proposition, disputes in society should be resolved by professional judges, not lay judges or lay jurors, who had been thoroughly trained in traditional techniques of legal analysis of the precedents found in published case reports. This alternative remained democratic because it recognized the plenary power of popular majorities, through legislation, to alter established law. Although the doctrine of judicial review prevented majorities from trampling thoughtlessly on the inherited rights of minorities, courts always had a duty to defer to the will of the people when the people through democratic processes extending over time interpreted the constitution differently than did the judges; of course, they also had to defer to supermajorities who amended the constitution.

Judicial review as practiced in the early nineteenth century was simply different from judicial review as it is practiced today. Judges then did not understand, as judges do today, that they had power to choose among competing visions of social policy. Policy choice was a democratic job for the people. Judges could, at most, resolve constitutional ambiguities or enforce preexisting constitutional norms until the people made a determined decision to reject what the judges had done. Nineteenth-century judges were not without power at the margins, but the people remained firmly in control—they could reject whatever judges did, and they alone had power to take constitutional law in fundamentally new directions.

Brown v. Board of Education changed everything. Half a century earlier, *Plessy v. Ferguson*,[52] which interpreted the ambiguities of the Fourteenth Amendment to allow legally mandated segregation by race, had insured that African Americans would remain in the same position of racial subordination in which they had always lived in America. Thereafter Jim Crow had remained settled practice throughout the South.

When *Brown v. Board of Education* overruled this settled practice and moved constitutional law in a new direction of racial equality, the Court was acting in a fashion in which it had never acted before. *Brown* did not resolve a constitutional ambiguity or defer to the political branches and take constitutional law in some new direction demanded by the people. Instead, it made a policy judgment that Jim Crow was so profoundly unjust that it had to be ended, whatever the will of the people.

With *Brown*, the rule of law ceased to be what it had been throughout the nineteenth century—a baseline that courts administered until the people changed it. Judicially created constitutional doctrine instead became an instrument that could overturn a settled line of constitutional practice, without action by and even in opposition to the will of the democratic branches of government. And with that, the aspiration of High Federalists for the judiciary rather than the people ultimately to rule—an aspiration rejected by John Marshall and the nineteenth century—assumed center stage in American constitutional thought.

Notes

1. 347 U.S. 483 (1954).
2. John Adams, quoted in L. Kinvin Wroth and Hiller B. Zobel, eds., *The Legal Papers of John Adams* (Cambridge, Mass.: Harvard University Press, 1965), vol. 1, 230.
3. Charles F. Adams, ed., *The Works of John Adams* (Boston: Little, Brown, 1852), vol. 3, 481.
4. John Adams, quoted in Wroth and Zobel eds., *Legal Papers*, vol. 1, 229.
5. 1 Bay 269 (S.C. 1792).

6. William Kent, *Memoirs and Letters of James Kent, L.L.D.* (Boston: Little, Brown, 1898), 112–113.
7. *Id.* at 117.
8. *Id.* at 113–114.
9. *Id.* at 117.
10. *Id.* at 117.
11. Fisher Ames to Christopher Gore, Feb. 24, 1803, in Seth Ames, ed., *Works of Fisher Ames* (Boston, 1854), vol. 321, quoted in Ellis, *The Jeffersonian Crisis*, 188.
12. Jesse Higgins, *Sampson against the Philistines, or the Reformation of Lawsuits; and Justice Made Cheap, Speedy, and Brought Home to Every Man's Door; Agreeably to the Principles of the Ancient Trial By Jury, Before the Same was Innovated by Judges and Lawyers* (1805), quoted in Ellis, *Jeffersonian Crisis*, 177.
13. John Jay to Rufus King, December 19, 1793, quoted in Haskins and Johnson, *Foundations of Power*, 115.
14. The Chief Justice and the Associate Justices of the Supreme Court of the United States to the Congress of the United States, February 1794, quoted in Haskins and Johnson, *Foundations of Power*, 115, 116.
15. John Marshall to William Paterson, April 19, 1802, quoted in Haskins and Johnson, *Foundations of Power*, 170.
16. Samuel Chase to John Marshall, April 24, 1802, quoted in Haskins and Johnson, *Foundations of Power*, 172, 177.
17. John Marshall to John Randolph, March 4, 1816, quoted in Del Dickson, ed., *The Supreme Court in Conference (1940–1985)* (New York: Oxford University Press, 2001), 33.
18. Joseph Story to Henry Wheaton, quoted in Dickson, *Supreme Court in Conference*, 34.
19. William Johnson to Thomas Jefferson, December 10, 1822, quoted in Dickson, *Supreme Court in Conference*, 35.
20. Francis Wharton, *State Trials of the United States during the Administrations of Washington and Adams* (Philadelphia: Carey and Hart, 1849), 336.
21. 3 U.S. (3 Dall.) 1 (1792).
22. This charge was reported in the Philadelphia *Aurora*, November 9, 1798, quoted in Maeva Marcus, ed., *The Documentary History of the Supreme Court of the United States*, (New York: Columbia University Press, 1990), vol. 3, 236 n. 24.
23. Samuel Chase's Charge to the Grand Jury of the Circuit Court for the District of Pennsylvania, April 12, 1800, in Marcus, *Documentary History*, vol. 3, 408–412.
24. Richard Peters to Timothy Pickering, quoted in Stephen B. Presser, *The Original Misunderstanding: The English, the Americans and the Dialectic of Federalist Jurisprudence* (Durham, N.C.: Carolina Academic Press, 1991), 110–111.
25. Testimony of Alexander Dallas before United States Senate in the Impeachment of Samuel Chase, reported in *Case of Fries*, 9 Fed. Cas. 826, 941, 943–944 (1799–1800).
26. *United States v. Callender*, 25 Fed. Cas. 239 (C.C.D.Va. 1800).
27. Wharton, *supra* note 34, at 708-12, quoted in James Morton Smith, *Freedom's Fetters: The Alien and Sedition Laws and American Civil Liberties* (Ithaca, N.Y.: Cornell University Press, 1956), 354.
28. 25 Fed. Cas. at 255.

29. *Id.* at 255, 256, 257.
30. Quoted in Ellis, *Jeffersonian Crisis*, 190.
31. *Cogswell v. Essex Mill Corp.*, 23 Mass. (6 Pick.) 94, 96 (1828) (argument of counsel).
32. *Gay v. Whiting*, Norfolk County Court of Common Pleas, Dec. 1810, quoted in William E. Nelson, *Americanization of the Common Law: The Impact of Legal Change on Massachusetts Society, 1760–1830* (Cambridge, Mass.: Harvard University Press, 1975), 165.
33. *Wait v. M'Neil*, 7 Mass. 261, 262 (1811).
34. John H. Morison, *Life of the Hon. Jeremiah Smith, LL.D.* 189-90 (1845), quoted in John Phillip Reid, *Controlling the Law: Legal Politics in Early National New Hampshire* 118 (DeKalb, Ill.: Northern Illinois University Press, 2004), 118.
35. 3 Johns. Cas. 339 (1804). The case is analyzed in detail in Julius Goebel, Jr., ed., *The Law Practice of Alexander Hamilton: Documents and Commentary* (New York: Columbia University Press, 1964), vol. 1, 775–867.
36. 4 Yeates at 322.
37. Roeber, *Faithful Magistrates*, 242–243.
38. The cases are discussed in detail in William E. Nelson, "The Province of the Judiciary," *John Marshall Law Review* 37 (2004), 325.
39. John Marshall to Samuel Chase, January 23, 1805, in Hobson, ed., *Papers of John Marshall*, vol. 6, 347.
40. 1 Brock. 212, 216 (Circuit Ct. Va. 1811).
41. Andrew M. Siegel, "'To Learn and Make Respectable Hereafter': The Litchfield Law School in Cultural Context," *New York University Law Review* 73 (1998), 2012, 2014.
42. 5 U.S. (1 Cranch) 299 (1803).
43. 5 U.S. (1 Cranch) 137 (1803).
44. See John Marshall to William Paterson, April 19, 1802, quoted in Haskins and Johnson, *Foundations of Power*, 170.
45. John Marshall to William Paterson, April 19, 1802, quoted in Haskins and Johnson, *Foundations of Power*, 170.
46. 28 Fed. Cas. 614 (D.C.D. Mass. 1808).
47. 14 Mass. 340 (1817).
48. The *Murray* case, which is unreported, is discussed in Nelson, *Americanization of the Common Law*, 107–108.
49. 6 Mass. 401 (1810).
50. This case, which is not officially reported, is discussed in Donald F. Melhorn, Jr., *"Lest We Be Marshall'd": Judicial Powers and Politics in Ohio, 1806–1812* (Akron, Ohio: University of Akron Press, 2003), 35–46.
51. 12 S. & R. 330, 344 (Pa. 1825).
52. 163 U.S. 537 (1896).

Bibliography

Cornell, Saul. *The Other Founders: Anti-Federalism and the Dissenting Tradition in America, 1788–1828.* Chapel Hill: University of North Carolina Press, 1999.

Ellis, Richard E. *The Jeffersonian Crisis: Courts and Politics in the Young Republic.* New York: Oxford University Press, 1971.

Haskins, George L., and Johnson, Herbert A. *Foundations of Power: John Marshall, 1801–1815.* New York: Macmillan, 1981.

Kramer, Larry. *The People Themselves: Popular Constitutionalism and Judicial Review.* New York: Oxford University Press, 2004.

Nelson, William E. *Marbury v. Madison: The Origins and Legacy of Judicial Review.* Lawrence: University Press of Kansas, 2000.

Nelson, William E. *The Roots of American Bureaucracy, 1830–1900.* Cambridge, Mass.: Harvard University Press, 1982.

Nelson, William E., "The Province of the Judiciary," *John Marshall Law Review* 37 (2004), 325.

Reid, John Phillip. *Controlling the Law: Legal Politics in Early National New Hampshire.* DeKalb, Ill.: Northern Illinois University Press, 2004.

Roeber, A. G. *Faithful Magistrates and Republican Lawyers: Creators of Virginia Legal Culture, 1680–1810.* Chapel Hill: University of North Carolina Press, 1981.

Wood, Gordon S. *The Creation of the American Republic, 1776–1787.* Chapel Hill: University of North Carolina Press, 1969.

Court Cases

Adams v. Howe, 14 Mass. 340 (1817).
Administrators of Moore v. Cherry, 1 Bay 269 (S.C. 1792).
Barnes v. First Parish in Falmouth, 9 Mass. 401 (1810).
Brown v. Board of Education, 347 U.S. 483 (1954).
Eakin v. Raub, 12 Serg. & R. 330 (Pa. 1825).
Georgia v. Brailsford, 2 U.S. 402 (1792).
Letcher & Arnold v. Woodson, 1 Brock. 212 (Circuit Ct. Va. 1811).
Marbury v. Madison, 5 U.S. 137 (1803).
Murray v. First Parish in Gloucester, unreported.
People v. Croswell, 3 Johns. Cas. 339 (1804).
Plessy v. Ferguson, 163 U.S. 537 (1896).
Rutherford v. M'Faddon, unreported.
Stuart v. Laird, 5 U.S. 299 (1803).
United States v. The William, 28 Fed. Cas. 614 (D.C.D. Mass. 1808).

2

JUDGES AND DEMOCRACY: THE CHANGING ROLE OF THE UNITED STATES SUPREME COURT

Cass R. Sunstein

THE SUPREME COURT OF THE UNITED STATES IS WELL over two hundred years old. In that time, the Court has issued thousands of decisions. Hundreds of those decisions involve central questions about democracy. In fact the Court has been centrally involved in both structuring and limiting the democratic process.

The Court has been asked to answer some of the most central questions about democratic practice. Must states respect a rule of one person, one vote? Are poll taxes acceptable? What about gerrymandering? Can young people, or convicted felons, be banned from voting? In answering these questions, the Court often adopts one or another set of ideas about democracy's preconditions. But there is much more. Often the Court blocks the democratic process, invalidating laws enacted by Congress or the states, or striking down attempted acts of presidential authority. On many occasions, the Court has ruled that the people's elected representatives may not intrude on people's rights. In that way, the Court seems to intrude on democracy.

The Court's rulings on democratic self-government can be organized in many different ways, but a common way to begin is with a distinction. Some judicial decisions uphold government actions; these decisions are often described as *deferential* or *restrained*. Deferential, restrained decisions can easily be understood as supportive of democracy, in that they represent an effort by the Court to give democratically elected officials a high degree of flexibility in performing their duties. Other judicial decisions invalidate government actions; these decisions are often described as *activist*. With activist decisions, the Court intervenes into democratic processes, concluding that a certain law or practice adopted by elected officials violates the Constitution.

But, as we shall see, some activist decisions nonetheless can be understood as important contributions to democracy itself. Freedom of speech and the right to vote, for example, are preconditions of democracy. When the Court vindicates these rights, it is very plausibly acting in democracy's service. Moreover, as Marie Provine shows in Chapter 12 in this volume, the American constitutional order aims to be more than a mere majoritarian democracy: it aspires to be a *deliberative democracy* that combines reason and reflection with a fair degree of political accountability. Perhaps some of the Court's decisions promote, rather than undermine, that aspiration. Indeed, this chapter will urge that some of the Court's most praiseworthy, and most lasting, decisions can be understood in exactly these terms. When the Court has properly embraced deference and restraint, it has done so with respect for the outcomes of political processes that are both deliberative and democratic. When it has acted aggressively, it usually has attempted to ensure reason-giving, accountability, or both.

Of course, the Supreme Court is but one actor on a large democratic stage. Its decisions are supplemented by what state courts do, and such courts often show considerable creativity. Indeed, we shall encounter one case (*Bush v. Gore*) involving an aggressive state Supreme Court that was interpreting its state constitution to protect the right to vote in a way that greatly exercised the United States Court. This is but a single example of the constitutional creativity of state judges.

In addition, the Supreme Court does not act in a legislative vacuum. The jurisdiction of the federal courts is set in large part by decisions of Congress. The various judiciary acts, enacted democratically, both constrain and empower the nation's Supreme Court. Throughout the nation's history, legislative enactments, defining the Court's authority, have played a major role in determining what the Court is permitted to do.

There is a final related point. If the country opposes what the Supreme Court is doing, the justices might well respond to the political opposition—and back off. This is partly because the justices are appointed by the president, who can and often does mold the Court's fundamental character. The conservative Court of the early twentieth century was radically altered as a result of appointments by Franklin Delano Roosevelt; the liberal Court of the 1950s and 1960s was fundamentally changed by the appointments of Richard Nixon and Ronald Reagan. And even when there are no new appointments, the Court usually tends to be cautious about running afoul of a clear popular consensus. In understanding the role of the Court, it is important to see that the justices rarely act, for a long period, in a way that the general public repudiates.

Judicial Restraint in the Nineteenth Century

For much of the nineteenth century, the Supreme Court remained faithful to Chief Justice Marshall's commitment in *Marbury v. Madison*[1] to decide only narrow issues of law and avoid second-guessing Congress's exercise of its political powers. Indeed, prior to mid-century, the Court never again held an act of Congress unconstitutional. On the whole, the Court behaved in a restrained fashion and stayed clear of political decisionmaking, which it left to the president and above all to Congress.

After an initial feint against the Court, Congress similarly acquiesced for most of the century in the legal role assumed by the Court. The feint was the impeachment of Justice Samuel Chase by the House of Representatives two years after *Marbury* was handed down—the only time a Supreme Court justice has ever been impeached in the nation's history.

From the late 1790s on, Chase had been a thorn in the side of the Jeffersonian Republican party, which had gained control of Congress in the 1800 elections and retained it thereafter. Like some other Federalist judges of his time, he had behaved in a partisan fashion against the Jeffersonians, although in a far more arrogant and overbearing fashion than any of his colleagues. The House's impeachment was a politically motivated effort at payback. But Chase almost certainly had not committed "high crimes or misdemeanors," which are the only grounds stated in the Constitution for impeachment. Crucially, the Senate refused to convict Chase, albeit on the implicit understanding that he and the other justices would refrain from partisan behavior. Hence he was permitted to stay on the bench to perform his judicial role.

Chase's acquittal by the Senate did much to establish the independence of the Supreme Court from Congress. In return, the Court, as it had promised in *Marbury*, deferred to the democratic branches of government, leaving them free to exercise their political powers as they saw fit.

One of the most important instances of this deference occurred a decade and a half after *Marbury*, when the Court was called upon to interpret a crucial clause of the Constitution, which gives Congress the power to enact all laws "necessary and proper for carrying into execution the foregoing powers, and all other powers vested by this constitution, in the government of the United States, or any department thereof." The meaning of this clause raises many questions about the relationship between courts and democracy itself. If the necessary and proper clause gives Congress a great deal of flexibility, then the elected representatives of the people, in the national government, have the authority to create a unified nation—a genuinely United States. But if the necessary and proper clause restricts Congress to what is, strictly speaking, "necessary," then the American system is more like a confederation of independent states.

This issue came to a head in *McCulloch v. Maryland*,[2] the greatest opinion of the Marshall Court, possibly ranking even above *Marbury v. Madison* in its impact on the constitutional framework and the operation of American democracy. The specific issue in *McCulloch* was Congress's power to create a Bank of the United States, one that would furnish loans to the federal government and help collect taxes. Congress's authority to create a national bank was sharply disputed in the nation's early years. James Madison, one of the most important thinkers behind the federal Constitution, argued that Congress had no such power. Alexander Hamilton, another important thinker, personally drafted the plan for the first Bank of the United States and vigorously defended its constitutionality. He argued that the bank was necessary and proper, in the sense of "useful" or "conducive," to the execution of explicit constitutional powers, including the power to collect taxes, to borrow money, to regulate commerce between the states, and to raise and support armies.

Writing for a unanimous Court, Chief Justice Marshall enthusiastically upheld the constitutionality of the Second Bank of the United States, on the basis of the arguments adumbrated by Hamilton in support of the First Bank. While emphasizing that the power of the national government "is supreme within its sphere of action," he acknowledged that the Constitution did not explicitly give that government the power to create a bank. But he insisted that the founding document did not have "the prolixity of a legal code" and that the powers of Congress should not be interpreted narrowly or ungenerously. The Constitution is a particular kind of document, one that is meant "to endure for ages to come, and, consequently, to be adapted to the various *crises* of human affairs." Its very nature required that "only its great outlines should be marked, important objects designated, and the minor ingredients which compose those objects deduced from the nature of the objects themselves." At this point Marshall offered an emphatic reminder: "In considering this question, then, we must never forget, that it is *a constitution* we are expounding." With this great phrase, Marshall urged that powers conferred on the people's democratically chosen representatives in Congress should be viewed expansively rather than grudgingly.

None of these general statements resolved the specific question of whether Congress could create a national bank. But Chief Justice Marshall insisted that the necessary and proper clause should be understood expansively—that Congress was not required to demonstrate absolute necessity and that it would have the power to choose whatever means it found appropriate. Marshall contended that if Congress were denied its choice of means, national government would not be possible. "Let the end be legitimate, let it be within the scope of the constitution, and all means which are appropriate, which are plainly adapted to that end, which are not prohibited, but consist with the letter and spirit of the constitution, are constitutional." The national bank satisfied this test, which has been quoted on numerous occasions in the nation's history.

More than any other decision of the early Court, *McCulloch v. Maryland* gave the young government the ability to create a genuine nation, rather than a mere collection of states. And the *McCulloch* decision is of enduring importance: It is invoked whenever members of Congress, or even presidents, seek to resist a crabbed understanding of their constitutional authority. The decision stands as a testimonial to the power of America's democracy to act freely and within broad limits.

Many other cases have followed *McCulloch* in displaying deference to the political branches of government. Two of the most important, the *Slaughter House Cases*[3] and *Munn v. Illinois*,[4] occurred in the aftermath of the Civil War and of the Reconstruction amendments to the Constitution, which imposed important new limits on the powers of the states. Both cases gave rise to a new issue related, nonetheless, to the issue in *McCulloch* of the Court's relationship to Congress. This new issue was one of how much the Supreme Court would interfere with the democratic output of state political institutions.

Two of the three Reconstruction Amendments, the Thirteenth and the Fifteenth, dealt almost entirely with issues of race. The Thirteenth abolished slavery, and the Fifteenth prohibited denials of voting rights on the basis of race. The Fourteenth Amendment, in contrast, was more vaguely written: it says that states must not deprive people of life, liberty, or property "without due process of law" and that state governments must provide all people with "equal protection of the laws." The issue in both *Slaughter-House* and *Munn* was how broadly this vague language cut. In particular, did the language of due process give the Supreme Court power to invalidate economic regulatory legislation adopted by democratically responsible state political bodies that was inconsistent with the Court's view of how the economy should be managed?

This issue first arose in the *Slaughter-House Cases*. The penning, slaughtering, and butchering of large animals, such as cattle and swine, produces offensive noises and odors, and in the nineteenth century, before the invention of modern refrigeration, also imposed health hazards on neighbors. Hence it would seem undesirable to maintain a slaughterhouse in the midst of a densely populated area, especially a hot, steamy, and unhealthy one like the City of New Orleans, Louisiana, was in the mid-nineteenth century. Thus, no one could have been too shocked when a 1869 law of Louisiana prohibited the slaughtering and butchering of livestock within the city limits of New Orleans.

But the Louisiana legislation went beyond this mere prohibition. It also chartered a corporation, the Crescent City Live-Stock Landing and Slaughter-House Company, and granted it a twenty-five-year monopoly over the slaughtering of animals in the three parishes or counties including and surrounding New Orleans. Historians have long debated whether the incorporators had a corrupt relationship with the Louisiana legislature, and they may well have. In any event, butchers who were not included in the monopoly and who feared their businesses would be destroyed brought suit to have it declared invalid under the newly ratified Fourteenth Amendment. Their specific claim was that the monopoly legislation deprived them of their property without due process of law.

The federal court that tried the butchers' claim sustained it. Sitting as circuit judge, Supreme Justice Joseph P. Bradley ruled that every American citizen, by virtue of the Fourteenth Amendment, enjoyed a judicially enforceable right "to adopt such lawful industrial pursuit . . . as he may see fit" and "to be protected in the possession and enjoyment of his property." Although states could impose "reasonable restrictions" on this right in order to promote "the general well being," judges ultimately had the duty to decide whether such democratically enacted state regulations were sufficiently reasonable to pass constitutional muster.[5]

When *Slaughter-House*, three years later, became the first case in which the Supreme Court interpreted the new Fourteenth Amendment, Justice Stephen J. Field agreed. The concluding sentence of his opinion declared, "That only is a free government, in the American sense of the term, under which the inalienable right of every citizen to pursue his happiness is unrestrained, except by just, equal, and impartial laws." Joined by Justice Joseph P. Bradley and two other justices, Field earlier had conceded that private rights were subject to reasonable regulation for the public good but also had implied that the range of regulation must be narrow and its reasonableness ultimately subject to judicial review. Field's and Bradley's opinions thus were activist in the extreme and severely intruded into traditional areas of democratic lawmaking by the states.

Justices Field and Bradley, however, were in dissent. Writing for a 5–4 majority, Justice Samuel Miller made it clear that he had no intention "to fetter and degrade the State governments." In his view, there was not in the Fourteenth Amendment "any purpose to destroy the main features of the general system" of American government—features that, among other things, insured judicial deference to the acts of democratically elected lawmaking bodies. He therefore read the amendment narrowly as an enactment designed only to insure equal treatment for formerly enslaved African Americans. He doubted "whether any action of a State not directed by way of discrimination against the negroes as a class, or on account of their race, will ever be held to come within the purview of this provision. It is so clearly a provision for that race and that emergency, that a strong case would be necessary for its application to any other."

Thus, the traditional power of states democratically to enact economic regulatory legislation was preserved. In its first foray into Fourteenth Amendment adjudication, the Supreme Court stayed on the same path of judicial restraint it had trod in *Marbury* and *McCulloch*, recognized the power of the people through democratic processes to determine the policies by which they would regulate their economies, and conceded to democratic state legislatures the same deference it had long conceded to Congress.

Of course, *Slaughter-House* was not the last word the Supreme Court would speak on the subject of state economic regulation. Merely four years later, the issue was again before the Court in *Munn v. Illinois*. Again the Court acted in a restrained, deferential fashion, although this time it did recognize that state regulation of private property could, in some instances, violate Fourteenth Amendment constitutional rights.

Fundamental changes in the economy of marketing grain had led to *Munn*. In the 1860s and 1870s railroads had penetrated deeply into the rich farmlands of the American Midwest and had begun collecting and shipping grain to storage points, where it was held in grain elevators, pending further shipment to its final destination. These new technologies reduced shipping costs, but also gave economic power to railroads and elevator operators, which used their power to keep most of the cost savings for themselves. When the Panic of 1873 led to falling grain prices while the charges of railroads and elevator operators remained high, the farmers who grew the grain were irate. As the dominant political force in the region, the farmers had no difficulty inducing their legislatures to enact statutes setting the rates that railroads and elevator operators could charge.

In *Munn v. Illinois*, the elevator operators challenged the state law regulating the rates of grain elevators. They claimed the law constituted a taking of property without due process of law. Writing for a 7–2 majority, Chief Justice Morrison Waite held that private property could be regulated as long as the regulation was reasonable. Moreover, when property became "clothed with a public interest" as a result of its use "in a manner to make it of public consequence, and affect the community at large," the reasonableness of the regulation was no longer subject to judicial review; once there was power to regulate property "affected with a public interest," the legislature was free to regulate however it saw fit. Waite recognized that such broad democratic power could "be abused; but that [was] no argument against its existence. For protection against abuses by legislatures the people must resort to the polls."

Although the highest courts of some states in the late nineteenth century struck down economic regulatory legislation as a taking of private property without due process of law, the federal Supreme Court, on the whole, followed *Slaughter-House* and *Munn* until near the century's end. The justices conceded that regulation could amount to a taking when it served no public purpose or was otherwise unreasonable. Routinely, however, the Court upheld regulatory programs enacted by state legislatures. With one notable exception about to be discussed, the pattern of judicial deference toward democratically elected lawmaking bodies proclaimed in *Marbury* and practiced in *McCulloch* thus persisted until nearly the end of the century.

The Court's Self-Inflicted Wounds

The Supreme Court has not, however, always deferred to the output of the democratic branches of government or acted with judicial restraint to facilitate the functioning of democratic processes. Indeed, since the middle of the nineteenth century, the Court has sometimes assumed a more activist role and has declared both federal and state legislation unconstitutional. Its early activist efforts were roundly criticized, however, and they did not successfully launch the Court on a new path of judicial activism. Indeed, in the first case after *Marbury* in which the Court held an act of Congress unconstitutional, *Dred Scott v. Sandford*,[6] the justices acted in such a flagrantly anti-democratic fashion that they inflicted a serious wound on the Court's prestige.

Dred Scott is almost certainly the most vilified Supreme Court decision in American history. It is vilified on three grounds: morality, law, and institutional hubris on the Court's part. It stands as a prime illustration of the risks of overreaching by the Court. Still it might be thought to mark a turning point not only in the history of the federal judiciary, but also in the history of the nation as a whole.

Dred Scott, a slave, was born in about 1799, several years after the ratification of the Bill of Rights. During childhood, Scott lived in Virginia with Peter Blow and his wife, Elizabeth. After Peter Blow's death, one Dr. John Emerson bought Scott, and in 1834 took him into service at Fort Armstrong, in Illinois, a nonslave state. They resided there for two years before moving to what is now Minnesota, then part of the Louisiana territory. In 1838 Emerson took Scott into Missouri, and Scott was sold as a slave to Sandford. Slavery was legal in Missouri, but it was prohibited in Illinois by the state constitution and in the Louisiana territory by the federal statute embodying the Missouri Compromise. Scott claimed that he had been made a free man by virtue of his sustained stays in Illinois and the Louisiana territory. Sandford responded that Scott was not free, because his former owner had a continuing property interest in him—that is what slavery meant—and because the federal government could not deprive an owner of property, including slaves, without due process of law. More dramatically still, Sandford claimed that Scott could not even sue in federal court, since Scott, as a slave, was not a citizen of Missouri, or indeed of any state.

The Supreme Court decided the case in 1857, a year in which the United States was profoundly split over the issue of slavery. Chief Justice Roger Taney's opinion for the Court held first that Scott was not a citizen of Missouri. Therefore the federal courts had no jurisdiction over the case. But Justice Taney did not rely on Missouri law. Instead he argued very broadly that no person descended from an African American slave could *ever* be a citizen for constitutional purposes. Under the Constitution, those descended from slaves "are not included . . . under the word citizen and can therefore claim none of the rights and privileges of citizens." Here Taney could not rely on the constitutional text, which did not support him. Instead he resorted explicitly and self-consciously to an understanding of original intentions. Thus he wrote:

> On the contrary, [descendants of Africans] were at that time considered as a subordinate and inferior class of beings, who had been subjugated by the dominant race, and whether emancipated or not, yet remained subject to their authority, and had no rights or privileges but such as those who held the power and the Government might choose to grant them.

At first glance, the Court's conclusion on this point should have been the end of the matter. If Scott was not a citizen of Missouri, the federal courts had no authority to hear Scott's complaint, and the case should have been over, at least for Chief Justice Taney. But the Court went on to consider the huge question of whether Scott remained a slave after living in the Louisiana territory. The Court said that he did. But why? Chief Justice Taney offered several arguments. First, he said that Congress could not abolish slavery in the Louisiana territory. The national legislature's authority to "make all needful Rules and Regulations respecting the Territory or other Property belonging to the United States" did not extend to territories not owned in 1789. Chief Justice Taney also offered a second point. He said that slavery was constitutionally sacrosanct, so that even if Congress had authority over new territories, it could not ban slavery there. "[T]he right of property in a slave is distinctly and expressly affirmed in the Constitution."

Finally, Chief Justice Taney added a third point, to the effect that Congress's power over the territories could not collide with other constitutional limitations. Congress could not, for example, eliminate freedom of speech in the territories. This point was decisive for the question at hand. A law that deprives someone of property because he has brought it into a particular place "could hardly be dignified with the name of due process of law." Thus the Court interpreted the Constitution's Due Process Clause not merely to give people a right to a hearing before their liberty or property is taken, but also to give people a substantive right to protection against undue government intrusions into the private domain.

The *Dred Scott* decision was of pivotal importance. Discussion of the case was the centerpiece of the Lincoln-Douglas debates of 1858, which, in turn, were central to Abraham Lincoln's obtaining the Republican presidential nomination in 1860 and to his electoral victory leading to secession and civil war in 1861.

According to Lincoln, Taney's statement that property in slaves was constitutionally protected eventually could lead to a ruling that not even free states could exclude slaves from their territory. As a result, Lincoln declared in both his 1858 and his 1860 campaigns that he would not, if elected, be bound by *Dred Scott*. Although he conceded that the Supreme Court's judgment bound the litigants before it, he stated in his inaugural address:

> If the policy of the government, upon vital questions affecting the whole people, is to be irrevocably fixed by decisions of the Supreme Court, the instant they are made, in ordinary litigation between parties, in personal actions, the people will have ceased to be their own rulers, having, to that extent, practically resigned their government into the hands of that eminent tribunal.

Lincoln, that is, refused to accept as binding on the nation as a whole a Supreme Court judgment at odds with the democratic will of Congress. And, when Congress in his first term enacted legislation prohibiting slavery in the territories—legislation that according to *Dred Scott* was unconstitutional—Lincoln promptly signed it into law.

The pattern of conflict with the judiciary to which the *Dred Scott* case led Lincoln and his fellow Republicans also manifested itself during the Civil War. The leading case was *Ex parte Merryman*,[7] where Chief Justice Taney, sitting as a circuit justice, issued a writ of habeas corpus on behalf of a prisoner in military custody and the Lincoln administration ignored the writ. Only Lincoln's 1864 appointment of a new Chief Justice, Salmon P. Chase, and his earlier nominations of four new associate justices led to the beginning of a rapprochement between the Court and the political branches.

More than any other case, *Dred Scott* is thus an example of how judicial intervention into democratic processes can end in disaster. Not incidentally, the case was also extremely doubtful as a matter of law. There was little basis for the Court's conclusion that freed slaves could not count as citizens. In fact, some freed slaves had participated in the ratification of the Constitution itself, and freed slaves had been allowed to vote in at least five of the colonies. The Constitution does not suggest that freed slaves do not stand on the same ground as everybody else. More generally, the original Constitution did nothing to entrench slavery. It recognized the existence of the institution but did little more than that.

Beyond the legal technicalities, the nation was in the midst of an extraordinary and wide debate about one of the central moral issues of the time. As history has shown, nine lawyers in Washington are most unlikely to be able to lay such issues to rest by appealing to the Constitution. Here, then, was a decision in which the Court attempted to settle an issue that was sharply dividing the nation; however, the Court's settlement, which was indefensible by reference to democratic ideals, could not last.

The consequences of the *Dred Scott* case endured for over a decade as Congress and the president used their power over appointments and over the structure and jurisdiction of the federal courts to keep the justices under control—and the justices acquiesced. First, by an act of 1862, Congress realigned the federal circuits, reducing from five to three the number of circuits that were essentially Southern in makeup. Along with the death of a justice from Virginia and the resignation of one from Alabama, the realignment allowed President Lincoln to appoint two new Northerners to the Court. Then, in 1863, Congress created a new tenth circuit for California and Oregon, as well as a tenth seat on the Court, to which Lincoln appointed Stephen J. Field, a Democrat supportive of the administration's war policies. When Salmon Chase replaced Roger Taney as Chief Justice in 1864, the Republicans found themselves in control of the Court.

But, with the assassination of Lincoln in April of 1865 and the growing divide between his successor, Andrew Johnson, and Congress, legislation was adopted in 1866 reducing the size of the Court to seven, although existing justices were allowed to retain their seats until death or resignation. This legislation had the effect of precluding Johnson from making any appointments to the Court. Then, when Ulysses S. Grant, whom congressional Republicans assumed they could control, became president in 1869, the number of justices was again raised to nine.

Meanwhile, Congress was manipulating the Supreme Court's jurisdiction. First, in 1867, it granted federal circuit judges power to issue writs of habeas corpus to anyone restrained in violation of the Constitution; under the 1867 act, orders either denying or granting the writ could be appealed to the Supreme Court. When a Mississippi editor named McCardle was arrested by the military for publishing libelous articles, he applied for habeas and, after his application had been denied by the circuit court, appealed to the Supreme Court.

The Supreme Court assumed jurisdiction of the appeal and heard argument on the merits. Then Congress reacted. Fearing that the Court might use McCardle's appeal to invalidate its legislation providing for military reconstruction of the South, Congress repealed so much of its 1867 act as authorized appeals to the Supreme Court and, in addition, deprived the Court of jurisdiction over any case that already had been appealed. In *Ex parte McCardle*,[7] the Court caved in. It upheld the constitutionality of the jurisdiction-stripping legislation, held itself to be without jurisdiction in the case, and declined to proceed further.

Only by returning in *Slaughter-House* and subsequent cases like *Munn v. Illinois* to the practice of deferring to the democratic branches of government was the Supreme Court able by the end of the nineteenth century to recovered its lost power and prestige. Ultimately, therefore, *Dred Scott* is best interpreted as an aberration rather than as a turning point away from the practice of judicial restraint. The same is true of the next two major cases in which the Court struck down federal and state legislation addressing economic matters and again got itself into deep trouble.

The first case, decided in 1895, was *Pollock v. Farmers Loan & Trust Co.*,[8] which addressed the issue of the constitutionality of a federal income tax. Federal taxes had been levied on incomes during the Civil War, but in 1872 the income tax had been allowed to lapse. But when Grover Cleveland was elected president in 1892 and his fellow Democrats gained control of both houses of Congress on a platform of tariff reduction, additional federal revenue was needed. The result was the income tax of 1894, which placed a two percent tax on all incomes over $4,000.

Several suits were brought to have the tax ruled unconstitutional, and the Supreme Court quickly agreed to accept three of them on appeal and to consolidate them for a hearing. Within two months, the Court heard oral argument, and one month later, it handed down its opinion. Justice Howell Jackson, who was ill, did not participate in the case.

The *Pollock* case presented many issues. On one, the Court was unanimous, holding that federal taxation of interest on state and municipal bonds unconstitutionally burdened the states and their subdivisions. This holding, however, was of minimal importance, since it is possible to craft a federal income tax that exempts interest on state and municipal bonds; indeed, today a tax with such an exemption exists.

By a vote of 6–2, the Court also ruled the income tax unconstitutional as applied to rent or other income from real property, on the ground that such a tax is a direct tax which must be apportioned among the states as provided in Article I, Section 2 of the Constitution. By a vote of 4–4, the Court split on the issue of whether invalidation of the income tax as applied to real estate and state and municipal bonds voided the entire act or only those portions specifically held unconstitutional. The Court also divided evenly on whether a tax on income from personal property was an unconstitutional direct tax and whether any income tax would be invalid, in whole or in part, because it could not be uniform.

Such a fragmented opinion, of course, was unsatisfactory as a means of disposing of major congressional legislature, and therefore the Court granted a rehearing of the case within days of handing down its opinion. Within a little more than a month, after hearing oral argument, it handed down its second opinion. This time it held the entire income tax unconstitutional by a 5–4 vote.

Many Americans were astounded and angry at the Court's decision. Although the particulars are too detailed for discussion here, many accused the majority of twisting precedent to reach its result. The two opinions also displayed some odd patterns of voting. Justice Jackson, who had not participated in the initial hearing of the case, was one of the four dissenters who, on rehearing, voted to uphold at least part of the tax. That meant that one of the four justices who had initially voted that the income tax was constitutional in part had switched positions and later voted it unconstitutional in its entirety. The lack of any explanation for the vote switch did not make the Court look good to those upset by *Pollock's* result.

Finally, as part of the decision following the initial hearing, there was a strident opinion by Justice Field, who was a member of the majority on the rehearing. He labeled the income tax "arbitrary and capricious and . . . fanciful" and then wondered: "[W]here is the course of usurpation to end? The present assault upon capital [i.e., an income tax] is but the beginning. It will be but the steppingstone to others, larger and more sweeping, till our political contests will become a war of the poor against the rich; a war constantly growing in intensity and bitterness."

The plain implication was that the Court needed to assume a far more activist role on behalf of the rich in order to protect them from the majoritarian democratic onslaughts by the poor.

The reaction to the Court's invalidation of the federal income tax in *Pollock*, which was replete with bitterness and intensity, in effect put the case on trial. And, with the adoption of an amendment to the Constitution—the Sixteenth—the authors of the *Pollock* majority lost. In retrospect, it seems clear that their challenge to democratic tax raising was not an unmitigated disaster only because it led to the insertion of the following language into the Constitution:

> The Congress shall have power to lay and collect taxes on incomes, from whatever source derived, without apportionment among the several States, and without regard to any census or enumeration.

The Court continued nonetheless to get into trouble in its leading cases. A mere decade after *Pollock*, in 1905, it decided *Lochner v. New York*,[9] a case that gave its name to a whole era of American constitutional law: the *Lochner* era.

At issue in *Lochner* was a New York law that banned employees from working "in a biscuit, bread or cake bakery or confectionery establishment for more than sixty hours in any one week, or more than ten hours in any one day." The central question was whether this provision took away the "liberty" of employers and employees without "due process of law." To answer that question, the Court had to say whether freedom of contract is an aspect of constitutional "liberty." The Court insisted that it is: "The general right to make a contract . . . is part of the liberty of the individual protected by the Fourteenth Amendment of the Federal Constitution." The Court acknowledged that freedom of contract is not absolute. The government is allowed to intrude on that freedom if it is acting under the "police power," which allows governments to enact both "labor laws" and "health laws."

The heart of the *Lochner* opinion is a lengthy discussion of why the maximum hour law cannot be justified as either. In the Court's view, it cannot be justified as a labor law because bakers are not children; they have full legal capacity. "There is no contention that bakers are not equal in intelligence and capacity to men in other trades or manual occupations." To protect workers, the government must show that the people involved are "wards of the state," without the ability to protect themselves. Bakers could not be so characterized.

The Court also held that the maximum hour law could not be defended as a "health law," because it could not be shown that bakers' health was particularly vulnerable from long hours of work. "We think there can be no fair doubt that the trade of a baker, in and of itself, is not an unhealthy one to that degree which would authorize the legislature to interfere with the right of labor." If certain work turned out to be particularly dangerous, then government could limit the total hours so as to preserve health. But the Court was not convinced that the work of baking produced any special danger. The Court hinted that the maximum hour law was, in reality, enacted from some motive other than the protection of health. Perhaps it was simply an interest-group deal; perhaps it was really an effort to help workers at the expense of employers. In any case it was unconstitutional.

Lochner was an enormously important decision. It stood for decades as a barrier to much legislation attempting to protect workers in the marketplace. The strongest statement of the position of the *Lochner* Court can be found in *Adkins v. Children's Hospital*,[10] a 1923 decision invalidating minimum wage legislation for women and children. In his majority opinion, Justice George Sutherland wrote: "To the extent that the sum fixed [by the minimum wage statute] exceeds the fair value of the services rendered, it amounts to a compulsory exaction from the employer for the support of a partially indigent person, for whose condition there rests upon him no peculiar responsibility, and therefore, in effect, arbitrarily shifts to his shoulders a burden which, if it belongs to anybody, belongs to society as a whole."

Thus the Court ruled that a minimum wage law interfered with voluntary agreements between employers and employees, creating a "compulsory exaction from the employer" by forcing him to support a poor person. It was unconstitutional for that reason.

The importance of *Lochner* extends well beyond the majority ruling. Its significance lies as well in the extraordinary dissenting opinion of Justice Oliver Wendell Holmes—an opinion that is often celebrated as the greatest in the entire history of American law. Justice Holmes issued a stirring call for judicial restraint; he complained that the *Lochner* majority had badly overreached. More generally, he insisted that "a constitution is not intended to embody a political economic theory." He contended that it "is made for people of fundamentally differing views, and the accident of our finding certain opinions natural and familiar or novel and even shocking ought not to conclude our judgment upon the question whether statutes embodying them conflict with the Constitution of the United States." In a much-quoted phrase, Holmes said, with evident sarcasm, that the "Fourteenth Amendment does not enact Mr. Herbert Spencer's Social Statics."

Holmes's dissenting opinion in *Lochner* has been invoked on countless occasions. Whenever the Supreme Court is tempted to accept a particular economic (or social) theory, the words of Holmes's dissent provide a strong note of caution.

Holmes's plea for judicial deference to the political process has been quoted against both liberal and conservative courts when they have intervened in the democratic domain.

Nonetheless, the *Lochner* decision persisted as good law for some three decades, into the administration of President Franklin Delano Roosevelt. But then, deep economic and political pressures forced the Court to retreat from the activism of *Lochner* and to cede to Congress and the state legislatures authority to regulate economic affairs. Since then, the Court has deferred to the judgments of the political branches as to regulation of the economy.

When Roosevelt assumed office in 1933, the nation was mired in the Great Depression. Unemployment rates had jumped to 25 percent. Poverty was widespread. The system of laissez-faire capitalism seemed on the verge of collapse. Whatever the Supreme Court had said in *Lochner*, Roosevelt promised a "New Deal" for the American people. A significant part of his New Deal consisted of efforts to help workers with minimum wage legislation, maximum hours legislation, and more. Often the Supreme Court stood in Roosevelt's way, striking down measures that he had strongly supported.

The conflict threatened to create a constitutional crisis. Frustrated by the Court's intransigence, Roosevelt proposed what has come to be known as the "court-packing plan," by which the president would be allowed to appoint an additional justice for every member of the Court who served past the age of seventy. The plan would have allowed President Roosevelt immediately to appoint six additional justices. Despite Roosevelt's popularity, the plan was widely criticized as an attack on judicial independence, and it was unclear during the spring of 1937 whether Congress would enact it. Thus, the nation was at a constitutional standstill until the Court decided the case of *West Coast Hotel v. Parrish*,[11] upholding the constitutionality of a minimum wage law for women. In that case, the Court essentially accepted the constitutional views of the Roosevelt administration and ratified the constitutionality of the New Deal—a decision often called "the switch in time that saved nine." When one of the four *Parrish* dissenters resigned at the end of the Court's term and Roosevelt replaced him with Hugo Black, a reliable New Deal supporter, the court-packing plan died.

The minimum wage law at issue in *West Coast Hotel* had seemed of doubtful constitutional validity under the Court's *Lochner* era "freedom of contract" precedents. Breaking dramatically from those precedents, the Court spoke in terms that could easily have been found in a Roosevelt era speech. "What is this freedom of contract? The Constitution does not speak of freedom of contract." The liberty protected by the Constitution, the Court said, "is liberty in a social organization which requires the protection of law against the evils which menace the health, safety, morals and welfare of the people." The Court went so far as to suggest that liberty, taken seriously, could even justify such protection: "the proprietors lay down the rules and the laborers are practically constrained to obey them." To avoid that constraint, the legislature could legitimately act. The legislature could also consider the fact that women's "bargaining power is relatively weak, and that they are the ready victims of those who would take advantage of their necessitous circumstances." The Court complained of "the exploiting of workers at wages so low as to be insufficient to meet the bare cost of living, thus making their very helplessness the occasion of a most injurious competition."

In a remarkable passage, the Court added a "compelling consideration which recent economic experience had brought into a strong light." This consideration had to do with the social effects of poverty. According to the Court,

> The exploitation of a class of workers who are in an unequal position with respect to bargaining power and are thus relatively defenseless against the denial of a living wage . . . casts a direct burden for their support upon the community. What those workers lose in wages the taxpayers are called upon to pay. The bare cost of living must be met. We may take judicial notice of the unparalleled demands for relief which arose during the recent period of depression and still continue to an alarming extent despite the degree of economic recovery which has been achieved. . . . The community is not bound to provide what is in effect a subsidy for unconscionable employers.

To avoid "a direct burden" on the community imposed by "unconscionable employers," it was permissible for government to require those employers to pay minimum wages.

West Coast Hotel changed the constitutional universe. While the decision focused on the particular issue of minimum wages for women and children, its rationale was very broad. After the Court's decision, most government regulation of the economy was constitutionally secure. Freedom of contract no longer stood in the way. Roosevelt's New Deal was vindicated.

Since the Court's decision, regulation of the relationship between workers and employers, if not of the economy as a whole, has been an issue for legislatures, not courts. *West Coast Hotel* signaled a large-scale retreat from the *Lochner* period and a return to the patterns of judicial deference and restraint that had governed Supreme Court jurisprudence through most of the nineteenth century. Indeed, as of 1940, it seemed the Court would never again assume an activist role of impeding the nation's attainment of democratic governance.

Enhancing the Functioning of Democracy

Writing in the aftermath of the New Deal, a political scientist named Robert McCloskey drew a distinction between economic and personal liberty. He asserted that the *Lochner*-era Supreme Court had overstepped its bounds and trampled on democratic values when it invalidated democratically enacted legislation in order to protect freedom of contract and property rights. Accordingly, he condemned judicial activism directed at the protection of economic liberty as inconsistent with democracy. In contrast, he argued that the Court should undertake an activist role in pursuit of personal rights. Underlying his argument is a theory—that the protection of personal liberty transforms people who lack rights into full-fledged citizens better able to participate in the democratic process. Judicial activism in pursuit of personal rights, on this view, enhances democracy.

On the whole, the Supreme Court has heeded McCloskey's distinction during the past half century, rarely invalidating either state or congressional legislation for the purpose of protecting freedom of contract or property rights, while holding that innumerable state and federal statutes violate constitutional rights to personal liberty. In protecting personal liberty the Court typically has assumed an activist, though pro-democratic, stance when, on subjects such as voting rights and freedom of expression, it has invalidated laws that restricted the free operation of the democratic process.

Although there had been some precursors, the turning point in the Court's new activism in pursuit of personal rights was *Brown v. Board of Education*,[12] which held unconstitutional Southern state laws explicitly requiring segregation on the basis of race. *Brown* quickly became the Supreme Court's most important decision in the twentieth century, if not in the entire history of the Court.

After the Civil War, the Constitution had been amended to forbid slavery and to prohibit states from denying any person "equal protection of the laws." But in its pivotal decision in the 1896 case of *Plessy v. Ferguson*,[13] the Court had held that racial segregation did not offend the Constitution. "Separate but equal" was perfectly permissible. With respect to racial segregation, the Court in the late nineteenth century thus assumed a posture of restraint, allowing state and local governments to do as they saw fit. Racial segregation had become a way of life in many Southern states, and the Supreme Court did not stand in the way.

Brown v. Board of Education was the culmination of a long process of undermining *Plessy*. The constitutional challenge was overseen by Thurgood Marshall, one of the greatest lawyers in American history, the leader of the Legal Defense Fund of the National Association for the Advancement of Colored People, and eventually a member of the Supreme Court. In a series of cases, Marshall attempted to show that "separate" was not really "equal" in practice. He argued, again and again, that white schools were far superior to schools for African American children, and that this was impermissible even under *Plessy*. The Supreme Court often agreed with him. But Marshall's implicit message, and what he ultimately hoped to establish, was broader: A democratic society could not provide equal citizenship if it segregated people on the basis of race, above all in the area of education.

There was an obvious obstacle to Marshall's challenge. Racial segregation was well-entrenched in places in which he meant to eliminate it. If the Court attacked segregation, it would be attempting to engineer a large-scale process of social reform. Would the Court really overrule its own decision in a way that would require judges to assume an aggressive role in American society?

A unanimous Court accepted Marshall's argument in *Brown*. The Court's opinion, written by Chief Justice Earl Warren, began by insisting that the history behind the Fourteenth Amendment was "inconclusive," partly because of dramatic changes in the status of public education between 1868 and the present. It was only in the twentieth century that free common schools, supported by public funds, fully took hold. "We must consider public education in light of its full development and its present place in American life throughout the Nation." And in the modern era, education has become "the very foundation of good citizenship." The Court added that "it is doubtful that any child may reasonably be expected to succeed in life if he is denied the opportunity of an education."

Of course, no African American child was entirely denied schooling. The real question was one of discrimination. On this point, the Court finally agreed that separate could never be equal. To separate school children "from others of similar age and qualifications solely because of their race generates a feeling of inferiority as to their status in the community that may affect their hearts and minds in a way unlikely ever to be undone." To support this point, the Court referred to psychological work suggesting that segregation did, in fact, endow African American children with a feeling of inferiority.

Brown v. Board of Education was a highly activist decision, one that invalidated a practice that state legislators had long endorsed. Not surprisingly, the Court's decision produced a firestorm of protest. Some people said that Earl Warren should be impeached. Many others called for disobedience to the Court's judgment, which, they said, lacked any constitutional basis. In fact, the courts alone were unable to produce serious desegregation. Ten years after *Brown*, the overwhelming majority of African American children in the South continued to attend segregated schools. It was not until the mid-1960s, when the Department of Justice became involved, that serious steps were taken to eliminate racial segregation in schools. In addition, Chief Justice Warren's opinion for the Court has been roundly criticized, not least because the Court relied on psychological work that was highly controversial at the time (and that is no longer accepted as authoritative).

But there is no question that *Brown v. Board of Education* has stood the test of time. More than that, it has become a symbol of how the Supreme Court might, in an important sense, protect democracy itself. By insisting on the idea of equality in education, the Court ruled that in the United States, no one is a second-class citizen. America, it suggested, is not a caste society, but a democracy—a polity, that is, in which all citizens are entitled to equal participation in government.

In the aftermath of *Brown*, the Supreme Court continued to pursue a new, activist role in service of the democratic process. Until that time, policing of the most fundamental of democratic rights—the right to vote—had been left largely in the hands of Congress and the state legislatures. For instance, the nineteenth century's two disputed presidential elections—those of 1800 and 1876—had been resolved by Congress in 1801 and by a special commission created by Congress and consisting principally of senators and representatives in 1877. While there were state election disputes that found their way into state courts, the Supreme Court and the lower federal courts had, in large part, kept themselves divorced from the voting process.

In the middle of the twentieth century, the Court's role changed, first and most importantly in the context of voting rights. As late as the 1950s, the principle of one person, one vote, was rarely honored. Voting was kept largely under the control of state governments, and many state voting systems gave more power to whites than to African Americans, to those who lived in underpopulated areas, or to those who lived in agricultural areas. By the middle of the twentieth century, such systems had, in fact, been in place for many decades. As a result, some people had more political power than others either by design or as a result of sheer chance.

In its most important voting rights decision, *Reynolds v. Sims*,[14] the Supreme Court ruled that under the Equal Protection Clause, states must follow the one person, one vote principle. In one bold stroke, the Court struck down the voting systems of Alabama, Colorado, Maryland, New York, and Virginia, each of which ensured that citizens in some areas would have less voting power than citizens in other areas. The Court ruled that under the Constitution, state authorities are not permitted to "provide that the votes of citizens in one part of the State should be given two times, or five times, or 10 times the weight of votes of citizens in another part of the State." The Court feared that without a principle of one person, one vote, electoral minorities would be able to entrench themselves, simply because the votes of the majority would be "diluted."

In *Reynolds*, the Court acknowledged that the United States Senate itself violates the principle it was imposing on the states. But it remarked that the national system was part of a complex compromise, in which some of the formerly independent states were guaranteed enhanced power that would protect them in a minority status as a condition for agreeing to the Constitution. No such compromise would justify political inequality within the states.

Reynolds v. Sims was exceptionally controversial in its time. Academic critics objected that *Reynolds* lacked anything like a clear basis in the Constitution. Certainly it is doubtful that the authors and ratifiers of the Fourteenth Amendment meant to impose the one person, one vote principle on state governments. But *Reynolds* rapidly achieved widespread public acceptance, even in the states that violated it. The decision now stands as the most prominent among a wide range of cases in which the Court has tried to protect the integrity of the political process by ensuring that no one is denied the right to vote. And *Reynolds* has had a huge practical impact as well, ensuring that state representatives are chosen according to the views of the political majority. Although it was an activist decision that struck down state laws and traditional voting practices, *Reynolds v. Sims* is today viewed as a democracy-enhancing decision that, at a minimum, ensures majority rule.

No less than the right to vote, the right to free speech is a cornerstone of democracy. But what does free speech include? No one really believes that the right to free speech is an absolute. The government is allowed to regulate perjury, bribery, fraudulent commercial advertising, and conspiracies to fix prices. None of these examples involves political dissent, which of course lies at the heart of the free speech principle; if the First Amendment is about anything, it is about democratic self-government.

But for many decades, the Supreme Court refused to give broad protection to political dissent, ruling that speech could be regulated if it had a "bad tendency"—a tendency to cause harm. Sometimes the Court allowed government to regulate speech that seemed to be part of a communist conspiracy.[15] Sometimes the Court allowed government to regulate speech that attacked the government during wartime.[16] In an early case, Justice Holmes suggested, for the Court's majority, that speech could be regulated only if it created a "clear and present danger"[17]—but the Court's majority did not take that standard very seriously. It permitted the government to regulate speech that posed merely a threat of harm.

All this radically changed with the Court's most important First Amendment decision, its remarkably brief and offhand opinion in *Brandenburg v. Ohio*.[18] Brandenburg was a member of the Ku Klux Klan. In a public speech, he had said, "We're not a revengent organization, but if our President, our Congress, our Supreme Court, continues to suppress the white, Caucasian race, it's possible that there might have to be some revengence taken." Brandenburg added, "Personally, I believe the nigger should be returned to Africa, the Jew to Israel." As a result of these statements, Brandenburg was convicted under an Ohio law making it a crime to advocate "the duty, necessity, or propriety of crime, sabotage, violence, or unlawful methods of terrorism as a means of accomplishing industrial or political reform."

The Supreme Court held that Brandenburg's conviction was unconstitutional. In so doing, the Court announced an exceedingly broad standard for protecting political dissent—one that made clear that dissent could be regulated only in the narrowest of circumstances. The Court went so far as to say that, in general, people were free to advocate violations of the law.

Governments could not "forbid or proscribe advocacy of the use of force or law violation except where such advocacy is directed to inciting or producing imminent lawless action and is likely to incite or produce such action." Because Brandenburg was engaged in mere advocacy, the Constitution would not allow him to be punished.

To understand the Court's test in *Brandenburg,* it is important to see that it has three separate elements. To be regulable, speech must (1) be directed at producing (2) imminent lawless action and also (3) be likely to produce such action. This is an exceptionally stringent and speech-protective version of Holmes's earlier clear and present danger test. In a case following *Brandenburg*, for example, the Court protected the ensuing statement during a political boycott: "If we catch any of you going in any of them racist stores, we're gonna break your damn neck."[19] In newspapers, on street corners, and on the Internet, political dissent is now protected, even if it advocates overthrowing the government and indeed even if it advocates terrorism. If lawless action is not both imminent and likely, the remedy is not censorship, but more speech.

Brandenburg stands as the crown jewel of the American commitment to freedom of expression. It protects speech in both war and peace. So long as it stands, it preserves the channels of political dissent—forcing government to allow speech by those who despise the government and wish it harm. By protecting speech that both officials and majorities find offensive and even threatening, it opens a great deal of space for the most intense disagreement and debate and hence for deliberative, democratic self-rule.

At first, the Court entered the thicket of electoral politics to foster democracy only in the two obvious repects we have discussed—insuring that the opponents of those in power could speak their views and protecting the right to vote. It avoided determining the winners and losers of elections. But, as is obvious, there is an analytical connection between protecting the right to vote and aggregating votes to determine a winner. That connection proved central to the Supreme Court's opinion in *Bush v. Gore*,[20] unquestionably a towering moment in the history of the relationship between the Supreme Court and democracy and perhaps a decisive one.

It is an understatement to say that the 2000 presidential election was exceedingly close. Vice President Al Gore won the popular vote by a narrow margin, but the outcome of presidential elections is settled by the Electoral College, and here everything turned on one question: Who won Florida? The initial judgment, based on machine counts, was George W. Bush. But Gore raised plausible doubts about the accuracy of the machine count in Florida, and he insisted that under Florida law, a manual recount was required to ensure an accurate tabulation. The Florida Supreme Court was highly receptive to Gore's arguments. It interpreted Florida law to require the Secretary of State to extend the statutory deadline so as to ensure a manual recount. In *Bush v. Gore*, Bush asked the United States

Supreme Court to reverse the Florida Supreme Court. Among other things, Bush objected that the Florida Supreme Court, referring simply to the "intent of the voter," had set out no standards to establish when and why a vote would be counted. As a result, similar voters would not be treated similarly, in violation of the Equal Protection Clause, the Due Process Clause, and even *Reynolds v. Sims*.

It is worth pausing over a central feature of the *Bush v. Gore* litigation. The stage was set by the decisions of the Florida Supreme Court, which had Florida law, including the Florida constitution, to interpret. The Florida Supreme Court sought to ensure that *every vote would count*—a goal that, on the court's view, was very much in the spirit of the Florida constitution itself. The Florida court's judgment in this regard helps illustrate an important general point: The state courts play an exceedingly important role in defining American democracy, one that complements the role played by the United States Supreme Court. Often the state courts go beyond the federal ones, ruling that their own constitutional principles impose requirements that are more protective of liberty and equality than the principles of the national Constitution. But on occasion, those state rulings will be challenged as violative of federal constitutional rights. And this is what Bush did in *Bush v. Gore*.

The Court accepted Bush's argument, stressing the Equal Protection Clause. Announcing its fundamental motivation, the Court wrote, "The right to vote is protected in more than the initial allocation of the franchise. Equal protection applies as well to the manner of its exercise. Having once granted the right to vote on equal terms, the State may not, by later arbitrary and disparate treatment, value one person's vote over that of another." The Court's major concern was that no official in Florida had generated standards by which to discipline the open-ended inquiry into "the intent of the voter." In the Court's view, "Florida's basic command . . . to consider the 'intent of the voter'" was "standardless" and constitutionally unacceptable without "specific standards to ensure its equal application. . . . The formulation of uniform rules based on these recurring circumstances is practicable and, we conclude, necessary." Without such rules, similarly situated ballots would be treated differently, and for no evident reason.

The Court offered some details on the resulting equality problem. "A monitor in Miami-Dade County testified at trial that he had observed that three members of the county canvassing board applied different standards in defining a legal vote." Standards even appeared to have been changed "during the counting process," with Palm Beach County beginning "the process with a 1990 guideline which precluded counting completely attached chads," then switching "to a rule that considered a vote to be legal if any light could be seen," then changing "back to the 1990 rule," and then abandoning "any pretense of a per se rule." A serious problem was that "the standards for accepting or rejecting contested ballots might vary not only from county to county but indeed within a single county from one recount team to another." This too was not mere speculation. "Broward

County used a more forgiving standard than Palm Beach County, and uncovered almost three times as many new votes, a result markedly disproportionate to the difference in population between the counties."

The Court also found a constitutional violation in the unequal treatment of "overvotes" (meaning ballots that machines rejected because more than one vote had been cast) and "undervotes" (meaning ballots on which machines failed to detect a vote, and which had been ordered to be reexamined). The Court objected that

> the citizen whose ballot was not read by a machine because he failed to vote for a candidate in a way readable by a machine may still have his vote counted in a manual recount; on the other hand, the citizen who marks two candidates in a way discernable by the machine will not have the same opportunity to have his vote count, even if a manual examination of the ballot would reveal the requisite indicia of intent. Furthermore, the citizen who marks two candidates only one of which is discernable by the machine, will have his vote counted even though it should have been read as an invalid ballot.

To this, the Court added "further concerns." These included an absence of specification of "who would recount the ballots," leading to a situation in which untrained members of "ad hoc teams" would be involved in the process. And "while others were permitted to observe, they were prohibited from objecting during the recount." Thus the Court concluded that the recount process "is inconsistent with the minimum procedures necessary to protect the fundamental right of each voter in the special instance of a statewide recount under the authority of a single state judicial officer."

The Court was aware that its ruling could have broad implications. If the Equal Protection Clause really means that each citizen has an equal chance to have his vote counted, then courts will be required to scrutinize many state elections, simply because different machines are often used in different areas of states. Hence the Court attempted to suggest that its principle might be limited to the particular setting of the case: "The question before the Court is not whether local entities, in the exercise of their expertise, may develop different systems for implementing elections. Instead, we are presented with a situation where a state court with the power to assure uniformity has ordered a statewide recount with minimal procedural safeguards."

The most obvious significance of *Bush v. Gore* lies in the fact that it promptly settled the 2000 election. The prompt settlement put to a halt a process that was becoming extremely heated and chaotic. Not surprisingly, the Court's decision produced sharply different reactions in the country, mirroring the electoral division between Bush and Gore. Almost everyone agreed that it would have been much better if the Court had been unanimous and that it was quite unfortunate that the Court was split along conservative/liberal lines. The process of continued vote counting was halted by the conservatives on the Court (Chief Justice William Rehnquist and Justices Sandra Day O'Connor, Antonin Scalia, Anthony Kennedy, and Clarence Thomas). Continued counting was supported by the more liberal members (Justices John Paul Stevens, David Souter, Ruth Bader Ginsburg, and Stephen Breyer). To say the least, the ideal of the rule of law is not furthered by a situation in which legal conclusions are so well-matched to political orientations. Hence *Bush v. Gore* was met by widespread claims that the Court had disregarded the law and "given" the presidency to George W. Bush. On the other hand, the principle behind the decision—of equality among voters—did have some appeal, and many people appreciated the fact that the Court brought an end to a controversy that was threatening to spiral out of control.

Perhaps the largest lesson of *Bush v. Gore* lies in its utter failure to damage the Court as an institution. The Court had entered into, and resolved, one of the most intense political battles in the nation's history—and it emerged unscathed from the process. Many people anticipated that the Court would lose credibility in the public eye, or at least that Gore supporters (one-half of the electorate!) would think that the Court had forfeited its electoral legitimacy. But this did not happen. There was no evidence that the Court had been even slightly weakened. Arguably, that was because the *Bush v. Gore* Court, in the end, came to be understood as acting in service of rather than in opposition to democracy.

Despite the immense transformations they have wrought in the role of the Supreme Court in American society, *Brown* and its progeny have remained faithful to *West Coast Hotel*'s abandonment of the idea of "substantive due process," the doctrine that authorizes the Supreme Court to strike down laws that intrude on liberty without sufficient justification. *Brown* rested on the Fourteenth Amendment's Equal Protection, not its Due Process, Clause. It and its progeny are about racial equality and the democratic functioning of the political process, not private liberty.

But in the 1960s, judicial activism to protect personal liberty under the guise of substantive due process enjoyed a surprising rebirth. Here the turning point was *Griswold v. Connecticut*,[21] in which the Court invalidated a law forbidding married people from using contraceptives. *Griswold* was the beginning of the modern "right to privacy," but the decision had a narrow reach: Connecticut's ban on the use of contraceptives within marriage was exceptionally unusual and palpably out of touch with existing public convictions. In *Roe v. Wade*,[22] the Court went much further.

The central question in *Roe* was whether the Due Process Clause protects the right to choose abortion as part of constitutional "liberty." The Court ruled that it does. It acknowledged that there is no explicit right to privacy under the

Constitution. But it insisted that liberty "is broad enough to encompass a woman's decision whether or not to terminate her pregnancy." The Court emphasized that if women are not allowed to choose, they will face a range of harms, including psychological distress, financial loss, and social stigma.

At the same time, the Court did not rule that the right to choose is absolute. It emphasized that the state has a legitimate interest "in protecting the potentiality of human life." After the fetus becomes viable outside of the womb, the state is permitted to prohibit abortion. But before that time, states could not deem fetuses to be "persons" so as to override the pregnant woman's right to choose. Before the end of the first trimester, state regulation would be entirely impermissible. During the second trimester, the state could regulate abortion in order to protect the health of the mother; but it could do no more. In this way, the Court appeared to write a kind of "how-to" guide for legislators attempting to regulate abortion. The Court's central ruling—the headline news—was that the woman's right to choose was subject only to narrow restrictions.

To say the least, the purely legal fallout from *Roe v. Wade* has been exceedingly complex. The Court has had to decide numerous cases clarifying the nature of the right that its decision protects. Is there a constitutional right to government funding for abortion? (No.)[23] May the state require the father to consent before an abortion is performed? (No.)[24] May the state require minor women to notify their parents that they plan to have an abortion? (Sometimes.)[25] More than any other case in the last forty years, *Roe v. Wade* has been challenged as an unacceptable exercise of judicial activism. Efforts have been repeatedly made to convince the Court to overrule *Roe*, but a majority of the Court has refused so far to depart from its essential holding.[26]

Defenders of the decision have argued that it should be seen as a kind of *Brown* for women, in the form of a ruling that forbids states from adopting a practice that turns certain people into second-class citizens. And some members of the Court have come to suggest that *Roe* turns not only on principles of liberty, but on principles of sex equality as well.[27] In their view, women's equality is promoted by the right to choose. But *Roe* has certainly failed to obtain the broad social consensus that now underlies *Brown*. A presidential candidate could not hope to win if he or she defended racial segregation, but a presidential candidate is not doomed if he or she questions *Roe*. The moral questions raised by abortion continue to split American citizens.

While *Roe* seems like *Brown* to its defenders, its critics contend that it is more like *Dred Scott*: an unsuccessful and morally abhorrent effort to use the Due Process Clause to settle large-scale moral issues. A much-disputed issue is whether *Roe* might be defended on democratic grounds. Can the decision be seen as an effort to ensure the democratic equality of women? Many people are skeptical.

Concluding Thoughts

How well has the Supreme Court adhered since *Marbury v. Madison* to Chief Justice Marshall's promise that it would serve rather than obstruct democratic processes and use law only to enhance democratic deliberation, not to impose its policy choices on an unwilling electorate? In the many cases, such as *McCulloch v. Maryland*, the *Slaughter-House Cases*, and *Munn v. Illinois*, in which it has deferred to and enforced policy decisions made by officials in the political branches, the Court's service of democracy has been unequivocal. In cases dealing with freedom of expression and the right to vote, such as *Brandenburg v. Ohio* and *Reynolds v. Sims*, the Court has elaborated democracy's internal morality. It has recognized that democracy does not simply mean majority rule and that at a minimum, a democratic system requires freedom of speech and the right to vote. *Bush v. Gore* and *Brown v. Board of Education* rest, in turn, on an understanding that democracy demands at least some form of political equality. The decision in *Bush* seems to recognize an equal right to have one's vote count—a right that might well be seen as required by the democratic ideal. And *Brown* struck down racial segregation, which was a device for subordinating African Americans, denying them equal citizenship, and converting them into a kind of lower caste. Thus, when the Court decreed an end to American apartheid, it was promoting a central democratic goal.

In *Dred Scott v. Sandford*, *Pollock v. Farmers' Loan & Trust Co.*, and *Lochner v. New York*, the Court took a temporary turn toward resolving controversial moral and economic policy issues and invalidating democratically enacted legislation at odds with its resolution. But the decisions in *Dred Scott* and *Pollock* have been reversed by subsequent amendments to the Constitution, and *Lochner* was effectively overruled by *West Coast Hotel v. Parrish*. Very few people defend these decisions today, and to do so is to mark oneself as out of the mainstream, even radically so.

The continuing controversy over *Roe v. Wade* further shows that the only legitimate role for the Supreme Court is to uphold the democratic process. Some people see *Roe* as a policy choice by the Court that was as morally abhorrent as the Court's choice in *Dred Scott*, and equally at war with the contrary choice made by the people through the democratic legislative process. They demand that it be overruled. Others see *Roe* as the foundation of democratic citizenship for women—as protecting a right of control over their own bodies without which women can be neither free nor equal. They demand that it remain on the books. Americans disagree, in short, about whether *Roe* promoted democratic equality or overruled democratic choice. But, beneath their disagreement, there seems to remain a broad consensus that the job assigned by the Constitution to the Court is to secure citizens in the equal rights they need to participate in democratic politics, not to make the policy choices that a properly functioning deliberative democracy must make for itself.

Notes

1. 5 U.S. 137 (1803).
2. 17 U.S. 316 (1819).
3. 83 U.S. 36 (1873).
4. 94 U.S. 113 (1877).
5. *See Live-Stock Dealers' & Butchers' Ass'n v. Crescent City Live-Stock Landing & Slaughter-House Co.*, 15 Fed. Cas. 649 (C.C.D. La. 1870).
6. 60 U.S. 393 (1857).
7. 17 Fed. Cas. 144 (C.C.D. Md. 1861).
8. 74 U.S. 506 (1869).
9. 57 U.S. 429 (1895), *opinion on rehearing*, 158 U.S. 601 (1895).
10. 198 U.S. 45 (1905).
11. 261 U.S. 525 (1923).
12. 300 U.S. 379 (1937).
13. 347 U.S. 483 (1954).
14. 163 U.S. 537 (1896).
15. 377 U.S. 533 (1964).
16. *Dennis v. United States*, 341 U.S. 494 (1951).
17. *Debs v. United States*, 249 U.S. 211 (1919).
18. *Schenck v. United States*, 249 U.S. 47 (1919).
19. 395 U.S. 444 (1969).
20. *NAACP v. Claiborne Hardware Co.*, 458 U.S. 886 (1982).
21. 531 U.S. 115 (2000).
22. 381 U.S. 479 (1965).
23. 410 U.S. 113 (1973).
24. *Maher v. Roe*, 432 U.S. 464 (1977).
25. *Planned Parenthood v. Danforth*, 428 U.S. 52 (1976).
26. *HL v. Matheson*, 450 U.S. 398 (1981).
27. *Planned Parenthood v. Casey*, 505 U.S. 833 (1992).

Bibliography

Cushman, Barry, *Rethinking the New Deal Court: The Structure of a Constitutional Revolution*. New York: Oxford University Press, 1998.

Fehrenbacher, Don E. *The Dred Scott Case: Its Significance in American Law and Politics.* New York: Oxford University Press, 1978.

Garrow, David J. *Liberty and Sexuality: The Right to Privacy and the Making of* Roe v. Wade. New York: Macmillan, 1994.

Kens, Paul. *Judicial Power and Reform Politics: The Anatomy of* Lochner v. New York. (Lawrence: University Press of Kansas, 1990).

Kluger, Richard. *Simple Justice: The History of* Brown v. Board of Education *and Black America's Struggle for Equality.* New York: Vintage Books, 1975.

Kutler, Stanley I. *Judicial Power and Reconstruction Politics.* Chicago: University of Chicago Press, 1968.

McCloskey, Robert G. *The American Supreme Court.* Chicago: University of Chicago Press, 1960.

Nelson, William E. *The Fourteenth Amendment: From Political Principle to Judicial Doctrine.* Cambridge, Mass.: Harvard University Press, 1988.

Paul, Arnold M. *Conservative Crisis and the Rule of Law: Attitudes of Bar and Bench, 1887–1895.* Ithaca, N.Y.: Cornell University Press, 1960.

Sunstein, Cass R. *After the Rights Revolution: Reconceiving the Regulatory State.* Cambridge, Mass.: Harvard University Press, 1990.

Sunstein, Cass R. *Democracy and the Problem of Free Speech.* New York: Free Press, 1993.

Sunstein, Cass R., and Epstein, Richard A., eds. T*he Vote: Bush, Gore, and the Supreme Court.* Chicago: University of Chicago Press, 2001.

White, G. Edward, with the aid of Gerald Gunther. *The Marshall Court and Cultural Change: 1815–1835.* New York: Macmillan, 1988.

Court Cases

Adkins v. Children's Hospital, 261 U.S. 525 (1923).

Brandenburg v. Ohio, 395 U.S. 444 (1969).

Brown v. Board of Education, 347 U.S. 483 (1954).

Bush v. Gore, 531 U.S. 115 (2000).

Debs v. United States, 249 U.S. 211 (1919).

Dennis v. United States, 341 U.S. 494 (1951).

Dred Scott v. Sandford, 19 Howard 393 (1857).

Ex parte McCardle, 74 U.S. 506 (1869).

Ex parte Merryman, 17 Fed. Cas. 144 (C.C.D. Md. 1861).

Griswold v. Connecticut, 381 U.S. 479 (1965).

HL v. Matheson, 450 U.S. 398 (1981).

Lochner v. New York, 198 U.S. 45 (1905).

Marbury v. Madison, 5 U.S. 137 (1803).

McCullough v. Maryland, 17 U.S. 316 (1819).

NAACP v. Claiborne Hardware Co., 458 U.S. 886 (1982).

Planned Parenthood v. Danforth, 428 U.S. 52 (1976).

Slaughter-House Cases, 83 U.S. 36 (1873).

Maher v. Roe, 432 U.S. 464 (1977).

Munn v. Illinois, 94 U.S. 113 (1877).

Planned Parenthood v. Casey, 505 U.S. 833 (1992).

Plessy v. Ferguson, 163 U.S. 537 (1896).

Pollock v. Farmers' Loan & Trust Co., 157 U.S. 429 (1895), 158 U.S. 601 (1895).

Reynolds v. Sims, 377 U.S. 533 (1964).

Roe v. Wade, 410 U.S. 113 (1973).

Schenck v. United States, 249 U.S. 47 (1919).

West Coast Hotel v. Parrish, 300 U.S. 379 (1937).

3

JUDICIAL INDEPENDENCE AND THE MAJORITARIAN DIFFICULTY

Kermit L. Hall

AT THE HEIGHT OF THE PROGRESSIVE ERA IN 1906, DEAN Roscoe Pound of the Harvard Law School urged the American bar to restore the independence of the judiciary. Pound's program of reform had several components, one of the most important of which was to make the judges of each states' highest appellate courts appointed rather than elected. "Putting courts into politics, and compelling judges to become politicians," he observed, "has almost destroyed the traditional respect for the bench."[1] Pound's plea paralleled similar demands by other Progressive reformers for a rational, expert-driven, and nonpartisan approach to public life. When Pound wrote, about eight in ten American state judges stood for election. Yet a century after Pound and the Progressives launched their attack on the popular election of judges, Americans continue to resort to this more rather than less democratic means to choose who will preside over their state courts. Today 87 percent of state judges stand for some form of election; 40 percent are selected on partisan ballots; and only three states appoint their judges and leave them to serve, as do federal judges, during good behavior.

Putting Courts Into and Out of Politics

By almost every standard, federal judges are the model of judicial independence and, for many like Pound, one to be embraced. Federal judges, including members of the Supreme Court of the United States, are appointed by the president with the advice and consent of the Senate, hold their offices during good behavior, enjoy salaries that cannot be reduced, and can be removed only through impeachment by a majority vote of the House of Representatives and conviction by two-thirds of the Senate. While appointment to the federal courts follows a decidedly political path, it is, in overwhelming contrast to most states, neither a popular nor a democratic journey.

The original rationale for appointing federal judges and their state counterparts turned on their vulnerability, not their might. Alexander Hamilton, one of the most forceful proponents of the federal judiciary, insisted in 1788 that there was no need to fear the judicial branch. It would be, according to him, "the least dangerous to the political rights of the Constitution . . . [and have] no influence over either the sword or the purse; no direction either of the strength or of the wealth of the society, and [it] can take no active resolution whatever [in settling public policy]."[2] An independent judiciary constituted the "citadel of . . . public justice and . . . public security." Hamilton's arguments were uncompromising. "Periodical appointments, however regulated, or by whomsoever made," he warned, "would, in some way or other, be fatal to [the judiciary's] necessary independence."[3] Half a century later, Alexis de Tocqueville, perhaps the most famous commentator on the relationship between law and democracy in America, recapitulated Hamilton's position. He warned that the emergent practice by some states of subjecting judges to periodic elections was tantamount to an attack on "the . . . republic itself."[4]

During the last two hundred years, American courts—both federal and state—have played an even broader role than Hamilton and Tocqueville anticipated. Courts are limited in their powers, of course. They generally do not set their own agendas; instead, they respond to real cases and controversies brought by real litigants. These litigants invariably mirror larger and conflicting social currents associated with developments as diverse as industrialization, immigration, changing gender roles, and attitudes toward race.

Whether, how, and to what degree courts should respond to the legal controversies generated by these demands roils contemporary politics. In April 2005, for example, House Speaker Tom DeLay of Texas proposed that Congress sharply reduce the jurisdiction of the federal courts in light of the judges' unwillingness to restore a feeding tube to Terri Schiavo, a brain-damaged woman in Florida. "Judicial independence does not equal judicial supremacy," DeLay proclaimed. "We [Congress] set the jurisdiction of the courts. They have run amok," Mr. DeLay said.[5] "We set up the courts. We can unset the courts."[6] There is no denying that the judiciary of Hamilton's era stands in the shadow of its much more significant counterpart today.

Judicial Review and the Countermajoritarian Difficulty

The history of the judiciary has been one of solidifying its sovereign authority, developing its independence, and extending its exercise of judicial review.

Judicial sovereignty means, in simple terms, that when courts, either state or federal, address constitutional matters, either state or federal, their views of what is constitutional are binding on the other branches and the public. Changes can be made through constitutional conventions, amendments, and even some forms of legislation, but in the American system the judiciary has come to enjoy the final word on what is constitutional. Judges also enjoy considerable although varying degrees of independence. This term means the ability of the courts to be free from coercion by the political branches.

Judicial review is the power of the courts to evaluate the actions of the other branches and, ultimately, rule on their constitutionality. During the nation's first seventy years judicial review was a controversial, slightly used power, both at the state and federal levels. Between the nation's founding and the outbreak of the Civil War in 1861, the Supreme Court of the United States struck down only two acts of Congress and only a handful of state laws. State courts invoked their powers of review with similar caution. When they did, the result was often contentious. In 1808, for example, the Ohio House of Representatives, dominated by Jeffersonian Republicans and acting on the precedent set by the impeachment of United State Supreme Court Justice Samuel Chase four years earlier, voted articles of impeachment against Federalist Judge George Tod of the Ohio Supreme Court. Tod's sin was writing the majority opinion that overturned a popular act of the legislature. While the Ohio Senate acquitted Tod by a single vote, the entire event weakened, for the next several decades, the claims of the Ohio judiciary to the exercise of judicial review.

What was once doubted and infrequently attempted today has become an essential and ubiquitous characteristic of the American judiciary specifically and American democracy generally. At the national level, judicial review promoted federalism, that constitutional principle that calls for the division of powers between the states and the nation. As Justice Oliver Wendell Holmes, Jr., once noted, "I do not think the United States would come to an end if we lost our power to declare an Act of Congress void. I do think the Union would be imperiled if we could not make that declaration as to the laws of the several States."[7] Keeping the federal courts generally and the Supreme Court especially free of direct state control was essential to the framers' constitutional scheme. Other older democratic nation-states, moreover, have replicated the American experience of relying on national courts to solidify the power of the central government.

The implications of judicial review go beyond matters of federalism, however. A vote by five of the nine unelected members of the Supreme Court can result in rejected federal and state legislation and reshaped public policies that affect millions of Americans. Critics cry foul at such an arrangement and point to what they call the countermajoritarian difficulty.

The constitutional scholar Alexander Bickel coined this phrase to describe one of the central problems of American constitutional democracy. The countermajoritarian difficulty concerns the exercise of power possessed by judges neither placed in office by the majority nor directly accountable to it. Bickel asked, in effect: How can a nonelective judiciary be justified in a democratic regime? If a law has been properly passed by the law-making branches of a democracy, why should judges, unelected judges in the case of the federal government and a few states, have the power to declare it unconstitutional?

The answer is that the American system is not a pure democracy. Instead, it is a constitutional democracy forged on two competing principles: a commitment to government founded on the will of the people and a simultaneous commitment to limit the potential excesses of popular will through resort to fundamental law. This latter concept holds that there are fixed rights guaranteed to each individual that cannot be undermined, even when they run counter to the will of the majority. The judiciary has emerged as the instrument to interpret that fundamental law and in theory the best hope for the rights of individuals and minorities. To preserve the balance in the constitutional system, judges must be free of direct political influence.

Recognizing the importance of independent courts able to exercise judicial review, however, does not settle the problem of how and to whom judges should be accountable. Certainly voting for judges would be one way to address the countermajoritarian difficulty. According to democratic theory elections bring officials into government committed to well-defined positions on major public issues to which an informed electorate holds them accountable. Theory and practice, however, have invariably diverged. Voters seldom have well-conceptualized positions on the issues; they often suffer from an acute inattentiveness to and ignorance of public affairs, including the candidates on the ballot. Yet ignorance does not mean that democratic accountability is irrelevant; to the contrary, elections are better understood as broad checks on the exercise of governmental power, of all kinds. To quote one of the leading authorities on electoral behavior: "The electorate does not decide policy; it accepts or rejects politicians associated with policies."[8] In this sense, elections indirectly impose democratic accountability on public officials.

Political parties have been one of the most important mechanisms through which voters have imposed accountability, including judicial elections. Paradoxically, partisan identification, the mechanism most essential to bring popular will to bear on the judiciary, has also been viewed as a threat to the independence of judges, whether state or federal.

The Importance of State Judiciaries

Most explanations of the American judicial system's relationship to democratic constitutionalism emphasize the federal judiciary and the countermajoritarian difficulty. The result is to obscure the importance of the state judiciaries, ignore the lessons of the states in selecting judges, and reflexively value independence over accountability. Yet, the diverse nature of the American courts actually underscores the centrality of elected state judiciaries and the vitality of state courts. The great body of day-to-day justice has taken place and continues to take place in the state and not the federal courts. Even more important, the American judicial system is centered in the states, not in the nation. For example, state courts of last resort, usually called supreme courts, have played the decisive role in shaping the major substantive areas of American law, such as torts, contracts, criminal procedure, property rights, and state constitutional rights. In areas such as the rights of the accused, state appellate courts have often lifted the ceiling of rights above the minimal floor set by the federal courts.

The decisions made by these state courts frequently have generated high levels of public controversy. In the last half of the twentieth century, one of the most contentious areas was financing of public education. More than one half of the high courts in the states have ordered state legislators to provide not only greater funding for but also guarantee a more equitable distribution of funds to all public schools. These state courts acted based on their own constitutions, not the federal Constitution, often with far-reaching consequences. For example, in *DeRolph v. Ohio*, 93 Ohio St.3d 309 (2001) the Ohio Supreme Court ordered the state legislature to spend more than a billion dollars to equalize support for public schools. The decision was greeted by calls for the removal of the several members of the court.

In other areas of law these appellate courts have been equally active and just as controversial. During the late nineteenth century state appellate courts established the doctrine of substantive due process and with it new guarantees permitting corporations to establish what they considered efficient hours and conditions of work. More recently, the Delaware Supreme Court held that a hospital could not refuse a person emergency medical treatment even if it had reason to believe the person could not pay for such care.

A Page of History, a Pound of Logic: State Courts and the Majoritarian Difficulty

Unlike the federal judiciary, where the central problem is the countermajoritarian difficulty, in most states the problem is the majoritarian difficulty. The question raised in the states today, where almost all appellate court judges face some form of election, is not how unelected/unaccountable judges can be justified in a political system committed to democracy, but how elected and hence popularly accountable judges can be justified in a system committed to constitutionalism. When those charged with checking the majority are themselves answerable to and thus susceptible to influence by the majority, the question arises how individual and minority protection is secured. Judges who safeguard a minority contrary to the wishes of a majority, for example, might be defeated in the next election and replaced by judges more attuned to majority will. Speaker DeLay, for example, at one point in the debate over Terri Schiavo suggested steps that would make appointed federal judges yield to popular pressure.

Nor is the majoritarian difficulty new. For more than a century and a half it has stood at the center of the constitutional politics of most states. Since the late 1840s the vast majority of state judges, unlike their federal counterparts, have come to and retained their positions on the bench through election, not appointment.

Oliver Wendell Holmes, Jr., once observed that "a page of history is worth a pound of logic."[9] With Holmes in mind, let's pose a simple question: Why did Americans start electing judges in the first place? The best answer: to grant those judges more power to exercise judicial review and to make them more independent of the political branches.

The history of electing judges is clear. In 1832, Mississippi became the first state to establish a statewide partisan judicial election process. Beginning with the New York constitutional convention in 1848 this approach gathered momentum, and from then until 1912 every new state entering the Union embraced it, as did a large majority of previously settled states. The traditional scholarly explanation of these developments insists that they were intended to reign in unaccountable, appointed judges and make them susceptible to direct popular pressure.

The argument, however, does not hold water. It underestimates the importance of the legal profession's almost total control of the movement to elect judges. It also misses the dramatic rise in the incidences of judicial review in the states following the adoption of the elective method. And it undervalues the majoritarian difficulty as a central problem of the American judiciary.

Popular election of judges was one, albeit an important one, of several items on the legal reform agenda of delegates to nineteenth-century state constitutional conventions. That agenda ranged over issues from improved court procedures to the costs of gaining justice. The control of this agenda was almost entirely in the hands of lawyer-delegates who overwhelmingly dominated the conventions' committees on law reform and the judiciary.

Simple self-interest drove some of their behavior. Lawyers knew the most about judges and courts and they had by far the most invested in the outcomes of any reforms. For them, change meant a more efficient administration of justice, greater status of the bench and bar, and an end to the penetration of partisan politics through the existing appointive method of judicial selection. Most importantly, reformers promised that the independence and authority of the judiciary would actually increase by granting it a popular base of support. Too often, lawyers at these conventions noted, the distribution of judgeships depended on "service to the party" rather than the "legal skills or judicial temperament" of appointees and turned the courts into "asylums for broken down or defeated politicians."[10] "Cliques and circles of a few politicians," another lawyer-delegate observed, dominated appointment of judges and meant lawyers who did "not belong to them, however well qualified . . . [could] never hope to rise to the bench."[11] Bishop Perkins, a lawyer and delegate to the 1848 New York convention, explained that appointed judges too frequently were "mere legal monks, always pouring over cases and antique tomes of learning."[12] According to Perkins, popular election promised an able, respected, enlightened, and active judiciary, one supported on a popular foundation through which it could impose an effective check on legislative power run amuck.

They found support, moreover, from nonlawyer delegates who had three other goals: control of the legislative branch, reduction in gubernatorial patronage, and the simplification of law. Some of those voices had a radical pitch. As the Ohio farmer Charles Reemelin noted in his state's 1850 constitutional convention, popular election of judges would reduce the "aristocratic tendencies of the bar" and prompt judges to be more attentive to public needs rather than the technicalities of the law.[13]

More moderate voices—the voices of lawyers—held sway. Far from limiting the power of state appellate judges, these lawyers understood that the adoption of popular election promised judges greater independence from the political branches by clothing them with the authority of the people to exercise judicial review. That power became increasingly important as these same delegates significantly lengthened state constitutions. By loading these documents with prohibitions and limitations, they became anchors rather than sails for the ship of state generally and the legislative branch in particular. Simply put, elected judges were given the task of making certain that legislators stayed in port.

These same lawyer-delegates also hedged their bets. They appreciated that the benefit of a stronger judiciary had to be balanced against the politicization of the bench. They specifically adopted measures designed to limit the full impact of direct election. These included holding judicial elections in off-years, requiring, often for the first time, that judges be lawyers, and placing limits on the terms of judges, ranging from six to twelve years. The Connecticut lawyer Simeon Baldwin, a future president of the American Bar Association, insisted that the term of office rather than the method of selection was the most important way to protect the judiciary while holding it accountable. Lawyers, like the public at large, had no interest in keeping incompetent judges.

The purpose of electing judges, then, was to make them command more rather than less power and prestige. And reformers got what they wanted. The incidence of judicial review soared in the second half of the nineteenth century as elected state judges replaced appointed ones.

The decision to elect rather than appoint judges had broad political consequences. By placing judges on the ballot they were made visible and, especially in two-party states, their pursuit of office became hotly contested. In Ohio between 1850 and 1920, for example, 20 percent of the incumbent supreme court judges went down to defeat, often after bruising campaigns. Ohio Supreme Court Justice Joseph R. Swan never even made it to the ballot in 1859. Republican party leaders at the state convention that year refused to renominate Swan because of his participation in a decision affirming the return of escaped slaves—a position that Ohio Republicans had repeatedly denounced.

Controversial issues could and did become part of judicial campaigns, and they frequently worked to the disadvantage of incumbent judges. In 1898, for example, William C. Van Fleet, a Republican, was defeated for reelection to the California Supreme Court by Walter Van Dyke, the Democratic candidate. Van Dyke had compiled an impressive record as a superior court judge, one admired by litigants and the bar of San Francisco. The campaign for Van Fleet's seat, however, turned on the judge's majority opinion in the case of *Fox v. Oakland Consolidated Street Railway Company*. Van Fleet overturned damages of $6,000 against the railway company in the death of a four-and-half-year-old boy run over by a train. In the midst of the 1898 campaign, the Democratic press reminded voters that "Van Fleet is the judge who rendered the Loren Fox decision, declaring that the life of a poor man's child is not nearly as valuable as that of a rich man's darling."[14] Van Fleet lost by nine thousand votes.

Accountability, Independence, and Power

The development and subsequent nineteenth-century history of electing state court judges warns against neatly dichotomizing the terms accountability and independence, terms that have multiple and to some extent overlapping meanings. Take the concept of independence. Roscoe Pound did not want judges free from all external influences, just political ones, and he preached consistently that judges should be accountable to the organized bar. By placing judges under the oversight of professionals, rather than naked public opinion, he insisted, an even-handed administration of justice was assured. In Pound's formulation, the professional trumped the personal; legal training and process tamed the capriciousness of politics. Professional accountability requires that judges acknowledge that the law is a separate authority with its own internal criteria, to which obedience must be paid. Since the bar is the repository of professional expertise, it, rather than the electorate, can best determine which judicial candidates most fully exhibit the necessary qualities.

The American Bar Association (ABA) and the American Judicature Society (AJS), for example, have historically insisted that the organized bar should dominate the judicial selection process. In their view, professional competence and judicial independence are intertwined; without a professionally qualified judiciary, they insist, it would be impossible to have both democracy and liberty. The

ABA has worried that even the process of appointing federal judges fails to take full account of the professional qualities of candidates. Since the early 1950s, an ABA committee has rated all candidates for federal judgeships based on their professional qualifications, with presidents paying varying degrees of deference to those ratings. Beginning in the 1930s the AJS pioneered the so-called merit selection of judges, which places great weight on the professional qualifications of candidates.

There is also conflict over whom judges should be independent of and accountable to. Nineteenth-century proponents of judicial election felt strongly that judges would be empowered through popular election to become the equals of the political branches. Others insisted that judges should never be directly accountable to the people, let alone to party officials, and that, given the technical nature of the law, the ultimate measure of their performance rests with the bar.

These varying claims about independence and accountability affirm that they are best understood not as ends in themselves, but as means to an end. The end is power, the perennial ghost at the American constitutional banquet. James Madison noted in the context of the nation's founding that the essence of government is power; and "power, lodged as it must be in human hands, will ever be liable to abuse."[15] Madison and others of the founding generation understood that the central issues involving the judiciary were neither its independence nor its accountability, although these were surely important. Instead, what counted was the terms under which judges were granted power, the ways in which they exercised that power, and the results that flowed from doing so.

Early American constitution makers knew the issues of power only too well. Having lived under the tyranny of an English system in which the king ruled and the judiciary stood constantly at risk, the framers of both federal and state constitutions learned that a judiciary too accountable was a judiciary too powerless. In the colonies, the king had absolute control over the appointment and removal of judges. The king's treatment of colonial judges appeared in the list of grievances in the Declaration of Independence: "He has made Judges dependent on his Will alone, for the tenure of their offices, and the amount and payment of their salaries."[16]

The response in the new American states, as was true at the national level, was to innovate. One of the most important innovations was the establishment of a separate judicial branch largely, but not completely, untethered from political control. The thirteen original states retained—but diffused—the appointive power. Eight of the thirteen adopted the appointive process, but placed it in the hands of one or both houses of the legislature; three provided for joint appointment by the governor and a council; and two provided for gubernatorial appointment subject to confirmation by a council. Some of these judges served terms during good behavior, some had limited terms, none were elected. For federal judges, the framers of the Constitution also retained the appointive power in the president, but diffused that power by requiring Senate confirmation.

This approach to judicial independence initially prevailed, but it did not triumph, as the experience in the states during the nineteenth century reveals. There were doubts even among those of the Founding generation most committed to the republic's future. Thomas Jefferson, for example, was a towering figure of the early nation, but he was also a critic of the judiciary. Should judges hold tenure during good behavior, he asked? No, Jefferson answered. "In truth," the third president wrote, "man is not made to be trusted for life, if secured against all liability to account."[17] And that was not the end of it. Jefferson called judges "sappers and miners," "worms," the "thieves of liberty," and a "body, like gravity, ever acting, with noiseless foot, and unalarming advance, gaining ground step by step, and holding what it gains," "ingulfing insidiously the special governments into the jaws of that which feeds them."[18] Jefferson warned that ultimately judges would end up being more political than legal, that the political would turn into the legal, and that judges would become over time powerful and therefore dangerous, contrary to the predictions of his arch rival Hamilton.

The Judicialization of Public Life

Jefferson's rhetorical attack on the judiciary was typically Jeffersonian, cogent but overwrought. Still, Jefferson's prophecy, to which Tocqueville subscribed, offers an insight into one of the most important developments in the judiciary: the tendency in the American constitutional system to judicialize public policy issues. This phenomenon became especially apparent during the same years in which states shifted from the appointment to the election of judges.

The term "judicialization" means that matters of public policy that might otherwise be left to resolution by the political branches—the executive and legislative—are instead settled by judges, they are "judicialized." As Tocqueville noted in the early nineteenth century, "[t]here is hardly a political question in the United States which does not sooner or later turn into a judicial one."[19] Today, politicians who find it hard to agree on anything, seem united in the view that judges are policy makers, even though some of those same politicians would insist that they should not be. Whether they believe judicialization of public life has been good or bad depends on whether they think the resulting public policy has been good or bad. In the space of a half century, for example, the critics of judicial activism from the New Deal era have now emerged in modern-day guise as the proponents of robust judicial intervention in a host of social issues. While Speaker DeLay rails against the power of the judiciary, his political opponents agree that judges are in fact powerful; where they disagree is over the appropriateness of such power.

There is more than a little irony in these developments. Advocates of judicial independence have insisted that accountability is ensured when judges remain bound to the law and its values and processes. At the same time, it is precisely this independence rooted in professional attributes that makes the courts such a welcome place to send the political buck.

The fate of slavery in the territories, during the 1850s, offers an example. Confronted with the vexing problem of whether slave owners should be allowed to take their human property into the new American territories, members of Congress of every political party in the 1850s decided that the judiciary was in the best position to settle the issue. President James K. Polk and Senators Stephen A. Douglas, Jefferson Davis, and Henry Clay were among the numerous antebellum political leaders who urged Congress "to leave the question of slavery or no slavery to be declared by the only competent authority that can definitely settle it forever, the authority of the Supreme Court."[20] President James Buchanan's inaugural address in 1857 explicitly declared that the status of slavery in the territories was "a judicial question, which legitimately belongs to the Supreme Court of the United States."[21] Lest jurisdictional problems bar judicial review, Congress after the Mexican War (1846–1848) routinely inserted measures facilitating judicial action on any question concerning the status of slavery in the territories. The famous Kansas-Nebraska Act of 1854 included a provision that permitted the immediate appeal to the Supreme Court of any case involving the hot potato issue of slavery.

Three years later the Supreme Court, with Chief Justice Roger B. Taney at its head, accepted the explicit invitation of Congress and the president to settle the issue. The Court, in the famous case of *Dred Scot v. Sandford* (1857), held that slave owners could not be prevented from taking their human property into the territories and by inference even into the settled states where slavery was prohibited by state law. Not long after the nation went to war with itself, in part over the issue of slavery in the territories.

On the eve of that war, President Abraham Lincoln punctuated his first inaugural address with the observation that "the representatives of the people have ceased to be their own rulers, resigning their government into the hands of" the unelected Supreme Court. Lincoln went on to urge his fellow politicians to reject the narcotic impulse of giving hard issues to the courts to make bad law. And he implored judges not to be seduced by the offer of a direct role in public affairs at the cost of their judicial credibility.

Some Realism about Lawless Powers?

Lincoln and other rule-of-law advocates in the mid-nineteenth century operated on two important assumptions, neither of which were wholly correct in their own time and which have since become increasingly suspect, but not discredited entirely. First, they insisted that the law provides a standard that can guide judicial decisions, and, second, that fidelity of judges to that law provides the appropriate baseline by which to assess their performance.

Since the later half of the twentieth century, however, both assumptions have been criticized. Some of this skepticism stems from the general decline in public trust toward all major institutions, including the courts. And some of it derives from the fact that the American public, tutored in the catechism of legal realism, has learned its lesson too well. That lesson teaches that judges, when they interpret constitutions and laws, bring their own ideology, preferences, and biases to bear, sometimes directly, more often covertly. The point of DeLay's attack on the federal judiciary was exactly that: judges were substituting their view of life and death decisions rather than following what the public wanted.

DeLay's attack, while clearly overwrought and in some ways misleading, nevertheless tapped a vein of popular sentiment. Most Americans have never been in a court, either the highest in the land or a local tribunal. Yet pollsters report that, while the public respects and in some instances reveres judges, it also believes that most courts do not mete out justice impartially and that judicial decisions are frequently based on other than legal merit. If judges are honored high priests of the law, a good part of the public view them as having interpretive feet of clay. Moreover, if judges act willfully, why should they be treated any differently than politicians?

Americans are also served a steady diet of legal realism that would lead even the most thoughtful person to conclude that the law is, at best, a lottery. To many Americans the law is the local personal injury lawyer on the television; Judge Lance Ito and O. J. Simpson's ill-fitting gloves; and John Grisham's fictional zoo of manipulative lawyers and well-meaning but hapless judges. To many Americans, as Oliver Wendell Holmes, Jr., once observed, "lawyers spend a great deal of their time shoveling smoke."[22] And most importantly, Americans regularly tell pollsters that green is the color of the law and that judges are mere bank tellers.

These overstated cultural stereotypes nonetheless are uncomfortable in their implications because they provide a vivid reminder about the consequences of judicializing public life. This judicialization has rendered the historically slippery surface of judicial politics all the more unstable. One need only scan the modern landscape of single-issue politics to appreciate the extent to which judges, through the exercise of their powers, have become part of the policy-making problem. What the framers of the federal Constitution once viewed as a closed process to be driven by elites has come to be substantially more open—to the media and special interest groups in particular.

Attention devoted to the appointment of federal judges has grown in proportion to their increasing role in shaping public policy. Controversy has followed as well. Robert Bork, President Ronald Reagan's failed nominee to the Supreme Court, has branded its members "a band of outlaws" who have "promot[ed] . . . anarchy and license in the moral order."[23] The political commentator Thomas Sowell described federal judges with the following words: "Far from restraining the lawlessness of those in power, judges have themselves become one of the lawless powers."[24] House Majority Leader DeLay has urged the impeachment of judges whom he regarded as too liberal, the withdrawal from the federal courts of their jurisdiction to hear matters of gay marriage, and the adoption of an amendment to the federal Constitution to undo the work of "four activist judges in Massachusetts" who concluded that gay persons had a right to marry. And these proposals, strikingly, came from a leader whose Republican party through the White House has appointed almost two-thirds of the current sitting federal judges.

From the political left, commentators have been equally critical. They have described the Supreme Court majority that settled the presidential election of 2000 in *Bush v. Gore* (2000) as the "felonious five," "transparent shills of the Republican Party," and, for good measure, "judicial sociopaths."[25]

The pattern is much the same in the states. Journalists have described various state appellate court judges as "idiots," "fuzzy headed buffoons," and even "stooges." Former Governor Gray Davis of California did little to undo these charges when he observed that, if judges he appointed to the bench took a position contrary to his, then they should resign. "My appointees should reflect my views. They are not there to be independent agents."[26] When the Vermont Supreme Court decided to deal with school funding issues, as had the Ohio Supreme Court, a constitutional amendment was introduced that would have forbidden them to do so.

Even judges who have tenure during good behavior are not necessarily free from the negative consequences of their decisions. New York federal district court Judge Harold Baer was strongly attacked for his decision and opinion throwing out evidence in a 1996 drug case. Republicans, again led by DeLay, urged his impeachment, and President Bill Clinton's press secretary intimated that Baer would be wise to resign. Baer ultimately reversed his decision. In 2000, Chief Justice David Brock of the New Hampshire Supreme Court was impeached (though not convicted) for alleged misdeeds concerning court procedures. But the real basis for the attack was his court's decisions mandating increased school funding and then rejecting legislative proposals to do so.

These examples notwithstanding, the concept of an independent judiciary, while sufficiently under attack to spark the American Bar Association to form task forces and issue reports, remains firmly entrenched. Lots of sound and fury, but so far only isolated instances of fundamental intrusion. However, any sensible attending physician would conclude that the patient's temperature is rising and the prognosis is, at best, guarded. And the reason, again, is the continuing spread of the underlying virus of the judicialization of public policy.

Judicial Elections and the Rule of 80: Americans Like to Elect Their Judges

The new era of democratic accountability in which state judges are selected and retained on the basis of their character, without tallying up their judicial votes, is a thing of the past. There is no way a state appellate court judge is going to be able to ignore the political consequences of certain decisions in an era of judicialized public policy. This modern form of accountability holds that judges must be answerable, not just to the profession from which they emerge, but to the public they serve and even more specifically to the special interests most affected by their decisions. At the same time, there have been concerted efforts to shore up judicial independence through greater accountability to the professional bar, not the people. The ABA, the AJS, the Century Foundation, and more than a dozen law reviews and journals have sponsored major studies and symposia on judicial independence. What has emerged is a grab bag of proposals for reform, some of them with roots going back to Pound a century earlier. The most significant of these proposals, however, turn on methods of judicial selection generally and the popular election of state judges, especially judges of the highest courts of the states.

There is enormous skepticism among the modern professional bar and many court reformers about the wisdom of electing judges. Charles Geyh, director of the American Judicature Society's Center for Judicial Independence and reporter to American Bar Association commissions on judicial independence, minced few words. As he bluntly put the matter: "judicial elections stink."[27] Geyh concluded that elections rob judges of their independence, reduce them to campaigning for offices that should be professionally earned rather than popularly won, subject courts to direct political pressures, and bring money to bear on campaigns that should be about the quality and character, not the fund-raising talents of judges. Taken together, Geyh and others argue, these problems threaten to shatter the independence of the courts and the legitimate exercise of judicial authority.

They support their case by invoking the so-called Rule of 80. That rule holds that 80 percent of the electorate does not vote in judicial elections; that 80 percent is unable to identify candidates for judicial office; that 80 percent believes that when judges are elected, they are subject to influence from their campaign contributors; and that, most strikingly, 80 percent of the public favors electing judges. In short, Americans love that which they know the least about and about which they appear to be the most cynical.

That most Americans like to elect judges and that they do not know what they are doing poses especially acute problems in light of the continued judicialization of public life. As those mid-nineteenth-century proponents of judicial elections understood, the ability of the judiciary to wield its power independently may ironically turn on its public and democratic legitimacy, a legitimacy won by an appropriate degree of popular accountability rather than by strict allegiance to the values of the legal profession. What seems on its face to be antithetical to the effectiveness of the judiciary is essential to its power. In an age of judicialized politics, judges should be independent, but not too independent. As those mid-nineteenth-century judicial reformers understood, state judges connected through election to the people they serve may actually be more rather than less independent of direct political pressures and more rather than less legitimate when they exercise their powers.

The Progressive Retreat from Democratic Accountability and the Rise of Merit Selection

The problems associated with the Rule of 80 have their roots not in the 1850s but in the Progressive movement and the rise of the organized bar in the early twentieth century. Roscoe Pound's experience again proves instructive.

Pound's call for reform in 1906 underscored how much and how little Progressive reformers and the leaders of the new bar associations shared in common. Both groups believed that greater efficiency, rationality, and order in public life necessitated changes that would diminish the control of political parties and remove untutored immigrants and the ignorant from the civic mix. They also, however, wanted to retain some base of popular authority for each branch of government. To that end, they touted the Australian ballot, the direct party primary, the initiative, referendum, and recall. But in the end, the organized bar would not go as far as Pound proposed, which was to adopt the federal scheme of judicial selection. A 1904 survey by the American Bar Association reported that on the question of judicial elections the group was almost perfectly divided. A poll of delegates to the 1910 Ohio State Bar Association convention revealed a similar even division, and a proposed constitutional amendment to appoint rather than elect judges failed even to reach the state's voters.

After a half century of experience with popular election, leaders of the ABA and state bar organizations called for radical change but ultimately accepted much less. They did so because they concluded that the particular method of selection was less important than the extent to which the bar could influence whatever process was followed. The only common ground on which Pound, the Progressives, and the organized bar could ultimately agree was the need to drive partisanship out of the election process. Ultimately, they accepted the continued election of judges but on nonpartisan tickets, although today about 40 percent of all judicial elections have a partisan basis.

The result was the bag of problems associated with the Rule of 80. Public participation in state judicial elections dropped; the failure rate of incumbents went down by more than one-half; turnout in judicial elections collapsed; and judicial campaigns increasingly lost their edge, especially in previously hotly contested two-party states.

One condition did persist. Judicial review by state courts continued its relentless expansion. Progressive reformers diminished the public accountability of judges but did nothing to limit these same judges' powers to intervene with the elected branches.

At the same time, the underlying environment for laws, courts, and judges was transformed. First proponents of sociological jurisprudence, such as Louis Brandeis, affirmed the value of explaining the law in terms of measurable results, not just formal doctrine. Beginning in the 1930s the legal realists went even further. Led by Jerome Frank and Karl Llewellyn, the legal realists offered a robust view of the interaction of law and society, insisting that the idea that judges interpreted the law was a fig leaf intended to cover the naked truth that they actually made it.

Pound lived long enough to become frustrated that so little changed. By 1944 he had adjusted and threw his considerable energies behind another project, the merit selection of judges. "Too much thought has been given to the matter of getting less qualified judges off the bench," he wrote in that year. "The real remedy is to put [better prepared ones] on."[28]

The merit selection process emerged as a way of having an independent yet democratically accountable judiciary. It called for a nominating commission, consisting of lawyers, non-lawyers, and sometimes judges, to recruit, investigate, interview, and evaluate applicants for judicial office. The nominating commission forwarded a short list of qualified candidates to the governor, from which he was required to make a selection. Judges served for specified terms but then stood, if they wished, unopposed for another term on a retention ballot.

The merit plan had its roots in the American Judicature Society, itself a product of the Progressive era, and in the crusading of Pound. Pound argued that the "most efficient causes of disaffection with the present administration of justice" included not only the partisan election of judges but disorganized and antiquated court systems that caused "uncertainty, delay and expense, and above all the injustice of deciding cases upon points of practice, which are the mere etiquette of justice."[29] AJS was formed in 1913 with the mission of improving the "efficiency" of the administration of justice. The Society's negative attitude toward the election of judges, for example, stemmed from a belief that partisanship was inefficient and that government, including the courts, should be run like a business. By 1928 the Society had formally endorsed a full-blown scheme of merit selection, and two years later the ABA jumped on board. In 1940 Missouri adopted it and since then the phrase "Missouri Plan" has become synonymous with merit selection.

Despite lingering doubts by some about merit selection's effectiveness in eliminating politics from judicial selection, and the lack of "hard" evidence that it produced better judges, the merit plan gained widespread acceptance. Today, thirty-four states and the District of Columbia use the merit plan for the selection of some or all of their judges. Since 1988, however, the pace has slowed, with only corruption-wracked Rhode Island adopting it. Proponents of merit selection have come to understand that in the new era of special interest politics and single issue elections, the costs of judicial elections, even ones designed to retain judges selected initially by commissions and governors, have soared.

For example, in 1986, groups opposing Chief Justice Rose Bird and two associate justices of the California Supreme Court spent almost $6 million to defeat them. In 1994 and 1996, the winning candidates for the Texas Supreme Court spent almost $10 million. In 2002 business groups affiliated with the Ohio Chamber of Commerce spent millions on ads for one supreme court race. And in Michigan almost $3 million was spent to fill vacant state supreme court posts. These sums dwarf previous spending patterns.

Costly and contentious judicial races have not been confined to states with partisan selection methods. Texas selects its judges in partisan elections, but Ohio and Michigan conduct nominally nonpartisan elections, and California reelects its merit-selected judges in retention elections. What is driving this behavior are not arcane debates over either the independence of the courts or the method of selection; instead, these races have become important because of the judicialization of public policy. These developments also mean that the formal rules of selection are important but so too is political culture, as a comparative view suggests.

Judicial Independence, Political Culture, and the Federal Judiciary

While Americans place great weight on the value of an independent judiciary, other democracies do not. Japan offers an example in part because American occupation authorities helped to write the modern Japanese constitution in the post–World War II period. That constitution vests the whole judicial power in the courts and provides explicitly for their independence. The constitution does, however, subject supreme court justices to a popular referendum every ten years and requires mandatory retirement at age seventy. In theory, then, Japanese high court judges have less independence than their American counterparts. Yet the Japanese Diet seldom impeaches judges and Japanese voters have never given any justice a negative vote greater than 16 percent.

What does make the difference in Japan is the system of politics. For most of its post–World War II history, the Liberal Democratic Party, or LDP, has dominated Japan, and it has found more subtle ways to deal with the judiciary, primarily through job assignments. Japan has a professional, civil-service like judiciary. Would-be judges apply for positions at the end of their legal training. If chosen, they receive an initial ten-year term. During this time they rotate through positions every two to three years. By controlling these assignments, the LDP historically controlled the judges. Industrious and orthodox judges received prestige appointments; the dilatory and more troublesome drew other, less rewarding, obscure assignments. Modern Japanese elections are highly competitive, but for half a century the LDP consistently won, and with winning came stability in judicial offices. Party leaders knew that they could control the judicial terrain and still not intervene directly in the actions of the judiciary.

This pattern contrasts sharply with the American experience, where national political parties historically have won erratically. Faced with this uncertainty, presidents and the Senate have followed two rules: hands-off sitting judges and prospective, up-front accountability. This means that in the federal system the face of the judiciary is shaped only at the moment of appointment, not during the term of service. The federal system has produced independent judges, but not necessarily consistent nor accountable ones. A recent study suggests that more than one-half of all Supreme Court appointees ended up taking policy positions at odds with the presidents that selected them.

The examples are legion. President Thomas Jefferson in 1804 appointed William Johnson who in his first major opinion held Jefferson's embargo of American ports illegal. Theodore Roosevelt selected Oliver Wendell Holmes, Jr., only to have Holmes side with the trusts in the famous *Northern Securities Cases.* Roosevelt said of Holmes: "I could carve out of a banana a judge with more backbone." Richard Nixon selected the conservatives Harry Blackmun and Warren Burger, the "Minnesota Twins," who delivered him the pro-abortion decision *Roe v. Wade.* President George H. W. Bush surely feels the same way about David Souter, and Republican President Gerald Ford, who had sought to impeach liberal Chief Justice Earl Warren, can not be happy to have his sole appointee, John Paul Stevens, emerge as the contemporary Court's most liberal justice. President Dwight D. Eisenhower summed matters up nicely at the end of his second term. Asked by the press what was the biggest mistake he made while in office, Ike purportedly responded: "Appointing Earl Warren was the biggest damn fool thing that I ever did." Asked to name a second, Eisenhower responded: "William Brennan."[30]

The justices understand entirely how the federal system of prospective accountability operates. Thurgood Marshall reportedly told one of his law clerks when Ronald Reagan was in the White House that "if I die while that man's president, I want you to just prop me up and keep me voting."[31]

Overt political manipulation of the federal selection system has often been met with stunning political reversals, ones that suggest that the informal norms that govern judicial independence are at least as important as the formal ones. The hands off the courts rule, which is a political reality rather than a constitutional requirement per se, often stimulates criticism of efforts to be too partisan. President Franklin D. Roosevelt, who had not been able to make a single Supreme Court appointment during his first term, in 1937 sought to pack the federal courts with his political supporters, only to be rebuffed by the members of his own party in Congress. Republican President Reagan was battered by

Democrats when he unsuccessfully put Robert Bork forward with the specific understanding that Bork would rearrange the constitutional landscape to fit Reagan's political picture frame. Speaker DeLay has suffered a similar rebuke and has backed away from his most strident positions.

The existence of these informal understandings makes bringing change to the federal judiciary essentially moot. There is little likelihood of electing federal judges; they are unlikely candidates for limited terms in office. Maintenance of American federalism and a commitment to protecting minority rights through fundamental law make such changes unlikely and probably unwise. While the countermajoritarian difficulty is a theoretical problem, in day-to-day practice it is essential to American-style constitutional democracy. The tools to hold these judges broadly accountable are few and ineffective. In more than two centuries only one Supreme Court justice, Samuel Chase in 1804, was impeached, and he escaped conviction. Between 1789 and 2004, the House initiated impeachment proceedings against only thirteen federal judges, out of more than five thousand who have served, although about an equal number of judges resigned just before formal action was taken against them. Of these thirteen cases, only five resulted in a conviction and removal from office.

Terms of Office and the Majoritarian Difficulty

The real action, then, is in the states, which have become the object of innovative recommendations meant to address the majoritarian difficulty. Some proposals lean toward Pound's model of professional qualifications and the influence of the bar. One scheme proposes to develop a training program for aspiring judges that would lead to a credential that identifies its holders as having the requisite judicial skills. Such an approach treats judges as public officials but even more significantly as legal professionals. It also reinforces Pound's idea that an independent judiciary is a professionally competent judiciary. Training of judges would also distinguish them from legislators and executives.

State appellate court judges would become a mix of something like civil servants in the United States and judges in civil law systems, who must be trained, credentialed, and selected on the basis of examinations. In France, for example, would-be judges must pass competitive written and oral examinations and then be admitted to the École Nationale de la Magistrature. After undergoing thirty-one months of classroom and apprenticeship training they assume positions at the bottom of the career ladder, with promotions on the basis of seniority and merit. In Germany, candidates for judgeships complete extended legal training in a university setting before taking their first state examination. If successful, they become temporary civil servants while receiving additional practical training. Only after completion of an apprenticeship of up to ten years can they hold a regular judicial position. Such an approach, however, would require not only wholesale changes in American legal education but further distancing judges from popular accountability at a time when public policy is becoming more judicialized.

While civil-law legal systems have transformed their judiciaries into a branch of the civil service, these same systems operated on the proposition that constitutional interpretation cannot be left entirely to technicians. In France, for example, the president of the Republic, the president of the Senate, and the president of the National Assembly each select three members of the French Constitutional Council. In Germany, the sixteen members of the Constitutional Court are selected by parliament, with eight members elected by a committee of the Bundestag (lower house of the national legislature), reflecting the proportional weight of parties in that chamber, and eight members directly elected by the Bundesrat (upper house of the national legislature), with a two-thirds vote required for selection.

These systems of judicial selection are manifestly political, even though the training of the judges follows a seemingly nonpolitical, professional process. Most importantly, these selection schemes reflect the reality that the task of a constitutional court differs from that of regular courts and that constitutional adjudication differs fundamentally from ordinary adjudication. Because the tasks are different, so too are the qualifications to perform those tasks.

Tempering the Majoritarian Difficulty

Like their counterparts in Europe, American state supreme court judges also engage in constitutional adjudication that often generates political controversy. As the constitutional scholar G. Alan Tarr has noted, the European experience points in the direction of a political, rather than an exclusively professionalized, selection process for the members of state high courts.[32] The way to temper the majoritarian difficulty while retaining a high level of popular accountability rests not with eliminating the election of judges, which Americans clearly prefer, but borrowing from the European experience with the length and non-renewability of their terms. Even merit selection plans require judges to stand periodically in retention elections. There is a broad consensus that short terms of office—six years or less—make judges vulnerable. Longer terms in office would mean that judges would not face reelection as often, they would not have to raise campaign funds as often, they would be less subject to the influence of contributors, and they could not be as easily intimidated by either the public or special interests. Longer terms also make holding a judicial office more attractive and, in theory, draw better qualified candidates to the bench.

The goal in a reformed American state system should not be, as Pound urged, the elimination of politics from the selection process, an unlikely outcome in any case, but to direct those politics in a different way. Doing so could be accomplished by blending the American preference for popular accountability with the European system of training judges, providing them with fixed terms, and, in the case of the constitutional courts, prohibiting them from seeking a second term. France, Germany, Spain, and Italy employ a mixed system of selection, with some judges named by the executive, some named by the judiciary, and some elected by super-majorities in parliament. Whichever system is employed, the key consideration is that the judge, once selected, serves a single nonrenewable term of office. In France, Italy, and Spain, the length of term is nine years, in Germany it is twelve years.

The American states might well formulate a hybrid, one in which judges would be elected initially and then hold office for an extended, nonrenewable period, perhaps twelve years, somewhat longer than the average eight years now served by state supreme court judges. Such a system would free judges to decide cases according to law, without fear of either electoral retribution or hope of favor from powerful interests. It would also free them from being targeted because of a few controversial decisions. Judges would, at the same time, still have the authority of the people who elected them, much as the mid-nineteenth-century reformers intended. Judicial candidates would still have to run for office initially, and there is every likelihood that contributions would still flow into campaigns, but the resulting accountability would not be a quid pro quo for giving money but a form of prospective accountability, in which the bar could participate, somewhat like the federal judiciary. Whatever the contributions a group makes to a judge's initial election, the judge would not have to return to that same group to keep office. The judges' initial supporters would not be able to take revenge at the polls if the judge adheres to law contrary to their interests. Again, the example of the federal courts is helpful. Aspirants to the federal bench cannot be successful without political support, but once on the bench judges know their independence is retained because they never have to go back to the political well again.

This proposal also acknowledges that there should be some turnover as a way of granting popular legitimacy to the judiciary. Given the public's clear preference for electing judges, an opportunity for periodic public input about the general direction of law and policy emanating from the states' highest courts may actually strengthen the judiciary. Once one acknowledges that state supreme court justices are involved in more than merely technical application of the law and are making decisions with broad societal consequences, the case for some popular accountability becomes compelling.

The arguments against this scheme of addressing the majoritarian difficulty are obvious. Distinguished lawyers might not be attracted to the posts because they could not be reelected. Once on the bench, however, judges would not have to engage in fund raising, perhaps making these positions, as is true in Europe, more rather than less attractive. Judges serving under this new dispensation might well see their term in office as the final stage in a legal career, rather than an intermediate stop. Even if the current average term of judges staying on the bench persisted, they would leave their service well equipped to re-enter the professional world of the law, with additional prestige and ability to generate revenue. Finally, there is a legitimate concern that a state might lose a talented judge prematurely. That loss has to be balanced against Paul Carrington's astute observation that "[t]here is no unobjectionable way to decide who shall judge or to judge those who do."[33] We already place term limits on many state legislators and governors, there are term limits on the service of the president of the United States, and in many states there are mandated retirement ages for judges. In any political system, change will be viewed by some as loss, the question becomes whether the benefits of that change outweigh the loss. A scheme that allows for the election of judges without the burden of reelection seems a way to moderate the majoritarian difficulty. Overcoming it entirely seems both unlikely and unproductive in an era of judicialized public policy.

Conclusion

When it comes to the legitimacy of the courts, we are stuck with what might be called a tale of two pities. The countermajoritarian one involves the appointive and largely unaccountable federal courts; the majoritarian one involves accountable but insufficiently independent state courts. Neither are susceptible to resolution without fundamentally altering the American constitutional system, an event that, while possible, is unlikely.

In the case of the state courts and the judicialization of American public life, care is warranted before concluding that electing judges "stinks." Reform is in order, but the political culture in most of the American states that currently elect judges makes it unlikely that wholesale change will be adopted. States are as unlikely to begin appointing their judges to terms of good behavior as the nation is to begin electing federal judges to fixed terms. Abandoning judicial elections altogether would be ill-advised, especially in the face overwhelming approval from the populace. The four components of the Rule of 80 are real, but the last of these—the public's strong wish to continue electing judges—effectively diminishes the possibility of addressing fully the other three.

Issues of judicial independence are nevertheless real and require attention. A comparative perspective on these matters encourages a moderate but important step toward blending the need for independent courts with democratically accountable judges. Adopting the European practice of granting judges of constitutional courts long, non-renewable terms in office would permit the American states to retain popular, prospective accountability while keeping judges from becoming hostages to the next election. Ironically, electing judges in an era of the judicialization of public policy is essential if state courts are to retain sufficient popular legitimacy to exercise their powers of judicial review.

As those nineteenth-century architects of judicial elections understood, the legitimacy of state court judges, unlike their federal counterparts, flowed significantly from an elective process that associated judges with the people in whose behalf they decided cases.

To perpetuate the American state judiciary and to make it more independent requires that it be publicly accountable, but not too accountable. The task ahead is to make judicial elections something other than the tail on the electoral kite. That means revitalizing the concept of a democratically accountable judiciary not beholden to any special interests and providing citizens with an appropriate means by which to calibrate the consequence of having judges so profoundly shape public policy and their lives. A century after Roscoe Pound and his fellow Progressives called for the end to election of state judges, perhaps even they would agree that the future of the American judiciary lies with the people and not just the law and its practitioners.

Notes

1. Roscoe Pound, "The Causes of Popular Dissatisfaction with the Administration of Justice," *Reports of the American Bar Association* 29 (1906): 404.
2. Alexander Hamilton, "Federalist 78," *The Federalist Papers*, edited by Clinton Rossiter (New York: New American Library, 1961), 464.
3. Ibid., 471.
4. Alexis de Tocqueville, *Democracy in America*, edited by J. P. Mayer, translated by George Lawrence (New York: Doubleday, 1969), 269.
5. *New York Times*, 8 April 2005, 21.
6. *New York Times*, 14 April 2005, 1.
7. As quoted in "Law and the Court," in *The Essential Holmes* by Oliver Wendell Holmes, Richard A. Posner, ed. (Chicago: The University of Chicago Press, 1992), 145.
8. Gerald M. Pomper, *Elections in America: Control and Influence in Democratic Politics* (New York: Dodd, Mead, & Co., 1973), 25.
9. Oliver Wendell Holmes Jr., *The Quotations Page*. Available at http://www.quotationspage.com/quotes/Oliver_Wendell_Holmes_Jr.
10. As quoted in Kermit L. Hall, "The Judiciary on Trial: State Constitutional Reform and the Rise of an Elected Judiciary, 1846–1860," *The Historian* 44 (May 1983): 347.
11. Ibid., 347.
12. Ibid., 346.
13. Ibid., 345.
14. *San Francisco Examiner*, 25 October 1898, p. 2., col. 2.
15. James Madison, "Speech before the Virginia State Constitutional Convention, December 1, 1829." Available at http://www.billofrightsinstitute.org/categories.php?op=newindex&catid=11.
16. "The Declaration of Independence," *Action of Second Continental Congress, July 4, 1776* (Washington, D.C.: Commission on the Bicentennial of the United States Constitution, 1992), 37.

17. Thomas Jefferson, "Letter to Monsieur A. Coray, October 31, 1823," *The Writings of Thomas Jefferson*, 20 vols., edited by Andrew A. Lipscomb (Washington, D.C.: Thomas Jefferson Memorial Association of the United States, 1904), vol. 15, 486–487. Available at http://www.bartleby.com/73/940.html.
18. Thomas Jefferson, "Letter to Thomas Ritchie, December 25, 1820," *The Writings of Thomas Jefferson*, 10 vols., edited by Paul L. Ford (New York: G.P. Putnam's Sons, 1892–1899), vol. 10, 170–171. Available at http://www.bartleby.com/73/943.html. And Thomas Jefferson, "Letter to Judge Spencer Roane, March 9, 1821," *The Writings of Thomas Jefferson*, edited by Andrew A. Lipscomb, vol. 15, 326. Available at http://www.bartleby.com/73/942.html.
19. Tocqueville, *Democracy in America*, edited by J. P. Mayer, translated by George Lawrence (1969). Vol. 1, part 2, chapter 8, 270.
20. *Cong. Globe*, 31st Cong., 1 Sess., 1154–1155 (speech of Henry Clay). See James K. Polk, Fourth Annual Message, in *Messages and Papers* 4, p. 642; *Cong. Globe*, 31st Cong., 1 Sess., App., 154 (speech of Jefferson Davis); *Cong. Globe*, 34th Cong., 1 Sess., App., 797 (speech of Steven Douglas).
21. James Buchanan, Inaugural Address in Richardson, ed., 5 *Messages and Papers of the President of the United States,* 431.
22. Oliver Wendell Holmes, Jr., *The Quotations Page*. Available at http://www.quotationspage.com/quotes/Oliver_Wendell_Holmes_Jr.
23. Quoted in Joan Biskupic, "Bork, Uncorked; The Judge Holds the Supreme Court in Contempt," The *Washington Post*, 16 March 1997, C01.
24. Quoted in Thomas Sowell, "Political Dangers," *Atlanta Journal-Constitution*, 9 January 2001. Available at http://www.brennancenter.org/programs/pester/pages/view _elerts.php?category_id=30&page=28.
25. Vincent Bugliosi, "None Dare Call It Treason," *The Nation*, 5 February 2001. Available at http://www.thenation.com/doc.mhtml?i=20010205&c=1&s=bugliosi. Quoted in Charles Gardner Geyh, "Why Judicial Elections Stink," *Ohio State Law Journal* 64, no. 1 (2003).
26. Quoted in Charles Gardner Geyh, "Why Judicial Elections Stink."
27. Ibid.
28. Roscoe Pound, introduction to Evan Haynes, *The Selection and Tenure of Judges* (New York: The National Conference of Judicial Councils, 1944), ix, xiv.
29. Roscoe Pound, "The Causes of Popular Dissatisfaction with the Administration of Justice," *Reports of the American Bar Association*, vol. 29 (1906), Part 1, 400–401. Available at http://www.law.du.edu/sterling/Content/ALH/pound.pdf.
30. The authenticity of these quotations remains in doubt, although they have become part of the lore that surrounds the Eisenhower presidency. There is little doubt, however, whether or not the words are entirely correct, that Eisenhower regretted his choices of both justices. See Henry J. Abraham, *Justices and Presidents*, 208–250.
31. Quoted in Jan Crawford Greenburg, "Justice Stevens' Retirement Would Shake Up Court Most," *Jewish World Review*, 25 June 2003. Available at http://www.jewishworldreview.com/0603/law_report.asp.
32. Tarr, G. Alan. "Selection of State Appellate Judges: Reform Proposals: Rethinking the Selection of State Supreme Court Justices." *Willamette Law Review* 39 (Fall,

2003): 1445–1470. A cogent critique of the current methods by which their judges are selected with a proposal for reform upon which I have relied.

33. Paul D. Carrington, "Judicial Independence and Judicial Accountability in the Highest State Courts," *Law & Contemporary Problems* 61 (1998): 79, 113.

Bibliography

Abraham, Henry J. *Justices and Presidents: A Political History of Appointments to the Supreme Court.* 3rd ed. New York: Oxford University Press, 1992. The best historical analysis of the process by which Supreme Court justices reach the best.

Baum, Lawrence. *American Courts: Process and Policy.* 5th ed. New York: Hougton Mifflin 2001. A brilliant overview of American courts and the ways in which they react with the political system.

Belknap, Michal R. *To Improve the Administration of Justice: A History of the American Judicature Society.* Chicago: The American Judicature Society, 1992. A history of the one of the nation's most important judicial reform organizations.

Bickel, Alexander M. *The Morality of Consent.* New Haven, Conn.: Yale University Press, 1975. An introduction to the issues of the countermajoritarian difficulty.

Bork, Robert H. *Coercing Virtue: The Worldwide Rule of Judges.* Washington, D.C.: AEI Press, 2003.

Burbank, Stephen B., and Barry Friedman, eds. *Judicial Independence at the Crossroads: An Interdisciplinary Approach.* New York: Sage, 2002. A path-breaking collection of essays from a strongly interdisciplinary perspective that identifies common myths in discussions of judicial independence.

Champagne, Anthony, and Judith Haydel. *Judicial Reform in the States.* New York: Rowman and Littlefield, 1993. An analysis of judicial elections in seven states.

Dahl, Robert A. *How Democratic Is the American Constitution?* 2nd ed. New Haven, Conn.: Yale University Press, 2003. A grand introduction to the contradictions that beset the American scheme of democracy.

Davis, Richard. *Electing Justice: Fixing the Supreme Court Nomination Process.* New York: Oxford University Press, 2005. A superb critique of the current practice of placing justices on the high court and what can be done to improve it.

Dubois, Philip L. *From Ballot to Bench: Judicial Elections and the Quest for Accountability.* Austin: University of Texas Press, 1980. The single best work on the relationship between judicial elections and accountability.

Ginsburg, Tom. *Judicial Review in New Democracies: Constitutional Courts in Asian Cases.* Cambridge, U.K., and New York: Cambridge University Press, 2003. An examination of three constitutional courts in East Asia, where law is traditionally viewed as a tool of authoritarian rulers.

Haley, John Owen. *Authority without Power: Law and the Japanese Paradox.* Reprint. New York: Oxford University Press, 1994.

Hall, Kermit L. *The Magic Mirror: Law in American History.* New York: Oxford University Press, 1989. A broad history of American law with a revisionist analysis of the rise and impact of popular election of judges.

Hurst, James Willard. *The Growth of American Law: The Law Makers.* Boston.: Little, Brown and Company, 1950. A seminal work on the development of courts and law making in the states.

Kommers, Donald P. *Judicial Politics in West Germany: A study of the Federal Constitutional Court.* New York: Sage, 1976. An excellent overview of the highest court of Germany.

Kramer, Larry D. *The People Themselves: Popular Constitutionalism and Judicial Review.* New York: Oxford University Press, 2004. A shrewd analysis of the interplay of popular will and judicial review on shaping constitutional principles.

Melhorn, Donald F. *Lest We Be Marshall'd: Judicial Power and Politics in Ohio, 1806–1812.* Akron, Oh.: University of Akron Press, 2003. This study links the development of judicial review to the politics of judicial selection during the first years of Ohio statehood.

Russell, Peter H., and David O'Brien. *Judicial Independence in the Age of Democracy: Critical Perspectives from around the World.* Charlottesville: University Press of Virginia, 2001.

Stone-Sweet, Alec. *Governing with Judges: Constitutional Politics in Europe.* New York: Oxford University Press, 2000. Focusing on France, Germany, Italy, Spain, and the European Union, the book examines the pan-European movement to confer constitutional review authority on a new governmental institution, the constitutional court.

Tarr, G. Alan, and Mary Cornelia Aldis Porter. *State Supreme Courts in State and Nation.* New Haven, Conn.: Yale University Press, 1988. An insightful study of the operations of highest courts in the states.

Thompson, Dennis F. *Just Elections: Creating a Fair Electoral Process in the United States.* Chicago: University of Chicago Press, 2002.

Upham, Frank K. *Law and Social Change in Postwar Japan.* Cambridge, Mass.: Harvard University Press, 1987. A brilliant analysis of the interaction of courts, politics, and social change in Japan since World War II.

Court Cases

Bush v. Gore, 531 U.S. 115 (2000).
DeRolph v. Ohio, 93 Ohio St.3d 309 (2001).
Dred Scot v. Sandford, 19 Howard 393 (1857).
Fox v. Oakland Consolidated Street Railway Company, 118 Cal. 55 (1897).
Northern Securities Co. v. United States, 193 U.S. 197 (1904).
Roe v. Wade, 410 U.S. 113 (1973).

SECTION II

COURTS IN THE CONSTITUTIONAL SYSTEM

4

THE JUDICIARY AND THE SEPARATION OF POWERS

Richard A. Brisbin, Jr.

DISTRUST OF GOVERNMENT IS DEEPLY ROOTED IN THE American character. When they first read the Constitution, some Americans detected a dangerous conspiracy to concentrate political power through a complicated mixing of powers. Also, because the framers ignored including in the Constitution the details of the checks and balances to be exercised by and upon the judiciary, the critics of the Constitution feared the appearance of a judicial aristocracy unresponsive to the people. As Patrick Henry commented, "no man on this earth can know its real operation."[1] What Henry found so maddeningly obscure was how the Constitution's framers had separated governmental powers among legislative, executive, and judicial branches. The framers had rejected an absolute separation as an overrated means for protecting liberty. They instead created a scheme of "mixed powers" and checks of each branch upon the others. This chapter addresses what has become of the judicial role in the mixed system of separated powers and checks and balances. Is it an unresponsive aristocracy or an essential component of modern American democracy?

To answer this question, the chapter argues that the original aim of the separation of powers and checks and balances was the prevention of governmental tyranny. Next, this chapter proposes that both legally binding judicial interpretations of the constitutional text made in response to lawsuits and congressional and executive branch "constructions," or elaborations of their constitutional powers, have engendered meaningful developments in the United States Constitution's separation of the branches and scheme of interbranch relations.[2] Because of imprecise text, omissions, and political developments, the judiciary has assumed independent authority to define the meaning of separated powers. However, as will be illustrated using the example of the federal judiciary, only at critical political moments has the judiciary risked its legitimacy and set its own seal on the meaning of separated powers. In new political contexts or to serve the political interests of their diverse constituencies, more commonly Congress and the president have constructed separated powers to produce consequential additions that specify the meaning or "fill in" the constitutional text. The upshot of these developments is that the American Founders' effort to prevent governmental tyranny through a "free government" that combined "stability and energy in government with a due attention to liberty and to the republican form" is always at issue.[3] Free government is the sovereignty of the people and popular rule or democracy. However, to protect the people's liberty against human fallibility, it also provides ongoing political dialogue and contestation among a judiciary with lifetime tenure, legislators eager to please diverse popular constituencies, and an executive driven by a vision of what he thinks America should be.

The Invention of Separated Powers and Checks and Balances

Before evaluating what separated powers means for contemporary American politics, it is important to explore the political concerns of the framers when they devised the separation of powers. The idea that governmental powers should be divided in some manner emerged in the ancient writings of Plato, Aristotle, and Polybius. They sought to include three separate social classes in politics—monarchy, aristocracy, and *demos* or citizens. In early modern England this three-class idea of government evolved into class-based institutional structures—the crown, the House of Lords, and the House of Commons—in what was labeled as a "balanced constitution" marked by "mixed government" and "rule of law." As described by John Locke and other seventeenth- and eighteenth-century writers, English government rested on the supremacy of the rule of just law. Law was to protect liberty from arbitrary exercises of political power. Although to prevent tyranny Locke sought independence for the executive, in practice the executive carried out the lawful commands of the House of Commons. Indeed, with the emergence of the supremacy of Commons in the eighteenth century, Britain abandoned separated powers.

In 1748 the Baron de Montesquieu, a French aristocrat, proposed a palliative for the arbitrary royal dictatorship of his homeland. Eager to establish a rule of law and foster a spirit of liberty, he contended that the unwritten English constitution divided power among legislative, executive, and judicial institutions. Through the establishment of legal boundaries on the authority of each branch, each had the limited capacity to restrain the others. Although Montesquieu's thesis became widely known in America, it was a bit of a muddle. He did not fully define a system of checks and balances or abandon the legacy of class-based governance. He assumed that executive power would best reside in a hereditary monarch. The legislature, he asserted, should be composed of an aristocratic class identified by virtues and honor as well as by their birth and riches. The judiciary would be from the same class as the accused and act in a manner consistent with the law.

The American Revolution drew upon an amalgam of an underlying faith in the rule of law, British political history, the English common law, and Montesquieu to reorganize politics. However, separation of powers underwent a revolutionary reconsideration in the New World. The immoral luxury and privilege that American revolutionaries associated with the British crown and the corruption of Commons became a source of disgust. In the new American politics, some revolutionaries thought that rank and privilege would disappear and the common sense and the virtues of a sovereign people would govern. As this idea of popular sovereignty evolved during and after the Revolution, Americans faced two threats to political liberty. The first threat was the reassertion of despotism with support from portions of the populace. Popular support for a despot might come in two guises—as minority or majority tyranny. Minority tyranny was the assertion of despotism by a class-based coup or "minority faction" adverse to the liberties of all. For example, many Americans worried that either British loyalists or an American officer corps might stage such a coup. Majority tyranny was the fear that a revolutionary popular movement would destroy the liberties of a minority such as property owners. Politically active Americans also recognized a second political problem: how to prevent public officials from lapsing into despotism or "governmental tyranny."

Although many Americans assumed that the solution to threats to liberty was the construction of laws that placed political power in the hands of the people's representatives, for years Americans experimented with the arrangement of governmental power. They did not want the concentration of power—"the definition of despotic government."[4] Although the revolutionary Congress adopted the Articles of Confederation, under the Articles, each state retained sovereignty and extensive political power. The power of the federal Congress did not rest on popular consent. Instead, state constitutional conventions served as a laboratory for experiments about the disposition of political power. At first, the states sought to diminish the immediate problem with British colonial governance—the power of royal governors. Pennsylvania drafted a constitution that replaced the governor with a twelve-member executive council. Other states opted for an executive who effectively served as chair of an elected executive board. In some states the legislature selected the executive. In most constitutions the executive lacked a legislative role or veto. Also, most states sought to curtail the power of officers who were formerly royal appointees, such as judges, by extending legislative control over their decisions, appointment, term of service, and salary.

Despite a drift toward popular sovereignty, the idea of a class basis for political institutions persisted. Particularly there existed a belief in a natural aristocracy—identifiable by its intellect or possession of property. To ensure the inclusion of persons of talent and wealth, some states, such as Maryland, selected their Senate through various procedures to ensure that men of talent and virtue held office. Most state constitutions opted for wealth or property ownership requirements for officeholders and voters. However, after 1780 most states included a redesigned executive in new or amended constitutions. Abuses of legislative power and political instability inclined the leaders of states such as Massachusetts, New Hampshire, and New York to adopt a popularly elected governor with increased independence from legislative control, a veto power, and the authority to enforce the laws. Arguments for greater judicial authority to protect the will of the people against legislative error also surfaced. The classical taxonomy of power based on social class gradually succumbed to the idea of having all elected public officials act for a sovereign public.

As a consequence of the states' experiments, by the time of the Constitutional Convention of 1787 most Americans had accepted popular sovereignty and some division of governmental functions. When adopted with public consent, the higher law of a Constitution defined proper uses of political power. To prevent lapses into corruption and despotism, the Convention solved—as best it could—the threat of popular support for tyranny through a complex scheme for the selection of representatives and officers. Desirous that virtuous leaders would hold office and temper popular sentiments adverse to the long-term security of the republic, they decided that there had to be a restraint on popular political sentiments. Therefore, the Convention determined that the people would directly elect only the House of Representatives. Additionally, the plan was that the large size and diverse population of the republic would make it unlikely that either a coup by a small faction or a mass movement would strip liberties from other persons.

Yet, the threat of governmental tyranny remained. Refining these efforts to control governmental tyranny through many constitutional conventions, today forty state constitutions have included a specific provision to protect departmental independence. Also, almost all state constitutions are much more specific in their definition of the scope and limits of powers than is the federal constitution. The consequence is that state judges have limited interpretive leeway in separation of powers cases and the other branches cannot construct new governmental arrangements.

Rejecting such a detailed legal definition of the powers of each branch, the framers of the federal constitution adopted an alternative approach. They offered a fresh, functional conceptualization of what James Madison called the "auxiliary precautions" against tyranny afforded by the separation of powers and checks and balances. The member of the Convention who wrote most cogently on the topic, Madison rested his support of the Constitution's separation of powers on three assumptions. First, because of their "fallen" status—the Judeo-Christian conception of human nature—mankind's virtue too often gave way to unpredictable passions and interests neglectful of the liberties of others. Second, to channel human nature to serve the civic good, the legal restraint of conflict among political interests could be achieved by the creation of separate and distinct departments. Third, political practices built into the Constitution would sustain restrained interbranch conflict. One practice was to prevent the unified support of officeholders for despotism by creating differences in "personal motives." The practice was to ensure that, "Ambition must be made to counteract ambition." The Constitution fostered such conflict by the creation of different duties for departmental officers and selection processes designed to energize officials to satisfy the sentiments of their diverse constituencies. Additionally, "constitutional means" or rules blending powers and instituting checks and balance would provide officials the opportunity to thwart despotic acts by officers of the other branches. It would necessitate the exercise of the virtues of dialogue, accommodation, and compromise.[5]

Madison's description of "personal motives" and "constitutional means" to prevent tyranny went beyond what he called a "mere demarcation on parchment of the constitutional limits of the several departments." Indeed, the Constitution does not specifically define the separation of powers. Instead, what emerged from the convention was a politics of separate governmental institutions sharing ill-defined powers—a "partial intermixture" of powers. Also, the Constitution provided for different ways of delegating power from the people to federal officers. The officers of the branches would then probably offer different perspectives on popular sentiments. In the Congress, the House of Representatives, directly elected by the people for short terms, would have "sympathy" with the interests of citizens in a local area. The Senate, selected by popularly elected state legislators, would be solicitous of the interests of the people of a state. The president and vice president, selected by the Electoral College, would represent the sentiments of the people as filtered by electors meeting away from the "heats and ferments" of the national capital. The appointment of the judiciary, Convention member Alexander Hamilton asserted, made it independent of specific constituents and inclined to follow the will of the people as stated in the Constitution. A unique feature of American federal constitutionalism, he declared that lifetime tenure of federal judges would secure the "impartial administration of the laws" that would serve as a barrier against the "despotism of the prince," and the "oppressions of the representative body." Together these arrangements for selection of officials and judicial independence promised that political conflicts among leaders representing many different constituencies would prevent governmental tyranny.[6]

To regulate the conflict among the branches, the framers created different blends of separate duties and powers for each branch *and* checks and balances scattered in provisions of the first three articles of the Constitution. The separation of powers enables each branch to claim powers and act to protect its powers and policies through acts of self-defense. Especially, each branch can attempt to defend its powers by the delegation of politically difficult issues to the other branches or by assigning blame for ambitious misuses of power, avarice, or errors of political judgment to another branch.[7] Therefore, unlike British and Canadian parliamentary government, in which the majority party in the legislature bears responsibility and blame for poor performance, the federal scheme affords each branch opportunities to avoid conflicts or to shift the blame for political errors to officials in another branch. However, to gain political credit, the checking and balancing function also allows each branch either the opportunity to sanction unpopular political decisions made by the other branches or to build a political consensus in support of its policies.

As Madison noted, however, it was "not possible to give each department an equal power of self-defense." Because he assumed that "the legislative authority necessarily predominates," to restrain congressional power the Constitution contains far more detail about the scope and limits of congressional powers. The "weight of legislative authority" also required the division of it between two houses rendered as "little connected with each other" as possible to double the security to the people's liberties.[8] Therefore both houses must concur on how to regulate the military and both must approve the declaration of wars. The House initiates appropriations for executive and judicial operations and can impeach the president, vice president, and judiciary. The House and Senate detail executive duties, define the appellate jurisdiction and number of members of the Supreme Court, and specify the duties of other federal courts. Yet, it is the Senate and not the House that advises and must consent to presidential executive and judicial appointments, consider the treaties negotiated by the president, and try impeachments. Each house of Congress must approve the legislation of the other. The president can approve their legislative actions or veto them, subject only to reversal by a two-thirds vote of both houses of Congress. He might also determine how to faithfully execute the acts of Congress. His checks on the judiciary include the nomination of judges and the enforcement of its rulings. But, save through the interpretation of laws in lawsuits, the federal Constitution offers little detail on the capacity of the judiciary to check and balance the other branches.

The Judiciary as Interpreter of Interbranch Relations

Although conventions in the states ratified the Constitution, a problem remained. Except for amendment the Constitution has no provision for the settlement of conflicts among the departments. The Constitutional Convention discussed how the judiciary or a Council of Revision might assume this duty.

However, with no site for the settlement of interbranch contests, the Constitution invited ongoing judicial interpretation and political constructions. Therefore, the single most important post-1787 addition to checks and balances is judicial review. It provides that legal interpretation by the judiciary will settle conflicts about the exercise of power by the branches. Judicial review rests on the recognition of the Constitution as the supreme law and supreme will of the people, of the judiciary as the institution best fit to interpret any form of law, and of the peculiar independence, professional knowledge, and duty to respect the Constitution that qualifies the judiciary for the interpretive task.[9] As an addition to the constitutional text, what is most amazing about judicial review is that the other branches have recognized the legitimacy of judicial review as an element of the rule of law. Today they remain quiescent even when in *Dickerson v. United States* (2000) Chief Justice William Rehnquist asserts that, "Congress may not legislatively supersede our decisions interpreting and applying the Constitution."

Despite its legitimacy, judicial interpretation of the separation of powers has produced continual political controversy and interbranch dialogue. First, there is a question of *when* judicial power should be asserted against the other branches to maintain the proper protection against governmental tyranny. The general answer is that federal judges have confined their interpretation of separation of powers to cases initiated by private parties or the government. The Supreme Court justices have acknowledged that risks for the legitimacy of their decisions exist when they interfere with the other branches. They have adopted practices of restraint to avoid some politically charged cases in which they might have to make controversial policy choices contrary to the interests of other powerful political forces. For example, they have refrained from judging matters they considered to be within the province of the "political" branches. The justices have deferred to congressional authority to revamp the appellate jurisdiction of federal courts. They have refused to provide legal advice for the executive. To prevent the adjudication of some constitutional claims against the Congress or the executive, they have developed rules on access to courts, such as the requirement of a direct injury to file a lawsuit and barriers against collusive suits. The federal judiciary consequently has rarely overturned congressional acts—only 160 provisions between 1789 and 2001.

When state judiciaries face the definition of their state's constitutional separation of powers, the constitutional and political features of the states militate against wide-ranging judicial oversight of the other branches. Because the distrust of judges was a powerful political idea in the early national period, state constitutional conventions placed limits on judicial powers. In several states, such as Kentucky and Ohio, even judicial review emerged only after considerable political controversy. Today in many states the legislature—rather than the state constitution—provides detailed rules on judicial powers, the structure of courts, and the selection of officers, such as the clerks, attorneys, and sheriffs that assist the judiciary. As discussed in the chapter by Kermit Hall in this volume, most states employ either elections to select judges or retention elections to evaluate the service of appointed judges. When coupled with the relative ease of adoption of state constitutional amendments that might overturn judicial interpretations of the powers of other branches, state judges appear to be even more constrained by official, interest group, and popular policy pressures than federal judges. Given frequent state judicial deference to the state's legislative majority, for much of the past century social, racial, or political minorities, criminal defendants, and women have secured their rights by challenging state legislative and executive actions in federal courts. Conversely, only when groups demanding equality in the financing of public schools had their claim rejected in federal court did they seek support for their interests in state courts.

Second, there is the question of *how* the judiciary is to construe the power of the other branches. Although they have usually interpreted the Constitution as they might any ordinary law, the U.S. Supreme Court justices have never settled on the standards to be used in interpretation of the Constitution and the acts of the other branches. With issues of separated powers the justices have relied on the intent of the framers, considering British and American history, political traditions, international law, and judicial precedents. However, the majority of separated powers cases feature a debate between two positions about the boundaries of the authority of each branch. There are justices who would permit creative or pragmatic interpretations of congressional and presidential powers. For example, in *Humphrey's Executor v. United States* (1935) the justices recognized that certain "independent" federal executive commissions could perform legislative or rulemaking functions and adjudicate "a wide range of controversies." They approve such adjustments of the structure of separated powers to ensure efficient or effective governance in line with the desires of the lawmaking majority. This choice is a pragmatic, risk-averse tactic that protects the legitimacy of the Court. Conversely, other justices argue that the enumeration of powers and procedures in the text of the Constitution provides a firm barrier against presidential or congressional efforts to claim implied or inherent powers. They would not permit Congress or the president to devise procedures to resolve political conflicts in ways that might blur the boundaries of powers between the branches. For example, in *Immigration and Naturalization Service v. Chadha* (1983) Chief Justice Warren Burger rejected a procedure called the legislative veto that was designed to secure congressional oversight of executive agencies. Arguing that "convenience and necessity are not the primary objectives—or the hallmarks of democratic government," he determined that the legislative veto violated "explicit and unambiguous provisions of the Constitution." Justices such as Burger bear the political risk of checks on their powers if they say no to the interests of the other branches.

However, in a large republic with many competing interests, this is an extremely risky political tactic only when the Court says no to the policies of a political coalition in control of both Congress and the presidency.

Most state supreme courts also have exercised judicial review cautiously. They have concentrated on interpretations of taxation, finance, and public education clauses in the state constitution. Despite evidence of more frequent use of judicial review to overturn state statutes since 1975, as indicated in the chapter by Paul Brace and Melinda Gann Hall in this volume, institutional variations and political differences among the states make it difficult to offer a general explanation about how and when a state judiciary will overturn statutes or administrative rules. In a small number of states the state's supreme court will provide advisory opinions on the constitutionality of actions proposed by the other branches, an activity that might preclude future conflicts among the branches. However, the other branches can ignore such opinions.

Additionally, the Constitution grants the federal judiciary the power to hear cases in equity. Equity permits judges, using "sound judicial discretion," to issue decrees to compel action, enjoin or prevent harms, cite parties for contempt of court, issue writs of habeas corpus to release detainees, and provide other forms of relief to parties who seek protection from injury. In separated powers cases, the Supreme Court has responded to parties seeking equitable relief to shape major statements about the powers of the branches. For example, the justices refused to enjoin President Andrew Johnson's enforcement of post–Civil War Reconstruction acts, but they upheld a federal court injunction when President Richard Nixon attempted to impose a pre-publication restraint on the publication of the secret Pentagon Papers. However, these exercises of judicial power occurred when the Court encountered a politically weakened president who posed little threat to their legitimacy and a congressional majority hostile to the president.

Third, there is the question of *whether* the legislature or executive might interpret the separation of powers—the so-called departmental theory of constitutional review. Although Congress and the president have not effectively exploited this option and made formal statements about the meaning of the Constitution, history suggests that judicial review does not necessarily preclude the Congress and the president from giving meaning to the separation of powers. Indeed, the president and Congress have often treated the Constitution as a framework to which they can informally add practices or modify meanings to meet diverse political needs. Often their actions have transpired without judicial involvement.

Although the twentieth-century expansion of federal mandates and the guidelines in federal grants of money to states have restricted the discretion of state legislatures, they remain important independent players in American politics. State constitutions have historically treated legislatures as residual delegates of the power of the people. Therefore, state judges have often deferred to legislative constructions of separated powers as indicative of the popular will. This means that state legislators construct the meaning of separated powers in many specific political controversies. State judges spend much of their time addressing cases about aspects of social and economic order within the policy parameters set by state legislative acts or statutes—crime, family matters, property disputes, contracts, transfer payments such as workers' compensation, and the like. State judges, however, wield greater policy-making authority in the domain of the judge-made or common law, such as in cases about personal and corporate liability for injuries. Also, there is some evidence that state courts have—more frequently than federal courts—asserted their power to ensure that executive agencies control their discretion and stay true to standards set by the legislature. However, such judicial policy interpretation has often invited legislation that reconstructs judicial power such as limitations on amounts of recovery for injuries and new laws that constrict agency discretion.

With a restrained use of judicial review, the ability to interpret the Constitution and other law to support the pragmatic use of power by Congress and the president or state legislatures, the limited use of equitable remedies in separated powers cases, and the opportunity for political constructions of separated powers, the judiciary appears to have adopted a defensive stance. It has created opportunities to avoid blame for many unpopular policies and to stay out of political conflicts. Although the chapters by Gregory Caldeira and Lynn Mather in this volume suggest that the legitimacy of the judiciary is deep enough that it expends little political capital when it resolves politically salient conflicts, history also indicates that the federal judiciary has not often bucked the political branches of the federal government, a point also discussed in the chapter by Keith Whittington in this volume. Its pose is one of prudence, for many justices sense that a politically aware and responsive judiciary avoids the risk of political criticism and threats to its independence.

The Contemporary Meaning of Federal Separated Powers

What has occurred with the interpretation and construction of separation of powers and checks and balances? Using the example of the federal government, the answer is that the branches have developed a potpourri of interpretations and constructions that do not rest on precise standards about the function of separated powers. Instead, as illustrated by the federal examples offered in this section, judicial interpretations and political constructions are often a pragmatic or crisis-driven construction of separated powers by the Congress and president. In many of these situations the Supreme Court has practiced prudence and avoided imposing checks on the other branches. Yet, despite its prudence, it has not just implemented the decisions of the political branches. Instead, it has actively participated in interbranch political dialogue and occasional turf warfare about the overlapping powers and duties of the branches.

Judicial Interpretations: Empowering the Congress and the Federal Agencies

In several respects the federal courts have interpreted the constitutional duties and power of Congress. First, the Supreme Court has rarely interfered in the internal operational procedures of the Congress. The judiciary has not ruled on the construction of majority party control of congressional leadership, the congressional committee system, rules of procedure, and traditions of congressional behavior that affect the inclusion of representatives' voices in lawmaking. However, when the House violated specific constitutional language on the expulsion of its members, in *Powell v. McCormick* (1969) the Court intervened to protect the affected member. The justices have construed the privilege from arrest for members during the sessions of Congress or during passage to the sessions as a protection against criminal arrest in those settings. The Court has read the Speech or Debate Clause to protect members and their aides against suits for libel or defamation for activity undertaken during a legislative session related to the consideration and voting on proposed legislation. Finally, the justices held that prosecution for bribery of a member is permissible as long as there is no inquiry into past legislative acts. These decisions make it clear that the judiciary will discipline congressional activity that violates constitutional text or that is criminal and harms the reputation of Congress with its constituents—decisions that are not especially politically risky for the judiciary.

Second, the Supreme Court has supported most uses of the legislative authority of Congress enumerated in seventeen paragraphs of Article I, section 8, of the Constitution. This has not always been the practice. During the century from 1837 to 1937 the justices often imposed restrictions on the use of congressional power to protect state governmental authority or the interests of property owners. Since 1937 the justices have affirmed the ample authority of Congress to tax to raise revenue and otherwise provide for the general welfare so long as they do not violate individuals' constitutional rights. Congress can spend revenues so long as the spending does not compel state governmental action or abridge an individual's constitutional rights. The justices have interpreted the Interstate Commerce Clause to authorize congressional regulation of economic activity that has a substantial economic effect on interstate commerce and to regulate various public health, safety, and moral problems that impede interstate commerce. Article I, section 8, also assigns Congress the power to "make all Laws necessary and proper for carrying into Execution the foregoing Powers." Since Chief Justice John Marshall's opinion in *McCulloch v. Maryland* (1819), Congress has used the clause to justify its construction of laws connected to enumerated powers—sometimes called implied or resulting powers. Using these powers and those in the enforcement clauses of constitutional amendments, Congress has established federal regulation of monetary and fiscal policy and political campaigns for federal office, and laws requiring compulsory military service and centralized federal budgeting. Related to implied powers is the claim that Congress has so-called inherited powers derived from the historical understanding of the duties of legislatures, such as the power to acquire territory recognized in *United States v. Kagama* (1886). With its enumerated, implied, and inherent powers broadly construed by the Supreme Court, Congress can claim credit for innumerable actions that benefit its constituencies.

Third, the Supreme Court has permitted the congressional delegation of its extensive enumerated and implied powers to the executive. Delegation of powers permits executive agencies to devise rules that lawfully supplement congressional legislation, to undertake measures to enforce the rules, and to adjudicate disputes over the meaning and enforcement of rules. The justices have approved almost all delegations of power, and, in recent years, they have disregarded any requirement that Congress precisely specify what powers are delegated. Thus, despite anti-bureaucratic sentiments among the American public, the judiciary has legitimized the expansion of national administrative power that began about 1900.

Using their delegated powers agencies can have enormous influence over the political agenda. They can "sell" Congress and the public on issues that need attention, devise regulations, and determine how to enforce them. The judiciary has assumed it can oversee the use of agencies' powers. However, judges commonly examine politically less conspicuous details of agency rulemaking procedures, the informal actions and enforcement practices of agencies, agency adjudicatory procedures, and the ethics of agency personnel. Evidence indicates that they defer to the administrative agency in the majority of disputes about these practices. Therefore, checking the agencies has become more a congressional than a judicial task. The judiciary has permitted Congress to use its implied powers to conduct investigations and compel persons to provide them with information. Congress then uses this power to oversee executive agencies and blame executive bureaucrats for policy errors made in the use of the powers it delegated to them. The Supreme Court has only restrained this power by requiring that congressional investigators provide a legislative purpose for the investigation and ask pertinent questions that do not violate the constitutional rights of persons that they question.

Consequently, the judiciary has seldom limited congressional power. It has let Congress legislate and claim credit for diverse policies undertaken to benefit its constituents. It also has let Congress shift rulemaking and enforcement power to federal executive agencies. Then, with judicial approval, Congress can investigate, hold hearings, and blame the executive branch for failed policies, inadequate enforcement of the laws, and specific abuses in the exercise of delegated power that upset its constituents.

Judicial Interpretations: Empowering the Presidency

Many of the framers envisioned the executive branch as essential for the enforcement of congressional legislation. However, key members of the convention secured constitutional language that did much more than address federal law enforcement. To secure "energy" in the office, Article II of the Constitution vested broad-ranging powers in the presidency. Today these powers mean that the president shapes the political agenda and responses to political crises. Nonetheless, how has the Supreme Court interpreted the powers of the presidency?

The most important decisions, those on executive privilege and immunity, have occurred when the president relied on English tradition to claim prerogative. John Locke defined prerogative as a "Power to act according to discretion, for the publick good, without the prescription of the Law, and sometimes even against it."[10] Although presidential use of prerogative often results in political conflicts, the Supreme Court has recognized some powers are inherent in the presidency. However, the justices have never suggested that the president can act against the law. For example, in *United States v. Nixon* (1974), the Court held that the president has an inherent executive privilege to protect confidential communications with his cabinet officers and aides and that judges must afford it great protection consistent with principles of the fair administration of justice. Because president and Congress normally negotiate conflicts about which communications are confidential to avoid litigation, so the judiciary has not said much more about this issue. However, the president cannot withhold such communications from the judiciary when they are required as the evidence essential for a fair criminal trial. Likewise, the Supreme Court has permitted Congress to regulate the release of presidential materials on official subjects after his term has ended. Furthermore, the president is immune from lawsuits that would impede the performance of his official tasks. Yet, he is subject to suits over private, unofficial conduct. His advisers have immunity only for confidential policy-making functions, and they forfeit immunity if they know or should know that they are violating an individual's constitutional rights. Thus, facing few direct threats to his power from lawsuits or congressional investigators, he can act decisively to advance his policy objectives.

Second, the Supreme Court has provided a similar message about the discretion of the president in the use of his enumerated powers in domestic politics. At the heart of presidential power is the Article II duty to "take care that the laws be faithfully executed." For example, the Supreme Court has allowed the president to appoint a bodyguard to protect a Supreme Court justice in the absence of legislation. Additionally, the *In re Neagle* (1890) decision exempted the bodyguard from state criminal prosecution for acts performed as a federal officer. The *In re Debs* (1895) decision permitted the president to use troops to break a strike to protect the mails and the freedom of other persons to engage in interstate commerce. This power also includes presidential discretion to determine the range of enforcement activities required by an act of Congress or a treaty approved by the Senate. Probably the president cannot refuse to execute a law. However, the effort that the executive must make to enforce it or the extent to which he can modify its intent during enforcement is still unsettled. The justices held in *Train v. City of New York* (1975) only that the president could refuse to spend appropriated funds only when Congress granted him such discretion. Also, many laws grant the president discretionary law enforcement authority. In the absence of constitutional claims, when Congress grants him the discretion to enforce laws his actions are not subject to judicial interpretation. For example, with judicial interference the Bush presidencies aggressively enforced federal obscenity laws while the Clinton presidency did little to enforce the same laws. Deference to extensive presidential powers also appears in judicial decisions about the presidential pardon power. The federal judiciary has held that the president can pardon—or pardon subject to conditions—any person for any federal criminal conviction, offense without conviction, or criminal contempt except impeachment.

The Supreme Court's interpretation of the appointment power has also drawn boundaries between the powers of presidency and Congress. In the *Myers v. United States* (1926) opinion of Chief Justice William Howard Taft, the justices held that the president could unilaterally remove executive branch officers appointed with the advice and consent of the Senate as an "incident of the power to appoint them." But, this opinion was limited by the decision in *Humphrey's Executor v. United States*, which concluded that the president's removal of an official of an independent regulatory agency, who had legislative and judicial as well as executive duties, had to have congressional approval. When Congress created other forms of commissions and offices that melded separate powers, the justices clarified the appointment power in cases about Federal Election Commissioners, independent counsels, the Comptroller General, and the United States Sentencing Commission. In these cases the president and Congress had created administrative offices that muddied the boundaries of separated powers. However, with the independent counsel and sentencing commission cases, the justices approved what amounts to an extension of appointment powers beyond the literal text of the Constitution in ways that augment the power of the president or Congress.

Third, the Supreme Court has deferred to the president's exercise of foreign policy-making power. Indeed, the justices have often confirmed the extensive inherent powers of the president in these policy arenas. The presidential foreign affairs power originates from the office's power to make treaties (subject to Senate approval by two-thirds vote for ratification) and appoint and receive ambassadors. Supreme Court interpretations have, however, indicated that it is much more. In *United States v. Curtiss-Wright Export Corporation* (1936) Justice George Sutherland concluded that the foreign affairs powers of the president were different in "in their origin and their nature" from the office's domestic powers. He held that the foreign affairs powers of the federal government resulted not from the Constitution but from its status as a sovereign nation. The Constitution, he further argued, gives the president the authority to act as "sole organ" for the nation in external affairs. Although the Constitution limits his power, it is "plenary and exclusive," exists with "a degree of discretion and freedom from statutory restriction," and permits him to apply congressional acts with a "broad discretion" in foreign affairs.

Relying on this conception of presidential power, the justices have approved executive agreements. Unilaterally concluded by the president, these agreements with other nations commit the United States to a course of action. Congress has required that it be notified of such agreements, and it can adopt legislation to support their enforcement. However, the Court has held that such agreements have the legally binding character of a treaty, and the agreements can void contravening state laws and forestall federal litigation of claims made by individuals. Additionally, the justices have deferred to presidential actions to revoke passports, ban travel to certain countries, and capture foreign nationals on the high seas to prevent their entry into the United States. In all of these cases the justices disregarded claims that individual rights to property, travel, or due process limited executive power.

In a similar vein the Supreme Court has deferentially interpreted the treaty powers. Pursuant to the Supremacy Clause, the justices have decided that treaties are superior over state laws. In *Goldwater v. Carter* (1979) they have declined to review whether a president can terminate a treaty. Presidents have terminated several treaties, and President George W. Bush even revoked the signature of President Bill Clinton to a treaty that established an International Criminal Court. Congress can affect foreign policy only through appropriations, restrictions on the authority delegated to executive agencies, and its ability to legislate on foreign commerce.

Consequently, judicial interpretation of the actions of the presidency has often resulted in the approval of unilateral presidential actions that extend executive powers. Judicial negations of presidential power on constitutional grounds are rare. Judges' decisions often respect the extensive powers inherent in the presidency. Their decisions therefore make the president the person accountable for bureaucratic management and foreign affairs. He can claim credit for success or bear the blame for failures of such policies. As occurred during the Nixon administration, the judiciary seems only willing to check presidential power when he has lost public and congressional support and poses few risks to the legitimacy of the courts.

Political Constructions: The President and Congress Adjust Domestic Powers

What arrangements have Congress and the president made about the construction of provisions for sharing power, and how has the judiciary reacted to these provisions? Joint presidential-congressional efforts to construct or reconstruct institutional interactions adjustment have occurred since the early days of the Republic. Some have received judicial approval, such as congressional delegations of power to executive agencies and the establishment of independent regulatory agencies. Nonetheless with very little judicial interpretation and with executive branch collusion, Congress has instituted presidential budget preparation (by the Office of Management and Budget) as a guide for its appropriations decisions and has established rules for executive agency advising and lobbying of its members and staff. It has developed entitlement programs such as Social Security and Medicare that require expenditures into the distant future. All of these actions improve the efficiency of Congress in responding to their constituents' interests in the funding of favorite programs or the public's worries about federal deficit spending.

The judiciary has seldom considered cases about congressional checks on the executive through the appropriations process or its oversight of executive branch operations. As noted above, executive responses to congressional investigations and executive enforcement of congressional appropriations acts have occasioned judicial interpretations. Nonetheless, judicial interventions have rarely forced senior executive branch officers to release materials to Congress or testify before Congress, required that the executive submit to congressional direction of the enforcement of laws, or regulated how the executive spends or "reprograms" appropriations for other purposes. Likewise, Congress's assignment of departmental reorganization power to the president and the creation of a civil service have taken place with little litigation. The executive veto and pocket veto have not received much consideration by the courts. This is also true of the president's duty to inform Congress and recommend legislation. Without judicial intervention Congress has twice impeached and tried the president. In both instances, the impeachments of Andrew Johnson and Bill Clinton, the Senate failed to achieve the two-thirds vote to remove the president. In part the failure can be traced to the blatant partisanship that accompanied the process.

The judiciary has also refrained from assessing the use of executive orders in domestic matters. Presidents most often use executive orders, a political construction of implied powers, to provide a written directive to the executive branch about the implementation of the law or presidential policy objectives. In recent decades the use of executive orders has justified unilateral executive branch and agency efforts in policy implementation as well as foreign affairs and civil rights policy. The Supreme Court has recognized that an executive order provides authority for an agency to adopt rules with the force of law. The judicial determination that an executive order violated the Constitution or act of Congress is rare. Other political constructions also sustain presidential unilateral direct action: (1) memoranda that direct administrative action; (2) proclamations, including George Washington's proclamation to justify actions against the

Whiskey Rebels of 1794 and Abraham Lincoln's Emancipation Proclamation, martial law, and militia mobilization proclamations; (3) national security directives to define foreign and defense policy; (4) presidential signing of statements that define his interpretation of the law or give directions for the administration of laws by executive agencies. The Supreme Court has not interpreted the constitutional status of memoranda and national security directives. It has determined that presidential proclamations are law, and the federal judiciary has permitted prosecutions for the violation of proclamations.

Despite this legacy of judicial deference to presidential and congressional adjustments of separated powers, three joint reconstructions of federal expenditure relationships—the legislative veto, a balanced budget procedure, and the line item veto—have failed to survive judicial scrutiny. In *Immigration and Naturalization Service v. Chadha* the Supreme Court held that the legislative veto, a statutory requirement that one or both houses of Congress can intervene to approve or disapprove enforcement actions or rules adopted by executive branch agencies, violated the constitutional requirement that legislative decisions be made by both houses of Congress and presented to the president for his consideration. By adopting the Graham-Rudman-Hollings Act of 1985, Congress and the president devised a mechanism to control deficit spending that, when spending exceeded spending ceilings set by Congress, required the Comptroller General to recommend spending reductions that the president must enforce. But, in *Bowsher v. Synar* (1986), the justices found that the role in the process of a congressional officer, the Comptroller General, violated the separation of powers. The Line Item Veto Act of 1996 permitted the president to cancel certain expenditures and limited tax benefits before he signed into law bills submitted to him by Congress. However, in *Clinton v. City of New York* (1998) the Supreme Court ruled that this procedure violated the veto process defined in the Constitution. In both cases, considerable congressional and academic opinion supported the justice's decisions, and the decisions had little direct effect on the public. Therefore, the Court did not face risks to its legitimacy or much political criticism for the decisions.

Political Constructions: President and Congress in War and Emergencies

The Constitution establishes civilian control of the military. The Commander-in Chief Clause gives the president the command of the military. Congress retains control over military appropriations, the declaration of war, military law and regulations, and provisions for the organization, arming, discipline, and deployment of the state militia to suppress insurrections and repel invasions. Congress has declared war only on five occasions, but the justices have left the declaration of an end to war to Congress—often years after the cessation of hostilities. The Supreme Court has supported congressional acts that allowed the executive branch to seize enemy property, to draft individuals into the armed forces, to call forth militia to thwart insurrections and invasions, and to operate a separate system of military justice.

Throughout American history the presidency nonetheless has extended its power beyond grants of authority by Congress to encompass the direction of armed forces in an undeclared war or military conflict. Also, as Chief Justice Rehnquist has written, "In time of war the government requires the necessary authority to conduct military operations successfully, and a concomitant of this fact is that individual freedom is accordingly circumscribed."[11] President Lincoln assumed the power to react to military action by the Confederate States by proclaiming a naval blockade and ordering the seizure of the property of Southern rebels captured by the navy. In *The Prize Cases* (1863) the Court upheld his action and indicated that he could act without a declaration of war when a military emergency existed. Other actions of Lincoln's administration also came before the Court. In *Ex parte Merryman* (1861) Chief Justice Roger Taney ruled that Lincoln's suspension of the writ of habeas corpus and the detention of Confederate sympathizers were unconstitutional because they contravened the text of Article I, but the administration ignored the order. Only after the war ended, in *Ex parte Milligan* (1866), did the justices hold unconstitutional Lincoln's order to try Confederate sympathizers before military courts when civilian courts were open. However, the justices supported other wartime measures authorized by Congress, including the issuance of paper currency and the seizure of Confederate's property.

During World War I, Congress approved executive control of rail and water transportation and telecommunications, the prohibition of the sale of alcohol, and new criminal laws to allow aggressive executive prosecution of espionage and sedition. The Supreme Court ruled that these actions were valid exercises of congressional power. During World War II, President Franklin Roosevelt and Congress extended their powers in new ways to support the war effort. The justices approved of the congressional delegation of far-reaching economic regulatory powers to the president, including price controls and product rationing. They permitted the executive to sanction violators of the guidelines. Despite a controversial dissenting opinion by Justice Frank Murphy that accused the Court's majority of racism, in *Korematsu v. United States* (1944) the justices upheld executive orders to register American citizens of Japanese ancestry and to isolate them in detention camps. Justice Hugo Black concluded that because of threats to national security the government had a compelling interest to detain the individuals without trial in the camps. However, once the government ascertained an individual's loyalty, the person had to be released from detention. Also, civilians charged with crimes outside the war zone had to be tried by civilian courts.

Also problematic is the use of military forces in combat without a declaration of war. Without declaring war, Congress appropriated funds to conduct combat operations against Native American tribes as early as 1789 and against French vessels between 1798 and 1800. The Supreme Court upheld the legality of the latter action. In skirmishes to defend American lives and property on the Barbary Coast and China, and military actions to restore order, seize pirates, terrorists, and criminals, or advance American political and economic interests in Afghanistan, several Caribbean and Central American nations, Lebanon, Iran, Mexico, Somalia, Sudan, and at sea, the president or local military commanders ordered the use of military force without a declaration of war and sometimes without congressional approval. The judiciary has recognized that Congress can restrict executive conduct of such military operations. However, when the president's secretly ordered military operations in Cambodia and Laos between 1965 and 1973 came to light, efforts by a member of Congress to enjoin the operations failed. In *Schlesinger v. Holtzman* (1973) the Supreme Court overturned lower court decisions granting the injunction.

Furthermore, acting as a signatory of the United Nations treaty, to enforce its Security Council Resolutions, American forces have engaged in large-scale combat operations in Korea (1950–1953) and Kuwait and Iraq (1991). The president commanded military action in Vietnam (1964–1975) and Iraq (2003 onward) under the authority granted by open-ended congressional joint resolutions—so-called area resolutions to conduct military operations in a region—but not declarations of war. The Supreme Court refused to review the constitutionality of the use of military forces in Vietnam. Lower federal courts also refused to consider the constitutionality of military actions in Kuwait and Iraq in 1991 initiated with United Nations approval and the military intervention in Yugoslavia undertaken during 1999 in concert with North Atlantic Treaty Organization nations.

The justices have determined that the president governs all conquered territory in his capacity as commander in chief. Absent congressional acts, his power is absolute, extensive, and cannot be questioned in the courts. He alone determines when to terminate the use of his powers. Although constrained by treaties, he has great discretion in the control of captured enemies. The justices have determined that military courts can try suspected enemy saboteurs and war criminals who serve in enemy armed forces, regardless of where they are captured. Although Congress authorized the detention of a U.S. citizen fighting for the Taliban against American forces in Afghanistan, when the military removed him to the United States the justices determined that the Constitution required due process. In *Hamdi v. Rumsfeld* (2004) they determined that he possessed a right to a meaningful opportunity to contest the basis for his detention before a neutral decision maker—which could be a military court. Additionally, in *Rasul v. Bush* (2004) the justices concluded that federal courts have jurisdiction to consider habeas corpus challenges to the legality of the detention of foreign nationals suspected of terrorism. The suspects were captured abroad and incarcerated at a military prison at Guantánamo Bay, Cuba. These decisions suggest that the judiciary will check presidential discretion in the "War on Terrorism" when it offends basic American constitutional values such as the Fifth Amendment's due process right to a hearing before incarceration.

The judiciary has not reviewed noncombat use of the armed forces. Thus, presidential decisions to deploy the military prior to the Mexican and Spanish-American Wars, the arming of merchant vessels prior to World War I, the occupation of Iceland, base construction in Greenland, and naval patrols to assist British forces in the North Atlantic prior to World War II all occurred without judicial consideration. The domestic powers of presidents during foreign affairs or military crises and emergencies are, however, open to question. The Supreme Court did not directly consider the embargo ordered by President Thomas Jefferson to avoid American evolvement in the Napoleonic Wars or Franklin Roosevelt's order for federal takeover of certain defense industries prior to American entry into World War II. The first exception to this pattern came about during the Korean conflict. In a controversial political maneuver in 1952 President Harry Truman ordered federal operation of the nation's steel mills to end a strike his administration deemed likely to threaten the war effort. Because he acted without congressional authorization or clearly stated constitutional power, by a 6–3 vote in *Youngstown Sheet & Tube Co. v. Sawyer* (1952) a badly splintered majority of the Supreme Court ruled that he could not take over the steel mills. Also, in *New York Times Co. v. United States* (1971), the Pentagon Papers case, the justices ruled that the president could not be granted an injunction to impose a prior restraint on the freedom of the press to publish classified materials about military operations, save when a grave threat to national security or the safety of military personnel could be shown.

Upset with its own ineptitude in controlling the executive's conduct of the Vietnam conflict, Congress adopted the War Powers Act of 1973. The act permits unilateral presidential use of military force to repel attacks on the United States or its armed forces and to rescue American citizens abroad. The president is to report such actions to Congress within forty-eight hours. The president can employ armed force for sixty days during which time Congress, if it is able to meet, can declare war or extend the use of the armed forces. With no congressional approval at the end of sixty days, the president has thirty days to end the use of forces. Since its adoption the Ford and Carter administrations notified Congress about uses of armed force. The Reagan administration informed Congress of actions in Grenada but not when it sent troops to Lebanon or conducted air strikes against Libya. The presidential administrations of George H. W. Bush, Bill Clinton, and George W. Bush deployed armed forces in Afghanistan, Haiti, Iraq, Kuwait, Panama, Somalia, and the Balkans without the invocation of the act. With these conflicts either Congress passed resolutions to support the use of force or the president justified the action as a fulfillment of treaty commitments. Arguing that courts lack the capacity to find facts about military actions, the federal judiciary has avoided considering the applicability of the act. In these and its many other decisions about military emergencies, it has avoided getting involved in the conflicts over decisions to put American troops in harm's way. Rather, it has let the president and—less so—Congress receive credit or blame for the nation's military operations.

Political Constructions: Checking and Balancing the Judiciary

What have the Congress and the president done to check or guide the powers of the judiciary? Congressional and presidential deference to Supreme Court decisions is the norm, even when the justices decide controversial issues such as the outcome of the 2000 presidential election. Possibly because the justices simply have seldom impeded a legislative majority for long periods or because the president and Congress respect the rule of law, the public and officials' support of the Court has remained substantial, even at times of intense political conflict. Also, because Congress can avoid political controversy by drafting ambiguous statutes that encourage litigation and leaving hot-button controversies, such as abortion, racial injustice, and school prayer to the courts, its members can avoid blame and potential electoral defeat. Thus, acting for its own political advantage, Congress empowers judges rather than checks judicial interpretations. In these circumstances the judiciary can react by either legitimating congressional and presidential action or bearing the blame for unpopular political choices and choices made when the president and Congress cannot reach a compromise.

Constitutionally, the most important presidential check on the judiciary is the power to nominate federal judges. It is a check that presidents have used to create a judiciary sympathetic to their policies and disinclined to confront them. For example, President George Washington nominated the first federal judges on the basis of their support for the new Constitution. Thereafter most presidents have attempted to nominate to the federal judiciary persons with kindred political party affiliation, ideology, or stance on political issues. The Senate must give its advice and consent to presidential nominations to the federal judiciary. Although the vast majority of nominees readily win consent, as discussed in the chapter by Joel Grossman in this volume, a few Supreme Court nominations have generated acrimonious debates in the Senate over the qualifications of the nominee or the nominee's ideology and record on controversial political controversies. These hearings permitted some senators, concerned about interest group support, to use procedural devices to delay or induce the withdrawal of presidential judicial nominations.

Also, through control of the Justice Department and the legal offices in various departments, the president shapes the docket of federal courts and, hence, the chance of politically contentious decisions. Executive branch lawyers initiate the civil and criminal actions filed against individuals, other governments, and private organizations and determine the cases they will appeal. They file friend of the court briefs or arguments. Because of a mix of skill in the selection of cases for review, its friend of the court briefs, and its prestige with the judiciary, the federal executive has succeeded more than other parties in convincing the judiciary of the soundness of its positions. The president thus can avoid judicial sanction or blame for his policies through skillful litigation tactics.

Although it is a check on the judiciary, presidents have infrequently urged Congress to change the size of the judiciary so a president could appoint political allies to the bench. Most famously, a Congress with a Jeffersonian majority adopted the Judiciary Act of 1802 and repealed the Judiciary Act of 1801 that the Federalist Party had enacted to place its loyalists in new federal judgeships. Conversely, Congress did not act on President Franklin Roosevelt's 1937 proposal to expand the size of the Supreme Court so that he could nominate justices favorable to his New Deal policies. Nonetheless, after Roosevelt's effort to "pack" the Court some of the justices became less hostile to congressional acts that advanced his New Deal policies. Thus, whether by action or threats of action on judicial membership, the other branches have influenced the judiciary.

Congress can independently seek to change the appellate jurisdiction of federal courts to define the kind of subjects or parties who can seek federal judicial relief. Most of the changes in jurisdiction have attempted to improve the efficiency of federal courts in the face of an expanding caseload. However, to penalize the judiciary for its past decisions, Congress has considered legislation to limit the topics the judiciary can consider. Congress has approved few such proposals in recent decades. Congress has recently adopted a controversial measure to ensure that federal judges abide by U.S. Sentencing Commission guidelines rather than exert independent discretion in sentencing. Much more frequently the Congress has passed a new law to abrogate judicial interpretations that its members thought contradicted the intent of its original legislation. Evidence indicates that such congressional overrides of judicial interpretations usually result in more consistent legislation or precise delegations of legislative power to agencies and, if there are further judicial interpretations of the law, judicial consensus with the revised intent of Congress. During the passage of the revised legislation members of Congress have the opportunity both to blame the judiciary for misreading their intentions and to appease constituencies by passing legislation that serves their interests.

Congress commonly directs its criticism of the judiciary at specific decisions. Much of the criticism is fodder to build support among constituencies important for its members' reelection campaigns and pass blame to the courts for unpopular defenses of the rights of criminal defendants and unpopular minority groups. There is little solid evidence that congressional critics have any direct influence over the Supreme Court or the rest of the federal judiciary. Also, Congress has considered constitutional amendments to overturn Supreme

Court decisions on controversial matters such as school desegregation, school prayer, and abortion, but the proposals were unsuccessful. Congress has impeached lower court federal judges on only eleven occasions, with seven of the trials resulting in the removal of judges from office and one in a resignation during proceedings. The only impeachment and trial of a Supreme Court justice, that of Samuel Chase in 1804, produced an acquittal. However, this impeachment indicated that Congress might not tolerate a partisan judiciary that ignored professional norms of legal interpretation and behavior. With judicial deference to its extensive powers the norm, the Congress has seldom needed to blame the judiciary for unpopular interpretations of the Constitution.

Although scholars have long recognized that the president's capacity to persuade and shape public opinion is one of his greatest powers, presidents have seldom sought to check judicial power by aggressively supporting constitutional amendments or legislation that might overturn decisions of the Supreme Court. Instead, presidents have used their "bully pulpit" to attack or support judicial decisions. For example, President Ronald Reagan repeatedly castigated the Supreme Court's restrictions on prayer in public schools. However, because of their influence on the composition of the judiciary and their ability to manage litigation, presidents have rarely had to confront a politically hostile judiciary. Consequently, they have not often had the opportunity to blame the courts for policy failures and political conflict. Indeed, evidence suggests that most congressional and presidential efforts to curb the judiciary or reverse its decisions have occurred in just four periods in American history—the early 1800s, the late 1820s, the 1860s, and the mid-1930s. In each of these periods a new partisan majority in control of the political branches enacted a bold new policy agenda, but it soon confronted opposition from a federal judiciary dominated by appointees of the defeated political party. In all four periods the new majority soon appointed justices or indirectly pressured the judiciary to support its policies. Threats by Congress or the president to sanction judicial independence soon waned. As with most examples cited in this section, the judiciary soon used its independent interpretive powers to support the policies of elected representatives.

An Assessment

After two centuries of interpretation and construction, do separated powers and checks and balances serve the framers' goal of limiting the despotic ambitions of public officials that might threaten the liberties of the people? The review in this chapter indicates that the federal and state judiciaries have reacted pragmatically to separation of powers conflicts. They have not propounded a unified constitutional theory of separated powers. The pragmatic understanding of separated powers emerged because of political realities. Whether appointed or elected, the

American judiciary normally shares perspectives on separated powers and other constitutional issues with dominant political voices in a state or the nation. Also, because of their limited reservoir of power, it appears that the federal and state judiciaries are often reluctant to address separated powers issues and face blame for controversial policy choices. Consequently, the judiciary often defers to the exercise of enumerated, implied, and inherent powers by the other branches. Additionally, it has legitimated many extra-constitutional political constructions that have reshaped the administration of public power, such as legislative delegation, presidential use of armed violence, and executive orders. For executive and legislative officers the result is that separated powers often serves as a tool to claim credit for popular actions and to shift or avoid blame when public policies adversely influence the sector of the public that comprises their constituency. Consequently the judiciary will usually avoid political risks and seek conformity with the sentiments of the partisan majority. It is not the aristocratic institution envisioned by critics of the framers but an institution responsive to other political institutions. However, these patterns of blame shifting and deference can subvert the framers' desire for political conflict among the branches as the way to contain governmental tyranny.

The U.S. Supreme Court justices' interpretations nonetheless have bounded some exercises of congressional and presidential power. They have diminished the threat of governmental tyranny when politically weakened presidents claimed prerogative or when legislation from a divided or irresolute Congress contradicted the constitutional text. These actions have tended to occur when the national political leadership is unpopular, such as with the Watergate tapes case, national leaders have adopted policy positions at variance with majority or elite sentiments, as with Truman's seizure of the steel mills, or the national leadership is locked in controversies that require immediate resolution but with no easy political solution, as with spiraling budget deficits. Also, by acting to empower minorities and women, the judiciary has abetted the broadening of the constituencies that offer political support to Congress, the president, and state officeholders. It has thus further democratized political debate about the performance of these institutions. Of course, in some intractable political conflicts among the branches that threaten the stability of the regime, the judiciary has acted as an independent policy maker. Separated powers and checks and balances thus works—sometimes—to ensure that American government responds to the people.

In 1788 James Madison commented that, "Justice is the end of government. It is the end of civil society." Justice, he added, must be pursued through constitutional government and the weaker individual must be protected against the violence of the stronger.[12] As indicated by evidence offered in this chapter, it is not clear that the politics of checking and balancing by the judiciary and the other branches will always achieve this lofty goal. Americans will realize the ambitions of the Founders only when the interpretation and construction of separated powers consistently works to proscribe violence against the weaker, when the powers of officeholders respect rather than attempt to manipulate the public's preferences, and when the public perceives that it is the master and not the subject of government. It also must function to protect against the new threats to free government posed by global corporations and terrorist cells. Consequently, popular sovereignty, democracy, and justice remain at risk.

Notes

1. Jonathan Elliot, ed. *The Debates of the State Conventions on the Adoption of the Federal Constitution, as Recommended by the General Convention at Philadelphia in 1787*, 2nd ed. (Philadelphia: J. B. Lippincott, 1866), vol. 3, 579.
2. Keith E. Whittington, *Constitutional Construction*, 1–19.
3. Alexander Hamilton, James Madison, and John Jay, *The Federalist* (No. 37), edited by Jacob E. Cooke (Middletown, Conn.: Wesleyan University Press, 1961), 233.
4. Thomas Jefferson, *Notes on the State of Virginia*, edited by William Peden (New York: W. W. Norton & Co., 1954), 120.
5. Hamilton, Madison, and Jay, ibid., 56–59 (No. 10), 323–353 (No. 47–51).
6. Ibid., 338 (No. 48), 445 (No. 66), 522 (No. 78).
7. The idea of shifting accountability or blame as an aspect of the practice of separated powers appears in Morris P. Fiorina, *Congress, Keystone of the Washington Establishment*, 2nd ed. (New Haven, Conn.: Yale University Press, 1989); and George I. Lovell, *Legislative Deferrals: Statutory Ambiguity, Judicial Power, and American Democracy* (Cambridge, U.K., and New York: Cambridge University Press, 2003), 1–41.
8. Hamilton, Madison, and Jay, 350 (No. 51), 418 (No. 62).
9. Ibid., 521–530 (No. 78); *Marbury v. Madison* (1803).
10. John Locke, *Two Treatises of Government*, edited by Peter Laslett (New York: Mentor Books, 1965), 422.
11. William H. Rehnquist, *The Supreme Court: How It Was, How It Is* (New York: William Morrow & Co., 1987), 158.
12. Hamilton, Madison, and Jay, 352 (No. 51).

Bibliography

Adams, Willi Paul. *The First American Constitutions: Republican Ideology and the Making of State Constitutions in the Revolutionary Era*. Translated by Rita Kimber and Robert Kimber. Chapel Hill: University of North Carolina Press, 1980.

Adler, David Gray, and Larry N. George, ed. *The Constitution and the Conduct of American Foreign Policy*. Lawrence: University Press of Kansas, 1996.

Barber, Sotirios A. *The Constitution and the Delegation of Congressional Power.* Chicago: University of Chicago Press, 1975.

Cooper, Phillip J. *By Order of the President: The Use and Abuse of Executive Direct Action.* Lawrence: University Press of Kansas, 2002.

Fisher, Louis. *Presidential War Power.* Lawrence: University Press of Kansas, 1995.

Fisher, Louis. *Constitutional Conflicts between President and Congress.* 4th ed. Lawrence: University Press of Kansas, 1997.

Fisher, Louis. *The Politics of Shared Power: Congress and the Executive.* 4th ed. College Station: Texas A&M Press, 1998.

Fisher, Louis. *Congressional Abdication on War and Spending.* College Station: Texas A&M Press, 2000.

Gwyn, W. B. *The Meaning of the Separation of Powers: An Analysis of the Doctrine from Its Origin to the Adoption of the United States Constitution.* Tulane Studies in Political Science, vol. 9. New Orleans: Tulane University, 1965.

Hamilton, Alexander, James Madison, and John Jay. *The Federalist.* Edited by Jacob E. Cooke. 1787–1788. Reprint. Middletown, Conn.: Wesleyan University Press, 1961.

Harriger, Katy J., ed. *Separation of Powers: Documents and Commentary.* Washington, D.C.: CQ Press, 2003.

Henkin, Louis. *Foreign Affairs and the United States Constitution.* 2nd ed. New York: Oxford University Press, 1996.

Lovell, George I. *Legislative Deferrals: Statutory Ambiguity, Judicial Power, and American Democracy.* Cambridge, U.K., and New York: Cambridge University Press, 2003.

May, Christopher. *In the Name of War: Judicial Review and the War Powers since 1918.* Cambridge, Mass.: Harvard University Press, 1989.

Mayer, Kenneth R. *With the Stroke of a Pen: Executive Orders and Presidential Power.* Princeton, N.J.: Princeton University Press, 2001.

Miller, Mark C., and Jeb Barnes, eds. *Making Policy, Making Law: An Interbranch Perspective* Washington, D.C.: Georgetown University Press, 2004.

Randall, James G. *Constitutional Problems under Lincoln.* Rev. ed. Urbana: University of Illinois Press, 1964.

Rozell, Mark J. *Executive Privilege: Dilemmas of Secrecy and Democratic Accountability.* Baltimore: The Johns Hopkins University Press, 1994.

Tarr, G. Alan. *Understanding State Constitutions.* Princeton, N.J.: Princeton University Press, 1998.

Thach, Charles C. *The Creation of the Presidency 1775–1789: A Study in Constitutional History.* Baltimore: The Johns Hopkins Press, 1923.

Vile, M. J. C. *Constitutionalism and the Separation of Powers.* Oxford, U.K.: Clarendon Press, 1967.

Whittington, Keith E. *Constitutional Construction: Divided Powers and Constitutional Meaning.* Cambridge, Mass.: Harvard University Press, 1999.

Court Cases

Bowsher v. Synar, 478 U.S. 714 (1986).

Clinton v. City of New York, 524 U.S. 417 (1998).

Dickerson v. United States, 530 U.S. 428 (2000).

Ex parte Merryman, F. Cas. 9487 (1861).

Ex parte Milligan, 71 U.S. 2 (1866).

Goldwater v. Carter, 444 U.S. 996 (1979).

Hamdi v. Rumsfeld, 124 S.Ct. 2633 (2004).
Humphrey's Executor v. United States, 295 U.S. 602 (1935).
Immigration and Naturalization Service v. Chadha, 462 U.S. 919 (1983).
In re Debs, 158 U.S. 564 (1895).
In re Neagle, 135 U.S. 1 (1890).
Korematsu v. United States, 323 U.S. 214 (1944).
McCulloch v. Maryland, 17 U.S. 316 (1819).
Myers v. United States, 272 U.S. 52 (1926).
New York Times Co. v. United States, 403 U.S. 713 (1971).
Powell v. McCormick, 395 U.S. 486 (1969).
Prize Cases, 67 U.S. 635 (1863).
Rasul v. Bush, 124 S.Ct. 2686 (2004).
Schlesinger v. Holtzman, 414 U.S. 1321 (1973).
Train v. City of New York, 420 U.S. 35 (1975).
United States v. Curtiss-Wright Export Corporation, 299 U.S. 304 (1936).
United States v. Kagama, 118 U.S. 375 (1886).
United States v. Nixon, 418 U.S. 683 (1974).
Youngstown Sheet & Tube Co. v. Sawyer, 343 U.S. 579 (1952).

5

JUDICIAL REVIEW AND INTERPRETATION: HAVE THE COURTS BECOME SOVEREIGN WHEN INTERPRETING THE CONSTITUTION?

Keith E. Whittington

IN A SERMON PREACHED BEFORE KING GEORGE I IN 1717 called "The Nature of the Kingdom," the controversial Bishop Benjamin Hoadly of Bangor, Wales, argued, "[W]hoever has an *absolute Authority* to *interpret* any written, or spoken Laws; it is *He*, who is truly the *Law-giver*, to all Intents and Purposes; and not the Person who first wrote, or spoke them." Hoadly's immediate point was theological, and this was a warning against giving the church hierarchy a privileged role in saying what the Scripture meant. If the bishops were to assume unchallenged authority to interpret the divine law and judge the "Consciences or Religion of his People," then the "*Kingdom of Christ*" would become "the *Kingdom* of those Men, vested with such *Authority*." The problem in the religious context is that the author of the Scriptures was not available to correct *ex cathedra* misinterpretations. The interpreters of the law could effectively become the sovereign, unless the original lawmaker was available to quell "the various and contradictory Opinions of Men."[1]

Hoadly's sermon caused a sensation, but he was already a well-known figure in the North American colonies as well as in Britain. A vigorous partisan of the Glorious Revolution, in which the Protestant Parliament had deposed the Catholic King James II, Hoadly had earlier published spirited attacks on the divine right of kings and defenses of the right of revolution against abusive governments. His later broadside against ecclesiastical authority and for individualism and religious toleration only enhanced his reputation as a political pamphleteer. American preachers, educators, and revolutionaries placed Hoadly alongside the famed British philosopher John Locke as one of the great torchbearers of republican liberty.

Hoadly's sermon before the king enjoyed renewed prominence in American legal circles in the twentieth century. Harvard Law School professor John Chipman Gray quoted the bishop three times in his influential treatise *The Nature and Sources of the Law*, but in doing so Gray turned Hoadly on his head. For Gray, along with other legal scholars of his era including Supreme Court Justice Oliver Wendell Holmes, it was a practical fact that judges, not legislators, were the true lawmakers. It was unavoidably the courts that "put life into the dead words of the statute"; "all the Law is judge-made law." Though the legislature is present in this world, its "statutes do not interpret themselves; their meaning is declared by the courts." Between the legislature and the judge, Gray and his colleagues pointed out, the judge has the last word.[2]

When considering its own role in interpreting the Constitution, the Supreme Court has echoed Gray's argument about statutes, raising the specter of a "government by judiciary" displacing democracy. Somewhat unfairly, Chief Justice Charles Evans Hughes's remark in an after-dinner speech that the "Constitution is what the judges say it is" has often been taken to symbolize the modern judicial mindset.[3] In a best-selling book on the Constitution, James M. Beck, President Warren Harding's solicitor general, praised the conservative Supreme Court of his era as a "continuing constitutional convention." Not long thereafter, Robert H. Jackson, President Franklin Roosevelt's attorney general and eventually a Supreme Court justice himself, used those same words in his own popular book to denounce that conservative Court.[4] Although the justices themselves have not been so bold as to compare the Supreme Court to a constitutional convention, they have reframed Charles Evans Hughes's remark as a constitutional requirement. In a series of prominent cases running from the 1950s through the close of the twentieth century, the Supreme Court has declared itself to be "the ultimate interpreter of the Constitution."[5] Once the Supreme Court has spoken, the justices have contended, all others are required to "end their national division by accepting a common mandate rooted in the Constitution."[6]

Although the founders shared Hoadly's sensibilities, they did not see the judicial authority to interpret the Constitution as raising especially difficult problems. From the perspective of the twenty-first century, it is surprising to discover that the courts and the power of judicial review received little attention in the debates over the drafting and ratification of the U.S. Constitution. The power of judicial review is nowhere mentioned in the text of the Constitution. The very term "judicial review" is a twentieth-century invention. Scholars who, in the late nineteenth century, began to look carefully at the question of whether the power of judicial review was even intended by the constitutional drafters were quickly frustrated by the lack of evidence bearing on the question either way.

No doubt part of the reason why the founders were relatively sanguine about constitutional interpretation by the judiciary was because they, like Hoadly, did not imagine the judiciary possessing an "absolute Authority to interpret." In explaining the power of judicial review fifteen years after the ratification of the Constitution, Chief Justice John Marshall contended in *Marbury v. Madison* that the authority to interpret the law was the particular province of the courts, part of the "duty of the judicial department to say what the law is," but his claims for the judicial authority to interpret the Constitution were fairly modest. He did not contend that the Court had privileged insight into constitutional requirements. Instead, somewhat disingenuously, he asked what the Court was to do if told to apply a law that was clearly in conflict with the terms of the Constitution. If Congress were to declare that a defendant could be convicted of treason on the testimony of only one witness, when the Constitution explicitly required two witnesses, Marshall asked, were judges to "close their eyes on the constitution, and see only the law?" He thought such a conclusion was too absurd to be true, too contrary to the entire purpose of a written constitution. Surely, "courts, as well as other departments, are bound by that instrument."[7] Judges, just like everyone else, were required to read and obey the dictates of the Constitution.

To consider how worried we should be about the possibility of the courts becoming sovereign when engaged in constitutional interpretation and judicial review, it will be helpful to think not only about the relationship between democracy and constitutionalism but also about our practical experience with courts and judicial review. Before getting to the practical checks on judicial power, however, we should recognize the different implications for democracy of judicial review depending on the kind of law at issue and nature of the constitutional questions to be decided. We will also review some prominent efforts to reconcile the practice of judicial review with democratic ideals.

Constitutionalism and Democracy

Alexander Hamilton famously regarded the judiciary as the "least dangerous" branch, with little ability to resist the exertions of the other branches of government.[8] Of far greater concern to many of the founders was the "impetuous vortex" of the legislature, as James Madison put it.[9] The danger, as they saw it, was that Congress would claim sole and absolute authority to interpret the Constitution, just as the British Parliament exercised sovereignty in the British constitutional scheme. If it did, Marshall contended, then the very purpose of a written constitution would be defeated. A legislature given the right to "interpret" the Constitution as it saw fit would be given "a practical and real omnipotence."[10] The Constitution would indeed be reduced to the "parchment barriers" that Madison had judged the early state constitutions to be.[11] Constitutional interpretation by the judiciary was needed to counterbalance constitutional interpretation by the legislature and to keep the legislature from slipping its constitutional fetters through creative interpretation of its own powers.

Later generations tended to view things in a somewhat different light. As judicial review was routinized, judges did not look like they were sounding the alarm for the sovereign people, who once alerted to a constitutional violation could, for example, throw the perfidious legislators out at the next election. Judges instead looked like they were governing from the bench. If judges sounded the alarm of constitutional violations, how would we know whether it was a false alarm? When it became evident that constitutional disagreements would be pervasive in the republic, then not everyone was likely to respond in the same way to the judicial alarm. Rather than protecting the people from the faithless legislature, the judges might simply join one side of a dispute within the legislature and among the people. This possibility seemed particularly stark when the Supreme Court intervened in the slavery dispute in the *Dred Scott* case in the last years before the Civil War. The congressional authority to prohibit slavery in the western territories was very much an issue within politics, and as a consequence the Court appeared to be irredeemably partisan when taking sides on that issue. It led Abraham Lincoln to warn, "If the policy of government, upon vital questions, affecting the whole people, is to be irrevocably fixed by the decisions of the Supreme Court . . . the people will have ceased to be their own rulers."[12]

Lincoln's response to the Court's exercise of judicial review in *Dred Scott* also highlighted the changed relationship between the legislature and the people and the problems that raised for the judicial authority to interpret the Constitution. John Marshall, and the Founders generally, imagined a clear distinction between the legislature and "the people," such that the courts could appeal to the latter when the former exceeded their will. Later generations, however, were much more likely to view the legislature as a simple extension of "the people." In that case, judicial obstruction of legislation was merely the obstruction of the popular will, preventing the people from being "their own rulers." Where constitutionalism and popular sovereignty were once linked, such that checks and balances were needed to prevent popular sovereignty from slipping into legislative sovereignty, they were now decoupled, such that "democracy" required giving effect to the will of the electoral victors. If democracy meant "a government of the people, by the people, for the people," then a strong judicial authority to interpret the law of the people and apply it against the people's representatives was problematic.[13] At the state level, judges were increasingly subject to election and constitutions were subject to popular revisions, to reflect this new sensibility. At the national level, judges remained distant from the people and the constitutional law remained hard to change by democratic means.

Democracy and constitutionalism are not entirely fixed targets, but the concepts as they have developed over the course of American history are in some tension, if not antagonism, with one another. In the eighteenth century, "democracy" evoked images of passionate mobs in ancient Greek city-states, all too likely to give the poisoned chalice to Socrates or fall under the sway of a silver-tongued dictator. The Founders preferred to think of America as an experiment in "republican" government, resting on the authority of the people but with popular sentiment filtered through representatives and the law. With the success of the experiment, however, democracy soon took on a more positive connotation and Americans embraced it as a description of their own political system. Democracy in this more modern sense came to be identified with "majority rule" and a relatively unfettered right of electoral and legislative victors to make government policy on matters of public concern. Likewise, elections were understood to be the vehicle by which the "will of the people" was to be identified, with electoral victors not merely occupying a legally defined office but also claiming a particular mandate to govern. The rise of "mass democracy" with universal suffrage was somewhat slower to take hold, but it dramatically altered the range of social interests to which government was expected to be responsive.

Whereas democracy was about empowering the government to act on behalf of the electorally expressed will of the people, constitutionalism was largely about reining it in. John Marshall emphasized in *Marbury* that a written constitution was meant to create legal checks on government officials. The Constitution specified what rights and powers particular officials might have and what processes they had to follow when exercising government power, and the courts were to see that those legalities were followed. From this perspective, the electorate contracted with a politician to exercise a particular public authority, and the courts were to insure that the politician did not exceed the terms of the contract by exercising more authority than he was entitled to. Over time a related feature of constitutionalism came to the fore, one which emphasized the protection of individuals and minorities. By the mid-nineteenth century, as the ideal and practice of democracy took hold and suffrage expanded beyond the wealthy elite, thinkers such as Alexis de Tocqueville and John Stuart Mill emphasized the characteristic danger of democracy, "majority tyranny." The abolition of slavery brought this concern into stark relief in the United States, prompting the passage of the Fourteenth Amendment to the U.S. Constitution and the launching of a much more aggressive era of judicial review.

Two Concerns about Judicial Review

The exercise of judicial review might be seen as coming into conflict with democracy in two distinct ways. The first is the "countermajoritarian" problem. If the actions of government in a properly functioning democracy reflect the will of the people, then the judicial nullification of government actions is the obstruction of the will of the people. At the same time, if not all citizens share the same interests, then the right to vote may not be sufficient to prevent a government controlled by an electoral majority from preying on the electoral minority. Judicial review, in this mode, is not about sounding the alarm for the people, but fundamentally about rejecting the results of the democratic process. It was relatively easy to embrace this judicial role when the paradigm case is the protection of a racial minority from slavery. Matters become more complicated when the issues become more controversial, as when, for example, the electoral majority seeks to impose a progressive income tax on a wealthy minority. Unsurprisingly, this populist critique of judicial review—that the judges were preventing the people themselves from governing—became common amid the political struggles accompanying industrialization in the late nineteenth century, and it has been with us ever since.

The second conflict between judicial review and democracy is the "government by judiciary" problem. The concern here is with judges "legislating from the bench" by making essentially discretionary decisions about public policy. While there are mechanisms for limiting judicial discretion, such as clear constitutional or statutory text and established precedents from earlier cases, judges in controversial constitutional cases often appear to make choices. The constitutional text, for example, supplies little guidance on how exactly to resolve many of the legal disputes that reach the Supreme Court. As Justice Robert Jackson once admitted, when acting under the Constitution's "majestic generalities," judges may not be able to provide a persuasive explanation for why they were legally compelled to reach the result that they did.[14] Judges interpreting the Constitution and exercising the power of judicial review may therefore appear antidemocratic not only because they obstruct the will of the electoral majority but also because they appear to be acting as law*makers*, addressing subjects that are not explicitly addressed in the Constitution or laying down rules that do not appear in the Constitution itself. Both of these antidemocratic concerns might be alleviated somewhat where, as in many states, judges are electorally accountable and thus have a certain visible democratic credential of their own. Even so, the strength of those democratic credentials are likely to be put to the test when courts must engage in particular exercises in constitutional interpretation and decide controversial cases.

Against What Majority?

The federal structure of the United States creates a serious complication for evaluating the conflicts between democracy and judicial review. If democracy requires governing in accord with the will of the electoral majority, then federalism complicates the situation by creating two levels of government that reflect the will of two distinct electorates. The state and national legislatures are matched by state and national judiciaries, which in turn interpret both state and national constitutions. If judicial review is charged with being antidemocratic for obstructing the will of the majority, it is not always obvious what majority is being obstructed.

The federal structure creates four basic combinations by which courts and legislatures might collide. One possibility that has begun to receive more attention in recent years is the judicial review of state laws by state judiciaries. State courts must interpret both state and federal constitutions when evaluating legislation that comes before them, though the more interesting cases arise when state courts interpret their own state constitutions. Here, at least, there is only one populace at issue, the people of the state in question. State courts reviewing state legislation then face a straightforward democratic concern, and over the course of American history state courts have become entangled in substantial controversy. State court judges were the first to try to exercise the power of judicial review in the United States, and in several states these early judicial claims to be able to assess the constitutionality of state laws led to legislative threats to remove the offending judges from office. Questions about judicial review in the early nineteenth century helped lead some states to begin to choose judges by popular election. In the late nineteenth and early twentieth centuries, it was often state courts that led the fight against progressive reforms such as the adoption of minimum wage and the legislative sanction of labor union activities.

More recently, state courts have grappled with their own distinct set of constitutional issues. After the U.S. Supreme Court in the 1970s turned aside challenges under the U.S. Constitution to state systems for financing public education, litigants pressed the case for reform in state courts. Many states rely on local financing to fund public schools, but this can result in wide disparities between those school districts with a strong tax base (e.g., wealthy suburbs) and those without (e.g., small towns, inner cities). Although the U.S. Supreme Court held that unequal spending on public schools did not violate the Equal Protection Clause of the U.S. Constitution, some state courts have since concluded that state constitutional requirements of "high quality" or "uniform and general" schooling required some form of school finance equalization. Such rulings have sometimes provoked extended battles between courts and the other branches of state government, as well as public outcry, as politicians struggle to develop more geographically equitable financing schemes. At minimum such reforms require higher taxes, limitations on spending, or both, in wealthier districts, and have sometimes initiated a wholesale reconsideration of the system of state and local finances. Governors and legislators have lost their jobs while struggling to respond to such judicial decisions. Such judicial rulings are all the more striking since they give legal teeth to constitutional language that legislators and voters had long been left alone to interpret, or ignore, as they thought appropriate. Not only are such judicial decisions often unpopular, but they necessarily draw judges in to the nitty-gritty of public finance, though most courts have been reluctant to simply dictate a constitutionally acceptable school funding system to state legislatures.

State courts have waded into an equally emotional dispute with rulings on same-sex marriage. Like the financing and operation of public schools, the recognition and regulation of marriage have traditionally been areas of state and local responsibility in the United States. Unlike the school equity cases, however, the gay marriage cases have generally involved state constitutional provisions that are closely analogous to the Equal Protection Clause of the Fourteenth Amendment of the U.S. Constitution. At first reading these state provisions independently of federal provisions and later reading them in light of U.S. Supreme Court decisions affecting the rights of homosexuals, judges in several states have forced public discussion of, and government action on, gay marriage and civil unions.

State policies on marriage have always implicated another aspect of federalism, the spillover effects of policies among states bound together in a common union. Unlike the school finance decisions, which had no direct impact on other states, even the threat of a favorable ruling in the same-sex marriage cases had immediate repercussions across the nation. Just as the relatively lenient divorce laws of states such as Nevada once allowed residents from others states to escape their more restrictive local statutes and get a "quickie divorce," so gay marriage rulings raised the possibility of homosexual couples bringing a marriage license home from a more lenient state. Unsurprisingly, courts in such relatively liberal states as Hawaii, Vermont, and Massachusetts were the ones that pushed ahead with such decisions. While such rulings were not necessarily welcomed even in their home states, they were even further out of line with public opinion in more conservative states. Even as such judicial deliberations led these state legislatures to consider statutory recognition of homosexual couples, the possible extraterritorial effects of such decisions forced state and national legislatures to scramble to find ways to legally shield more conservative states from them.

The national effect of the gay marriage cases points toward the second possible combination of courts and legislatures, state courts reviewing the constitutionality of national laws. This combination is relatively rare, in part because the constitutional design seeks to minimize the opportunities for local political majorities to frustrate the policies of national political majorities. Unlike the preceding Articles of Confederation, the U.S. Constitution created a government with its own power of taxation and enforcement so as to make the federal government a freestanding government that was not reliant on the cooperation of the states to act on national policy. Many of the Federalist supporters of the Constitution feared that state judges would not be sufficiently sympathetic to the new national government and might hinder its operation. The first statute creating the federal judiciary anticipated that state courts might declare federal laws unconstitutional and gave the U.S. Supreme Court the authority to hear and reverse those state court decisions. When the Virginia courts asserted in the early nineteenth century that the Supreme Court did not have the constitutional authority to review and overturn state court decisions, the Supreme Court quickly and emphatically reasserted its authority. "Public mischiefs" were bound to occur, the Court reasoned, if the interpretation of the Constitution were left in the hands of the several state courts, who might render "jarring and discordant judgments." The Constitution could not "be different in different states" or left subject to "state prejudices . . . and state interests."[15] A few years later when the state of Maryland imposed punitive taxes on the federally chartered Bank of the United States, arguing in part that Congress did not have the constitutional authority to incorporate a bank, the Supreme Court elaborated further on the logic of limiting the ability of state governments to interfere with the laws of the national government. When a state acting alone claimed the authority to set aside the constitutional judgments of the national legislature, then it "acts upon measures of government created by others as well as themselves, for the benefit of others in common with themselves." There was a difference, the Court explained, between the "action of the whole on a part, and the action of a part on the whole," and the government of the whole people could not be held hostage to the judgments of merely local majorities.[16] A federal hierarchy in constitutional interpretation reinforced the supremacy of national majorities over local majorities.

Judicial Review of State Laws by the Federal Courts

This has also been true when state laws are at issue, as in the third combination of state laws being reviewed by national courts. These are the most visible, the most common, and often the most controversial occasions for the exercise of judicial review. Over the course of its history, the U.S. Supreme Court has held state or local ordinances unconstitutional in over twelve hundred cases. Just in the latter half of the twentieth century, these cases have included some of the most notable decisions the Court has ever rendered, including the abolition of the racial segregation of the schools, the finding of a right to an abortion, the prohibition of organized prayer in public schools, the extension of free speech rights to include the burning of the American flag, and the legalization of sodomy.

The limitation of the power of state governments is one of the central goals of the Constitution. Even though James Madison was unable to win support for a congressional veto over state legislation, the text of the original Constitution does include several restrictions on the states and instructed judges that the terms of the Constitution were to be regarded as supreme over any conflicting state laws or constitutional provisions. Supporters of the Constitution were motivated in part by a concern that state legislatures, too responsive to local majorities, were insufficiently attentive to the rights of individuals. In the states, Madison thought, "the stronger faction can readily unite and oppress the weaker." He hoped that shifting some issues into national politics would make it harder for oppressive majorities to form. The variety of interests represented in the national legislature would make it more likely that "a coalition of a majority of the whole society could seldom take place on any other principles than those of justice and the general good."[17] Madison himself was slow to accept the usefulness of the judiciary as a check against the problem of majority tyranny. He preferred to find a democratic solution to the problem of majority tyranny rather than turn to the "precarious security" of "creating a will in the community independent of the majority" (the primary example of which, to Madison, was a hereditary aristocracy).[18] But after the Civil War, there was more political will to impose national, legally enforceable limits on the states, and federal judicial review became an increasingly important mechanism for securing liberty within them.

The supporters of the Constitution in 1787 were also motivated by a concern that state legislatures would, if left to themselves, enter into dangerous conflicts with one another. With some states, such as New York and New Jersey, laying punitive taxes on each other's goods, and other states, such as Connecticut and Pennsylvania, squabbling over disputed boundaries, civil war among the states was widely feared at the time of the constitutional convention. Of course, the boundary between the authority of the state and federal governments was likewise vague and heavily contested. Madison spoke for many in noting that a tribunal, such as the Supreme Court, for peacefully resolving such disputes "is clearly essential to prevent an appeal to the sword and a dissolution of the union."[19] More than a century later, Supreme Court justice and thrice-wounded Civil War veteran Oliver Wendell Holmes concluded, "I do not think the United States would come to an end if we lost our power to declare an Act of Congress void. I do think the Union would be imperiled if we could not make that declaration as to the laws of the several States."[20]

Although the Court's interpretation of the Constitution when striking down state laws is often controversial, the Supreme Court's decisions are often a closer reflection of the views of the majority of the nation than are the state laws they are invalidating. At the turn of the twentieth century, the justices doubted that state legislators were the best judges of whether, for example, the commercial rights of out-of-state insurance companies were adequately protected when they were barred from insuring ships and cargo in the port of New Orleans. In the mid-twentieth century, the justices were skeptical of the claims of southern states that inadequate and racially segregated schools met the Constitution's requirement that states give their citizens equal protection of the laws. While such laws might have met with the approval of local electoral majorities, they held little favor with national electoral majorities, and evaluating whether the Court was displacing the rule of the people in such cases requires some consideration of which majority was entitled to rule.

Other cases cannot be set aside so easily. Often when the Court acts to strike down a state law as unconstitutional, it is acting against a policy prevailing in only one or a few states, such as Louisiana's maritime insurance law, the South's racial segregation laws, or Connecticut's beleaguered law prohibiting the sale of contraceptives at the dawn of the sexual revolution. On occasion, however, when the Court decides against one state in a single case it is simultaneously casting a legal shadow over the laws of many other states. Although the Texas abortion law at issue in *Roe v. Wade* was, in 1973, more conservative than the reform laws that had been recently adopted by some other states, the Court's opinion had the effect of invalidating the abortion laws then on the books in all fifty states. When the Court held in 1972 that the prevailing means of imposing the death penalty violated the Constitution, it affected the laws in three-quarters of the states, though most actual death sentences were imposed and carried out in the South. When the Court concluded that the Texas conviction of Gregory Lee Johnson for burning the U.S. flag violated the constitutional protection of free speech, it had the effect of nullifying similar laws in nearly every state. In cases such as these, the policies that the Court displaces are favored by national, and not merely local, majorities, and the public and political response is often immediate and national in scope.

Judicial Review of Federal Laws by Federal Courts

The final combination, of national courts invalidating national laws is less common, but seemingly clearer in posing the conflict between judicial review and democracy. Over its history, the Supreme Court has struck down federal statutory provisions as conflicting with constitutional requirements in just over 150 cases, and though these cases pitted the Court against a coequal branch of the national government, relatively few of them could be said to raise concerns for the status of democracy. The celebrated 1803 case of *Marbury v. Madison*, in which the Supreme Court first announced its power of judicial review, is interesting in this regard. Though Chief Justice John Marshall used the occasion to assert the Court's important role in interpreting the fundamental law and in insuring that the national legislature did not exceed its constitutional commission, the action it took—ruling out one interpretation of a technical provision in the Judiciary Act of 1789—was less than dramatic and not of much concern to either legislative or electoral majorities.

In other cases in which the Court has been called upon to review the constitutionality of the federal government's actions, the policies at stake are more important. Abraham Lincoln's remonstrance against the judicial displacement of democracy was in reference to just such a case. In the 1857 *Dred Scott* case, the Court reached the question of whether Congress had the authority to prohibit slavery in the territories. The states had largely settled for themselves whether they would allow slavery within their borders or not, but the status of the new western territories, and their likely political future as states, had been a central issue in American politics since the 1820s. The established political parties, the Whigs and the Democrats, were riven by the issue, and a new political party, the Republicans, was being formed around it. The Court hoped to squelch the increasingly violent agitation over slavery and end the Republican threat to the established party system by setting out a clear, though extreme, resolution of the issue, by taking the matter out of the hands of Congress and guaranteeing the right of slaveholders to carry their slaves into the territories. In fact, the Court was unable to resolve the controversy and only succeeded in marking itself as the enemy of the ascendant Republicans and their antislavery principles.

The Court has also notably refrained from obstructing the actions of the federal government, sometimes to its later regret. When the Federalist Party under John Adams passed the Sedition Act and used it to attempt to silence their Jeffersonian critics prior to the election of 1800, federal judges turned a deaf ear to cries that the act violated the First Amendment's guarantees of freedom of speech and the press. When the justices strengthened First Amendment protections in the twentieth century, history's judgment of the Sedition Act was very much on their minds. More recent decisions by the Court to uphold federal action have led to similar regrets. In 1942, Congress authorized the president, acting through military commanders, to impose restrictions on the activities of civilians in a "military zone," under threat of imprisonment. President Franklin D. Roosevelt in turn issued an executive order requiring "every possible protection against espionage and against sabotage," and authorized military commanders to remove American citizens of Japanese descent from their homes on the West Coast and intern them in camps during the war with Japan. In the 1944 case of Toyosaburo Korematsu, who had been convicted of violating such a civilian exclusion order, a majority of the Court refused in "the calm perspective of hindsight" to gainsay the military judgment "in a critical hour" of the commander-in-chief who did not believe it possible to try to separate those who posed true security risks from those who did not, and chalked the case up to the "hardships . . . of war."[21] When called upon to evaluate the constitutionality of President George W. Bush's order to detain indefinitely an American citizen captured in Afghanistan without a hearing to test the military's claim that he was, in fact, an "enemy combatant," the current justices took pains to identify themselves with the *Korematsu* dissenters in concluding that it would not "infringe on the core role of the military for the courts to exercise their time-honored and constitutionally mandated roles of reviewing" the factual basis for such continuing detentions.[22]

The Basic Structures of Government and the Fundamental Liberties of the People

As this brief review shows, federalism complicates the evaluation of the antidemocratic quality of constitutional interpretation by the courts, depending on the strength and scope of the political majority being obstructed by judicial review. The implications of judicial review for democratic government are also complicated by the kind of issue at stake in a case that comes before the Court. In particular, we can distinguish between what we might call structural, or process, issues on the one hand and liberty, or substantive, issues on the other.

Most of the text of federal and state constitutions is concerned with laying down the structure and processes of government. The main body of the U.S. Constitution, for example, primarily establishes the three branches of the national government, details the powers of each, specifies the relationship between the national government and the state governments, and provides for the ratification and amendment of the Constitution itself. The meaning of most of these constitutional provisions is fairly clear and a tradition of government practice built up over time has further elaborated what the constitutional organization of government looks like. Even so, disputes do arise over what these aspects of the Constitution require, and judges are sometimes called upon to help resolve those disputes and clarify the meaning of the Constitution.

Such cases can be extremely important in their political and policy consequences and in their implications for the maintenance of the constitutional design, but they are rarely the exemplary cases of the countermajoritarian problem. Cases focusing on the structures of government can sometimes be of substantial popular interest and resonant with democratic concerns, such as the Court's mid-twentieth-century dismantling of "rotten boroughs" that severely reduced the influence of urban voters in state legislatures or the Court's rejection in the 1990s of state-imposed term limits on U.S. congressmen. In other cases, such as *Marbury*, the structural questions at issue are fairly esoteric and of only limited concern to those outside professional politics. Interpreting the structural features of the Constitution also allows the Court to play the role of a neutral umpire. As a young clerk to a Supreme Court justice, William Rehnquist took a jaundiced view of the Court's history in deciding on matters of rights and values, but he thought the Court's record was better on structural issues. "Where theoretically co-ordinate bodies of government are disputing, the Court is well suited to its role as arbiter." In the "less emotionally charged" realm of government organization, the Court could "determine the skeletal relations of governments to each other without influencing the substantive business of those governments."[23] As a justice on the Court, William Rehnquist has generally urged his colleagues to avoid invalidating legislative decisions on the basis of controversial rights claims, but he has been quite willing to side against Congress in disputes within government or between different levels of government. Structural decisions are more likely to tell government officials how and by whom policy decisions are to be made than to tell them that certain policies may not be adopted at all. Decisions that reject the congressional effort to give the president an effective "line-item veto" to strike out certain provisions of a bill while allowing the rest of the bill to become law or that indicate that only states and localities but not the federal government may regulate the possession of firearms near public schools, for example, may complicate the policymaking process and make certain kinds of policy results more difficult to achieve, but they rarely rule some policy goals off limits to democratic decision-making.

Probably the most publicly visible parts of the Constitution concern liberty issues, or matters of policy substance. The Bill of Rights is the most famous source of rights provisions limiting government power, but there are also important substantive constraints contained in the original body of the Constitution, the post–Civil War Fourteenth Amendment to the Constitution, and various other constitutional amendments as well. State constitutions have their own bills of rights, but they are more distinctive in also containing often quite specific policy commitments, such as constitutional provisions requiring the states to provide systems of public education or public support for the infirm. It is in interpreting these constitutional clauses that judges come into the most direct conflict with legislatures and political majorities, for it is on these issues that judges often instruct legislators that a constitution has permanently placed some policies beyond their political reach. These are also often the issues around which legislative and electoral politics turn. In the mid-nineteenth century, the Supreme Court found the rights of slaveholders trumped the power of the federal or territorial governments. In the late nineteenth and early twentieth centuries, the Court pointed to various property rights that precluded legislators from, for example, setting railroad rates, imposing a minimum wage or maximum working hours on employers, prohibiting child labor, or requiring employees to join a labor union. In the latter part of the twentieth century, the Court has emphasized other sets of rights that have, for example, barred racially segregated public schools and limited government use of racial affirmative action, required local governments to issue parade permits to Nazis and Klansmen and to prohibit student-led prayers at high school football games, and recognized freedom of individual choice in acquiring abortion services or in performing a wide array of consensual sexual acts. State courts have sometimes led and sometimes aggressively followed the lead of the U.S. Supreme Court on these issues and more, whether protecting cigar manufacturing in apartment houses in nineteenth-century New York or safeguarding fully nude exotic dancing in twentieth-century Pennsylvania. It is most often on these issues that the courts have been accused of displacing the sovereignty of the people.

Strategies for Resolving Democracy and Judicial Review

Over the course of the long debate over the scope and legitimacy of judicial review in a democracy, three basic strategies for escaping the countermajoritarian difficulty have been developed. Each strategy has its own implications for how the courts should go about the task of constitutional interpretation and how the power of judicial review should be exercised. One response is simply to embrace the countermajoritarian potential of the courts as a positive good. From this perspective, the very purpose of constitutionalism is to preserve the liberty of individuals and minorities against the encroachment of government officials and popular majorities. It is the very insulation of courts from democratic influences that makes them so distinctive and so valuable within an otherwise democratic system. This response might also note that the power of judicial review is, in fact, only one of many mechanisms within the American constitutional system to limit the power of overbearing majorities. Madison's efforts to nationalize some policy decisions and take them out of the hands of local political majorities, the relatively long terms of U.S. senators, the equal representation of heavily and scarcely populated states in the Senate, the presidential veto, and the Senate filibuster, among other features of American politics, are all designed to temper majoritarian pressures. Moreover, the desirability of democracy is itself rooted, in part, in the recognition of the equal worth and dignity of every individual, which also underlies the constitutional commitment to rights. Especially when contrasted to such twentieth-century alternatives as fascism and Communism, the concept of democracy became identified not only with institutions of popular government but also with the recognition and protection of human rights. Where Judge Learned Hand once worried that judges could become like "a bevy of Platonic guardians," his former clerk, legal philosopher Ronald Dworkin, countered that great matters of constitutional principle should not be left to depend "on the weight of numbers or the balance of political influence."[24] Where Justice Robert Jackson, who helped lead the Court's retreat from the conservative activism of the early twentieth century, admitted that the "task of translating the majestic generalities of the Bill of Rights . . . into concrete restraints on officials . . . is one to disturb self-confidence," Justice William Brennan, who helped lead the Court's advance into an era of liberal activism in the 1960s, chastised those who would shy away from the judicial "challenge of working with the majestic generalities" of the Constitution.[25] If the courts become sovereign when interpreting the Constitution, then this approach would argue that this simply reflects the ultimate sovereignty of the individual over the coercive power of the state.

A second strategy to escape the countermajoritarian problem is to obscure it by noting the ways in which the courts might help secure democratic values and reinforce democratic institutions. The Founders hoped that representative democracy would avoid some of the turmoil and danger of classical direct democracy, as well as allow the possibility of extending popular government beyond the narrow confines of a Greek city-state to the broad tracts of a modern nation. In doing so, however, it also creates new incentives for those in power to seek to manipulate the tools of government in order to remain in power, for the representatives to turn against those they represent. Thus, government officials may seek to censor the information that reaches the electorate so as to silence critics or to regulate the financing and conduct of campaigns so as to disadvantage electoral challengers. They may prefer that administrative proceedings or criminal prosecutions be shrouded in secrecy so as to obscure their actions. Legislators may draw electoral boundaries to preserve their own hold on office, or to enhance the power of their own particular constituencies. Judges may enhance the sovereignty of the people by "policing the process of representation" and by employing the Constitution to prevent politicians from entrenching themselves in power and sheltering themselves from democratic accountability.[26] By focusing on the process of constitutional decision-making, judges might be able to interpret the Constitution without impeding democratic outcomes.

A third strategy for escaping the countermajoritarian problem is to limit the problem by finding a democratic mandate for the constitutional efforts of judges. This was John Marshall's strategy when he emphasized that the Court in interpreting the Constitution did nothing but attempt to hear the voice of "we the people" over the cacophony of the normal legislative process. By adhering faithfully to the Constitution's commands, the judiciary could be said to be respecting and preserving the sovereign authority of the people, even if that required disregarding the lesser authority of their feckless legislative agents. This approach to reconciling judicial review with democracy requires accepting the democratic pedigree of the Constitution and adopting an interpretive approach that emphasizes that pedigree. While John Marshall could count on his readers readily admitting that the Constitution spoke with the voice of the sovereign people, readers in later generations may not be as willing to grant him that assumption. Both the sheer passage of time since the Constitution's adoption and changing conceptions of democracy complicate the idea that the Constitution better captures the political will of the people than do legislative provisions. To effectuate this strategy for legitimating judicial review, judges must also take care to insure that their interpretations of the Constitution are persuasive as faithful renderings of the sovereign command. Some would add that this claim would be more persuasive if judges refrained from setting aside legislative acts in all but the clearest cases of constitutional violation. Judges might be modest enough to recognize that legislators are capable of reading the Constitution as well and that judges should only move against them when legislators appear not merely to have adopted a different reading of the Constitution than the one favored by the judges but when they appear to have ignored constitutional mandates entirely. By faithfully interpreting the Constitution, proponents of this strategy would argue, judges do not become sovereign but rather uphold the sovereignty of the people as constitution-makers, capable of writing constitutional limitations on government officials with the expectations that judges will help prevent transgressions of them.

Formal Checks on Judicial Power

The theoretical problems associated with judicial review are complex and interesting ones, but they only become pressing if in fact the judiciary seems to threaten popular control of constitutional meaning. The theoretical discussion leaves open the question of whether the judges have, in fact, become sovereign when interpreting the Constitution. We have seen that the issue is more troubling in some contexts than in others. Judicial arbitration of structural disputes and the national correction of local majorities may be less threatening to democratic values than judicial imposition of favored values against jurisdictionally comparable majorities. Even then, we cannot lose sight of Bishop Hoadly's initial expectation that there may be sufficient checks on secular judges to prevent their exercising absolute authority over constitutional meaning.

We might consider first the formal checks on overreaching judicial efforts to interpret the Constitution. The most basic question here is how easily judicial interpretations of the Constitution can be overturned. The U.S. Constitution makes this very difficult. More concerned with preventing frequent challenges and revisions to the hard-won and finely tuned terms of the Constitution than with facilitating the authoritative correction of judicial error, the Founders set the bar for constitutional amendment very high. Just how high may not have been evident to them. The Articles of Confederation required that any revisions to it receive the unanimous consent of every state, which proved to be a fatal defect. Many state constitutions of the revolutionary era included no explicit mechanism for amendment at all, necessitating the assembly of a new constitutional convention to consider any proposals for change to the fundamental law. By those standards, the amendment process laid out in Article V of the Constitution seemed rather flexible. Indeed, within sixteen years of the Constitution's ratification it had already been amended twelve times. But over time the Constitution's requirement of the approval of two-thirds of each chamber of Congress and three-fourths of the states has proven very difficult to meet. When the U.S. Supreme Court interprets the Constitution, it is hard to overrule it.

The U.S. Constitution was one of the first written constitutions in the world. Its example as to amendment procedures has not generally been followed. Judging by the procedural obstacles to successful amendment and the historic experience with amendment efforts, the U.S. Constitution is perhaps the most difficult to amend of any constitution currently in use. State constitutions in the United States are universally easier to amend than is the federal Constitution. This gives rise to a robust history of legislators and voters writing new constitutional text in response to state judicial decisions, giving voters rather than judges the last word on what the state constitutions will mean.

A second formal method for overturning the constitutional interpretations of judges is some form of legislative override. That is, rather than altering the constitutional text to correct a perceived judicial misinterpretation, legislators may be empowered to formally set aside a judicial ruling on the constitutionality of a statute. Canada provides one example of such a mechanism. Following the British model, Canada had long gone without a written constitution and the power of judicial review. In 1982, however, Canada adopted the Charter of Rights and Freedoms, which was subject to judicial interpretation and enforcement against the provincial and federal parliaments. But a clause of the Charter allows Canadian legislatures to declare laws valid for up to five years "notwithstanding" their apparent conflict with some constitutional provisions, sheltering them from judicial review. The province of Quebec employed the clause, for example, to protect its "French only" requirement for outdoor signs from free speech challenges, and Alberta used the clause to protect its ban on homosexual marriages from judicial review. In the early twentieth century, at the same time that many American states were adopting initiative and referendum procedures and constitutional decisions by conservative judges were being severely criticized, there were numerous proposals for "judicial recall." Some states did adopt constitutional provisions allowing individual judges, among other kinds of government officials, to be "recalled" before the regular end of their term of service. Even more radical was the proposal advocated by former president Theodore Roosevelt and others to "permit the people themselves by popular vote, after due deliberation and discussion, but finally and without appeal, to settle what the proper construction of any constitutional point is." Roosevelt had come to believe that "the power to interpret is the power to establish; and if the people are not allowed finally to interpret the fundamental law, ours is not a popular government," and thus it must be well within their means to override the constitutional interpretation of judges with which they disagree.[27] Those proposals were not adopted.

A different kind of formal check on judges relates to how easy it is for them to issue authoritative interpretations of a constitution. The U.S. Constitution is silent as to the procedure that the justices of the Supreme Court must use for ruling on a constitutional, or any other, issue. Unsurprisingly, the justices have adopted majority rule, such that with its current composition of nine justices five votes are required to declare a law unconstitutional. This is the common procedure adopted to govern the exercise of judicial review elsewhere as well, though in many countries the actual vote of the judges in a case is never made public.

One common proposal in the early twentieth-century United States for judicial reform was to require something more than a majority of the justices to agree before a law could be invalidated. Just as supermajority requirements for constitutional amendments make it more difficult for legislators or voters to alter a judicial interpretation of the Constitution, so a supermajority requirement for judicial review would make it more difficult for judges to overturn the constitutional judgment of the legislature and strike down a statute. Another means for making it harder for judges to make controversial interpretations of the Constitution is to write a clearer, more specific constitutional text. There is no mystery as to why the Supreme Court has spent a great deal of time discussing such "majestic generalities" of the Constitution as the requirement of "equal protection of the laws" or the prohibition on laws "abridging the freedom of speech" and very little time elaborating what the Constitution means when it says that "no Person shall be a Senator who shall not have attained the Age of thirty Years." Unfortunately, such constitutional abstractions are very hard to avoid, and while most constitutions are far more detailed and verbose than the U.S. Constitution, they all contain similarly vague phrases.

Finally, it is possible to limit judicial interpretation of a constitution by restricting the caseload and jurisdiction of judges. The most obvious way to do that is to deny judges the authority to interpret a constitution at all. In the United State, all judges, from the trial court to the Supreme Court, may interpret the Constitution and declare a statute void. In reaction to the American experience, but with a desire to create some form of judicial review, the Austrian Federal Constitution of 1920 provided an alternative model that has become common in Europe and elsewhere. In this European model, regular judges are not allowed to interpret the constitution; only a single and specialized constitutional court may do so. Such a constitutional court may be designed to be more, or less, independent than the regular judiciary, and access to the constitutional court may be restricted in various ways. For example, the French Constitution of 1958 created a constitutional court but allowed it to review the constitutionality only of proposed bills and only upon the request of the leadership of the government. At the opposite extreme, anyone anywhere can request a constitutional interpretation from the Hungarian constitutional court.

Informal Checks on Judicial Power

There are also informal means to limit the ability of judges to interpret a constitution. The more accountable judges are to others the less aggressive they are likely to be in constitutional interpretation. The most direct form of accountability comes in the terms and conditions of the tenure of judicial office. The U.S. federal government is again unusual in the degree of independence that it grants its judicial interpreters of the Constitution. Once appointed, federal judges hold lifetime tenure unless impeached and removed by Congress for "high crimes and misdemeanors," a difficult and rare procedure. State judges in the United States are usually easier to remove. Some legislatures may remove state judges not only by impeachment but also "by address," which normally requires only a simple majority of the legislature and does not require any particular reason for removal. State judges are also frequently subject to "recall" or "retention" elections. Unlike federal judges, state judges hold fixed terms of office, though they usually are eligible for reelection or reappointment. Judges with the responsibility for constitutional interpretation in other countries likewise usually have limited terms of office. Judges may also be held accountable through threats to their budgets. Although judges in the United States usually have constitutional protections against their salaries being reduced, that guarantee is not common in the rest of the world. Even if their own salaries are protected, judges everywhere are subject to financial restrictions that affect their working conditions. At the extreme judges might be threatened not only with the loss of clerical and legal staff but even with the loss of an office in which to work and paper on which to write.

As detailed elsewhere in this volume, methods of judicial selection can vary widely and have consequences for constitutional interpretation. The judicial selection process is an important mechanism for carrying politically popular understandings of constitutional meaning onto the bench. The selection of judges might be highly insulated from the political process. In some countries, for example, the judges sitting on the highest courts may fill vacancies on their bench themselves. The European model is designed precisely to allow for a more politicized selection process to the constitutional court, while maintaining a more bureaucraticized, nonpolitical selection process for regular courts. In Germany, for example, an informal process has developed such that each major political party controls particular seats on the constitutional court. In some American states, judges are chosen through partisan popular elections, in which case constitutional interpretation by judges can be expected to follow electoral sentiment fairly closely. Federal judges in the United States are nominated by the president and confirmed by a majority of the Senate. While individual judges hold lifetime appointments, vacancies open in the judiciary on a fairly regular basis, allowing each president to put his own stamp on the constitutional opinions that hold sway in the judiciary.

Finally, judges are affected by their education and training and experience in the world. Sometimes, their experience and training as lawyers may lead judges to hold rather different constitutional views than the general public. Lawyers as a group, for example, may be more tolerant of political dissent than is the public as a whole, and thus may give rights of free speech a more liberal interpretation than would others. Critics of recent judicial decisions on social issues affecting religion and sexuality have often suggested that the judiciary is drawn from the "cultural elite," who may not share the same values as the average citizen. Other aspects of their background may also have significance for the constitutional views of judges. The conservative judges of the early twentieth century, for example, had often built their careers working as attorneys for large corporations. The liberal Justice Louis Brandeis, on the other hand, was a controversial appointment in part because of his background as a leading lawyer for labor unions. Reflecting on the judicial process, Justice Benjamin Cardozo once noted that judges "do not stand aloof on these chill and distant heights. . . . The great tides and currents which engulf the rest of men do not turn aside in their course and pass the judges by."[28] Judges are likely to share many of the same values, prejudices, and crazes that are common to their time and place. Judges are people too.

The Judicial Record

With all these checks on the judiciary, what is the record on constitutional interpretation? Have the judges become sovereign when interpreting the Constitution? There are of course always exceptions, but for the most part the historical record should be fairly reassuring to those concerned with judges trampling over popular majorities (and perhaps less reassuring for those who imagine judges standing alone against the crowd).

Judges often work within the political and constitutional mainstream. That is not to suggest that their rulings will not be controversial, or that they may not occasionally venture further out on their own, but simply that judicial understandings of the Constitution will resonate within a broader community that shares those basic understandings. That mainstream in the federal judiciary is often defined by the dominant political party, and often the presidential wing within that party. Thus, the nationalism and economic conservatism of the federal courts in the late nineteenth and early twentieth century were extremely controversial, drawing vocal denunciations from populist and progressive activists and political candidates in both major parties and several minor parties. At the same time, those judges were being consciously selected and publicly praised by the winning presidents who emerged out of the more conservative wings of the two major parties. When Franklin Roosevelt and the New Deal Democrats won repeated and decisive victories during the Great Depression and World War II, the courts soon reflected his more progressive agenda. When the Supreme Court under Chief Justice Earl Warren reached its peak of liberal activism in the 1960s, it enjoyed the warm support and encouragement of the administrations of John Kennedy and Lyndon Johnson.

On major issues, the Court is also usually not too far out of line with considered public opinion. The Supreme Court probably reflected public opinion in the North with its first tentative steps against Jim Crow in cases brought in the

1920s, 1930s, and 1940s by the NAACP, but the Court was unwilling to take more significant action on black civil rights until the 1950s and 1960s when national majority opinion had turned more sharply against the southern caste system and national political leaders were lobbying the Court to take action. The mainline religious denominations were supportive of the Court when it ruled against school prayer in the 1960s, though more conservative churches were hostile to the ruling. The Court seemed to be moving in the same direction as public opinion when it ruled in favor of abortion rights and against the death penalty in the early 1970s, but public opinion (and the Court) soon reversed course on the death penalty, and criminal justice issues generally, and over the next two decades the Court felt its way along with public opinion toward a more moderate position on abortion. Studies have shown that across the broad sweep of Supreme Court decisions, the Court more often than not aligns itself with dominant public opinion.

When interpreting the Constitution, the Court is often engaged in bringing national sentiment to bear on local outliers. Court decisions in the early nineteenth century striking down Maryland's anti-bank tax, dismantling New York's steamboat monopoly, or requiring Virginia to recognize a British subject's right to inherit valuable Virginia farmland were unpopular locally but won plaudits from neighboring states and national officials. When making a recommendation to President James Monroe for a vacancy on the Court, Attorney General William Wirt, with such cases in mind, reminded the president, "The local irritations at some of their decisions in particular quarters . . . are greatly overbalanced by the general approbation with which those same decisions have been received throughout the Union."[29] In the late nineteenth century, the Court, along with the other branches, was busy facilitating the creation of a national economy by clearing out populist obstructions erected in the South and Midwest against railroads, interstate corporations, and out-of-state creditors. In the mid-twentieth century, the Court turned its attention to the racial segregation, outmoded police practices, and traditional moralism of the South.

Where the Court shows true independence in constitutional interpretation, it is more often acting in the absence of real majorities than bucking a settled majority. Neither of the two established political parties was keen on taking a firm position of their own on the slavery question when the Court handed down *Dred Scott*, and in the years leading up to the decision party leaders trying to straddle the sectional divide all but begged the Court to take the issue out of electoral politics. While the affected politicians were unhappy with the Court's requirement of legislative reapportionment in the mid-twentieth century, the general public was content with a decision that promised to shift legislative power toward the majority of the electorate. When public opinion on homosexuality was still fairly conservative, the Court upheld Georgia's sodomy law in 1986. After years of growing public acceptance of homosexuality and legislative repeals of many such laws, the Court was ready to revisit the issue and overturn a Texas statute in 2003. The Court probably underestimated the public's emotional reaction to its decision that flag-burning was protected political expression, but the squelching of flag-burning was not high on the public's agenda either before or after the decision and the public remained committed to the tolerance of dissent even if it did not always like what that sometimes required in practice.

The Court is one voice among many attempting to give meaning to the Constitution. Although judges have a particularly powerful voice in the constitutional dialogue, they cannot monopolize the conversation. The courts listen for direction from others, and often try to take small steps forward rather than giant leaps. Having issued one judgment on an issue, they are often provoked, prodded, and challenged to revisit the issue again from a different angle and in a different light. After the Court struck down the death penalty in 1972, the justices were quickly met with a welter of reformed death penalty statutes. Having approved those reform measures, they have been pressed ever since to consider new applications and new questions about the application of capital punishment. Similarly, the Court was quickly faced with an endless stream of statutes and executive orders directly confronting or raising new questions about the Court's understanding of abortion rights, forcing the Court to walk a winding path, adhering to aspects of its initial decision while compromising others. Even when striking down provisions of federal statutes, the Court has rarely created insuperable obstacles to congressional policy objectives. When Congress is still interested in the policy at issue, and sometimes the legislative majorities that supported the initial statue are long gone by the time the Court considers it, it has usually been able to find the means to achieve what it wanted while satisfying the Court's constitutional objections.

The possibility of a sovereign judiciary seemed unlikely at the time of the Founding. Though courts were exceedingly important as sites of governance, their understanding of the law was in principle contingent on legislative agreement. The creation of a judicially cognizable written constitution altered that formal dynamic, but political practice and predominant conceptions of constitutionalism and popular government minimized its initial significance. By the twentieth century, however, both the political practice and our understanding of constitutionalism and democracy had significantly changed. The threat of "government by judiciary" seemed quite pressing, and our basic ambivalence about how best to balance the twin virtues of constitutionalism and democracy has not gone away. The tensions between democracy and constitutionalism suggest the need for caution on the part of judges in the exercise of their power of constitutional interpretation so as to minimize the danger of judges substituting their own vision of society for that of the people under the guise of interpretation. At the same time, however, we should recognize that in practice the courts have more often leaned with than leaned against the political winds. Judges are more apt to reflect the constitutional sensibilities of the people than to displace them.

Notes

1. Benjamin Hoadly, *The Nature of the Kingdom, or Church, of Christ: A Sermon Preached Before the King* (London: Knapton and Childe, 1717), 8.
2. John Chipman Gray, *The Nature and Sources of the Law* (New York: Columbia University Press, 1909), 120, 162.
3. Charles Evans Hughes, "Speech before the Elmira Chamber of Commerce, May 3, 1907," in *Addresses and Papers of Charles Evans Hughes* (New York: G. P. Putnam's Sons, 1908), 139. In context, then-Governor Hughes was trying to make a point about the importance of the judiciary and the need to preserve its independence in order to protect constitutional liberties.
4. James M. Beck, *The Constitution of the United States* (New York: George H. Doran Company, 1924), 221; Robert H. Jackson, *The Struggle for Judicial Supremacy* (New York: Vintage, 1941), x.
5. *Baker v. Carr,* 369 U.S. 186, 211 (1962); *Powell v. McCormack*, 395 U.S. 486, 521 (1969); *United States v. Nixon*, 418 U.S. 683, 704 (1974); *Miller v. Johnson*, 515 U.S. 900, 922 (1995). See also *Cooper v. Aaron*, 358 U.S. 1, 18 (1958); *United States v. Morrison*, 529 U.S. 598, 675 n7 (2000).
6. *Planned Parenthood v. Casey*, 505 U.S. 833, 867 (1992).
7. *Marbury v. Madison*, 5 U.S. 137, 177, 178, 180 (1803).
8. Alexander Hamilton, "No. 78," in Alexander Hamilton, James Madison, and John Jay, *The Federalist Papers*, edited by Clinton Rossiter (New York: New American Library, 1961), 465.
9. James Madison, "No. 48," in *The Federalist Papers*, 309.
10. *Marbury v. Madison*, 178.
11. James Madison, "No. 48," in *The Federalist Papers*, 308.
12. Abraham Lincoln, "First Inaugural Address," in *Abraham Lincoln*, edited by Roy P. Basler (New York: Da Capo Press, 1990), 585–586.
13. Abraham Lincoln, "Gettysburg Address," in *Abraham Lincoln*, 734.
14. *West Virginia State Board of Education v. Barnette*, 319 U.S. 624, 639 (1943).
15. *Martin v. Hunter's Lessee*, 14 U.S. 304, 347 (1816).
16. *McCulloch v. Maryland*, 17 U.S. 316, 435–436 (1819).
17. James Madison, "No. 51," in *The Federalist Papers*, 324, 325.
18. Ibid., 324, 323.
19. James Madison, "No. 39," in *The Federalist Papers*, 246.
20. Oliver Wendell Holmes, "Speech at a Dinner of the Harvard Law School Association of New York, February 15, 1913," in *Collected Legal Papers* (New York: Harcourt, Brace, and Company, 1921), 295–296.
21. *Korematsu v. United States*, 323 U.S. 214, 216, 217, 218, 224, 219 (1944).
22. *Hamdi v. Rumsfeld*, 159 L. Ed. 2d 578, 603 (2004).

23. William H. Rehnquist, "A Random Thought on the Segregation Cases," reprinted in Senate Judiciary Committee, *Nomination of Justice William Hubbs Rehnquist: Hearings before the Committee on the Judiciary*, 99th Cong., 2nd sess., 1986, 324.
24. Learned Hand, *The Bill of Rights* (Cambridge, Mass.: Harvard University Press, 1958), 73; Ronald Dworkin, "Learned Hand," in *Freedom's Law: The Moral Reading of the American Constitution* (Cambridge, Mass.: Harvard University Press, 1996), 344.
25. *West Virginia Board of Education v. Barnette*; William Brennan, "Constitutional Adjudication and the Death Penalty: A View from the Court," *Harvard Law Review* 100 (1986): 326.
26. John Hart Ely, *Democracy and Distrust*, 73.
27. Theodore Roosevelt, "A Charter of Democracy: Address before the Ohio Constitutional Convention at Columbus, Ohio, February 21, 1912," in *Progressive Principles*, edited by Elmer H. Youngman (New York: Progressive National Service, 1913), 49–50, 75.
28. Benjamin N. Cardozo, *The Nature of the Judicial Process* (New Haven, Conn.: Yale University Press, 1921), 168.
29. William Wirt, quoted in John Pendleton Kennedy, *Memoirs of the Life of William Wirt*, vol. 2 (Philadelphia: Lea and Blanchard, 1850), 134.

Bibliography

Ackerman, Bruce. *We the People: Foundations*. Cambridge: Harvard University Press, 1991. Theory of American constitutionalism that links judicial review to democratic politics.

Barnett, Randy E. *Restoring the Lost Constitution: The Presumption of Liberty*. Princeton, N.J.: Princeton University Press, 2004. Defense of an active judicial review on behalf of a libertarian understanding of the Constitution.

Bickel, Alexander M. *The Least Dangerous Branch: The Supreme Court at the Bar of Politics*. Indianapolis: Bobbs-Merrill, 1962. Influential formulation of the tensions between democracy and judicial review.

Bobbitt, Philip. *Constitutional Interpretation*. Oxford, U.K., and Cambridge, Mass.: Basil Blackwell, 1991. Primer of the ways in which the courts interpret the Constitution.

Devins, Neal, and Louis Fisher. *The Democratic Constitution*. New York: Oxford University Press, 2004. Overview of the ways in which democratic politics shapes constitutional interpretation.

Dworkin, Ronald. *Taking Rights Seriously*. Cambridge, Mass.: Harvard University Press, 1978. Defense of expansive judicial review to protect individual rights.

Elster, Jon, and Rune Slagstad, eds. *Constitutionalism and Democracy*. New York: Cambridge University Press, 1988. Collection of essays examining the relationship between democracy and constitutionalism in the United States and elsewhere.

Ely, John Hart. *Democracy and Distrust: A Theory of Judicial Review*. Cambridge, Mass.: Harvard University Press, 1980. Defense of judicial review as a means for preserving the functioning of democratic institutions.

Gillman, Howard. *The Constitution Besieged: The Rise and Demise of Lochner Era Police Powers Jurisprudence*. Durham, N.C.: Duke University Press, 1993. History of judicial review in the late nineteenth and early twentieth centuries.

Klarman, Michael J. *From Jim Crow to Civil Rights: The Supreme Court and the Struggle for Racial Equality*. New York: Oxford University Press, 2004. Politically sensitive history of racial civil rights in the twentieth century.

Kramer, Larry D. *The People Themselves: Popular Constitutionalism and Judicial Review*. New York: Oxford University Press, 2004. Examination of the early history of judicial review and constitutionalism in the United States and defense of popular control over constitutional meaning.

McCloskey, Robert G. *The American Supreme Court*. 4th ed., revised by Sanford Levinson. Chicago: University of Chicago Press, 2005. Accessible overview of history of constitutional interpretation by the Supreme Court.

Peretti, Terri Jennings. *In Defense of a Political Court*. Princeton, N.J.: Princeton University Press, 1999. Accessible overview and defense of the political influences on the Supreme Court.

Stone Sweet, Alec. *Governing with Judges: Constitutional Politics in Europe*. New York: Oxford University Press, 2000. Examination of the emergence and practice of constitutional review in Europe.

Sunstein, Cass R. *The Partial Constitution*. Cambridge, Mass.: Harvard University Press, 1993. Defense of judicial review and constitutional interpretation to advance public values and deliberation.

Waldron, Jeremy. *Law and Disagreement*. New York: Oxford University Press, 1999. Philosophical critique of judicial review and constitutional rights.

Whittington, Keith E. *Constitutional Interpretation: Textual Meaning, Original Intent, and Judicial Review*. Lawrence: University Press of Kansas, 1999. Defense of the original meaning of the Constitution as a guide to judicial review.

Court Cases

Baker v. Carr, 369 U.S. 186 (1962).

Cooper v. Aaron, 358 U.S. 1 (1958).

Dred Scot v. Sandford 60 U.S. 393 (1857).

Hamdi v. Rumsfeld, 159 L. Ed. 2d 578 (2004).

Korematsu v. United States, 323 U.S. 214 (1944).

Marbury v. Madison, 5 U.S. 137 (1803).

Martin v. Hunter's Lessee, 14 U.S. 304 (1816).

McCulloch v. Maryland, 17 U.S. 316 (1819).

Miller v. Johnson, 515 U.S. 900 (1995).

Planned Parenthood v. Casey, 505 U.S. 833 (1992).

Powell v. McCormack, 395 U.S. 486 (1969).

Roe v. Wade, 410 U.S. 113 (1973).

United States v. Morrison, 529 U.S. 598 (2000).

United States v. Nixon, 418 U.S. 683 (1974).

West Virginia State Board of Education v. Barnette, 319 U.S. 624 (1943).

6

PATHS TO THE BENCH: SELECTING SUPREME COURT JUSTICES IN A "JURISTOCRATIC" WORLD

Joel B. Grossman

ONE OF THE MOST IMPORTANT DEVELOPMENTS IN THE late twentieth and early twenty-first centuries has been the rise of courts and the enhanced role of judges in democratic governance. Ran Hirschl has called this development a move "towards juristocracy."[1] Law and courts, especially constitutional courts, are looked to increasingly as protectors of rights and engines of social change, and as regular participants in the policy-making process. Indeed, as Hirschl has noted, "An American-style rights discourse has become a dominant form of discourse in [these] countries."[2] While there is considerable evidence that these expectations may be overstated, and that courts by themselves cannot achieve such goals, they are persistent nonetheless.[3]

That courts and constitutions have an important role to play in a democracy seems to be an idea that has taken hold, with considerable fervor, in other countries even more than in the United States, where there is still much adherence to the claim that courts risk their legitimacy by posing a "countermajoritarian difficulty."[4] Nevertheless, there cannot be much doubt that juristocracy—the constitutionalization of rights, the establishment of activist judicial review, and generally the empowerment of courts and judges as essential ingredients of governance—is a popular American innovation and export. At the same time, Americans themselves remain somewhat ambivalent about the proper role of courts, and this ambivalence helps to explain both the wide range of methods by which judges are selected in the United States, and the escalating salience and controversy that accompany many judicial contests.

Critics of the rise of judicial governance decry the convergence of law and politics. While they may not be seeking a return to the long rejected philosophy of legal autonomy and formalism, they do allege that activist judging is an illegitimate incursion into the prerogatives of elected and politically accountable representatives, that it *weakens* the fragile structure of democracy and delegitimizes the courts, and that it is, in any case, an inefficient and ineffective way to make public policy.

Debate about the function and proper role of courts in the United States has once again become a hot button issue. It heats up whenever the Supreme Court, or any court, makes a controversial decision, and increasingly when there are key judicial vacancies to be filled. Such issues played a prominent role in the 2004 presidential election. But such debate, though now more intense, is certainly not new. Supporting the ratification of the Constitution, Alexander Hamilton in *The Federalist* No. 78 drew a distinction between law and politics, between will and judgment, and assured citizens that the new federal judiciary would be the "least dangerous branch."

This duality was also echoed by John Marshall in *Marbury v. Madison* (1803). But it was, at best, a disingenuous claim at the time; and certainly one that could not be defended today. Hamilton used it to promote the new constitution and the establishment of federal courts, and to assuage the doubts of those who feared the new national government that the Constitution created. And Marshall used it to protect the Supreme Court from its enemies—while often ignoring it when convenient. Controversy about the newly formed Supreme Court, and the federal court system that was to be created in 1789, was continuous and heated.

While the United States Constitution was a great new experiment in governance, with boundary lines not clearly marked, constitutions, and the need for judges to interpret them, were not. Judicial review was in common practice in the states prior to the Constitution (though not widely approved and not yet central to political life and democratic lawmaking). Marshall made it abundantly clear that the meaning of the Constitution was rarely self-contained and obvious, and that those who interpreted it—a role he staked out for the federal courts but one that did not reach its full flowering until the mid-twentieth century—made a difference. It took more than 150 years for the Supreme Court to fully accept and apply Marshall's dictum that "it is the province and duty of the judicial department to say what the law is." But those words have become the mantra of liberal and conservative courts alike. Where Marshall appeared to accept some limits on when and how the Court could "say what the law is" in the context of the *Marbury* case, the modern Court seems disposed to taking and applying those words literally.

This chapter focuses on the selection of Supreme Court justices, but it does so in a comparative context that also describes how other federal judges, state judges, and judges in foreign countries are chosen. This comparative perspective will be especially important when, in the final section, proposed alternatives and reforms are discussed.

Paths to the Bench: A Comparative Perspective

Who becomes a judge, and how that choice is made, are vital to understanding the role of courts in a democratic society. Judicial selection norms and practices reflect a society's values, political limits and aspirations, the clash of competing political forces, and the political organization of the society. How judges are selected, and who is selected, are good barometers of the values of a political system.

Eliot Slotnick has noted that judicial selection is also a "rare interface in American politics where all three branches of government come into play at the same time and enter the public stage at the same time."[5] Thus, judicial selection, particularly at the federal level, should not be seen merely as routine, but as a reflection of key institutional relationships and the clash of public values. Indeed, federal judicial selection now is a real-time indicator of the evolving democratization of our political institutions, seismic shifts and divides in the political culture, a consequent mainstreaming of the judicial role, and the changing expectations people have of courts and the law. As Howard Gillman has so presciently noted, judicial selection is not just about judges; it is also about patronage, and party, and presidential values, strategies, and agendas.

Judicial selection, at both the state and national levels, is now big time politics, an occasion for the mass mobilization of both elites and ordinary citizens, for sharp political maneuvering and debate, for big-money fund-raising and spending and political look-alike scenarios of intrigue and power politics. The successful attack on the nomination of Robert Bork to the Supreme Court in 1987 may have been an unusually full flowering of the democratization and politicization of judicial selection. Of course it was a Supreme Court appointment, and the nominee, if confirmed, would have changed the ideological balance on the Court. Further, it got embroiled in national politics—the controversial nomination of a lame duck president whose influence was diminishing, considered by a Senate controlled by the opposition party in a bitterly divided government, and a candidate with outspoken and inflexible views and a confrontational manner. All of these factors, taken together, made the stakes uniquely high. And the consequent explosion reverberated throughout the system.

Not all judicial selection events will engage the political system that way, but the Bork controversy (and outcome) demonstrated why judicial selection matters and why it has become a central and divisive political issue. Judge Bork, who complained bitterly about his rejection, never understood that choosing judges had become a much more democratic and public process. The stalemate in the Senate over President George W. Bush's judicial nominees, amid the more general polarization of the electorate, suggests that intense controversy may now be the regular order of the day for Supreme Court and many federal appeals court nominations.

Selecting judges is an inherently political and dynamic process, a hybrid of professional and political concerns, as well as a curious amalgam of beliefs about the role judges should play, democratic/populist norms, majority rule, and the rule and autonomy of law. And reflecting this ambivalence, Americans select their judges in a number of ways that draw on both populist and professional concepts. All *federal* judges are selected by executive nomination and Senate confirmation, although there are substantial differences in practice between Supreme Court and lower federal court nominations. Article III of the Constitution delegated to Congress the authority to create a system of inferior federal courts, and Congress did so immediately in the Judiciary Act of 1789. It also chose a uniform system of selecting federal judges and rejected the constitutional option to "vest the appointment of such [judges] in the President alone, in the Courts of Law, or in the Heads of Departments" (the latter, in the case of federal judges, presumably the Supreme Court).

Among the states there are basically five selection methods in use, with many states employing a different system for different levels of courts. Judges are chosen by partisan election, nonpartisan election, executive appointment (with or without legislative confirmation), election by the legislature, and variations of the so-called merit selection or "Missouri Plan." Under that plan (with many variations)[6], a judicial nominating commission is chosen for each court level, usually by the governor and the bar. That commission then presents the governor with a short list of nominees for the vacant position, and the governor must choose from that list. In some states, senatorial confirmation is also required. The judge chosen by the governor serves for a short term, usually a year, then is "presented" to the voters in a noncontested election. A judge who is "retained" by the electorate serves the prescribed term of office, and then stands again for retention. Voters are asked to assess the judge's record only; there are no opponents. It is more of a referendum than an election. And there are usually no term limits; retention elections thus produce perennial incumbents—not quite the same as life tenure, but close. At best the Missouri Plan system might be regarded as "election-lite." It must be noted also that a substantial number of state judges are chosen initially by gubernatorial appointment to fill a vacancy, but then have to be "re-chosen" for a full term by whatever system that state employs.

Electing judges is a uniquely American phenomenon. Prior to 1787, before it became a state, only Vermont chose any of its judges by election. Georgia, in 1812, was the first state to provide for judicial election, but the trend toward electing judges then accelerated rapidly, nourished by western expansion and populist Jacksonian Democracy, and again at the beginning of the twentieth century, by the Progressive movement.[7] By the time of the Civil War, twenty-four of the thirty-four states elected most of their judges (in partisan elections). Dissatisfaction with the partisan election of judges began to develop, however, and by 1927 twelve states had adopted some kind of nonpartisan system.[8] The "Merit Plan" was endorsed by the ABA in 1937, and Missouri became the first state to adopt it, in 1940.

If all these selection systems were superimposed on a map of the United States, the pattern would look as follows: gubernatorial and legislative appointive systems, and some partisan elections, prevail in the older, eastern, states. As one moves west, the trend is toward nonpartisan elections and variations of the Missouri Plan. The map has been fairly stable for some time, but almost all recent shifts have been toward some form of the Missouri Plan.

Two Models of Judicial Selection

One way to conceptualize judicial selection options is to view them as two models or "ideal types" on a continuum. At one end is a cluster of variables that might be designated the *professional-independent* model. At the other end is a cluster that might be labeled the *responsive-accountable-political* model.

The professional model exists in its purest form in most non-British European systems. Prospective judges follow a career track and receive separate training and apprenticeship experiences from those law graduates who aspire to prosecutorial positions or private law practice. Judging is a separate vocation, and is centrally organized along bureaucratic lines. It is a relatively closed system in which judges (of all but constitutional courts) are "trained" and gain experience as they move up the judicial ladder; there is virtually no political involvement, and no issues of "democracy" or individual judges' political ideology. Compatibility with democratic norms is simply not an issue. Judging is an autonomous profession.

As described by Epstein, Knight, and Martin:

> [In Germany] the Judiciary is a distinct profession. One must be a university graduate with the equivalent of an undergraduate major in law, pass with exceptionally high marks a set of professional examinations, undergo several years of training that combine further study with apprenticeship, and finally sustain another set of rigorous examinations administered by the government. Once in the judicial profession, judges follow career paths similar to civil servants, moving slowly up the hierarchy from less important to more important courts if they receive good fitness reports from senior jurists.[9]

Transplanted across the ocean, this professional model loses much of its distinctiveness. American judges are lawyers first; they receive no special pre-bench training, are not chosen exclusively by lawyers (or other judges), and they move back and forth among the bench, the bar, and the political world. Judging is not a separate profession, but a subspecies of the legal profession.

Among the systems in use in the United States, Missouri Plan derivatives are the most "professionalized," although they would rank far below the continental systems on any scale of professionalism. The emphasis is on the selection of judges by the bar (nominations generated by nominating commissions, and appointment by the governor). The process is lawyer driven. That there must be an electoral role, as already indicated, has long been reluctantly conceded, but it is conceptualized and structured in the Missouri Plan to be as "nonpolitical" and nonintrusive as possible.

Missouri Plan–type selection is the exclusive province of the states. But for a brief time it also operated at the federal level. President Jimmy Carter created a judicial nominating commission (with thirteen regional panels) to nominate candidates for the federal courts of appeals. He argued that it would produce better judges by a more objective and less political process. And perhaps even more important, it would be the vanguard of a movement to diversify the federal bench by nominating increased numbers of women and minorities. A similar effort at the district court level was only partially successful; federal district court nominating commissions were created in thirty states; but many senators (who sometimes individually utilize mini-commissions that *they* have appointed to suggest judicial nominees) were unwilling to relinquish their patronage authority.[10]

This experiment was, in any case, terminated abruptly by the Reagan administration. Whether it produced "better" judges is difficult to discern. It did produce the intended substantial increase in the appointment of minorities and women. And, not unexpectedly, since the commission members were chosen largely by the White House), the plan also produced mostly Democrats. As a way out of the current confirmation gridlock, Senator Patrick Leahy proposed a similar reform, with less White House control of the nominating commissions. It has received little attention or support.

The Missouri Plan approach is also designed to emphasize the more technical aspects of judging. Judges should be chosen not for partisan or political reasons, but for professional criteria such as experience, training, education, age, and judicial temperament. In other words judges should be chosen who will make the system work the way the ABA thinks it should—in a nonpolitical, predictable, fashion. While the Missouri Plan cannot escape all political connections, it has the best chance of being seen as a relatively nonpolitical event. It masquerades as non-partisan, but ultimately it cannot be nonpolitical.

To further "protect" a process that already has moved substantially away from its ideal model, the ABA and some state bar associations have attempted to place limits on campaign rhetoric, spending, and fundraising in those states in which judges are elected. In the words of the ABA's Commission on the 21st Century

Judiciary, "the time has come to inoculate America's courts against the toxic effects of money, partisanship, and narrow interests."[11] But traditional limits on judicial campaign speech (including attack advertising) have recently been challenged by the Supreme Court's 2002 decision in *Republican Party of Minnesota v. White*,[12] and thus it is not clear what, if any, limits can be placed on or enforced against judicial election candidates (particularly incumbents).

"Real" elections require some kind of discourse about relevant issues to educate the public and engage its interest. Limits on out-of-control spending in judicial elections are difficult to maintain. States may have to consider public funding for judicial elections. Thus the ABA Report is no doubt correct in fearing that *its* interests are in jeopardy. But there are also pressures, in those states where judges are elected, to make judicial elections more meaningful by opening up discourse rather than stifling it. How can citizens vote intelligently if they have little information on which to base those votes?

The alternative responsive-accountable-political model is also found nowhere in its pure form. But relatively speaking, selection systems that can be identified with it embody a more open and flexible view of the role of courts, a greater sensitivity to democratic norms and goals, and a corresponding distrust of lawyer control and legal formalism. In this model, courts belong to the people and should be accountable and responsive to their needs. Law and politics are seen as interdependent rather than mutually exclusive; judicial policymaking is inevitable and not necessarily undesirable. It is thus appropriate for judges to be selected, by one means or another, through the political system. Elections are not necessarily the preferred means, but they are acceptable—*nonpartisan* elections in particular. And if elections are employed, judicial candidates have to meaningfully communicate with voters on the issues and the merits of the candidates.

It should be noted that "responsive" and "accountable" are different but mutually supportive concepts. Responsiveness implies a greater openness to concepts of justice, equality, and fair play, and some level of agreement with various constituencies on critical issues involving competing values and principles. The rule of law is important, but to be effective it cannot be hidebound and unchanging.

Accountability implies an act of judgment. No one believes it appropriate for the electorate or a legislative body to review and possibly overrule a particular decision. But, according to this view, a judge can and must be accountable more generally for his or her behavior on the bench—however that is conceived. On a strict professional model view, the notion of judicial accountability is an oxymoron—a judge is only accountable to "the law" and to his conscience. Nevertheless, as Robert McCloskey once noted, there is an inherent and inescapable tension between the rule of law and popular sovereignty.[13] This is not necessarily unhealthy. To be legitimate, courts must be seen as part of the governing structure of a society, but also separate and distinct, and not merely as an autonomous enterprise. Although federal judges, strictly speaking, cannot be held "accountable" since they hold office for life and can be removed only by impeachment, they do exhibit varying degrees of responsiveness to issues of individual rights and justice, as they see them.

Judicial accountability is promoted, and judicial independence allegedly undermined, by the rise of judicial ethics concerns and the establishment of judicial disciplinary commissions. Beginning with California in 1961, every state established, by various names, a judicial disciplinary commission. And in 1980, Congress passed the Judicial Conduct and Disability Act, which provides a mechanism to determine if a federal judge "has engaged in conduct prejudicial to the effective and expeditious administration of the business of the courts," or is physically or mentally unable to perform his or her duties. In the states, either the commissions, or the state supreme court acting on the motion of the commission, may discipline, suspend, or remove a judge convicted of misconduct or found to be unable to perform.

Congress delegated a similar oversight function to the Judicial Conference, but because of Article III ("the judges shall hold their offices during good behaviour") limits, and because federal judges are subject to impeachment, it did not authorize the administrative *removal* of offending judges. Instead, federal judges convicted of misconduct or found to be disabled may be at least temporarily "separated from their dockets"—meaning that they remain as judges, with full pay and perquisites, but lose their authority to hear and decide cases.[14]

The "standards" of judicial conduct contained in the law apply to all federal judges, including Supreme Court justices.[15] The Supreme Court, however, was explicitly exempted from the enforcement provisions. Thus when Justice Antonin Scalia, in 2004, was accused of a conflict of interest in a politically sensitive case, and his recusal demanded, he was under no obligation to recuse and no one else had the authority to require him to do so.[16] By contrast, no state immunizes its highest court justices from its disciplinary standards and procedures.

Whether subjecting judges to ethics accountability and oversight compromises their "independence" is a matter of debate and definition. Sitting federal judges are already subject to impeachment and/or criminal charges. The prevailing—but not unanimous—view seems to be that serious misconduct should not be protected, that its deleterious effects on the prestige and legitimacy of the courts more than warrants at least some mark of official displeasure short of removal. Likewise, the serious disability of a judge undermines the judicial function and places extra burdens on other judges. But there remains an uneasiness that such interventions might undermine the independence of judges, and that courts would fall prey to internal jealousies and rivalries, to say nothing of latent partisan paybacks.

What exactly is meant by "judicial independence"? In debates about the role of courts, and the qualities to look for in choosing judges, the concept looms especially large. It has become a central part of the established rhetoric of judicial legitimacy. But in achieving iconic status its meaning has blurred. Clearly, individual judges should be impartial and objective in their decisions, but independence surely does not preclude appellate review any more than it immunizes criminal conduct. No one would argue that a judge has a right to be dishonest or engage in misconduct, but how should such behavior be addressed?

The framers believed that impeachment was the only individual oversight mechanism consistent with preserving the independence of federal judges. Congress, as we have seen, has concurred in this judgment.[17] But judges and the Supreme Court are under constant oversight by Congress and the president in other ways. The latter expresses his views through the selection process, and by his public support (or nonsupport) of important Supreme Court decisions. Congress has the power to pass constitutional amendments to overturn unpopular constitutional decisions, the authority to overrule the Court on statutory interpretations, and, at least arguably, the right to curb the Court's jurisdiction over cases or issues Congress does not trust the Court to make.

Only Congress may impeach a federal judge, although it has not done so for political reasons in a very long time.[18] And, more mundane but not irrelevant, while Congress may not reduce the compensation of federal judges, it can deny them a pay raise to express its unhappiness with a particular decision. This happened in the 1960s, although the lost pay raises were eventually restored. All of this suggests that judicial independence is a variable and contingent concept that rests uneasily on a precarious structure of legitimacy and good will.

In an earlier and simpler day there was little concern or even debate. But as Peter Russell has noted, the growth of judicial power in well-established liberal democracies has triggered a new level of concerns about judicial independence. As judges become more activist and autonomous in checking other branches of government, and become involved in hotly contested policy issues, they attract considerably more attention; their official acts, as well as their private lives, are inevitably scrutinized more intensively. As courts become more connected to a society's political system, they became more vulnerable to political oversight, and risk losing some of that independence (that may or may not have actually existed).[19]

The pressures on individual judges facing re-election (or re-selection) are obviously strong, but the evidence does not support the most extreme claims of judicial vulnerability. Russell may well be correct, however, in noting that pressures are likely to be felt most at the structural level, and particularly at the point of closest contact between the courts and the people—the selection system. Martin Shapiro, whom Russell quotes, characterized judicial independence as secure at "'retail,' but not at 'wholesale.'"[20] But even at wholesale there is at best mixed evidence of courts bowing meekly to political overlords, or judges feeling excessively accountable to those who have chosen them. "Judicial independence" is an old concept with new and evolving meanings. Although it needs to be reconceptualized and reconfigured to bring it into alignment with the modern role of courts, it remains a major issue in assessing how judges should be chosen.

Although this chapter focuses on the American experience, judicial selection—like constitutions, constitutionalism, and judicial review—is now a near universal experience. And it is predicated on a common theme—that as the nature of courts has evolved into more complex forms and political connections, our thinking about judges necessarily changes as well. As courts have come to play more important political roles, the selection of judges has become increasingly complex and divisive. When people perceive that judges will have an increased impact on their lives, they will want to have a greater role in choosing those judges.

We have come a long way from the indigenous judges in Martin Shapiro's *Courts,*[21] who in the basic triad of dispute resolution are chosen by the parties, or who are community or religious elders. In Russell's words:

> The one point common to all the countries we have looked at is a growth in the power of the judiciary. In constitutional democracies, both new and old, judiciaries have become visible centers of power not only providing a credible adjudicative service for increasingly litigious societies but also exercising considerable leverage on controversial issues of public policy. This development has required an ironic trade-off. A judiciary cannot be powerful unless it enjoys a high level of institutional independence and its individual members are free from internal as well as external direction of their decision making. But the price to be paid for such power is close and continuous public scrutiny and contentious debate do as well as increasing demands that their selection, promotion, education, and discipline be subject to more open and representative processes.[22]

The "New Politics" of Choosing Supreme Court Justices

In 1789, President George Washington, anticipating that he would have an entire Supreme Court to fill—six "vacancies" as it turned out—was prepared to act immediately when Congress authorized those positions. On the very day that he signed the Judiciary Act of 1789 into law, the president sent Congress six Supreme Court nominations. And the Senate confirmed them all *two days later,* without any debate.[23] How things have changed! All were Federalists. Washington initially encouraged those interested in a Supreme Court appointment to write to him, and he then discussed his options with friends. The final decisions were his alone.

Nominations

Nominating Supreme Court justices today is, of course, vastly more complex, but certainly no less political. Most presidents (but not all) have shared Washington's determination to nominate those with comparable policy views—usually but not always from the same party. But some presidents have appointed their friends and given little attention to politics and policy matters. In general, it could be said that in one combination or another, Supreme Court nominations are marked by the president's pursuit of personal, policy, and political/partisan goals.[24] The enhanced role of the Court today has elevated Supreme Court nominations (and courts of appeals nominations) to the first rank of policy and political importance. No president can afford to be as casual—or careless—as Harry Truman, who consulted with few others and made his own decisions quickly. He was not hurt by them politically (as a president would be today), but the Court had to endure years of mediocrity. There was little Senate scrutiny and not much public interest at the time.

Presidents are not always "successful" in their nomination choices. Dwight D. Eisenhower offered the chief justiceship to Earl Warren, and then nominated William Brennan without knowing that he would become one of the most liberal judges of the twentieth century.[25] Between them they were the backbone of the liberal Warren Court, and Eisenhower is reputed to have said later that his two greatest mistakes as president were sitting on the bench. Nixon would certainly have been grieved by Harry Blackmun's metamorphosis from a midwestern conservative to, at the time of his retirement, the Court's most outspoken liberal. Nixon was extremely agitated, and perhaps surprised, when three of his four appointees voted against him in the *Nixon Tapes* case.[26]

Presidents Ronald Reagan and George H. W. Bush similarly guessed wrong on some of their nominees. Reagan did not realize that Sandra Day O'Connor was "soft" on abortion and affirmative action; and Bush, relying on advice from his assistants and Senator Warren Rudman of New Hampshire, failed to detect David Souter's latent liberal tendencies. And Bill Clinton could not have appreciated that his two appointees, Ruth Bader Ginsburg and Stephen Breyer, joined a unanimous Court, in *Clinton* v. *Jones* (1997),[27] in ruling that the president does not have even temporary immunity from private civil suits while in office.

Presidential strategies of nomination differ. According to David Yalof, different decisional frameworks can be pursued: an "open" framework in which all factors and candidates for a particular vacancy are pursued; a "single-candidate focused" framework, in which the identity of the likely nominee has been decided in advance of the vacancy; and a "criteria" driven framework in which a president and his advisors establish specific criteria that prospective nominees must meet.[28] Within these frameworks, considerations of patronage, personal loyalty, and ideological/policy preferences loom especially large.

Harry Truman's nominations were, as we have seen, rewards for loyalty and friendship, and his choices were largely personal, with apparently little regard for policy consequences. Few others were consulted. Eisenhower exemplified the third category. Responding to Truman's "cronyism," after his nomination of Earl Warren to be chief justice, Eisenhower established strict rules and standards. He was also the first president to formally consult with the ABA Committee on Federal Judiciary.

Warren had been chosen largely as payment for a political debt for his support of Eisenhower at the 1952 Republican Convention. He was offered the solicitor generalship, which he accepted, and was also promised the next vacancy on the Court. Before the nomination was made officially, however, Chief Justice Frederick Moore Vinson died. Warren then assumed that he would either get that position, or an associate justiceship if someone on the Court was promoted to chief justice. Not wanting to promote from within the Court, Eisenhower somewhat reluctantly offered the chief justiceship to Warren, and put him on the Court immediately with a recess appointment. After that, Eisenhower required that all his nominees have prior judicial experience, which Warren did not have.

Warren was neither the first nor the last potential nominee to have a hand in his own nomination. Ruth Bader Ginsburg's nomination was largely orchestrated by her law professor husband. And it is not uncommon for the friends and supporters of potential nominees to use all of their connections and media opportunities to push for their preferred candidate. Sitting justices have also been known, privately of course, to lobby a president on new appointments. Chief Justices William Howard Taft (1921–1930) and Warren Burger (1969–1986) were especially active in this regard. As a federal judge on the court of appeals, Burger waged a scarcely concealed and successful campaign to be appointed chief justice.

Eisenhower was determined to avoid Truman's cronyism, and succeeded. Indeed, with one glaring exception, his Supreme Court appointments were of very high quality (Warren, Brennan, John Marshall Harlan II, Potter Stewart). The one exception was Charles Whittaker, a true disaster, whose nomination was more political than policy or loyalty driven; he left the Court after only six years. Kennedy and Johnson operated very differently. They took personal control of Supreme Court nominations, and in three of their four selections, chose political supporters who also happened to be highly qualified—Arthur Goldberg, Byron White, and Fortas. Johnson's choice of Thurgood Marshall was a historic appointment. Johnson maneuvered Marshall into line for the Court by first appointing him Solicitor General. Coming as it did at the height of the civil rights movement, the nomination was clearly intended as a major symbolic act. Other than Marshall, none of these appointees had prior judicial experience.

Richard Nixon understood that selecting Supreme Court justices was critical to his image of being tough on crime, and to his "southern strategy." His choices of Warren Burger and Harry Blackmun to replace Warren and Fortas were a symbolic repudiation of the Warren Court. Blackmun, a mainstream midwestern Republican federal judge, was Nixon's third choice after the Senate rejected his efforts to appoint a southerner, first Clement Haynsworth and then G. Harrold Carswell. When Hugo Black and Harlan left the Court in 1971, several of Nixon's initial choices were deemed unqualified by the ABA. He responded with the nominations of Lewis Powell and William Rehnquist, neither of whom he knew personally. Both had demonstrable conservative credentials.

Ronald Reagan understood the linkage between the Court and his political and ideological goals; his nominations—of O'Connor, Rehnquist as chief justice, Scalia, Bork, and Anthony Kennedy—were directed toward those goals. Reagan took a completely hands-off approach, relying very substantially on his assistants until the search process neared its conclusion. He was not tempted to choose his friends; perceived ideology was paramount.

The most recent presidents to make Supreme Court nominations, George H. W. Bush and Bill Clinton, emphasized both ideological and symbolic concerns—particularly in Bush's appointment of Clarence Thomas to succeed Marshall, and Clinton's appointment of Ruth Bader Ginsburg. Clinton said later that he would not have chosen Ginsburg if she had not favored abortion rights. Bush and Clinton also emphasized "confirmability" of their nominees; they wanted to make compatible nominations without expending too much capital. In this respect, of course, Bush guessed wrong with Thomas, whose confirmation was one of the ugliest and most divisive in memory. And he probably did not appreciate quite how conservative Thomas was. Bush worked with a small group of trusted advisers; Clinton was unwilling to delegate significant power to subordinates.

Nomination decisions must be based on information about a candidate. Today these investigations, conducted by the FBI, are incredibly intensive and intrusive. Some are offended, but there is little margin for error. If the FBI does not find some damaging information, one can be sure that opponents will, and that it will be made public. Attorney General John Mitchell's sloppy investigation of G. Harrold Carswell, for example, failed to turn up several racist incidents that, when revealed at confirmation, contributed to his defeat and sorely embarrassed the Nixon administration. Likewise, no one in the Justice Department found the memo—*opposing Brown v. Board of Education* (1954, 1955)[29]—that William Rehnquist, as a clerk just out of law school, wrote for Justice Robert Jackson. That memo would haunt Rehnquist's two nominations, particularly when he claimed that he had written the memo as a draft exposition of *Jackson's* views rather than as a statement of his own beliefs. When strong evidence to the contrary surfaced, Rehnquist simply repeated his story. It sullied his nominations, but did not defeat them.[30]

The Role of the ABA

From the mid-1950s to 2001, presidents submitted their potential Supreme Court (and other federal court) nominees to a committee of the American Bar Association for a confidential assessment before a nomination was made. Sometimes a single name was submitted, at other times an informal list of several potential nominees. The ABA Standing Committee on Federal Judiciary then rated the potential nominees as well qualified, qualified, or not qualified, based on its assessment of judicial temperament, professional competence, and personal integrity. The ABA was thus privileged to have access to the process before a final choice had been made. The president would then have the benefit of both the ABA and FBI reports before making that decision. After a nomination was announced, the ABA report was communicated to the Senate Judiciary Committee, and the ABA chair usually testified at the hearings.

Ginsburg and Breyer (and many others before them) received "well qualified" endorsements from the ABA, and this did not hurt their easy confirmations. But four committee members—a significant minority—rated Robert Bork as not qualified; and Clarence Thomas received two negative votes. Several potential nominees of Richard Nixon, including California judge Mildred Lillie, were deemed unqualified by the ABA, leading Nixon eventually to abandon those nominations and choose Rehnquist and Powell instead.

In 2001 the administration of George W. Bush decided to dispense with the ABA's privileged role. Some Republicans felt that the ABA Committee, once very conservative, had become too liberal. The ABA Committee, and other interest groups who regularly investigate and evaluate judicial nominees, are now given the name of an actual nominee at the same time as it is presented to the Senate for confirmation. The ABA committee then investigates and reports its findings and evaluations to the Senate Judiciary Committee, as do other interest groups. But the ABA no longer has the benefit of a special role and the chance to conduct an inquiry before a nomination is announced. It is now simply one of the many interest groups that routinely have become deeply engaged in selection and confirmation politics.

There is no single, or sure, strategy for nominating Supreme Court justices. But all recent presidents have, to a greater or lesser extent, emphasized ideological compatibility, "correctness" on certain key issues valued by the president or his supporters, the impact of a particular nomination on the president's (or his party's) political fortunes, the need to please a president's supporters, and confirmability, which in turn depends on which party controls the Senate and by how comfortable a margin. Most, but not all, nominees are from the president's party. Recent presidents have also given preference to "younger" rather than older nominees, who can be counted on to defend the ideological ramparts for an extended period of time. Most recent nominees have been drawn from the federal courts of appeals—a subject discussed in more detail below.

Confirmation by the Senate

When a Supreme Court nomination is announced, it is officially transmitted to the Senate Judiciary Committee, which holds public hearings, and then votes on whether or not to submit the nomination to the entire Senate. The Senate, after further debate, decides by majority vote whether to "consent." This process, and particularly the hearings, have become "prime time" media events. The Bork nomination, to which we have already referred, is perhaps an extreme example of how this process has evolved, but it is nonetheless useful to examine it first.

Just before the Senate, in 1987, rejected his nomination to be an associate justice of the Supreme Court, Judge Bork angrily denounced the proceedings he had just endured:

> The process of confirming justices for our nation's highest court has been transformed in a way that should not and indeed must not be permitted to occur again. The tactics and techniques of national political campaigns have been unleashed on the process of confirming judges. This is not simply disturbing, it is dangerous. Federal judges are not appointed to decide cases according to the latest opinion polls. They are appointed to decide cases according to law. But when judicial nominees are assessed and treated like political candidates, the effect will be to chill the climate in which judicial deliberations take place, to erode public confidence in the impartiality of courts and to endanger the independence of the judiciary.

Notwithstanding its rhetorical excess, Bork's lament is descriptively accurate. The stakes are higher and the process of selecting Supreme Court justices has become unabashedly open and overtly political. The selection process has become more politicized, more public, more intense, more divisive, and more democratic. But it is not only the Court's role and the judicial recruitment process that have evolved from what the framers conceived, or indeed, from the pre–New Deal days. The entire political system and our political culture has become more democratic and more open, and the selection of judges is inevitably part of that transformation.[31]

Emblematic of these changes in the politics of Supreme Court recruitment has been the extraordinary efforts by interest groups across the political spectrum to support or oppose confirmation. In so doing they have substantially changed the dynamics of the process. Their efforts clearly drove the outcome of the Bork nomination, but interest groups had become increasingly active in *all* Senate confirmation hearings for many years. If the Bork nomination was different it was because of the intensity of interest group activity, the costs of attacking and defending the nominee, the media coverage, the no-holds-barred savagery of attacks, and some new strategies as well. The Bork affair was a far cry from the lower key in which even controversial prior nominations had been considered.

It appears, according to the Senate Postmaster, that the "Bork controversy drew more mail than any issue in recent memory."[32] Fund raising and expenditures, especially by anti-Bork groups, reached new heights. Groups focused not only on members of the Senate, and particularly the Judiciary Committee, but waged what amounted to a grass roots war over public opinion to influence senators indirectly by creating constituent pressure.[33] Indeed the battle over Bork's nomination led to a new, now widely used slogan: "getting Borked." New levels of interest group activity, and spiraling costs, were not the only markers of this new confirmation process. Another is the length of the confirmation process, which in controversial cases, may last for many months, particularly in or near election years, when emotions and stakes are very high.[34]

Was the Senate's rejection of Bork consistent with constitutional intent? Does the Senate have the right to reject a nomination solely for ideological reasons? In the Constitutional Convention of 1787, debate focused on the Virginia Plan, which called for the congressional selection of judges, and the New Jersey Plan, which would have assigned that power to the executive. The Senate was originally assigned the sole power to appoint members of the Supreme Court. The delegates considered but rejected the idea of vesting the appointment power solely in the executive. But then in a last minute compromise the power was divided—the president was given the power to nominate, and the Senate the power to "advise and consent." It was thought that a divided appointment power would promote responsibility through the president's role, and "security" (against executive intrigues) through the Senate's. While it was not expected that the Senate would compete with the president over whom to nominate, it *was* assumed that it would exercise independent judgment as to the suitability of the president's nominees.

Although not without ambiguity, Alexander Hamilton's views in *Federalist* Nos. 76 and 77 can be read to support this interpretation. They are especially persuasive because it was Hamilton who originally suggested the joint executive-Senate appointment plan. In *Federalist* No. 76 Hamilton argued that the Senate could deny confirmation if there were "special and strong reasons for the refusal." The Senate's power to deny confirmation "would have an excellent check upon a spirit of favoritism in the president, and would tend greatly to prevent the appointment of unfit characters from State prejudice, from family connection, from personal attachment, or from a view to popularity."

While Hamilton did not directly advocate an unlimited Senate role (and some have argued that he was advocating a limited one), there is nothing in his words to suggest the kind of limits on senatorial consideration that Judge Bork articulated. Indeed, Professor Henry Monaghan, a Bork supporter, concluded that the Senate had no obligation to confirm. "Rather (and to my surprise), all the relevant historical and textual sources support the Senate's power when and if it sees fit to assert its vision of the public good against that of the President."[35] The best interpretation is that the words of Article II, Section 2 (and the intent of the framers) permit, if they do not require, the Senate to play an aggressive *checking* role. That includes consideration of a nominee's ideology, values, and prior decisions as well as how a particular nomination might affect the Supreme Court's political balance.

If the framers had intended the Senate merely to "concur" in nominations they could have used the language of the previous clause in Article II, regarding treaties. That they did not suggests that they had something else in mind—perhaps some kind of collaborative effort between the president and the Senate. But as it evolved, it has become the president's sole responsibility to nominate, and the Senate's institutional responsibility to approve or deny, for any reason. Individual senators of the president's party, however, have claimed and generally been accorded more of an advisory and clearance function with nominees from their own states, enforced by norms of senatorial courtesy. No single senator can block a Supreme Court confirmation, however, as is the case with the "blue slip" process to enforce senatorial courtesy that is used with lower federal court nominations.

The last Supreme Court appointment was that of Judge Stephen Breyer in 1994, by President Bill Clinton. All told, there have been 148 Supreme Court nominations, and 120 appointments, some of whom never took the oath of office (four were appointed and confirmed twice, eight declined appointment or died before beginning service on the Court, and twenty-eight were not confirmed). Breyer is the 108th justice to serve on the Court. Of the twenty-eight nominees not confirmed, twelve were formally rejected, six nominations were withdrawn, and the Senate failed to act on ten.[36]

Prior to 1900 the Senate rejected approximately one-quarter of all Supreme Court nominations. In the twentieth century, the Senate rejected six nominations.[37] From 1900 to 1968, however, evidencing a new trend, only one nomination out of forty-three was rejected by the Senate—President Herbert Hoover's choice of Judge John Parker in 1930. His defeat was not only unique in that period, but also noteworthy because the ideological opposition to him was expressed overtly.

Several other nominees—Louis Brandeis, Harlan Stone, Charles Evans Hughes, and Black—also faced intense (but unsuccessful) ideological opposition. Opposition to Brandeis was laced with scarcely concealed anti-Semitism. But it was also during these years that a fairly strong presumption of confirmation began to develop. Until 1968, most senators publicly opposed a nominee only for a lack of professional qualifications, or for the commission of some impropriety. Ideology was always a hidden agenda. But that norm was clearly changing, and it certainly is no longer controlling today.[38]

That the Senate's role was limited to determining whether or not a nominee was "qualified" was certainly the view expressed by President Nixon in 1970, bitterly decrying what he believed to be unwarranted Senate interference with *his constitutional responsibility* to choose Supreme Court justices. Nixon was wrong on the Constitution, but his reading of the political tea leaves was more outdated than wrong. The Senate's rebuff of his first two nominations—Carswell and Haynsworth—was, following the earlier defeat of Fortas by Republicans, the beginning of a new order and of a much more aggressive and active Senate confirmation role that reached new heights in the Bork debacle.[39] It also marked the beginning of a new executive branch countertactic: intensive "candidate preparation" by the White House staff, and intensive lobbying. Senate Judiciary Committee hearings, on both sides, are now carefully scripted.

During this period, several other nominees besides Bork faced intense ideological opposition—in particular Rehnquist in 1971 and 1986, and Thomas in 1991. Rehnquist's nomination as chief justice by President Reagan received the most negative votes ever for that position; and Thomas received more negative votes than any successful nominee. And all nominees, even those who received little formal opposition, nonetheless had to endure long delays and intense Senate interrogation and scrutiny.[40] Clearly, the confirmation process, now a nationally televised spectacle, has become much more than a check on a nominee's qualifications. In many cases it may not be much about the nominee at all, but more about executive-legislative politics. When a Republican justice is replaced by a Democrat, and vice versa, the Senate's rejection rate doubles. And to further emphasize how politicized Supreme Court confirmations have become, they have the highest reject rate among *all* Senate confirmations—about 20 percent. One might accurately describe Supreme Court confirmations now as "nasty, brutish, and *long.*"

Reviewing the "new politics" of Supreme Court selection, the Twentieth Century Fund Task Force on Judicial Selection concluded, in 1988, that the "problem" with the confirmation process for Supreme Court nominees is that "it is too visible and attracts too much publicity. . . . It has become very much a national referendum . . . that distracts attention from, and sometimes completely distorts, the legal qualifications of the nominee. . . . It is dangerously close to looking like the electoral process."[41]

The Task Force recommended depoliticizing the process by no longer *requiring* nominees to appear personally before the Senate Judiciary Committee. The confirmation decision would then be based, the Task Force argued, "on a nominee's written record and the testimony of legal experts as to his competence." This would, in theory, restore the basic purpose of confirmation hearings "to ensure that we select competent, impartial, and thoughtful judges . . . [and it would] restore public confidence in the appointment process, the Supreme Court, and the federal judiciary . . . and restore the complete independence of the courts of justice, [which] is an indispensable prerequisite for the judiciary in a democratic polity."

No action was ever taken on these proposals, despite the eminence of the Task Force members. None is likely, because the idea of depoliticizing Supreme Court confirmations and conducting them in secret is scarcely conceivable. It is difficult to imagine the crisis or changed political circumstances that might produce such a result. The Supreme Court's role, and the appointment of Supreme Court justices, is now firmly and inextricably embedded in the political system.

The evolving confirmation process has had diverse impacts. First, it shapes presidential strategies of nomination, with a new emphasis on timing and "confirmability"—which in turn depends on whether the Senate is controlled by the president's party. It is no accident that all recent nominations—and most since 1970—have gone to federal appeals judges. They have passed through the Senate at least once before, and their views are likely to be on record and well known. Presidents may shape their choices to insure confirmation, favoring candidates who, from either the right or left, tend toward the moderate center, or eliminating those most likely to provoke heated opposition and thus use scarce resources needed for other political projects. Second, as Baum has noted (although this is hard to prove), the prospect of a long and bitter confirmation battle may deter some prospective nominees. Finally, the confirmation experience may affect a justice's behavior on the bench, inducing him or her to be more liberal or conservative (or more moderate) than he or she might have been. Thomas's confirmation ordeal may well have hardened his conservative instincts against the views of his liberal adversaries.

Who Becomes a Supreme Court Justice?

The Constitution establishes no formal qualifications for appointment to the Supreme Court or the lower federal courts, as it does for members of Congress and the president. Congress, despite periodic proposals to do so, has never proposed a constitutional amendment or attempted to legislate judicial qualifications using the Necessary and Proper Clause of Article I, Section 8. Nevertheless, certain norms have developed that have the same effect. All justices have been lawyers (by the standards of their time), and at least since the New Deal all have had law school training,[42] most at one of the nation's prestigious law schools. Among the current justices, Rehnquist and O' Connor were classmates at Stanford; Breyer, Scalia, Souter, and Kennedy went to Harvard; Ginsburg began at Harvard but received her degree at Columbia; Stevens graduated from Northwestern and Thomas from Yale. In the last fifty years, only three justices did not graduate from ranked law schools: Charles Whittaker graduated from the University of Kansas City Law School, Thurgood Marshall received his degree from Howard University, and Chief

Justice Warren Burger graduated from the William Mitchell College of Law in St. Paul, Minnesota.

Until the 1970s, religion and geography were important factors in who was nominated to the Court. Brandeis, the first Jewish justice, was appointed in 1916. The practice of a "Jewish seat" lasted until Fortas's departure, with Felix Frankfurter and Arthur Goldberg holding it after Brandeis. But the practice has disappeared, although two of the current justices, Breyer and Ginsburg, are Jewish. Likewise there was once thought to be a "Catholic seat," but when Brennan was replaced by Souter, a non-Catholic, it was not much of an issue. Three current justices are Catholic—Scalia, Thomas, and Kennedy—and there seems to be no reason any more to "reserve" a special seat for any particular religion. It was also important once for the Court to reflect geographic balance (particularly given the justices' early circuit riding duties), but that norm also has largely disappeared.

At the same time, however, race and gender have become politically important recruitment criteria. Thurgood Marshall, appointed by Lyndon Johnson, was the first African American justice—a truly historic appointment. President George H.W. Bush thought it necessary to replace Marshall with another black justice, and chose Clarence Thomas. Sandra O'Connor was Ronald Reagan's choice to fulfill his campaign pledge to appoint the first woman justice. Scalia was the first justice of Italian descent, and it seems very likely that a Hispanic justice will be appointed in the near future. As new groups win political strength and recognition, they too will seek and receive the symbolic recognition of a Supreme Court appointment. While presidents, especially these days, give precedence to policy considerations, they cannot be oblivious to concerns of ethnic and gender representation and diversity. One can expect that, sometime in the future, those factors will also cease to be an issue, as minorities and women are selected for the Court in the normal course of events, and gender and ethnicity will no longer merit special consideration. Perhaps other concerns will rise in their place.

Until the 1960s, it could be said that America's Supreme Court justices "looked alike." All were white men, and the preponderance were men of means who had attended prestigious colleges and law schools (according to the standards of their time), who were (or had been) highly regarded lawyers and either knew the president and/or shared his political views. Mostly they also came from the same political party as the president. Their trajectory to the Court often included prior service as a judge and high level political positions. But some came with no such experience; they were primarily politicians, lawyers in private practice, or they may have been law teachers.

Since the 1960s, the Court has come to look a little bit more like America, although it is certainly is not a mirror of the nation's cultural, ethnic, and religious diversity. Nine positions can only be divided up in so many ways. But slowly the old attributes have given way to a richer mosaic.

In the 1950s and 1960s, conservative critics of the liberal Warren Court often claimed that what had led the Court "astray"[43] were too many justices without "prior judicial experience." Frequent targets of this criticism were Felix Frankfurter, William O. Douglas, and, of course, Earl Warren. "Impeach Earl Warren" signs littered the nation's roads. Bills were introduced in Congress to require prior judicial experience, albeit without success. There is a strong countervailing argument, however, that the Court, given its mission, benefits from justices with a wide range of experiences.

Ironically, just as the Court was becoming more diverse in some respects, it has become less so in others. As Epstein, Knight, and Martin have shown, prior service on a federal court of appeals has now become nearly a de facto qualification. The last justice who came directly from private practice was Lewis Powell in 1971; the last to be a sitting cabinet secretary was Arthur Goldberg in 1962.[44] One has to go back to 1945 to find a sitting legislator (Harold Burton) elevated to the Court. Thus career experience on the Court has become substantially more uniform.[45] Indeed, Epstein and colleagues conclude that "at no other time in American history has the Court been composed of justices so alike in terms of their career experience."[46] While this may be too strong a conclusion, there seems to be one common path to the Supreme Court today, and it runs through the courts of appeals.

Chief Justice Rehnquist, the only member of the current Court to have *no* prior judicial experience, has warned that the Court will in time "too much resemble the judiciary in civil law countries." Rehnquist has argued that courts staffed primarily if not exclusively by career judges, "simply do not command the respect and enjoy the independence of ours."[47] These judgments seem too harsh, or at least premature. But there can be no doubt, based on substantial evidence, that while the "lawyer is not necessarily father to the judge," career experiences are a critical factor in influencing how justices understand and decide cases. The fact that the justices divide so often in key cases belies the notion that there is no difference between them, or that they can be defined by their prior service as appellate judges.

Leaving the Bench, Creating Vacancies

The U.S. Constitution places no limits on how long a federal judge may serve "during good behaviour." Members of Congress, however, are limited to specific terms subject to re-election, although there is no mandatory retirement age. The Supreme Court invalidated attempts by several states to place term limits on members of Congress from those states.[48] And the president is limited to being twice elected and serving for a maximum of ten years by the Twenty-second Amendment. About two-thirds of the states have mandatory retirement provisions for their judges, which the Court upheld when they were challenged under the federal age discrimination statute.[49] And, as we have seen, all of the states and the federal government have provisions for dealing with incompetent or disabled judges, although a federal judge, disabled or otherwise, can only be removed by impeachment.

"Leaving the Bench" provisions and practices are important for several reasons. How and when a justice departs has come to be intimately connected with the selection of his or her successor—what Artemus Ward has called "succession politics."[50] Dealing with disabled justices while maintaining the institutional integrity of the Court is also a problem of some importance.

How have justices left the bench? In the early days, when there were no retirement provisions and circuit riding was burdensome and dangerous, justices did not last long; virtually all left by resignation or death (John Marshall being a notable exception). In the years since 1954, with more than ample retirement provisions in force, *every* justice but one has departed by retirement. The exception was Abe Fortas, who resigned to avoid likely impeachment. Of the justices who retired, many were thought (or known) to be no longer able to function effectively.[51] Ward argues that partisan considerations have become a dominant factor in retirement decisions—timing one's retirement to enable a president of the same party to nominate a replacement.

Thus, in a very real sense, a retiring justice may control, if not actually designate, his or her successor. Sometimes justices in declining health will postpone the inevitable in the hope of facilitating a politically friendly successor. This does not always work: a stroke-impaired Justice Douglas continued to participate in the Court's business in the vain hope of denying a Republican president—Gerald Ford—the opportunity to replace him; likewise, a seriously ailing Thurgood Marshall remained on the bench in an ultimately futile effort to deny Presidents Reagan and George H.W. Bush the right of replacement.

On the current Court, Justice Stevens has made it clear he will not willingly allow president George W. Bush to replace him; and Sandra O'Connor apparently contemplated retirement if and when Bush was elected in 2000. When it appeared that the Democratic candidate, Al Gore, would win the election, O'Connor was heard to say "this is terrible," and her husband to add that they had been planning to retire to Arizona. But President Bush has now been re-elected, and Justice O'Connor has not (yet) retired. This practice of "succession politics" is no longer novel; indeed it is assumed that all justices think this way (which is probably not true). But some critics argue that it is an unwarranted intrusion by individual justices into the constitutional selection process.

The disability issue, raised by the Douglas affair in particular, is potentially more important. When, following his stroke, Douglas insisted on participating although he was clearly unable to do so, seven of the remaining eight justices agreed to let him believe he was participating, but in fact decided not to count his vote in any case where it determined the outcome. They also agreed, as apparently had been done with Charles Whittaker years before, that a fifth vote would be required to grant certiorari if Douglas's vote was one of the four cast in favor. Justice White protested that this was a violation of the Constitution, which gives neither one's colleagues nor anyone else the right to make such a decision for another justice. Eventually all the other justices persuaded Douglas to retire, using a carrot and stick approach.[52] As mortality ages increase, and the justices, like all people, live longer, disability problems of this kind are likely to multiply, and could have an adverse effect on the institution. How long can the Court do its business with an impaired judge on the bench? Other than the kind of informal arrangements that marked the Douglas case, the only present solution to serious disability is impeachment—a drastic and certainly inappropriate remedy —and one never used for that purpose.

There are three possible reform options to deal with judicial disability, all imperfect. Congress could pass a constitutional amendment establishing a mandatory retirement age for Supreme Court justices (or all federal judges). Second, an amendment could provide for the appointment (or election) of justices to nonrenewable fixed terms. These are not mutually exclusive. Third, Congress could implement the existing statutory judicial disability provisions by first making them applicable to the Supreme Court, and second, establishing some procedure–perhaps within the Court itself—for determining disability and removing disabled justices. A constitutional amendment would be required, however, to avoid serious separation of powers concerns.

Article III's life tenure provision made more sense in 1787 than it does today. Life expectancy was much lower, and thus the likelihood of Supreme Court justices serving for a *very* long time remote. Since the average retirement age of justices since 1970 is now 78.8 years, and the average length of service 25.5 years,[53] there is increased concern that the Court has fallen out of touch with the political system, and that some way to prevent judicial coagulation is needed. FDR echoed similar thoughts in 1937 when he proposed his infamous "court packing" plan. But age is no ironclad barometer of judicial performance. A significant number of justices have been intellectually vital and wrote some of their best opinions past the age of seventy-five, while some were no longer functioning effectively at a much earlier age. Any specific retirement age, would, like life itself, be arbitrary. Douglas, as a young justice, had supported a retirement age for justices, but his views changed with increasing age and declining health. Nevertheless, the Supreme Court is nearly unique in its life tenure among high courts in its life tenure provisions. Only Rhode Island, among the states, provides life tenure for its supreme court justices. And virtually no other constitutional democracy does so.

Establishing fixed term limits would also dramatically alter the dynamics of the Court. If the terms were set at eighteen years and staggered and a new justice was appointed every two years, presidents would constantly be making appointments, to the detriment of any concept of judicial independence, to say nothing of separation of powers. The opportunity for executive meddling would be greatly exacerbated. And the Court's institutional stability might be threatened if it had to "remake" its internal dynamics every two years. On the other hand, giving each president a minimum of two nominations per term might defuse the crisis atmosphere that now attends irregular and often long awaited opportunities.

The third proposal—a workable judicial disability plan—would also require an amendment to make it compatible with the good behaviour clause, but there might always be objections that any limits of this kind would intrude unavoidably on judicial independence. Such objections would underscore the need for a coequal institution to enforce constitutional rights and boundaries *from* political majorities, but whether an externally imposed plan would actually have that effect remains to be seen.

An interesting alternative would be for the Supreme Court itself to establish some internal procedures for dealing with disability, but even that option could not include formal removal as a solution. It would have to be redone every time a new "Court" was formed with the addition of a new justice. And it could only function with continued unanimous consent; compliance by each justice individually would always be voluntary.

The current health problems of Chief Justice Rehnquist, his reduced participation in the Court's work, and his determination to reveal as little as possible about his illness, have been the subject of much concern. The justices themselves might ward off more serious inroads into their independence by agreeing to undergo annual health exams with the results revealed publicly, following the lead of the president and vice president. But the Court is a much more secretive institution, and it seems unlikely that all the justices would agree to this (and it would be an individual, not an institutional, decision, in any case).

Conclusions

The selection of Supreme Court justices is a microcosm of the political system, and a reflection of the great importance of the Court in that system. The stakes are uniquely high and the outcomes of enormous consequence. As other options that the framers created to limit the judiciary, such as impeachment, have fallen into limbo, a selection event takes on even greater salience. The Court has become a central force in the post–New Deal governance system; its activist role is deeply embedded in the political structure. It is a key point of entry and influence for important political forces, and a vital and very useful forum for the rational discussion of, and possible resolution of, emotionally charged issues, particularly so at a time when there has been a breakdown of consensus norms in the political community and its other institutions. Given the Court's enhanced political role—judicial activism is now deeply embedded in our political fabric—it does not seem inappropriate to maintain the political selection of the justices. It is one of the Court's main ties to democracy.

There has been no change on the Court in nearly eleven years, and one or two appointments could produce radical doctrinal shifts on key issues. The prospect of an escalating confrontation, with a stalemate that obstructs the Senate and perhaps the entire government, may be an important determinant of whom the president nominates. The Democratic minority in the Senate seems prepared to use the most extreme tactic yet devised to block Supreme Court nominations it opposes—the filibuster—in which a nomination is blocked, and effectively defeated, if a 60 percent majority for cloture cannot be attained.

This tactic was used ("tried out") successfully to block a number of President Bush's court of appeals nominations in 2003–2004. It is not an entirely new tactic, however. Young Republicans in the minority bucked their leadership and blocked the nomination of Abe Fortas as chief justice in 1968. And it has been used sporadically (but mostly unsuccessfully), by both parties, to oppose other courts of appeals nominees. But never before has it been used so aggressively, so successfully, or with such rancor.

Republicans have argued that the filibuster, as applied to judicial nominations, is unconstitutional because it undercuts the provision for a majority vote on confirmation. But unless the filibuster is unconstitutional generally, there seems no reason to suppose it is so only for judicial nominations. Republicans have threatened to use either a "fast track" process or the so-called nuclear option to break a Supreme Court confirmation filibuster. But any change in the rules, such as "fast tracking" judicial nominations, would itself be subject to a filibuster.

The nuclear option would escape this requirement. Under it, a point of order could be made by a Republican senator to the presiding officer (Vice President Cheney) for a ruling that filibusters could not be used to block judicial nominations. The expected favorable ruling from the chair, sustaining the point of order, would then, if challenged, be upheld by a majority, and the Democratic minority would be bypassed. A filibuster cannot be used on such a procedural matter, which is nondebatable under the Senate rules. The label "nuclear option" refers to the extreme measures the Democrats have promised to employ to protest this maneuver, such as shutting down the Senate to all non-emergency business.[54] The possibility of such an unseemly and destabilizing scenario is itself a reason for caution on both sides.

In May 2005 the Senate narrowly avoided such a confrontation by adopting a temporary compromise. The Democrats would allow a vote in the full Senate on several courts of appeals nominations that they were blocking in return for at least a temporary postponement of the "nuclear option" strategy by the Republicans. The option for employment of a filibuster was maintained. Whether this compromise can withstand the hydraulic pressures of an expected

Supreme Court nomination to replace the ailing chief justice is doubtful, unless it persuades President Bush to make a more centrist and mainstream appointment that Democrats can accept. Absent such a concession by the president, the Senate seems destined to continue on a collision course with itself. The fallout from that collision is likely to produce significant but as yet unpredictable changes in the process by with by which Supreme Court justices are chosen.

If the Senate "went nuclear" on the next Supreme Court nomination, however, calls for reform, already plentiful, would increase. We have already discussed some of those reforms, since they are proposed periodically: a retirement age for justices, fixed term or terms of office, specification of qualifications for service on the Court, some form of the Missouri Plan idea in which a bipartisan commission would present the president with a list of names from which the nominee would be chosen *or* election of the justices by region, and/or changes in the confirmation process such as those recommended in the Task Force Report.

There are three problems with these proposals. The first is that they presume that the system is broken and in need of repair. The second is that those who are proposing them do not have the same interests or expectations; and they might not work as intended. And the third is that they might! The fact that the selection system has evolved as it has is not necessarily a sign of malfunction. It is reasonably predictable. One could make the argument that it fits well within, and reflects, the changing structure of the entire political system, for better or worse. Life tenure is certainly not perfect; and if new constitutional arrangements were in order, it might not have many supporters. But most who call for change are not concerned so much with the process as with its outcomes. No one can be sure whether, or how, retirement ages or fixed terms, or any of the listed reforms, would work, what the consequences would be, and who would be the beneficiaries.

Unless we devise some clear consensus about what is needed and appropriate, and doable, reform for its own sake will be futile, and possibly dysfunctional. Take the Task Force proposal, which was designed to "depoliticize" the confirmation process. Not only is that not possible—we can not go back to Washington's first six appointments—but it seems quite undesirable when one considers the alternatives. If not choice by the political system, then choice by whom? Selecting judges is a quintessentially political act, even (or especially) in a juristocracy; how can it be otherwise? Balanced against the problems and uncertainties of the current selection system, would any of the proposed reforms produce better results?

Notes

* I am indebted to Eric Wolkoff for extraordinary research assistance on this project.

1. See Ran Hirschl, *Towards Juristocracy*. See also Robert Bork, *Coercing Virtue: The Worldwide Rule of Judges* (Washington, D.C.: AEI Press, 2003).

2. Hirschl, ibid., p. 1.
3. See Gerald Rosenberg, *The Hollow Hope*; Stuart A. Scheingold, *The Politics of Rights: Lawyers, Public Policy, and Political Change,* 2nd ed. (Ann Arbor: University of Michigan Press, 2004); and Michael J. Klarman, *From Jim Crow to Civil Rights* (New York: Oxford University Press, 2004).
4. See Alexander M. Bickel, *The Least Dangerous Branch: The Supreme Court at the Bar of Politics,* 2nd ed. (New Haven, Conn.: Yale University Press, 1986).
5. Eliot Slotnick, "A Historical Perspective on Federal Judicial Selection," *Judicature* 86 (2002), 13–16.
6. There are many bewildering and largely inexplicable variations as well. For example, Michigan and Ohio chose their judges in nonpartisan elections, but judicial candidates are nominated in party primaries.
7. After the Revolution all other states chose judges by appointment, eight by the legislature, four by various combinations of executive appointment and legislative confirmation.
8. Larry Berkson, "Judicial Selection in the United States: A Special Report" *Judicature* 64 (1980), 176–193. Updated by Seth Anderson.
9. Lee Epstein, Jack Knight, and Andrew D. Martin, "The Norm of Judicial Experience," *University of California Law Review* 91 (2003), 938–939.
10. President Carter wrote to each Democratic senator asking them to establish similar nominating commissions in their respective states for federal district court appointments. Senator Lloyd Bentsen of Texas is alleged to have responded, "I am the merit commission for the State of Texas." See Slotnick, "A Historical Perspective," note 5, p. 15.
11. "Justice in Jeopardy, Report of the American Bar Association Commission on the 21st Century Judiciary" (2003), p. 102.
12. 536 U.S. 765 (2002).
13. Robert McCloskey, *The American Supreme Court,* 4th ed., rev. by Sanford Levinson (Chicago: University of Chicago Press, 2005).
14. See *Chandler v. Judicial Council of the Tenth Circuit,* 398 U.S. 74 (1970); and *McBryde v. Committee to Review Circuit Council Conduct and Disability Orders of Judicial Conference of U.S.*, 278 F. 3d 29 (D.C. Cir. 2002); cert denied 537 U.S. 821 (2002).
15. Section 455(a), Title 28, U. S. Code. Judges are prohibited from engaging "in conduct prejudicial to the effective and expeditious administration of the business of the courts," and they can be sanctioned if they are "unable to discharge all the duties of office by reason of mental or physical disability." It says further that "any justice, judge, or magistrate judge of the United States shall disqualify himself in any proceeding in which his impartiality might reasonably be questioned."
16. Justice Scalia's mea culpa memorandum opinion is at 124 S. Ct. 1391 (2004).
17. Although one can make a respectable case that Congress had the authority to provide for a separate enforcement mechanism for the "good behaviour" clause by employing the Necessary and Proper Clause. There is nothing in the language of the impeachment clause that mandates its exclusivity. Congress was presented with this option when it considered the 1980 Judicial Conduct and Disability Act, however, and rejected it. Federal judges thus cannot be subject to periodic review of their per-

formance except by appellate courts. Few are impeached. Many decisions are reversed on appeal but there is no penalty for reversal except to reputation. Of the eight federal judges impeached in the twentieth century, all were charged with criminal misconduct offenses. The last (and only) Supreme Court justice impeached was acquitted by the Senate in 1805, although Justice Abe Fortas, accused of various improprieties in 1969, might well have been impeached had he not resigned. On the other hand, in those states which employ elections (or retention elections) there is an additional oversight mechanism—review by the voters.

18. Of course there are always political considerations in the mix, even if not formally considered as such. The two most recent impeachments, of federal judges Alcee Hastings and Walter Nixon, were nominally about misconduct but also politically charged.
19. Peter H. Russell, "Judicial Independence in Comparative Perspective," in *Judicial Independence in the Age of Democracy: Critical Perspectives from around the World*, edited by Peter H. Russell and David A. O'Brien (University Press of Virginia, 2001), 301.
20. Quoted in Russell, "Judicial Independence in Comparative Perspective."
21. Martin Shapiro, *Courts: A Comparative and Political Analysis* (Chicago: University of Chicago Press, 1981), chap. 1.
22. Russell, "Judicial Independence in Comparative Perspective," note 19, p. 307.
23. See Maeva Marcus, "George Washington's Appointments to the Supreme Court," *Journal of Supreme Court History* 24 (1999). Five of the six nominees had held top level judicial appointments in their respective states. All told, Washington made thirteen nominations and eleven appointments to the Supreme Court. In the twentieth century, Franklin Roosevelt made nine appointments, Eisenhower five, Truman, Nixon, and Reagan, four each. Jimmy Carter had no appointments to make, and George W. Bush had none in his first term; the last previous president not to have a Supreme Court appointment was Andrew Johnson! It might also be noted that only four of Washington's six appointees showed up when the Court was organized in the spring of 1789; one declined the appointment, another (Rutledge) simply never showed up and after three years resigned to become the chief justice of South Carolina. See McCloskey, *op. cit.*, note 13, p. 2.
24. Sheldon Goldman, *Picking Federal Judges*, p. 3.
25. Eisenhower wanted to appoint a Democrat and a Catholic to "balance" the Court. Brennan, a New Jersey Supreme Court justice, fit the bill, and he came highly recommended by the respected Republican chief justice, Arthur Vanderbilt.
26. Burger, Blackmun, and Powell. Rehnquist did not participate. Of his four appointees, Nixon, ironically, would have been most pleased with Rehnquist, whom he didn't like; he disparagingly commented that "he looked Jewish," could never remember his name (he called him "Renchberg" or "Rensler"), and chose him only because a preferred candidate, Howard Baker, declined. See John Dean, *The Rehnquist Choice: The Untold Story of the Nixon Appointment That Redefined the Supreme Court* (New York: Free Press, 2001).
27. 520 U.S. 681 (1997).
28. David Yalof, *Pursuit of Justices*, p.6.
29. 347 U.S. 483.

30. Dean, *The Rehnquist Choice*, note 26. Dean's conclusion, based on additional evidence found after Rehnquist's second confirmation, is that he was not truthful.
31. For example, the Seventeenth Amendment democratized the Senate, making it more responsive (eventually) to popular and constituent opinion and the pressures of single interest groups. That led to the demise of the old seniority system and well defined institutional relationships. As Lyndon Johnson learned from the successful Republican filibuster of Abe Fortas's nomination to be chief justice, a president could no longer rely solely on the assurance of senior Senate leaders (often of both parties) that a particular nominee would be confirmed. The Nineteenth Amendment, enfranchising women, and the 1965 Voting Rights Act, plus many Supreme Court decisions enfranchising blacks and other minorities, also contributed to a vast expansion, and more diversity, in the electorate. The phenomenon of divided government, currently in hiatus, also contributed to the politicization of Supreme Court recruitment by disrupting the rough balance of consensus recruitment politics. An added engine of change has been the information revolution and its technology, which insures that no element of a nominee's life or career will pass unnoticed or unchallenged.
32. Quoted in Lauren C. Bell, "Senate Confirmations in an Interest Group Age," *Extensions* (Spring 2004), 21. Also see Forrest Maltzman, "Advice and Consent: Cooperation and Conflict in the Appointment of Federal Judges," in *Institutions of American Democracy: The Legislative Branch*, edited by Paul Quirk and Sarah Binder (New York: Oxford University Press, 2005); and Roy B. Flemming et al., "Witnesses at the Confirmations: The Appearances of Organized Interests at Senate Hearings of Federal Judicial Appointments, 1945–1992," *Political Research Quarterly* 51 (1998), 617–631.
33. Ibid. See also Robert A. Katzmann, *Courts and Congress* (Washington, D.C.: The Brookings Institution Press, 1997), p. 35.
34. Charles R. Shipan and Megan L. Shannon, "Delaying Justice(s): A Duration Analysis of Supreme Court Confirmations," *American Journal of Political Science* 47 (2003), 654–668.
35. Henry Monaghan, "The Confirmation Process: Law or Politics," *Harvard Law Review* (1988), 1202–1212, at 1204. See also Michael Gerhardt, *The Federal Appointments Process*, pp. 15–38. It took only a few years for the Senate to first reject a Supreme Court nominee, John Rutledge, at least partly for his political views; this established the precedent that the Senate's responsibility was to examine *all* of a nominee's qualifications.
36. According to the foremost authority on Supreme Court appointments, Lawrence Baum. See Baum, *The Supreme Court*, 8th ed. (New York: CQ Press, 2004), p. 28 and passim.
37. Parker, Fortas (to Chief Justice), Haynsworth, Carswell, Bork, and (Douglas) Ginsberg. Not included is Judge Homer Thornberry, who was (informally) nominated by President Lyndon Johnson to replace Fortas after he was elevated to chief justice. But the Fortas nomination was withdrawn to avert a Republican filibuster and certain defeat, and since there was no longer a vacancy, Thornberry was never formally nominated or considered by the Senate.
38. See John Anthony Maltese, "The Selling of Clement Haynsworth: Politics and the Confirmation of Supreme Court Justices," *Judicature* 72 (1989), 338–347.

39. As late as 1971, although practices were clearly changing, senators were still hesitant to *openly* advocate a purely ideological judgment. For example, in response to the first Rehnquist nomination, Senator Jacob Javits argued that a nominee could be rejected if he did not have, besides the expected qualifications of intellect, competence, experience, and integrity, "a high commitment to freedom, dignity, and justice for all citizens." Senator William Proxmire responded that the Senate should confirm a nominee of obvious intellectual ability (such as Rehnquist), without consideration of any substantive views which he might hold "unless it could be shown that the nominee did not understand or would not support the Bill of Rights." Javits' views closely paralleled those expressed by Professor Charles L. Black, Jr., in his influential article "A Note on Senatorial Consideration of Supreme Court Nominees" *Yale Law Journal*, 79 (1970), 657–664. Black wrote that: "A senator properly may, or even at some times in duty must, vote against a nominee . . . on the ground that the nominee holds views which, when transposed into judicial decisions, are likely . . . to be very bad for the country." Black's views played a significant role in mobilizing opposition to Carswell, and later to Bork.
40. The following markers suggest the evolution of the Senate's confirmation role: 1873: hearings of Senate Judiciary Committee closed; 1916 (Brandeis) first public hearing on a nominee; 1925: first nominee (Stone) to appear personally before the Committee; 1930: first full public hearing; 1949: limited television coverage; 1955: beginning of practice whereby all nominees testified; 1969: practice began of nominees "visiting" offices of Senate leaders and committee members to pay a "courtesy call"; 1981: since then *all* hearings have been nationally televised; 1950s–2001: ABA Committee on Federal Judiciary investigated and evaluated all nominees before formal nomination. Since then only after nomination.
41. David M. O'Brien, *Judicial Roulette: Report of the Twentieth Century Fund Task Force on Judicial Selection* (New York: Priority Press Publications, 1988).
42. Justice Robert Jackson attended Albany Law School for a year, then "read law" as an apprentice law clerk. He was the last Supreme Court justice appointed not to have graduated from law school. Justice Stanley Reed, appointed to the Court three years before Jackson, attended the University of Virginia Law School for a year (and another at Columbia University), and also did not graduate from law school. But since Reed remained on the Court three years longer than Jackson, he was the last "serving" justice not to have graduated from Law School.
43. These decisions, which offended right wing Republicans and southerners, included *Brown* and a series of allegedly "pro-communist" decisions. See C. Herman Pritchett, *The Political Offender and the Warren Court* (Boston: Boston University Press, 1958).
44. Though not a cabinet member, Rehnquist was an assistant attorney general when nominated.
45. Epstein et al., "The Norm of Judicial Experience," note 9, pp. 908–909. Indeed, "limiting" the Supreme Court only to those who have served on the courts of appeal, is likely to have an unusually limiting effect. Success on the Supreme Court is not necessarily dependent on being able to "think like a judge." And the courts of appeal, as presently constituted, are still a fairly limited source of minority candidates. But history also shows that appointment to the Supreme Court can have a lib-

erating effect, leading some justices to begin to think "out of the box."

46. Ibid., p. 908.
47. Ibid.
48. *U.S. Term Limits v. Thornton*, 514 U.S. 779 (1995).
49. *Gregory v. Ashcroft*, 501 U.S. 452 (1991) upheld Missouri's mandatory retirement age for state supreme court judges.
47. Artemus Ward, *Deciding to Leave*, chap. 1.
51. According to Ward, quoting David Garrow, that list would include Sherman Minton, Charles Whittaker, Hugo Black, William O. Douglas, Lewis Powell, and Thurgood Marshall. Ibid., p. 244.
52. Ibid., 229–237 and Appendix B.
53. The average age at retirement, from 1789 to 1970, was 68.5 years; the average length of service for that same period was 15.2 years. Justice William Douglas holds the record for service of 36 years, 6 months, and 25 days.
54. Maltzman, "Advice and Consent," note 32.

Bibliography

Abraham, Henry J. *Justices, Presidents, and Senators: A History of U.S. Supreme Court Appointments from Washington to Clinton*. Rev. ed. Lanham, Md.: Rowman and Littlefield, 1999.

Atkinson, David N. *Leaving the Bench: Supreme Court Justices at the End*. Lawrence: University Press of Kansas, 1999.

Bickel, Alexander M. *The Least Dangerous Branch: The Supreme Court at the Bar of Politics.* New York: Bobbs-Merrill, 1962.

Dean, John. *The Rehnquist Choice*. New York: Free Press, 2001.

Gerhardt, Michael. *The Federal Appointments Process: A Constitutional and Historical Analysis.* Durham, N.C.: Duke University Press, 2001.

Goldman, Sheldon. *Picking Federal Judges: Lower Court Selection from Roosevelt through Reagan*. New Haven, Conn.: Yale University Press, 1997.

Grossman, Joel B. *Lawyers and Judges: The ABA and the Politics of Judicial Selection*. New York: John Wiley & Sons, 1965.

Hirschl, Ran. *Towards Juristocracy: The Origins and Consequences of the New Constitutionalism*. Cambridge, Mass.: Harvard University Press, 2004.

Maltese, John Anthony. *The Selling of Supreme Court Nominees*. Baltimore: Johns Hopkins University Press, 1995.

Rosenberg, Gerald. *The Hollow Hope: Can Courts Bring about Social Change?* Chicago: University of Chicago Press, 1991.

Silverstein, Mark. *Judicious Choices: The New Politics of Supreme Court Confirmations*. New York: W. W. Norton, 1994.

Ward, Artemus. *Deciding to Leave: The Politics of Retirement from the United States Supreme Court.* Albany: State University of New York Press, 2003.

Yalof, David Alistair. *Pursuit of Justices: Presidential Politics and the Selection of Supreme Court Justices*. Chicago: University of Chicago Press, 1999.

Court Cases

Brown v. Board of Education (I), 347 U.S. 483 (1954).
Brown v. Board of Education (II), 349 U.S. 294 (1955).
Chandler v. Judicial Council of the Tenth Circuit, 398 U.S. 74 (1970).
Clinton v. Jones, 520 U.S. 681 (1997).
Gregory v. Ashcroft, 501 U.S. 452 (1991).
Marbury v. Madison, 5 U.S. 137 (1803).
McBryde v. Committee to Review Circuit Council Conduct and Disability Orders of Judicial Conference of U.S., 278 F. 3d 29 (D.C. Cir. 2002); cert denied 537 U.S. 821 (2002).
Republican Party of Minnesota v. White, 536 U.S. 765 (2002).
U.S. Term Limits v. Thornton, 514 U.S. 779 (1995).

7

IS JUDICIAL FEDERALISM ESSENTIAL TO DEMOCRACY? STATE COURTS IN THE FEDERAL SYSTEM

Paul R. Brace and Melinda Gann Hall

WHEN IT COMES TO AMERICAN COURTS, MANY PEOPLE have a perspective like the famous *New Yorker* magazine rendering of a New Yorker's view of the world. According to this view, a New Yorker looking west sees the George Washington Bridge, a vast wasteland, and a tiny Los Angeles in the distance. Similarly, in popular, journalistic, and even scholarly treatments of courts and law in the United States, there is the massive United States Supreme Court building in Washington, D.C., populated by nine towering figures, with only a huge, unknown, and under-appreciated wasteland beyond. On one level, this is not too surprising. Supreme Court justices have at times been towering legal intellects, and many of the Court's decisions are publicly salient and dramatic, with far-reaching consequences. At the same time, however, just as there is much of consequence going on between the George Washington Bridge and Los Angeles (or so some believe), there also is a tremendous amount of legal terrain beyond the United States Supreme Court that needs to be recognized, understood, and appreciated. State courts are at heart of this enterprise.

This chapter considers the fascinating realm of state judicial politics, dividing discussion into two separate but highly related parts. First, the historical development of state courts is described within the context of several core issues in democratic theory that state courts have helped to resolve. Second, more practical matters are examined through a discussion of the operating characteristics of contemporary state court systems, including the extraordinary diversity among these institutions. These discussions highlight the direct impact of state courts, especially state courts of last resort, on the landscape of contemporary American politics.

Because of the presentation below of some exciting new data on state supreme courts, this chapter is quite distinct from others in the volume. Using the recently released State Supreme Court Data Project, which contains an extraordinary array of information about the decisions reached in every state's highest court from 1995 through 1997, this chapter will present a series of graphs to depict a wide variety of ways in which these institutions resolve the cases on their dockets. This decidedly empirical focus will serve to illustrate dramatic state-to-state differences and will place in stark relief the legal and political significance of state judiciaries in the federal system.

Overall, this comprehensive examination of historical, theoretical, and contemporary issues about state judicial politics argues that state court systems in the United States have promoted democracy in two fundamental and interrelated ways. First, courts, especially state courts, provide an important forum for dispute resolution in a manner generally viewed as legitimate and authoritative. Without this, especially in large democracies, the dissatisfaction that arises from injustice or unresolved disputes would only serve to fuel conditions for rebellion or government oppression. Second, for the various reasons detailed below, courts prevent more conventional majoritarian processes from being overtaxed, which would result in factionalism or cyclical and unstable outcomes. Throughout U.S. history, state courts have played an important role in reducing the volume of disputes and the number of alternatives in conventional majoritarian politics. In the end, by virtue of the volume of disputes they resolve and the comparatively high esteem they receive from the public, state courts promote respect for the rule of law and the rights of citizens, two critical components of the fabric of a functioning democracy.

By design, very few conflicts in society spill over into the realm of majoritarian politics. However, this does not mean these conflicts do not exist, nor does it mean that they are not addressed to a reasonable degree of satisfaction. For many Americans involved in important conflicts over property, rights, or privileges, justice is sought not at the ballot box but in court, and overwhelmingly the forum for resolution of these significant conflicts is state courts. In a typical year, state trial courts handle *over three hundred times* as many cases as federal district courts. State intermediate appellate courts process *over three times* as many appeals as the U.S. Courts of Appeals. And state supreme courts address *over seven hundred times* as many cases as the United States Supreme Court. Clearly, when it comes to the volume of disputes handled in the United States, the state court systems are the backbone of the American judicial system.

By settling a huge number of important disputes each year (currently over 100 million filings per year in the trial courts alone), state court systems effectively remove many issues from majoritarian electoral or legislative politics. Courts generally, and state courts specifically, resolve disputes over important economic, social, and explicitly political issues. From tort litigation to privacy rights to ballot access and the permissibility of ballot measures, these courts influence our more traditional electoral political agenda. Specifically from the perspective of democratic theory, it has been well understood for about three centuries now that majoritarian processes suffer inherent problems that promote instability, and that these problems become even more pronounced when many alternatives are addressed. If unsettled grievances spilled over into majoritarian processes, society would be much more fractious, jeopardizing the stability and predictability necessary for democratic governance.

Undoubtedly, state court systems operate with certain biases. Certainly gaining access to these courts is not a minor affair, and there are many in our society with grievances against the government, a firm, or a private individual who never have their day in court. Yet, even though many never find themselves in courts, state or federal, huge proportions of the population, certainly more than have ever been in court, express tremendous confidence in their state court systems, as documented below. If citizens did not have confidence in these courts they would not abide by their rulings, which would put further burdens on other government institutions.

State courts, like their federal counterparts, have no power of enforcement. As a consequence, courts have found it crucial to nurture and maintain mass support. Because state courts have a high degree of legitimacy in the public's eyes, these institutions can address the huge volume of disputes before them authoritatively. By gaining and maintaining the public's confidence, state courts are able to solve many problems in democratic society in nonmajoritarian ways. State courts have, in essence, gained majoritarian support for a process, not an outcome, and this is a critical contribution to American democracy.

A Brief History of Courts in American Political Development

To appreciate better the contemporary role of state courts in American democracy, it is useful to trace the historical development of courts in the political processes. Writing about the America of the 1830s, Alexis de Tocqueville appreciated the instability of majoritarian processes and the importance of courts in American democracy.[1] He saw legislatures as very responsive to majoritarian impulses and commented extensively on the instability in law that this could produce. Alternatively, courts could affect law only within the context of particular cases before them. By rendering decisions that would bear upon the interests of the particular parties before them, courts would thus slight the law only incidentally. Consequently, laws produced through majoritarian impulse could be diminished slightly or completely if there were repeated cases before courts.

Courts united the trial of the individual with the trial of the law, subjecting law to narrow corrections but protecting it from wholesale assault. To Tocqueville, it was this practice of American courts that operated to protect liberty and secure public order. Similarly, it is worthy to note that Tocqueville thought the insulation of courts from majoritarian pressures was vital, and thus Tocqueville was highly critical of the "experiments" of states to elect rather than appoint judges.

Stephen Skowronek reiterated the importance of courts to American political and economic development in his influential *Building a New American State*.[2] Skowronek saw courts as playing a very fundamental and even decisive role in our early political development. In the antebellum period, the state of the republic was defined by political parties and federal courts. Political parties, through aggressive use of patronage and distributing other spoils, were massively effective in gaining control of the apparatus and rewards of government. State and local political organizations defined a clear and irresistible discipline for gaining and manipulating political power and would ultimately provide the cement to hold together the highly fragmentary government designed by the Constitution. Political parties were successful in mobilizing majorities that facilitated working relationships within and among the branches and levels of government and sewed diverse geographical and institutional elements together in the pursuit of the distribution of the government's valuable goods and services. However, courts were the only institutions that stood outside direct party domination and, according to Skowronek, provided the essential counterbalance to the voracious electoral machines of the era. In many important ways, courts put the brakes on the highly partisan operation of politics in this period. Courts at each level of government nurtured and defined the state's prerogatives over the economy and society, promoting the sanctity of contracts and defining the grounds for corporate charters. Eventually, American judges embraced a pragmatic and positive view of themselves as policymakers, adopting an instrumental outlook.

While Skowronek emphasized the importance of the federal bench in this period, several authoritative studies point to the growing power and scope of state court systems. Morton Horowitz notes that decision by decision, state court judges in the early nineteenth century began the process of making new law and new legal rules that he characterizes as "instrumentalism," reshaping private law so that it may serve as "a creative instrument for directing men's energy toward social change."[3] Hence, to effect social change within a common law tradition inherently biased against change required both a transformation of legal rules and the role of judge-made law in society. He believed that courts generally, and state courts particularly, shed their passivity to the point of assuming a quasi-legislative role. He argues that early nineteenth-century judges understood that legal rules matter and that "different sets of legal rules would have differential effects on economic growth, depending both on the distribution of wealth they produced and the level of investment they encouraged."[4]

Kermit Hall also notes the emergence of legal instrumentalism that came to displace the older conception of law as precedent bound rules that judges applied mechanically.[5] Appellate courts emerged as both lawmaking and law-finding institutions as states retreated from the post-revolutionary emphasis on legislatures. It was also in this era that state constitutions shifted from organic law to voluminous treatises intended to reign in legislatures. As Lawrence Friedman notes, the wordy and excessive text of state constitutions that would appear in this era were made to order for an aggressive judiciary. The many constitutional controls over sloppy, corrupt, and selfish legislation played into the hands of litigants and courts.

By the Civil War, judges were not only administering the rule of law but were increasingly called upon to mediate among the growing number of competing interests crowding the political scene. The appellate judiciary built upon this legacy after the Civil War, expanding its power in response to the distributive political decisions of the party period beginning in the 1830s.[6] This period witnessed a dramatic growth in the range and scale of judicial activity, with courts deciding an ever-increasing number of private disputes and determining public policy. As Hall notes, "judges had a large and active hand in the governance of a rapidly changing society."[7] To deal with burgeoning case loads, state court systems would grow more dense and complex in this period, commonly adopting a three-tiered system with trial, intermediate appellate, and an appellate court of last resort.

Friedman also notes that the period between the Civil War and the end of the century was characterized by the prevalence of activist judges. The variety of jurisdictions offered by American federalism induced responsiveness in the law. While the states might act as laboratories of social legislation, they were also competing sellers of jurisprudence in a vast federal matrix, and easy laws drove out harsh ones. Like their federal counterparts, state appellate courts would develop a doctrine of substantive due process to place limits on legislative power. In some instances, they would use this doctrine to strike down state legislation that had the effect of creating monopolies. At other times, it might be used to overturn state legislation intended to regulate health, safety, or welfare. Horowitz argues that courts transformed the law after the Civil War by developing new common law doctrines that subsidized American economic expansion and benefited the wealthy. It is in this period that legal formalism emerged, which held that judges should restrict themselves to abstract reasoning rooted in laissez-faire economic principles.

By the beginning of the twentieth century, a more sociological and liberal approach to judging began to develop. Judges began to recognize that extra-judicial materials could be useful in understanding intentions of legislators or the social implications of law. As a judge of the New York Court of Appeals, Benjamin Cardozo would write *The Nature of the Judicial Process,* in which he stated that judges were more than simple machines.[8] Cardozo believed that judges created laws, but he remained wedded to the notion that justice demanded respect for precedent or litigants would lose faith in the courts. Faced with vexing social problems, the duty of judges was not to find law but to create it in a manner that was bound by then-contemporary views of science. Cardozo called for a scientific analysis of social needs to pursue the law's ultimate end of achieving social justice. Like-minded judges in the 1920s and 1930s remained devoted to precedent but also pressed for a new social vision to avoid injustice. These judges would work to undermine the classical legal order that protected property and modified the law to fit emerging social needs. Nineteenth-century attitudes would disintegrate as judges came to view their role as one of social policymaking.

The broadened role of state courts called for heightened concerns about their integrity. Commenting on the changes in New York, William Nelson believes the "disintegration of shared values and the collapse of the doctrine of precedent . . . made it necessary to convince the public, and perhaps even the judges themselves, of the special dignity and integrity of the bench."[9] To be viewed as legitimate, the courts had to take ethics and discipline very seriously, and Nelson observes a dramatic increase in disciplinary actions in the 1960s and 1970s. The public might not always believe in the correctness of court decisions, but with attention to ethics, they could at least have faith in the integrity of the decision-making process.

Without institutional legitimacy, courts could not function as consequential partners in governance. State courts have pursued legitimacy throughout U.S. history but the approach has differed from one era to the next. In the contemporary era, much ink is spilled regarding the politics of judicial selection, the increasing role of money in judicial elections, and judicial ethics. Judges need to be seen as above conventional politics at a time when their decisions reach beyond precedent to create law. In another era, the quest for legitimacy was also pervasive but, as Friedman notes,

> late 19th century judges stressed very strongly that they did not make law. . . . There were ample reasons why the judges assumed so docile a posture. For one thing, it provided magnificent camouflage. It disclaimed responsibility for unpopular opinions. It was the one reason why judges, even though elected, did not stand naked before the partisan public. . . . The flight into technicality and personality was only apparently a flight toward a more humble, self-effacing role. . . . They claimed the expert's privilege of monopoly control of their business and insisted that what they did, like all experts' work, was value-free. These were valuable postures of self-defense.[10]

Because they have nurtured their legitimacy over time, state courts, like their federal counterparts, have been able to be active participants in governance, withstanding partisan tides while taking controversial stands. For much of U.S. history, state courts have performed like safety valves, taking on mediating functions between competing or conflicting social and economic interests, and they have done so authoritatively because they have promoted an image of propriety and legitimacy. This image has allowed them to make adjustments in policy in less visible ways than conventional majoritarian politics, reducing the agenda of more open political processes to manageable proportions.

State Courts: Part of the Method of Democracy

The choice to become a democratic republic over two centuries ago raised many important issues about governance that still are unresolved to this day. The term "republic" is derived from the Latin term *res publica*, or "public affair," and implies ownership or control of the state by the population at large. From this perspective, democracy is a system that promotes participatory decision making, either directly or through elections. Democracy is much more than this, however. William Riker observed that there is no single, authoritative definition of democracy. Instead, democracy is comprised of properties "found in these documents . . . [that are] elements of the democratic method . . . [and that] are means to render voting practically effective and politically significant, and all the elements of the democratic ideal [that] are moral extensions and elaborations of the features of the method that make voting work."[11]

From this perspective, democracy is not simply the opportunity to vote in elections but also is a broader methodology that renders voting practically effective and politically significant. For this to occur, not all issues can be subject to voting. Agendas must be set and alternatives must be narrowed.

Creating opportunities for voting and participation was not the primary preoccupation of the framers of the U.S. Constitution. Quite the contrary, most of the framers were much more concerned with the instability and factionalism that could arise from mass participation in governance. Most notably, James Madison, commonly considered the architect of the Constitution, was preoccupied with the instability that could accompany a democratic system. He is perhaps most remembered for his observations concerning the mischief of faction: since conflict is sewn in the nature of man, how do we manage conflicts without destroying liberty? Like other theorists of democracy, Madison also was troubled that a key element of most democratic systems—majority rule—has some undesirable properties other than rampant factionalism. Madison was very familiar with the Marquis de Condorcet's seminal *Essai* where the French philosopher observed that for any option that might be chosen by a majority of voters, there is usually some other option, preferred by a different majority, which can upset it.[12]

For Madison and the other framers, there were thus both practical and theoretical reasons to devise a government that did not depend on simple majority rule. Factionalism could undermine the rights of all, and cyclical voting could produce destructive instability. It was imperative that very few issues were subject to majority rule. The result was a system of checks and balances between branches of government and a division of power between levels of government. It is a system of government that allows expression of popular sentiment on a limited number of issues at differing levels of government while, at the same time, removing many issues and alternatives from the public agenda. The resulting system places greater emphasis on stability than on responsiveness to mass preferences. As Madison noted in *Federalist* 37, "stability in government is essential to national character."[13]

It was not until almost two centuries later that scholars came to appreciate the vital role of government's structural arrangements in promoting stability. Nobel Prize economist Kenneth Arrow sought to discover which democratic voting rules or procedures for collective decision-making would be able to aggregate existing individual preference rankings into a single consistent collective outcome. He demonstrated that no such rules or procedures appear to be available and showed that democratic decision-making processes cannot be both fair and rational. Arrow's core insight is known as the voters' paradox. That paradox, the one initially noted by Condorcet and familiar to Madison, lay dormant until Arrow and others rediscovered it in the 1950s. The paradox indicates that decision making by the time-honored democratic practice of majority vote can produce nothing but perpetual cycling among the various options. The problem only worsens when expanded to large, real world settings where there are many more than three policy options available and far more than three individuals entitled to participate.

Given Arrow's insight, it is clear that democratic processes alone cannot produce definitive stable outcomes, and one must wonder what imparts the high degree of stability observed in the United States. Left only to majoritarian processes, rampant instability or factionalism should result. So why does this does not occur? The answer is simple: because the structure, rules, and procedures of the democracy reduce, divide, and distribute conflicts between branches and levels of government, subjecting only a small proportion of issues to anything like broad majoritarian processes.

Americans vote for their legislators from geographic subunits, not from the nation at large. As the nation was reminded in 2000, the president is selected by electors and not by the popular vote. Statewide voting for the United States Senate, state officials (including some state supreme court justices), and referenda or initiatives are the majoritarian processes of the largest scale in American politics. The evolution of the U.S. two-party system has, for the most part, narrowed the viable alternatives down to two candidates for most offices. One need only to reflect on the presidential election of 2000 to appreciate how more alternatives (e.g., Pat Buchanan, Ralph Nader) contribute to uncertainty or instability. Ballot measures in states with initiative processes remind us, too, that there are impassioned groups in American society striving to impose their values on the values of others. Even in the twenty-first century, there are indications that chaos might lurk just below the surface of the seeming stability.

State Courts and Democratic Processes

What if Americans had more alternatives to consider? As far back as the election of 1800 to as recently as the election of 2000, having more than two candidates for an office has lead to confusion and ambiguity in outcomes. In large measure, the U.S. two-party system narrows choices for elective office down to the nominees of the two major parties. They do not do this without a little help, however. State party organizations have succeeded over the years in passing legislation that makes ballot access difficult for any but the two major parties. Ballot access requirements make it difficult for third party or independent candidates to run in many states. However, ballot access laws are litigated, frequently finding their way into both federal and state courts. State courts thus play a major role in shaping the terms of engagement for political parties in this country and the number of alternative candidates from which voters can choose. This process of controlling alternatives can determine outcomes, precisely in the same manner understood by Condorcet, Madison, and Arrow.

To appreciate this fundamental point, consider this example about the 2004 presidential election. Recently, state or county court judgments in Arizona, Florida, Iowa, Michigan, Nevada, New Hampshire, Oregon, Pennsylvania, and West Virginia determined whether Ralph Nader appeared on the presidential ballot in these states. If the 2004 election were even remotely like the 2000 election, Nader's presence or absence on one or a few state ballots would have played a decisive role in determining the president of the United States.

What if Americans participated more in direct democracy? As it is, there is considerable activity in this area but there might well be much more if not for the courts. For example, in the 2002 election, there were 202 statewide ballot measures in forty states. Voters approved approximately 62 percent of them. In 2004, ballot measures on issues as varied as gay marriage, the minimum wage, and immigration appeared on state ballots. Voters considered whether to place caps on medical malpractice awards in a number of states. Florida voters cast ballots regarding parental notification before a minor receives an abortion and whether to raise the minimum wage above the national standard.

Over time, initiative and referenda processes bring many rights and privileges of Americans into play, and state courts frequently are being asked to invalidate these initiatives before or after they are passed. State courts also are being asked to rule on conflicts over the conditions for allowing initiatives to gain entry to the ballot in the first place. For example, a simple Lexis-Nexis search of California cases involving "ballot measure" reveals that these types of issues have appeared in over one hundred court cases since 1984. Of course, California may be an extreme example, but the fundamental point remains. State courts shape the frequency and scope of ballot initiatives in states where initiatives are allowed, thereby ultimately influencing the character of public policy in doing so.

Throughout U.S. history, state courts have played a fundamental role in keeping a lid on majoritarian impulses. They have tinkered with the particulars of majoritarian outcomes by resolving disputes and restricting alternatives. State courts have done this commonly in obscurity but with the confidence of the American people. It could reasonably be argued that this lid is too tight because political processes in America do not offer alternatives that are attractive to many Americans.[14] Alternatively, a much more expansive but chaotic process could ensue if barriers to the ballot were reduced, if opportunities to use the initiative process were more open, or if courts were more deferential to laws passed through ballot measures. Depending on one's values, the limits to third parties and initiative measures enforced by state courts may be viewed as a good or a bad thing. Most assuredly they cannot be ignored as unimportant. Directly or indirectly, state court actions shape the scope and direction of popular participation in American politics and play a decisive role in the democratic methodology. At best, settling disputes concerning ballot access or the acceptability of ballot initiatives is a rare but nonetheless important aspect of state court activity. Much more of their effort is devoted to handling routine criminal cases and civil disputes. To be effective, a democratic system must allow the peaceful articulation of demands and resolution of competing claims in a manner that promotes a sense of justice and social unity.

If public opinion polls are any indication, state court systems perform this role very well. In a 2002 national survey, 77 percent of those polled expressed some to a great deal of confidence in their state court system, while only 22 percent said they had just a little or no confidence in these courts. Only between 6 to 12 percent felt their state courts were doing a poor job, 61 percent thought the judges were independent, and 79 percent believed they were qualified.[15] While somewhat short of the support expressed for the United States Supreme Court, these levels exceed support for high courts in European countries, suggesting that state courts enjoy a high degree of legitimacy.[16]

Based on the sheer bulk of criminal and civil disputes addressed in state courts, it is evident that these courts provide the dominant means through which many demands are articulated and many rights are protected. Citizens obey the law based on perceptions of fairness or unfairness.[17] This respect for the rule of law is essential for democracy, and state courts play a vital role in this process not only by dispensing with a mountain of legal disputes, but doing so in a manner that promotes the widespread perception of fairness and legitimacy. It is easy to imagine how the seeds of rebellion could be sewn if significant numbers of citizens felt they were treated unfairly and quit obeying laws. Anarchy or ever-harsher government actions would seem to be a likely consequence. Clearly, state court systems are a vital component of the delicate balance of democracy.

All this is not to suggest that the public never challenges the authority of state courts. However, these incidents have been rare. For example, presumably because voters felt that judges were too lenient, voters in Washington passed a referendum in 1993 calling for "three strikes and you're out" mandatory sentencing. In practice, the referendum was designed to remove judges' discretion when sentencing criminal defendants ever convicted of three cumulative felonies by requiring mandatory life sentences for these defendants. In 1994, California followed suit with similar legislation, and by 2004 twenty-six states had some form of sentencing law like the one initially enacted in Washington in 1993. Thus, even though state courts generally enjoy substantial support from the public, the widespread fear of crime prompted the residents of many states to reduce the latitude of state courts in sentencing decisions.

Similarly, but within the context of civil law, in response to the perception that liability insurance coverage was becoming more costly and less available, most states enacted legislation in the mid-1980s that reformed common law rules and other court procedures involving tort litigation. Further, tort reform remains an active issue in many states.

In sum, "three strikes" rules and recent forms of tort reform indicate that even though the public expresses high amounts of general trust and confidence in their state court systems, the fear of crime and perceptions of leniency or excessive generosity can, and have, fueled popular efforts to circumscribe court actions. Nonetheless, while popular movements to make courts tougher on crime or to end the so-called lawsuit lotteries have gained voter support in many states, courts have remained very trusted and esteemed institutions. By sizable majorities, the American public believes that state courts administer justice in a fair and impartial manner, and mass movements to circumscribe judicial choice are rare. It is easy to imagine a distrustful public passing many laws to limit state court discretion if Americans did not have confidence in these tribunals. In practice, state courts have substantial latitude in most areas of law, making relatively quiet and minute adjustments to democratic outcomes or procedures in relative obscurity.

Courts in Practice

As discussed, state courts play a critical role in resolving disputes for individual litigants but also serve to stabilize the democratic political system. Now it is important to shift to a detailed description of some important dimensions of state judicial politics related to the earlier discussion. At this point, the focus is on state supreme courts, for a number of important theoretical and practical reasons.

First, as described, state courts are enormously important legal and political institutions, with the awesome responsibility for resolving the vast majority of the nation's legal disputes. As the courts of last resort, state supreme courts have the final authority on these issues most basic to citizens' daily lives. Furthermore, in rendering decisions, state supreme courts exercise extraordinary discretion. They interpret not only state laws but also federal laws and, in the process, contribute significantly to public policy. Finally, as power continues to devolve from the federal government to the states, state courts are assuming an increasingly central role in litigation and politics, making discussions of these institutions particularly timely.[18] Assessing the nature of state courts, their idiosyncrasies, and the latest developments within, is an important task. In fact, the failure to understanding the states results in a very incomplete understanding of American politics. From a practical standpoint, the recently completed State Supreme Court Data Project provides comprehensive and systematic data about the decisions of the states' highest courts from 1995 though 1997, a resource that simply does not exist for other state courts.

The exercise that follows with the State Supreme Court Data Project involves simple description and should not be mistaken for commentary or criticism. Also, the patterns to be presented are fascinating and clearly beg for explanation. Nonetheless, while critically important to seek to explain why the various patterns and variations to be described actually occur and with what political implications, such a task is well beyond the scope of this chapter. In fact, such an enterprise will demand considerable time and scholarly focus over the next several years if not the next decade.

With those caveats duly noted, consider the fact that within state supreme courts are individual decision makers with highly diverse backgrounds, experiences, and values. Moreover, because of the sheer volume of cases, these courts address virtually every legal issue and fact pattern likely to arise at the appellate level. Similarly, in resolving this vast array of issues, state supreme court justices interpret and apply a variety of constitutional provisions, statutes, and other types of law. State supreme courts also present a wide array of institutional features and configurations, both in terms of structures, and external and internal rules and procedures. Finally, the American states, the environments within which state supreme courts operate, are diverse politically, economically, and culturally. Therefore, within the context of state supreme courts, the range of judicial authority in the United States and the variety of ways in which these important institutions contribute to democracy can clearly be seen.

The Work of State Supreme Courts in the American Democracy

State supreme courts manifest extraordinary differences in the nature of their dockets, the propensity to favor or disfavor certain categories of litigants, the extent to which they supervise and correct the lower courts, their willingness to engage in the process of separation of powers by invalidating the actions of the other branches of government and citizen initiatives on constitutional grounds, and the degree to which individual justices are willing to step in front of the purple curtain and dissent from decisions of the court majority. These important and often dramatic variations across states reflect significant differences in the fundamental functions of these courts and in the exact nature of the role of the judiciary in state and national politics. In the aggregate, these variations have substantial impacts on access to government and on the distribution of wealth and power in the United States.

State Supreme Court Dockets

Consider Figure 1, for example, which describes state supreme court dockets from 1995 through 1997 (n = 21,296). In this graph, miscellaneous cases consist of a variety of specialized issues, such as juvenile cases and certification, that fall outside the usual range of criminal and civil disputes.

As Figure 1 illustrates, state supreme courts on average decide more civil cases than criminal. In fact, civil litigation occupies 60 percent or more of the

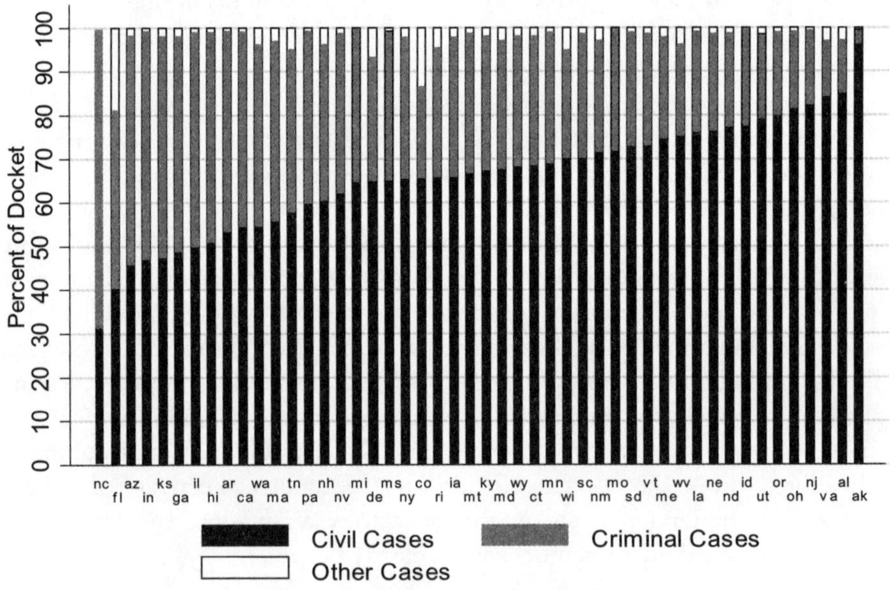

NOTE: Oklahoma and Texas have two supreme courts and have been excluded from this graph.

SOURCE: State Supreme Court Data Project 1995–1997.

Figure 1

dockets in all but thirteen supreme courts. However, state supreme courts vary dramatically in the extent to which they specialize in matters of criminal or civil law.

At one extreme, the high court in Alaska hears virtually no criminal cases and instead focuses its attention almost exclusively on civil matters. Less than 5 percent of the docket in Alaska involves criminal law and other cases, while about 96 percent of the docket is civil. Alabama is a close second, devoting 85 percent of its docket space to civil litigation. At the other extreme, almost 70 percent of the cases in North Carolina are criminal, with only 31 percent devoted to civil issues. Florida is quite similar to North Carolina, dedicating only about 40 percent of its docket to civil matters. These dramatic differences in docket composition across the states suggest that supreme courts play very different functional roles within their respective judicial systems and states. State supreme courts can function largely either to strengthen or weaken the coercive arm of the state against convicted criminals, or to interject judicial authority into the relationships among a variety of classes of public and private litigants. These choices have the consequence of providing varying levels of access to judicial power to different groups in society and, depending on the nature of the decisions, play a decisive role in determining how power and wealth are allocated in the states.

These different roles are further evidenced in the specific components of the criminal and civil dockets. Figure 2 illustrates the proportion of criminal cases that involve murder, the most serious and publicly salient crime, and also distinguishes murder cases in which the death penalty actually was imposed by the trial court from all other murder cases.

Generally, seven state supreme courts devote over 50 percent of their criminal dockets to murder cases, while nine states spend less than 10 percent. At the extremes, North Carolina dedicates a whopping 91 percent of the criminal docket to murder cases, making these about the only type of criminal case reviewed by this court, while Maine hears almost none. Recall from the previous figure that only about 31 percent of North Carolina's docket involves civil matters; thus, taken together, North Carolina emerges as a state supreme court which largely is a forum for reviewing murder cases, which constitute 63 percent of the court's overall docket.

Regarding the death penalty, seventeen states have no death penalty cases on their dockets, either because the state did not authorize capital punishment from 1995 through 1997 (Alaska, Hawaii, Iowa, Maine, Massachusetts, Michigan, Minnesota, North Dakota, Rhode Island, Vermont, West Virginia, and Wisconsin) or because there are no capital cases to review (Kansas, New Hampshire, New Mexico, New York, and Wyoming). On the other hand, states like Virginia and Arizona hear mostly capital cases, of the murder cases on their dockets. In fact, in Florida and Arizona, about half of the criminal docket involves capital murder. In

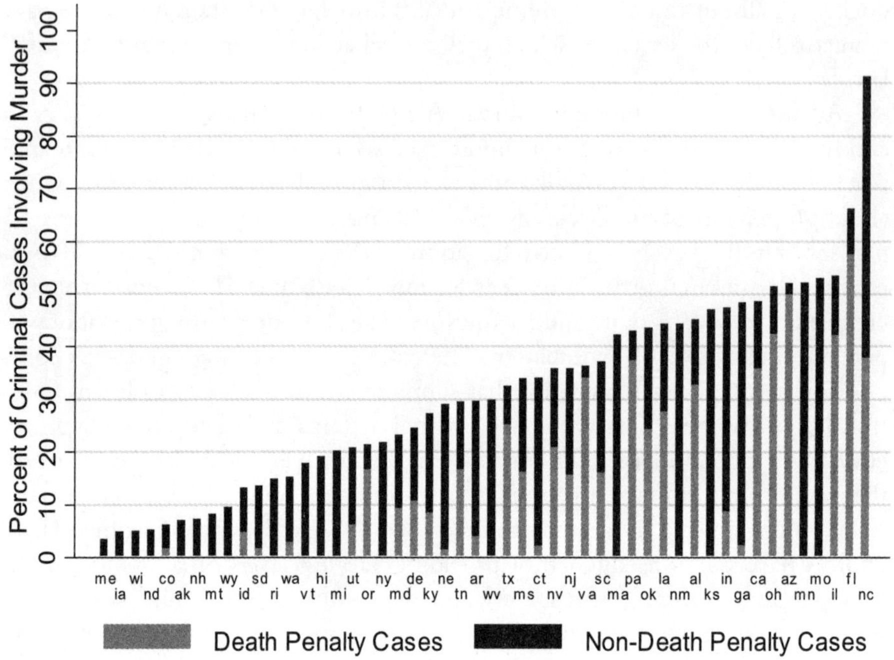

SOURCE: State Supreme Court Data Project 1995–1997.

Figure 2

these states, among other things, the justices, who are retained in elections, should be in a more precarious position with voters in their states, who could react negatively at election time to prior decisions overturning death sentences.

When considering the characteristics of civil dockets, recall from Figure 1 that most state supreme courts focus on civil litigation. Figure 3 illustrates the extent to which civil actions, which compose over 60 percent of most supreme courts' dockets, involve torts. Again, the substantial diversity among states is apparent. At one end of the spectrum, states like Georgia, Florida, Indiana, and Oregon devote only a small fraction of their civil dockets to tort cases, while Alabama, Illinois, Michigan, and Tennessee focus about half of their total civil dockets on torts. In fact, given the large percentage of civil cases on the Alabama Supreme Court docket and the considerable percentage of tort cases therein, the Alabama Court spends much of the time operating as a distributive arena. Recall that this stands in stark contradistinction to North Carolina at the other end of the spectrum, which is heavily loaded with capital cases. In fact, it appears that the job of supreme court justice is vastly different between these two states, along with the types of interests drawn to these courts and the typical stakes involved in the cases.

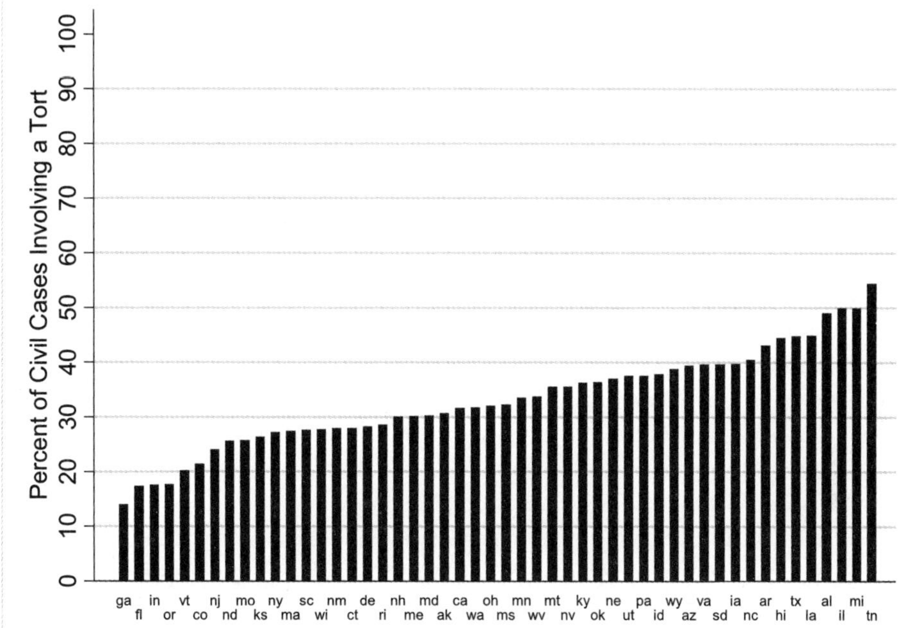

SOURCE: State Supreme Court Data Project 1995–1997.

Figure 3

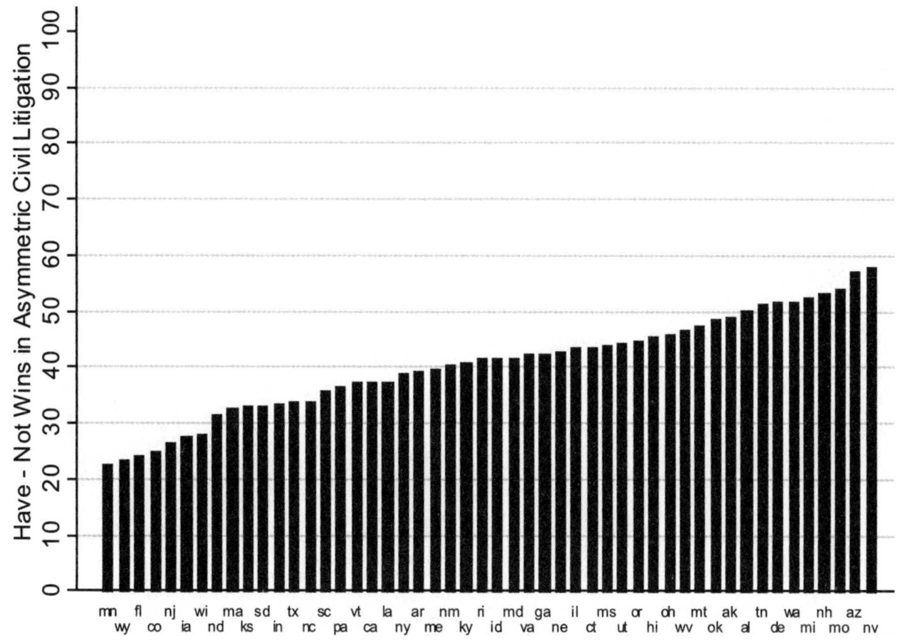

SOURCE: State Supreme Court Data Project 1995–1997.

Figure 4

Who Wins in State Supreme Courts

The extent to which courts favor "haves" (i.e., businesses, governments, groups) over "have-nots" (i.e., individuals) in civil litigation has been debated extensively in the scholarly literature, with lots of claims and counterclaims about the ability of courts to protect the downtrodden versus protecting the wealth and power of the entrenched economic and political elite. Figure 4 illustrates the extent to which have-nots win in state supreme courts in all civil cases involving these two sets of litigants. As Figure 4 documents, the states vary substantially along this dimension. In general, state supreme court decisions are skewed against have-not victories; individuals win less than half the time in all but nine states in cases involving more powerful litigants. Have-nots are most unsuccessful in Minnesota, Wyoming, and Florida, where have-nots win less than 25 percent of the time in these cases. However, have-nots have a slight advantage in Tennessee, Delaware, Washington, Michigan, New Hampshire, Missouri, Arizona, and Nevada.

Figure 5 examines who wins in criminal cases, revealing some intriguing patterns. State supreme courts vary tremendously in their willingness support defendants in criminal cases, either by reversing convictions or sentences. Concerning convictions, in Colorado, Kansas, Arkansas, Wyoming, and Ohio, for example, defendants prevail in about 5 percent or less of their appeals, while in Oregon and

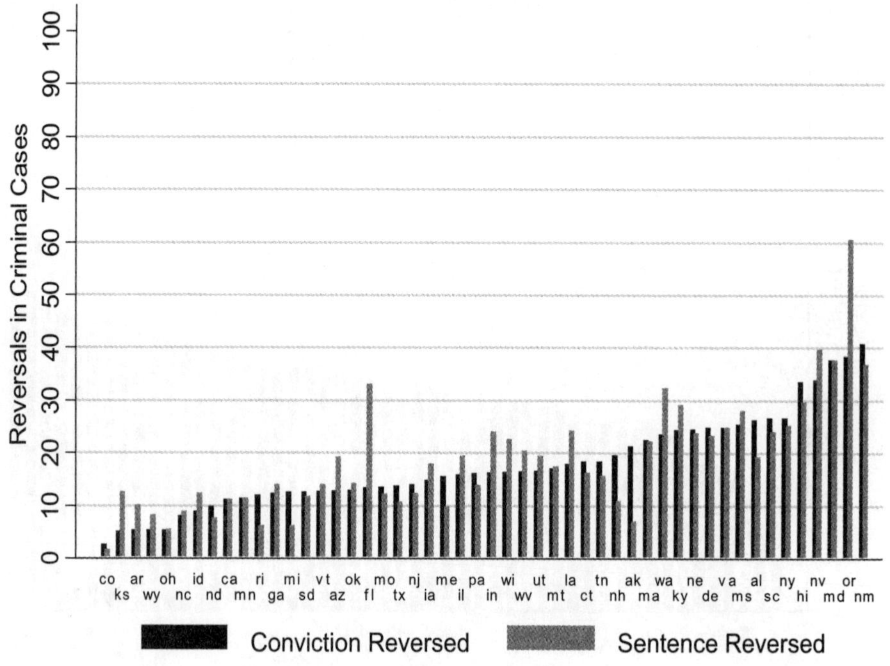

SOURCE: State Supreme Court Data Project 1995–1997.

Figure 5

New Mexico they are successful in about 40 percent. Concerning sentences, many states are more likely to reverse sentences than convictions, with Oregon really standing out by overturning just over 60 percent. In fact, states like Oregon can be viewed as being quite active in supervising the decisions of the lower courts in matters of criminal law and, more broadly speaking, in checking the power of government to deprive individuals of important rights and freedoms.

Supervision of the Lower Courts

Concerning general propensities to reverse the lower courts, Figure 6 illustrates these tendencies among state supreme courts. Like the previous figures describing other dimensions of state supreme court decision making, Figure 6 portrays the incredible variation among courts of their willingness to reverse, along with the somewhat surprising result of the extent to which they do so. In this and all subsequent graphs, the two supreme courts in Texas and Oklahoma are considered separately. The civil courts of last resort, the Texas Supreme Court and Oklahoma Supreme Court, are designated as "txs" and "oks" in the graphs. Similarly, the criminal courts of last resort, the Texas Court of Criminal Appeals and the Oklahoma Supreme Court, are labeled as "txc" and "okc."

As Figure 6 illustrates, twenty-six state supreme courts reverse the lower court, either fully or in part, in at least half of the cases on their dockets. The

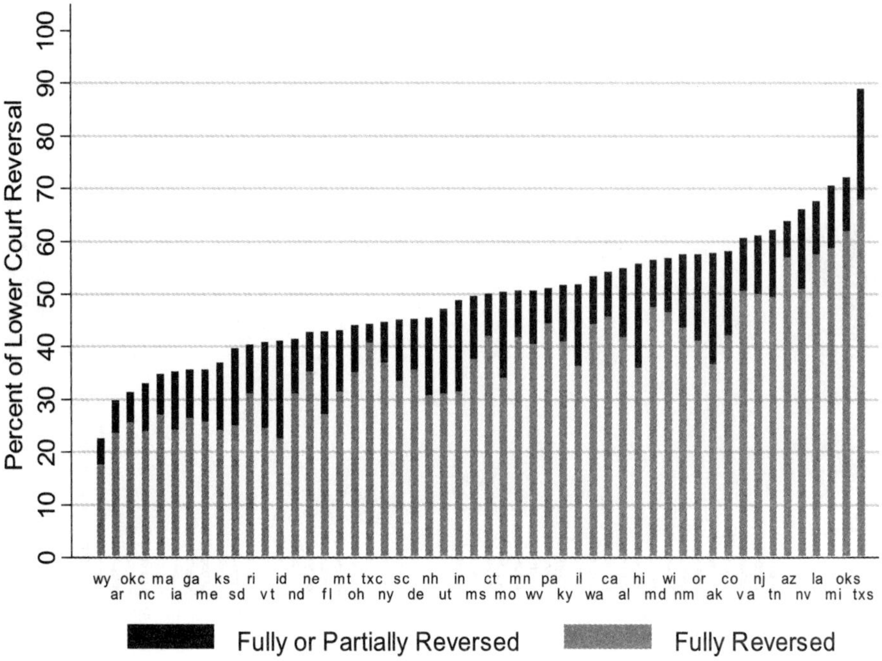

SOURCE: State Supreme Court Data Project 1995–1997.

Figure 6

Texas Supreme Court leads the pack with a reversal rate of almost 90 percent, while Wyoming secures the opposite end of the spectrum with a reversal rate of about 22 percent. Clearly, the supervisory role of state supreme courts in the state judicial system differs considerably from state to state. Also fascinating are the differences between the civil and criminal courts of last resort in Texas and Oklahoma. While the Texas and Oklahoma Supreme Courts have the highest lower court reversal rates of all state courts of last resort, the two criminal courts of last resort in these states are below the median. In fact, the Oklahoma Court of Criminal Appeals has one of the lowest reversal rates. Obviously, much is at play in these two sets of courts to produce such different outcomes on this crucial dimension of judicial decision-making.

State Supreme Courts in the System of Separation of Powers

Figure 7 displays the percentage of cases on each court's docket involving constitutional challenges under the state or federal constitution to a statute, executive order, or ballot initiative. In most courts (forty-seven of fifty-two), these cases do not occupy much docket space, constituting 10 percent or less of the overall docket. However, some states decide substantial proportions of these cases. At the

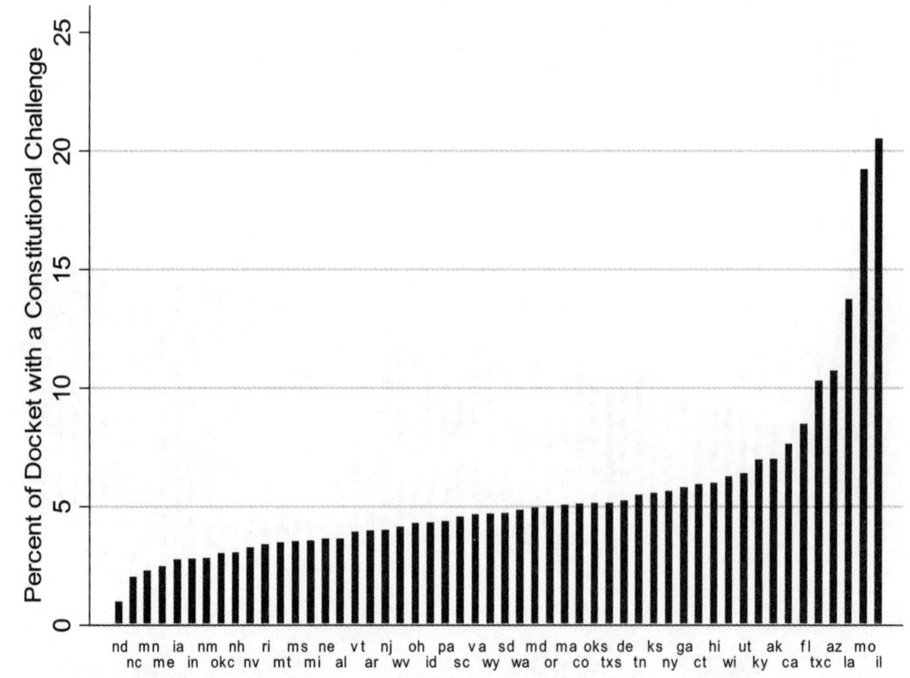

SOURCE: State Supreme Court Data Project 1995–1997.

Figure 7

extreme, about one of every five cases in Missouri and Illinois asks the court to rule on the constitutionality of the actions of other actors in the political system. Keep in mind, however, that these are likely to be highly salient cases politically, so that even a few of these per term can place the state high court in the political spotlight.

How do other actors fare in constitutional litigation? Figure 8 presents these data, which are in some sense quite surprising. Although most states have few of these cases on their dockets, in some states the tendency to invalidate on constitutional grounds is significant. Fifteen state high courts invalidate in at least 30 percent of the cases raising issues of constitutionality. Clearly, in a sizable proportion of states, supreme courts are very active players in the system of separation of powers. From a different perspective, when one considers states like Missouri and Illinois with relatively larger proportions of these cases on their dockets, a reversal rate over 20 percent, which both of these courts have, means that the supreme court is spending a considerable amount of time taking on the legislature and voters, even though the court does not have a general tendency to invalidate on constitutional grounds. Considering the exercise of judicial review as a counter-majoritarian action, these data reveal that courts in some states are most willing to perform this function.

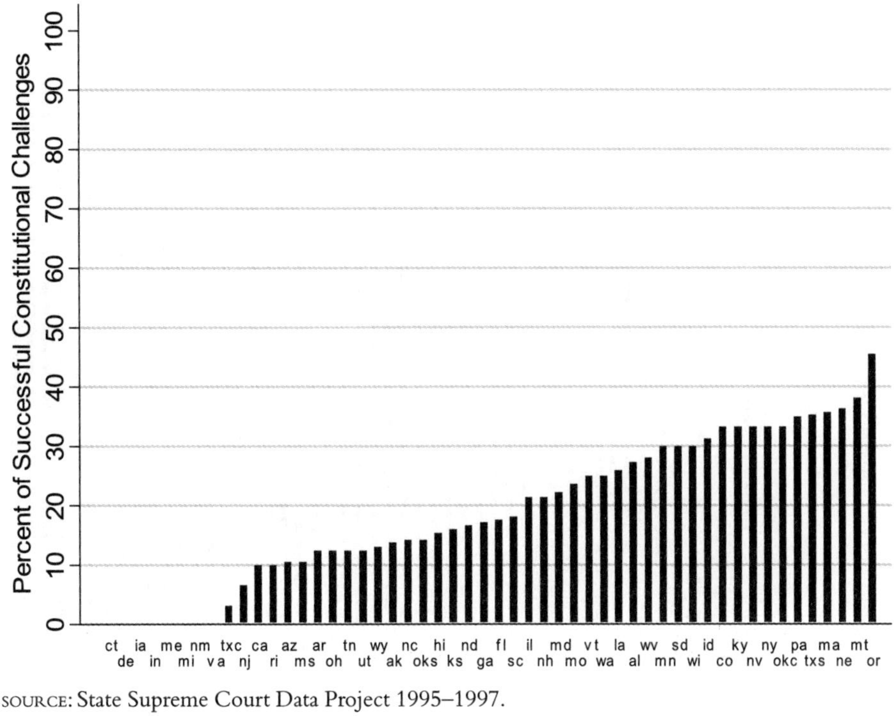

SOURCE: State Supreme Court Data Project 1995–1997.

Figure 8

On the other hand, the courts in some states did not invalidate on constitutional grounds at all during the period being considered. The high courts in Connecticut, Delaware, Indiana, Iowa, Maine, Michigan, New Mexico, and Virginia failed to find constitutional fault with any statute, ordinance, or ballot initiative from 1995 through 1997.

Factionalism in State Supreme Courts

Finally, the degree of dissent in state supreme courts is considered. Dissent rates are determined by a number of factors, including, but certainly not limited to, ideological disagreement among the justices of a court. However, dissent can have political consequences. Unanimous decisions may be perceived as more legitimate and, for the individual justice, can shield an unpopular decision with the power of the court. Dissent, on the other hand, represents factionalism of some sort and has the opposite consequences of those just described. Thus, dissent can be problematic for a court or for individual justices, depending on the extent to which it occurs, and in which cases.

Figure 9 illustrates dissent rates in state supreme courts from 1995 through 1997. As these data document, most states have unanimity rates that exceed 70

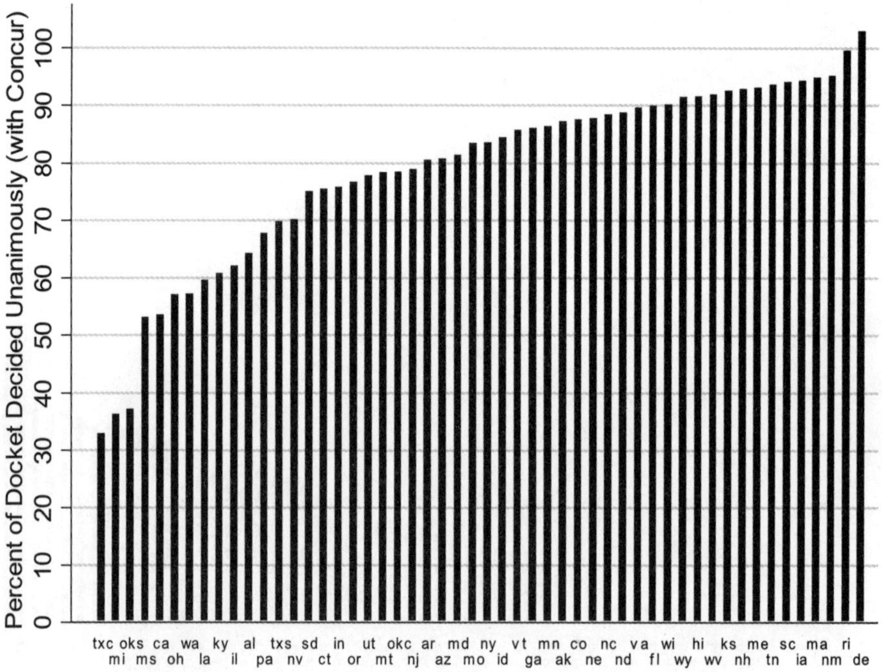

SOURCE: State Supreme Court Data Project 1995–1997.

Figure 9

percent, demonstrating a high level of formal consensus in these courts. Only three courts (Texas Court of Criminal Appeals, Michigan, and the Oklahoma Supreme Court) have dissent in more than half their cases. Thus, in most state supreme courts, many decisions do not reflect the kind of factionalism that can raise issues of legitimacy for the court or cause difficulty for individual justices who deviate from popular decisions, but there certainly are exceptions to this general rule.

Democratic Processes and State Supreme Courts: The Special Case of Electing Judges

One intriguing way in which democratic processes and courts clearly intersect is in the realm of judicial selection. In the American states, most judges are elected and must face voters regularly to retain their seats. While debates over judicial selection are complicated and cannot be summarized effectively in a single essay, one important concern is whether electing judges undermines judicial legitimacy by requiring judges to raise campaign funds and engage in other activities that mar the image of impartiality. There is another perspective, however, that suggests that elections might serve to enhance the legitimacy of courts by giving voters control over the composition of the bench and by serving to sensitize judges to the preferences of constituencies on those matters of law that more clearly involve public policy making than application of settled rules of law. Regardless of which system of selection might be best overall, there are numerous ways in which elections interject democratic pressures into the process of judging and complicate the normative goal of judicial independence.

As studies of elections to many different types of offices have established, electoral competition forges observable linkages between citizens and government, enhancing the representative function. Among other things, incumbents chosen in relatively competitive races are more likely to defer to the preferences of their constituencies when casting votes on controversial issues rather than choosing policy alternatives that better reflect their own personal preferences. Moreover, tighter margins of victory increase the likelihood of future electoral challenge and possible electoral defeat, thus promoting another cycle of competition to enhance the incumbent-constituency connection. Finally, some challengers actually do win, and the resulting turnover in personnel can serve to bring the institution more in line with public preferences generally.

Regarding judicial elections, one of the most important questions about this relationship between democratic processes and judicial decision making is whether judicial elections really have the sort of competitive nature that could provoke such a response. Some basic information about state supreme court elections from 1990 through 2000 provide some preliminary answers. Generally speaking, there are lots of reasons to think that they might.

Consider, for instance, reelection rates over the past decade for the United States House of Representatives, United States Senate, statehouses, and state supreme courts. From 1990 through 2000, reelection rates were, respectively, 94.1 percent, 89.3 percent, 85.1 percent, and 84.1 percent.[19] Thus, the likelihood of electoral defeat in state supreme courts is on average at least equivalent to, if not higher than, the electoral threat for other important state and federal offices. In fact, seats in the House of Representatives, the quintessential representative institution, are considerably safer on average than seats on state supreme courts.

Further, competition in the form of challengers has been increasing in state supreme court elections, particularly in nonpartisan elections. In 1990, only one of every three justices (37.5 percent) in nonpartisan states was forced face challengers, but by 2000 two of three (68.0 percent) were challenged for reelection. At the same time, partisan elections have a challenge rate of 81.2 percent and now are virtually guaranteed to produce challengers for justices seeking reelection to the state high court bench. Thus, while there are differences between partisan and nonpartisan elections regarding competition, both potentially could serve to interject democratic politics into judicial decision making.

Finally, although state supreme court justices are more likely to be challenged in partisan elections than nonpartisan elections, in contested races the margins of victory are about the same in these two types of elections. The average percentage of the vote in contested nonpartisan elections from 1990 through 2000 is 57.08 percent (n=74) while the average margin in contested partisan elections is 55.04 percent (n=65).[20] Generally speaking, elections won by 60 percent of the vote or less are considered marginal, and a substantial portion of contested supreme court seats can be so classified. Thus, overall, electing judges might not only give voters direct control over the composition of the bench but also might have substantial consequences for the choices justices make under competitive electoral conditions. Whether this is a desirable or undesirable consequence is left to the evaluation of the reader.

A Note on Membership Change

Aside from elections, frequent membership change is the norm on the state high court bench. In fact, it is critical to observe that state courts differ dramatically from their federal counterparts in this respect. Consider, for example, that the last appointment to the United States Supreme Court was Stephen Breyer in 1994. However, from January 1994 through May 2000, nine justices in Nebraska left the bench (representing complete membership replacement), while New Mexico and West Virginia each had eight turnovers. On average, from January

1994 through May 2000, each state supreme court had between seven and eight natural courts (i.e., periods of stable membership).

Stated differently, a time span of approximately six and one-half years (January 1994–May 2000) produced substantial changes due to death, resignation, retirement, and electoral defeat in state supreme courts, resulting in *385 natural courts* in the fifty-two courts of last resort during that period. This is a period in which there were only *two natural courts* on the United States Supreme Court. Because of the high turnover on these courts, short periods of time nonetheless produce membership changes comparable to many decades on the United States Supreme Court. This extraordinary rate of change has consequences relevant to the courts' legitimacy and connection to democratic majorities. Generally speaking, courts should be kept in line, or brought back into line, with majority preferences through the process of membership replacement, and it appears that substantial opportunities for this important process exist in state supreme courts.

Conclusion

This theoretical and practical look at state courts has highlighted their critical importance to American democracy and, more specifically, to the maintenance of order and stability in the United States. At the broadest theoretical level, state courts remove choices from majoritarian politics and thus curb the kind of instability that can result from unrestricted agendas.

Similarly, state courts, particularly state supreme courts, engage in politics in different ways and thus influence political access and outcomes in different ways. While all courts are a forum for dispute resolution and generally enjoy a great deal of legitimacy with the public, courts vary in the extent to which they are able or willing to consider certain types of issues, provide access to particular groups, rule in favor of certain classes of interests, supervise the lower courts and thus control outcomes within the state judicial hierarchy, take on legislatures and voters in the game of separation of powers, and demonstrate factionalism within the ranks of the justices. Further, courts are connected to democratic processes to varying degrees through various alternative processes for selecting and retaining judges, and through the incentives or disincentives for service on the bench. In other words, courts not only serve democracy, courts also are controlled to varying degrees by democratic processes, normative ideals of judicial independence aside.

Given the incredible variation among the states' highest courts, one scarcely can imagine how a single court system could provide the sorts of democratic alternatives described while simultaneously responding, at least to some extent, to political pressures that promote legitimacy and guard judicial power. Regarding courts, one size does not fit all, and the republic has survived in part because federalism allows these critical variations.

Notes

1. Alexis de Tocqueville, *Democracy in America*.
2. Stephen Skowronek, *Building a New American State: The Expansion of National Administrative Capacities* (New York: Cambridge University Press, 1982).
3. Morton J. Horowitz, *The Transformation of American Law, 1780–1860*, 1.
4. Ibid., xvii.
5. Kermit Hall, *The Magic Mirror*, 107.
6. Kermit Hall, *The Magic Mirror*.
7. Ibid., 227.
8. Benjamin Cardozo, *The Nature of the Judicial Process* (New Haven, Conn.: Yale University Press, 1921).
9. William E. Nelson, *The Legalist Reformation*, 345.
10. Lawrence M. Friedman, *A History of American Law*, 333.
11. William H. Riker, *Liberalism against Populism*, 49.
12. Marquis de Condorcet, *Essai sur l'application de l'analyze à la probabilité des decisions rendues à la pluralist des voix* (Essay on the Application of Analysis to the Probability of Majority Decisions). Dennis R. McGrath, "James Madison and Social Choice Theory: The Possibility of Republicanism" (Ph.D. diss., University of Maryland, College Park, 1983).
13. Alexander Hamilton, James Madison, and John Jay, *The Federalist Papers,* 26.
14. E. E. Schattschneider, *The Semi-Sovereign People: A Realist's View of Democracy in America*.
15. Deborah Goldberg, Samantha Sanchez, and Bert Brandenberg, eds., *The New Politics of Judicial Elections: How 2002 Was a Watershed* (New York: Justice at Stake Campaign, 2002).
16. James L. Gibson, Gregory A. Caldeira, and Vanessa A. Baird. "On the Legitimacy of National High Courts," *American Political Science Review* 92 (June 1998), 343.
17. Tom Tyler, *Why People Obey Law*.
18. Ronald Weber and Paul Brace, "States and Localities Transformed," in *Change and Continuity in American State and Local Government*. edited by Ronald Weber and Paul Brace (New York: Chatham House, 1999).
19. House and Senate data are calculated from Paul R. Abramson, John H. Aldrich, and David W. Rohde, *Change and Continuity in the 2000 Elections* (Washington, D.C.: CQ Press, 2002), for gubernatorial elections from Richard M. Scammon, Alice McGillivray, and Rhodes Cook. *America Votes 24: A Handbook of Contemporary Election Statistics* (Washington, D.C.: CQ Press, 2001), and for judicial elections from Melinda Gann Hall and Chris Bonneau. "Does Quality Matter? Challengers in State Supreme Court Elections," *American Journal of Political Science* 50 (January 2006), forthcoming.
20. Melinda Gann Hall and Chris Bonneau. "Does Quality Matter? Challengers in State Supreme Court Elections," *American Journal of Political Science* 50 (January 2006), forthcoming.

Bibliography

Cardozo, Benjamin. *The Nature of the Judicial Process.* New Haven, Conn.: Yale University Press, 1921.

Condorcet, Marquis de. *Essai sur l'application de la analyze à la probabilité des decisions rendues à la pluralist des voix.* Paris: De l'Imprimerie royale, 1785.

de Tocqueville, Alexis. *Democracy in America.* Edited and translated by Harvey C. Mansfield and Delba Winthrop. Chicago: University of Chicago Press, 2000.

Friedman, Lawrence M. *A History of American Law.* New York: Simon and Schuster, 1973.

Hall, Kermit. *The Magic Mirror: Law in American History.* New York: Oxford University Press, 1989.

Hamilton, Alexander, James Madison, and John Jay. *The Federalist Papers.* New York: New American Library, 1961.

Horowitz, Morton J. *The Transformation of American Law, 1780–1860.* Cambridge, Mass.: Harvard University Press, 1977.

Nelson, William E. *The Legalist Reformation: Law, Politics and Ideology in New York, 1920–1980.* Chapel Hill: University of North Carolina Press, 2001.

Riker, William H. *Liberalism Against Populism: A Confrontation between the Theory of Democracy and the Theory of Social Choice.* San Francisco: W. H. Freeman, 1982.

Schattschneider, E. E. *The Semi-Sovereign People.* New York: Holt, Rinehart and Winston, 1960.

Skowronek, Stephen. *Building a New American State: The Expansion of National Administrative Capacities.* New York: Cambridge University Press, 1982.

Tyler, Tom. *Why People Obey Law.* New Haven, Conn.: Yale University Press, 1990.

8

AMERICAN COURTS AND DEMOCRACY: A COMPARATIVE PERSPECTIVE

Donald P. Kommers

FROM THE NATION'S FOUNDING UNTIL TODAY, COURTS have been a mainstay of American democracy. They settle legal conflicts between private parties, protect the legal rights of citizens generally, and supervise the administration of ordinary law. But most importantly for present purposes, they possess the power to invalidate laws when found in violation of the Constitution. This power of constitutional judicial review has transformed federal and state courts—the United States Supreme Court in particular—into major political institutions. It could hardly be otherwise in the U.S. system of separated and divided powers. By enforcing limits *on* popular government while reinforcing popular representation *in* government, they play key roles in protecting human rights and preserving self-government. In short, they serve as essential sprockets in the twin wheels of constitutionalism and democracy.

In the years following World War II, the fledgling democracies of Western Europe and Japan established similar courts of judicial review, a development largely inspired by the American experiment. By the year 2000, in what must count as one of the most fascinating political developments in the last half century, nearly all of the world's constitutional democracies, including the emerging states of post-communist Eastern Europe, had established constitutional courts of one kind or another. These tribunals are now virtually synonymous with constitutional democracy. Several have blossomed into judicial institutions comparable in power and prestige to the United States Supreme Court. Among these tribunals, the European Court of Human Rights stands out as the world's leading international constitutional court. The expansion of judicial power almost everywhere in the democratic world has resulted in the globalization of constitutional review—with all that this implies for the range and depth of cross-national influences in judicial structure and policy.

This chapter explores the relationship between American courts and democracy. It seeks to illuminate this relationship by comparing American courts with judicial systems in selected foreign jurisdictions and the extent to which they reflect and support democracy. Its focus is on the democratic character of these systems, whether they inhibit or advance democracy, and what influence they might or should have on each other's organization, procedures, and policies. It also asks whether the American scheme of courts represents the best way to support democracy and whether Americans would enhance the democratic legitimacy of their courts by selectively borrowing from the practices of other nations. Although this chapter considers judicial systems as a whole, its main targets of analysis—apart from the U.S. Supreme Court—are the high courts of judicial review in Germany, Canada, and South Africa.

Courts and Democracy: Preliminary Remarks

A threshold question needs to be addressed: What is democracy and where do courts fit into the structure of government in an age of democracy? For present purposes, democracy may be defined as a political order that combines popular government with a system of entrenched rights enforceable by independent courts of law—in short, a constitutional democracy. A democracy implies a government in which power is vested in the people and exercised by them through regular elections and representative institutions, mechanisms designed to produce laws and policies supported by popular majorities. A *constitutional* democracy, by contrast, places procedural and substantive limits on majority rule. Certain procedural limits are actually calculated to reinforce democracy, often by defending or expanding rights of political participation. Courts reinforce democracy, for example, whenever they strike down laws or practices that deny equal voting rights to minorities, impose unreasonable burdens on a minor party's access to the ballot, or interfere with a group's ability to engage in political association or communication.

A constitutional democracy also imposes substantive limits on popular majorities. These limits are of two kinds: The first embraces a governmental system of checks and balances; the second demands respect for basic human rights. Both are designed to promote liberty. As James Madison wrote in *Federalist* 47, the establishment of separate executive, legislative, and judicial departments is "an essential precaution in favor of liberty." "The accumulation of all powers . . . in the same hands," he continued, "may justly be pronounced the very definition of tyranny." For this reason, he insisted—in *Federalist* 48—that each of the coequal departments should be "checked and restrained by the others." As for human rights, they seek to promote the values of dignity, equality, pluralism, justice, tolerance, and fairness. These values, like participatory rights, also support democracy. They are two sides of the same coin. Democracy empowers persons to govern themselves but self-government is impossible without the enjoyment of personal liberty.[1]

In the received opinion of today, the realization of democracy—as defined—requires independent courts of law empowered to invalidate majoritarian laws and policies when found to be unconstitutional. As a general principle, this is a plausible proposition. But is it totally convincing? Owen M. Fiss, a prominent constitutional scholar at Yale University, has remarked that "[a]n independent judiciary can be a threat to democracy," and "in a democracy it must be acknowledged that too much independence is a bad thing."[2] Courts do make terrible mistakes; and they occasionally take sides in political disputes under the guise of judicial impartiality. Many Americans think this is what happened when the U.S. Supreme Court, in *Bush v. Gore* (2000),[3] decided the outcome of the presidential election. Judicial independence, like the principle of constitutionalism itself, is doubtless compatible with democracy, but as Professor Fiss suggests, they must be reconciled to preserve the values of both.

The question is this: How independent of popular control should courts be? The modern world of constitutional democracy has tried, appropriately, to shield court systems from the power of political majorities. But judicial independence does not imply total insularity from the popularly controlled institutions of government. After all, the court systems under discussion in this chapter are the products *of* democracy, they operate *in* democracy, and for this reason they cannot properly be removed *from* democracy's influence. Courts should and must be insulated from the power of transient majorities but not from popular accountability to the broader public they serve. In an age of democracy, given the expansion of judicial power around the world, courts are expected to have some degree of popular legitimacy.

The jurisdictions covered in this chapter differ in the ways they structure the relationship between democracy and their judicial systems. Several of these systems were established long before the global expansion of judicial power in our time. But they no longer exist in isolation from one another. Judges from different countries often confer with one another in face-to-face meetings, they cite one another with increasing frequency, and they have formed what is no less than an international community of constitutional interpreters. The global conversation relates not only to judicial policy and common problems of constitutional interpretation, but also to judicial organization, staffing, training, and decisional procedures. The democratic pedigree of these structures and processes is the main subject of the next section.

Judicial Systems: A Comparative Overview

One way of measuring the democratic pedigree of the American judicial system is by comparing it to the judiciaries of other durable democracies. The comparison might begin by distinguishing between Anglo-American and European models of judicial organization. The first belongs to the common law, the second to the civil law legal tradition. Broadly speaking, the common law system prevails in nations rooted in English law and institutions, whereas the civil law system—again broadly speaking—predominates in continental Europe. Significant variations in judicial structure and administration within each of these families of law make them inviting targets of comparison with the United States. In this short space, however, it is impossible to do justice to all these variations. Instead, the United States will be compared mainly with Canada, Germany, and South Africa: Canada because that country's judiciary is based almost entirely on the English experience; Germany because of its far-reaching influence on the organization and power of courts in the civil law world; and South Africa because of the hybrid nature of its legal system and its effort, as one of the world's new democracies, to create a court system marked by judicial impartiality and democratic accountability. In addition, these four jurisdictions represent common examples of judicial power and organization found in the contemporary democratic world. Finally, where appropriate, the European Court of Human Rights will be added to the mix, for it represents the most prominent example of a transnational constitutional court. The discussion in this section, however, focuses on court systems generally. Each nation's highest court of constitutional review, along with the European Court of Human Rights, will be taken up in greater detail later.

Competing Versions of Judicial Power and Organization

Before continuing, more should be said about the common and civil law traditions as they relate to judicial power and organization. The modern civil law tradition is associated with the European legal codes of the nineteenth and early twentieth centuries. Collected and systematized by legal scholars, these legislative codes represent comprehensive bodies of rationally ordered rules and principles founded on the belief that they are sufficient to regulate all private legal relationships. The common law, on the other hand, is judge-made law. Often called "unwritten" law, it derives its rules neither from statutes nor comprehensive codes. Common law judges make the law on the basis of morality and custom and their accumulated precedents constitute the basis of further growth in the law. Accordingly, common law judges enjoy far greater law-*making* power than the typical civilian judge. And in the United States, where this power extends to deciding constitutional disputes between levels and branches of government, judicial power has reached, at least until recently, a level unmatched in European civil law countries.

In the civilian tradition, courts are largely under the control of the executive, just as their judges are selected, trained, and promoted within the judicial bureaucracy. Correspondingly, the judges regard themselves not as lawmakers but rather as state officials entrusted with administering the law *as written*; they tend to emphasize the judiciary's *separation* from the political branches rather than as part of a complex system of political checks and balances. Common law courts assumed a slightly different character. Originally, in England, they were set up in geographical units called "circuits" to administer the king's justice. Later on, a separate system of equity courts emerged under the authority of the Lord Chancellor (the king's agent) to hear cases, in accordance with principles of "fairness" or "natural justice," beyond the reach of the common law. Accordingly, the appointment of common law judges was an executive—or royal—prerogative, a practice continued by other common law countries such as the United States, Canada, and Australia.

The common law's trademark, however, is the prominent role played by practicing lawyers skilled in advocacy before the courts. Lawyers, most of whom were independent practitioners outside of government, were known for their specialized knowledge of judicial precedents. Judges depended on their expertise and advocacy as aides in the development of the law. In common law countries, therefore, and not unsurprisingly, judges were—and are—recruited mainly from among these practitioners and usually after many years of experience at the bar. (In England, one must have practiced law for at least ten years as a barrister before being eligible for a judicial appointment.) In contrast to the civil law system, bench and bar were—and are—united in a common enterprise.

This contrast in the status of civil and common law judges corresponds, even today, to certain political system characteristics. The European version of separation of powers, which was heavily influenced by the French Revolution, drew a hard and fast line between legislative and judicial authority. Judges were part of the landed aristocracy and beholden to the monarchs who appointed them. As the expression of the popular will under the new revolutionary dispensation, parliament was seen as the soul of democracy, whereas courts were reduced to apolitical civil service–like agencies entrusted with enforcing law as enacted by legislative majorities. In the United States, by contrast, courts are part of the political system and thus capable, at least since *Marbury v. Madison* (1803), of checking executive or legislative power when it exceeds the limits of the constitution. In addition, unlike the European post-revolutionary perspective, the American founders were suspicious of popular democracy. In their complex system of checks and balances, independent courts of law—common law courts—were bound to play a critical role in the governing process.

Four Judicial Systems

COURT ORGANIZATION. Although the four nations under review are federal or quasi-federal political systems, each structures its judicial system differently. In the United States, fifty autonomous state court systems, staffed by around 30,000 judges, parallel a separate system of federal courts composed of 850 judges. Each set of courts hears cases involving, respectively, separate bodies of state and federal law. The Canadian judiciary, on the other hand, combines national and state courts in a single system. Provincial or state courts, consisting of 3,500 judges, hear all cases arising under both local and national law, whereas the federal supreme court serves as a general court of appeal for all civil and criminal cases initiated in the provincial courts. Thus, there is no separate system, as in the United States, of general trial and intermediate courts of appeal at the federal level. And in the typical common law system, as in Canada and the United States, all tribunals are courts of *general* jurisdiction—one measure, incidentally, of the immense influence of these courts. A notable exception is the Canadian Federal Court, a tribunal of twenty-five judges divided into trial and appellate divisions with jurisdiction over specialized areas of administrative law, thus allowing the Supreme Court to exercise more easily its supervisory control over the provincial courts.

Federal and state courts are unified to an even greater extent in Germany except that the judiciary includes separate hierarchies of administrative, social, finance, and labor courts as well as ordinary courts of civil and criminal jurisdiction. All lower and intermediate courts of appeal in each area of specialization are state courts. Although established and staffed by the states, federal law defines their structures and procedures along with the qualifications and legal status of their judges. The final courts of review in each of these hierarchies are federal courts. (Standing apart from and above all these tribunals in matters of constitutional interpretation is the Federal Constitutional Court, to be discussed below.) South Africa, finally, with the adoption of its 1996 Constitution, retained the hierarchical court structure inherited from the Union Constitution of 1910. The courts within the traditional hierarchy include, from bottom to top, magistrate courts, which handle most civil and criminal disputes, a system of superior courts—now called high courts—with general jurisdiction as defined by Parliament, and the Supreme Court of Appeal, the court of last resort for non-constitutional appeals. The great innovation under South Africa's new constitution was the creation of the Constitutional Court, the court of last instance over constitutional matters.

JUDICIAL TRAINING AND SELECTION. The four systems also feature variations in the selection and training of judges. In the United States, state and federal judges are chosen by radically different methods. Federal judges are appointed by the president for life subject to the advice and consent of the Senate. State judges, by contrast, are chosen for limited terms of office (typically six to ten years) under a variety of selection methods. The prevailing methods for selecting state supreme court judges, for example, include legislative appointment, partisan and nonpartisan elections, gubernatorial appointment with senate confirmation (the federal model), and gubernatorial appointment from a list submitted by a nonpartisan judicial nominating commission, a procedure followed, after the expiration of a judge's term of office, by a nonpartisan retention election in which he or she is retained in office if supported by a majority of voters. All other state judges are chosen by a similar—and bewildering—variety of methods and procedures. That twenty-two states select their highest judges in partisan and nonpartisan elections has raised serious questions about their independence and impartiality.[4] Interestingly, no other constitutional democracy elects any of its important judges by popular vote.

Like American federal and some state judges, Canadian judges receive their appointments from the executive but the process lacks the democratic check of legislative confirmation. In addition, the federal executive appoints the judges of the provincial general trial and intermediate appellate courts, a scheme originally designed to shield the selection of these judges from local influences inasmuch as they were also entrusted with the enforcement of federal law. Beneath these levels of the judiciary is another layer of tribunals consisting of provincial courts of *limited* jurisdiction whose 2,500 judges receive their appointments from the provinces themselves. The provincial attorneys general make the appointments but usually after the candidates have been proposed or screened by an independent, nongovernmental recruiting committee, a practice borrowed from the judicial nominating committee system used in many American states. The judges of the "upper" provincial judiciary, like the judges of the Federal Court, are known for their competence and independence, but the selection process has been heavily criticized for its lack of transparency and the role played by party politics. These judges are also unrepresentative of the larger society. Few claim working-class origins; many are the sons and, more recently, the daughters, of judges and lawyers. Compulsory retirement at the age of seventy does, however, add a democratizing element to the selection process.

Turning to Germany, we would note that around 22,000 judges staff Germany's lower and intermediate courts of appeal, some 17,000 of whom sit on the courts of ordinary civil and criminal jurisdiction. The remaining judges preside over the various labor, social, finance, and administrative courts. (These figures do not include some 350 judges who staff the federal courts which, as noted earlier, constitute the final courts of appeal in each specialized area.) In a recent essay, Edward Blankenburg, a German law professor, argued that the German judiciary "has become a separate institution emphasizing autonomy from politics at the same time that it has gained considerable political power."[5] He supported this claim by citing (1) the "tight control" state justice ministries wield over legal education, judicial recruitment, and promotion of judges, (2) the high number of professional judges relative to the population, (3) civil litigation rates that are among the highest in the world, and (4) a mode of judicial review that "binds public decision-makers to the letter of the law."

But whether these are good measures of judicial power is unclear. Needless to say, German judges are no longer classified as civil servants and they enjoy more autonomy than under any previous constitution. But their power fails to measure up to the authority of common law judges. The principle of separation of powers, as understood in Germany, bars ordinary judges from questioning the decisions of the political branches, just as it seems to require specialized courts to review the legality of state activity in the narrow bands of the civil public law world. Nor, finally, are ordinary judges in Germany's climate of legal positivism suited, by training or temperament, as Blankenburg suggests, to question the supremacy of written law, a perspective highlighted by the infrequency with which ordinary judges certify constitutional questions to the Federal Constitutional Court.

Yet German judges are as fully independent as common law judges in the United States and Canada. Their salaries cannot be diminished and they enjoy comparable guarantees against being transferred, suspended, or removed from office, although they are required to retire at the age of sixty-five. The general profile of German judges, however, is different from their common law peers. As in civil law systems generally, the former enter the judiciary at the outset of their careers, but only after they have completed seven years of training and passed two major state examinations, one after finishing their university studies and the other after apprenticing in various courts, administrative agencies, and law offices. If accepted, they enter a probationary period of three years under the supervision of tenured judges. The survivors receive full-time judicial appointments, usually at the lowest court levels, with all the security this implies in terms of tenure, salary, benefits, and prestige.

The initial appointments are based mainly on merit and have little to do with politics. But upward movement within the judiciary may well depend on a judge's political acceptability by the ministry responsible for his or her advancement or promotion. Most judges see themselves as legal technicians insulated from politics but, interestingly, judges are permitted to become members of political parties and even to speak out on political issues so long as they exercise the restraint necessary to maintain public confidence in their independence. It is hard for Americans to reconcile judicial independence with active participation in political activities, and such activity would be regarded as highly improper in England and Canada as well as in the United States. The German perspective, however, is one that sees judges as citizens with the same right as other Germans to participate fully in the life of the democracy they have sworn to uphold under the Basic Law. Indeed, German judges aspiring to membership on one of the federal courts, which would be the high point of a judicial career, might well be advised to join a political party and cultivate the right bureaucratic and political friendships.

Far more politicized is the selection of federal judges, and their numbers are large. (The Federal Court of Justice alone, which is the highest court of appeal for ordinary civil and criminal jurisdiction, has some 130 members, most of whom sit on five-judge panels.) Federal judges are selected by a committee made up of executive and parliamentary representatives. If, for example, a judge is being selected for the Federal Court of Justice, the selection committee includes the Federal Minister of Justice, all sixteen state ministers of justice, and an equal number of parliamentary representatives. The result is a tribunal more diversified politically and professionally than at the state level. Many of these judges have backgrounds in parliament and the civil service, but they are required to have all the qualifications required for judicial office. Some critics have deplored the influence of party politics in their selection; yet it would be difficult to show that American or Canadian federal judges, who are also selected largely on the basis of their political affiliations, are any less independent or competent than Germany's federal judges. It should be pointed out, finally, as noted later on, that the judges of the Federal Constitutional Court are chosen by a process even more overtly political—and democratic—than other federal judges.

The status of South African judges, finally, has undergone a major change in the aftermath of the apartheid regime. All judges under the old regime were appointed by the government, and they were overwhelmingly white. The judges of the magistrate courts, the workhorses of the judicial system, had the rank of ordinary public servants subject to the disciplinary control of the executive. Needless to say, under the old system of parliamentary supremacy, these and other judges played a major role in upholding the legality of apartheid laws. Since then, the system has been transformed. Magistrate courts are now independent of the civil service, and the system of judicial selection has been reformed to achieve greater accountability and representation. For example, a new magistrates commission has been established to monitor the selection of judges, to train magistrates in the values of democracy and human rights, and to insure greater representation of women and blacks in their courts.

There has also been a major effort to democratize the appointment of higher court judges. Prior to 1994, these judges were presidential appointees and, as in the England, they tended to be drawn from the ranks of the senior practicing bar. Executive appointment has continued under the new constitution, notwithstanding efforts to shift this responsibility to parliament. Created instead was a twenty-three-member Judicial Service Commission (JSC) consisting of ten members of parliament, the Minister of Justice, and four members appointed by the president after consulting with party leaders in the National Assembly—that is, fifteen political appointees—along with eight representatives of the legal profession and the judiciary. No presidential appointment to the higher judiciary can be made without consulting with the JSC. Finally, the constitution itself requires that the "racial and gender composition of South Africa must be considered when judicial officers are appointed" (Article 174 [2]).

Models of Constitutional Justice

As noted at the beginning of this chapter, the most dramatic postwar development in judicial power and organization has been the global expansion of constitutional review. What was once a unique feature of the American governmental system has become an aspect of constitutional governance almost everywhere in the democratic world. Equally dramatic—and fascinating—has been the impact that courts of constitutional review have had on each other. Faced with common problems of governance in an age of globalization, they have relied on each other's jurisprudence for guidance in the interpretation of their respective constitutions.[6] In addition, the expansion of judicial power that has accompanied the adoption of constitutional review has tended to narrow the differences between civil and common law court systems. Yet the two systems have responded differently in their efforts to reconcile judicial independence with democratic accountability. As we shall see, these differences range from constitutional doctrines flowing from the principle of separation of powers all the way over to organizational matters such as the nature of the court exercising the power of judicial review and the selection, appointment, tenure, and removal of its judges.

Constitutional review has assumed a variety of institutional forms. Again, we can distinguish roughly between the European and American models of judicial review. The American model empowers all courts to hear and decide constitutional cases and controversies. Any judge, state or federal, may nullify any law he or she finds unconstitutional. More precisely, judicial review in the United States includes the power of federal or state judges to void state laws on state or federal constitutional grounds. As Keith Whittington remarks in this volume, this diffusion of judicial review creates serious conflicts between democracy and constitutionalism, although at the state level, he suggests, the conflict "might be alleviated" by the popular election of judges.

The European model, by contrast, concentrates judicial review in a specialized court of constitutional review outside of and apart from the structure of the regular judiciary. In the world today, some fifty nations—twenty-six of them in Europe—have adopted the European model. The world's major common law democracies (e.g., Ireland, India, New Zealand, Australia, and Canada), together with Israel and several Latin American nations, have adopted the American model by lodging judicial review in the general court system. (Still other nations have adopted mixed systems by concentrating judicial review in their highest courts of general appellate review but denying other courts the competency to decide constitutional issues. The following sections deal mainly with the highest courts of *constitutional* review.

United States

Already in 1835, Alexis de Tocqueville observed that judges are among "the major political powers in the United States." This power derives from the authority of courts—all courts—to declare laws—any law—unconstitutional. From Tocqueville's day to the present, the power of judicial review has found its most prominent institutional representation in the Supreme Court. But the Court's power to pronounce laws invalid on constitutional grounds is not laid down in the Constitution. The doctrine of judicial review traces its origin to *Marbury v. Madison*,[7] the famous case in which Chief Justice John Marshall inferred the doctrine from the Constitution's language and structure. Marshall's reasoning caught on; for the principle of judicial supremacy in the interpretation of the Constitution evolved into a unique and generally accepted feature of American constitutionalism. Judicial review continued to advance and expand in the twentieth century and by 1975, in decisions such as *Brown v. Board of Education* and *Roe v. Wade*,[8] the Supreme Court's influence over American life and law had reached new levels of control—and controversy—triggering anew old debates about the compatibility of judicial review with democracy.

From the beginning, the Supreme Court has been fully aware of its counter-majoritarian character, but its reputation for independence has helped it to withstand the cyclones of criticism it has faced over the years for striking down federal and state laws favored by legislative majorities. The Constitution's framers secured the Court's independence by granting federal judges lifetime appointments—subject to good behavior—and salaries that may not be diminished during their time in office. In addition, they cannot be removed from office except by the cumbersome route of legislative impeachment. But the Court is not without some degree of democratic legitimacy. The president, elected by all the people, appoints the justices subject to the advice and consent of a popularly elected Senate, while the Constitution empowers Congress to regulate the Court's membership, calendar, and appellate jurisdiction.

In recent decades, however, appointments to the Supreme Court have become highly politicized affairs. As the nominations of Robert Bork and Clarence Thomas showed, Senate confirmation hearings have evolved into titanic—and, some would add, unseemly—ideological battles over a judicial nominee's political and judicial views. The stakes in these battle are high because appointments to the Supreme Court are for life and because the Court itself is sharply divided between its so-called liberal and conservative wings. (The same knock-down-drag-out fights have taken place over presidential nominations to the lower federal courts.) Have these public battles over judicial nominees, in which political interest groups have also played an increasing role, compromised the Supreme Court's independence or impartiality? Are the Canadian, German, and South African schemes to be preferred? These questions will be addressed in due course.

Out of respect, finally, for the political judgments of the other branches of the federal government—and, more generally, for the principle of democracy—the Supreme Court has recognized that the Constitution limits the range and scope of its power. These limits are well-known, and they include, as Whittington notes, certain canons of restraint or strategies of avoidance by which the Court seeks to avoid unnecessary confrontations with the political branches. The Court is also empowered to determine its own workload, for it enjoys full authority to take only those constitutional cases it wants to decide. Of course, this ability to decide what it wants to decide is a source of power. But it also serves as a tool for avoiding explosive issues that could hurl the Court into the center of another political storm.

Canada

With the adoption of its Charter of Rights and Freedoms in 1982, Canada created its own juridical democracy along the lines of the American model. Before 1982 Canada, like its English parent, adhered to the principle of parliamentary supremacy. Majoritarian democracy was in the Canadian bloodstream, and judges had historically deferred to the judgments of legislative majorities. Judicial review was exercised mainly to resolve conflicts between federal and provincial governments, but an otherwise valid law enacted by either government could not be contested on constitutional grounds.

The Charter of Rights and Freedoms was a revolutionary document. Unlike the U.S. Constitution, it *expressly* empowered Canadian courts to overrule parliamentary legislation, provincial or federal, if in conflict with any of the Charter's rights or freedoms. But the Charter is a document unlike the American Bill of Rights in that it seeks to protect collective as well as individual rights. Moreover, it requires the courts to interpret the Charter "consistent with the preservation and enhancement of the multicultural heritage of Canadians."[9] Accordingly, communitarian interests may well trump a claim to *individual* liberty, as when the Supreme Court sustained a federal law criminalizing hate propaganda.[10] Equally important, the Charter contains a limitation clause subjecting guaranteed rights to "reasonable limits prescribed by law as can be demonstrably justified in a free and democratic society" (Sec. 1). No such limitation clause appears in the American Bill of Rights. In short, although the Canadian Supreme Court has vigorously enforced Charter liberties against legislative majorities, it has not accepted the anti-statist culture of individualism that permeates the civil liberties decisions of the U.S. Supreme Court.

As these Charter provisions may suggest, parliamentary supremacy in Canada is not yet dead. The Charter's "override" section represents one effort to reconcile the principles of parliamentary and judicial supremacy. It permits the federal or a provincial parliament to declare that one of its laws shall remain in force up to a period of five years "notwithstanding" its incompatibility with one of the Charter's legal or equality rights. The override mechanism has been used no fewer than sixteen times—mainly by Quebec—although in only two instances was the override successfully invoked in response to a decision of the

Supreme Court. All remaining invocations of the override were written into statutes prior to their passage, thus preempting judicial declarations of unconstitutionality at both provincial and federal levels. The override mechanism is of great symbolic importance for Canadians opposed to American-style judicial review. As Canadian scholar Peter Hogg has remarked, "So long as the last word remains with the competent legislative body, there can be no acute or longstanding conflict between the judicial and legislative branches, and much of the American debate over the legitimacy of judicial review is rendered irrelevant."[11]

To what extent is Canada's Supreme Court organized to reflect its independence and democratic legitimacy? A bizarre feature of Canadian court organization is the Supreme Court's creation by statute in 1875. Thus, unlike the American Supreme Court, which is established directly by the Constitution, it could be abolished tomorrow. History explains the situation. Although designed as a general court of appeal, the Canadian Supreme Court was not until recently a national court of last resort. Until 1949, the Privy Council of England's House of Lords served as Canada's final court of appeal under the British North American Act of 1867—the imperial statute that created the Canadian Confederation. All this changed, along with the nature of judicial power in Canada, with the abolition of Privy Council appeals in 1949 and the subsequent "patriation"—that is, conversion—in 1982 of the BNA Act into an independent Canadian constitution which, as noted, now includes a new charter of rights and liberties.

Constitutionally founded or not, the Canadian Supreme Court has evolved into a major court of constitutional review whose reputation for independence is no less real than that of the U.S. Supreme Court. But the Court's expanded powers have triggered demands for more transparency in the appointment of its members. The justices are effectively appointed by the prime minister, with or without consulting with his cabinet. Early on, patronage played a crucial role in the appointment process. But commentators agree that professionalism has overtaken party politics. All justices are now drawn from the legal profession and must have at least ten years of experience as a practicing lawyer or judge. Most, however, have served as judges of the Federal Court, a provincial court of appeal, or a provincial superior court. Geographic balance also marks the Court's membership. Tradition dictates that three justices will be appointed from Quebec (a French civil law province), three from Ontario (an English common law province), two from the western provinces, and one from the maritime provinces. In recent years at least three of the justices have been women. Justices, however, are required to retire at the age of seventy-five, and they can only be removed by a complex procedure involving all three branches of the national government, rendering their tenure as secure as American federal judges.

Yet, even within these constraints, the prime minister is in a position to unilaterally mould the Court's ideological make-up, and there is no parliamentary check on his selections. This situation has led to a major effort to change the method of selecting and screening justices. Judicial reformers have advanced several proposals for change, including advisory screening committees to vet the qualification of nominees and making the provincial legislatures rather than the prime minister responsible for judicial nominations. The most popular proposal would establish a parliamentary judicial review committee to hold hearings on the qualifications of prime ministerial nominees. This would not be the equivalent of the "advice and consent" procedure in the U.S. Senate, but it would expose to public view aspects of a nominee's public record and personal history that a prime minister might ignore at his risk. Many Canadians, however, oppose any adoption of what Peter Russell calls "American-style confirmation hearings."[12]

Germany

Germany's Federal Constitutional Court (FCC) ranks as one of the world's most prominent and powerful constitutional tribunals. Following Europe's civil law model, it is a specialized court of constitutional review and the only court in Germany authorized to hand down binding interpretations of the Constitution. The FCC's express jurisdiction under the Basic Law includes the power to adjudicate conflicts between branches and levels of government, to settle electoral disputes, to declare political parties unconstitutional, and—in what is called an abstract judicial review proceeding—to resolve mere *doubts* about the constitutionality of a statute immediately after its passage at the request of the federal or a state government or one-third of the members of parliament. Many of the FCC's published opinions, however, consist of concrete review cases—cases in which judges are required to refer their "serious doubts" about the constitutionality of a law under which a case arises to the FCC for resolution. In exercising these and other constitutionally prescribed powers, the FCC has had a profound influence on Germany's political system.

The Court's "political" jurisprudence, a characterization commonly accepted by constitutional commentators, is original and compulsory. Cases may not be withdrawn unless the FCC consents. One must bear in mind that the FCC represents the public interest and not that of the judges or political officials who initiate the proceeding. The general public is the entity with the main stake in the clarification of constitutional issues. In the German public mind, the definitive resolution of serious doubts about the constitutionality of laws and statutes is part of what it means to be governed by the rule of law. Accordingly, strategies for avoiding constitutional decisions, such as the American political question doctrine, have no place in German constitutional law.

The wide-ranging powers and frequency with which state and federal laws have been invalidated have turned the FCC into a virtual fourth branch of government. Well aware of this possibility, German legislators enacted tenure and recruitment policies designed to alleviate the "countermajoritarian" problem that Whittington highlights in his discussion of American judicial review. First, the judges are appointed for nonrenewable terms of twelve years, and they are required to retire at the age of sixty-eight, regardless of whether they have completed their terms. Second, the Basic Law requires the parliamentary election of its sixteen judges—federal law divides the FCC into two senates of eight judges each—one-half of whom are elected respectively by the Bundestag and Bundesrat. A two-thirds vote is required in both houses to elect a justice, although in the Bundestag a judicial selection committee of twelve members, in which the political parties are represented proportionate to their overall parliamentary strength, chooses its eight judges, a procedure that requires a multiparty consensus on judicial appointees, often necessitating, in addition, negotiations between the two parliamentary bodies. The process has resulted in the election of judges broadly representative of German political life and culture. These procedures have contributed to the enhancement of the FCC's democratic legitimacy, which helps to explain the enormous trust Germans have shown in their highest court of constitutional review.

South Africa

The creation of South Africa's constitutional court symbolizes the nation's passage from parliamentary to constitutional supremacy. Accordingly, judicial review is a major linchpin of South Africa's new constitutional order, one that has borrowed elements from the German and American systems. Owing to lingering suspicions of the judiciary's commitment to constitutional values, South Africans were initially reluctant to authorize courts generally to exercise American-style judicial review. But under the 1996 Constitution, all tribunals except magistrate courts—the workhorses of the judiciary—are able to address constitutional questions; yet, certain disputes are reserved for the exclusive jurisdiction of the Constitutional Court (CC). Apart from their suspicion that the regular courts could not be fully trusted with the exercise of judicial review, South Africans felt that a separate constitutional tribunal was needed to highlight the importance and visibility of constitutional adjudication. But having magnified judicial power beyond anything known before, they also sought to establish a constitutional tribunal marked by independence and accountability.

The South African Constitution follows the example of Germany's Basic Law by specifying the CC's powers. Its exclusive authority includes the power to review constitutional disputes between the highest organs of the state, to determine whether a constitutional amendment is constitutional, and to decide whether under certain conditions a parliamentary *bill* is constitutionally valid. The CC also has the final say on whether a national or provincial *law* conforms to the Constitution. Actually, the CC is required to confirm a high or appellate court decision declaring a law unconstitutional before an order of invalidity can go into effect. And, as in Germany, a third of the members of the national parliament may ask the CC to review the constitutionality of a parliamentary law, but such a request must be made within thirty days of the president's signature. Finally, the CC serves as the final court of appeal in all other constitutional matters.

These powers are awesome, and they express the popular trust South Africans expect the CC to personify. To this end, the Constitution limits judicial tenure and circumscribes the president's appointment power by requiring him (or her) to follow an elaborate process of consultation with the cabinet, the National Assembly's party leaders, the chief justice, and the Judicial Service Commission (JSC). As in Germany, constitutional judges are appointed for non-renewable terms of twelve years or until they reach the age of seventy. (It takes a parliamentary law to extend the term of a CC judge.) South Africans, however, declined to follow the German lead on parliamentary selection. Instead, they continued the old system of presidential appointment. Under the apartheid regime, the president on the advice of the Justice Minister selected all higher court judges, a secretive process that resulted in what the South African *Sunday Times* characterized as a "virtually all-male, all-white, all middle-class and largely Afrikaan speaking" bench.

Under the new dispensation, the JSC plays a pivotal role in selecting higher court judges, including constitutional judges. An independent body composed of high judicial and executive officials, along with representatives of the legal profession, parliament, and opposition political parties, the JSC recruits, screens, and interviews candidates. The vetting process, however, is closed to the public. Under the Constitution, the JSC prepares a short list of nominees from which the president is expected to fill a judicial vacancy. Despite objections that the president is empowered to appoint key executive and judicial officials to the JSC, the Constitutional Court, in certifying the constitutionality of the 1996 Constitution, declared the system fully compatible with the required constitutional principle of judicial independence.[13] The process has resulted in the recruitment of many black judges, but few are women and most continue to be recruited from a narrow social and education background. The JSC's role notwithstanding, the system continues to be criticized for its lack of transparency and the extent to which the president is still able to exert leverage over the selection process.

Judicial Review and Democracy

The proliferation of constitutional courts in Europe and elsewhere in the aftermath of World War II resulted largely from the influence of American constitutionalism. The very idea of constitutionalism was in several respects an American export. First, the American experience taught postwar constitution-makers to treat their constitutions as supreme law, superior to ordinary law, and thus binding on all branches and levels of government. Second, it taught them that courts could—and should—play a crucial role in the protection of both democracy and human rights. But as we have seen in many of the world's new democracies, specialized constitutional tribunals were the institutions of choice to play this role. Civil law countries among these nations rejected the American model of diffuse judicial review, just as they adjusted the scope of judicial review to their distinctive legal cultures and parliamentary political systems. Finally, to reconcile judicial review with democratic theory, countries such as Germany and South Africa sought refuge in policies on judicial selection, tenure, and security in office.

American Constitutionalism Abroad

Judicial doctrine was the most important American influence on foreign courts of judicial review established after 1945. It is easy to see why. First, the American Supreme Court had more than 150 years of experience in constitutional interpretation, having built up impressive bodies of decisional law on basic rights and liberties, federalism and separation of powers, criminal procedure, and the applicability of constitutional limitations in times of crises. Second, in each of these areas, and increasingly in fields such as privacy, minority rights, gender equality, right to life matters, and fair and effective political representation, constitutional governments, especially advanced democracies like the United States, were facing similar problems of governance. These and related problems required courts to adjudicate conflicting claims of constitutionalism and democracy or, relatedly, to reconcile the tensions between the values of liberty and order (or equality). Third, the postwar constitutions discussed in this paper feature human rights provisions, many of which are similar to those found in the U.S. Bill of Rights. Judges interpreting these provisions for the first time, in the absence of an indigenous body of constitutional doctrine, relied naturally on American judicial precedents in the interpretation of their own constitutions. Years later these courts were still drawing inspiration from the decisions of the United States Supreme Court.

The judges of numerous courts around the world have acknowledged the Supreme Court's influence. As Chief Justice Aharon Barak of the Israeli Supreme Court recently remarked, "United States public law in general, and United States Supreme Court in particular, have always been, to me and to many other judges in modern democracies, shining examples of constitutional thought and constitutional action."[14] Helmut Steinberger, a justice of Germany's Federal Constitutional Court from 1975 to 1987, has acknowledged the influence of American constitutional law as it applies to "functionally equivalent . . . methodological approaches and substantive solutions [to human rights issues], although their articulation and the ways and means to arrive at them may differ." Similarly, Claire L'Heureux-Dubé, a justice of the Canadian Supreme Court from 1987 to 2002, has underscored the frequency with which the Canadian tribunal has "cited United States precedent in setting forth principles of interpretation for the Charter [of Rights and Liberties]." The same is true of South Africa's Constitutional Court. It repeatedly consults American and other foreign law in the interpretation of the 1996 Constitution. Interestingly, the libraries of each of the major courts covered in this chapter have full sets of the *United States Reports*.

By the 1990s, however, the world's leading constitutional courts had created bodies of constitutional jurisprudence comparable in range and sophistication to the work produced by the United States Supreme Court. This was notably true of Germany's Federal Constitutional Court and the European Court of Human Rights, and since 1982 and 1993, respectively, it has been true of the Canadian Supreme Court and South Africa's Constitutional Court. These courts have been particularly active in safeguarding constitutionally guaranteed rights and in monitoring the democratic political process. In playing this role, they have followed the lead of the United States Supreme Court in defending fundamental rights and reinforcing representative democracy. Yet foreign judicial outcomes have not always coincided with the result in the American cases. It is not unusual for these foreign courts to reach results different from the U.S. Supreme Court—for example, in free speech cases—when applying common values such as liberty, equality, personhood, privacy, human dignity, or democracy. Then too these values are often defined, weighed, or balanced differently in the United States than in other advanced constitutional democracies. Relying increasingly on their native legal and political traditions, these courts have begun to map their own paths through the forests of human rights and political democracy.

The remarks of Justice L'Heureux-Dubé are particularly relevant here: "[A]s courts look *all* over the world for sources of authority, the process of international influence has changed from *reception* to *dialogue*. Judges no longer simply *receive* the cases of other jurisdictions, particularly the United States, and then apply them or modify them for their own jurisdiction. Rather, cross-pollination and dialogue between jurisdictions is increasingly occurring."[15] And so it is. The influence of American constitutional case law on the rest of the world is still very substantial, but in today's world of dialogue and instant communication across national borders, the Supreme Court is just one among several judicial voices competing for the attention of the world's constitutional courts. Often, the influence of the American Supreme Court is negative rather than positive. Foreign courts continue to cite, consider, quote from, or review the American jurisprudence but then often decide to march to a different tune in accord with the music they hear coming from their own constitutions or traditions.

Examples of such influences, both positive and negative, abound. In the field of criminal procedure, American precedents continue to be cited with approval in scores of Canadian and South African cases, perhaps because these jurisdictions share the tradition of the common law. One exception concerns the death penalty. In *State v. Makwanyane* (1995),[16] the famous case that struck down the constitutionality of the death penalty in South Africa, the Constitutional Court examined at great length *Gregg v. Georgia* (1976),[17] the equally important American case upholding the validity of the death penalty. The South African Court examined the case sympathetically, even suggesting that the American result may have been driven by the "due process of law" language of the Fourteenth Amendment, words that appear to support the death penalty as a matter of principle. The Court then turned its attention to Justice William Brennan's dissenting opinion in *Gregg*, finding his argument more convincing than the majority opinion. "The weight given to human dignity by Justice Brennan," wrote the Court, "is wholly consistent with the values of our Constitution and the new order established by it." The allure of Justice Brennan's opinion underscores another point about the influence of American constitutionalism abroad, and that is the rich lodes of constitutional thought and theory that foreign courts have found in American dissenting and concurring opinions.

Interestingly, both the American and South African tribunals sought to reconcile their death penalty decisions with democracy. Both courts acknowledged that public opinion and legislative majorities appeared to support the death penalty in their respective countries. How relevant this should be in determining whether capital punishment is cruel and degrading treatment in violation of the Constitution was an issue before both tribunals. The United States Supreme Court concluded that it would be abusing its power by interfering with the democratic political *process* that led the state legislature in question to install the death penalty. South Africa's Court, by contrast, adopted a *substantive* view of democracy, holding that a "democratic society based on freedom and equality" requires the protection of "the social outcasts and marginalized people of our society." The death penalty, said the lead opinion, "destroys life" and "annihilates human dignity," a procedure which in the eyes of the South African Court cannot be tolerated in a genuinely *democratic* society, no matter how much public opinion or legislatures may favor it.

Freedom of speech is yet another jurisprudential field in which American and foreign constitutional tribunals have differed in their conceptions of democracy. Yet it is no exaggeration to say that the American emphasis on *freedom* of speech as the *sine qua non* of democracy has been influential all over the democratic world. The jurisprudence of the foreign courts under discussion is studded with references to American free speech doctrine. Seminal free speech decisions in Germany, Canada, and South Africa have all taken their main cue from Benjamin Cardozo's oft-quoted remark that freedom of speech is "the matrix, the indispensable condition of nearly every other form of freedom."[18] Yet, while foreign constitutional tribunals have relied heavily on American speech cases for the interpretation of their constitutions, they have not always accepted the latter's conclusions.

New York Times v. Sullivan (1964),[19] a famous American freedom of the press case described by a leading authority on freedom of speech (Harry Kalven) as an "occasion for dancing in the streets," is a prominent example of a judicial decision that foreign courts have extensively examined but seldom followed. *Sullivan* insulated newspapers against libel actions for uttering false statements about public officials unless the plaintiff can show that the statements were made with "actual malice" or with utter disregard for the truth. The decision is flush with quotable passages in celebration of free speech. Each of the courts under discussion has been moved to consider *Sullivan*'s compelling argument in favor of what it called "breathing space" for the press when sued for slandering a public official. *Sullivan*'s tracks are clearly visible in the defamation jurisprudence of Germany's Constitutional Court, Canada's Supreme Court, and the European Court of Human Rights. It will suffice to consider Canada's treatment of *Sullivan*.

In *Hill v. Church of Scientology* (1995),[20] a crown attorney sued the church for making false statements about his conduct in a criminal action he had filed against Church of Scientology. In its defense, the church invoked *Sullivan*, arguing that the common law of defamation violated the Charter's free speech guarantee. The Canadian Supreme Court discussed *Sullivan* in great detail, finding it "instructive" in several respects, but concluded that its reasoning could not be adopted in Canada. The Court's comparative assessment did not stop here. It reinforced its analysis by reviewing the criticism of *Sullivan* by American judges and academic writers and by pointing out that the American case had not been followed in the United Kingdom or Australia. Turning *Sullivan* on its head, the Court suggested that in a democracy, "[t]hose who publish statements should assume a reasonable level of responsibility."

The promotion of hatred against readily identifiable racial and ethnic groups is another area of free speech law that has prompted foreign tribunals to engage the reasoning of the U.S. Supreme Court. In the United States, the Supreme Court has tended to strike down bans on hate speech in the absence of narrowly drawn statutes aimed at words that inflict real harm on real persons. Liberty is the driving force behind the American perspective, one that envisions "uninhibited" speech as democracy's essential core. In Germany and South Africa, by contrast, the courts have taken an alternative view that sees democracy in a different light, one that elevates the competing principle of human dignity to the highest rank in the constitutional order. Before closing out this section on the influence of American constitutionalism abroad, we might also mention *Keegstra v. Regina* (1990),[21] the well-known Canadian case that rivaled *Hill* in the attention it gave to American decisional law.

Keegstra was brought by a high school teacher convicted of unlawfully promoting hate propaganda against Jews, a conviction unlikely to have survived constitutional analysis in the United States. Writing for the majority, Chief Justice Dickson cited or reviewed more than a dozen American cases, remarking that "the practical and theoretical [importance of this jurisprudence] is immense, and should not be overlooked by Canadian courts." But he went on to say that "we must examine American constitutional law with a critical eye." "It is only common sense," he continued, "to recognize that, just as similarities will justify borrowing from the American experience, differences may require that Canada's constitutional vision depart from that endorsed in the United States." But after acknowledging the U.S. Supreme Court's "strong aversion to content-based regulations of expression," he was not altogether sure—not as sure as many American commentators—whether Canada's policy on hate speech would contravene the First Amendment. His was a fascinating "spin" on the collective meaning of American case law. Chief Justice Dickson resurrected an old American case—*Beauharnais v. Illinois* (1952)—that sustained a group libel statute, suggesting along the way that the case had not lost its legitimacy, notwithstanding later cases that appeared to undermine its vitality. At the end of the day, however, the majority found hate propaganda incompatible with the Canadian vision of a free and democratic society.

This discussion should not give the impression that foreign constitutional courts are always unanimous in their disagreements with the U.S. Supreme Court. Occasionally, these courts disagree with each other even when applying the basic values of their respective constitutional systems. One example may suffice. As James Q. Whitman has pointed out in a 2004 article in the *Yale Law Journal*, the United States and Europe feature different "cultures of privacy."[22] Both cherish the values of liberty and dignity, but in considering conflicts between privacy and freedom of the press, the former tilts toward liberty and the latter toward dignity. But even in their application of a common *dignitarian* value, European courts occasionally differ among themselves. But like their treatment of American constitutional doctrine, they exhibit considerable hospitality toward one another's reasoned pronouncements.

Foreign Law in the Supreme Court

Speaking before a German-American constitutional law conference in 1989, the chief justice of the U.S. Supreme Court, William Rehnquist, remarked:

> For nearly a century and a half, courts in the United States exercising the power of judicial review had no precedents to look to save their own, because our courts alone exercised this sort of authority. When many new constitutional courts were created after the Second World War, these courts naturally looked to the decisions of the Supreme Court of the United States, among other sources, for developing their own law. But now that constitutional law is solidly grounded in so many countries, it is time that the United States courts begin looking to the decisions of other constitutional courts to aid in their own deliberative process.[23]

As noted in the previous section, foreign constitutional courts have relied heavily on American legal precedents in the interpretation of their own constitutions. And they continue to do so, particularly when applying constitutional provisions and values equivalent to those found in the Bill of Rights. South Africa's constitution is unique in that it specifically authorizes courts " to consider foreign law" in promoting the values incorporated into its bill of rights.

To what extent have American courts—notably the Supreme Court—taken Chief Justice Rehnquist's advice to heart? Several justices have expressed their willingness to learn from foreign decisional law. Justice Sandra Day O'Connor, for example, speaking before the Southern Center for International Studies in Atlanta, Georgia, on 28 October 2003, conceded that foreign decisions "should at times constitute persuasive authority in American courts," a practice she described as "transjudicialism." She added: "I suspect that with time, [the Supreme Court] will rely increasingly on international and foreign law in resolving what now appear to be domestic issues, as we both appreciate more fully the ways in which domestic issues have international dimension, and recognize the rich resources available to us in the decisions of foreign courts." Justices Stephen Breyer and Ruth Bader Ginsburg have uttered similar statements.

It might be added parenthetically that references to foreign law in American judicial decisions is not new. Early on in American history, English common law, civil and criminal, was actually regarded as part of American law. But more important for present purposes are the appeals to Roman precedents and "ancient law" in *The Federalist Papers* and in early Supreme Court decisions. Recourse to natural law in constitutional cases such as *Calder v. Bull* (1798) and to admiralty law in various state and federal courts was a common occurrence. Justice Joseph Story's approving reference in the famous case of *Swift v. Tyson* (1842) to Cicero's commercial jurisprudence as "in great measure, not the law of a single country only, but of the commercial world" (also quoted in Latin no less),[24] is yet another example of civilian legal influences in American law. So when members of the current Supreme Court cite the decisions of modern constitutional courts, they are following a long-standing tradition in American legal history.

In recent years, however, international human rights and foreign decisional law have played a minor role, at best, in the Supreme Court's jurisprudence. The relative failure to engage the reasoning of non-American constitutional courts has disappointed some foreign judges. The criticism of Justice Claire L'Heureaux-Dubé of Canada is particularly severe. In 1998, she remarked: "The United States Supreme Court seems to operate almost totally in a legal isolation booth. The failure of the justices of the Rehnquist Court to take part in the international dialogue among the courts of the world is contributing to a growing isolation and diminished influence. The failure is a loss for American jurisprudence, and for the development of human rights around the world." Chief Justice Aharon Barak of Israel, after acknowledging his Court's reliance on American constitutional law, regretted that "the United States Supreme Court makes very little use of comparative law." Justice Ginsburg, writing in 2003, was equally blunt. "We are the losers," she wrote, if we do not both share our experience with, and learn from others" in this "world [of] increasingly porous borders."[25]

A survey of Supreme Court decisions over the last ten years (March 1995 to February 2004) reveals twenty-eight cases in which international or foreign law had been cited. But in eighteen of these cases the cited materials appeared mainly in dissenting opinions, eleven of which were written by Justice Breyer who, as noted, is among the justices most apt to seek inspiration from abroad. Six additional dissenting or concurring opinions citing foreign materials were written by Justices Stevens, Ginsburg, or Breyer. Interestingly, seven of the eighteen opinions involved the death penalty. In only ten of the twenty-eight cases were foreign legal materials cited in majority or plurality opinions. Six of the ten dealt with minor procedural issues or the interpretation of international treaties or arbitration agreements. Only four cited the decisional law of other high courts of judicial review, but in none of these cases was there any real engagement with the reasoning of these courts. The foreign decisions were cited simply to show that the Supreme Court was in step with the ethical standards of other advanced democracies.

In two of these cases, however, the majority's references to foreign decisional law produced dissents on and off the Court. In striking down a state law criminalizing homosexual sodomy in *Lawrence v. Texas*,[26] Justice Anthony Kennedy invoked a decision by the European Court of Human Rights nullifying a similar Northern Ireland statute, a decision that is now authoritative, he noted, in the forty-five nations belonging to the Council of Europe. Similarly, in *Atkins v. Virginia*,[27] which invalidated the death penalty as applied to a mentally retarded criminal, a six-person majority embellished its opinion with a footnote citing several amicus briefs advocating reliance on European judicial cases and European opinion in general. The footnote, which sought to bolster the majority's view that Americans have come increasingly to regard the death penalty as a "cruel and unusual" punishment, prompted strong dissents from Chief Justice Rehnquist and Justice Antonin Scalia. Both questioned the relevance of foreign law and opinion for the interpretation of the U.S. Constitution. Scalia's *Lawrence* dissent was more blunt; he described the reference to the European Court's case law as "meaningless dicta," echoing his view in an earlier case—responding to Justice Breyer's dissent in *Printz v. United States*[28]—that "comparative [constitutional] analysis [is] inappropriate to the task of interpreting a constitution," although he conceded that it might be relevant to writing a constitution.

Three standard arguments have been marshaled to support the views of Chief Justice Rehnquist and Justice Scalia. The first is that American history, culture, and traditions are different from other countries and thus there can be no real common ground on issues such as capital punishment and homosexuality or even on the broader issues of federalism or separation of powers. The second is that late twentieth-century constitutions have little in common with a two-hundred-year-old document grounded in and surrounded by the gloss that life, history, and untold hundreds of established precedents have written upon it. The third and related argument is that heavy American reliance on original history or the intentions of the founding fathers has no equivalent in the interpretive approaches of modern constitutional courts. The arguments suggest that the American experience is exceptional or unique among the world's democracies. Some would argue that America's more individualistic, more anti-statist, more pluralistic, and more heterogeneous society would resist the grafting of foreign transplants into the American body politic.

Many commentators, however, find these arguments less than convincing. In today's globalized world, advanced constitutional democracies face common problems of governance in subject-areas from free speech and affirmative action to partisan gerrymanders and criminal procedure, and they do so under constitutional provisions similar to equivalent words and phrases in the U.S. Constitution. Each of the tribunals under study in this chapter have had to define the meaning of liberty, equality, democracy, and human dignity—often weighing them against one another—in resolving conflicting constitutional claims. In addition, and like the U.S. Supreme Court, each of these courts has had to deal with the perennial tension between majority rule and minority rights (i.e., democracy and constitutionalism), just as each has had to consider its relation to the political branches of government and the propriety of overruling their decisions or settling their conflicts.

It would be carrying American "exceptionalism" too far to suggest that foreign constitutional reflections on these matters, particularly in comparable democracies committed to political freedom and the judicial enforcement of guaranteed rights, has *no* relevance to constitutional interpretation in the United States. In *United States v. Then*, Judge Guido Calabresi rightly noted that several post-1945 systems of judicial review are America's "constitutional offspring," prompting him to say that "[w]ise parents do not hesitate to learn from their children."[29] Even Chief Justice Rehnquist and Justice Scalia, who objected to the use of foreign precedents in the death penalty and homosexual sodomy cases, seem willing to learn from their children. In 1999, at a Georgetown University symposium on comparative constitutional law, the chief justice repeated his observation, quoted earlier, that the time has arrived for U.S. courts to begin looking "to the decisions of other constitutional courts to aid in their own deliberative process." As for Justice Scalia, he, like the chief justice, has participated in several conferences and symposia on comparative constitutional law involving judges and scholars from other countries. And, as already noted, resort to comparative law in addressing legal issues is a familiar practice in American judicial history.

Democracy and the American Judicial System

How does the American judicial system stand up to the courts of the other democracies when measured by the standards of independence and democratic accountability? In particular, does the American scheme represent a better balance between these values than found in the foreign judiciaries examined in this chapter? The question is not easily answered. Each foreign system is embedded in historical, political, and cultural traditions different from those prevailing in the United States. Civil and common law jurisdictions, although beginning to converge in many respects, feature different systems of judicial recruitment and organization with correspondingly different patterns of independence and accountability. In European civil law systems, ordinary judges are recruited at a young age, usually on the basis of merit, by the judicial bureaucracy itself, and they preside over courts of specialized jurisdiction within which they are sheltered for the duration of the careers. In Germany, state ministers of justice, often assisted by judicial selection committees, play key roles in the selection process. In the United States, by contrast—as in some other common law democracies—national and local judges are recruited by political elites, and they preside over courts of *general* jurisdiction, both civil and criminal. Unlike civilian judges, they are also empowered to address constitutional issues raised in the normal course of litigation.

Yet, as suggested, generalizations as to which system is superior is difficult to make. As for judicial independence, both the civil and common law judges considered in this chapter are protected by laws and policies related to salary guarantees, judicial tenure, and the institutional autonomy of their courts. It may be slightly harder to remove or punish a judge in a civil law country than in the United States. German law, for example, reinforces the independence of local—that is, non-federal—judges by permitting their dismissal, suspension, or transfer pursuant only to a *judicial* decision, whereas many American judges can be removed *politically* either by impeachment or a recall election. Additionally, in some American states, judges who hand down unpopular decisions occasionally suffer retaliation in the voting booth. Does this violate the principle of judicial independence? Probably not, at least for Americans who feel that courts are *ultimately* responsible to the larger public for what they do. In this sense, American judges are subject—and appropriately so—to a larger measure of democratic political control than German judges.

Accordingly, German judges are less accountable than in the United States to *political* decision-makers. For the manner in which they administer justice, they are held accountable by their peers and superiors within a self-governing judicial establishment. Their judicial and off-the-bench behavior must of course conform to the democratic values of the Constitution and to the professional standards of conduct explicitly laid down in the law. The closer connection between judicial and political establishments in the United States with regard to judicial recruitment seems necessarily and properly related to the broad policy-making roles of American courts. These courts play a crucial role in the American system of separated powers, especially when on constitutional grounds they require political actors and other branches of government to account for their actions. The tradition of electing judges in mid-career, usually after considerable experience in politics or in the practice of law, seems fully consistent with the nature of judicial power in America. The selection and removal of judges by political elites covers the judiciary with the veneer of democratic legitimacy seemingly required in a constitutional *democracy*. So the American system of judicial selection seems decidedly more open or transparent than in the bureaucratic judiciaries of civil law systems such as Germany.

In many American states, however, where judges are popularly elected for short terms or forced to submit themselves to nonpartisan retention elections, politics may threaten the independence of the judiciary, undermining the ability of courts vigorously to enforce constitutional rights or limits on the political branches of government. While there seems to be no real evidence to show that appointed judges are more competent or independent than elected judges, there is a wide consensus among legal and judicial scholars that an elected judiciary—particularly judges chosen in partisan elections—is a bad thing. That no other advanced democracy elects its judges by popular vote would seem to sustain this thesis. On the other hand, as the experience of Canada and South Africa would suggest, executive control of the judicial recruitment process, in the absence of significant legislative or other public participation, makes the system less open or accountable than in the fourteen American states in which their highest judges are chosen by the legislature or by the governor with the consent of the legislature's upper house or from a list submitted by a judicial nominating commission.

In switching the scene to the models of constitutional justice described earlier in this chapter, Americans can justly pride themselves in the contribution their diffuse system of judicial review has made to constitutional politics in the United States. That state and federal courts have historically addressed and decided constitutional issues has invigorated the American system of separation of powers by engaging legislators and executive officials in constant dialogue over the scope and limits of governmental power. The dispersion of judicial power in America, as suggested by one commentator, has "enhance[d] the system's overall capacity for self-correction," just as it "better provide[s] for political stability by establishing more avenues for the expression of opposition" to executive and legislative authority.[30] The sharp division between judicial and legislative power in civil law countries, on the other hand, helps to explain why judicial review has been withheld from ordinary courts and placed in the hands of specialized tribunals outside the regular judicial structure. In parliamentary systems with no clear separation of executive and legislative power, the specialized constitutional court seems an appropriate way of instituting a judicial check on legislative majorities and, through the medium of concrete judicial review—as in Germany—of imposing unity on a fragmented judicial system.

Parliamentary governments also prevail in Canada and South Africa. But because they are also common law systems, their courts address constitutional as well as other legal issues. Judicial review in South Africa, however, is only partially diffuse. Magistrate courts have been denied the power to decide constitutional issues and constitutional decisions of higher courts require the approval of the Constitutional Court before they can go into effect. South Africa felt compelled to establish a separate constitutional court on the German model to place a sharp spotlight on constitutional values in the post-apartheid era as well as to serve as a check on parliamentary majorities. The president, assisted by a Judicial Selection Commission largely controlled by judges and lawyers, remains dominant in the appointment of its members, but a measure of political control over the court's members results from their limited tenure. In Canada, where diffuse judicial review functions as it does in the United States, executive control is also predominant in the selection of judges, and these judges too, as in South Africa, tend to be politically unaffiliated members of the practicing bar. Under the new Charter of Rights and Freedoms, their power is immense, but the power of provincial and federal courts to disallow parliamentary legislation is democratically tamed by the ability of legislatures to override constitutional decisions.

Each of the highest courts of judicial review under study in this chapter has in its own way adopted strategies and techniques to reconcile judicial review and democracy. But on the whole, particularly with respect to the various modes of judicial review and approaches to constitutional interpretation, there seems little that Americans could usefully borrow from the practices of these tribunals. Some Americans may feel that the judicial tendency to balance the values of dignity and liberty in Canada and Germany manifests greater respect for legislative judgments—and thus for prevailing social values—than the more categorical or libertarian judgments of the Supreme Court, especially in the domain of First Amendment freedoms. Here certain judicial outcomes are preferred to others, but outcomes as such are not easily transplanted to another political or legal culture. Moreover, such outcomes depend on philosophical and moral perspectives around which judges unite and divide in all major constitutional democracies, and it is highly unpredictable how the values of liberty and dignity will be applied by a particular court in a given country.

On the other hand, Americans could enhance the democratic legitimacy of their Supreme Court—and the national judiciary in general—by abolishing life tenure for federal judges. Permanent tenure is of course cemented into the Constitution, and this would be extremely difficult to change. But if Americans were given the chance to rewrite their Constitution, they would almost certainly follow the lead of most other advanced democracies and urge, as they have in advising constitution-makers in other nations, the adoption of limited terms of office. The original rationale for lifetime judges—that permanent tenure is a necessary condition of judicial independence—no longer holds true. The experience of Germany, South Africa, and Canada clearly shows that judicial independence can be equally and solidly secured by limited, nonrenewable terms of twelve or more years or by the imposition of a compulsory retirement age. Judicial acumen not only declines with age; too often in the American experience, justices appointed a generation earlier lose contact with new political and social realities that bear on the process of constitutional interpretation.

In recruiting Supreme Court justices, finally, Americans might also reflect on how foreign practices could enhance their democratic legitimacy. Of interest is that the jurisdictions considered here have rejected American-style confirmation hearings that often result in pressure-group dominated, ideological infighting over judicial nominees, a process Germans and Canadians believe collides with the principle of judicial independence. In Germany, parliamentary nomination of constitutional court judges, along with the two-thirds vote required for their confirmation, produces cross-party consensus candidates fairly representative of the polity. In the United States, of course, parliamentary selection, as opposed to confirmation, would conflict with the Constitution. But a constitutional amendment might not be required to institutionalize by law a two-thirds rule for confirming Supreme Court nominees. In this event, the president would have to confer with the leaders of both political parties before nominating a candidate and the parties would be compelled to negotiate their differences. In the unlikely event that such a reform could ever be instituted, the president would be well advised to follow South Africa's practice by choosing judicial nominees from a list of candidates screened ahead of time for their competence and political acceptability by a committee of experts broadly representative of the nation's legal, social, and political life.

Notes

1. Aharon Barak, President of Israel's Supreme Court, has advanced what is perhaps the most persuasive argument rooting the judicial protection of human rights in democratic theory. He recently remarked that "[d]emocracy has its own internal morality, based on dignity and equality of all human beings." Accordingly, in his words, a "democracy cannot exist without the [judicial] protection of individual human rights—rights so essential that they must be insulated from the power of the majority." See "A Judge on Judging: The Role of a Supreme Court in a Democracy," *Harvard Law Review* 116 (November 2002): 39.
2. Owen M. Fiss, quoted in "The Right Degree of Independence" in Irwin P. Stotzky (ed.), *Transitions to Democracy in Latin America: The Role of the Judiciary* (Boulder, Colo.: Westview Press, 1993), 58.
3. 531 U.S. 98 (2000).

4. For a detailed breakdown of these systems of selection and retention, see *The Book of the States* (The Council of State Governments, 1998), Volume 32, 129–148.
5. See "Changes in Political Regimes and Continuity of the Rule of Law in Germany" in Herbert Jacob et al., *Courts, Law, and Politics in Comparative Perspective*, 249.
6. The modern tendency of constitutional courts to cite, receive, consult, or borrow from the constitutional law of other national and transnational courts has led to an explosion of scholarship in comparative constitutional law. The publication of two major casebooks in the last five years reflect the growing importance of this field. See Vicki C. Jackson and Mark Tushnet, eds., *Comparative Constitutional Law: Cases and Materials* (New York: Foundation Press, 1999), and Norman Dorsen, Michel Rosenfeld, Andras Sajo, and Suzanne Baer, *Comparative Constitutionalism: Cases and Materials* (St. Paul, Minn.: West Group, 2003).
7. 5 U.S. 137 (1803).
8. See, respectively, 347 U.S. 483 (1954) and 410 U.S. 113 (1973).
9. Canadian Constitution (Constitution Act, 1982), Part I (Canadian Charter of Rights and Freedoms), Sec. 27.
10. See, for example, *Keegstra v. The Queen* [1996] 1 S.C.R. 458.
11. Peter W. Hogg, *Constitutional Law of Canada*, 4th ed. (Toronto: Carswell, 1997), 916–917.
12. Peter H. Russell, "Reform's Judicial Agenda" in Paul Howe and Peter H. Russell, eds. *Judicial Power and Canadian Democracy* (Montreal: McGill-Queens University Press, 2001), 121.
13. *In Re Certification of the Constitution of the RSA, 1996.* 1996 (4) SA 744, 814-815.
14. Barak, "A Judge on Judging," 27.
15. Claire L'Heureux-Dubé, quoted in "The Importance of Dialogue: Globalization, the Rehnquist Court, and Human Rights" in Martin H. Belsky (ed.), *The Rehnquist Court: A Retrospective* (Oxford University Press, 2003), 234.
16. 1995 (3) SALR 391 (CC).
17. 428 U.S. 153 (1976).
18. *Palko v. Connecticut*, 302 US 319, 327 (1937).
19. 376 U.S. 254 (1964)
20. [1995] 2 S.C.R. 1130.
21. [1990] 3 S.C.R. 697.
22. James Q. Whitman, "Two Western Cultures of Privacy: Dignity Versus Liberty," *Yale Law Journal* 113 (April 2004): 1151–1221.
23. Ruth Bader Ginsburg, "Looking beyond Our Borders: The Value of a Comparative Perspective in Constitutional Adjudication." 40 *Idaho Law Review* 1–10 (2003).
24. Paul Kirchhof and Donald P. Kommers, eds., *Germany and Its Basic Law: Past, Present, and Future* (Baden-Baden: Nomos, 1993), 412.
25. 41 U.S. (16 Pet.) 1, 19.
26. 123 S. Ct 1406 (2003).
27. 536 U.S. 304 (2002).
28. 521 U.S. 898 (1997).
29. 56 F.3d 464, 469 (2d Cir. 1995) (concurring).

30. Jeffrey Seitzer, *Comparative History and Legal Theory* (Westport, Conn.: Greenwood Press, 2001), 122.

Bibliography

Brewer-Carías, Allen R. *Judicial Review in Comparative Law*. Cambridge, U.K., and New York: Cambridge University Press, 1989.

Cappelletti, Mauro. *Judicial Review in the Contemporary World*. Indianapolis: Bobbs-Merrill, 1971.

Cappelletti, Mauro. *The Judicial Process in Comparative Perspective*. Oxford, U.K., and New York: Clarendon Press, 1989.

Corrado, Michael Louis. *Comparative Constitutional Law: Cases and Materials*. Durham, N.C.: Carolina Academic Press, 2005.

Devlin, Patrick. *The Judge*. Oxford, U.K.: Oxford University Press, 1979.

Greenberg, Douglas, et al., eds. *Constitutionalism and Democracy: Transitions in the Contemporary World*. New York: Oxford University Press, 1993.

Guarnieri, Carlo, and Patrizia Pederzoli. *The Power of Judges*. Oxford, U.K., and New York: Oxford University Press, 2002.

Jacob, Herbert, et al., eds. *Courts, Law, and Politics in Comparative Perspective*. New Haven, Conn.: Yale University Press, 1996.

Koopmans, Tim. *Courts and Political Institutions: A Comparative View*. Cambridge, U.K.: Cambridge University Press, 2003.

Landfried, Christine, ed. *Constitutional Review and Legislation: An International Comparison*. Baden-Baden: Nomos Verlag, 1988.

L'Heureuz-Dubé, Claire. "The Importance of Dialogue: Globalization, the Rehnquist Court, and Human Rights." In *The Rehnquist Court: A Retrospective*, edited by Martin H. Belsky. Oxford, U.K., and New York: Oxford University Press, 2002.

Majone, Gian Andrea. *Independence vs. Accountability? Non-Majoritarian Institutions and Democratic Government*. Florence: European University Institute, 1994.

Merryman, John Henry. *The Civil Law Tradition: An Introduction to the Legal Systems of Western Europe and Latin America*. 2nd ed. Stanford, Calif.: Stanford University Press, 1985.

Models of Constitutional Jurisdiction. Council of Europe, Strasbourg, 1993.

Neubauer, D. W. *Judicial Process, Law, Courts, and Politics in the United States*. 2nd ed. Fort Worth, Tex.: Harcourt Brace College Publishers, 1997.

Russell, Peter H., and David M. O'Brien. *Judicial Independence in the Age of Democracy: Critical Perspectives from around the World*. Charlottesville: University Press of Virginia, 2001.

Shapiro, Martin. *Courts: A Comparative and Political Analysis*. Chicago: University of Chicago Press, 1981.

Schmidhauser, John R., ed. *Comparative Judicial Systems*. London and Boston: Butterworths, 1987.

Steinberger, Helmut. "American Constitutionalism and German Constitutional Development." In *Constitutionalism and Rights: The Influence of the United States Abroad*, edited by Louis Henkin and Albert J. Rosenthal. New York: Columbia University Press, 1990.

Stone Sweet, Alec. *Governing with Judges: Constitutional Politics in Europe*. Oxford, U.K.: Oxford University Press, 2000.

Stotzky, Irwin P., ed.. *Transition to Democracy in Latin America: The Role of the Judiciary*. Boulder, Colo.: Westview Press, 1993.

Tate, C. Neal, and Torbjörn Vallinder. *The Global Expansion of Judicial Power*. New York and London: New York University Press, 1995.

Court Cases

Atkins v. Virginia, 536 U.S. 304 (2002).
Beauharnais v. Illinois, 343 U.S. 250 (1952).
Brown v. Board of Education, 347 U.S. 483 (1954).
Bush v. Gore, 531 U.S. 98 (2000).
Calder v. Bull, 3 U.S. 386 (1798).
Gregg v. Georgia, 428 U.S. 153 (1976).
Lawrence v. Texas, 123 S. Ct 1406 (2003).
Marbury v. Madison, 5 U.S. 137 (1803).
New York Times v. Sullivan, 376 U.S. 254 (1964).
Palko v. Connecticut, 302 U.S. 319, 327 (1937).
Printz v. United States, 521 U.S. 898 (1997).
Roe v. Wade, 410 U.S. 113 (1973).
Swift v. Tyson, 41 U.S. 1 (1842).
United States v. Then, 56 F.3d 464, 469 (2d Cir. 1995) (concurring).

SECTION III

COURTS, CULTURES, AND PUBLICS

9

COURTS IN AMERICAN POPULAR CULTURE

Lynn Mather

ON A HOT SEPTEMBER NIGHT IN 1925, A WHITE MOB IN Detroit attacked the house of a young black doctor hoping to force him and his family out of their new neighborhood. Ossian Sweet, grandson of a slave, had moved north, graduated from college and medical school, and worked hard to buy the lovely brick house that his wife, Gladys, adored. But their second night in the house ended in violence and chaos, with a white neighbor dead and the Sweet family and their friends hauled away in a paddy wagon. Eleven blacks were charged with first-degree murder. Historian Kevin Boyle recreates the sensational trial that followed in his award-winning book, *Arc of Justice: A Saga of Race, Civil Rights, and Murder in the Jazz Age.*[1]

Clarence Darrow, a celebrated defense attorney, had just finished arguments in the Scopes trial when he agreed to come to Detroit to help defend the Sweets. The 1925 courtroom drama riveted the city and was covered by newspapers around the country, especially those papers aimed at black readers. Through the events and issues at trial, the public learned about the violence of racism and the daily threats faced by educated, middle-class blacks; the rallying power of the Ku Klux Klan, which had substantially expanded its activities in the North; the newly formed community "improvement" associations designed to institutionalize residential segregation; orchestrated perjury by police and witnesses to the shooting; and the creation of a new organization, the NAACP, to advance the dignity and power of African Americans. An ambitious young trial judge, Frank Murphy (who later was appointed to the U.S. Supreme Court by President Franklin Delano Roosevelt), presided over the trial and the jury verdict was delivered by twelve white men.

Seventy years later, a wealthy black man went on trial in Los Angeles for murdering his wife. The O. J. Simpson case combined race and gender politics, sex and violence, an ambitious trial judge and flamboyant defense lawyer, and allegations of police racism and perjury. Like the Ossian Sweet case, the O. J. trial commanded extraordinary media attention, but now there was television in the courtroom to create a national audience for the proceedings. The Cable News Network (CNN) devoted a total of 631 hours to the case and an estimated 95 million in the United States alone viewed the trial's opening day.[2] The country's fault lines of race, gender, and class were revealed at the daily water cooler rehashing of courtroom testimony and arguments. Women's organizations sought to use the case as a vehicle for raising consciousness about domestic violence. Other groups stood by O. J. in his defense. Finally, a racially mixed jury of men and women delivered the verdict.

Regardless of what one thinks of the jury acquittals in these two cases, the courts in both provided arenas for conflict resolution and also for broader public debate about divisive social issues. Debate within the court was structured through legal rules and procedures with legal advocates speaking to a judge for the state, a jury of laypersons, and a public audience. Those who were unhappy with the verdicts—and there were many in both cases—voiced their disapproval but also acquiesced in the outcome. By examining the role of trial courts in American popular culture, we will see how popular depictions of trials may promote democratic participation and respect for law. Yet we will also see the reverse, whereby the image of the courtroom proceedings simply reinforces for the public the class and racial bias of the legal system and thereby inhibits democracy.

The history of courts in American culture and society supports both views. There is evidence of lawyers and judges who exemplified civic virtue and independence, of legal decision making based on principle and reason, and of jurors who upheld the rule of law by applying judicial instructions to the facts before them, and only deviated as needed to accomplish justice. Yet there have also been biased and corrupt judges, lawyers motivated by self-interest rather than their clients' problems or the tenets of professionalism, laws and legal procedures that discriminated based on race and gender, and jurors who followed popular sentiment not law. Rather than seeing the history of American courts as either continuous progress or unmitigated decline, I will point out trends in both directions.

Similarly, I take issue with contemporary critics of law on television and film who suggest that these new media have undermined the rule of law by their stereotyped, sensational reporting or their image-based accounts of cases. Such depictions create false expectations in the citizenry and blur the line between fact and fiction, writes legal critic Richard Sherwin.[3] The image-based logic of TV clashes with the legal principles of logic and reason, eroding law's legitimacy and weakening courts as a bulwark against popular majorities. In this view of the system's failings, the problem lies not with the judiciary, legal profession, or citizenry but with the skewed images of law in modern American culture. This critique has been expressed by earlier generations, however, as observers denounced lurid depictions of violent crime or biased accounts of trials in newspapers. Indeed, it is not easy to represent legal conflicts in ways that reserve judgment and express fidelity to law yet will also appeal to a popular audience. The audience expects a point of view as an expression of community values and norms. And whatever details are selected for the TV image or whichever written words are chosen to describe a case, both will necessarily impose meaning on the legal case. Thus I see the problems of cultural representation as endemic, and of long standing, for the judicial system.

Further, as political scientist Martin Shapiro points out, the basic triadic form of conflict resolution, which characterizes American adjudication, is inherently unstable.[4] Although it is common for two parties in dispute to seek the help of a third party, as soon as the third party rules in favor of one side, the losing side will resent the two-against-one situation. In order to ensure acceptance of adjudicated case outcomes, societies often encourage mediation or compromise to resolve disputes. And thus, despite the formal ideal of a zero-sum outcome from an adversary trial, there are always pressures on lawyers and judges to promote negotiated case settlements. Societies also avoid two-against-one problems by insisting that both parties give prior consent to abide by the decision of the third party. In complex societies, such consent is provided by citizens' agreement to respect the decision of the judge and the judge's interpretation of the law. However, as Shapiro suggests, the creation of the office of judge and of rules of law creates new tensions for conflict resolution. It places courts squarely in the business of social control and thus lessens the independence of judges, since judges now have a vested interest in preservation of the government that gave them their position. In short, once courts are situated within a political system, the basic social logic of turning to a third party for assistance in conflict resolution is undermined.

Trial Courts and American Democracy

This chapter examines the place of courts in popular culture and their role in advancing American democracy. Without delving into what exactly "American democracy" requires, I propose a few basic principles to which I will return throughout the chapter. Successful democratic governance requires an open society in which all citizens can exercise voice and have a reasonable chance of being heard. We typically think of voice in terms of elections and voting, but the concept can also be applied to courts. Do they provide open and accessible institutions for raising grievances, asserting rights, and resolving conflicts? Second, American democracy proclaims a rule of law, with expectations of fair, impartial decision making based on law. To what extent do court processes and legal decision makers follow the rule of law? Third, the constitutional guarantee of trial by jury means that American democracy contains a strong element of populism embedded within its legal institutions. How do courts combine legal decision making with the popular voice of lay jurors? These questions provide a backdrop for my investigation of courts in American society and popular culture.

In view of the emphasis on appellate courts elsewhere in this volume, this chapter will pay particular attention to trial courts, especially state trial courts. The material that follows is organized around two central questions: How do Americans *see* courts? And what do they *know* about courts? To answer these questions I begin with the physical and cultural representations of courts. What do courts look like? How are legal actors and court proceedings depicted in the media? That is, in newspapers, television news, court reality shows on TV, and in fictional dramas? In the last part of the chapter, I explore the impact of these representations on the construction of popular legal knowledge. How do the images and narratives of law shape legal consciousness? Do they encourage democratic participation and the use of courts for conflict resolution? Or discourage it? Do they educate citizens and promote the rule of law? Special attention will be given to courtroom trials, juries, and their audiences. By exploring what the public sees and knows about courts, this chapter seeks to help us understand the role that courts play in strengthening or impeding American democracy.

Physical Representations of Courts

What do Americans see when they look at their courts? Despite the ubiquity of courts on television, we should not overlook people's actual experiences as they drive by a court, walk through its metal detector, or show up for jury duty. Indeed, direct personal experience with courts actually ranks higher as a source of information than school or the media, according to a 1998 national survey by the American Bar Association (ABA). When asked *where* they got their knowledge of the justice system, most respondents named personal experience, school or college, and the mass media, in that order. Personal experience with courts included acting as a plaintiff, defendant, witness, or observer, and it was rated as the most important source of information about the justice system (63 percent), just ahead of school or college (59 percent) or jury duty—another form of personal experience (57 percent)—and considerably higher than television news (41 percent) or newspapers (local, 36 percent; national, 35 percent). A different recent survey, conducted by the National Center for State Courts (NCSC), found just over half of respondents reported "personal involvement" in courts; most of those had been observers (40 percent) or jurors (24 percent).

Interestingly, direct court involvement has increased significantly over the past few decades. For example, the percentage of adults reporting they had served as a juror was 27 percent in the 1998 ABA survey and 24 percent in the 1999 NCSC survey compared to only 6 percent in a national survey taken in 1977.[5] What explains this dramatic increase in jury participation given that jury trials actually declined during this period? Why was the jury that decided Ossian Sweet's case so different in its social makeup than the one that acquitted O. J. Simpson? The answer lies in major changes in jury selection and operations. The Supreme Court ruled in 1975 that automatic exemptions for women were unconstitutional and later decisions held that peremptory challenges could not be based on race. By imposing constitutional standards on jury selection, the Court made juries far more demographically diverse than they had ever been before. Local courts also expanded their selection pools to include registered voters, licensed drivers, taxpayers, and even unemployment lists, all in an effort to broaden the pool of eligible jurors. Finally, many courts reduced the time expected for jury service, instituting a "One Day or One Trial" system, which made it easier for those summoned to serve. Although jury participation is still far from universal, the fact that roughly one in four Americans has served as a juror shows remarkable improvement even since the mid-1970s, let alone since the nineteenth century. This change has also brought many people into a courthouse for the first time. They not only saw the buildings but they entered them as participants in the legal process.

American Courthouses

Court buildings themselves reflect society's expectations and ideals and, once constructed, they influence the role that courts play within society. As British Prime Minister Winston Churchill said, "We shape our buildings, and afterwards, our buildings shape us."[6] Visitors to the U.S. Senate today are shocked to see the small and modest basement room where the Supreme Court functioned from 1810 to 1860. But those quarters reinforced a particular role for the Court in American government. The grand neoclassical structure of the Supreme Court's current building, to which it moved in 1937, certainly suggests the larger and more powerful institution that the Court would become in the years that followed. The tall white columns, great marble stairs, and majestic decorations define the Supreme Court as a symbol of law for the nation.

Trial courts, particularly the county courts that handle major crimes and civil cases and often serve as administrative centers of local government, also define law for Americans. Indeed, as the country expanded in the nineteenth century, landowners in different towns competed over the location of the county seat, knowing that it would bring prestige and business to the town. Often located in the geographic middle of the county, the county seat attracted farmers, ranchers, and tradesmen on a regular basis. The courthouse in the square provided a physical location to facilitate economic and social contacts, while also constituting a cultural and political symbol for the community. Often with park-like surroundings, courts served, and continue to serve, as a gathering place for picnics and civic celebrations, as well as a place to record significant events in citizens' lives—births, marriages, land purchases, bankruptcies, and deaths. American county courts thus furthered nineteenth-century democracy by fostering direct connections between residents and local government, offering a forum for conflict resolution and enforcement of rights, and a location to construct community across some (though by no means all) social groups.

The architectural style of court buildings generally reflects fashions of the era and the region. Whether Federal, Grecian Vernacular, Romanesque, Colonial Revival, Neo-Classical, or Art Nouveau, historic county court buildings blazed with civic pride—and expense. The extraordinary details and fine building materials used in pre-1950 courthouses conveyed the majesty of law and the importance of the courthouse in civic life. Historic court buildings usually featured a tall clock tower. In the nineteenth century, only the affluent could afford pocket watches so the courthouse clock tower provided what was considered to be the official time. Inside these historic courtrooms one finds high ceilings, intricately carved decorations, ornate moldings, life-sized statutes, elegant light fixtures, and fine woods and stone. Legal historian Michael Kammen explores why nineteenth-century Americans built such grand temples of justice given their experience of courts as oppressive institutions in the eighteenth century. The answer lies in the prestige that a grand edifice could bring to a county seat and also the security that a neighboring town could not steal the county seat away.[7]

Interestingly, a number of books, pamphlets, and Web sites now celebrate the history and architecture of courthouses in each state. See, for example, Kathleen M. Wiederhold's *Exploring Oregon's Historic Courthouses* or the glossy coffee-table book *Wisconsin's Historic Courthouses* by L. Roger Turner and Marv Balousek. Some of these resources come from local history buffs, the courts themselves run others, and tourist offices distribute others. Kansas touts its court architecture alongside of directions to golf courses and pheasant hunting. A Pennsylvania Web site displays color photos of their courthouses to allow visitors to "send an email post card" with a picture of any Pennsylvania local court, courtesy of the Pennsylvania Visitors Network. This love of courthouses must seem strange to those in countries where courts represent authoritarian or even highly centralized rule, but this cultural promotion of courthouse architecture in the United States can be understood as an expression of its legal ideals.

Symbols or slogans of law and justice frequently adorn court buildings. The U.S. Supreme Court proclaims, "Equal Justice Under Law," and other court buildings similarly etch their ideals in stone. Above the entry to the 1921 Stearns County courthouse in Minnesota are the words, "Where Liberty Ends Tyranny Begins" and "The Pedestal of Liberty Is Justice." Even the names of some trial courts reflect the connection between democracy and rule of law—as in Los Angeles County Court's "Hall of Justice" or Philadelphia's "Court of Common

Pleas." Historic court buildings have added symbols to embrace local heroes and to commemorate local history. On the lawn in front of courthouses, one finds cannons, plaques, and memorials to honor the military or famous regional figures. The historic Sharkey County courthouse in Rolling Fork, Mississippi, even has a gazebo and marker celebrating the famed blues artist Muddy Waters. Added to the 1902 courthouse in 1988, the memorial states, "In Honor of Muddy Waters. Born near Rolling Fork in 1915 as McKinley Morganfield." Other courts publicly commemorate historic trials that occurred there, such as the somber portrait and bronze plaque in Canandaigua, New York, for the 1872 trial and conviction of Susan B. Anthony for voting.

While the iconography of nineteenth-century courthouses announced principles of law and justice, the legal experience of women, blacks, and men without property was vastly different. They lacked access to the legal system, which was run by and for white men with property. The recent courthouse markers have attempted to transform the racist and sexist history of a court's past through contemporary signals of the openness of courts to all residents. Judges and administrators are painfully aware of the exclusive history of their courts, a history that denied blacks and women the right to serve on juries and that, in the South, segregated courtroom seating by race.

Resistance to creating open and fully accessible courts remains, however. In a recent case from Tennessee, a paraplegic who refused to leave his wheelchair and crawl up the courthouse stairs to the second floor to answer a traffic complaint was subsequently arrested for "failure to appear." He challenged his conviction and ultimately won before the U.S. Supreme Court. The Court ruled that the Americans with Disabilities Act required states to provide equal access to their courts. The Supreme Court underscored the symbolic importance of its decision to extend rights to handicapped citizens by announcing the *Tennessee v. Lane* decision on 17 May 2004, exactly fifty years to the day after their ruling in *Brown v. Board of Education* (1954).

Courthouses constructed more recently have lost much of the dignity and exalted nature of traditional court buildings. Rather than the majestic courthouse in the center of the public square, the post-1950 courts are often indistinguishable from office buildings and located in a newer part of town. In a comparison of building styles of past and present American courts, political scientist John Brigham echoes Churchill's comment about the shape of buildings and argues for the symmetry of form and function: "In local courts . . . an architecture of efficiency has taken over the architecture of justice represented by the Supreme Court."[8] Contemporary trial courts resemble large, highly secure, offices and act like them as well, routinely processing a high volume of cases and projecting a fortress-like image. Compare, for example, the original Stearns County courthouse in St. Cloud, Minnesota, built in 1921, with its adjacent 1991 addition.

Figure 1 Stearns County courthouse (Minnesota) 1921

Figure 2 Stearns County courthouse (Minnesota) 1991

The contrast between historic trial court buildings and the newer ones visually emphasizes their different functions. The exterior of the 1921 Stearns County courthouse has a grand entrance, inviting all up its wide stairs, while the 1991 exterior appears impenetrable, designed to keep the accused inside and the public outside. Courtroom security and social control have displaced everyday conflict resolution.

Specialized Courts

The history of crime and punishment oscillates between periods of leniency and severity. While contemporary courthouse architecture reinforces public policies of crime control and harsh sentencing that expanded in the 1990s, the recent development of specialized problem-solving courts reflects concern for the rehabilitation of individual offenders. Beginning in 1989 and spurred by generous federal funding in the 1990s, drug courts for those with substance abuse problems now number over one thousand and exist in every state. Drug courts combine a belief in treatment and therapy with an expansion of state surveillance over offenders and a reduction in due process protections (since offenders must waive their rights in order to obtain treatment). Judges become therapists and social workers, and defendants become clients, in drug courts, mental health courts, domestic violence courts, and others.

The drug court movement today has a disturbing parallel to urban courts in the early twentieth century, during what historian Michael Willrich calls "America's First War on Crime" in his book *City of Courts: Socializing Justice in Progressive Era Chicago*. Today's therapeutic jurisprudence, like its nearly century-old predecessor, sociological jurisprudence, looks at the social impact and consequences of law on criminal offenders. Specialized courts in the Progressive era, such as "The Morals Court," "The Court of Domestic Relations," and "The Boys Court," offered help to poor defendants through middle-class social workers assisting them with health care, employment, education, family support, and the like. But as Willrich suggests, this "new vision of urban courts, as social tribunals that would expose the root causes of criminality, bankrolled an unprecedented and often coercive extension of legal and disciplinary power into the social and domestic lives of working-class city-dwellers."[9] Offenders in today's drug courts are largely young, poor, and often minorities. Everyday details of their lives are open to state inspection and weekly urine samples are required as a condition for remaining in the program. Supporters of the courts praise the constructive recovery and rehabilitation they provide, a pointed contrast with incarceration. But critics have asked why judges—who are mostly middle class—have become so intimately involved in defendants' lives. "At what point do you say, 'O.K., we have enough poor people under court control'?" asked one New York defense attorney.[10] In both historic periods, the move away from severity meant that specialized trial courts assumed ever-greater responsibilities for social regulation, thus compromising the independence of judges by aligning them so closely with particular political interests and class values.

Courts in the News and on Television

If courthouse architecture and specialized courtrooms provide one kind of representation, news reporting, television, and film provide others. Cultural representations of law and courts can also contribute to American democracy. They identify key legal actors and institutions, define rules and processes of law, provide symbols of justice and a discourse for discussing social conflicts, and spur individuals and organizations to care about those conflicts and engage in civic life. Of course, not all courtroom images are so laudable. Indeed, as the following materials suggest, much of the coverage of legal action shows it to be distorted, inaccurate, and sensationalized in ways that are highly detrimental to democracy. The coverage stifles minority voices and discourages equal participation in law and civic affairs.

Newspaper Coverage of Courts

Published reports of crime and trials are found in the earliest historical records of the colonies, ranging from the detailed reports of witchcraft trials to highly abbreviated accounts of legal actions in the mid-seventeenth century. Journalism scholar Robert E. Drechsel examined a number of local newspapers between 1700 and 1900 and found a remarkable consistency in reporting on court cases over those two centuries. Coverage of criminal cases generally outweighed that of civil cases, a pattern that has also been observed in contemporary studies of both newspaper and television coverage of courts.[11] Specialized publications in the nineteenth century printed lengthy reports of criminal cases, full of sensational and lurid details much like today's televised coverage of crime on the local news. And just as contemporary critics deplore the biased news reporting that lavishes so much detail on violent crime, so did writers in the past. In *Walden*, published in 1854, Henry David Thoreau complained about the attention given to inconsequential legal events: "If we read of one man robbed, or murdered, or killed by accident . . . we never need read of another."[12] And Thoreau attacked the public's indifference to political events such as the hanging of John Brown for leading a raid to further the antislavery cause.

It is no accident that we would find such differences in news coverage between crime and civil cases, and between individual conflicts and broader public issues. Journalists have their own goals such as selling papers and staying in business, which require printing stories that will appeal to the masses and not challenge local values. News stories with a broad thematic focus are far less common than those that focus on specific events or individuals. And the latter are less likely to engender calls for major policy change. William Haltom explains that civil lawsuits receive less news coverage than criminal ones because they typically involve less drama and greater complexity, they seem private compared to the inherently public criminal cases, and they are harder for reporters to cover intelligibly. Civil cases usually lack experienced spokespersons who can talk with the press and provide background information, in contrast to prosecutors and law enforcement officials who deal with the press on a regular basis.[13]

Newspapers tend to cover certain parts of court cases more than others. Thus, one sees the beginnings and endings of cases far more than the competing legal arguments in the midst of a trial. One study of newspaper reporting found that 41 percent of all criminal case coverage occurred on the pretrial stage, including arrest, filing of charges, and arraignment. And a similar pattern of news coverage existed in civil cases with more attention to the initial case filing and verdict than to stages in the middle.[14] The famous case involving spilled hot coffee at McDonald's persuasively illustrates the problems created by selective reporting. William Haltom and Michael McCann systematically analyzed newspaper coverage of the case and found that most articles focused on the jury's $2.7 million verdict in punitive damages against McDonald's for serving their coffee so hot that it burned an elderly woman. Readers did not learn the crucial facts presented at trial that had persuaded the jury to reach such a figure—facts such as the scientific evidence on burns, the severity of the victim's injuries, the seven hundred previous complaints against McDonald's for similar injuries and the company's indifference to them. In addition, newspapers devoted little coverage to the judge's decision after the jury verdict, which drastically reduced the punitive damage award by almost 80 percent. As a result of how the media reported these issues, the public developed a distorted impression of the legal system.[15]

Television News

Compared to print journalists, TV reporters pay even less attention to what goes on in courts. But, like newspapers, television also devotes considerably more coverage to criminal cases than to civil ones. Television's need for dramatic visual images results in disproportionate attention to murders, rapes, kidnappings, and other violent crime. Viewers rarely see traffic cases, petty thefts, drug cases, or burglaries on television news. The mass media follow journalistic conventions such as "if it bleeds, it leads" and "dollars holler." Hence the court stories featured both on broadcasts and in print overemphasize violent crimes and large financial awards in civil cases. Most Americans in the NCSC survey said that they rely regularly on TV news (73 percent) as their primary source for news as compared to newspapers (58 percent), or radio (49 percent). Television and newspapers are providing skewed and incomplete information to the general public about court processes and judicial proceedings when they show far more criminal than civil cases, emphasize violent crime and large financial verdicts, focus on the filing of charges and on verdicts but without the processes in between, and when they ignore the out-of-court negotiations and settlements that characterize most cases.

The medium of television also does poorly with its coverage of appellate courts, including the Supreme Court. Appellate proceedings typically lack the drama of an individual narrative with good guys and bad guys, they have few visual images, and they contain debates over important legal principles but expressed in technical legal language. What is a TV reporter to do? The answer has been to ignore them—even the oral arguments of the U.S. Supreme Court. Elliot Slotnick and Jennifer Segal systematically examined television coverage of the Supreme Court and found that 74 percent of the Court's decisions in 1989 received *no* coverage whatsoever on any of the three major networks.[16] Rulings on constitutional issues such as abortion, affirmative action, free speech, and the like, received far more coverage than did statutory legal issues (which tend to be complex and technical). Interestingly, television reporters also devoted more attention to cases where interest groups had filed friend of the court briefs to advocate a particular outcome. In such cases, reporters could interview experienced advocates to help provide "spin" or "color" to the stories.

What the public sees in court through newspaper and television coverage reflects the systematic biases and limits of the media. The need to sell papers and reach viewers leads to overemphasis on crime, dramatic individual stories, and visual imagery. Limits on reporters' ability to translate legal issues for a mass public and to quickly gather the necessary background facts for a good story further distort court coverage. Consequently, the public knows less about legal cases now than they did in the days when the local court provided a major source of public entertainment. The solution suggested by some is to open the courts to cameras and live broadcasting.

Cameras in the Courtroom

Allowing cameras and television broadcasting to cover court proceedings requires judicial balancing of two competing constitutional principles: the defendant's right to a fair trial and the freedom of the press to cover that trial. At first the Supreme Court tipped the scale in favor of defendants' rights and prohibited states from allowing cameras in court to broadcast criminal trials. The primitive broadcasting equipment created a circus atmosphere with bulky cameras and sound mikes everywhere, thus depriving defendants of their right to a fair trial, the Court said. But that changed in the 1980s with improved technology and a shift in political attitudes. In *Chandler v. Florida* (1981) the Supreme Court endorsed the societal benefits of opening courts to a wider audience and held that television cameras did not automatically violate the defendant's rights. Cameras could be used even over the defendant's objections. Ever mindful of the cultural image of law, the justices expressed their concern for the appearance of justice. In so doing they drew on a centuries-old English legal principle, "justice must not only be done, it must be seen to be done." Since the *Chandler* ruling, nearly all the states have changed their rules to allow television broadcasting and still cameras in court. Most states, however, give judges wide discretion to ban such equipment from individual proceedings, as they deem appropriate. Increasingly, trial judges are using that discretion to keep cameras out of their courts, especially in criminal cases and high-profile trials.

The federal judiciary has been much more skeptical of cameras and television than state judges have been, a difference that may lie in the greater need that state judges feel to be accountable to their constituencies, compared to their more independent federal brethren. Federal courts currently prohibit cameras and television broadcasting, even after what most acknowledged was a successful experiment with television in selected lower federal courts. The results of televising state trials have added fuel to both sides in the debate among the federal jurists. Broadcasting holds out the promise of greater civic education, enhanced knowledge of law, and more informed public discussion about important and complex issues. But TV also leads to selective and perhaps distorted coverage of those issues (for instance, through its use of sound bites) and may have a deleterious impact on the legal process. Some federal judges also worry that public confidence in the judiciary could decrease as a result of opening up their proceedings. That is, ironically, perhaps some of the current legitimacy and respect for the federal courts stem from their mystery and lack of visibility.

When the Florida Supreme Court heard oral arguments in the 2000 presidential election case, a large television audience saw for the first time what a state appellate court hearing was like. Given the high stakes of the case—the outcome of the presidential election—many viewers tuned in with intense interest. But the legal discourse and focus on technical details seemed to obscure issues that partisans on both sides saw as straightforward. Conflicting interpretations of law provided by different legal experts further confused TV viewers. The U.S. Supreme Court has a long-standing policy against any form of cameras in its courtroom. But when the extraordinary 2000 election case reached the justices for its second hearing, the Court was faced with incredible pressure from the media and the public to open its doors. How could a democratic government allow a court to decide the outcome of an election and *not* share with the public the arguments and questions on which the decision would be based? The Supreme Court took the unusual step of allowing audio (though not video) broadcast of the *Bush v. Gore* (2000) oral arguments immediately following the hearing. Almost three years later, the Court again released an audio broadcast immediately after arguments in the 2003 University of Michigan affirmative action cases. These two experiences, along with expanded use of audio recordings (now made possible on the Web and used in many schools and college classes) are allowing a wider public audience to see the Supreme Court at work.

But the current justices—ever mindful of the sensational, popularized coverage of state court trials—adamantly oppose letting cameras in.

Court TV

Once the broadcasting ban on state courts was lifted, television soon took advantage of the opportunities. In 1991 a new cable network, Court TV, began operations, promising live coverage of criminal and civil trials with expert legal commentary. Court TV quickly grew in popularity during the 1990s, featuring celebrity drama and social issue trials such as the Menendez brothers' murder trial, the "tobacco conspiracy case," and the trial that put the network on the map, the O. J. Simpson case. When the verdict was announced in October 1995, the country paid attention: energy use soared as TV sets were turned on; long distance phone calls dropped 58 percent; and trading on the New York Stock Exchange dropped by 30 million shares. Even the Supreme Court was not immune. As the justices sat on the bench listening to oral arguments, a note was circulated with the news of the jury's acquittal of O. J. Simpson.[17]

The televised O. J. trial created a national dialogue over what in earlier times might simply have been a crime of local or regional interest. The images and symbols from the case (Nicole's frantic phone call to 911, the glove that didn't fit, Johnny Cochran versus Marcia Clark) and the political fault lines of the trial (a case of domestic violence or of racist police) constituted a cultural representation of crime for the entire nation, not just for Los Angeles. And that representation continues to shape our understanding of defendants, victims, legal rules, criminal lawyers, judges, and trials. Although O. J. was a superstar before his trial, in other cases, defendants (or victims) are constructed as celebrities by the media. Indeed, when the 2004 Scott Peterson murder trial was moved out of Stanislaus county because of prejudicial pretrial publicity, a number of other California counties volunteered to "host" the trial (much like cities bidding to host a convention, or countries bidding to host the Olympics). County leaders were candid with reporters about the economic benefits of having the trial in their towns, given the number of newscasters and Court TV reporters it would attract. Thus, it is not so surprising, as John Brigham writes, that we now "think of law as a cultural industry that is linked to celebrity and the popular representation of legal institutions."[18]

Like any other industry, however, the televised image of law followed the market—or in this case, the Nielsen ratings. Since the year 2000, Court TV has more than tripled its audience by showing more crime dramas and shows about forensics, and fewer actual trials. And the lead commentator who now presides over the network's daily trial coverage is a former prosecutor who proudly speaks for crime victims and expresses contempt for defense attorneys. Court TV reporters used to be forbidden to express a position on the trials they were covering, but ever since Time-Warner bought Court TV in 1997, loud and passionate opinions have become commonplace. In short, while Court TV initially created a national audience and dialogue about legal cases, the network's potential for civic education and the dramatization of democratic values seems to have given way to a one-sided spectacle of crime and punishment.

Reality Courts

When *The People's Court* began in 1981, it pioneered a new television genre. With a "real" judge and "real" litigants who brought their complaints to a television studio rather than to small claims court, the program became so successful that by the late 1980s, six times more Americans could identify Judge Wapner by name than could identify Chief Justice William Rehnquist. Before his stint on *The People's Court*, Judge Joseph A. Wapner served for twenty years as a trial judge in California, at one point presiding over the largest trial court system in the country (Los Angeles County). In his book *A View from the Bench*, Judge Wapner recounts some of his favorite cases and explains his judicial philosophy as a mix of caring, firmness, and respect for people's stories: "When Americans leave a courtroom feeling that their cries have been heard, we should all share pride in the fact that our legal system works as well as it does."[19]

Since around 2000, somewhere between seven and eleven different reality court programs have been aired daily, most featuring former jurists such as "Judge Judy" (New York), "Judge Mathis" (Detroit), and "Judge Joe Brown" (Memphis).[20] *Judge Judy* garnered the highest ratings and became one of the top ten syndicated programs in the nation just one year after the show began in 1996.[21] Judges' personalities and styles vary but all the programs show a strong judge who actively questions the parties and does not hesitate to challenge and interrupt them, sometimes quite rudely. Indeed, the dominant judicial style has shifted from Judge Wapner's avuncular one to something far more shrill. Disputing parties are unrepresented in court, and on some programs there are no witnesses. Recent surveys underscore the importance of court reality TV shows. The 1999 NCSC survey found that 61 percent regularly or sometimes obtained information about courts from TV dramas and 40 percent said the same about court reality shows. These survey figures were higher for African American and Hispanic respondents, and viewer demographics consistently demonstrate a disproportionately female and minority audience for court reality programs (which air on daytime TV). Indeed, a study of TV advertising by the 2004 presidential candidates revealed that *Judge Judy* was among the top programs selected by Democrats for ad placement, whereas *Law and Order* and *NYPD Blue* were among the top shows for the Republicans.[22] Although some argue for the educational benefits of reality courts, others raise concerns about the visual picture of courts that these TV programs provide. Law professor Taunya Lovell Banks compared the racial and gender composition of judges on these shows with the composition of the American judicial system. Of the nine judges on syndicated reality court programs in 2000–2001, four were black men; two were black women; two, white men; and one, a white woman. Yet, overwhelmingly, American judges today are white men. Only 3 percent of the judges are black, and this distortion by TV, Banks argues, "may actually undermine popular support for increased racial and gender diversity on the bench by suggesting that our nation's benches are already diverse . . . the presence of women and non-white judges in integrated settings [may] reassure viewers that justice in the United States is meted out impartially."[23] An alternative, more positive interpretation, of judicial diversity on these shows would suggest that they might build trust and confidence in the legal system, particularly for a viewing audience of women and minorities. That is, they could encourage an expectation of justice and fairness before the law, which could lead to a willingness to assert legal rights and engage our democracy rather than cynically giving up on it.

Fictional Representations of Courts on TV and Film

Just like judges on the reality court series, the gender and racial demographics of legal actors on contemporary law-based dramas construct a reassuring visual image of an integrated legal system. Programs centering on crime and legal conflict have a long history in the popular media. But we have moved from *Dragnet*'s two white men as police partners in the 1950s to the ubiquitous white and black police pair on more recent cop shows. The regular cast of series such as *L.A. Law*, *Ally McBeal*, or *The Practice* presents a mixed image of American law offices by gender and race, but only occasionally do these programs address the career problems that women and minority lawyers face.

Televised images of law and courts from the 1990s show several other shifts from earlier TV series. First, legal dramas expanded from the always-popular criminal conflicts to include civil law cases. And, in so doing, for example, *L.A. Law* re-centered law, locating more of the legal action in the boardroom and in individual lawyer's offices rather than the courtroom.[24] By showing the pretrial process, with discovery, motions, and negotiations, and introducing some of the everyday dilemmas of legal practice, this program received considerable praise even from legal scholars. Nevertheless, with affluent Beverly Hills clients, the types of civil cases shown hardly represented an accurate picture of the civil docket, and the law was considerably less important than personalities and romantic relationships.

In dramatic crime series in the 1990s, the prosecutor displaced the defense attorney as hero, argues media scholar Elayne Rapping.[25] In popular court shows of the 1960s and 1970s, the defendant was usually innocent, and dramatic conflict centered on the investigative and rhetorical skill of the defense attorney to free the hapless defendant who had been trapped by an unjust legal system. Contemporary crime dramas now focus on the victim in need of protection, with law enforcement and prosecutors as the heroes who locate and convict the guilty offenders. Stories end with incarceration and harsh punishment to separate the evil wrongdoer from the good society. Crime control, not due process or the evils of racial discrimination, is the underlying message.

Contrast the *Law and Order* message with the story of a white accuser and innocent black defendant in the classic 1962 film *To Kill a Mockingbird*. As the heroic defense attorney Atticus Finch says to the jury: "I have nothing but pity in my heart for the chief witness for the State. She is a victim of cruel poverty and ignorance. But my pity does not extend so far as to her putting a man's life at stake, which she has done in an effort to get rid of her own guilt."[26] Consider also the Henry Fonda character in *Twelve Angry Men* who, as the lone holdout against conviction, ultimately persuades his fellow jurors to put aside their ethnic prejudice and stereotyping to examine the facts presented at trial and vote for acquittal. The liberal slant of those films has been replaced by conservative representations today that pay more attention to victims than to defendants, sympathetically portray police and prosecutors, and rarely show defense lawyers in a positive light.

Cultural studies of law and legal actors have increased in academic circles and even the legal academy is beginning to pay close attention to the impact of cultural representations. Some of this new work has developed from earlier scholarship on law and literature, while other scholars have come from the social sciences, law, or media studies. How we see others deal with their disputes, and how we see police, lawyers, judges, and juries respond, influence what we know about courts. That knowledge, in turn, figures prominently in the role courts play in society.

Common Knowledge of Law and Courts

Law's power resides not only in formal actions such as judicial decisions or jury verdicts, but also in the power to construct social reality. Law provides a set of normative frameworks and institutions for understanding and interpreting human relationships and conflicts. Analysis of law and courts in society thus requires studying what socio-legal scholars call "legal consciousness" or "the common knowledge of law."[27] That is, how do people understand and use law? How do cultural representations of legal actions construct different kinds of legal knowledge? How does the trial, as a special form of court performance, generate moral and political lessons and directly engage citizens in democracy?

Legal Processes and Their Representation

Televised portrayals of legal processes can teach citizens about law and how courts work. Perhaps the best example of a positive educational benefit of television is knowledge of the *Miranda* warnings. When the Supreme Court made its highly controversial five-to-four decision on police interrogation practices in 1966, the majority opinion concluded with detailed instructions for law enforcement officers about the warnings that they must recite to arrested suspects before questioning could begin. These instructions conveyed important constitutional rights to defendants, rights that were hardly part of common knowledge in the mid-1960s. But as a result of crime dramas on TV, millions of Americans now know that, if arrested, they have the right to remain silent and the right to a lawyer.

Key to enforcement of the *Miranda* warnings is the exclusionary rule that makes any illegally obtained confession or evidence inadmissible at trial. That rule, along with other procedural safeguards, became part of the legal knowledge of millions of viewers of the O. J. Simpson trial. Despite the excesses and posturing for cameras during the trial, the case created an extraordinary conversation about how the legal system works. Indeed one survey found that 55 percent of Americans said that they learned a great deal about the justice system from watching the O. J. trial.[28] When O. J.'s preliminary hearing began, viewers all over the country were engaged in a civics lesson about the difference between a grand jury indictment and a preliminary hearing, and about the definition and significance of probable cause. After O. J.'s acquittal at the criminal trial, commencement of his civil trial instructed viewers about the meaning of double jeopardy and the different burdens of proof required for civil and criminal trials. In fact, one public survey attributed the surprisingly high percentage of respondents who knew that an offense could result in both civil and criminal charges to publicity about the O. J. case.

Televised representations of the criminal justice system also convey misleading information to viewers, however. Americans tend to overestimate rates of violent crime and recidivism and to hold inaccurate perceptions of the racial identities of crime perpetrators and victims. Although most murders and assaults are committed by friends and family, televised images depict strangers as the assailants, which fuels the public's fear of crime and increases support for punitive sentencing. Criminal justice practices are also misrepresented in popular culture. For example, the frequency of *Miranda* warnings given on TV undoubtedly exceeds that by police in real life. Many real crimes are never solved, unlike the televised ones that always manage to reach resolution right at the end of the hour. Contrary to the image on TV, police do not routinely test for fingerprints. Relatively few crimes are solved by the defendant voluntarily breaking down and confessing. And most criminal cases end with guilty pleas, not trials. These realities of criminal law enforcement and case disposition can frustrate victims and their families who come to court with expectations created by TV. Even the dramatic images of jury deliberation shown on television and film overestimate the amount of give and take and shifting of votes compared to what occurs on actual juries. Psychologists find that jurors in criminal trials rarely reverse their initial verdict preferences. And minorities of one, such as Henry Fonda in *Twelve Angry Men*, "almost never succeed in converting everyone else."[29]

When judges on court reality programs question disputants about key issues or problems with their stories, they provide viewers with some basic legal concepts and ideas. But by presenting such active judges who run their courtrooms in an inquisitorial manner, these series portray a distorted picture of the trial process. A study of small claims courts found that litigants had quite unrealistic expectations of what would occur in court. They expected the judge to actively help them construct their cases rather than passively waiting for the litigants' presentations. Another study found that frequent viewers of court reality programs were twice as likely as nonviewers to believe that judges should act aggressively, ask questions during trial, express displeasure about testimony they did not like, and have opinions about the verdict.[30]

Court reality programs on TV may also be influencing public expectations about the importance of legal representation. There is no question that there has been an increase in *pro se* (self) representation in civil courts in recent years. Reasons for this trend include the high cost of lawyers and the inaccessibility of legal services, as well as efforts by courts to simplify legal processes by providing easy-to-use forms and information to facilitate self-representation. Court reality TV series suggest that litigants can easily present their own cases and in the end, half of them win. Viewers learn through such shows that perhaps lawyers are not necessary for a success in court. In fact, an astounding six out of ten Americans "believe that it would be possible to represent themselves in court if they wanted to."[31]

There are two ways to look at the disparity between TV images of legal practices and their realities. Most commonly, critics lambaste the representation for its misleading images or distorted information. How can lawyers and judges do their jobs properly if the citizenry has been socialized by television and film to have false expectations? On the other hand, to the extent that legal actors in court and in popular culture mutually influence each other, then the disparity may be less problematic. After all, both are continually in flux. As litigants demand easier access to courts and more intelligible legal processes, courts respond with forms, Web sites, information officers, and other ways of breaking down the distance between courts and communities. On TV, court reality programs flourish, showing everyday citizens explaining their complaints in plain language to a judge, without the help of a lawyer. Both images, in turn, encourage people to see the courts as accessible institutions for problem solving, at least in minor cases. And as rates of self-representation increase, courts cope as best they can. Trial judges may become more proactive, like Judge Judy, simply because they find that it is expected of them, and because they no longer have lawyers present in the courtroom to explain the process to litigants. In fact, when one party appears in court with a lawyer and the other does not, some judges now will bend the rules to help the unrepresented party simply to preserve fairness and level the playing field.[32]

The Function of Trials

The trial occupies a particular place of significance in American popular culture. Revered in myth as an ideal mechanism for conflict resolution, the trial in practice is hardly an efficient way to resolve conflict. Since the win-or-lose format of trial is bound to leave one party dissatisfied at the outcome, it is not surprising that many parties seek resolution by alternative processes such as negotiation, mediation, or arbitration. According to a NCSC study of state courts in 2002, only 7 percent of civil cases and 3 percent of felony criminal cases were disposed of by bench or jury trial. The importance of trials in society lies less in their contributions to dispute settlement than to social control. A public trial provides a stage for the performance of law, rhetoric and persuasion, teaching moral lessons, and engaging popular passions and the emotional involvement of a lay audience of citizens. The trial flourished in the Classical era of Greece and Rome and has defined any number of dramatic legal moments—the religious trials of Joan of Arc and the "witches" of Salem, the trial of Irish playwright Oscar Wilde for homosexuality, the prosecution of John Scopes for teaching evolution, and the trials of kidnappers (Bruno Hauptmann), spies (the Rosenbergs), and political protesters (the Chicago Seven), and numerous others. Consider how often we hear the media proclaim that an upcoming case may be the next "Trial of the Century."

In 1935, the distinguished legal realist Thurman Arnold wrote *The Symbols of Government*, describing the trial as one of those crucial symbols:

> It is a common belief that courts are an efficient way of enforcing the law, and of settling disputes. This is because these are two of the important ideals of the judiciary, not because it is actually true. . . . Law as a philosophy is the property of scholars; as a technique it is the property of lawyers. . . . To the great mass of people the language of the theories of law is unknown. It is not the doctrine but the public judicial trial which symbolizes for them the heaven of justice which lies behind the insecurity, cruelty, and irrationality of an everyday world. . . . The judicial trial thus becomes a series of object lessons and examples. It is the way in which society is trained in the right ways of thought and action, not by compulsion, but by parables which it interprets and follows voluntarily.[33]

Trials perform law for the public through dramatic conflict between two parties, with a third party judge or jury representing the state as arbiter. Trials involving celebrities (e.g., Claus von Bulow, William Kennedy Smith, Winona Ryder, Martha Stewart, Michael Jackson) have always been popular because they combine a theatrical court performance with a voyeuristic look at the rich and famous ensnared by their own transgressions. Political trials also attract wide audiences because they provide symbols that represent competing positions in political or social conflicts. Abstract principles become intelligible through individual people and events. For instance, the trials of antiwar protestors during the Vietnam conflict became public debates over the correctness of America's military presence there. The Ossian Sweet trial focused attention on residential segregation by race and the rights of blacks to defend themselves against racial violence. Popular and political trials, particularly when they receive extensive coverage in the media, thus further democracy by engaging the citizenry directly in discussion of the meaning of law or the validity of government action. Such discussion is structured and contained through the formal conventions of the trial process.

THE AUDIENCE. Further, the constitutional guarantee of a *public* trial ensures that judges cannot hermetically seal themselves off from the community to hear arguments and reach a verdict. The community as audience plays a key role in the trial performance, setting expectations for the judge and jury. In criminal trials, in which the state furnishes players for both the prosecutor's and the judge's roles, the public audience may provide a brake against unduly harsh sanctions. In the seventeenth and eighteenth centuries, whippings, confinement in the stocks, and execution of convicted criminals always occurred in the public square. Such spectacles provided public entertainment, but more importantly, they implicated the community in the punishment. The watchful public could try to resist or intervene if they believed that the authorities had gone too far.[34]

Today's public audience includes those within the courtroom, those following a trial through TV, the Internet, or the newspapers, and those interested in a case solely for the legal or political issues raised. Critics complain about the lack of congruence between different representations of the same event but the difference should not be surprising given the diverse aims of those involved. Good performers (including trial lawyers, reporters, politicians, interest group leaders) know that, "if you change the audience, you change the performance."[35] And thus each will portray or spin the trial narrative to further its own goals. Midway through Scott Peterson's double murder trial in California, in July 2004, the *New York Times* reported: "There are two trials under way here over the killings of Laci Peterson and her unborn son. One is the quiet proceeding inside the four walls of the town courthouse . . . all but bereft of drama and hard to follow. . . . The other trial takes place in the hallways and on the esplanade in front of the courthouse, where a spin zone relentlessly churns before television cameras, which are barred from the courtroom itself."[36] In the "second" trial, TV pundits suggested initially that the prosecution was losing to the more persuasive and emotional performance of the defense attorney. Yet a third trial was also underway as spokespersons for anti-abortion groups presented the case as a poster child to promote the cause of fetal rights. The trial functions as an adjudication between competing discourses in society, with the audience reaction to a verdict an integral part of the process through which a community defines itself and its laws.[37]

JURIES. Trial by jury directly promotes American democracy in several ways. First, the very fact of receiving a summons, being questioned as part of a venire, and then serving on a jury, imposes direct political participation. Historically, restrictions by race, ethnicity, sex, and class sharply limited those who were called for jury service. But, as noted above, recent surveys that report one in four Americans having served on a jury reflect a heartening trend. Second, the political independence of juries can be seen in jury nullification, the power of jurors to ignore formal law if necessary to reach a verdict that comports with their sense of justice. Although no longer authorized by law as it was in the nineteenth century, the power of juries to nullify unpopular laws exists informally and is illustrated by jury acquittals of defendants during Prohibition, in trials of Vietnam war protesters, and in several trials of Dr. Kevorkian for physician-assisted suicide.

Third, juries give meaning to law by the very process of fact-finding and applying legal categories to those facts. In deciding whether a defendant acted with "reasonable care," or whether a killing was done with "intent and malice aforethought," in setting amounts for civil damage awards or deciding which murderers deserve the death penalty, jurors are drawing on ideas and values from their common knowledge. Fourth, by infusing the law and legal decisions with that common knowledge, jury verdicts set powerful benchmarks for the settlement of future cases. As litigants and their lawyers weigh the value of a negotiated compromise, they compare that settlement to how much better (or worse) they expect to do at trial. That calculation depends upon trends in jury verdicts about "what a case is worth." Juries thus act as the populist voice of our legal system, expressing the will of the people about law and justice.

Nevertheless, as in other parts of American government, checks and balances exist over juries. Trial judges can set aside or reduce individual jury verdicts, and appellate judges can modify them as well. Legislatures can restrict the discretion of jurors by removing certain decisions from their purview or setting limits on the penalties or awards available to them (e.g., statutory caps on punitive damages). Two very recent Supreme Court decisions illustrate appellate oversight of jury discretion through constitutional interpretation. In the 2003 case of *State Farm Mutual v. Campbell*, the Court imposed limits on juries in civil cases by ruling that a ratio of punitive damages to compensatory damages greater than 4-to-1 might be excessive and thus beyond constitutional bounds. Instead of having a free hand in awarding punitive damages, juries are now more strictly limited. Tort reform groups praised the Court for reining in "runaway" juries. Yet the decision also weakens the ability of jurors to express the laypersons' judgment in cases of egregious or reckless misconduct.

In criminal law, however, the Supreme Court has been moving in the opposite direction, that is, to expand jury discretion in criminal sentencing. In the 2004 *Blakely v. Washington* decision, the Court struck down one state's sentencing guidelines because they allowed judges at the time of sentencing to establish facts that would increase a defendant's sentence. The Court said that the jury, not the judge, must find any fact that is essential to punishment in cases of upward departure from legislatively set guidelines. In *U.S. v. Booker* (2005), the Court extended the *Blakely* doctrine, ruling that the federal sentencing system, which Congress created in 1984, was an unconstitutional violation of defendants' rights to trial by jury. The sentencing guidelines could still be used, the Court said, but only as an advisory to federal judges, not a requirement on them. This decision empowers the popular voice of the jury and restricts prosecutorial power, tempering what many observers (including a number of federal judges) contended was an overly rigid and harsh federal sentencing system.

Conclusion

Much of American politics consists of moving issues from one sphere of government to another. The framers designed the system that way and enterprising policy entrepreneurs routinely take advantage of the multiple options available to them. Thus, the populism of juries does not usually remain unchecked for long. At the end of the nineteenth century, a system of workman's compensation replaced jury decision making to resolve and compensate victims of industrial accidents. Some contemporary critics today urge a similar removal of tort cases from the court system. We have seen that civil trials receive little news coverage in newspapers or on TV. Consequently, debates over tort reform are waged through the mass media with oversimplified cases, anecdotes, and advertising. Popular depictions of tort lawsuits appeal to deeply held cultural values of individual responsibility and distrust of lawyers. Counternarratives, pointing to a decline in tort filings and the rarity of punitive damage awards, have been relatively less successful. Laws are made and interpreted to respond to public problems. But who defines the problems and their "public" nature? It is in this critical area that the interplay between popular culture, courts, and democratic lawmaking becomes especially significant.

Individuals and groups mobilize the law when they go to the police, a lawyer, or the court for help in resolving their problems. Contrary to popular folk wisdom and images of petty lawsuits on court reality shows, turning to law is not the first response of most people. Victims of crime do not routinely report the occurrence to the police, whether from fear, shame, a desire to handle it themselves, inconvenience, or distrust of police and courts. Similarly, when facing problems that could be civil lawsuits, people's first response is to do nothing or handle the problem on their own, not to seek a lawyer. The cost of legal representation is prohibitive for people with ordinary civil legal problems. Unlike criminal cases, in which one has a constitutional right to a lawyer, no such right exists for civil matters and a major complaint about the American justice system centers on the cost of legal services. TV shows such as *L.A. Law* may highlight the disparity between the glamorous law offices in Hollywood and the inaccessibility of those services for many Americans. Yet shows like *Judge Judy* may promote the opposite, encouraging ordinary folk to use the legal system to resolve disputes.

Popular knowledge about law and courts affects legal mobilization by defining the kinds of cases for which law is perceived to be the appropriate response. That knowledge varies enormously according to the values and beliefs of different communities. Just as "all politics are local," one could say that "all law is local" as well. The diversity of courthouse architecture in county courts across the country visually underscores this point. Residents of some towns would never dream of using law for problems that are routinely found in courts elsewhere, just as prosecutors have divergent standards as to which cases merit filing in criminal court. Local legal cultures are shaped by variation in state law, local history and politics, and community knowledge and values. The nationalization of the media, however, from television to *USA Today*, can dislocate local cultures by presenting images and representations of law that clash with community narratives and experiences. These legal images may encourage citizens to see courts as more accessible than they really are and to assert their legal rights. But other images, such as those of violent crime on TV, may polarize communities by reinforcing racial stereotypes and fostering distrust of fellow citizens. Even in areas with low crime rates residents often report high fear of crime because of what they have seen on TV. Centralization of the mass media through consolidation of newspapers and the creation of media conglomerates threatens democracy by diminishing local variation in legal knowledge.

Common knowledge of law varies by social location as well as by geography. Racial minorities and women have different histories and experiences with American courts than do white men, leading to disparate understandings of the value of legal mobilization. Sociologist Laura Beth Nielsen found such differences in her research on people's attitudes toward urban street harassment. People of color and white women are far more likely than white men to experience the ugly taunts and curses that characterize offensive public speech. But while all groups generally opposed the use of law to regulate such speech, differences in their reasoning reveal much about legal consciousness. White men tended to disfavor legal intervention because it would violate "traditional First Amendment values," African American men disfavored it because of their "distrust of authority and a cynicism about law generally," and white women were more likely to oppose it "both because it is 'impractical' to do so and because regulating it may present them as victims and further undermine their social status."[38] Such variation in beliefs about the value of law for addressing problems may reflect the experiences of different social groups and also their portrayal in popular culture.

Survey data reinforce the relationship between social identity and perceptions of law and courts. African Americans in particular express deep distrust of the legal system and a belief that individuals are not equal before the law. Two-thirds of African Americans polled in the NCSC survey believe that "people like them" are treated somewhat or far worse than other people in court, compared to 83 percent of all Americans who feel that "people like them" are treated better or the same. Other surveys show a similar racial division between the attitudes of African Americans and whites toward the legal system, with Hispanics falling usually somewhere in between. Most Americans also believe that wealth influences how one deals with the law. Ninety percent of respondents in the ABA survey strongly agree or agree that "wealthy people or companies often wear down their opponents by dragging out the legal proceedings," and only one-third felt that courts treated people alike regardless of wealth.[39] Those who use the legal system on a regular basis possess a common knowledge of law that advantages them over litigants who are appearing in court for the first time. Repeat players know the rules and can structure transactions to take advantage of them; they have ongoing working relationships with court staff and ready access to specialists and to specialist legal counsel; they can settle cases or not with an eye toward longer-term gains and also toward rule change. Empirical research on the outcomes of court processes generally supports the advantages of repeat players. It is not only wealth and organizational capacity, but also their experience with courts that makes businesses powerful legal adversaries.[40] For example, through decisions to resolve certain cases out of court but to resist on others, employers have been able to develop legal doctrine in family leave policies that favors their interests over those of employees. For another example, tobacco companies have created a formidable obstacle to lawsuits against them. They marshaled legal expertise and their own specialists, took advantage of legal rules (e.g., the health warnings on cigarette packages were part of their defense), vastly outspent any adversaries, drew on cultural scripts of individual responsibility, and adhered to a firm "no settlement" policy. But a few key jury trials provided arenas for popular participation and challenge to the power of Joe Camel. Ordinary citizens on various juries around the country awarded millions of dollars in damage awards against tobacco manufacturers.

The federal system provides numerous opportunities for those seeking legal change. Individuals and groups that cannot win in the legislative or executive arena see if they can do better in the courts. Each of the different courthouses described at the outset of this chapter, and each local community with its own legal culture, may provide a site for new legal ideas. Opportunities for change in public policy often stem from individual legal problems. Examples range from finding liability for tobacco harms or allowing gay marriage to posting the Ten Commandments in the courthouse or protecting fetal rights through targeted prosecution. Media coverage of litigation in such cases can stimulate public debate and discussion and thus connect law to ordinary citizens and their everyday lives. In so doing, the image of law and courts furthers democracy by promoting the openness and accessibility of law.

Notes

1. Kevin Boyle, *Arc of Justice.*
2. Elayne Rapping, *Law and Justice as Seen on TV*, 124.
3. Richard K. Sherwin, *When Law Goes Pop.*
4. Martin Shapiro, *Courts.*
5. ABA survey data is from "American Bar Association Report on Perceptions of the U.S. Justice System," reprinted in *Albany Law Review* 62 (1999), 1307. The NCSC survey data is from *How the Public Views the State Courts: A National Survey, National Center for State Courts.* Available at: http://www.ncsconline.org/WC/Publications/Res_AmtPTC_PublicViewCrtsPub.pdf (1999), 16.
6. The California Judicial Council Web site introduces California's historic courthouses with this quotation. See www.courtinfo.ca.gov/courts/trial/historic/.
7. Michael Kammen, "Temples of Justice: The Iconography of Judgment and American Culture," in *Origins of the Federal Judiciary*, edited by Maeva Marcus.
8. John Brigham, "From Temple to Technology: The Construction of Courts in Everyday Practice," in *Everyday Practices and Trouble Cases*, edited by Austin Sarat et al. (Evanston, Ill.: Northwestern University Press, 1998), 208. See also John Brigham, *The Cult of the Court.*
9. Michael Willrich, *City of Courts*, 319.
10. Robin G. Steinberg, quoted in Leslie Eaton and Leslie Kaufman, "In Problem-Solving Court, Judges Turn Therapist," *New York Times*, April 26, 2005.
11. Robert E. Dreschel, *News Making in the Trial Courts.* See also William Haltom, *Reporting on the Courts: How the Mass Media Cover Judicial Actions*; and Steven M. Chermak, "Police, Courts, and Corrections in the Media," in *Popular Culture, Crime and Justice*, edited by Frankie Y. Bailey and Donna C. Hale (Belmont, Calif.: Wadsworth Publishing, 1998).
12. Thoreau, quoted in Adam Cohen, "Walden at 150: What Would Thoreau Think of the 24-Hour News Cycle?" *New York Times*, August 22, 2004.
13. William Haltom, *Reporting on the Courts.* See also Shanto Iyengar, *Is Anyone Responsible? How Television Frames Political Issues* (Chicago: University of Chicago, 1991).
14. Haltom, *Reporting on the Courts*, and Chermak, "Police, Courts, and Corrections in the Media," also found the largest proportion of criminal case coverage to be at the pretrial stage.
15. William Haltom and Michael McCann, *Distorting the Law.*

16. Elliot E. Slotnick and Jennifer A. Segal, *Television News and the Supreme Court.*
17. George Gerbner, "Cameras on Trial: The 'O.J. Show' Turns the Tide," in *Journal of Broadcasting & Electronic Media* 39 (1995), 562. Personal interview with Joan Biskupic, Supreme Court reporter.
18. John Brigham, "Representing Lawyers: From Courtrooms to Boardrooms and TV Studios," *Syracuse Law Review* 53 (2003), 1165, at 1198.
19. Joseph A. Wapner, *A View from the Bench* (New York: Simon and Schuster, 1987), 21.
20. According to one analysis, there were nine reality court shows in the 2000–2001 television season, eight in 2001–2002, and seven in 2002–2003. Taunya Lovell Banks, "Will the Real Judge Stand-Up: Virtual integration on TV Reality Court Shows," *Picturing Justice: The On-Line Journal of Law & Popular Culture* (January 2003). Available at: http://www.usfca.edu/pj/realjudgebanks.htm. Another study of reality court programs reports eleven such shows airing in 2002. See Kimberlianne Podlas, "Blame Judge Judy: The Effects of Syndicated Television Courtrooms on Jurors," *American Journal of Trial Advocacy* 25 (Spring 2002), 557.
21. Kimberlianne Podlas, "Should We Blame Judge Judy?: The Messages TV Courtrooms Send Viewers," *Judicature* 86 (July-August 2002), 38.
22. Jim Rutenberg, "Campaigns Use TV Preferences to Find Voters." *New York Times,* July 18, 2004.
23. Banks, "Will the Real Judge Stand-Up."
24. Brigham, "Representing Lawyers."
25. Rapping, *Law and Justice as Seen on TV.* See also Connie L. McNeely "Perceptions of the Criminal Justice System: Television Imagery and Public Knowledge in the United States," in *Interrogating Popular Culture: Deviance, Justice, and Social Order,* edited by Sean E. Anderson and Gregory J. Howard (Guilderland, N.Y.: Harrow and Heston, 1998).
26. Harper Lee, *To Kill a Mockingbird* (Philadelphia: Lippincott, 1960). Full quote available at: http://www.americanrhetoric.com/MovieSpeeches/moviespeechtokilla-mockingbird.html.
27. See, for example, Sally Engle Merry, *Getting Justice and Getting Even: Legal Consciousness among Working-Class Americans* (Chicago: University of Chicago, 1990); Patricia Ewick and Susan S. Silbey, *The Common Place of Law.*
28. Sandra F. Chance, "Considering Cameras in the Courtroom," *Journal of Broadcasting & Electronic Media* 39 (Fall 1995), 555.
29. James P. Levine, *Juries and Politics,* 153.
30. William M. O'Barr and John M. Conley, "Lay Expectations of the Civil Justice System," *Law & Society Review* 22 (1988), 137. And Podlas, "Should We Blame Judge Judy?," at 41.
31. NCSC survey, *How the Public Views the State Courts: A National Survey,* 25. For discussion of the rise in *pro se* representation in family law, see Lynn Mather, "Changing Patterns of Legal Representation in Divorce: From Lawyers to *Pro Se,*" *Journal of Law and Society* 30 (March 2003), 137.
32. Lynn Mather, Craig A. McEwen, and Richard J. Maiman, *Divorce Lawyers at Work.* Jona Goldschmidt, "How are Courts Coping with *Pro Se* Litigants?" *Judicature* 82 (1998), 13.
33. Thurman Arnold, *The Symbols of Government,* 128–129.

34. Lawrence M. Friedman, *Crime and Punishment in American History*. Michel Foucault *Discipline and Punishment: The Birth of the Prison* (New York: Pantheon Books, 1977). Austin Sarat, *When the State Kills: Capital Punishment and the American Condition.*
35. Gerbner, "Cameras on Trial," 563. See also Lynn Mather and Barbara Yngvesson, "Language, Audience, and the Transformation of Disputes," *Law & Society Review* 15 (1980), 775.
36. Sharon Waxman, "TV 'Experts' Have a Verdict in the Laci Peterson Case," *New York Times*, July 29, 2004.
37. Robert Hariman, "Performing the Laws: Popular Trials and Social Knowledge," in *Popular Trials*, edited by Robert Hariman.
38. Laura Beth Nielsen, "Situating Legal Consciousness: Experiences and Attitudes of Ordinary Citizens about Law and Street Harassment," *Law & Society Review* 34 (2000), 1055, at 1085–1086.
39. For the racial data quoted here see NCSC survey, *How the Public Views the State Courts: A National Survey*. See also ABA, "American Bar Association Report on Perceptions of the U.S. Justice System," and Tom R. Tyler and Yuen J. Huo, *Trust in the Law*. The differences by wealth reported here are from the ABA survey.
40. Marc Galanter developed the concept of repeat players and their advantages in "Why the 'Haves' Come Out Ahead," *Law & Society Review* 9 (1974), 95. See also Herbert M. Kritzer and Susan S. Silbey, *In Litigation.*

Bibliography

Arnold, Thurman. *The Symbols of Government*. New York: Harcourt, Brace, & World, 1962. Originally published in 1935.

Boyle, Kevin. *Arc of Justice: A Saga of Race, Civil Rights, and Murder in the Jazz Age*. New York: Henry Holt and Company, 2004.

Brigham, John. *The Cult of the Court*. Philadelphia: Temple University Press, 1987.

Drechsel, Robert E. *News Making in the Trial Courts*. New York: Longman, 1983.

Ewick, Patricia, and Susan S. Silbey. *The Common Place of Law: Stories from Everyday Life*. Chicago: University of Chicago Press, 1998.

Friedman, Lawrence M. *Crime and Punishment in American History*. New York: Basic Books, 1993.

Greenhouse, Carol J., Barbara Yngvesson, and David M. Engel. *Law and Community in Three American Towns*. Ithaca, N.Y.: Cornell University Press, 1994.

Haltom, William. *Reporting on the Courts: How the Mass Media Cover Judicial Actions*. Chicago: Nelson-Hall Publishers, 1998.

Haltom, William, and Michael McCann. *Distorting the Law: Politics, Media, and the Litigation Crisis*. Chicago: University of Chicago, 2004.

Hans, Valerie P. *Business on Trial: The Civil Jury and Corporate Responsibility*. New Haven, Conn.: Yale University Press, 2000.

Hariman, Robert, ed. *Popular Trials: Rhetoric, Mass Media, and the Law*. Tucsaloosa: University of Alabama Press, 1990.

Kritzer, Herbert M., and Susan S. Silbey, eds. In *Litigation: Do the 'Haves' Still Come Out Ahead?* Stanford, Calif.: Stanford University Press, 2003.

Levine, James P. *Juries and Politics*. Belmont, Calif.: Brooks/Cole Publishing, 1992.
Marcus, Maeva, ed. *Origins of the Federal Judiciary: Essays on the Judiciary Act of 1789* Oxford, U.K, and New York: Oxford University Press, 1992.
Mather, Lynn, Craig A. McEwen, and Richard J. Maiman. *Divorce Lawyers at Work: Varieties of Professionalism in Practice*. Oxford, U.K., and New York: Oxford University Press, 2001.
Merry, Sally Engle. *Getting Justice and Getting Even: Legal Consciousness among Working-Class Americans*. Chicago: University of Chicago Press, 1990.
Rapping, Elayne. *Law and Justice as Seen on TV*. New York: New York University Press, 2003.
Sarat, Austin. *When the State Kills: Capital Punishment and the American Condition* Princeton, N.J.: Princeton University Press, 2001.
Shapiro, Martin. *Courts: A Comparative and Political Analysis*. Chicago: University of Chicago Press, 1981.
Sherwin, Richard K. *When Law Goes Pop: The Vanishing Line between Law and Popular Culture*. Chicago: University of Chicago Press, 2000.
Slotnick, Elliot E., and Jennifer A. Segal. *Television News and the Supreme Court: All the News That's Fit to Air?* Cambridge, U.K., and New York: Cambridge University Press, 1998.
Tyler, Tom R., and Yuen J. Huo. *Trust in the Law: Encouraging Public Cooperation with the Police and Courts*. New York: Russell Sage, 2002.
Wiederhold, Kathleen M. *Exploring Oregon's Historic Courthouses*. Corvallis: Oregon State University Press, 1998.
Willrich, Michael. *City of Courts: Socializing Justice in Progressive Era Chicago*. New York: Cambridge University Press, 2003.
Zimring, Franklin E., Gordon Hawkins, and Sam Kamin. *Punishment and Democracy: Three Strikes and You're Out in California*. Oxford, U.K., and New York: Oxford University Press, 2001.

Court Cases

Blakely v. Washington, 542 U.S. ___ (2004).
Brown v. Board of Education, 347 U.S. 483 (1954).
Bush v. Gore, 531 U.S. 98 (2000).
Chandler v. Florida, 449 U.S. 560 (1981).
State Farm Mutual v. Campbell, 537 U.S. 1102 (2003).
Tennessee v. Lane, 541 U.S. 509 (2004).
U.S. v. Booker, 543 U.S. ___ (2005).

10

WHAT AMERICANS KNOW ABOUT THE COURTS AND WHY IT MATTERS

Gregory A. Caldeira and Kevin T. McGuire

FROM OUR MODERN PERSPECTIVE, THE FRAMERS OF THE U.S. Constitution seem to have been remarkably wary of democratic government. Their principal concern was devising a strong central government with diffused power whose members would act on behalf of the body politic—a republic—rather than establishing popular supervision and control of public policymaking. To that end, the framers placed the federal government at a distance from its citizens. Presidents were to be selected by state electors who would, because of their presumptive awareness and appreciation of the national political scene, make more enlightened choices than the populace of each state. Likewise, under the framers' design, members of the U.S. Senate were named to the Congress by their respective state legislatures. After all, state legislators would be far more likely than everyday citizens to comprehend both the needs of a national legislature and the skills necessary to serve effectively in that office. Only in the case of the House of Representatives, whose members were expected to be sensitive to public opinion, were voters entrusted with the responsibility of selecting members of the national government.

Perhaps nowhere was the framers' distrust of democratic government greater than in their mechanism for selecting members of the federal judiciary. The power of choosing justices of the Supreme Court and other federal judges was quite far removed from direct popular control. Nominations were to be made by a president, who was to be selected indirectly through a college of electors, and confirmation was left to the Senate, whose members were equally removed from popular input, themselves selected by state legislators. In short, federal judges were selected by other federal officers, none of whom answered directly to the voters.

Knowledge of the courts and opinions about its personnel and policies were presumed to be limited. Since the framers were generally skeptical of entrusting authority to citizens as a whole—there was, after all, no guarantee that the public would appreciate what sorts of qualities would be essential for an effective judge—removing the federal judiciary from popular oversight and placing it into the hands of the president and Senate would, according to Alexander Hamilton, "promote a judicious choice of men for filling [these] offices. . . ."[1] What is more, providing life tenure for federal judges ensured that the judiciary would not be subject to the inflamed passions of the day. Thus, public opinion was not expected to govern directly the federal courts.

Over time, however, the framers' Constitution has become substantially more democratized. Americans have made formal changes to the Constitution; the Seventeenth Amendment placed the selection of the U.S. Senate into the hands of the electorate, for instance. No less significant, informal changes have also opened up the political process; for example, even though the president is still formally chosen by the electoral college, Americans as a practical matter select the chief executive in a national election. As a consequence, what the American public thinks about politics matters much more today than it did in 1787.

The federal courts have not been immune to the movement toward greater democratic control of policy. Indeed, the political process now allows a good deal of direct popular input into both the selection of federal judges and into their decision making. Who should serve on the U.S. Supreme Court is a topic on which Americans have strong opinions. Nominees are called to testify before publicly televised sessions of the Senate Judiciary Committee, and interest groups representing various cross-sections of society try to mobilize mass opinion to influence both a president's choice of a nominee and the Senate's decision on confirmation.

At the state level, similar shifts toward popular oversight of judges have taken place. In the formative years of the republic, state judges were selected indirectly, most often by state legislatures. By the early 1800s, however, the practice of placing the selection of judges into the hands of state electorates had begun to take root. Under the leadership of President Andrew Jackson, who was distrustful of political elites and believed that the direction of government ought to controlled by everyday citizens, states began to adopt elections as a primary means of keeping their judges in check.[2]

Because so many state judges are now elected, Americans are expected to go regularly to the polls to evaluate the qualifications of both would-be and sitting judges. Today, voters in most states have some form of direct control over who gets to serve on the state bench. In light of the broad popularity of elections, states seem to have assumed that their citizens are willing to take an active interest in the composition and behavior of their judicial officials.

Of course, Americans' direct knowledge of the courts is also a function of the types of issues that they consider and the policies that they develop. Americans have paid particular attention to the courts at least since the 1950s, when judges began to address highly salient legal questions. As a consequence, issues that have come to perennially divide Americans—abortion, affirmative action, the death penalty, the rights of the accused, to name a few—are ones that, in one way or another, trace their origins to the decisions of judges. Today, whether courts decide highly personal issues, such as the right to die or the validity of gay marriage, or issues of broad consequence for the nation, such as the disposition of a presidential election, the decisions of judges can generate substantial public reactions.

In a very real sense, then, the United States has democratized its courts and thereby the courts' policies. Over time, Americans have come to play a much more direct role in the selection of all kinds of judges. Moreover, those judges—either by willingness or necessity—now labor over policies that are central to the lives of many Americans.

These changes invite some probing questions, however. If Americans have assumed more democratic control of their judges, have they become informed enough to make responsible decisions? After all, an informed citizenry is one of the assumptions underlying any democratic government. If the public is to take an active role in the selection of its public decision makers and the evaluation of their policies, then it ought to possess the kind of information necessary to make rational decisions. How well do Americans measure up to this standard in the case of the judiciary? To the extent that Americans do demonstrate an adequate understanding of the courts, what consequences does that knowledge have for the governmental process? In short, what do Americans know about the courts, and why does it matter?

Knowledge and Assessment of the Courts

At first glance, evaluating what Americans think about their judicial system presents a seeming paradox. On the one hand, citizens seem to hold fairly favorable opinions about the judiciary. On the other hand, they seem to know little about the courts and their functions. How can they support something about which they seem to know so little?

Federal Judiciary

The U.S. Supreme Court provides the most glaring example in this regard. Compared to the elected branches, the Court is an especially well regarded institution, and over and over again, polls show that Americans have more confidence in the Court than either the president or the Congress. In evaluating the Court's authority, most Americans think that it is exercising about the right amount of political power, and more often than not they believe that the Court is doing a good job. Yet Americans seem to know surprisingly little about the Court, its members, or its policies. By most accounts, the public has little specific knowledge of the decisions that the Court issues, and few if any can name a single person who sits on the Court.

These sorts of findings, however, hide a good deal of complexity. Within the population, there is variation in how attentive individuals are to matters of politics. Some people follow the news from Washington with great interest, others are less concerned with national affairs. Those who are more attentive to the business of government have a keener sense of the policymaking process and how institutions must interact and make trade-offs. As a result, Americans who have a better understanding of the how the Court operates within the political system and those who pay attention to its decisions are much more likely than others to hold the Court in high esteem.

At the same time, support for the Court also seems to spring from a more general set of core democratic values. Those who are committed to broad democratic values—support for tolerance and free speech as well as respect for minority rights and due process of law—are among the most likely to affirm the Court and its mission.[3]

Judged by democratic standards, these lessons are encouraging. They suggest that there is a strong connection between an informed citizenry and how that citizenry thinks about the judiciary. Even though the Supreme Court is, as has been so often observed, a counter-majoritarian institution, Americans nevertheless evaluate it as they might other political institutions. Those who understand the Court's role and who are committed to the values that the Court often protects are the very citizens who view the Court in the most favorable light.

Of course, the justices are not democratically accountable in the strictest sense. Despite the increased attention to and popular input in the selection of the justices, the Court's members once confirmed are insulated from direct electoral control. But this scarcely prevents the public from evaluating the Court as if it were. Like other policymakers, the justices can make unpopular decisions, and such decisions naturally alienate public support.

As a general matter, when the Court's decisions deviate from the prevailing public mood, support for the institution tends to wane. If the leading policies of the Court go left when popular opinion turns right, the public begins to lose confidence in the Court's capacities.[4] This has been illustrated in a number of specific contexts: the justices' support for the rights of criminal defendants, various restrictions on abortion rights, and the right to burn the American flag have all cost the Court some measure of public esteem.[5]

Whatever the level of knowledge and support for the Court, it takes on magnified importance when one looks at those who are directly affected by the Court's decisions. To be sure, the Supreme Court is a national policymaker, but individual cases arise in specific contexts and affect different constituencies. Studies reveal that citizens are extremely attentive to the decisions in which they have a direct stake. Far from being indifferent to the Court, for example, the residents of the communities in which originated several different cases—issues of religious establishment, free exercise of religion, state encroachment upon Indian affairs, and the federal protection of endangered species—all were keenly aware of the policies that the justices handed down. Not only that, their evaluation of those policies was governed by the extent to which the decisions were consistent with their own preferences.[6]

These findings serve as a reminder that the demands of political knowledge made in a democratic government can occasionally be too high. In order to be informed, the public needs to be sufficiently motivated to acquire information and have the opportunity to get it.[7] One would scarcely be surprised if voters in textile states followed congressional legislation affecting clothing imports but knew little of legislation affecting national parks, the automotive industry, or off-shore oil operations. Few judicial policies fall with equal weight across the nation. Thus, it makes sense that any test of civic knowledge with regard to the courts should, at least in part, look to those who have an interest in judicial outcomes.

State Judiciaries

Local attitudes have the potential to take on even greater relevance when one considers how Americans think about the courts in their individual states. Here, there are a good many factors that distinguish state judges from their federal brethren. Most notably, state judges are typically subject to direct electoral control and enjoy only limited tenures. Greater democratic supervision of state courts would consequently carry with it a heightened expectation of public awareness of judicial actors and processes.

Ironically, one of the complications of democratic control of state judiciaries is that citizens—even the conscientious ones—are at a loss for information. Judicial elections are elections of fairly low visibility, which can make ferreting out information about the candidates a difficult enterprise. To complicate matters, states have often regulated the extent to which judges may actively campaign, thereby frustrating the ability of office-seekers to explain their positions to the voters. Recently, the U.S. Supreme Court struck down such regulations in *Republican Party of Minnesota v. White* (2002), but there is no guarantee that judicial office-seekers will take advantage of the opportunity to campaign. Policies that permit rather than restrict behavior often have only modest consequences.[8] So, even though they may have secured the legal right to advocate their candidacies, many running for judicial offices will undoubtedly continue to see active political campaigns as a distasteful enterprise that calls into question their objectivity.

In light of such low levels of information, the reservoir of public knowledge of judicial candidates is very shallow. Prior to election day, voters often know little about the individuals running for office, and perhaps not surprisingly they express no preferences among the various candidates. On Election Day, many simply refrain from voting, and those that do vote have few objective criteria upon which to base their vote choice. Voters in judicial elections will often put to use whatever basic indicators are available. In the absence of most other kinds of information, for example, the party identification of the candidates can have a great deal of influence on the vote choice.[9]

This lack of knowledge of judicial candidates does not necessarily mean that citizens have no basis for evaluating their respective state judiciaries. If poll numbers are any indication, many Americans who are attentive to the policies of the U.S. Supreme Court would be hard pressed to name one its members. If familiarity with the Court as an institution—that is, understanding of its policies, as opposed to its membership or having a direct stake in its policy decisions—explains how individuals evaluate the Court, then similar familiarity at the state level might well determine how Americans evaluate state courts.

Indeed, at the state level, there seems to be a clear connection between familiarity with the courts and the level of support that those courts enjoy. Unlike their relationship to federal courts, Americans are more likely to have some kind of direct experience with the judicial process in their respective states. State judicial systems are perceived as more fair by those who have some type of direct contact with them. To take one prominent example, citizens are frequently called for jury duty, and those who have served on juries tend to form favorable opinions of the courts.[10]

For others, this direct experience involves going to court. Traffic accidents, property damage, disputes with landlords, divorce, and other common complications of American life bring large numbers of Americans to the steps of their local courthouses. Whatever the outcome, the judicial process itself seems to leave a positive impression on those who participate in its decision making. That such direct involvement induces support is not surprising, considering that media reports of outlandish cases help to form a perception of courts as peculiar, perhaps irrational institutions. For many, expectations are undoubtedly low. As one study explains, "If what citizens encounter in the court house is considerably better than what they expect walking in the door, it is not surprising that they rate the experience in relative positive terms."[11] Once citizens receive a firsthand understanding of how the machinery of the judiciary actually runs, they express confidence in its operations.

These various findings paint a picture of a consistent linkage between the level of knowledge of courts and how Americans evaluate them. From the nation's highest tribunal to its more humble local courts, the judiciary receives its greatest support from those who are best informed about the role that courts play in American life. Not all Americans fully understand the operations of their courts, of course, but this is hardly unique to the judiciary; many in the mass public reveal uncertainty or confusion about the workings of other components of the political system. To the extent that there is an informed citizenry that is reasonably attentive to the business of the judiciary, sympathetic to its institutional mission, and perhaps even directly involved in its operations, Americans have justified their expanded democratic supervision of the courts.

Public Opinion and Democratic Consequences

To this point, we have considered how Americans think about and judge their courts. That story, by itself, is certainly important in the context of a political system that now facilitates direct citizen involvement in both the selection of judges and the monitoring of their policies. Still, that story remains incomplete. In a democratic system, the values of citizens are supposed to be transmitted into policy by their governmental institutions. So, leaving aside whatever their own preferences might be, public officials are expected to heed the opinions of their various constituencies. To what degree are courts democratic in this sense? Do judges take public opinion into account when making decisions?

At the same time, public opinion is not just a constraint on decision makers. Its relevance does not end after it has guided policy into place. There is important feedback in a democratic system. Policy choices provoke public reactions, both positive and negative, and this foment of public response gets channeled back to decision makers. How, then, does the public react to the decisions that judges make?

In the abstract, it is easy to envision the flow of public opinion, governing policy outputs which themselves stimulate public reaction as it circles back to guide the development of subsequent policies. Thinking about these causal links in the context of the courts, however, is somewhat more complicated. Unlike elected representatives who are obligated to follow and act upon the wishes of the voters, judges are not usually thought to be servants to the public will in the same sense. True, the public scrutinizes many federal judges at the time of their appointment, and of course, in order to be elected or to maintain their positions, state judges must surely consider how the values they might claim to represent (such as fairness, common sense, or humility) or that decisions they make will affect potential supporters on Election Day. Nevertheless, judges are, on balance, far more removed from popular control than members of the legislative and executive branches. Moreover, judges are ultimately supposed to maintain a fidelity to the U.S. Constitution and the laws written under it, regardless of the direction of the winds of public sentiment. In evaluating how public opinion affects the courts—as well as how the courts affect public opinion—it is important to bear these distinctions in mind.

Popular Checks on Judicial Policy

In framing the Constitution, the founders created a judiciary that was institutionally weak. In trying to allay fears that the Supreme Court might use its authority to take advantage of the other branches, Alexander Hamilton offered his now famous assurance that the Court had "neither FORCE nor WILL, but merely judgment." Quoting Montesequieu, the French political thinker whose notions of the separation of powers were put to direct use by the framers, Hamilton summed up the relative strength of the Court in blunt terms: "Of the three powers . . . the judiciary is next to nothing."[12] Judges would have to depend upon elected officials, he explained, to put their judgments into effect.

For this reason, the Supreme Court would be obligated to test the waters before adopting its most preferred policies and try to gauge the likely public reaction. If the justices anticipate that the decisions they are disposed to make will generate sufficient public discord, then they should adjust their policies in ways that are more likely to meet with popular approval. Alexis de Tocqueville was one of the first observers to take note of the Court's reliance upon popular sentiment. As he explained, "The power of the Supreme Court Justices is immense, but it is power springing from opinion. They are all-powerful so long as the people consent to obey the law; they can do nothing when they scorn it. . . . The federal judges therefore must not only be good citizens and men of integrity . . . but must also be statesmen; they must know how to understand the spirit of the age, to confront those obstacles that can be overcome and to steer out of the current when the tide threatens to carry them away, and with them the sovereignty of the Union and obedience to its laws."[13]

Modern scholarly support for Tocqueville's elegant observation has been somewhat mixed. Some doubt that a Court with unelected, life-tenured justices would ever pay any attention to public sentiment, and many analysts have been unable to document any consistent effects of public attitudes on the Court. Still, there is a growing body of evidence, the most recent of which demonstrates that, across such leading policy areas as criminal procedure and civil liberties and rights, the justices have in fact paid a great deal of attention to changes in the public mood over roughly the last half-century. When popular opinion has been liberal, it has pulled the Court's policies to the left, just as conservative moods within the public have drawn the Court to the right.[14]

This does not mean that the Court is explicit about its sensitivity to popular opinion. As Justice Felix Frankfurter once explained, "To a large extent, the Supreme Court, under the guise of constitutional interpretation of words whose contents are derived from the disposition of the Justices, is the reflector of that impalpable but controlling thing, the general drift of public opinion."[15] Looking at the particulars of individuals cases, therefore, it may be hard to discern any sensitivity to public preferences. In the aggregate, though, clear patterns emerge, showing responsiveness to mass opinion.

Seen in this way, public opinion serves as a very real democratic check on the potential excesses of the Court. Since the Court cannot put its rulings directly into effect, it cannot afford to alienate the average American for very long. Without a basic undercurrent of support for their actions, the justices cannot expect that their decisions will be taken seriously by elected officials who, in the end, are the ones who must translate the Court's rulings into action.

Among the members of the federal judiciary, the Supreme Court is scarcely alone in its consideration of public opinion. Trial judges also make decisions with an eye toward satisfying local opinion. Like their counterparts on the Supreme Court, these federal judges enjoy lifetime tenure, but unlike the justices, they make decisions in a very different type of environment. Whatever psychological protections the High Court enjoys by its isolation in Washington, no such security is available to federal trial judges, who live and work within the specific areas over which they exercise jurisdiction. Consequently, they are less likely to deviate from what they perceive to be the public sentiment within their communities.

One very visible illustration of this phenomenon can be seen in how federal trial judges in the South responded to the U.S. Supreme Court's command for racial desegregation of the public schools. Resistance to the Court in the South was especially pronounced, and the federal judges responsible for supervising desegregation there displayed various levels of enthusiasm for carrying the High Court's policies to full effect. Leaving aside the practical obstacles to desegregation—more populous school districts made the process difficult as a technical matter, as did having to reassign the very large numbers of African Americans within some school districts—judges whose courts were physically located within the school districts they were monitoring showed much greater reluctance to desegregate than judges who were not members of the communities under their supervision.[16] In terms of democratic responsiveness, the lesson here is obvious; fearful of popular backlash, federal judges who each day had to face—literally face—a skeptical public reluctant to abandon its traditional education policies felt pressure to stall the process of integrating their schools.

Similar results obtain in other areas of the law, as well. During the United States' involvement in military conflict in Vietnam, for instance, young men opposed to the war and compulsory military service were frequently prosecuted for various draft offenses. In cases of conviction, the federal judges hearing these cases had a good deal of discretion in the severity of the punishments that they could impose. Interestingly, the stringency of those punishments was closely related to the public's growing disaffection for the Vietnam War. As more and more Americans concluded that entering the hostilities was a mistake, federal judges pronounced significantly more lenient sentences. According to this view, judges do not make decisions in a political vacuum. Rather, they exist in and are influenced by the changing patterns of public opinion.[17]

Desegregation and the Vietnam-era draft are highly salient issues, and in that respect they are atypical of most the cases that federal judges decide. It is hard to say, therefore, whether their apparent democratic responsiveness in these contexts is representative of how they make decisions more generally. To find that judges are constrained by public opinion in cases involving issues on which large numbers of Americans have intense views is perhaps not surprising. A more rigorous test would explore the impact of public opinion in less prominent areas of judicial policymaking.

Taken together, however, the evidence from the U.S. Supreme Court and the federal district courts makes a fairly dramatic point: judges who are not electorally accountable often behave as if they were. Despite the absence of formal democratic controls, federal judges seem to sense that, in order to ensure that their policies will be taken seriously by elected officials and those whom they represent, they cannot afford to ignore public sentiment.

If public opinion guides the behavior of life-tenured judges, it has all the more impact on state judges who must face the voters directly on a regular basis. Where states have put into place institutions that require direct, democratic accountability, the relevant political actors behave rationally by taking steps to satisfy their constituents and thereby secure their reelection, and state judges are no exception. Many of the same circumstances that make legislators especially responsive to their constituencies hold equal sway with elected judges. Just as the votes of legislators on policy are guided by public sentiment, so too are the votes of judges when they decide cases.[18]

Among others things, judges elected by narrow margins vote in ways that they perceive to be consistent with public preferences. Sensing their electoral vulnerability, these judges—no less than their legislative counterparts—are loath to alienate the voters and seek to satisfy the electorate's political dispositions, rather than their own.

Furthermore, legislators often make politically costly decisions early in their terms of office, using the remainder of the time until reelection to secure the voters' goodwill. As their terms draw to a close, however, legislators can ill-afford to cast unpopular votes. Again, elected judges manifest similar behavior. At the end of their terms, these judges shift their votes toward the prevailing views of the electorate and minimize the potential ammunition that might be used against them on Election Day.

Quite apart from the necessities of electoral expedience, some elected officials are simply more adept at the business of political representation than others. Regardless of whether they sit in the statehouse or on the state supreme court, elected officials are politicians, and those who have honed their political instincts before seeking higher office are invariably advantaged over other candidates. For this reason, elected judges who come to the bench having already developed a sense of how to be responsive to constituents readily recognize the need to act strategically and adjust their votes so as to maximize their chances of reelection.

It is scarcely a wonder that when states structure their institutions to induce democratic responsibility, this is precisely what they get. What is striking, however, is these representational effects are not dependent upon the character of the elected office. From the perspective of electoral accountability, judges are in some ways no different from legislators. Invoking many of the scholarly insights into legislative behavior, one of the leading students of state judicial elections explains, "Elected judges under restricted conditions may seek to reduce the risk of electoral defeat by engaging in representational behavior, such as projecting the image that the decisions of the judge comport with the basic values of the voters or casting votes to accommodate perceived constituent preferences."[19]

In varying degrees, both federal and state judges are constrained by democratic forces. Perhaps the mechanisms operate in somewhat different ways. Federal judges know that the efficacy of their policy choices is dependent upon public support. Elected state judges know that, if their decisions do not sit well with the voters, they can be replaced. In either context, the values held by citizens are filtered and reflected in judicial policy.

Legitimacy

The success of any democratic institution is a function of its acceptance by those over whom it exercises authority. When everyday citizens value the mission of that institution, regardless of the content of its policies, it can lay claim to legitimacy. Because, as Thomas Jefferson explained, government derives its "just powers from the consent of the governed," the authority of American courts is conditioned by popular opinion.

In a broader context, both national and international courts seek public acceptance of their respective missions. Across the countries of Europe, for example, national high courts enjoy varying levels of institutional support. Greater public awareness of and satisfaction with these national courts combine with the age of these several tribunals to elevate their public esteem.[20]

In the United States, the legitimacy of the courts has been variously tested. The outcomes of high-profile cases frequently dismay various segments of the American public; the acquittal of former football star O. J. Simpson on murder charges or the successful insanity defense of John Hinckley, the would-be assassin of President Ronald Reagan, are two examples. No less likely, the decision of courts *not* to become involved can be costly; the refusal of various courts to intervene and prevent the removal of a feeding tube from a woman named Terri Schiavo, who had for years been in a vegetative state, provoked a firestorm of public criticism. Decisions such as these generate vocal calls for reform of the judicial system. Still, the nation's courts seem to have diffuse support sufficient to weather these occasional storms.

Perhaps the most visible test of judicial legitimacy occurred in the fall of 2000, when the outcome of the presidential election between George W. Bush and Al Gore was settled by judicial intervention in what turned out to be an ambiguous process of ballot counting and certification in Florida, the crucial state upon which hinged the presidency. The U.S. Supreme Court's decision in *Bush v. Gore* (2000) had the practical effect of settling the election. Its order to put an end to the recounting of Florida's ballots resulted in Bush ascending to the presidency.

Aside from settling the election, the decision also generated a massive outpouring of public criticism. Everything from the justices' decision to consider the dispute to the various rationales that the Court offered in its written opinion was subject to some form of condemnation, as critics assailed the Court on charges of partisan policymaking. Given the sheer volume of vituperation, many observers of the Supreme Court were quick to conclude that the majority in *Bush v. Gore* had done deep and perhaps irreparable harm to the institutional reputation of the Court. The public, it was argued, had lost faith in the institution. In other words, the decision had apparently come at the cost of substantial legitimacy.

But did the decision actually undermine the Supreme Court's institutional support? Close inspection of public opinion data reveals that it did not.[21] Indeed, it turns out that, rather than the decision in *Bush v. Gore* affecting the Court's legitimacy, it was this very legitimacy that determined how the public reacted to the ruling. Those who held the Court in high esteem regarded the Court's decision as objective, fair, and based upon the law, while those who had less loyalty to the Court as an institution concluded that the decision was more likely a product of simple partisanship.

To be sure, after the decision, there was an ideological component to how individuals evaluated both the decision and the Court itself. So, for example, members of the public who were supportive of George Bush, not surprisingly, expressed faith in the Court as an institution and believed *Bush v. Gore* was a decision based upon the legal merits of the case. Such ideological considerations notwithstanding, both Democrats and Republicans who had a preexisting faith in the Court's capacities perceived the justices as acting in a fundamentally fair way in the election dispute.

The larger lesson is that institutional loyalty and support are important commodities for courts in a democratic system. In a government that adheres to majority rule while maintaining respect for minority rights, courts will inevitably render decisions that will alienate assorted segments of society, some large and some small. So long as judges operate in an environment of public confidence, they can continue to make what are, by their lights, responsible policy choices, even choices that provoke widespread disaffection. Thus, legitimacy in the eyes of the public helps to preserve the basic mission of the judiciary in a democratic government.

Structuring Democratic Alternatives

Policymakers lead, as well as follow, public opinion. By their attention to specific issues and the positions that they take on those issues, national officeholders help frame the debates that take place within American politics. What about the courts? Do the individual policies adopted by judges in turn affect how the mass public thinks about those issues?

One place where the judiciary's influence on public debate can be seen is in the nation's trial courts. As the initial referees in most legal disputes, trial judges can serve as agenda setters. Because judges at this level must often consider whether cases are frivolous, they act as a kind of filter through which they allow to pass only cases that raise issues of sufficient legal merit. Not only that, their adoption of specific policies in the cases that they do decide often provide the specific terms for popular debate.[22]

Shaping the issues for public discourse is one thing, but changing the public's opinion on those issues is quite another. Some have argued that, given its visibility and authority, the U.S. Supreme Court can act as an opinion leader by crafting policies that will instruct and persuade the mass public. According to this view, the justices offer a kind of public education, one in which they "transfer to the minds of the citizens the modes of thought lying behind legal language and the notions of right fundamental to the regime."[23] By this mechanism, the Court imbues the citizenry with a sense of how the fundamental rule of law underwrites and supports democratic government.

The evidence that the Court has been able to play this role—that is, to function as a "republican schoolmaster"—is not especially strong. The public seems to react largely on the basis of its preexisting views on the issues before the Court, rather than how the Court handles them.[24] To be sure, polls often reveal broad swings in public opinion on an issue after the Court renders a decision, but those changes in mass opinion are just as likely to reflect shifts away from the positions adopted by the Court as they are to measure movement toward the justices' policies.[25] Stated simply, the Supreme Court seems to alienate as many people as it attracts.

Of course, not all of the Court's decisions are of equal relevance to the public, and thus attention to the Court varies from one issue to the next. When we look to individuals who are fully informed about a particular case and how it was resolved, we find that the Court is quite capable of persuading the public. So, for example, when the Court considered whether a public school's denial of the use of its facilities by a religious group violated the group's right to free expression and free exercise of religion, the residents of the area surrounding the school were well informed about this case of obvious local interest. After the Court issued its ruling striking down the school's prohibition, the residents of the community, as might be expected, were unpersuaded by the Court; they lost their case, after all. Nearby residents, however—who were also well-informed about the case—evidently took the Court's lesson to heart. Their attitudes changed, and their support for open access for religious groups increased significantly. This illustration suggests something more general: so long as it does not perceive that it has a direct stake in the outcome of a case, the attentive public shows remarkable receptivity to the justices' message.[26]

Although the Supreme Court can act as a republican schoolmaster, the consequences of its public instruction can be somewhat more complex. Indeed, for some constituencies, the justices' policies have a polarizing, rather than a persuasive effect. Instead of producing attitude change, the Court can serve to crystallize the public's existing attitudes, increasing their intensity. If one were to compare, for example, public support for abortion in surveys taken before and after the decision in *Roe v. Wade* (1973), one would find little difference. People who favored abortion (or opposed it, as the case may be) before the *Roe* decision expressed the same preference after the decision.

What did change, however, was the intensity of the support and opposition. Some Americans, such as those with higher levels of education, tended to favor abortion prior to *Roe*, and the strength of their support only increased after the Court endorsed abortion rights. Other Americans, such as Catholics, were opposed to abortion before the *Roe* ruling, and this was an opinion that they held far more intensely in the wake of the justices' decision. In effect, the convictions of each groups were only strengthened by the Court. So, rather than changing the direction of public opinion, the Court did change its magnitude. This effect is by no means unique to abortion. As in *Roe*, when the Court issues a landmark ruling in other salient areas of the law, such as capital punishment, the public responds to the Court in similar ways.[27]

There seems little doubt that judicial decisions frame how Americans think about various political issues. Not only do courts provide structure to the policy alternatives, in many instances they condition the public's reaction to them. Precisely how the courts affect the public's thinking is not entirely straightforward. Taken as a whole, judicial decisions seem not to make an extensive impression on the American mind. Opinions on issues that confront the courts do change, but it is not at all clear that courts are responsible for these shifts in opinion. Among attentive publics, however, the judiciary can and does change how they think about issues, yet these are changes that can bring people together as well as drive them apart.

Conclusions

American courts are democratic institutions. Their principal responsibility, of course, is to interpret the law, but that interpretation is moderated—sometimes directly, sometimes indirectly—by public opinion. In the short term, the selection of judges, their votes in individual cases, and the implementation of their decisions can be conditioned by prevailing public opinion. Over the long haul, courts show a more general responsiveness to changes in public mood, a connection that is important since their effectiveness is tied to popular support for their institutional mission. For these reasons, it is especially important to look with some care at how the public thinks about the judicial system.

For many in the mass public, who judges are and what they do are not issues of much concern. To the extent that the public comprehends the courts, however, that knowledge will underwrite public confidence in the capacities of judicial institutions. Such legitimacy is scarcely trivial for courts. Indeed, it is vital to their effectiveness as policymakers; when courts are taken seriously by the public, so too are their policies.

The complex ways in which public opinion is tethered to the judicial system makes broad generalizations somewhat difficult. Some of the linkages between citizen attitudes and the courts apply to relatively small and often diverse groups. Moreover, the observed impact of courts on public opinion differs across different constituencies and across distinct issues. Since our knowledge is frequently derived from studies of atypical policies areas—such as abortion or desegregation—we cannot say with authority whether our assessments carry equal weight in less visible domains. Likewise, our understanding is derived from a disproportionate focus on the U.S. Supreme Court. Much less is known about how other courts engage the public mind. Regardless of the policies or the courts under scrutiny, most analyses provide only limited snapshots taken at one or perhaps two points in time. Scholars have only begun to untangle the longer-term relationships between courts and public opinion. Much simply remains unknown.

Still, one of the significant lessons that can be gleaned from surveying the evidence is that Americans bring to their courts many of the same expectations that they bring to the other institutions of government. The public evaluates them based upon their performance, reacting in predictable ways to the policies in which they have an interest. In addition, the public expects judges to be mindful of popular preferences, and for their part courts can and often do serve this representative function by sensing public mood and adjusting their decisions accordingly. Naturally, we are mindful of the various institutional features that make courts distinctive. As long as Americans expect judges to lead public opinion as well as be guided by it, however, courts will preserve their fundamental democratic character.

Notes

1. Alexander Hamilton, "Federalist No. 76," in *The Federalist Papers,* edited by Garry Wills. New York: Bantam Books, 1982), 384.

2. Walter F. Murphy, C. Hermann Pritchett, and Lee Epstein, *Courts, Judges, and Politics: An Introduction to the Judicial Process*, 5th ed. (Boston: McGraw-Hill, 2002), 148.
3. Gregory A. Caldeira and James L. Gibson, "The Etiology of Public Support for the Supreme Court," *American Journal of Political Science* 36 (1992), 635–664.
4. Robert H. Durr, Andrew D. Martin, and Christina Wolbrecht, "Ideological Divergence and Public Support for the Supreme Court," *American Journal of Political Science* 44 (2000), 768–776.
5. Gregory A. Caldeira, "Neither the Purse Nor the Sword: Dynamics of Public Confidence in the Supreme Court," *American Political Science Review* 80 (1986), 1209–1226; Robert H. Durr, Andrew D. Martin, and Christina Wolbrecht, "Ideological Divergence and Public Support for the Supreme Court"; Anke Grosskopf and Jeffery J. Mondak, "Do Attitudes toward Specific Supreme Court Decisions Matter? The Impact of Webster and Texas v. Johnson on Public Confidence in the Supreme Court," *Political Research Quarterly* 51 (2000), 633–654.
6. Valerie J. Hoekstra, "The Supreme Court and Local Public Opinion," *American Political Science Review* 94 (2000), 89–100.
7. Michael X. Delli Carpini and Scott Keeter, *What Americans Know about Politics and Why It Matters* (New Haven, Conn.:Yale University Press, 1996).
8. Lauren Bowen, "Attorney Advertising in the Wake of *Bates v. State Bar of Arizona* (1977)," *American Politics Quarterly* 23 (1995), 461–484.
9. David Klein and Lawrence Baum, "Ballot Information and Voting Decisions in Judicial Elections," *Political Research Quarterly* 54 (2001), 709–728.
10. Susan M. Olson and David A. Huth, "Explaining Public Attitudes towards Local Courts," *Justice System Journal* 20 (1998), 41–61.
11. Herbert M. Kritzer and John Voelker, "Familiarity Breeds Respect: How Wisconsin Citizens View Their Courts," *Judicature* 82 (1998), 59–64, at 63.
12. Hamilton, "Federalist No. 78," 394.
13. Alexis de Tocqueville, *Democracy in America*, edited by J. P. Mayer and Max Lerner, translated by George Lawrence. (New York: Harper & Row), 137.
14. Kevin T. McGuire and James A. Stimson, "The Least Dangerous Branch Revisited: New Evidence on Supreme Court Responsiveness to Public Preferences," *Journal of Politics* 66 (2004), 1018–1035.
15. Felix Frankfurter, *Law and Politics: Occasional Papers of Felix Frankfurter*, edited by Archibald MacLeish and E. F. Prichard, Jr. (New York: Harcourt, Brace and Co.), 197.
16. Michael W. Giles and Thomas G. Walker, "Judicial Policy-Making and Southern School Segregation," *Journal of Politics* 37 (1975), 917–936.
17. Beverly B. Cook, "Public Opinion and Federal Judicial Policy," *American Journal of Political Science* 21 (1977), 567–600.
18. Melinda Gann Hall, "Electoral Politics and Strategic Voting in State Supreme Courts," *Journal of Politics* 54 (1992), 427–446.
19. Ibid., 429.
20. Gregory A. Caldeira and James L. Gibson, "The Legitimacy of the Court of Justice in the European Union: Models of Institutional Support," *American Political Science Review* 89 (1995), 356–376; James L. Gibson, Gregory A. Caldeira, and Vanessa A.

Baird, "On the Legitimacy of National High Courts," *American Political Science Review* 92 (1998), 343–358.

21. James L. Gibson, Gregory A. Caldeira, and Lester Kenyatta Spence, "The Supreme Court and the U.S. Presidential Election of 2000: Wounds, Self-Inflicted or Otherwise?" *British Journal of Political Science* 33 (2003), 535–556.
22. Lynn Mather, "Policy Making in State Trial Courts," in *The American Courts: A Critical Assessment*, edited by John B. Gates and Charles A. Johnson (Washington, D.C.: CQ Press, 1991).
23. Ralph Lerner, "The Supreme Court as Republican Schoolmaster," in *1967 Supreme Court Review*, edited by Philip B. Kurland (Chicago: University of Chicago Press, 1967), 180.
24. Larry R. Baas and Dan Thomas, "The Supreme Court and Policy Legitimation: Experimental Tests," *American Politics Quarterly* 12 (1984), 335–360.
25. Thomas Marshall, "The Supreme Court as Opinion Leader," *American Politics Quarterly* 15 (1987):, 147–168.
26. Valerie J. Hoekstra and Jeffrey A. Segal, "The Shepherding of Local Public Opinion: The Supreme Court and Lamb's Chapel," *Journal of Politics* 58 (1996), 1079–1102.
27. Charles H. Franklin and Liane C. Kosaki, "Republican Schoolmaster: The U.S. Supreme Court, Public Opinion, and Abortion," *American Political Science Review* 83 (1989), 751–771; Timothy R. Johnson and Andrew D. Martin, "The Public's Conditional Response to Supreme Court Decisions," *American Political Science Review* 92 (1998), 299–309.

Bibliography

Berkson, Larry C. *The Supreme Court and Its Publics: The Communication of Policy Decisions.* Lexington, Mass.: Lexington Books, 1978. The volume explores the level of awareness of the Supreme Court's decisions among various groups affected by several of the Court's policies.

Canon, Bradley C., and Charles A. Johnson. *Judicial Policies: Implementation and Impact.* 2nd ed. Washington, D.C.: CQ Press, 1999. As part of a larger analysis of adherence to the policies of courts, these authors discuss how the details of judicial decisions are transmitted and understood by the mass public.

Ely, John Hart. *Democracy and Distrust: A Theory of Judicial Review.* Cambridge, Mass.: Harvard University Press. A modern classic on how judges should approach the interpretation of the U.S. Constitution, this book highlights some of the difficulties that the Supreme Court faces when using public opinion as a guide for making decisions.

Erikson, Robert S., Michael B. MacKuen, and James A. Stimson. *The Macro Polity.* New York: Cambridge University Press, 2002. This sophisticated volume examines broad trends in governmental responsiveness to public preferences over time, including several assessments of the Supreme Court.

Hoekstra, Valerie J. *Public Reaction to Supreme Court Decisions.* New York: Cambridge University Press, 2003. This fascinating book researches the opinions and reactions of the residents of communities in which the U.S. Supreme Court's cases originate.

Lasser, William. *The Limits of Judicial Power: The Supreme Court in American Politics*. Chapel Hill: University of North Carolina Press, 1988. An historical examination of the Supreme Court's power in which the author argues that the Court's power has not been limited by adverse public reaction to its decisions.

Marshall, Thomas R. *Public Opinion and the Supreme Court*. Boston: Unwin Hyman, 1989. A comparison of how public preferences on a variety of salient issues compare to the U.S. Supreme Court's resolution of those issues.

Murphy, Walter F. *Elements of Judicial Strategy*. Chicago: University of Chicago Press. 1964. The classic volume on how sophisticated justices take into account a variety of constraining forces, including public opinion, while seeking to maximize their own legal and policy goals.

Slotnick, Elliot E., and Jennifer A. Segal. *Television News and the Supreme Court: All the News That's Fit to Air?* New York: Cambridge University Press, 1998. The best and most systematic examination of how the electronic media cover the Supreme Court and thereby affect what Americans know the justices' policies.

Court Cases

Bush v. Gore, 531 U.S. 98 (2000).

Republican Party of Minnesota v. White, 536 U.S. 765 (2002).

Roe v. Wade, 410 U.S. 113 (1973).

11

THE IMPACT OF COURTS ON AMERICAN LIFE

Gerald N. Rosenberg

Courts are everywhere. Virtually every level of government in the United States has courts, from the smallest village to the federal government itself. On the local and state level there are traffic courts, small claims courts, family and domestic relations courts, divorce courts, juvenile courts, criminal courts, probate courts, and so on. In New York City there is a housing court. Other states have water courts, workers' compensation courts, tax courts, and administrative courts.[1] On the federal level, there are the U.S. district courts, the U.S. courts of appeals and, the most famous U.S. court, the Supreme Court of the United States. But that is just the beginning. There are a plethora of specialized federal courts including, for example, U.S. Bankruptcy Court, the U.S. Court of Appeals for the Federal Circuit, the U.S. Court of Appeals for Veterans' Claims, the U.S. Court of Federal Claims, the U.S. Court of International Trade, the U.S. Tax Court, and the U.S. Foreign Intelligence Court.[2] There are also court-like structures in many organizations that adjudicate disputes and grievances. On the federal level examples include the National Labor Relations Board (NLRB), the Federal Communications Commission (FCC), and the Federal Trade Commission (FTC). Americans may still eat apple pie, but perhaps the well-known saying should be changed from "as American as apple pie" to "as American as a court of law."

The presence of courts is also felt throughout American culture. Americans think in terms of procedural fairness and deciding issues "according to law." Judges and courts are a deep part of this sense of fairness. Consider, for example, that the United States has popular television shows about courts such as *The People's Court* and *Judge Judy*. In contrast, in France, one of the most popular television shows has been a book review show (*Apostrophe* and later *Bouillon de culture*). And the language of courts, the language of rights, is an integral part of American society. The claim "I have a right to . . . " is deeply tied up with the prevalence of courts in American society.

Courts in the United States, unlike courts in most other countries (at least until very recently), are forums for major policy debates. Questions of race and gender discrimination, abortion, criminal procedure, university admissions, dangerous and unhealthy products, and so on, are often litigated. In the year 2000 the U.S. Supreme Court even decided the outcome of the presidential election. As Alexis de Tocqueville noted in the nineteenth century, "there is hardly a political question in the United States which does not sooner or later turn into a judicial one."[3]

This essay explores the ways in which courts impact upon the lives of Americans. Do courts affect Americans in deep and long-lasting ways or tangentially or not at all? Do courts only affect particular classes of Americans such as racial minorities, or manufacturers of unsafe products, or those who break the law? Or do courts affect all Americans in both routine and subtle ways? Do all Americans have equal access to courts or do courts favor the wealthy? And are the effects of courts on American life changing over time? This essay also explores what the answers to these questions may mean for democracy in the twenty-first century. Is democracy weakened by the use Americans make of courts, or is it strengthened by it? Or is the reality of the relationship somewhere in the middle? The material that follows cannot answer all of these questions, but it can highlight some of the many ways in which Americans interact with courts and the many and varied impacts courts have on American democracy and American life.

Working Definition of Democracy

In order to explore the relationship between the use of courts by Americans and American democracy, a working definition of democracy is necessary.[4] On its most basic level democracy requires that adult citizens determine, at least indirectly, what their government does. Adult citizens must have the right to vote to select their government officials in free, fair, and frequent (regularly scheduled) competitive elections. These in turn require political equality among citizens, the right to learn about candidates and government actions through a free press, the right of all people to express their political views publicly, and the right of all citizens to run for elective office. Thus, in a democratic political system the most important decisions facing the country must be decided by the people themselves through their power to elect their government and to remove it from power if it acts contrary to the people's wishes.

As basic as these rights are, they are insufficient to produce a democracy. A democratic political system is also one that protects fundamental political and civil liberties. While the extent of these liberties is contested, at the very least a democratically elected government that stifles speech critical of its actions, or persecutes racial and ethnic minorities, is not democratic in any meaningful sense. This is largely because such actions make it difficult or impossible for all citizens to participate in the democratic process.

A final requirement of a democracy is that a democratic government is bound by the rule of law. It can not take away citizens' rights or property arbitrarily, without due process of law, without having its actions examined by an independent decision maker. In addition, citizens must be protected not only from government, but also from organizations and bureaucracies with concentrated economic or political power, and from each other. The rule of law requires that there be institutions for settling disputes that are independent of both the government and the parties who appear before them. In the American democratic political system these are found in the judicial system. A judicial system in a democracy requires that all citizens must be equal before the law. Their race, gender, wealth, age, and the like, must be irrelevant. In the United States, the symbol of the judicial system, the blind goddess of justice, represents these features. She is blind because she takes no notice of who is before her, whether they are rich or poor, minority or white, male or female, powerful or weak. She focuses only on the requirements of the law and the facts of the case. She is a goddess because she dispenses justice, insuring that the law as enacted by government is followed and that citizens' rights are protected. Finally, citizens must have equal access to the courts and the ability to be represented by lawyers. Without the rule of law, the ability of citizens to participate equally, freely, and effectively in selecting their governmental officials and influencing their actions is compromised. Without the rule of law, democracy cannot exist.

Direct Involvement with Courts

The number and percentage of Americans who have had direct involvement with courts is astounding. Interestingly, the more famous the court, the least direct contact it has with citizens. On the one hand, very few Americans have had direct contact with the U.S. Supreme Court. On the other hand, millions of Americans are directly involved in local court cases every year. The following section provides the data that can help us gain perspective on the impact of courts on American life.

Federal Courts

At the apex of the American judicial system sits the U.S. Supreme Court.[5] It is the best known American court and many of its decisions are reported in the media. Interestingly, however, it hears and decides very few cases. In recent years it has issued written opinions in fewer than one hundred cases a year. In the year

2000, for example, although nearly nine thousand cases were brought to it, the U.S. Supreme Court heard oral arguments in only eighty-six cases and issued written opinions in only eighty-three. While Supreme Court decisions can have important effects on all Americans (discussed below), direct involvement in the Supreme Court is minuscule.

The U.S. courts of appeals are the intermediate level of courts in the federal system. They sit below the U.S. Supreme Court and above the U.S. district courts, hearing appeals from the latter. In the year 2000, there were 54,697 appeals commenced in these courts.[6] The majority of these were civil; criminal appeals totaled only 9,162.

There is a good deal more interaction with the U.S. district courts, the trial courts of the federal judicial system. Situated in every state, U.S. district courts are open to litigants who meet certain requirements. The basic requirements are stated in Article III of the U.S. Constitution and include jurisdictional as well as substantive requirements. For example, U.S. federal district courts are open to citizens of different states who have a dispute and to litigants who make a legal claim based on the U.S. Constitution or federal law. When a legal action is commenced dealing with money, such as a contract dispute, a tort claim for compensation for an injury, and so on, current law requires that the amount of money in dispute be at least $75,000. U.S. district courts are also the forum in which the United States brings criminal prosecutions.

How often are cases filed in U.S. district courts? In the year 2000, 263,049 civil cases were commenced. Approximately 61 percent of these cases were based on statutes and approximately 16 percent involved claims for compensation due to injuries. The number of cases filed dropped somewhat in 2001, to 253,354, but rebounded in 2002 to 268,071.

There are fewer cases involving criminal law than civil law on the federal level, although the numbers have been growing very rapidly in the last decades of the twentieth century. As the twentieth century came to a close, for example, the Department of Justice reported 115,589 arrests for violations of federal law. These arrests led to 83,251 federal prosecutions, resulting in 68,156 convictions and 50,451 people sent to prison.

Considering these data as a whole, in the year 2000 approximately 400,000 cases were filed by individuals, businesses, governments, and others organizations in the U.S. federal courts. While that is a lot of cases, as a percentage of adult Americans it is tiny, approximately one-seventh of 1 percent. If the only courts in the United States were federal courts, then Americans would not have much direct interaction with courts.

State and Local Courts

Federal courts are not the only courts in America.[7] Every state has a separate legal system and it is in these state and local courts where Americans most often have direct involvement. In the year 2002, there were a staggering 96.2 million civil and criminal cases filed in state and local courts. That number is the equivalent of one case for every three people. Removing the approximately 2 million cases dealing with juveniles, the number of cases filed is a whopping 44 percent of the number of all adult Americans, the equivalent of nearly one case for every two adults.

These figures are put in some perspective by the fact that 60 percent of these cases (57.7 million) dealt with traffic infractions. The National Center for State Courts, which painstakingly compiled these data, found that approximately 16.3 million cases (16.8 percent) dealt with civil disputes, 15.4 million (16 percent) involved criminal law, 4.6 million (4.8 percent) dealt with domestic relations (divorce, child custody, etc.), and 2 million (2.1 percent) concerned juveniles. And these numbers have been growing. Over the ten-year period that ended in 2002, the number of cases in every category except traffic cases grew by double digits, led by a 19 percent increase in criminal cases, a 16 percent increase in juvenile cases, and a 14 percent increase in domestic relations cases. All of these rates are higher than the growth of the U.S. population over the same period.

These data, taken as a whole, show that many Americans have had direct involvement with courts. Much of this involvement has been relatively light, such as paying a traffic ticket, while other involvement, such as divorce, child custody, and imprisonment, has affected lives in fundamental ways. It is clear that courts play a major role in the life of Americans.

The Impact of Direct Involvement with Courts

The purpose of litigation is to resolve disputes and exercise social control. Most people, most of the time, follow the law as announced by a judge or a jury. When traffic fines are assessed, they are usually paid. When divorces are granted, the formerly married individuals lead independent lives and are free to marry again. When criminal penalties are assessed, they are carried out. These outcomes are in accord with the underlying notion of the rule of law as an essential part of American democracy. But the impact of courts on the lives of Americans, even those directly involved in litigation, is not always that simple or straightforward.

Civil Suits

There are not good data on what happens to the parties in civil suits after disposition, either through verdicts being reached or settlements being achieved. Given the large number of courts, and huge number of cases, data-gathering is difficult. Further, most cases are settled prior to trial, and settlements need not be made public. Under the concept of the rule of law that is essential to a democratic society, the losing party should fulfil whatever obligations are imposed upon it. But does that happen? American courts do not have mechanisms to insure that verdicts are carried out. Indeed, they do not even have formal mechanisms for becoming informed about what happens when the parties leave the court. The only formal way a judge can discover that a verdict is not being implemented is for one of the parties to return to court to complain. This imposes a burden on many litigants who lack the resources to return to court.

By way of illustration, consider the rather ordinary case of *Fullerton Lumber Co. v. Torborg* (1955), from Wisconsin, dealing with an employment contract between a lumber company and one of its employees. The facts were straightforward. Albert C. Torborg was hired by the Fullerton Lumber Co. to manage one of its lumber yards. As part of his employment contract, he agreed that if and when he left Fullerton's employment he would not work for any competing business located within a fifteen-mile radius of the lumber yard for a period of ten years. However, several years later he quit his job and opened a competing lumber yard in the same town, within a fifteen mile radius of Fullerton's lumber yard, and he hired three of Fullerton's employees to work in his new lumber yard. The Fullerton Lumber Co. sued Torborg for violating his contact and asked the court to issue an injunction ordering him to stop working for the new lumber company. After two separate decisions of the Wisconsin Supreme Court, the Fullerton Lumber Co. won and the trial court held that Torborg was restrained from competing with the Fullerton Lumber Co. for three years.[8] In a later decision Torborg was ordered to pay $9,500 in damages to the Fullerton Lumber Co. In the best American tradition, a legal dispute had been brought to court and, after several appeals, the court had issued a clear decision.

However, it appears that the decision was never implemented in any meaningful way. Although Albert C. Torborg resigned as secretary-treasurer of the lumber company he started, one Betty Torborg, with the same home address as Albert and apparently his wife, became vice president. The company continued to operate. When the injunction ended, the secretary-treasurer was listed as A. C. Torborg, presumably Albert C. Torborg. As for the $9,500 in damages owed by Torborg to the Fullerton Lumber Co., Albert C. Torborg successfully filed for bankruptcy. The major debt wiped out by the bankruptcy was the $9,500 owed to Fullerton Lumber Co.[9]

Is this story unique? The best, though tentative, answer, is no. From the existing data it appears that court decisions are unevenly implemented. In a review of tort cases, for example, Haltom and McCann conclude that "awards go partially or completely unpaid and uncollected far more often than most people would guess."[10] There are also data from domestic relations courts that suggest that in about half of all cases those ordered to pay child support pay less than the ordered amount and sometimes pay nothing at all. According to data collected by the U.S. Department of Health and Human Services, only about one-half of custodial parents due child support receive the full payment the court ordered. About one-quarter receive partial payment and about one-quarter receive nothing at all.[11] Considering that in both the year 2000 and 2001 nearly 1.2 million new child support orders were issued by courts, many children and parents are affected by this nonpayment or underpayment. Indeed, by the first year of the twenty-first century, custodial parents were owed more than $88 billion in back payments of which only $5.7 billion had been paid.[12]

These data raise serious questions about the rule of law that is fundamental to a democratic society. They suggest that in some large number of cases the decision of the court is not carried out and the obligations imposed by settlements are not fulfilled. In the case of nonpayment of child support, the lack of judicial impact keeps millions of children in poverty. This may not be the fault of courts but the results are the same; the rule of law is not followed and the impact of courts is uneven. And it is the poor who suffer the most from the uneven implementation of law.

Criminal Law and Criminal Courts

The image that many Americans have of a criminal court is of a trial with eloquent and righteous lawyers arguing for justice in front of a wise and learned judge and a rapt jury listening to every word. The defendant's guilt or innocence hangs in the balance and the power of the state is checked by the requirements of law. It is the stuff of great movies and novels, but it does not bear any resemblance to what Americans actually experience in criminal courts.

To start, it is indisputable that "trials are relatively rare events."[13] Nationwide, only 4 percent of all criminal cases with convictions are the result of jury trials. The typical criminal process is for the defendant to plead guilty in return for a lighter punishment. This has been the case for many decades. In the late 1970s Malcolm Feeley examined 1,640 criminal cases in New Haven, Connecticut, over a several month period. Among his findings was the absence of trials. Trials, Feeley concluded, are "rare events."[14] As a long-time criminal defense lawyer summed up the way in which the criminal justice system reaches decisions, the "overwhelming majority of convictions in criminal cases (usually over 90 percent) are not the product of a combative, trial-by jury process at all, but instead merely involve the sentencing of the individual after a negotiated, bargained-for plea of guilty has been entered."[15]

While there are many reasons for the lack of trials, chief among them is the lack of resources on the part of both the judicial system and most defendants (discussed below). In many large urban areas criminal court facilities are sometimes dilapidated with inadequate space and equipment. Caseloads are enormous and judges and prosecutors are under pressure to move cases along. In addition to creating pressure for plea bargaining, the lack of resources also leads to criminal courts that are often "chaotic and confusing."[16] Thus, criminal courts can behave more like bureaucracies processing cases than like courts carefully weighing guilt or innocence and dispensing justice. On its face, the current criminal justice system fits uneasily into the rule of law that is essential to democratic government. And when the lack of adequate legal representation is added to the picture (discussed below), the fit is even more tenuous.

Prisons

One of the most direct impacts of courts on peoples' lives occurs when people are found guilty of a crime and either sent to prison or put under supervision (probation). In 2003 nearly 6.9 million people were under the control of the criminal justice system, approximately 3.2 percent of the adult population in the United States, or one in thirty-two adults. This included 691,301 people in local and county jails, 1,387,269 in state and federal prisons, 4,073,987 on probation, and 774,588 released from confinement and on parole. And all of these figures grew from the preceding year. The number of people on probation grew 1.2 percent and the number of people on parole grew by 3.1 percent, the largest increase in a decade. In terms of those incarcerated, there was a 3.9 percent increase in the jail population and a 2.3 percent increase in the prison population.

Leaving prison does not end one's involvement with the judicial system. In 2003, 38 percent of those who were discharged from prison were re-incarcerated, either because of a technical violation like failing a drug test or because they were charged with committing a new crime. An additional 9 percent failed to keep in contact with their parole officers and could not be located. Of the 2.2 million people discharged from probation in 2003, three out of five met the conditions of their supervision. Another 16 percent were jailed because of a rule violation or a new crime, and 4 percent becoming fugitives.[17]

These figures are staggering. The United States has the highest rate of incarceration of any nation in the world.[18] In addition to the psychological and emotional costs and any social stigma that may attach to being found guilty of a crime, there are economic and political costs as well. Prisoners cannot earn a living and help support a family. They are not part of the workforce and they do not pay taxes. Housing and caring for prisoners costs billions of dollars. In 2001, for example, the fifty states together spent $38.2 billion on their prison systems and the United States spent $3.8 billion.[19] When prisoners are released, they often have a difficult time finding employment because many employers are unwilling to hire them. In addition, by the end of the twentieth century all levels of government were imposing restrictions on felons. On the federal level persons convicted of state and federal drug crimes may be denied a broad range of federal benefits and assistance programs. In some states convicted felons are barred from voting. Forty-eight states and the District of Columbia prohibit inmates from voting while incarcerated for a felony. Thirty-five states prohibit felons from voting while they are on parole and thirty-one of these states prohibit those on felony probation as well. Seven states deny the right to vote to all ex-offenders who have completed their sentences. The result is that an estimated 4.7 million

Americans, or one in forty-three adults, have currently or permanently lost their voting rights as a result of a felony conviction. There is also a heavy racial disparity in these numbers. 1.4 million African American men, or 13 percent, are disenfranchised, a rate seven times the national average. In six of the states that deny the vote to ex-offenders, one in four black men is permanently disenfranchised.[20] The impact of the criminal justice system on the lives of Americans is profound, particularly on racial minorities.

Delay

The discussion above has documented the uneven implementation of judicial decrees, the apparently rushed and chaotic nature of many criminal courts, and the disparate impact of courts on minorities and the poor. Given the number of judges in the United States, and the demands made upon them, these results should not be surprising. The approximately thirty thousand state judicial officers, and the more than nine hundred federal judges, are confronted with nearly one hundred million cases a year, a figure that averages out to over three thousand cases per judicial officer per year. The bulk of these cases occur at the state level. On the federal level, in the early years of the twenty-first century, approximately five hundred new cases were filed each year per judge, or approximately 1.4 new cases per judge per day. In 2003 the average caseload per three-judge federal appellate panel reached 1,090, the highest level ever. As a representative of the Judicial Conference told a congressional subcommittee in June 2003, the federal judiciary cannot meet "current workload needs" without more judges.[21]

A distressing result of these numbers is the delay between the filing of a case and its adjudication. In the federal system, for example, the median time from the filing of a civil case to the end of a trial is nearly two years (twenty-one months). In some areas it is even longer. One study of the U.S. Equal Employment Opportunity Commission found that the median time from the filing of a lawsuit alleging workplace discrimination to the commencement of the trial was two and one-half years.[22] If the old saying "justice delayed is justice denied" has any truth, then there is a good deal of denial of justice in the American judicial system.

The situation described above is particularly troubling because there is little that judges can do to remedy it. There simply are neither enough judges nor enough money being spent to cope with the demands Americans place on the judicial system. The problem lies with the political process and the unwillingness of elected officials to spend the money required to meet the demands placed on the judicial system. While virtually all agencies of government assert they need more resources, the judicial system belongs in a different category. The judicial system and the rule of law it works to guarantee is fundamental to democracy. Without adequate resources for the judiciary, a robust democratic life is threatened.

Equal Access and Representation

Nowhere is the judiciary's lack of resources more powerfully felt than in its impact on the poor. In order for the rule of law to protect and enhance democracy, all people must have equal access to, and equal rights in, the judicial system. If they do not, then justice is unevenly distributed among citizens, and democracy is more of an aspiration than a reality.

Criminal Courts

The Constitution of the United States provides all those arrested with a set of guarantees fundamental to the rule of law and democracy. These include, among others, the right to a jury trial and the right to be represented by counsel. And in a series of landmark decisions the U.S. Supreme Court has held that people cannot be sent to prison without the assistance of counsel which must be provided to the poor at government expense.[23] These rights are based on the requirement at the heart of democracy that all citizens are equal before the law.

These basic requirements for a democratic political system are not met in the criminal justice system. As noted earlier, trials are relatively rare events. Courts have neither the resources nor the time to provide them. It is thus in their interest to encourage plea-bargaining with poor criminal defendants, who often see little choice but to accept the bargain. Perhaps more importantly, poor people are either not represented by counsel or receive inadequate and ineffective representation. The problems start as early as the decision about whether or not to release an arrested person on bail. It is estimated that 500,000 people remain in jail each day not because they have been found guilty of a crime or determined to be a threat to society but because they can not afford to post bail.[24] Lawyers can make a difference even at the bail stage. An analysis of two groups of randomly selected defendants charged with similar nonviolent offenses and having comparable backgrounds found that two and one-half times as many defendants represented by lawyers were released on recognizance than unrepresented defendants. Further, twice as many defendants represented by a lawyer had their bail reduced to an affordable amount compared to those not represented.[25]

In court, the pattern is similar. In his sample of 1,640 criminal cases in New Haven, Connecticut in the late 1970s, Feeley found that only one-half of all defendants had a lawyer. Twenty percent of those charged with felonies, and one-third of those receiving jail sentences, were not represented by counsel, in direct violation of constitutional requirements.[26] Twenty years later, and clear across the country, little had changed. Watching 1,600 misdemeanor arraignment hearings in southern California in the 1990s, Meyer and Jesilow noted that "few of the defendants we studied were represented by counsel."[27]

Numerous commentators have noted that the mere physical presence of counsel is far from the substantive promise of the effective assistance of counsel.

This point is powerfully made in a nearly four-hundred-page study of the criminal defense of the poor in New York City. The very first sentence of the text sets the tone, stating that indigent criminal defendants in New York City "receive ineffective assistance from lawyers who . . . fail to provide competent adversarial representation."[28] A 2000 *Harvard Law Review* article sums up the situation this way:

> there is a broad consensus that criminal defense systems are in a 'state of perpetual crisis.' . . . '[T]he grave inadequacy of existing systems for serving the indigent is widely acknowledged and widely discussed.' In fact since the 1963 *Gideon* decision, a major independent report has been issued at least every five years documenting the severe deficiencies in indigent defense services. The evidence is unambiguous and telling. Lawyers representing indigent defendants often have unmanageable caseloads that frequently run into hundreds, far exceeding professional guidelines. These same lawyers typically receive compensation at the lowest end of the professional pay scale. . . . [I]t has become trite to lament the sometimes shockingly incompetent quality of indigent defense counsel in American today.[29]

American democracy is undermined by the unequal treatment of the poor in criminal courts.

Civil Courts

Although lack of access to lawyers in civil courts does not lead to prison, it, too, violates the basic requirements of a democratic political system by putting those without sufficient resources at a disadvantage in making their case. There is little doubt that poor people in America lack equal access to the civil courts. There is also little doubt that their need for legal representation is as great as, if not greater than, the need of wealthier Americans. In the year 2000 there were over thirty million Americans living below the poverty line, approximately 11 percent of the American population.[30] If judicial resources were distributed evenly across the country, then approximately 11 percent of lawyers would be working on behalf of the poor. Since in the year 2000 the U.S. Census reports 929,000 lawyers, then approximately 102,000 lawyers should be working on behalf of the poor.[31] This is not the case. Writing in 1991, Smith found that only about 4 percent of lawyers were employed by legal aid or public defender programs.[32] There is no evidence that much has changed. A 1999 survey by the magazine *American Lawyer* of lawyers at the one hundred highest-grossing firms found that they spent approximately eight minutes per day on pro bono cases. Assuming a five-day work week and a month's vacation over the course of a year, this adds up to approximately thirty-two hours a year, well below the minimal fifty hours per year the American Bar Association urges lawyers to spend working with the poor. In New York State, one-half of all lawyers do no pro bono work at all.[33]

Maryland provides a case study of attempts to help the poor gain access to courts since its access to justice for the poor is "widely recognized as the national model."[34] However, Maryland's efforts fall far short of meeting the needs of all its poor citizens. Depending on the methodology used, in the year 2000 Maryland legal services addressed somewhere between 33 percent and 73 percent of the estimated legal needs of its poor citizens. In terms of funding, Maryland spent between 29 percent and 65 percent of the estimated funds necessary to provide equal access to the poor. While these ranges are large, and are based on estimates of need, they provide an indication of how large is the unmet need.

Nationally, Robert Kershaw writes, the "best estimates are that 20 percent of [the legal] needs [of the poor] are adequately addressed, a percentage essentially unchanged since the 1990s." Comparing the per capita pro bono resources in both Maryland and the U.S. to similar spending in other Western democracies, Kershaw finds that the U.S. lags "their per capita or percent of GNP expenditures for legal services to the poor by a factor of two or three times."[35]

Democracy requires that citizens have equal access to the justice system. As America enters the twenty-first century it is clear that poor people lack equal access. In testimony before the Commission on the 21st Century Judiciary of the American Bar Association, Stephen Bright put the point bluntly: "We're going to come to a reckoning here very shortly where we are going to have to either sandblast 'Equal Justice Under Law' off the Supreme Court building or we're going to have to do something about access to justice for people who don't have any money."[36]

American democracy is undermined when tens of millions of citizens lack the financial resources to enjoy the protections of the rule of law and the judicial system that are essential to any democratic society. Providing equal access to the judicial system for poor Americans is one of the biggest challenges facing the judicial system in the twenty-first century.

Diversity

America in the twenty-first century is increasingly racially diverse. As the American Bar Association's Commission on the 21st Century Judiciary noted, by mid-century half of all Americans will be persons of color. It has always been the case that roughly half of all Americans are female. However, when Americans interact with courts they appear before judges who are predominantly white and male. On the state level, for example, only approximately 8 percent of judges are minorities.[37] On state supreme courts only one-quarter of the judges are women.[38] In the federal system, approximately 21 percent of judges are female, 6 percent African American, and 2 percent Hispanic.[39] While these numbers roughly track the percentages of lawyers who are women and minorities, they fall far short of the demographic make-up of American society.

In theory this should not matter. In a democratic society governed by the rule of law judicial outcomes should not depend on the race or gender of judges. In practice, however, a predominantly white and male judiciary, at the very least, raises the issue of potential bias. The report of the American Bar Association's Commission on the 21st Century Judiciary warned that if the judiciary does not "reflect the diversity of the society in which we live," then "the legitimacy of the courts and the judicial system will be called into question with increasing frequency."[40] The commission was "convinced that the continued failure to meaningfully diversify the courts will work to the detriment of the 21st Century judiciary's overall health, quality, and level of public support."[41] That, in turn, will weaken the democratic system.

Indirect Involvement with Courts

The preceding sections have presented and considered data showing that very large numbers of Americans have direct involvement with courts. The data also show that minorities and the poor lack equal access and face unequal treatment. The data raise serious questions about the way in which the direct involvement of Americans with courts sits with the fundamental requirements of democracy. But courts also affect Americans indirectly through rulings in individual cases that influence policy nationwide. Thomas Burke notes that "the range of matters that can be litigated in the United States is broader than in other nations and growing each year."[42] These matters include litigation over allegedly defective, unsafe, or dangerous products, cases stemming from accidents, judicial interpretations of statutes, and judicial interpretations of the U.S. and state constitutions. Supporters of such litigation claim that it protects the health, safety, and basic rights of American citizens, contributing to and furthering democracy. Critics vehemently disagree, arguing that courts are preventing citizens from making fundamental decisions about the way Americans live, making the United States considerably less democratic. I turn now to consider how courts influence American life in these areas.

Torts and Product Liability

In the last several decades of the twentieth century courts became deeply involved with issues of products liability, allegedly unsafe or unhealthy products, and claims of legal liability for accidents and unexpected outcomes. From asbestos to silicon breast implants to the temperature of coffee served at fast food restaurants to the design of cars to the health effects of cigarette smoking to medical malpractice, courts have had an impact on American life. What is the extent of that impact? What is the relationship between this kind of litigation and the practice of democracy? This section examines these questions.

In the early twenty-first century there appears to be a common view that in all these areas courts have become dangerously powerful. There is, Marc Galanter writes, the perception that people are suing each other indiscriminately about the most frivolous matters, and juries are capriciously awarding immense sums to undeserving claimants. The system is arbitrary, unpredictable, berserk, demented; it has spun out of control. The resulting "litigation explosion" is unraveling the social fabric and undermining the economy.[43]

Elaborating on this view, its adherents further contend that unscrupulous and greedy lawyers encourage people to bring questionable lawsuits against wealthy defendants in the hope of making millions of dollars. Often, the alleged injured party is uninvolved since the aim of the litigation is to enrich the lawyers, not compensate the named plaintiff for any wrong. Faced with juries that are generally sympathetic to the "little person," and thus ready to believe that the defendant corporation or rich doctor was at fault, defendants are often willing to settle even nonmeritorious suits to avoid potentially huge liability. This, in turn, leads to the removal of good products from the market, and sometimes the bankruptcy of good companies. It stifles innovation. It results in the reduction of medical services as doctors, rather than pay soaring malpractice insurance premiums, curtail their practices or move. The cost of paying enormous sums of money in these cases, is passed on to consumers through higher costs. American companies lose their competitive edge to foreign manufacturers who do not face the litigation threat to the same extent, and jobs are lost. Finally, by allowing this kind of litigation courts weaken democracy by removing from citizens the ability to make fundamental decisions about the way in which they lead their lives.

On a less extreme note, Robert Kagan argues that the "adversarial legalism" of the United States does not serve its citizens. In contrast to other democratic countries, Robert Kagan argues, the United States relies more heavily on litigation to resolve disputes and set policy than on regulation and bureaucratic administration. Judicial authority is fragmented among many courts located in many different jurisdictions. There is only weak hierarchical control and the system is driven by lawyers. The result is an inefficient and unpredictable system that imposes high costs on society. It ill serves accountability, efficiency, and individual fairness.[44]

This is a powerful indictment of the impact of courts on American life. Is it true? A major challenge in understanding and assessing the effect of tort and product liability litigation on American life is that it is difficult to gather accurate data about how many cases are filed and with what outcomes. This is largely due to the decentralized American legal system, the large number of nonpublic settlements, and the politicization of the issue. Given the large financial stakes involved, many so-called studies and reports are little more than paid propaganda. That being said, the indictment appears to be overstated. After reviewing these and similar claims, and a myriad of scholarly studies, William Haltom and Michael McCann conclude, "there is a lot of bunk out there."[45]

Consider, for example, the area of medical malpractice. A major study sponsored by Harvard University found that out of every one hundred injuries caused by negligent medical practice, only about a dozen claims are made. Further, among those who suffer major permanent injuries resulting in at least partial disability, only about one in six file claims.[46] Filing a claim, of course, does not necessarily mean damages will be awarded. Neil Vidmar reviewed more than a dozen studies of medical malpractice litigation and found that the median win rate for plaintiffs was "around 29 percent."[47] As for the alleged sympathy of jurors toward the plaintiffs, Vidmar found that "multiple sources of data strongly indicate that, on the whole, juries do not favor claimants over doctors, and do not make negligence judgements based on the depth of defendants' pockets or the severity of patients' injuries."[48] As for settlement, Vidmar found that "insurers tend to settle cases where defendant liability is clear and to contest cases where they conclude there is no liability."[49]

What is true of medical practice appears to be true in other areas as well. "Research typically shows Americans rarely take their disputes to court."[50] In the late 1970s, for example, the Civil Litigation Research Project at the University of Wisconsin found that on average only one in twenty grievances developed into litigation.[51] More specifically, the study found that of every one hundred Americans who believed they had lost more than $1,000 because of illegal conduct, only five filed suit.[52] As the twentieth century was coming to a close, a major study by the Institute for Civil Justice at the Rand Corporation found similar results. Focusing on serious injuries, it found that those injured made claims in about 44 percent of automobile injuries but in only 7 percent of injuries at work and only about 3 percent of other injuries. Overall, the Rand study found that out of every one hundred people who suffered a disabling injury, eighty-one took no action and only two filed a lawsuit.[53] With some exasperation, Haltom and McCann note that "[s]cholars have repeatedly demonstrated what *a minuscule proportion of disputes even approaches a courthouse, let alone a courtroom.*"[54] As Burke sums up the data, "Far from a nation of litigators, the United States seems to be filled with 'lumpers,' people inclined to lump their grievances rather them press them."[55]

There are many possible reasons why few grievances or injuries become court cases. Obvious ones include the time, resources, and emotional commitment involved in going to court. Less obviously, lawyers screen cases, rejecting those which they think they are unlikely to win or in which their litigation costs are likely to be greater than any recovery. In addition, individuals are at a disadvantage in suing defendants such as insurance companies, large corporations, and government. In a noteworthy 1974 article Marc Galanter argued that these "Haves" are endowed with multiple resources that allow them to prevail more often than not in litigation. These resources include judicial experience and expertise that come from being "repeat players" in litigation, financial resources that allow them to outspend and outlast their opponents, and the ability to play by the rules rather than needing to change them. Empirical studies of the U.S. Courts of Appeals and state high courts have supported Galanter's argument.[56]

The data just presented are clearly at odds with the general perception that in the torts area courts are having a large and negative impact. Part of the reason for this general perception is the way in which some critics have publicized alleged examples of apparently absurd judicial outcomes. Perhaps the most famous example is that of the woman who spilled a cup of McDonald's coffee on her lap and was awarded almost $2.9 million by a jury. Critics use the case as the poster-child of a court system run amok. Because this case has become the "best known contemporary legal legend"[57] it is worth looking at a bit more closely.[58]

The case involved a seventy-nine-year-old woman, Stella Liebeck. On February 27, 1992, while riding in a car driven by her grandson, she purchased a cup of coffee at a McDonald's drive-through window in Albuquerque, New Mexico. Her grandson pulled the car away from the window and brought it to a complete stop by a curb in the parking lot. In order to steady the cup to add sugar and cream, Liebeck put the cup between her legs and removed the top. Unfortunately, the cup tipped, spilling the coffee on her. Rather than a mere annoyance, however, the coffee burned her very badly. At the hospital doctors found that the coffee had caused third degree burns on 6 percent of her body, including her thighs, buttocks, genitals, and groin area, and caused lesser burns that eventually left permanent scarring on 16 percent of her body. She spent a week in the hospital and subsequently underwent a series of painful skin grafts.

As a result of her ordeal, Liebeck asked McDonald's to reimburse her for her medical expenses, which amounted to about $20,000. In response, McDonald's offered her $800. Liebeck declined the payment and sued. The court appointed a mediator who recommended that the parties settle the dispute for $225,000. Although Liebeck agreed, McDonald's did not. In preparing the case her lawyer discovered that over the previous decade McDonald's had received over seven hundred complaints about the temperature of its coffee and had paid nearly three-quarters of a million dollars to settle such complaints. At trial it was revealed that McDonald's served its coffee about twenty degrees hotter than the standard in the trade.[59] The company's own expert admitted at trial that coffee that hot could not be drunk and would cause burns if it was. Although the jury awarded her $160,000 in damages and $2.7 million in punitive damages (an estimate of McDonald's profits from two days of coffee sales), the judge reduced the punitive damages to $480,000 (three times the amount of the damages). The judge then ordered another conference at which the parties reached a confidential settlement.

Was the case rightfully decided? There may be room for honest disagreement. But given the horrific burns Liebeck suffered, the numerous complaints McDonald's had received about the temperature of its coffee and its prior payouts, and the eventual settlement at an amount substantially less than the nearly $2.9 million initially awarded by the jury and presumably less than the reduced amount ordered by the judge, it is difficult to see the case as a travesty of justice or an example of a judicial system run amok. Even so, the case still may be unusual because Liebeck apparently won a large judgment. As Haltom and McCann sum up the literature, "scholarly experts have documented that plaintiffs rarely win large judgements against corporations for defective products."[60]

As a policy matter the question of the temperature at which coffee should be served at fast-food restaurants is trivial. American courts have been involved in much more important policy issues. Even if few Americans litigate, there clearly are cases that are litigated and that impact the broader society. One example is the litigation over tobacco. The evidence that cigarette smoking has adverse health effects has been widely known since at least 1964 when the U.S. Surgeon General issued a report linking cigarette smoking to various illnesses. However, despite the fact that there were between forty-eight and fifty-three million adult smokers each year in the 1960s, 1970s, and 1980s, Americans did not bring lawsuits against tobacco companies in large numbers. While the first lawsuits brought by dying smokers and their families against the tobacco companies were filed in the late 1950s,[61] by 1992 there had only been twenty-three trials, resulting in two victories for the plaintiffs, both of which were overturned on appeal.[62] Starting in 1993, however, the picture changed.

From 1993 through June 1998 there were 807 legal actions commenced against the tobacco industry. These were brought not only by individuals seeking damages for injuries to themselves and others, but also included fifty-five class action lawsuits and lawsuits by attorneys general from forty states and Puerto Rico seeking to recover monies spent by states to care for sick smokers.[63] As a result of this litigation, hundreds of billions of dollars were awarded to the plaintiffs, and billions of dollars to their lawyers around the country. The most important and monetarily largest outcome was the Master Settlement Agreement reached between the tobacco industry and the states with the help of the U.S. Congress. Among other provisions, it required the industry to pay the states $206 billion over twenty-five years.[64]

Did the use of courts to deal with cigarettes serve democracy? The answer is not clear, and both supporters and critics of massive product liability litigation can point to various data supporting their position. On the one hand, several hundred billion dollars was paid by the tobacco companies to states for health care costs and antismoking campaigns. The money will come from increases in the purchase price of cigarettes, and perhaps from shareholders' profits. On the other hand, the democratic political process was not involved in the decision about how to deal with the health effects of tobacco. After the litigation tobacco companies continued to produce and sell cigarettes, which they were as unhealthy after the settlement as they were before it. A small group of lawyers became very rich. The effect on the number of cigarette smokers is not clear either, although it appears negligible. In 1993, when the successful litigation started, there were 46.4 million adult smokers. In 2002, there were 45.8 million adult smokers, a minor change. In comparison, back in 1965 there were 50.1 million adult smokers. As a percentage of adults, however, while 42.4 percent were smokers in 1964, that percentage dropped to 25 percent by 1993, several years before the litigation against the tobacco companies succeeded. In 2002, the percentage dropped further, to 22.5 percent. These data suggest that the percentage of adult Americans smokers has been dropping steadily since the 1960s, with the largest drops occurring well before the tobacco litigation succeeded. Among teenagers and young Americans, the incidence of smoking is actually higher after the litigation than before it. In 2003, 22.9 percent of high school students in the United States were current cigarette smokers, as were 28.5 percent of eighteen to twenty-four year olds, the highest percentage for any age group. This latter figure is an increase of 3 percentage points over the 1993 figure and nearly 6 percentage points higher than the 1990 rate.[65] In sum, a major result of litigation over tobacco was the enormous financial cost to the tobacco industry and an equivalent cash payment to the states. There has apparently been little effect on the number and percentage of adult smokers. The issue of how to deal with health effects of smoking remains.

The history of tobacco litigation shows that in the area of torts and product liability courts can have large impacts on the lives of Americans. But are these impacts good? Do they threaten democracy or strengthen it? The Civil Litigation Project of the Rand Corporation has attempted to answer these questions. In a large project at the end of the twentieth century on class action litigation, Deborah Hensler and her colleagues interviewed over seventy individuals in more than forty law firms, corporations and other organizations including "many of the leading class action practitioners, on both the plaintiff and defense sides."[66] They also selected ten recently filed class action lawsuits for intensive study including six consumer class action cases, two mass product damage cases, and two mass personal injury cases.[67] These are precisely the kinds of cases that critics charge are undermining democracy. Perhaps unsurprisingly, the results were mixed.

On the positive side, the study notes that "[m]any believe that these [kinds of] lawsuits serve important public purposes by supplementing the work of government regulators whose budgets are usually quite limited and who are subject to political constraints." Surprisingly, some of the corporate representatives who were interviewed concurred, saying that such lawsuits have "played a regulatory role by causing them to review their financial and employment practices." In addition, "some manufacturer representatives noted that heightened concerns about potential class action suits have had a positive influence on product design decisions."[68] The ten cases they examined provided some support for these statements. In all six consumer cases, for example, the litigation was associated with changes in the defendants' business practices.[69] While the study doesn't state whether these changes strengthened or weakened the businesses, other studies, Galanter notes, have "found little evidence of any significant effect on America's prosperity or competitiveness."[70]

On the negative side, the authors could not decide whether all the claims were meritorious or not, leaving the possibility that some were trivial and trumped up.[71] Further, in some of the cases the plaintiffs' lawyers appeared "simply interested in finding a settlement price that the defendants would agree to" rather than assessing the actual damages to their clients. In addition to questions of fairness, the authors also note that this behavior undermines the social utility of these suits in deterring wrongful or harmful practices.[72] Overall, the study concludes that "[d]amage class actions pose a dilemma for public policy because of their capacity to do both good and ill for society."[73]

What, then, is the relationship between this kind of litigation and the practice of democracy? In a perfect world, there would be no such litigation because all products would be completely safe. Potentially dangerous products would be stopped by government regulators long before they reached the market. All businesses would be scrupulously honest and no citizen or lawyer would seek financial gain under the guise of questionable injuries. In the real world, however, this is not possible. Honest people make mistakes and dishonest people take advantage of others. The challenge America faces is that as society becomes increasingly complex, citizens need a way of verifying the safety of products or the veracity of the claims made about them. Government regulators often lack the resources, and sometimes lack the political will, to vigorously insure product safety and enforce the law. If a requirement of democracy is that citizens must be protected from organizations and bureaucracies with concentrated economic or political power, then the involvement of courts in product liability and tort cases may strengthen democracy. On the other hand, if another requirement of democracy is that adult citizens determine, at least indirectly, what their government does and decide the most important decisions facing the country, then these kinds of cases may weaken democracy by removing at least some important policy decisions from elected officials and, indirectly, voters. In addition, the tort system is inefficient and unpredictable, and it privileges those with deep pockets. There is a tension here that may only be resolved in practice. The use of courts in torts and products liability cases may sometimes produce outcomes that protect citizens and strengthen democracy and may sometimes produce outcomes that ignore or harm citizens and weaken democracy.

Constitutional Litigation

Nowhere is this tension between the role of courts and democracy more starkly presented than in constitutional litigation. The most well-known court decisions in America are constitutional decisions of the U.S. Supreme Court. As the highest court in the land it presumably has the last word on constitutional requirements. To a lesser extent the same is true of the supreme court of each state when it interprets its state constitution. In a democratic political system governed by a constitution, and operating under the rule of law, constitutional decisions of high courts are binding. This potentially gives courts the power to make policy. But in a democracy, policy making is the prerogative of the elected branches of the government, whose officials serve at the pleasure of the citizens. What happens, then, when courts issue constitutional decisions dealing with contested issues? From the mid-twentieth century on, the U.S. Supreme Court did just that at an increasing rate, deciding, for example, questions of race and gender discrimination, abortion, criminal procedure, and university admissions. State high courts have acted as well. In 1999, for example, the Vermont Supreme Court held that the Vermont Constitution required that same-sex partners be given "all or most of the same rights and obligations provided by the law to married partners" (*Baker v. Vermont*, 1999). In 2003 the Supreme Judicial Court of Massachusetts interpreted the Massachusetts Constitution to require the state to issue marriage licenses to same-sex couples (*Goodridge v. Department of Public Health*, 2003). What is the impact of constitutional decisions like these on American life and on democracy in America?

Supporters of the role of the courts in deciding constitutional issues claim such decisions bring democracy to life by protecting the rights of those least able to protect themselves. These might include groups such as racial minorities, the poor, pregnant women, criminal defendants, and gays. The political process may fail minorities because of discrimination, institutional blockages created by seniority and inert bureaucracies, the hesitancy of elected officials to take a stand on contentious issues, the lack of political power of these groups, and their lack of popularity. Thus, supporters argue, constitutional decisions strengthen democracy.

In contrast critics believe that "for much of the second half of the twentieth century, America's courts—state and federal—have injected themselves willy nilly into fundamentally moral and political disputes"[74] where they do not belong. The role of courts is to decide legal issues, not to chose sides in moral and political debates. In a democracy, they argue, it is the people who must be the ultimate arbiters of morality and policy. Robert Bork sums up the critique this way: "The Court is removing from democratic control the most important moral, political, and cultural decisions that affect our lives."[75] Constitutional decisions, the critics argue, weaken democracy.

Regardless of who is correct, it is important to note that there is much that courts don't do. There are a large number of important policy areas where courts play little or no role. A list might include foreign policy, the military, economic policy including budgets, taxation, social welfare, growth, health policy, housing, and so forth. Clearly judicial decisions can and do impact these areas but on the whole they remain outside of judicial involvement.

It is also important to note that much of what courts do in terms of policy is to interpret legislation. In the first three years of the twenty-first century, for example, nearly two-thirds of civil filings in U.S. district courts were brought under statutes.[76] A court is typically asked to consider whether a statute covers a particular dispute After the decision the legislature can, and sometimes does, rewrite the statute to make it clearer, expand its reach, reject the court's interpretation, and so on. An excellent example deals with the question of whether a disability plan that excludes coverage for pregnancy and childbirth violates Title VII of the 1964 Civil Rights Act. In *General Electric Co. v. Gilbert* (1976) the Supreme Court held that it did not. In response, Congress, in October 1978, enacted the Pregnancy Discrimination Act amending Title VII to make pregnancy discrimination a type of forbidden sex discrimination.

When courts engage in statutory interpretation they often play an influential policy role. This is largely because they are working within already established bureaucracies with resources and commitments. The very fact that the courts are interpreting a statute means that government has acted, committing resources to achieve a particular goal. And since the legislature has the ability to modify or overturn the court's interpretation if it so chooses, control of policy remains with the elected branches. Although people may not always agree with a judicial interpretation of a statute, this kind of judicial action fits comfortably within democracy.

Returning to constitutional decisions, one can distinguish between at least four different kinds. The categories are not hermetically sealed and some decisions could be placed in more than one category. The distinction is made because their impact on American life and American democracy differs.

There is one kind in which courts simply uphold governmental action against charges of unconstitutionality. For example, in two 1964 cases (*Heart of Atlanta Motel v. United States*, 1964; *Katzenbach v. McClung*, 1964), the U.S. Supreme Court upheld the constitutionality of the 1964 Civil Rights Act against legal challenges. In 2003 the U.S. Supreme Court upheld the constitutionality of an affirmative action plan at the University of Michigan Law School (*Grutter v. Bollinger*). These kind of decisions simply allow the status quo to continue. In that sense they have little impact; life goes on as before under the policy-setting role of the legislature and other governmental actors.

A second kind of constitutional decision involves disputes between different branches of government. For example, a state may contend that the federal government is overstepping its constitutional limitations and usurping state powers. Starting in the earliest years of the United States, in the 1790s, and continuing throughout American history, disputes between the federal and state governments over which government has the constitutional authority to act have been brought to the courts. For example, in *New York v. United States* (1992), the Court invalidated part of a federal law that required states to provide for disposal of internally generated low-level radioactive waste. The Court held the Congress could not "commandeer the legislative processes of the States by directly compelling them to enact and enforce a federal regulatory program."

Other decisions at the end of the twentieth century limited the power of Congress in favor of the states on issues such as violence against women (*United States v. Morrison*, 2000), guns in school zones (*United States v. Lopez*, 1995), and the application of the Americans with Disability Act to state governments (*Board of Trustees of the University of Alabama v. Garrett*, 2001).

The Supreme Court has also become involved in constitutional disputes between the branches of the federal government. A famous example is *Youngstown Sheet & Tube Co. v. Sawyer* (1952) which pitted the U.S. Congress against the president of the United States. At issue was whether the president had the constitutional authority to order the United States to take control of several steel mills in order to maintain steel production during the Korean War. The Court held the president lacked the authority and could not act without Congress first passing legislation. The president and the judiciary have also clashed. In *United States v. Nixon* (1974) and *Clinton v. Jones* (1997) the Supreme Court held that presidents were not entitled to automatic immunity from legal process.

Although deciding which branch of government has the constitutional authority to decide an issue is very important, most people are more interested in the substantive result of such decisions. Thus, the impact of many of these separation-of-powers type decisions is not noticed by most Americans. But they can matter a great deal to the lives of Americans. For example, during the first thirty-seven years of the twentieth century the Supreme Court limited the power of the federal government to regulate the economy in favor of the states. These sorts of decisions limit the ability of the national government to act, removing important policy decisions from democratic choice.

A third kind of constitutional decision tells government that it must stop what it is doing or refrain from taking certain actions. In the first three decades of the twentieth century, for example, the Supreme Court held that under the Constitution neither the states nor the Congress could establish minimum wages or maximum hours for workers. In 1973, in *Roe v. Wade*, the Supreme Court held that the Constitution did not allow government to interfere with a pregnant woman's decision, in consultation with a doctor, to terminate a pregnancy during the first two trimesters of pregnancy. A twenty-first century example is *Lawrence v. Texas* (2003) in which the Supreme Court held that states could not make private, consensual, sexual conduct between adults a crime. This "nay-saying" kind of constitutional decision can have important effects on the lives of American citizens. A decision like *Lawrence* protects citizens from arrest and criminal prosecution. A decision like *Roe* gives pregnant women the legal right to obtain a safe abortion. While supporters of such decisions celebrate them for extending rights and allowing individuals to participate fully in the broader society, critics argue that they usurp the rights of democratic majorities to decide the moral values of society.

The fourth kind of constitutional decision is one in which the courts *require* government to take affirmative steps, to change behavior. For example, *Brown v. Board of Education* (1954) held that schools must end segregation which meant, in effect, that they must desegregate. *Miranda v. Arizona* (1966) held that before police question a suspect they must read him or her a set of rights. *Argersinger v. Hamlin* (1972) held that poor people cannot be sent to prison without the assistance of counsel, which must be provided at government expense. A host of decisions required prisons, hospitals, mental health institutions, and other large governmental bureaucracies to change their practices, sometimes in major ways. These "yea-saying" kind of decisions invariably support the relatively disadvantaged who lack the political resources to change practice through the political process.

These "nay-saying" and "yea saying" decisions are often politically controversial. As noted above, critics charge that they substitute judicial decision-making for legislative and political deliberation, weakening democracy. In contrast, supporters praise them for extending rights and allowing more people to participate fully in democratic life. Indeed, to a large extent the so-called "culture wars" of the late twentieth and early twenty-first century revolve around this debate. What both sides have in common is an assumption that the implementation of constitutional decisions is unproblematic. Are they right?

The Implementation of Constitutional Decisions

When American courts require governmental institutions to change their behavior to remedy a constitutional failing, they are in an unusual position.[77] This is largely because courts lack the resources to implement their decisions. As Robert McCloskey put it, "one of the Supreme Court's [and the broader judicial system's] peculiar characteristics is that it attempts to decide questions of policy without the advantage of conventional political resources."[78] The judicial system was particularly structured this way, perhaps reflecting the framers' fear of judicial power. Alexander Hamilton noted this structural weakness in "Federalist No. 78" where he famously wrote that the judiciary has "no influence over either the sword or the purse . . . and must ultimately depend upon the aid of the executive arm even for the efficacy of its judgments."[79] Lacking the ability to control budgets or call out the military, the courts depend on the executive branch to implement their decisions. These structural constraints on courts suggest that implementation of constitutional decisions may not be straightforward.

This is indeed the case. Constitutional decisions are implemented unevenly. Consider, for example, two of the most controversial constitutional decisions of the U.S. Supreme Court, *Brown v. Board of Education* (1954), holding racial segregation in public schools unconstitutional, and *Roe v. Wade* (1973), finding a constitutional right to abortion. Starting with *Brown*, it may come as a surprise that a decade after *Brown* little had changed for most African American students living in the eleven states of the former Confederacy that required race-based school segregation by law at the time of the decision. For example, in the 1963–1964 school year, barely one in one hundred (1.2 percent) of these African American children was in a nonsegregated school. That means that for nearly 99 of every 100 African American children in the South a decade after *Brown*, the finding of a constitutional right changed nothing.

There was a slow but steady rise in the number of legal abortions performed in 1973 and the years following *Roe v. Wade*. However, legal abortions are unevenly available across the United States. Each year, hundreds of thousands of women must travel considerable distances to obtain abortion services. This is largely because most hospitals, the existing institutions that provide medical care and childbirth services, have refused to implement the decision. Implementation has been left to private abortion clinics. But in places where political leaders or large segments of the population oppose abortion, there are few or no clinics. Considering that the U.S. Supreme Court has held that women have a fundamental constitutional right to obtain abortions, and that abortion is the most common surgical procedure performed on American women today, the uneven availability of abortion demonstrates the problematic nature of the implementation of constitutional decisions.

Another way in which constitutional decisions may affect Americans is through their symbolic effects. When the U.S. Supreme Court finds a constitutional right to something, it is suggested, it has a particularly powerful effect on how Americans think about the issue. The problem with this seemingly plausible claim is that it lacks empirical support. That is, there is not much evidence that Court decisions on controversial issues change many minds.[80]

Overall, the impact of constitutional decisions on the lives of Americans and on American democracy is mixed. In particular, decisions supporting minorities and the poor are not always fully implemented. There is no straightforward and simple answer to the questions about how court decisions affect the lives of Americans.

What Americans Think about Courts

The evidence presented in this chapter has shown that the impact of courts on the lives of Americans is varied and uneven. In particular, racial minorities and the poor lack the same access to the judicial system as the wealthy and receive unequal treatment. Are Americans aware of this? Several polls of the American public conducted at the end of the twentieth and the beginning of the twenty-first century illustrate that Americans are aware of these discrepancies and have mixed views of the judicial system and its role in the democratic system.

To know American courts is not necessarily to love them. Starting on the positive side, a 1998 public opinion survey of one thousand randomly selected adults sponsored by the American Bar Association (ABA) found that 80 percent of respondents agreed with the statement that the American justice system is the best in the world.[81] Fifty percent of the respondents said they were extremely or very confident in the Supreme Court. However, after that, the level of support dropped. Only 34 percent of respondents were extremely or very confident in federal judges other than Supreme Court justices and only 28 percent chose that category for state and local courts. As for the "U.S. Justice System in General," only 30 percent were extremely or very confident compared to 27 percent who were slightly or not at all confident.[82] Overall, 51 percent of respondents believe that the "justice system needs a complete overhaul."[83]

In November of 2001 the Justice At Stake Campaign also completed a national survey of one thousand randomly selected adults. While the survey focused on issues dealing with the selection of state judges, it contained a number of questions relevant to the impact of courts on the lives of Americans. In terms of support for the job being done by state courts, slightly over 50 percent rated it as excellent or good compared to over 40 percent who rated the job just fair, or poor.[84] Although nearly two-thirds of respondents (63 percent) thought the word "impartial" described judges well or very well, over half (52 percent) thought the words "controlled by special interests" did so too. Similarly, when asked how well the word "political" described judges, a whopping 76 percent of respondents answered "very well" or "well."[85] Part of these results may be driven by respondents' nearly unanimous belief that policy groups were turning to the courts to try to further their political agendas. Eighty-eight percent of respondents agreed that "Special interest groups are trying to use the courts to shape policy on everything from taxes and education to health care and the environment" and 91 percent agreed that "Special interest groups are trying to use the courts to shape policy on everything from the death penalty and abortion to affirmative action and gun rights."[86]

Respondents were also dissatisfied about the costs involved in litigation and the length of time it takes to reach a resolution of legal disputes. Seventy-seven percent of respondents agreed that it costs too much to go to court and 78 percent agreed that it takes too long for courts to do their job.[87] These data show that Americans believe courts favor the wealthy and the powerful, violating a key requirement of the rule of law essential to democracy.

Judicial Bias

A fundamental part of the rule of law that is crucial to democratic government is the equality of all citizens before the law. The symbol of the blind Goddess of Justice represents this core belief. But majorities of survey respondents do not believe the American judicial system treats people equally in terms of wealth, race, and gender. In terms of gender, for example, where respondents thought there was the least amount of bias, "only about half of the respondents agree that men and women are treated equally" by the judicial system.[88] The ABA survey also found that overall women had less positive attitudes about the justice system than men.[89]

Respondents perceived even more bias with race. When asked if they agreed with the statement that, "In most cases, the courts treat all ethnic and racial groups the same," only 39 percent did, while 47 percent disagreed (the remaining 14 percent took no position).[90] This perception of racial bias was corroborated by a poll of 1,001 lawyers, approximately half white and half black, carried out by the *ABA Journal* and the *National Bar Association Magazine*. It found that the lawyers' perceptions of racial bias were similar to the perceptions of the national survey except that in some cases the perception of bias was even stronger.[91]

The perception of bias is stronger still with wealth. When asked if "Courts try to treat poor people and wealthy people alike," a cardinal requirement of the legal system, 55 percent disagreed and only 33 percent agreed.[92] The Justice At Stake survey reported a similar result. Only one-third of its respondents thought that the justice system works equally for all citizens compared to 62 percent who agreed that "there are two systems of justice in the U.S.—one for the rich and powerful and one for everyone else."[93] And 90 percent of respondents to the ABA survey concurred that wealthy people or companies wear down their opponents by dragging out legal proceedings.[94] As the American Bar Association's Commission on the 21st Century Judiciary put it, "The perception of two forms of justice—one for the wealthy and one for the poor—is widespread."[95]

Many of these findings reinforce the data presented earlier in the chapter. They show that Americans believe that the judicial system sometimes and perhaps often fails to provide the rule of law necessary for democracy. This is particularly the case with questions of equal access and bias. The perceptions Americans hold about the judicial system do not fit comfortably with the requirements of democracy.

Conclusion

The impact of courts on the lives of Americans and on the practice of American democracy is both widespread and uneven, positive and negative. Americans bring disputes to courts in extraordinary numbers, validating the rule of law. But they do not always abide by the outcomes. The judiciary lacks the racial, ethnic, and gender diversity of the broader society, and large percentages of Americans believe it is biased against women, people of color, and especially the poor. The judicial system does not provide equal access to all Americans, making justice unevenly distributed and democracy more of an aspiration than a reality. These are harsh words, but the data support them.

Courts play a major role in policy making. Through statutory interpretation, tort and product liability cases, and constitutional adjudication, courts are involved with issues that have the potential to affect all Americans. Decisions in such cases may strengthen democracy by protecting and enhancing the rights of all citizens, or they may weaken democracy by removing from public debate and democratic choice issues of moral and substantive importance. Perhaps they do both for there is no consensus on this point.

The American democratic system has a built-in tension between popular sovereignty and the role of courts. This is because democracy requires both that policy decisions be made by elected officials and that rights be guaranteed and protected by the rule of law. This tension creates the virtual certainty that there will be times when judges, elected officials, and segments of the population disagree. In turn this means that the impact of courts on American life and American democracy is constantly changing and is not susceptible to any one definitive characterization.

As the twenty-first-century United States becomes increasingly complex, and increasingly diverse, it is likely that Americans will continue to bring disputes and grievances to courts. How courts respond, and how those responses affect American society, are largely political questions. In the end, courts are only one among many institutions that have the ability to influence policy and strengthen or weaken democracy. Courts, and the decisions they make, are part of a dynamic, complex, and fluid society in which political, economic, and cultural forces interact. Courts will have only as much influence as the political system allows. And since all Americans have the ability to influence the political system, the impact of courts on American life in the twenty-first century ultimately depends on all of us.

Notes

* Thanks to Lynn Mather, Marie Provine, Judge Tom Phillips, Paul Carrington, Judge Judith Billings, and the editors for helpful comments. In particular, Lynn Mather provided detailed, thoughtful, and insightful comments. My chapter is the worse for not having incorporated all the comments I received.

1. Stumpf and Culver, *The Politics of State Courts*, 21.
2. Smith, *Courts and Trials: A Handbook*, 171.

3. de Tocqueville, *Democracy in America*, 270.
4. For further reading on the basic requirements of a democracy, see Robert A. Dahl, "The Moscow Discourse: Fundamental Rights in a Democratic Order," *Government and Opposition 15* (1980): 3–30; and Dahl (1979), Dahl (1971).
5. Unless otherwise noted, the data cited in this section come from the U.S. Department of Justice Programs, Bureau of Justice Statistics. Available at: http://www.ojp.usdoj.gov/bjs/. Data can also be found in the *U.S. Census Bureau, Statistical Abstract of the United States: 2003* (123rd ed.) (Washington, D.C.: GPO, 2003), and earlier editions.
6. Carp, Stidham, and Manning, *Judicial Process in America*, 53.
7. Unless otherwise noted, the data cited in this section come from the National Center for State Courts. Available at: http://www.ncsconline.org/.
8. Danzig, *The Capability Problem in Contract Law*, 53.
9. Macaulay, "Supplementary Comments," 54–65.
10. Haltom and McCann, *Distorting the Law*, 99.
11. U.S. Department of Health and Human Services, Administration for Children and Families, Office of Child Support Enforcement, "Child Support Enforcement Twenty-Third Annual Report to Congress," available at: http://www.acf.hhs.gov/programs/cse/rpt/annrpt23/index.html.
12. U.S. Department of Health and Human Services, Administration for Children and Families, Office of Child Support Enforcement, "FY 2001 Annual Statistical Report," available at: http://www.acf.dhhs.gov/programs/cse/pubs/2003/reports/statistical_report/index.html.
13. Smith, *Courts and Trials*, 170.
14. Feeley, *The Process Is the Punishment*, 3.
15. Blumberg, "The Practice of Law as Confidence Game," 64.
16. Feeley, *The Process Is the Punishment*, 3.
17. Lauren E. Glaze and Seri Palla, "Probation and Parole in the United States, 2003," U.S. Department of Justice, Office of Justice Programs, Bureau of Justice Statistics Bulletin (July 2004 NCJ 205336). Available at: http://www.ojp.usdoj.gov/bjs/pub/pdf/ppus03.pdf.
18. International Centre for Prison Studies, "Entire World—Prison Population Rates per 100,000 of the National Population," Kings College London (2004). Available at http://www.prisonstudies.org. See also Roy Walmsey, "World Prison Population List" (5th ed.), Home Office, United Kingdom. Available at: http://www.homeoffice.gov.uk/rds/pdfs2/r234.pdf.
19. James J. Stephan, Bureau of Justice Statistics, Special Report, State Prison Expenditures, 2001 (June 2004, NCJ 202949). Available at: http://www.ojp.usdoj.gov/bjs/pub/pdf/spe01.pdf.
20. Sentencing Project, "Felony Disenfranchisement Laws in the United States," May 2004. Available at: http://www.sentencingproject.org/pdfs/1046pdf.
21. Office of Judges Program, Statistics Division, Administrative Offices of the United States Courts, "Federal Judicial Caseload Statistic" (March 31, 2003). Available at: http://www.uscourts.gov/caseload2003/contents.html.

22. Lewis L. Maltby, "Private Justice: Employment Arbitration and Civil Rights," *Columbia Human Rights Law Review* 30 (1998): 29–64.
23. See *Gideon v. Wainwright* (1963); *Argersinger v. Hamlin* (1972).
24. Carp, Stidham, and Manning, *Judicial Process in America,* 215.
25. See Douglas L. Colbert, Ray Paternoster, and Shawn Bushway, "Do Attorneys Really Matter? The Empirical and Legal Case for the Right of Counsel at Bail," *Cardozo Law Review* 23 (2002): 1719–1793.
26. Feeley, *The Process Is the Punishment*, 9, 9–10.
27. Meyer and Jesilow, *"Doing Justice" in the People's Court*, 111.
28. Michael McConville and Chester L. Mirsky, "Criminal Defense of the Poor in New York City," *New York University Review of Law and Social Change* 15 (1987): 581–979.
29. Note, "Gideon's Promise Unfufilled: The Need for Litigated Reform of Indigent Defense," *Harvard Law Review* 113 (2000): 2062–2079.
30. U.S. Census Bureau, *Statistical Abstract of the United States: 2003*, 43.
31. Ibid., 399.
32. Smith, *Courts and the Poor*, 137.
33. See Susan Saulny, "Volunteerism among Lawyers Surges, Encouraged by Slumping Economy," *New York Times* Web edition, February 19, 2003.
34. Robert B. Kershaw, "Access to Justice in Maryland—A Visionary's Model," *Maryland Bar Journal* (May/June 2004): 50–53.
35. Kershaw, "Access to Justice in Maryland," 50–51.
36. American Bar Association, *Justice in Jeopardy*, 47.
37. American Bar Association, *Justice in Jeopardy*, 60.
38. Carp, Stidham, and Manning, *Judicial Process in America,* 99.
39. According to the U.S. Census Bureau (2003, 399), in 2002 women were 29.2 percent of lawyers, African Americans were 4.6 percent, and Hispanics were 3.1 percent. See gendergap.com.
40. American Bar Association, *Justice in Jeopardy*, 12.
41. American Bar Association, *Justice in Jeopardy*, Appendix A.
42. Burke, *Lawyers, Lawsuits, and Legal Rights*, 3.
43. Marc Galanter, "An Oil Strike in Hell: Contemporary Legends About the Civil Justice System," *Arizona Law Review* 40 (1998): 717–752. Galanter refers to this as the "jaundiced view," and rejects it as lacking credible evidence.
44. For thoughtful critical commentary on Kagan's argument, see "Review Symposium on Kagan's *Adversarial Legalism: The American Way of Law*," *Law & Social Inquiry* 28 (2003): 717–872.
45. For a review of scholarly studies, see Haltom and McCann, *Distorting the Law,* chapter 3, 73–110.
46. Cited in Haltom and McCann, *Distorting the Law,* 83. See also Burke, *Lawyers, Lawsuits, and Legal Rights,* 3.
47. Vidmar, *Medical Malpractice and the American Jury*, 38, 39.
48. Ibid., 265.
49. Ibid., 43.
50. Burke, *Lawyers, Lawsuits, and Legal Rights,* 3.

51. Cited in Haltom and McCann, *Distorting the Law*, 79.
52. Cited in Burke, *Lawyers, Lawsuits, and Legal Rights*, 3.
53. Cited in Haltom and McCann, *Distorting the Law*, 83.
54. Haltom and McCann, 86; emphasis in original.
55. Burke, *Lawyers, Lawsuits, and Legal Rights*, 3.
56. See Donald R. Songer, Reginald S. Sheehan, and Susan Brodie Haire, "Do the 'Haves' Come Out Ahead over Time? Applying Galanter's Framework to Decisions of the U.S. Courts of Appeals, 1925–1988," *Law & Society Review* 33 (1999): 811–832; and Donald J. Farole, Jr., "Reexamining Litigant Success in State Supreme Courts," *Law & Society Review* 33 (1999): 1043–1058.
57. Galanter, "An Oil Strike in Hell," 731.
58. The discussion that follows is based on Haltom and McCann, *Distorting the Law,* chapter 6, 183–226; and Galanter, "An Oil Strike in Hell," 731–733.
59. McDonald's defended this practice by arguing that since most of its coffee customers take their coffee with them to drink later, selling it at a dangerously high temperature produced a suitably warm cup of coffee later when it was eventually drunk.
60. Haltom and McCann, *Distorting the* Law, 7.
61. Lynn Mather, "Theorizing about Trial Courts: Lawyers, Policymaking, and Tobacco Litigation," *Law & Social Inquiry* 23 (1998): 897–940.
62. Haltom and McCann, *Distorting the Law*, 236.
63. Mather, "Theorizing about Trial Courts," 910, 911.
64. Haltom and McCann, *Distorting the Law*, 239 note 20.
65. Centers for Disease Control and Prevention, National Center For Chronic Disease Prevention and Health Promotion, Tobacco Information and Prevention Source, *Morbidity and Mortality Weekly Report*. Various years, available at: http://www.cdc.gov/tobacco/index.htm.
66. Hensler et al., *Class Action Dilemmas*, 4.
67. Ibid., 12, 13.
68. Ibid., 8–9.
69. Ibid., 20.
70. Galanter, "An Oil Strike in Hell," 738.
71. Hensler et al., *Class Action Dilemmas*, 16.
72. Ibid., 8
73. Ibid., 25.
74. Watson, "Introduction—Courting Disaster," ix.
75. Bork, "Courts and the Culture Wars," 5.
76. U.S. Census Bureau, *Statistical Abstract of the United States,* 214.
77. The following discussion is based on Rosenberg, *The Hollow Hope*; and Rosenberg, "The Real World of Constitutional Rights."
78. McCloskey, *The American Supreme Court*, 47.
79. "Federalist No. 78," 465.
80. See Rosenberg, "The Irrelevant Court."
81. American Bar Association, *Perceptions of the U.S. Justice System* (1999), 38. Available at: http://www.abanet.org/media/perception.html.

82. American Bar Association, *Perceptions of the U.S. Justice System*, 32.
83. Ibid., 40.
84. Justice at Stake, *National Survey of American Voters* (2002), 3. Available at: http://faircourts.org/files/JASNationalSurveyResults.pdf.
85. Justice at Stake, *National Survey*, 5.
86. Ibid., 11.
87. American Bar Association, *Perceptions of the U.S. Justice System*, 43.
88. Ibid., 8.
89. Ibid., 43.
90. Ibid., 41.
91. Ibid., 8.
92. Ibid., 41.
93. Justice at Stake, *National Survey*, 7.
94. American Bar Association, *Perceptions of the U.S. Justice System*, 41.
95. American Bar Association, *Justice in Jeopardy*, ix.

Bibliography

American Bar Association. *Justice in Jeopardy: Report of the American Bar Association Commission on the 21st Century Judiciary*. Chicago: American Bar Association, 2003.

Bork, Robert H. "Courts and the Culture Wars." In *Courts and the Culture Wars*, edited by Bradley C. S. Watson, 3–14. Lanham, Md.: Lexington Books, 2002.

Blumberg, Abraham S. "The Practice of Law as Confidence Game: Organizational Cooptation of a Profession." In *Law & Society: Readings on the Social Study of Law*, edited by Stewart Macaulay, Lawrence M. Friedman, and John Stookey, 63–85. New York: W. W. Norton, 1995.

Burke, Thomas F. *Lawyers, Lawsuits, and Legal Rights: The Battle over Litigation in American Society*. Berkeley: University of California Press, 2002.

Carp, Robert A., Ronald Stidham, and Kenneth L. Manning. *Judicial Process in America*. 6th ed. Washington, D.C.: CQ Press, 2004.

Dahl, Robert A. "Procedural Democracy." In *Philosophy, Politics, and Society*, 5th series, edited by Peter Laslett and James Fishkin, 97–133. Oxford, U.K.: B. Blackwell, 1979.

Dahl, Robert A. *Polyarchy: Participation and Opposition*. New Haven, Conn.: Yale University Press, 1971.

Danzig, Richard. *The Capability Problem in Contract Law: Further Readings on Well-Known Cases*. Mineola, N.Y.: Foundation Press, 1978.

de Tocqueville, Alexis. *Democracy in America*. Edited by J. P. Mayer. Garden City, N.Y.: Anchor Books, 1969.

"Federalist No. 78" (A. Hamilton). *The Federalist Papers*, edited by Clinton Rossiter. New York: Mentor/New American Library, 1961.

Feeley, Malcolm M. *The Process Is the Punishment: Handling Cases in a Lower Criminal Court*. New York: Sage, 1979.

Haltom, William, and Michael McCann. *Distorting the Law: Politics, Media, and the Litigation Crisis*. Chicago: University of Chicago Press, 2004.

Hensler, Deborah R., et al. *Class Action Dilemmas: Pursuing Public Goals for Private Gain.* Santa Monica, Calif.: Rand Institute for Civil Justice, 1999.

Kagan, Robert A. *Adversarial Legalism: The American Way of Law.* Cambridge, Mass.: Harvard University Press, 2001.

Macaulay, Stewart. "Supplementary Comments." In Richard Danzig, *The Capability Problem in Contract Law*, 54-65. New York: Foundation Press, 1978.

McCloskey, Robert G. *The American Supreme Court.* 4th ed. Chicago: University of Chicago Press, 2005.

Meyer, Jon'a, and Paul Jesilow. *"Doing Justice" in the People's Court: Sentencing by Municipal Court Judges.* Albany: State University of New York Press, 1997.

Rosenberg, Gerald N. *The Hollow Hope: Can Courts Bring about Social Change?* Chicago: University of Chicago Press, 1991.

Rosenberg, Gerald N. "The Irrelevant Court: The Supreme Court's Inability to Influence Popular Beliefs about Equality (or Anything Else)." In *Redefining Equality*, edited by Neal Devins and Dave Douglas, 172–190. New York: Oxford University Press, 1998.

Rosenberg, Gerald N. "The Real World of Constitutional Rights: The Supreme Court and the Implementation of the Abortion Decisions." In *Contemplating Courts,* edited by Lee Epstein, 390–419. Washington, D.C.: CQ Press, 1995.

Smith, Christopher E. *Courts and Trials: A Reference Handbook.* Santa Barbara, Calif.: ABC-CLIO, 2003.

Smith, Christopher E. *Courts and the Poor.* Chicago: Nelson-Hall, 1991.

Stumpf, Harry P., and John C. Culver. *The Politics of State Courts.* New York: Longman, 1992.

U.S. Census Bureau. *Statistical Abstract of the United States: 2003.* 123rd ed. Washington, D.C.: GPO, 2003.

Vidmar, Neil. *Medical Malpractice and the American Jury: Confronting the Myths about Jury Incompetence, Deep Pockets, and Outrageous Damage Awards.* Ann Arbor: University of Michigan Press, 1995.

Watson, Bradley C. S. "Introduction—Courting Disaster: Jurisprudence as Moral Philosophy." In *Courts and the Culture Wars*, edited by Bradley C. S. Watson. Lanham, Md.: Lexington Books, 2002.

Court Cases

Argersinger v. Hamlin, 407 U.S. 25, 37 (1972).

Baker v. Vermont, 744 A.2d 864, 886 (1999).

Board of Trustees of the University of Alabama v. Garrett, 531 U.S. 356 (2001).

Brown v. Board of Education, 347 U.S. 483 (1954).

Clinton v. Jones, 520 U.S. 681 (1997).

Fullerton Lumber Co. v. Torborg, 270 Wis. 133, 70 N.W.2d 585 (1955).

General Electric Co. v. Gilbert, 429 U.S. 125 (1976).

Gideon v. Wainwright, 372 U.S. 335 (1963).

Goodridge v. Department of Public Health, 440 Mass. 309, 798 N.E.2d 941 (2003).

Grutter v. Bollinger, 539 U.S. 306 (2003).

Heart of Atlanta Motel v. U.S., 379 U.S. 241 (1964).
Katzenbach v. McClung, 379 U.S. 294 (1964).
Lawrence v. Texas, 539 U.S. 558 (2003).
Miranda v. Arizona, 384 U.S. 436 (1966).
New York v. United States, 505 U.S. 144 (1992).
Roe v. Wade, 410 U.S. 113 (1973).
United States v. Lopez, 514 U.S. 549 (1995).
United States v. Morrison, 529 U.S. 598 (2000).
United States v. Nixon, 418 U.S. 683 (1974).
Youngstown Sheet & Tube Co. v. Sawyer, 343 U.S. 579 (1952).

12

JUDICIAL ACTIVISM AND AMERICAN DEMOCRACY

Doris Marie Provine

THE UNITED STATES STANDS OUT FROM THE REST OF THE world in its reliance on lawyers, courts, and litigation. We open up an extraordinarily broad range of human action to legal remediation, and we make litigation affordable with contingency fees and class-action suits. Rights consciousness runs deep in the United States. Policy-oriented lawsuits are commonplace. The "rights industry" is well developed, encouraged by legislation establishing new grounds for litigation and by the structure of American government, which makes it easy to challenge administrative action. We give broad, unqualified power to judges at every level to overturn legislation and executive action on constitutional grounds. Our common-law tradition envisions judge-made law, and legal training encourages lawyers and judges to be creative. The tendency for political questions to become legal questions became apparent early in this country. Alexis de Tocqueville noted it in 1835 in his famous study of our system of governance, *Democracy in America*.

Judges are both venerated and disparaged in our system. Their engagement in politics has been controversial since the founding era. President Andrew Jackson reportedly reacted to an 1832 Supreme Court decision with the comment that "John Marshall has made his decision. Now let him enforce it." By the close of Marshall's tenure as chief justice, Congress had tried nearly every measure possible to reduce the Court's power. Efforts to curb judicial activism remain a regular feature of American politics. They include threats of impeachment, proposed constitutional amendments to reverse decisions, bills withdrawing jurisdiction or requiring super-majorities for decision, and budget cuts. Congress nearly stripped the federal courts of power to hear cases involving Communism in 1958, for example, and it significantly limited the access of prisoners to the federal courts in the 1990s. Opponents of integration proposed impeachment for Chief Justice Earl Warren after *Brown v. Board of Education* (1954).

With so much happening in the courts, some people think that democratic governance is out of balance. Judicial decisions outlawing prayer in schools, permitting abortion, and giving new trials to the criminally accused have evoked loud complaints about out-of-control judges. Judicial supervision of prisons, schools, hospitals, and other facilities feeds resentment about the power of "unelected judges." Overactive courts are blamed for the penetration of legal concerns into the workplace, sexual intimacy, religious expression, and death and dying. Business complains of its vulnerability to costly damage suits.

Critics tend to blame judges, rather than the political system that makes judges powerful and litigation commonplace. Opponents rally to the charge that judges have become too "activist." But they generally stop short of suggesting that the system be overhauled, in part because the idea of judicial guardianship of basic values enjoys considerable public support. Americans are taught that judges must be independent and that they must have the power to overturn legislation to safeguard democracy and the rule of law. We are eager to convince the rest of the world of this basic truth. Judicial power is, in this respect, like other important features of the American democratic experiment—federalism, regulation of the economy, presidential authority, national security—accepted in the abstract, but controversial in implementation.

It is easy to dismiss complaints about activist judges as personalized invective against disliked decisions. But there is more to the argument than the most highly advertised complaints might suggest. Democratic nations that respect the rule of law and the need for a judiciary free of direct political influence have options. Judicial independence can be maintained without necessarily giving judges the last word in interpreting the constitution; France is an example. Nor should judicial independence be treated as an all-or-nothing concept—there are in every system degrees of independence. Constitutional democracies that invest judges with broad powers of judicial review create real tensions between the branches of government that can be productive, or possibly destructive.

Nations should also consider the cost of relying heavily on the adversarial process to resolve policy issues. Litigation is expensive, creating costs and inefficiencies. Lawsuits cannot do much to change a nation's choices regarding income distribution or punitive public policies. Yet, judicial power is growing, not just in the United States, but also globally. The number of metanational and international courts and tribunals has increased dramatically since World War II. New democracies are investing their courts with significant authority. Judges are an important part of a human-rights revolution that is occurring around the world.

Are judges going beyond their proper bounds and expounding too much law? This deceptively simple question calls for a clear understanding of what is at stake. The discussion here begins by defining the issues and exploring the variety of complaints about overactive courts. The next section of the essay considers the extent and pattern of litigation at the domestic and international level. The final section evaluates the issues as courts grow in significance, both domestically, and at the global level.

It will become clear in this analysis that growing judicial authority arises, not so much out of self-aggrandizing tendencies of individual judges, but rather from legal, social, and economic forces that tend to create lawsuits. One such force is the size and spending of government. Government now spends more in a few hours than it did in a year two hundred years ago. Just as important are changes in what people expect from government and from courts. Americans expect more from both than they did in earlier generations. They expect justice when they feel they have been wronged and recompense for injuries and loss. Critics of courts, Lawrence Friedman suggests, have their causal arrows wrong—courts have not caused society to become more litigious; it is changes in society that have forced courts to behave differently.[1] Courts become involved in public policy, not out of self-initiated activism, but because legislation provides opportunities to involve courts in policy making. The expanding role of the judiciary has made courts more visible and more obviously a player in struggles over policy change, but it has not eliminated their fundamental passivity—judges in the United States do not create cases, nor do they design the tools available to resolve them.

Overactive Judges?

The expanding role of courts and tribunals at every level all over the world has evoked a surprisingly impoverished political debate in the United States. The focus of criticism remains fixated on judges, lawyers, and litigants. Changes in legislation that make more lawsuits possible—and technological, administrative, and social developments that make them more likely—have virtually escaped notice. Also virtually invisible in this debate is the growth of the administrative sector, with its tendency to blur traditional lines between branches. Government now operates with millions of administrative personnel—courts are an important check on their activities, and court-like bodies within the administrative sector are a significant phenomenon in their own right.

Even in the context of particular legal disputes, the tendency has been to focus on the character of the judge, rather than the law involved. "Judicial activist" is the favored term of opprobrium. The *Devil's Dictionary* offers this lighthearted definition: Someone who refuses to overrule *Roe v. Wade,* but excluding Supreme Court justices who claimed the power to determine the 2000 presidential election. The "activist" epithet is not a technical term—it cannot be found in most legal dictionaries, but it does have a veritable heritage in controversies about courts. An "activist" judge goes beyond the proper boundaries of office to reach decisions more properly within the scope of the popular branches of government. The underlying criticism is that judges have become political strategists, using their power to shape law in the direction of their preferences, and in the process damaging our democracy and endangering the rule of law. This section takes a brief look at the terms of this critique.

Democracy, American Style

Democracy is government by the people. Regular elections and representative institutions that operate by majority rule are typically part of the formula, as is an independent judiciary to ensure the rule of law. Constitutional democracy, as others in this volume have noted, is a more complicated aspiration that places limits on popular authority through a written or unwritten constitution. Some of these limits may actually reinforce democratic principles, for example, those that require full participation in the political process. The American system of constitutional government features checks and balances that limit the scope of government and force cooperation among the executive, legislative, and judicial branches. Our system creates an additional layer of complexity by providing for both a national and a state level of governance, each with separate constitutional mandates. The complicated, carefully delimited, overall plan suggests that founders were interested in restraining governmental power. Hamilton's famous description of the judiciary as "the least dangerous branch" should be read to suggest a concern, not just with judicial power, but with the dangerous potential of the whole government.

In creating a constitution with detailed powers and a bill of rights, the founding generation clearly anticipated judicial review of legislative and executive action. The matter was not particularly controversial, perhaps because the founders were more afraid of legislative, than judicial, tyranny. The judiciary, it was thought, would represent the popular will and prevent legislative overreaching (see Whittington in this volume). This changed as the franchise expanded and Americans grew more accustomed to representative government. Lifetime appointments for judges began to seem unwise in the nineteenth century and many states moved toward election of judges. Frederick Grimke's 1848 treatise on democratic governance recommended election of judges to keep them in touch with the people.[2] Concerns about unelected judges did not necessarily arise from their power to declare legislation unconstitutional. Only two federal statutes were declared unconstitutional between the nation's founding and the Civil War in 1861. For Grimke, the issue was the quasi-legislative power that judges exercise when they interpret and apply ordinary law. These cases become precedents for future decisions. Books containing judicial decisions, he noted, were much more numerous than statute books.

As the federal government grew during and after World War II, and as popular expectations about its capacities grew, the power of courts to determine policy became more obvious. Decisions requiring racial desegregation and setting standards for police work brought home the message that courts can create policy. Courts were at the same time growing more involved in important nonconstitutional issues involving statutory interpretation and implementation of broad federal mandates in the environment, mental health, public facilities management, and other matters that local and state governments had in the past managed without interference. Courts relaxed their procedural rules, allowing access to litigants on the basis of ideological concerns, and Congress facilitated this movement by providing for legal challenges to the agencies charged with implementing government policies. These changes were part of a "rights revolution" that culminated in the 1960s (see Epp in this volume). In this process, the judiciary became more intimately a fixture in American politics.

Black-Robed Politicians

The case against policy-making judges can be succinctly stated. The principle of separation of powers reserves lawmaking to legislators; judges are charged with applying law, not making it. We insulate judges from public accountability, not to enable them to overturn legislation they dislike, but to protect the judicial function from inappropriate influences. Critics charge that judges have taken advantage of their independence from the accountability of the ballot box, making policy as they see fit. Professor Lino Graglia states the problem in bold terms: "The paradox is that, although judicial policymaking is both oxymoronic and unconstitutional, it is one of the most prominent and distinguishing features of our present system of government. Asking whether judges have a policymaking role in the American system of government is like asking whether gravity has a role in the solar system."[3] Professor Graglia's critique can be applied to a broad range of judicial action, from Supreme Court decisions invoking individual-rights protections under the Constitution, to judicial elimination of common-law barriers against tort recovery.

Treating judicial policymaking as something judges could stop if they respected the proper limits of their authority tends to draw attention toward judicial personality and ethics, and away from the ambiguities of law and its (sometimes intentional) vagueness. Supporters of judges, and many judges themselves, counter with arguments stressing law's uncertainties. As Aharon Barak, President of Israel's Supreme Court points out, law often speaks with "a number of voices." An appellate judge's most important duty in a democracy is to reduce those multiple voices to one. This is, necessarily, a creative act: "Law is not mathematics. Law is a normative system. So long as we cannot predict the future, so long as language does not enable generalizations that extend to all relevant situations, so long as we cannot overcome human limitation, we will have to live with uncertainty in law."[4]

Critics like Professor Graglia accept the idea of ambiguity in law to a point, but suggest that law's ambiguity gives judges interpretative options, and that this freedom tempts them to become policy makers. Law schools and the national media, Graglia argues, help move judges in this direction: "It is not the plodding, law-applying judge whose face adorns national magazines, whose life becomes the subject of admiring television shows, and who is invited to speak at law school symposia."[5] Judges, he fears, will tend to impose their views on the rest of us unless they are forced to stay within proper bounds.

Judicial Activism in the Prism of Politics

Those disappointed by judicial rulings have always complained that judges departed from the true law in reaching them. These complaints came from liberals in the 1930s when the Supreme Court overturned New Deal legislation, and from conservatives in the 1970s who were distressed at the rise of protections for women, the environment, and prisoners arising out of federal judicial decisions. Criticism of state judges is no less intense and can be more effective because the state bench is less insulated from electoral pressures. (Hall in this volume notes that 87 percent of state judges stand for election, 40 percent of them on partisan ballots.)

Judges, whether at the state or federal level, make easy targets for criticism—their work is abstruse, and they tend to remain stoically silent in the face of political attacks, even the fierce rhetoric that characterizes our highly partisan era. Jibes at judicial willfulness and alleged disdain for democratic process are commonplace, with judges routinely described as "despots," "elitists," and "high-handed." There are calls for limits on the jurisdiction of courts, for de-funding enforcement orders, for monitoring the bench, and, in some cases, for impeachment. When the Massachusetts Supreme Court issued a decision supporting same-sex marriage, Congress responded with a hearing entitled "Judicial Activism v. Democracy," implying that the two are on a collision course. Such criticism is remarkable in the face of the actual infrequency with which the Supreme Court declares laws unconstitutional. The Court found one federal and one state law unconstitutional in 2003, out of eighty opinions issued. In the five-year period 1999–2003, the Court found five federal and twelve state statutes unconstitutional.

The theme of elitist, anti-democratic judges sits, somewhat uncomfortably, in tandem with veneration of a few precedent-setting cases. *Brown v. Board of Education* is a particularly awkward case for those who criticize judicial activism because it is undeniably an activist decision, representing a complete break with previously applicable law on novel constitutional grounds. Yet, with the passage of time, *Brown* has come to symbolize right thinking about race. The political complexities were apparent on May 18, 2004, *Brown*'s fiftieth anniversary. President George W. Bush gave a speech celebrating the decision on the same day that he issued a press release criticizing the Massachusetts Supreme Court on the grounds that: "The sacred institution of marriage should not be redefined by a few activist judges."

Specific decisions have always played an important role in the argument against activist judges. They may, in fact, *be* the argument for many people. The public is not very aware of courts except when a case gets the attention of the media. Unpopular cases not only arouse indignation; they link judges to a broader political agenda. Organizations select their illustrative cases carefully. The religious right chooses cases that suggest a dangerous turning away from common-sense moral values, while corporations feature extravagant awards that burden free enterprise. The approach tends to make courts look more politically freewheeling than they are.

The New Right on Judicial Activism

The most hyperbolic criticism of activist judges comes from the New Right, which uses every available opportunity to express its dismay with decisions that limit the reach of popular Bible-based moral principles. The Center for Reclaiming America, for example, puts judges at the center of its anti-abortion message: "This is the heart of the pro-life battle—if we lose the courts, and especially the Supreme Court, we will lose the abortion war!"[6] The organization's Web page features a Judicial Watch section that updates readers on court battles of interest to readers, such as the effort to bring creation science into public schools and the struggles over the display of the Ten Commandments. Not surprisingly, the Center strongly opposed a Florida court's June 2003 decision authorizing removal of a feeding tube from Terri Schiavo, a case that went on to became a world-wide *cause célebrè* among religious activists and those who support an independent judiciary. The case revealed the readiness of some conservative Christian groups—and their supporters in government at the local, state and federal levels—to denounce judges in strong, even threatening, terms. The case can also be interpreted as a signal of the vitality of judicial independence in the face of hostile legislative and executive action. Despite these attacks, the state and federal judiciary stood firm in its interpretation of the power of judges to have the final word on matters within their jurisdiction, providing the nation with a lesson in the power of judicial review.

Robert Bork, a one-time Reagan nominee for the U.S. Supreme Court, is perhaps the best-known spokesman for the position that "America is moving from the rule of law to the rule of judges." He denounces "the virulent judicial activism that increasingly calls into question the authority of representative government and the vitality of traditional values as they evolve through non-judicial institutions, public, and private."[7] Bork criticizes the liberal left, not just for its commitment to "coerced virtue" through litigation, but because of its alleged bias toward godlessness, immorality, and socialism. He is suspicious of the rise of international tribunals and dismayed at the increasing power of courts in democracies. Having studied the rise of judicial power in Canada, Israel, and other countries, he concludes that tyranny by a judicial elite is endemic wherever courts are endowed with the power of judicial review: "The crucial question for all nations that desire to remain self-governing is how to tame and limit the anti-democratic aggressions of their judiciaries and of the international tribunals and forums we are so blithely and thoughtlessly creating."[8]

Conservative organizations like the Heritage Foundation sustain and give shape to the New Right critique by sponsoring lectures and publications by outspoken and well-placed critics of "activist" courts. Their message is populist: Courts should not interfere with the will of the people, particularly in matters of morality, where even the least sophisticated citizens have life experience to guide them. Judicial interference is harmful because it weakens popular morality and damages the political processes that should be dominant in a democracy.

A Contrasting View: Principled Activism

Some conservatives are deeply critical of the New Right's attack on judicial review, seeing it as "a new majoritarianism and a fundamental narrowing of judicial protections for individual rights" that would shift power to legislative majorities and change the meaning of citizenship in the United States.[9] These observers see promise in the proper exercise of judicial review, or "principled judicial activism." They believe that judges have been too reluctant to exercise their power to overturn unwarranted legislative initiatives in the economy and in regulating social relations, for example, by requiring bilingual education. At the same time, they urge judicial restraint in creating new remedies like affirmative action and busing. Libertarian-leaning legal foundations like the Cato Institute implement this approach with coordinated litigation agendas. The Federalist Society assists by organizing events for judges, lawyers, and law students and by lobbying for judicial appointments.[10]

The enthusiasm for constitutional litigation comes from conviction that the founding generation wanted a constitution based on maximum freedom for individuals, with a very limited central government and strong controls on legislators. Judges were to be guardians of this framework, a bulwark against the excesses of the other two branches. The Cato Institute criticizes both Congress and the courts for exceeding their delegated powers, recommending appointment of judges who will employ judicial review to protect economic liberties. Stephen Macedo, an articulate spokesperson for this position, argues in *The New*

Right v. the Constitution that the founding generation's experience with chaos and political strife made it suspicious of legislative tyranny: "Judicial review is not an anomalous blotch on a democratic scheme of government. Contrary to what the [New Right] conservatives hold, judicial review is an integral part of a scheme of constitutionally limited government."[11]

The Corporate Perspective on Excessive Litigation

Criticism of overactive courts also comes from the corporate sector, which sometimes feels the impact of large damage awards for product defects, production problems, and corporate misbehavior. Doctors complain of high medical malpractice insurance costs, which their insurers blame on courts and greedy claimants. These interests have worked hard to convince the public and legislatures of the need for tort reform and other changes in the courts that will make injury litigation less attractive, and they regularly sponsor many bills to effect these changes. More recently, some corporate interests have begun to contribute heavily to state races for judicial office.

The corporate emphasis on inefficiency and unfairness is distinctive from both the New Right and the libertarian-leaning positions. The corporate campaign is not about judicial overreaching per se, but about the tendency of judges to allow new causes of action and to give too much scope to juries, both of which work to the detriment of the "deep pockets" who get sued. Business groups offer data of varying quality to suggest the seriousness of the problem, and lobbyists use it to push for tort-curbing legislation at the state and federal level. State legislatures have been quite responsive; most have enacted damage caps and many have mandated alternative means of dispute resolution.

The corporate-sponsored effort involves a continuing public-relations campaign designed to arouse indignation at "runaway" jury verdicts and sue-happy contingency fee lawyers. It is silent about the large economic stakes of those advocating this position. This effort has received a lot of help from the mass media, which has uncritically absorbed the corporate view that the cost of injuries in America as a problem created by courts and greedy litigants, rather than the absence of affordable health care and an adequate system for delivering it.[12]

The theme of individual greed and judicial naiveté resonates in American society. Professor Thomas Burke, who has studied the movement in detail, sees stories about lawsuits over a broken date or spilled coffee as "parables about a fundamental breakdown in American society. The prerequisites for peaceful community life, the stories suggest, have evaporated. Greed, individualism, and contentiousness are winning out."[13] The fact that most of these stories are exaggerated, or even factually incorrect, does little to weaken their impact. The reason, Burke suggests, is that they are moralistic and they speak to a more general worry that there are few "litigation free" zones in our contemporary society.

Executive Branch Concerns about National Security and the Courts

Republican administrations since the Reagan era have generally supported court-curtailing efforts, whether they have arisen out of New Right conviction, corporate bottom-line thinking, or libertarian beliefs about the evils of big government. Since the September 11, 2001, World Trade Center bombing, the executive has a new reason to argue for judicial restraint. Preoccupation with national and domestic security puts the executive branch on a collision course with the judiciary. The decision of the Supreme Court to consider the claims of persons who had been captured during the fighting in Afghanistan and then indefinitely confined at the Guantánamo Bay Naval Base was a sharp blow to the Bush administration, which fought hard to keep the courts out of this matter. Veteran Supreme Court journalist Linda Greenhouse describes the conflict as "a moment long in coming: the imperial presidency meets the imperial judiciary."[14]

The Guantánamo decision is only the tip of an emerging judicial iceberg of concern with affairs the executive would prefer to keep out of sight. The American Civil Liberties Union and other organizations are bringing suit and using their power to discover the other side's facts to gain access to information about interrogation techniques. They publicize this information as part of their broader effort to change U.S. policy toward detainees. The executive branch cannot complain too sharply about these judicial incursions into military and executive arenas because public opinion is divided on the tactics appropriate in these cases. Besides, there are risks to the legitimacy of both branches when they conflict too openly with each other.

The executive campaign against judicial involvement in matters of national security is better fought in the context of security legislation, like the Patriot Act. Advocates outside the administration, such as the Washington Legal Foundation, can be more openly confrontational: "Ideological lawyers have convinced some federal courts that unelected judges, and not our Commander-in-Chief, should have the last word on how our military can detain captured terrorists. . . . While judges and activists quibble over legal niceties, our despicable enemies are pondering how to take advantage of their newly created constitutional rights in the next attack."[15]

Evaluating the Debate

The corporate campaign has been the most continuous effort to rein in courts and the most successful in terms of legal reform, most of which has occurred at the state level. Other constituencies critical of the direction of contemporary court decisions have focused most on the federal level. Bills to limit jurisdiction over issues that are obviously within the province of courts, for example, whether the Ten Commandments can be displayed in a government facility, generally fail, but the negativity toward activist judging carries weight in debates over judicial appointments and funding for courts. Efforts to cut off access to courts, particularly to vulnerable populations, have also been successful.

The "too much judging" position is popular with politicians because it combines a high-minded concern with the fate of democracy with a platform that appeals to business, conservative Christians, wealthy Republicans, and other secular constituencies who vote. It also resonates with a broad-based concern in American society about excessive individualism, obsession with individual rights, softness on crime, and the breakdown of community. Mary Ann Glendon expresses this concern and its connection to the foundations of democratic governance in her 1991 book, *Rights Talk*: "Our simplistic rights talk regularly promotes the short-run over the long-term, sporadic crisis intervention over systematic preventive measures, and particular interests over the common good. . . . By infiltrating the more carefully nuanced languages that many Americans still speak in their kitchens, neighborhoods, workplaces, religious communities, and union halls, it corrodes the fabric of beliefs, attitudes, and habits upon which life, liberty, property, and all other individualized social goods ultimately depend."[16]

Not everyone agrees with Glendon's juxtaposition of rights against community. Supporters of courts argue that rights consciousness and a strong system for vindicating them can help a community function better. Some of these constituencies, aroused by the conservative attacks on courts during the second Clinton presidency, have organized to fight for judicial independence. Their position is that courts must be supported and allowed to function without political interference. Other reasons for supporting courts focus on whom they serve. Courts offer access and visibility to individuals and groups who are not wealthy. Litigation, even when it is unsuccessful, can be a strategy for raising consciousness and developing support for new rights claims, like comparable worth, disability rights, school finance equalization, and freedom from sexual harassment.[17] Such policies attract support, not so much because they provide new benefits, but because they appeal to the American sense that wrongs should be punished and their injuries should be addressed. Whatever nostalgia Americans feel for communal, religious, and family-based morality, those beliefs appear to be mixed with a desire for justice administered through courts.

The debate about activist judges is an example of what Stuart Scheingold, in another context, has dubbed "the politics of rights," a way of mobilizing for change that uses America's strong feelings about justice and the rule of law to push for practical social change. Usually such campaigns are positive, using popular support for rights to advance a progressive cause. But in this case, it is negative feelings about courts that are highlighted and the objective is to discourage litigation. The symbolism is dramatic: high-handed judges and greedy lawyers; selfish litigants who will press their rights to the hilt; endless legal red tape and high fees; spurious legal reasoning; and costly judgments that can bankrupt humble communities.

Rhetorical devices that befit a highly symbolic campaign are part of the struggle over whether courts are doing "too much": narratives with heroes and villains; "typical" stories that are not in fact typical; metaphors that dichotomize judicial choice into the catch-all categories of "activism" and "restraint"; intentional ambiguity designed to elicit support from diverse groups. What, after all, is "judicial activism" except a term developed for the purposes of policy change? Even less emotional appeals that emphasize efficiency and fairness, for example, mandatory diversion of cases to binding arbitration, have a political purpose. Such arguments are based on a vision of how competing interests should be organized, and create winners and losers in the policy-making process.[18]

Is Judicial Influence Growing?

The institutional power of courts, particularly of the federal courts, has been increasing over the years. There were sixty-one federal judges in 1869—now there are over one thousand. The federal courts are twice as large as Congress, and more expensive to operate. The growth pattern at the state level, which is by far the larger element in the American judiciary, has also been impressive. The subject-matter range of courts at both the state and federal levels is enormously broader than it was a century ago.

The institutional transformation of the U.S. Supreme Court, standing at the apex of the system, has perhaps been most dramatic. It began as a circuit-riding court with no regular courthouse, scant resources, a largely mandatory agenda, and few people who wanted to serve. The modern Supreme Court has magnificent facilities, chooses its own agenda, and has the institutional resources to make its voice heard, which increases its overall impact. Service on the Supreme Court has become a very high honor that few would refuse. Indeed, the current contentiousness over Supreme Court appointments can be explained by the enormous importance of these lifetime appointments.

Concern that the courts are becoming more powerful thus appears to be well founded. The number of cases filed or adjudicated is one indication. The crux of the question, however, is whether judges are taking over what legislators used to do—and do better. The question should be raised, not just at the domestic level, where most of the political heat is, but also at the international level, where the increasing authority of judges is most marked. Globalization makes these two levels ever more intertwined. This section opens with a brief look at domestic caseloads, and then proceeds to issues raised by the rise of public-interest litigation, particularly that directed at institutional reform. At the international level, the focus is on the increasing number of courts and court-like tribunals and their growing responsibilities for the protection of individual rights against the popular will.

Growing Caseloads

Most litigation in the United States occurs in state courts, which have jurisdiction over most crimes and civil cases, including traffic offenses. Federal courts handle less than 3 percent of the total U.S. caseload. The numbers, at first glance, are startling. Over 96 million new cases were filed in the nation's 15,500 state courts in 2002, according to the National Center for State Courts. But traffic cases make up over half of that volume. Still, this represents a lot of litigation. What can the pattern of filings tell us? Looking at federal and state general-jurisdiction trial courts in the fifteen-year period between 1987 and 2001, three patterns are clear:

- Criminal filings are increasing at both the state and federal level, particularly felony cases, which increased 47 percent in the state courts and 83 percent in the federal courts in this period.
- Civil filings (excluding tort) are also up, but less so. They have increased 17 percent in the state courts and 5 percent in the federal courts. (Note that the U.S. population increased about 15 percent during this period.)
- Tort filings are down, both in state and federal courts, a surprising pattern considering warnings about exploding rates of litigation over personal injuries and medical malpractice. The drop is 7 percent in the state courts and 22 percent in the federal courts over the past fifteen years.

Appeals from trial-court judgments have grown, but slowly in the past fifteen years. At the state level, appeals increased about 7 percent over the ten-year period between 1992 and 2001, but they seem to have stabilized at about the same level they reached in 1995. The average increase in federal appeals has been 1 percent per year in recent years. The growth in federal appeals has been uneven since the 1970s; in a few years the number has dropped. Over 80 percent of federal appeals are decided without full publication to avoid invocation as precedent.

The bottom of the dispute resolution pyramid is also changing. After filing more and more cases are being settled through alternatives to trial, which have been strongly promoted by the courts and government grants. The reduction in trials since the 1960s has been dramatic, both on the civil and criminal side, particularly in the federal courts. Less than 2 percent of federal civil cases now go to trial, down from 11.5 percent in the 1960s. The percentage of criminal trials dropped from 15 percent to less than 3 percent in the same period. The Federal Sentencing Guidelines, which took effect in 1987, had a dramatic effect on the rate at which federal criminal cases went to trial because they permitted enhancement of sentences after a finding of guilt. Accused people plead guilty rather than risk these penalties. The Supreme Court cast the future of the Guidelines in doubt in a series of decisions in 2004–2005.[19]

There is no evidence of a litigation explosion here. Nor did we suffer an explosion of litigation in the 1970s and 1980s, another period of much-publicized distress about hyperactive courts hamstringing business and clogging the courts. Per capita rates of litigation were growing then, but not dramatically, and they never reached historic highs, which were set in the nineteenth century. Most claims then, as now, were quickly settled.

What the 1970s marked was not a dramatic rise in cases, but a rise in elite disillusionment with the civil justice system. Professor Marc Galanter traces this disillusionment to two developments. One was the expansion of remedies to include new members of the body politic. In the 1970s, for the first time, legislation and constitutional interpretation created legal rights for consumers, injured workers, blacks, women, the disabled, and prisoners. The other change was less visible and more gradual. Galanter noted that the twentieth century brought a growing predominance of "purposive corporate organizations"—local governments, businesses, organizations—over more spontaneous groupings like families and neighbors. These corporate and governmental actors increasingly organize our lives and dominate the legal system, where they enjoy great advantages because of their scale and organizational rationality. Individuals enter the legal domain only briefly in life emergencies.[20]

The real locus of concern about over-functioning courts, in short, lies in anxieties created by what courts are doing, rather than in the amount of judicial activity per se. And what courts are doing is paying more attention to the have-nots and non-elites, because they have more capacity to sue than they did in the past. It should not be surprising that there is disgruntlement among the business interests, professionals, government officials, and other entities that they sue. Ironically, it is these large organizational actors that helped to make courts seem the appropriate venue for effecting change because of their own heavy reliance on lawyers and litigation.

The Rise of Public-Interest Litigation

The 1960s and 1970s marked a turning point in social activism directed at courts. Lawyers began to talk about litigation as a fulcrum for reform and started to bring suits designed to vindicate the public interest. A new type of case law began to develop. One important line of development concerned government benefits like welfare and disability payments. Lawyers argued, successfully, that such "new property" should be protected like the "old property" of land, goods, and cash in the bank.[21] Courts got into the business of achieving racial balance in schools in the wake of *Brown v. Board of Education*. At about the same time, prisoners, inmates in mental-health facilities, and even school children established individual rights within institutions. The environment became a source of reform-minded litigation. Government at every level was under pressure to justify its performance.

Public-interest law was born in this period. Abram Chayes described the key features of this type of litigation in a famous 1976 article. He notes several salient differences from traditional litigation:

- Unlike traditional one-on-one lawsuits, public-interest litigation deals with many interested individuals and groups at once.
- The litigation is forward looking because the purpose is to shape public policy, not to compensate individuals for past violations.
- The judge is active, not passive, with responsibility to organize and shape the litigation to ensure a just outcome.
- A court's judgment does not end the litigation, as in a traditional case; it marks the beginning of the institutional-reform effort.
- Remedies are based on considerations of policy, not on traditional measures of harm.[22]

A public-interest lawsuit often ends with a consent decree or injunction binding all of the parties to take certain actions. The terms of these decrees are worked out among the lawyers for both sides, sometimes aided by experts appointed or approved by the court. Often the decree requires an infusion of public money to improve the functioning of the institution. In 2004, for example, a New York court ordered New York City to spend $5.9 billion more on its public school system. Localities must respond to these orders, under pressure of the court's contempt power, which involves fines and even imprisonment for officials who defy a valid court order. This puts local officials in an awkward position. If they spend in accordance with a court's order, they are reallocating public money away from priorities established by local democratic processes. This was, after all, the purpose of the suit—to win by judicial decision what would not otherwise be forthcoming.

Institutional Reform Litigation—A Threat to Democracy?

If the United States were a simple democracy, and not a constitutional, federal republic, a consent order requiring local officials to spend local tax revenues would be a clear case of judicial over-reaching. But constitutional requirements and the power of the Congress under federalism are important considerations in this evaluation. While a ruling based on a general constitutional provision—as some prison lawsuits are—could raise questions about the proper scope of judicial review, a ruling based in congressional legislation raises no such questions. Our federal system envisions that the popularly elected representatives at the national level will sometimes tell the popularly elected representatives at the local level what to do. Courts are simply the vehicle for carrying out that mandate.

Much of the litigation that engages judges in policy making arises out of this kind of congressional standard setting. The foundation for litigation might be laid by a well-organized public-interest constituency that seeks legislation to reach a popular goal, for example, environmental protection or better schools. Congress responds with an "unfunded mandate," a law that sets forth detailed processes and obligations designed to reach the desired goal. The necessary money is expected to come from the state or local government. Interested parties are given authority to sue to ensure that localities do what the legislation requires.

Ross Sandler and David Schoenbrod, two public-interest lawyers who became disenchanted with this approach to social reform, produced a decade-by-decade accounting of major federal statutes regulating state and local governments. They found almost no activity until the 1960s, when nine statutes were adopted to address environmental quality, food and agriculture, and civil rights. In the 1970s, there were twenty-five statutes ranging over a broader gamut that included flood prevention, anti-aging, and occupational health and safety. The 1980s and 1990s each produced twenty-one new statutes. "Congress," they conclude, "went from regulating state and local governments hardly at all, to regulating them in detail. . . . In statutes enacted between 1970 and 1991, Congress preempted more states' laws than it had from 1789 to 1969."[23]

Not all institutional-reform litigation arises from a federal statute setting forth detailed standards and authorizing enforcement suits. Litigants sometimes base their challenges on state or federal constitutional standards. An example is litigation to equalize public-school spending. The conditions of life under imprisonment have proven another particularly fertile ground for this kind of litigation. When prison conditions slip below a level that can be justified under normal administrative practice, a judicial determination that constitutional requirements are violated is a real possibility. Lack of medical facilities, the prevalence of violence in a prison, even torture by prison guards—all are examples of the kinds of findings that have proven constitutionally actionable. Prison officials may welcome this intervention as a way to unlock the public purse, which of course highlights the conflict between court and legislature.

What keeps judges within appropriate bounds when they are asked to overturn democratically arrived-at preferences on constitutional grounds? Malcolm Feeley and Edward Rubin examined this question and noted a somewhat reassuring pattern. The wave of prison-reforming decisions that began in the 1960s, they found, was not the work of a few judges, but of the judiciary as a whole. Hundreds of judges participated in reaching decisions, in upholding or modifying decisions on appeal, and in the process examining each other's justifications for intervention. Still, the role trial judges play in these cases is far from conventional. They act more like a national administrative agency in setting aside local preferences. Feeley and Rubin see this new role, not as a departure from the rule of law, but as an adjustment to the emerging realities of governance in a complex, globalizing, administratively developed, and rights-conscious nation.

Judicial Policy Making as the Norm, Not the Exception

The argument that judges are expounding too much law starts from the assumption that policy making is not part of the judicial role—the proper role of the judiciary is to passively apply the law as agent of the designated lawmakers. The Constitution, it is argued, offers the only ground for upsetting the democratic will, and it should be read to ascertain its original intent, not as a "living constitution," which would leave too much to the subjective preferences of the judge. A problem with this analysis is that judging is an inherently creative activity, particularly in a common-law system that trains lawyers and judges to apply precedent with broader general principles in mind.

The common-law system of adjudication, which is fundamental to Anglo-American legal systems, arose before the age of statutes and constitutions. It accepts judges as policy makers. Even Justice Antonin Scalia, a harsh critic of judicial policy making, admits this: Lawyers are educated to admire the judge who, like Holmes or Cardozo, "has the intelligence to discern the best rule of law for the case at hand and then the skill to perform the broken-field running through earlier cases that leaves him [sic] free to impose that rule: distinguishing one prior case on the left, straight-arming another on the right, high-stepping away from another precedent about to tackle him from the rear, until (bravo!) he [sic] reaches the goal—good law."[24]

Justice Scalia contends that the age of common-law adjudication is over; statutes now spell out legal obligations and duties. Scalia fails to note, however, that legislators are not always willing to create clear rules and back them up with spending. Vagueness that leaves nettlesome details to the courts can be a winning legislative strategy that satisfies diverse constituencies. Adequate funding for broad social-welfare reform is another problem. It is tempting to create rights and benefits without setting aside the funds to implement them. This spawns litigation, whether judges welcome it or not.

Applying the mandates of our two-hundred-year-old constitution raises another set of difficulties. There is only rudimentary agreement on how to ascertain and honor the historical meaning of the document. Whatever judges do will be subjected to intense scrutiny and criticism—Americans are accustomed to casting moral and political debates in constitutional terms.

Whether or not one approves of judicial policy-making, it should be clear that the interdependence of the elements of our system is already well established. Policy emerges from an iterative process that involves all three branches.

As government takes on more issues, so must courts. New forms of government action call forth new procedures for vindicating the rights. Upon occasion government itself brings suits against business or individuals or other governments to effect policy change. A recent example is the decision by New York City to sue gun manufacturers for "unnecessary" murders in its jurisdiction. The multibillion-dollar settlement of state litigation against the tobacco companies is another case of judicial policy making at the behest of government.

Judges engage in policy making, in short, because of the way our system is designed, not because they are prone to arrogant interventionism. Congress and state legislatures have helped this process along with legislation authorizing class-action suits, with quick-review procedures, and other incentives that promote litigation. The problem, if there is one, is basically structural, and not amenable to significant change through more conservative judicial appointments. Such judges may side less often with criminal defendants, civil plaintiffs, and advocates of liberal causes like environmentalism, but they will not issue fewer lawmaking opinions.

The debate over activist judges is misleading in another way as well. It suggests a higher level of confrontation between branches than actually exists. There are, of course, judicial decisions that challenge the will of the popularly elected branches, but the number is smaller than popular rhetoric about activist judges might lead one to expect. Even in these high-profile cases, the courts often have significant popular support for their position. American judges typically have a background in public life that disinclines them to "damn the torpedoes" with their decisions. They have developed doctrines that enable them to avoid unpopular positions on legal issues. Nor do legislators necessarily mind being second-guessed by courts. Congress sometimes uses vagueness to strategic advantage in drafting statutes or rewriting them to achieve a majority. The permeability of Congress to special interests is somewhat offset by the relative insulation of the federal courts.

Does this networked system of diffused power serve the United States well? Critics point to its cost and inefficiency. Another problem is the loss of focus that can occur when judges narrow legislatively created rights. Policy making through litigation also has the potential to spawn doctrines that are impractical and unwise. Many have criticized the Supreme Court for stymieing campaign-finance reform on constitutional grounds, for example. Policy making through litigation elevates the stakes when judges must be chosen. Judicial elections are becoming harder fought and partisan battles over lifetime appointments are growing fiercer in part because judges are important in the policy-making process.

With these defects come some important advantages. Litigation serves as an equalizer, providing opportunities for participation that would otherwise not be available. It also accommodates a deep-seated American distrust of politicians and bureaucrats. Most important, perhaps, judicial engagement, with its aura of reasoned decision and dispassionate appreciation for all sides in a dispute, lends legitimacy to other government operations.

Globalizing Justice

The influence of judges in the formation and implementation of policy appears to be increasing worldwide. National courts in many countries are expanding their jurisdiction, taking on new kinds of disputes, and referencing decisions from other nations to support their growing power. Regional and specialized courts and tribunals are becoming more common, and they are taking an increasingly active part in resolving problems created by economic interdependence and concerns about human rights.[25] The European Court of Justice has become a significant player in determining how economic integration will proceed in Europe, partly through its own decisions, and partly through the radiating effect it has on national courts. A somewhat similar pattern has developed in the realm of human rights through the European Court of Human Rights. Founded in the aftermath of World War II to prevent such a disaster from ever happening again, the court has grown in power and prestige over the years. Since the 1980s, this court has been deluged with petitions complaining of government decisions infringing on individual rights. Decisions of this court, binding on member nations, are cited all over the world.

The impulse to create metanational courts is not limited to Europe. The horrors of genocide and violence that crosses international borders have provoked war-crimes tribunals in Rwanda and Bosnia, and, most recently, an International Criminal Court with global jurisdiction. Regional human-rights courts have been established in Latin America and in Asia. Economic integration has brought specialized tribunals with varying jurisdiction based on trade conventions and treaties, including NAFTA (the North American Free Trade Agreement), and the WTO (World Trade Organization). Much dispute-resolving activity occurs in the shadows of these international and bilateral agreements.

Economic integration, cultural dislocation, and a growing concern for human rights ensure a steady flow of change-oriented litigation at the international level, even in the absence of world government. In fact, the lack of world government helps explain why meta-national courts have been established: they fill a void. Some of these new courts can be used by individuals and by a vast and growing array of nongovernmental organizations to promote reform.[26] Growing lines of communication among judges also facilitate the trend toward an international jurisprudence. Judges from all over the world are meeting in seminars and training sessions and judicial organizations and finding that they have common concerns. They are reading, and increasingly citing, each other's opinions, which they can access electronically.[27]

The powerful nations of the world back some, but not all, of these developments. These nations are wary of being held to international human-rights standards declared by judges from other nations. Most of these powers have opted out of compulsory jurisdiction of the oldest international tribunal, the International Court of Justice in The Hague. The court, which operates under United Nations auspices, was founded shortly after World War II by some of the very nations who are distancing themselves from it.

The behavior of the United States has been most extreme in this regard. The United States grew disenchanted with the International Court of Justice when it lost a case brought by Nicaragua to end the mining of its harbors in 1984. Its approach to the new International Criminal Court has been similar. The U.S. government at first promoted its development, but then declined to submit to its jurisdiction. Currently the United States has gone further, threatening to withdraw foreign aid from nations that refuse to exempt the United States from suit in this court. At the time of this writing, ninety-six countries, mostly small developing nations, had signed on to these immunity deals. Even reference to foreign judgments by American courts is suspect in the current political environment. A 2004 resolution criticizing the Supreme Court for citing foreign judgments attracted dozens of sponsors in the House of Representatives. The principal sponsor of this resolution threatened impeachment for judges who base decisions on foreign precedents.

Even trade courts, which are the outgrowth of economic treaties, cause concern in Congress. When the WTO issued a ruling against U.S. subsidies to the cotton industry, congressional representatives from both parties were enraged. Some asked whether the United States should remain in an organization that issued rulings that call domestic programs into question. Reaction was even more negative to the decision by a NAFTA panel that a Mississippi court had denied a Canadian party a fair trial. The United States had never before lost such a dispute, and many people saw for the first time a potential foreign threat to American judicial independence. In the words of one observer, "If Congress had known that there was anything like this in NAFTA, they would never have voted for it."[28]

Courts and Democratic Governance

Where is the persuasive middle ground in the debate over activist judges? The issue is much broader than the scope of judicial review under the Constitution. What does the participation of courts in so many endeavors—including provocative new claims of injury, for example, of obesity from dining on fast food—do to democracy? At its broadest, the issue is whether government regulation, which always includes courts, should be involved in a particular private activity at all. Advocates of the legalization of marijuana argue, for example, that government has no legitimate interest in this area. Government did take this position in the nineteenth century, leaving the matter of drug control to doctors and even to individual consumers. If government is going to be involved, the next question is whether independent review of its actions should be available; the consensus, particularly in recent decades, has been that it should.

The amount of judging that occurs, in other words, is not entirely under judicial control. Congress and the state legislatures are major players in determining how much judges will be engaged in policy making. Legislators have the power, not just to create new rights, but also to create new courts, new judgeships, new layers of review, and new means of litigating, like class actions. Over the past two centuries, for example, Congress has used its power to vastly expand the network of federal courts. In the 1960s and 1970s Congress and some state legislatures focused on expanding the reach of the courts to social problems, including civil rights, disability rights, and the environment. By the same token, when legislators become disillusioned with courts, they often cut back on judicial power. Frances Zemans describes the current struggle between legislatures and courts:

> Legislation restricting judicial review of habeas corpus petitions, sentencing guidelines that include mandatory minimums that severely limit judicial discretion, the Civil Justice Reform Act of 1990 that imposed oversight by district-level committees and mandated alternative dispute resolution programs, and the Prison Litigation Reform Act of 1995 have all been adopted. . . . There have been continuing efforts to cap punitive damages through a federal products-liability statute, and bills in the 105th Congress included a number of restrictions, such as requiring three-judge panels to review state laws adopted by referendum. At the same time the judiciary had not received even a cost-of living increase for several years. . . . State judiciaries have also faced limits imposed by legislatures, including sentencing guidelines, three-strikes laws, and a variety of tort-reform measures.[29]

The federal courts have resisted some of these efforts to constrain their jurisdiction. Chief Justice Rehnquist has complained regularly about unfilled judicial vacancies, salary erosion, the harsh rhetoric Congress directs at courts, and the failure to consult with judges before adopting restrictive legislation. The imposition of mandatory sentencing guidelines caused a major uproar, dividing the bench over their constitutionality until the Supreme Court settled the matter. Sentencing authority continues to be a point of tension between the two branches. In his 2003 address, for example, the chief justice was sharply critical of the Protect Act, which requires any federal judge who gives a lighter sentence than that prescribed by the federal sentencing guidelines to report to the Senate Judiciary Committee."[30]

Analogous struggles over the scope of judicial authority occur in the states. In Arizona, for example, legislators are considering proposals to replace merit selection with election, and to give the legislature final authority over procedural and evidentiary rules. The separation of powers allows for such politicking about jurisdiction, the method of selection, and resources, but legislatures can go too far. Professor Zemans draws a useful distinction between the institutional and decisional independence of courts, arguing that the system of divided powers allows for efforts to curb the courts as an institution, but not for efforts to curb decisional independence.[31] When legislators use their funding power to punish particular courts for decisions they do not like, which is quite possible in some state systems, they have gone beyond the proper bounds of their authority.

Legislative Norms and Judicial Independence

Aside from punishing judges for particular decisions, which seems clearly inappropriate, are there any legitimate bounds on legislative or executive initiatives to curb judicial power? Constitutional language, necessarily vague and dated, gives no definitive answers, contrary to what some advocates claim. Public opinion is an uncertain guide, particularly in light of media attention that distorts what courts do. Legislators should support judicial decision-making to the extent that they believe democracy will function better if they do. Courts create new channels for political debate, and new players. They are an important part of a functioning democracy for this reason.[32] Their effectiveness in actually producing social change is, to some extent, beside the point.[33] In public-interest litigation, their value may lie in bringing issues to the public's attention. In private litigation, the value lies in giving a second look to the exercise of government power and giving claims an airing.

At one level, Thomas Burke observes, the litigation debate is about who decides: "Do we need the tort system to police pharmaceutical companies, or can we trust a bureaucracy, the Food and Drug Administration? Should the handling of a toxic waste dump be decided through local politics, a federal bureaucracy, or litigation? Is disability a problem to be solved by rehabilitation professionals, welfare programs, or rights-based litigation? Are the decisions made by administrative agencies worthy of deference, or should courts step in and take a "hard look"? Should malpractice-damaged newborns be compensated through tort litigation or social insurance programs?"[34] Americans have relied on courts in many of these situations because they trust them more than the alternatives. The United States, traditionally suspicious of big government, has not developed a strong, well-organized bureaucratic sector. Courts are the politically feasible alternative. The allocation of judging should be evaluated with such realities in mind.

Familiar principles of justice provide some guidance on the proper boundaries of judicial power. The starting point should be that judicial oversight is valuable to those who can avail themselves of it. It is a scarce public good that should be distributed by principles that can be called fair, not by bargaining responsive to the highest bidder. Discussion of what will and will not be subject to review by courts should take account of who is receiving this good, as well as why. Too often, debates about the limits of review or "frivolous lawsuits" are carried on as if they were unconnected to the people who claim injury.

Some legislative initiatives of recent years can be criticized as insensitive to any recognized principles of fairness. The off-again on-again treatment of legal access for the poor is an example. In recent years, the anti-access movement has gone much further than it did in the past when it cut off funds for certain types of litigation. Legislatures have taken the more fundamental step of eliminating the right to sue in many situations that poor people face. Federal laws now prescribe automatic deportation of immigrants for minor offenses, automatic eviction from subsidized housing when family members are involved in drug offenses, automatic exclusion from food stamps, and other penalties. Legislatures have reduced judicial discretion with mandatory minimum sentencing laws and three-strikes legislation. Juveniles have lost the individualized oversight that courts provide with automatic assignment to adult courts and zero-tolerance policies in schools. These policies effectively reduce the critical oversight of judges, even when groups have adequate legal representation.

Conclusion

Aristotle observed that there would be no need for justice if all men were friends. It should be a matter of concern when those with whom our nation is least friendly get the least justice. Limits on prison-reform litigation, for example, drew accolades in some conservative circles. But such limits are nothing to be proud of in a nation that imprisons over two million people, and keeps many of them in crowded, unsafe conditions. Legislatures are limiting judicial review in order to please powerful constituencies who desire to punish or to reject others in our society. The mean-spirited emotional rhetoric that swirls around courts in Congress and in many state legislatures reflects an unfortunate breakdown in institutional norms of fairness and decency for all sectors of our society.[35] Political control over the jurisdiction of courts was part of the constitutional plan, but the founders expected legislatures to be even-handed in exercising this power.

The rhetoric about judicial despots, grasping lawyers, and selfish litigants deflects us from the debate we should be having about fairness in the allocation of judicial oversight within the United States. The emotional tenor of this debate also prevents us from seriously grappling with the costs and inefficiencies of our current system. We have, as one critical observer remarked, "a system that will not only execute a poor man, but will also spend $2,000,000 trying to determine whether that man was represented adequately by a court-appointed drunkard who was paid $500 for his services."[36] There are good arguments for strengthening capacity to make fair and final decisions through clear legislation, adequate support for legal services, and state-federal cooperation.

These observations also apply to the international level. Our own experience with courts suggests that international tribunals will grow stronger over time.[37] Metanational courts will attract increasing numbers of litigants seeking to effect policy change, and courts will become more skilled in dealing with these suits. The accumulation of decisions will help these courts achieve credibility by giving them precedents with which to fashion new, more persuasive decisions. As they gain in institutional legitimacy, these new judicial voices will grow louder in world affairs. The colloquy they provoke is part of a larger global trend in which individual rights are gaining ground at the expense of traditional hierarchies and political bodies.

The United States has been of mixed minds about these developments, supporting human-rights arguments, but avoiding committing itself to international adjudication whenever possible. We are a great power torn between maintaining world hegemony and submitting to an international regime of rights that places limits on military and economic power. As in the domestic sphere, we have emotionalized the debate, and in the process overestimated the capacity of courts to alter the global movement toward individual rights. The United States should take a more positive stance, acknowledging that international courts give voice to concerns that would otherwise be submerged and thereby promote world peace.

Notes

*A number of helpful critics read and commented upon this chapter, and Gregory Broberg, a graduate student in the School of Justice and Social Inquiry at Arizona State University, assisted in its production. Those who commented upon the manuscript include: Lawrence Baum, Paul Carrington, Malcolm Feeley, Susan Goldsmith, Kermit Hall, Roger Hartley, Richard Lempert, Kevin McGuire, Kenneth Miller, Konstance Plett, Gerald Rosenberg, Stuart Scheingold, and Michael Shelton.

1. Lawrence Friedman elaborates this point in *Total Justice*.
2. John William Ward, ed., *The Nature and Tendency of Free Institutions* (Cambridge, Mass.: Harvard University Press, 1968).
3. Lino Graglia, "Do Judges Have a Policy-Making Role in the American System of Government," *Harvard Journal of Law and Public Policy* 17 (1994), 119–130.
4. "The Role of a Supreme Court in a Democracy," the Justice Matthew O. Tobriner Memorial Lecture at the University of California, Hastings College of Law, September 24, 2001, published in *Hastings Law Journal* 53 (2002), 1205–1216.
5. Graglia, "Do Judges Have a Policy-Making Role," 121.

6. The Center for Reclaiming America, "Stand in Support of Pro-Life Judges and Justices!" Available at: http://cfra.info/73/1b.asp.
7. Robert Bork, *Coercing Virtue: The Worldwide Rule of Judges* (Washington, D.C.: AEI Press, 2003), 53.
8. Bork, *Coercing Virtue,* 139.
9. Quoted from Steven Macedo, *The New Right v. The Constitution* (Washington, D.C.: Cato Institute, 1986), 1. See also Lee Cokorinos, *The Assault on Diversity: An Organized Challenge to Racial and Gender Justice* (Lanhan, Md.: Rowman and Littlefield, 2003), and James A. Dorn and Henry G. Manne, *Economic Liberties and the Judiciary* (Fairfax, Va.: George Mason University Press, 1987). The argument for courts as a bulwark against too much democracy resonates with Ran Hirschl's study of campaigns to establish stronger access to judicial review in Canada, New Zealand, South Africa, and Israel (*Toward Juristocracy: The Origins and Consequences of the New Constitutionalism* [Cambridge, Mass.: Harvard University Press, 2004]). He concluded that pressure to strengthen judicial review in those nations came from elites concerned about losing power, particularly large businesses and landowners who feared democratically inspired interference with their property and trade opportunities. These elites favor a strong judicial branch because they believe judges generally support policies that promote a liberal, free-market-oriented society. Their fear, in short, is of excessive democracy
10. Clint Bolick, *Changing Course: Civil Rights at the Crossroads* (New Brunswick, N.J.: Transaction Books, 1988).
11. Macedo, *The New Right,* 36–37.
12. For a detailed analysis see William Haltom and Michael McCann, *Distorting the Law: Politics, Media, and the Litigation Crisis* (Chicago: University of Chicago Press, 2004).
13. Thomas F. Burke, *Lawyers, Lawsuits, and Legal Rights,* 2–4, 171. Also, see Lawrence M. Friedman, *Total Justice* (Boston: Beacon Press, 1985).
14. Linda Greenhouse, "Chief Justice Attacks a Law as Infringing on Judges," *New York Times* (January 1, 2004), A6–14.
15. Washington Legal Foundation paid advertisement in the *New York Times* (March 22, 2004), A27.
16. Glendon, *Rights Talk,* 15.
17. Michael McCann, *Rights at Work: Pay Equity Reform and the Politics of Legal Mobilization* (Chicago: University of Chicago Press, 1999). Also see Stuart A. Scheingold, *The Politics of Rights: Lawyers, Public Policy, and Political Change,* 2nd ed. (Ann Arbor: University of Michigan Press, 2004).
18. See especially *United States v. Booker* 125 S. Ct. 738 (2005) and *Blakely v. Washington* 125 S. Ct. 21 (2004).
19. See Deborah Stone, *Policy Paradox: The Art of Political Decision Making* (New York: Norton, 2001), especially 371–376.
20. Marc Galanter, "An Oil Strike in Hell: Contemporary Legends about the Civil Justice System," *Arizona Law Review* 40 (1998), 716–752, and see "The Day after the Litigation Explosion," *Maryland Law Review* 46 (1986), 3–39.
21. See Charles Reich, "The New Property," *Yale Law Journal* 73 (1964).
22. Abram Chayes, "The Role of the Judge in Public Law Litigation," *Harvard Law Review* 89 (1975–1976), 1281–1316; 1302. Chayes lays out the key features of public-

interest litigation. Remarkably prescient and still a good description of this type of lawsuit. Also see Ross Sandler and David Schoenbrod, *Democracy by Decree: What Happens When Courts Run Government* (New Haven, Conn.: Yale University Press, 2003), 115.

23. Ross Sandler and David Schoenbrod, *Democracy by Decree: What Happens When Courts Run Government* (New Haven, Conn.: Yale University Press, 2003), 21–23.
24. Cited in Lee Cokorinos, *The Assault on Diversity*, 9.
25. Alec Stone Sweet, *Governing with Judges: Constitutional Politics in Europe* (Oxford: Oxford University Press, 2000), discusses this trend. See also Mary L. Volcansek, *Law Above Nations: Supranational Courts and the Legalization of Politics* (Gainesville: University Press of Florida, 1997).
26. Charles Epp explores the conditions for rights mobilization in *The Rights Revolution: Lawyers, Activists, and Supreme Courts in Comparative Perspective* (Chicago: University of Chicago Press, 1998).
27. Anne-Marie Slaughter, "A Global Community of Courts," *Harvard International Law Journal* 44 (2003), 191.
28. The speaker is Judge Abner Mikva, former federal appellate judge and congressman, and one of the three judges in the case. His view was echoed by several legal scholars, one of whom described the case as "the biggest threat to United States judicial independence that no one has heard of and even few people understand." For the chief justice of the California Supreme Court it was "rather shocking that the highest courts of the state and federal governments could have their judgments circumvented by these tribunals." Quotations from *New York Times*, April 18, 2004, 1–19.
29. Frances Kahn Zemans "The Accountable Judge: Guardian of Judicial Independence," *Southern California Law Review* 72 (1998–1999), 625–656; 629. Roger Hartley and several colleagues have explored issues of judicial independence in state and federal courts from an empirical perspective. See Robert E. Hartley and Lisa M. Holmes, "The Increasing Senate Scrutiny of Lower Federal Court Nominees," *Political Science Quarterly* 117 (2002), 259–278, and James W. Douglas and Roger E. Hartley, "The Politics of Court Budgeting in the States: Is Judicial Independence Threatened?" *Public Administration Review* 62 (July/August 2003), 441–454.
30. Chief Justice William Rehnquist, *2003 Year-End Report on the Federal Judiciary*, Supreme Court of the United States (January 1, 2004), 2. His 2004 year-end report developed a similar theme, criticizing congressional threats of impeachment for controversial decisions. See *New York Times*, January 1, 2005, p. A10.
31. Robert E. Hartley and Lisa M. Holmes, "The Increasing Senate Scrutiny of Lower Federal Court Nominees," *Political Science Quarterly* 117 (2002), 259–278; and James W. Douglas and Roger E. Hartley, "The Politics of Court Budgeting in the States: Is Judicial Independence Threatened?" *Public Administration Review* 62 (July/August 2003): 441–454. Congress frequently gets the "last word" on issues that have already been resolved by courts. In *Overruled? Legislative Overrides, Pluralism, and Contemporary Court-Congress Relations* (Stanford, Calif.: Stanford University Press, 2004), Jeb Barnes studied the pattern of overrides. He concludes that the override process has a positive effect—it usually opens up policy making to a larger number of players and lends clarity to ambiguous legal rulings.

32. Teri Jennings Peretti, *In Defense of a Political Court* (Princeton, N.J.: Princeton University Press, 1999). See also Susan Burgess, *Contest for Constitutional Authority: The Abortion and War Powers Debates* (Lawrence: University of Kansas, 1992).
33. The question of whether courts are capable of producing significant social change has provoked a fascinating scholarly literature that began in 1957 with an article by Robert Dahl, "Decision-Making in a Democracy: The Supreme Court as a National Policy Maker," *Journal of Public Law* 6 (1957), 279–295, arguing for their ineffectiveness. Charles Johnson and Bradley Canon attempted to provide an even-handed assessment of the policy impact of courts in *Judicial Politics: Implementation and Impact* (New York: Congressional Quarterly, 1984). Gerald Rosenberg provided a series of case studies that supported this position in *The Hollow Hope: Can Courts Bring about Social Change?* (Chicago: University of Chicago Press, 1991). A recent article showing that, under some circumstances, courts can be quite effective, is by Paul Frymer, "Acting When Elected Officials Won't: Federal Courts and Civil Rights Enforcement in U.S. Labor Unions, 1935–85," *American Political Science Review* 97 (2003), 483–499.
34. Burke, *Lawyers, Lawsuits, and Legal Rights*, 199. See, to the same effect, Kagan, *Adversarial Legalism*.
35. The pattern of blocked appointments and retributive behavior is about a decade old, Michael Tolley observed in a recent analysis of the history of disputes over judicial selection in the U.S. Congress ("Legal Controversies over Federal Judicial Selection in the United States: Breaking the Cycle of Obstruction and Retribution over Judicial Appointments," a paper prepared for the annual meeting of the International Political Science Association in London, January 29–30, 2004.) In each of his annual addresses on the state of the judiciary from 2000 on, Chief Justice Rehnquist has complained of the number of unfilled vacancies in the federal judiciary.
36. Paul Campos, *Jurismania: The Madness of American Law* (New York: Oxford University Press, 1998), 24.
37. Kevin T. McGuire makes this argument in relation to the U.S. Supreme Court in "The Institutionalization of the U.S. Supreme Court," *Political Analysis* 12 (2004): 128–142.

Bibliography

Burke, Thomas F. *Lawyers, Lawsuits, and Legal Rights: The Battle over Litigation in American Society.* Berkeley, Calif.: University of California Press, 2002. Introduces the concept of "litigious" policies and explains why Congress produces them.

Feeley, Malcolm, and Edward Rubin. *Judicial Policy Making and the Modern State: How the Courts Reformed America's Prisons.* New York: Cambridge University Press, 1998. This book is a tour de force in discussing how courts became involved in reforming prisons and the political implications of this involvement. A useful review of the book is by Daniel Farber, "Stretching the Adjudicative Paradigm: Another Look at Judicial Policy Making and the Modern State," *Law and Social Inquiry* 24 (1999): 751.

Friedman, Lawrence M. *Total Justice: What Americans Want from the Legal System and Why.* Boston: Beacon Press, 1985. A good, brief introduction to American legal culture and how it has changed over time.

Glendon, Mary Ann. *Rights Talk: The Impoverishment of Political Discourse.* New York: Free Press, 1991. A critique of rights consciousness from a communitarian and international perspective by a thoughtful legal scholar.

Kagan, Robert A. *Adversarial Legalism: The American Way of Law.* Cambridge, Mass.: Harvard University Press, 2001. Describes how the American legal system could be more efficient and fairer in criminal, civil, and administrative dispute resolution.

Kagan, Robert A., and Lee Axelrad, eds. *Regulatory Encounters: Multinational Corporations and American Adversarial Legalism.* Berkeley: University of California Press, 2000. Conversations with multinational corporate officials about their legal encounters in different nations convinced the authors that adversarial legalism is a peculiarly American phenomenon.

Kozlowski, Mark. *The Myth of the Imperial Judiciary: Why the Right is Wrong about the Courts.* New York: NYU Press, 2003. A thorough unpacking and debunking of many conservative claims about over-active courts.

McCann, Michael W. *Rights at Work: Pay Equity Reform and the Politics of Legal Mobilization.* Chicago: University of Chicago Press, 1994. A case study in the power of litigation to change beliefs about entitlements.

Miller, Mark C., and Jeb Barnes, eds. *Making Policy, Making Law: An Interbranch Perspective.* Washington, D.C.: Georgetown University Press, 2004. A useful series of essays suggesting that American public policy should be viewed as a collaborative effort between various agencies of government acting as equals, rather than a legislative product to be implemented by courts.

Rosenberg, Gerald N. *The Hollow Hope: Can Courts Bring about Social Change?* Chicago: University of Chicago Press, 1991. A classic in the political-science literature on courts because it challenges those who believe that judicial pronouncements invariably lead to social change. Rosenberg persuasively demonstrates that usually courts are ineffective without support from other quarters.

Sandler, Ross, and David Schoenbrod. *Democracy by Decree: What Happens When Courts Run Government.* New Haven, Conn.: Yale University Press, 2003. These authors take an up-close look at a few expensive institutional reform suits and see a major problem in the way resources can be deflected from reasonable and democratically supported ends to purposes that work for the litigants involved, but no one else. They concede the significance of institutional reform litigation, but offer a number of practical reforms to improve it. The book is most valuable for showing how active Congress has been in creating opportunities for suit.

Scheingold, Stuart A. *The Politics of Rights: Lawyers, Public Policy, and Political Change,* 2nd ed. Ann Arbor: University of Michigan Press, 2004. Distinguishes general belief in rights from practical activity to accomplish political change. The new edition incorporates recent developments in the study of rights litigation.

Volcansek, Mary L., ed. *Law above Nations: Supranational Courts and the Legalization of Politics.* Gainesville: University Press of Florida, 1997. A good introduction to the growing significance of metanational courts in human rights and economic regulation.

SECTION IV

RIGHTS, LIBERTIES, AND DEMOCRACY

13

COURTS AND THE RIGHTS REVOLUTION

Charles R. Epp

IN THE SECOND HALF OF THE TWENTIETH CENTURY, THE United States experienced a fundamental and pervasive rights revolution, and the continuing gay rights movement indicates that it has not yet run its course. The depth, scope, and nature of the rights revolution may be illustrated by a job advertisement from 1952 for an audiovisual librarian at a large public university in the Midwest:

> Sex—female;
> Church preference—Protestant;
> Race preference—white;
> Other specifications—Preferably single; if married preferably no children; or children of school age.[1]

The extent of discrimination on the basis of race, sex, and religion in an earlier era is now breathtaking. In many states, African Americans were excluded by law or custom from jobs; restaurants, hotels, swimming pools and other public accommodations; schools and universities attended by white students; voting in party primaries and general elections; from marriage with whites; and on and on. In an earlier era, in some states married women's wages were the property of their husbands; husbands but not wives were allowed to divorce on grounds of adultery; in many states women were excluded from juries and from holding state office; women were, by law, paid less than men when employed as public schoolteachers; and married women had limited rights to conduct business.

Such discriminatory laws and policies reflected a pervasive exclusion of some people from full membership and equal dignity in the political community. If an African American woman could not vote, could not send her children to her local school, was barred by explicit employment policy from many jobs, and could not serve on juries, there was little doubt that she was, at best, a second-class citizen by virtue of both race and sex. In the space of half a century, in other words, American society's fundamental assumptions about status and membership in the polity have been transformed.

The legal transformation in membership and status, moreover, has directly influenced a host of areas of the law, among them criminal procedure, freedom of speech and association, the establishment of religion, and sexual privacy. Thus the Supreme Court expanded the rights of freedom of expression and association in order to protect participants in the civil rights movement from censorship by southern officials, which led, in turn, to broad expansions of constitutional protection for freedom of speech and association more generally. Similarly, the Court, pressed by civil rights advocates and others, expanded the due process rights of criminal defendants in part in order to address the persistent problem of racial discrimination by police and criminal courts. For similar reasons, in order to address racial discrimination in the application of state welfare policies, the Court expanded the due process rights of welfare recipients, which led to a cascade of changes in governmental procedures governing a host of government benefits ranging from licenses to jobs. As the Court developed its newfound commitment to eradicate racial status from American law, it turned to related issues, among them complaints by members of minority religious groups that many state and local policies effectively established dominant religious views as the official policy of government. And, as the Court's commitment to equality of citizenship, freedom of expression, and religious freedom from government-imposed religion grew, its justices began to expand a right to sexual privacy that had long been a demand of the women's rights movement. Taken as a whole, these developments contributed to a rights-based transformation of American law, which will be referred to here as the rights revolution. The rights revolution was a sustained development, centered on individual rights to equal respect and voice, that progressively has broadened the concept and practice of membership in the American political community.

Virtually all of the rights revolution's key policies grew out of a request, dating to the years before the Civil War, by African Americans and women to be included as full and equal members of the American political community and economy. Their demands for full inclusion gained great strength as their movements grew during the middle decades of the last century, a point that will be discussed later. The popular base for the rights revolution tells us something about the nature of the new rights. Although rights are often thought to be protections for *individual liberty* against democratic majorities, many of the key rights created by the rights revolution are *democratic rights*, particularly rights to full and equal participation in the democratic polity and economy. Civil rights, as

Orlando Patterson, a leading sociologist and historian of slavery and freedom has argued, have typically been a rhetorical claim of the oppressed, of those who demand to be treated on an equal basis with the powerful.

Although courts are often seen as the central players in the rights revolution, the legal basis for the transformation is broader than the pronouncements of courts alone. Key advances in rights have been created as well by presidential executive orders, congressional statutes, state statutes, local ordinances, federal administrative rules, state administrative rules, and such mundane authorities as agency employment handbooks. Many U.S. cities, for instance, have antidiscrimination ordinances that are significantly more protective of some groups, particularly gays and lesbians, than are federal statutes or court decisions. In other words, judicial decisions, often thought to be the key source of the new rights, were but one mode of their creation. During the rights revolution, new rights flowed from all of the myriad law-creating sources in the governmental process, and courts, in some respects, followed the rest of government.

American courts, nonetheless, are intimately connected, in the public mind and in their institutional development, with the rights revolution. That association brings to the American judiciary a coalition of defenders and a broad degree of popular support—but it also has exposed the courts to withering criticism. Thus, President George W. Bush, in calling for a constitutional amendment banning same-sex marriage, declared that the amendment was made necessary by decisions of "activist judges" to redefine the law of marriage. The president's comment reflects a common view that the American courts are undemocratic, even antidemocratic institutions, and, particularly, that they led the rights revolution and thereby imposed on an unwilling country a host of illegitimate individual rights.

That view, as suggested here, misunderstands the relationship between judicially created rights and the broader processes of political and social change. But the president's comment also reflects a deep relationship between courts and the rights revolution. Both the depth of that relationship and the general tendency of judicially created rights to follow social and political change merit recognition.

Courts and the Social and Political Organization of Rights

There is, undoubtedly, a grain of truth in the critics' claims: the American judiciary is more intimately associated with the rights revolution than are state legislatures, governors, the U.S. Congress, and the presidency. For one thing, American courts, of course, participated in creating many of the rights revolution's key policies, most prominently by striking down race and sex discrimination in public life. But courts did so at the behest and with the support of powerful social movements and key elements of the U.S. government.

The Affinity between Courts and Social Movements

Courts are attractive venues for such groups as African Americans and women who are excluded from full participation in public life. Particularly in the United States, such groups have viewed their most fervent aspirations not as mere goals, policies, or law, but as moral or higher-law *rights* to equal status in the community. African Americans, women, and others have viewed their claims to equality of status as properly guaranteed by the key rights-based amendments to the Constitution, particularly the Bill of Rights and the Thirteenth, Fourteenth, Fifteenth, and Nineteenth Amendments. The Fourteenth Amendment, in particular, guarantees equal protection before the law. It was adopted at the behest of a political coalition aiming to constitutionalize the aspirations of the abolitionist movement, and its fate has been tied ever since to the legacy of that movement. The federal courts, and especially the U.S. Supreme Court, as the contributions by William Nelson and Keith Whittington in this volume attest, increasingly have claimed a nearly exclusive authority to interpret the meaning of the Constitution, and in so doing have staked a claim to being *the* official arbiters of such rights claims.

The affinity between courts and rights-based social movements does not end there. Most of the key constitutional rights amendments and the main federal statutes protecting civil rights declare those rights in language that is notoriously general and ambiguous. Constitutional and statutory ambiguity, of course, is the natural product of compromises among political factions. But general and ambiguous legal language becomes a dead letter unless given life through interpretation and enforcement by courts, and so social movements demanding their "rights" have naturally turned to the courts for clarification and support. Additionally, constitutional and statutory ambiguity seems to enhance the utility of such statutes for social movement organizers, as it gives them the room to creatively interpret ambiguous provisions in ways congenial to their interests.

For groups excluded from the right to vote or speak, the courts, and especially the Supreme Court, may appear to be the only branch of government that might hear and act on a demand for inclusion. Federal courts undoubtedly follow the course of dominant trends in public opinion and electoral realignment for the simple reason that their members are replaced over time by dominant political coalitions. Nonetheless, courts have an unusual degree of independence from more short-term electoral calculations and consequently are often the last hope for groups whose requests for a political voice have been ignored by legislatures and elected executives. More than enough examples exist of judicial action at the request of excluded groups and in the face of apparently dominant majority opposition in order to give such groups an enduring hope for justice in the courts. The Jehovah's Witnesses religious sect, for instance, for whom the compulsory flag salute was a violation of deeply felt religious principles, won a landmark right, at the height of World War II, for school children to be free not to participate in such salutes. No legislature at the time had responded to such concerns. Similarly, in the 1930s, when there was no realistic chance that Congress would adopt civil rights legislation—indeed, opponents had blocked even anti-lynching bills—the dean of Howard University's School of Education observed that it is "no longer a question of whether Negroes *should* resort to the courts, they must resort to the courts. They have no other reasonable, legitimate alternative."[2]

Additionally, the Supreme Court's individuality and broad jurisdiction lend to it an air of unusual prominence and symbolic significance; its small number of decisions gives to each a greater symbolic weight. In comparison to presidential executive orders, which are often lost from public view, and other presidential pronouncements, which are buried under the pile of yet more presidential pronouncements, Supreme Court decisions can stand out as prominent statements. In comparison to the legislative output of Congress, which is contained in complex bills full of compromise provisions—and increasingly consists of single massive "omnibus" appropriations bills containing provisions spanning the entire policy waterfront—the output of the Supreme Court can be remarkably simple and clear. Thus when, in a pair of cases in 1989 and 1990, the Supreme Court examined whether flag-burning as a form of expression is a protected form of expression, the news media covered the Court's decisions to hear the cases, the oral arguments in the cases, and then nearly every newspaper, television, and radio station in the country reported the Court's final decisions, which may be reduced to a one-line pronouncement: flag-burning is protected by the Bill of Rights. The common goal of many social movements, of ultimately gaining a decision by the Supreme Court, is therefore eminently reasonable: few single decisions of other governing institutions, in this country or elsewhere, are as nationally prominent and symbolically resonant.

There is yet another reason why the courts are attractive forums for excluded groups. Although there is only one Supreme Court, the number of American courts is truly enormous. These myriad courts, moreover, are divided into separate state and federal judicial systems. The profusion of courts and their jurisdictional divisions serve social movement organizers and other policy entrepreneurs, particularly by offering the possibility of "forum shopping," or strategically choosing the most favorable court in which to file a case. Thus plaintiffs may strategically seek a sympathetic judge or jury pool. Defendants against rights lawsuits typically have less ability to move a lawsuit filed against them into a more sympathetic court.

Finally, even when movement organizers lose a lawsuit in the end, they may have gained other things of benefit. Perhaps the most obvious and important is publicity. The news media contribute very directly to the appeal of courts for social movements for a simple reason: plaintiff victories in court are publicized at higher rates than plaintiff losses. It is the victorious rights plaintiff, not the victorious organizational defendant, who is attractive to the media, and, as political scientist Michael McCann has observed, litigation and judicial decisions—even decisions rejecting a movement's claims—may be very useful to movement organizers in encouraging people to join the movement.[3] Similarly, a lawsuit asserting a right can encourage excluded groups to recognize that they *have* rights. Thus, as long ago as the early 1930s, it was reported that civil rights litigation had "the psychological effect upon Negroes themselves . . . of stirring the spirit of revolt among them."[4] Additionally, lawsuits, even if ultimately lost by the rights plaintiff, may be used to encourage legislatures or businesses to adopt reforms. Thus, after women's rights litigants lost a Supreme Court decision on the subject of pregnancy discrimination, they succeeded in using the case as a springboard for mobilizing a coalition in Congress to amend the Civil Rights Act of 1964 to prohibit employment discrimination on the basis of pregnancy.

Judicial "Follower-ship"

It has long been observed, nonetheless, that the Supreme Court's agenda follows broad trends in American politics, and this is especially true of the Court's agenda on rights. The Supreme Court, as Gerald Rosenberg and Michael Klarman have observed, lacks the organizational power of the Congress and the presidency, and the justices undoubtedly recognize limits on their power.[5] Over its history, the Court has rarely stepped far beyond public opinion and rarely fights for long against determined political majorities.

Particularly regarding rights, several institutional and structural conditions limit the capacity of American courts, and especially the Supreme Court, to truly lead. The U.S. judicial hierarchy and the Supreme Court's approach to selecting cases contribute to slow and deliberate examination of issues, typically ensuring that no decision will be issued until after a long process of prior deliberation in lower courts. In the U.S. judicial system, in contrast to the courts in many other countries, there is only one national supreme court and it has final legal authority over all areas of the law; the range and number of petitions for certiorari, or requests to hear a case, brought to the Supreme Court each year is thus unusually large. Yet the Court's capacity to decide cases is limited and so it decides a mere hundred or so cases per year.

As a consequence, the Court's justices share a strong preference for allowing a new legal issue to "percolate" in lower courts before deciding the issue. That is, the justices prefer hearing cases involving legal conflict among lower courts, particularly when a number of courts have rendered decisions favoring each side of the issue. Conflicting lower court decisions help to clarify the nature of the issues and interests at stake and the best reasons that can be marshaled on behalf of the opposing positions. After sufficient percolation, the justices seem to plausibly believe, their ultimate decision is likely to have greater policy impact than if the legal disputes were less fully developed, and, moreover, their decision is unlikely to be subject to unanticipated criticisms. Additionally, the Court's justices prefer to use the appropriate "vehicle"—the right case—for rendering a decision. Those favoring a shift in judicial policy prefer to do so with a case in which the facts are friendly to their position and in which there are no complicating issues that blunt the communication of their message. Justices thus may prefer to defer judgment on a matter to a later time rather than render a decision via an inappropriate case. And, of course, the opponents of a policy change are likely to favor deferring the issue as well. Indeed, because of the large number of certiorari petitions brought to the Court each year, in the words of a Supreme Court clerk, "there is enormous pressure not to take a case."[6] For this reason, early certiorari petitions on an issue are likely to be denied. As a clerk observed, "it's going to come up again if it's really an important issue. In fact a test to see if an issue is really important is to see if it comes up again."

The Court's institutionalized preference to wait for sufficient "percolation" and the appropriate "vehicle" means that issues are seriously considered for decision only after a significant period of development through litigation in lower courts. With the exception of some highly unusual cases having particular national significance, the delay between the emergence of a legal dispute in lower courts and decision of it by the Supreme Court is often measured in years and sometimes in decades. The Court virtually never decides a disputed issue in the first case raising that issue to reach the Court. Only some kinds of issues, therefore, survive the vetting process to reach the Court's agenda. They are issues supported by widespread litigation spanning a number of federal judicial circuits.

The Supreme Court, in sum, rarely decides a major issue, particularly a major rights issue, in the advance of broad legal mobilization in support of policy change. In this sense, the Court is a follower, not a leader, of trends in legal mobilization. The Court, although undeniably supreme, is embedded in an ongoing process of legal development in which coalitions of litigants play key roles. Litigants provide the Court's docket with cases; they provide the Court's jurisprudence with fully ripened arguments; they are the Court's enforcement arms.

Conditions for Broad Legal Mobilization around Rights

The foregoing discussion is more important for understanding the Court's role in the rights revolution than in virtually any other area of policy. That is because in many other areas of policy significance, the natural constituencies for judicial policies have little difficulty generating the level of lower-court litigation that satisfies the Court's "percolation" requirement. Thus, businesses and governments have the financial and organizational capacity to generate litigation on an ongoing basis, and they do so as a regular part of pursuing their day-to-day interests.

The natural constituencies for civil rights and liberties, however, historically have developed the necessary levels of litigation with greater difficulty. Although civil rights have great symbolic value, their monetary value to an individual litigant rarely compensates for the financial cost and time of the lawsuit. Put another way, although rights are "public goods" (they benefit many people in addition to the individual winner in a rights case), their benefits to the individual plaintiff almost always are monetarily too little to justify the actual cost of the litigation. For the same reasons, the contingency fee system in the United States, which allows plaintiffs' attorneys to gain their compensation from the damage award granted to the plaintiff, does not, on its own, provide the necessary financial support and incentives for pursuing rights litigation. If the damage award is not sufficient to cover a plaintiff's costs, there is no incentive for lawyers to take up the case on a contingency fee basis. Successful rights litigation, in sum, generally consumes a level of resources that is beyond the reach of ordinary individual plaintiffs.

In order to achieve success in the judicial arena, then, groups asking for better protection of their rights have had to develop an infrastructure of organizations, sources of financing, and legal expertise capable of supporting rights litigation in the absence of a financial pay-off. The development of such an infrastructure contributed to a democratization of access to the judicial agenda. Foremost, rights-advocacy organizations, among them the American Civil Liberties Union and the NAACP–Legal Defense Fund, provide expert legal counsel, help to coordinate legal research as well as other supporting research, aid in the development of legal strategies, help to provide financing and aid in finding other sources of financing for test cases, and provide networks of communication that facilitate the exchange of ideas. Few such organizations existed before 1920, and their growth in the middle decades of the century provided a key foundation for the rights revolution.

Some governmental rights-enforcement agencies have played a role similar to that of private rights-advocacy organizations, albeit with much greater resources. The U.S. Department of Justice has at times provided key support for civil rights cases, in particular by helping to coordinate legal research and strategy, as well as filing amicus curiae ("friend of the court") briefs in the Supreme Court.

Institutional sources of financing, from individual philanthropists, private foundations, and government-supported legal aid programs, also have proven to be crucial for the development of the rights revolution. After the NAACP–Legal Defense Fund's victory in *Brown v. Board of Education*, for instance, the Ford Foundation contributed millions of dollars to the development of similar rights-supportive litigation organizations. The Supreme Court also contributed directly to the resource base for rights litigation in a series of decisions beginning in 1961.

In addition to organizational support and financing, the availability and degree of organization of sympathetic, skilled lawyers, of course, is a necessary condition for the development of rights cases. In particular, the degree of race and sex diversity in the legal profession affects the availability of lawyers who are sympathetic to rights claims. In the 1960s and 1970s, the U.S. legal profession grew dramatically and began to diversify as women and members of racial minorities increasingly became lawyers, providing support for civil rights litigation.

The major rights-focused social movements of the last century have all developed such infrastructures of support for litigation. Thus, the civil rights movement built upon, but also contributed to, the development of organized support for civil rights litigation; the movement drew out significant financial support from such institutions as the Ford Foundation; the black community's growing political clout encouraged the U.S. Department of Justice to provide support for civil rights; and the movement cultivated a growing body of sympathetic attorneys. Similar developments occurred, in varying degrees, in relation to the women's rights movement and the gay rights movement. Conservative groups, too, increasingly have cultivated organizational and financial support for litigation favoring conservative legal causes.

Although the courts are notoriously weak in their powers to enforce and implement their decisions, the fact that Supreme Court decisions on rights typically follow the development of an infrastructure of organizations, lawyers, and government agency support has worked, at least partly, to fill in the gap left by those weak powers of enforcement. The Court's decisions rarely end dispute over an issue and rarely command automatic compliance. But, in the context of full legal mobilization in favor of several alternative positions on key issues, as is typically present in cases before the Supreme Court, the Court's decisions grant authoritative legal resources to some interests and withhold them from others. The "winners" may take these resources, attempt to interpret them even more fully in their favor, and then use them in lower courts and in negotiations outside of court to achieve shifts in policy. The "losers" gain no such direct resources for leveraging favorable policy changes. But they may seek to exploit ambiguities in the Court's decisions to slow or undercut the pressure for policy change. Thus in an important sense, even the Court does not "own" its decisions: the legal doctrine that they create is almost always a choice among competing alternatives, each of which has been richly developed by litigants and lower courts, and, just as importantly, once issued, the Court's opinions become subject to renewed rounds of interpretation and development by mobilized groups. These renewed rounds of interpretation typically discover and exploit ambiguities and implications of the Court's decisions in ways that generate further ambiguities and conflicts in lower courts, thereby virtually forcing the Supreme Court to take up additional cases in order to attempt to bring clarity and order to the law.

The American Judiciary and the Rights Revolution

An inclusive vision of rights dates to the antebellum era, particularly the abolitionist movement and the radical republican political movement. In the midst of the political instability in the wake of the Civil War, those movements pressed for formal, legal recognition of rights for the freed slaves, demanding, in particular, that freed slaves be granted equality of participation in the marketplace and in the political community. The principal products of their efforts were the Civil War amendments, the Thirteenth, Fourteenth, and Fifteenth Amendments to the Constitution. Those amendments banned slavery, guaranteed equal protection before the law, and guaranteed the right to vote regardless of race. More fundamentally, the movement for equal constitutional rights resonated broadly in popular culture. As the eminent American historian Eric Foner has observed, "the conception of [the freed slaves] as equal citizens of the American republic galvanized blacks' political and social activity during Reconstruction."[7]

White majorities worked rapidly to limit the scope of the new constitutional rights and then to fundamentally undercut them. At the outset, even though women had played crucial roles in the abolitionist and radical republican movements they were excluded from many of the benefits of the new rights. Thus, although Senator Charles Sumner gave women much of the credit for passage of the Thirteenth Amendment banning slavery (the movement, indeed, in very short order had generated supportive petitions containing over 400,000 signatures), the congressional majority refused to include women in the Fifteenth Amendment's right to vote.[8] To compound the injuries, that amendment explicitly discriminated on the basis of sex for the first time in the Constitution by basing congressional representation on the number of "male" citizens.

The Supreme Court further narrowed the scope of the new constitutional rights, essentially siding with the view that the Civil War amendments did not greatly alter the states' traditional authority over individual rights. In a string of landmark cases beginning within a few years after passage of the Civil War amendments, the Court undercut their practical value for African Americans and entirely excluded women from their key protections. In the first such case, the Court ruled that the amendment's privileges and immunities clause created no new constitutional rights.[9] Immediately thereafter, the Court in *Bradwell v. Illinois* (1873) rejected a woman's argument that the Fourteenth Amendment protected her right to equal employment opportunity, specifically her right to enter the legal profession, and two years later, in *Minor v. Happersett* (1875), the Court (endorsing the view of Congress) unanimously rejected a claim that the Fifteenth Amendment extends to women the right to vote. A year later, in *United States v. Reese* (1876) and *United States v. Cruikshank* (1876), the Court so narrowed the right of African American men to vote that it became practically meaningless.

Then in 1883, in the *Civil Rights Cases,* the Court issued a profoundly important decision that haunted efforts to protect civil rights for almost a century: it struck down parts of the Civil Rights Act of 1875 that had banned racial discrimination in hotels and other public accommodations, declaring that Congress's authority to enforce the Fourteenth Amendment extended only to actions by state and local governments and their officials, and not to actions by private individuals and businesses. The notorious *Plessy v. Ferguson* (1896) added the final nail to the Civil War amendments' coffin by allowing states and localities to enforce segregation by race.

The Supreme Court thus directly repudiated many of the dearest aspirations of the major social movements of the era. Yet the vestiges of those movements carried on and renewed their demands for inclusion as full and equal members of the political community. "Indeed," as historian Hendrik Hartog has observed, "particular groups may have voiced 'their' constitutional rights most intensely at times when constitutional textual authority contradicted their constitutional understandings."[10]

The Civil Rights Movement

With the collapse of Reconstruction in the South and the unfriendly decisions of the Supreme Court, African Americans faced an increasingly hostile climate. White majorities took away their right to vote; white terrorist groups, particularly the Ku Klux Klan, used violence in an attempt to quell their attempts to organize; police officers and juries acted in biased and even abusive ways in the criminal justice process; rental housing and real estate sales were segregated by race; schools were segregated by race; job opportunities often were segregated by race; and, when African Americans succeeded in organizing under the banner of the National Association for the Advancement of Colored People (NAACP), that organization faced legal attacks aimed at driving it out of operation.

The NAACP became the primary organizing force in fighting these forces of exclusion. Formed in 1909, it developed a legal strategy that sought to erode legal support for each of the particular engines of exclusion. The NAACP legally fought and eventually defeated the principal mechanisms for denying to blacks the right to vote; fought and defeated the principal mechanisms for enforcing housing segregation; fought and eventually eroded racial segregation in public schools; successfully defended against attacks on its own existence, in the process contributing to a great expansion in the rights of association and expression; and challenged and eventually eroded the worst police and trial abuses in the area of criminal justice. The NAACP's efforts contributed fundamentally to many of the main elements of the rights revolution.

Changes in several conditions beyond the court system and outside of the control of any organized movement made these legal changes possible. Perhaps most fundamentally, as Doug McAdam, a leading analyst of the civil rights movement, has shown, shifts in economic and social conditions greatly enhanced the political clout of the African American community.[11] Before 1930, with their population concentrated in rural areas of the South, African Americans had little electoral influence, few legal resources, and few political allies. Many were virtual serfs of large cotton-growing interests. Northern industrial interests favored a steady supply of cotton, and either acquiesced in or fully supported southern cotton growers' efforts to maintain order and productivity among black farm laborers. Because few blacks lived outside of the South, disfranchisement in that region eliminated the black political voice from the entire nation. After 1930 those key conditions began to change. The market for cotton had collapsed, economic opportunities in northern cities had grown, and many blacks began moving from the rural South to seek jobs in northern cities where, coincidentally, their right to vote was not as restricted. As a consequence, African Americans' political clout increased substantially. Their vote at the national level contributed to Democratic presidential victories as early as 1936 and became critical to Democratic success by the election of 1948, and African Americans began playing an increasingly important role in the Democratic coalition. By the early 1940s, as the United States entered World War II, the country's leadership increasingly identified the U.S. mission as defending human rights and democracy. President Franklin Roosevelt, in his famous "Four Freedoms" address, declared in ringing tones, "Freedom means the supremacy of human rights everywhere. Our support goes to those who struggle to gain those rights and keep them." Yet such hopeful declarations clashed with the record of racial discrimination throughout much of the country.

Under increasing pressure, Presidents Roosevelt and Truman began providing symbolic (and some practical) support to African Americans' political demands. Political scientist Kevin McMahon observes that as African Americans became central to the New Deal coalition, the Supreme Court's hostility to New Deal legislation and its partial acceptance of the white primary in the South served to unite the NAACP and the Roosevelt administration in a common cause aimed at expanding protections for the civil rights of African Americans.[12] Roosevelt therefore began nominating justices to the Supreme Court who supported both his legislative program and civil rights; in all, he nominated nine justices, eight of whom were committed to expanding constitutional protections for civil rights. Roosevelt also replaced his conservative Attorney General with Frank Murphy, a racial liberal (subsequently nominated by Roosevelt to the Supreme Court).

Attorney General Murphy created the Justice Department's Civil Rights Section in 1939 (apparently upon the urging of President Roosevelt) and used it to expand federal power to protect civil rights against discrimination and violence in the states by both officials and private individuals. In particular, Murphy gave the new Civil Rights Section the responsibility of enforcing long-dormant Reconstruction-era federal civil rights statutes, which it pursued through a campaign of test-cases brought to the Supreme Court on the problems of lynching, police brutality, and involuntary servitude and peonage in the South. In Murphy's words, the federal government, through the work of the Justice Department, was to become "a powerful bulwark of civil liberty" against racially exclusionary policies and practices in the states.

African Americans also increasingly gained the economic, organizational, and political resources that served eventually as the basis for the civil rights movement. In black churches, soon to be among the key hubs of the civil rights movement, the average membership, resources, and educational training of ministers increased substantially. Similarly, in black colleges, another base of the civil rights movement, enrollment and resources grew dramatically after the early 1930s. The number and organizational strength of southern chapters of the NAACP, the leading civil rights organization in the country, also grew significantly after the early 1930s.

In the context of these developments, as legal historian Mark Tushnet has documented, in the early 1930s the NAACP began supporting litigation against key racially exclusionary forces: restrictions on the right to vote, racism in the criminal justice process, housing segregation, and school segregation.[13] With regard to voting rights, in a string of cases in 1921, 1927, and 1932 the Supreme Court had supported the NAACP's claim that Texas's exclusively white primaries violated the Fourteenth Amendment. But at the height of constitutional controversy over the New Deal in 1935, the Court, in *Grovey v. Townsend*, had unanimously upheld Texas's latest attempt at preserving the white primary. In that case, the Texas legislature had simply left party membership criteria to the full control of party officials; the Court reasoned that the Texas Democratic Party's decision to exclude blacks was thus a purely "private" decision and therefore was beyond the reach of the Fourteenth Amendment. In a one-party state, as was Texas at the time, such a decision effectively denied to blacks the right to vote. In response, the Justice Department's Civil Rights Section (CRS) supported a test case arguing that the right to vote under the Constitution's Article I covered primary elections, and that officials interfering in this right may be prosecuted under Reconstruction-era civil rights statutes; in 1941, in *United States v. Classic*, the Supreme Court agreed. The NAACP built on this precedent to challenge the constitutionality of white primaries run independently of state authorization, and the Court agreed with the challenge, striking down racially exclusive primaries of any sort once and for all in *Smith v. Allwright* (1944). Southern racists' efforts to exclude African Americans from voting, as a result, became increasingly limited; they were left with such methods as poll taxes, literacy tests, and terrorist violence. The NAACP and the CRS supported test-case litigation against these other exclusionary devices. But the Supreme Court, after having unanimously rejected a constitutional challenge to poll taxes in 1937, declined to hear a new challenge in the 1940s, eventually striking down state employment of poll taxes in 1966 in *Harper v. Virginia State Board of Elections,* after a delay of several decades and passage of the Twenty-fourth Amendment in 1964, which barred the use of poll taxes in federal elections.

With regard to racial discrimination and abuses in the criminal justice process, the NAACP supported a number of cases to the Supreme Court. In *Powell v. Alabama* (1932), the Supreme Court created the constitutional right to free legal counsel in capital cases if the defendant cannot afford a lawyer. The case involved the classic hot-button issue of southern racial exclusion: the "Scottsboro Boys," as they were called, were charged, on the basis of dubious evidence, with the rape of two white women, and were initially convicted and sentenced to death without benefit of legal counsel while a mob threat of lynching hung over the trial should "justice" prove to be too slow. After the Supreme Court created the new right to state-supported legal counsel in capital cases, the NAACP continued to support cases challenging racial discrimination by the police and criminal courts over the following years. By the 1940s, the organization had gained the support of the Justice Department's Civil Rights Section. Their combined efforts ran against significant barriers in the legal system as southern grand juries refused to indict suspected members of lynch mobs, and when, in 1945 in *Screws v. United States*, a police brutality case, the Court set a high standard for criminal conviction under federal law of government officials charged with violating civil rights. Efforts to gain clear judicial support for a campaign against racial discrimination in the criminal courts remained only partially successful until the criminal procedure revolution of the 1960s, to be discussed shortly.

With the flagging of progress in the criminal justice arena, the NAACP and the Justice Department put increasing effort into attacking racially exclusionary practices through the civil courts. In the area of housing and school segregation, the NAACP's campaign gained significant strength in the late 1940s after the Truman administration began providing support to those causes in court challenges. The impetus for Truman's renewed effort lay in two developments: the threat that he might lose black voter support and with it reelection in 1948, and, as historian Mary Dudziak has shown, growing international attention to America's racial segregation and racist abuse.[14] Indeed, by early 1948, Truman's political advisers favored taking significant steps to generate support among black voters, and by the late 1940s, the State Department steadily warned the administration that support for the United States in the cold war was threatened by the nearly worldwide perception that American domestic policy was thoroughly racist and out of step with the country's claim to be the world's champion for human rights. Notably, African Americans mobilized pressure on the Truman administration in both areas.

Truman responded with appointment of a Committee on Civil Rights, charged with drafting a report focusing on ways to better protect the civil rights of African Americans in the South. Its landmark report, *To Secure These Rights*, issued the first clear official statement of the rights revolution's aspirations: it called for "elimination of segregation, based on race, color, creed, or national origin, from American life." Moreover, the report lamented the limited enforcement tools remaining in the judicially shredded Reconstruction-era civil rights statutes and called for new civil rights legislation. Acknowledging the unlikelihood that Congress would act on that request, the report also, for the first time, outlined what McMahon calls a "court-centered strategy," "a call for the Court to act without the benefit of a new statute."[15] The report declared, "when the clauses of the Constitution contain language from which substantial power to protect civil rights may reasonably be implied, we believe the Supreme Court will be as ready to apply John Marshall's doctrine of liberal construction as it has been in dealing with laws in other fields." Immediately upon publication of the report, the Solicitor General's office drafted its first amicus curiae brief on behalf of a private civil rights litigant, in the case *Shelley v. Kraemer* (1948), challenging the constitutional validity of judicial enforcement of racially restrictive covenants in real estate contracts (a practice that had greatly contributed to racial segregation in housing). The Supreme Court sided unanimously with the NAACP and Justice Department position, striking down any judicial enforcement of racially restrictive real estate covenants. Philip Elman, an official in the Solicitor General's office, later observed that after the Supreme Court's decision, "the rewards that came were very great. . . . We were now in business looking for Supreme Court civil rights cases in which to intervene as *amicus curiae*."[16]

The NAACP–Legal Defense Fund, with the support of the Justice Department, next turned its full attention to racial segregation in public schools. The NAACP had supported a series of earlier cases, but its big breakthrough came in the 1950s. In one, the Justice Department's supporting brief was the first request to the Supreme Court to overturn entirely the *Plessy* separate-but-equal doctrine. In two other crucial cases, the Solicitor General supported the NAACP's challenges to racially segregated, substandard educational facilities offered by southern states to black graduate students. When the Supreme Court agreed, in *Sweatt v. Painter* (1950), that a separate law school for African Americans, even if the equal of a law school for whites in tangible respects, would be inherently unequal in its symbolic prestige, it was increasingly clear that the Supreme Court might be amenable to a fundamental challenge to the separate-but-equal doctrine.

In this context, the NAACP–Legal Defense Fund developed the cases culminating in *Brown v. Board of Education* (1954), in which the organization for the first time asked the Court to declare segregation in public schools to be unconstitutional. The Court heard arguments in the case in 1952, but the justices remained so sharply divided that they postponed the decision pending a rehearing the following year. They also asked the Justice Department for the views of the new Eisenhower administration on the subject (having received the outgoing Truman Justice Department's explicit support for overturning segregation). Then, in the summer of 1953, Chief Justice Frederick Moore Vinson, among those hesitant to reach a sweeping decision striking down segregation in thousands of schools, died unexpectedly, and President Dwight D. Eisenhower nominated Earl Warren to the seat. After intense internal discussions, the Eisenhower Justice Department issued an amicus brief that avoided taking a position on segregation—but, during the oral rehearing, the department's representative responded to a justice's question by siding with the NAACP's call for the Court to strike down school segregation. With explicit support for striking down racial segregation in public schools from both the old Truman administration and the new Eisenhower administration, Chief Justice Warren worked with great dedication to achieve a unanimous decision to that effect, and he famously succeeded. But, in order to achieve unanimity, Warren compromised on implementation of the decision, postponing the matter until after a rehearing on the question of enforcement. A year later, the Court issued its decision on enforcement. The case, *Brown II* (1955), ordered enforcement at "all deliberate speed," and left the matter of interpretation of this crucial, ambiguous criterion to lower federal court judges. In a series of very brief unsigned decisions over the next few years, the Court struck down state-mandated racial segregation in parks, recreation areas, and public transportation.

Many southern whites and much of the white political establishment in the South responded with shock to the *Brown* decision and shortly mounted a campaign of "massive resistance" against desegregation. Although schools (and other public facilities) began desegregating in border states and the North, for almost a decade after *Brown*, segregation remained virtually unchanged throughout the South.

The first organized actions of the civil rights movement shortly followed the *Brown* decision. In McAdam's view, the Supreme Court's decision in *Brown* provided a key indicator to African Americans that the federal government might indeed be open to fundamental change on civil rights and therefore that organized pressure might succeed. It is noteworthy that the first organized steps in the civil rights movement consisted of efforts by local NAACP chapters to enforce the Court's decision in *Brown*, a strategy that grew out of an NAACP meeting five days after the decision was announced. Within months of the *Brown II* decision, blacks in Montgomery, Alabama, started that city's famous bus boycott, generally credited as the first mass action of the civil rights movement. Martin Luther King, Jr., and his organization, the Southern Christian Leadership Conference (SCLC), quickly emerged as the national leader of the movement. By 1960, other groups, particularly the Student Nonviolent Coordinating Committee (SNCC), generated myriad locally focused civil rights actions, among them the famous lunch-counter sit-ins that spread rapidly throughout the South.

Both civil rights activity and violent resistance to it reached a searing pitch in 1963. SNCC mounted a number of actions in Birmingham, Alabama, and the police responded with dogs, spray from fire hoses, and the use of clubs. Other similar confrontations occurred elsewhere. President John F. Kennedy, in response, asked for passage of a federal civil rights statute. At the end of August 1963, several hundred thousand civil rights advocates participated in the bellwether event of the civil rights movement, the March on Washington, where Dr. Martin Luther King gave his celebrated "I Have a Dream" speech. The juxtaposition of the civil rights movement's democratic aspirations and their opponents' violent response crystallized sympathy for the movement among many northern voters. That fall President Kennedy was assassinated.

Under intense pressure for change from the public and President Johnson, Congress passed the Civil Rights Act of 1964, the most significant piece of civil rights legislation since Reconstruction. The act banned discrimination on the basis of race, color, sex, religion, and national origin in public accommodations (Title II), among them hotels, restaurants, bars, and recreational facilities, and in all aspects of employment (Title VII), particularly hiring, promotions, pay, and dismissal.

The following spring, King and the SCLC organized a march from Selma, Alabama, to Montgomery, the state capital, to protest the state's continuing denial of the right to vote for the vast majority of its black citizens. The marchers never made it out of Selma, as police mounted on horseback drove them back with clubs and tear gas. The spectacle of vote-seeking citizens beaten by police on horses brought streams of civil rights supporters to Selma, where they organized for another march. President Johnson called on Congress to pass new voting-rights legislation, and Congress shortly acted, adopting the Voting Rights Act of 1965. The act immediately banned throughout most of the South the remaining mechanisms used to keep blacks from the polls, among them literacy tests (which were discriminatorily applied) and poll taxes. The act also required the states covered by its provisions to seek pre-clearance from the Justice Department for any changes in state or local voting laws.

The Civil Rights Act of 1964 and the Voting Rights Act of 1965, themselves key pieces of the rights revolution, served further to forge an institutional link between that revolution and the federal courts. The Supreme Court quickly upheld broad interpretations of both acts against challenges that they were beyond the legitimate authority of Congress, thereby authorizing a significant expansion of Congress's authority to address racial discrimination.[17] The Supreme Court and federal courts generally, moreover, played key roles in enforcing the provisions of both acts. With regard to the Civil Rights Act of 1964, for instance, the Supreme Court's decision in *Griggs v. Duke Power District*

(1971) interpreted the act's ban on employment discrimination to cover not only intentional job discrimination but also practices that, whether intentionally or not, produce disparities in employment by race and sex.

In the wake of passage of Civil Rights Act and the Voting Rights Act, it was clear that all branches of the federal government had linked arms in support of the civil rights movement. In 1968, fourteen years after the *Brown* decision, the Supreme Court finally squarely addressed continuing southern efforts aimed at retaining racial segregation in the schools. Southern states, with their efforts to retain segregation by law under increasing attack, had turned to an old and well-used tactic to evade civil rights enforcement: they removed official support for racial segregation, leaving to parents the "freedom of choice" as to where their children would attend school. The approach echoed Texas's final effort to retain the white primary by leaving primary elections entirely in the "private" control of political party officials. Under Virginia's "school choice" plan, all white parents in New Kent County chose to send their children to the school formerly established by law as a white school, and most black parents sent their children to the school for black children. The NAACP–Legal Defense Fund (LDF) challenged Virginia's "school choice" law on the grounds that, in the context of social and economic pressures to retain racial segregation, it simply continued school segregation by other means. The Supreme Court, in *Green v. County School Board of New Kent County* (1968), agreed, demanding that state and local officials must engage in efforts to achieve racial integration in public schools. The decision led lower courts and school officials to turn toward school busing.

Legal Spin-offs from the Civil Rights Movement

Upon full development of the civil rights movement, the Supreme Court came to its aid in a number of significant ways, as historian Michal Belknap has observed, many of which produced landmark decisions that generated new directions for the rights revolution.[18] At the narrowest level, the Court acted to shield individual movement participants from routine criminal prosecutions for movement-related activities, in the process overturning scores of convictions of civil rights activists during the 1950s and 1960s.

When southern opponents of desegregation attacked the NAACP through criminal prosecutions, state bar association ethics investigations, and legislative investigations of communist ties, the Court consistently acted to shield the organization in a string of key decisions.[19] The Court's close support for the civil rights movement, moreover, generated a wide range of cases in other areas of the law, particularly regarding freedom of association and expression. *NAACP v. Alabama* (1958), rejecting an attempt by the state of Alabama to obtain the membership records of the state NAACP chapter, was the origin of modern law on freedom of association, a constitutional right that the Court expanded in the 1960s and 1970s.

Freedom of expression, according to many observers, is the quintessential American constitutional right. Without it, other rights are meaningless. In a number of cases arising from the civil rights movement, the Supreme Court significantly expanded protections for freedom of expression. Perhaps the most significant of the freedom of expression cases arising from the civil rights movement was the landmark decision in *New York Times v. Sullivan* (1964). The case grew out of an advertisement in the *New York Times* taken out by civil rights organizers alleging repressive actions by local officials in Montgomery, Alabama. Several inadvertent factual inaccuracies in the ad exposed the newspaper and those who paid for the ad to a lawsuit for libel for falsely damaging the reputation of the Montgomery officials. The Court's landmark decision protects critics of public officials from libel actions unless the criticism is deliberately false or made with reckless disregard for the truth. The right to criticize public officials without fear of being sued over inadvertent errors is now a bedrock principle of First Amendment law. Likewise, political demonstrations have become a standard feature of the American political landscape, and, as political scientist Lucas Powe observes, "virtually the entire law of mass demonstrations came from [the Warren Court's] civil rights [decisions]."[20]

In retrospect, it is increasingly clear that the Court's criminal procedure revolution, too, grew out of the broader context of the civil rights movement. By the early 1960s, civil rights organizers had long criticized state and local police officers for racially discriminatory practices and outright abuse. The Court had heard an increasing number of cases but, until 1961, had stopped short of bringing the broad range of state and local policing activities under federal judicial oversight, reasoning that they were matters assigned by the Constitution to state control. The Court began shifting decisively in favor of federal oversight with the case of *Monroe v. Pape* (1961), which revived Section 1983 of the Civil Rights Act of 1866, thereby allowing victims of local official misconduct to sue for civil damages in federal court. The case involved a black man who, along with his family, was subjected in the early morning hours in their home to a warrantless strip search, harassment, and physical abuse by Chicago police officers acting on a false tip that the man had committed a murder. In *Monell v. Department of Social Service* (1978), the Court held that municipalities may be liable for the actions of their employees, thereby creating an incentive for cities to ensure that employees do not violate citizens' rights. The Court's decisions in *Monroe* and *Monell* provided the key mechanism for redress still used today by plaintiffs alleging abuse by police and other officials.

In the same term, the Court began a revolution in criminal procedure in the case of *Mapp v. Ohio* (1961), ruling that evidence obtained by police illegally—that is, in violation of constitutional standards of due process—may not be used in court. The Court soon rapidly expanded constitutional rights to due process for criminal defendants in a broad range of cases. In the landmark decision

Gideon v. Wainwright (1963), the Court extended the principle established three decades earlier in the *Powell* case, holding that defendants charged with a felony must be provided with a defense lawyer if they cannot afford to hire one. The Court's criminal procedure revolution reached its fullest extent in *Miranda v. Arizona* (1966), where the Court held that the constitutional right against self-incrimination requires that any information obtained by police officers from a criminal suspect may not be used against him in court unless the officers had first notified the suspect of his constitutional right against self-incrimination and his right to an attorney, and unless the suspect waives those rights. In the 1980s, the Court chipped away at *Mapp*'s exclusionary rule but ultimately left it largely intact. In the1990s, critics of the *Miranda* rules mounted a growing campaign to reverse the decision but, in *Dickerson v. United States* (2000), by a 7–2 majority, the Court strongly reaffirmed its commitment to *Miranda*.

Near the height of the civil rights movement, organizers began developing a nascent welfare rights movement among the poor and attempted to gain judicial declarations of a fundamental right to welfare. They ultimately failed to achieve that broadest of goals but the cases they brought to the Supreme Court produced very significant new directions in the rights revolution that are still felt today. In *Shapiro v. Thompson* (1969), the Court struck down state laws requiring a minimum period of residency (typically of about a year) before a woman could receive welfare, on the grounds that such laws infringed on the fundamental right to travel. And in *Goldberg v. Kelly* (1970), the Court held that if welfare agencies intend to cut off benefits to a person, she must be given adequate notice of that intent and a chance to contest it in a hearing prior to the cut-off, on the grounds that welfare benefits constitute a property interest protected by the Constitution. The decision was soon extended to any "entitlement," understood as such benefits as a license or government job that, by statute, may not be rescinded except for good cause. The line of Supreme Court decisions begun by *Goldberg v. Kelly* thus generated the "due process revolution" in administrative procedure, which, for many Americans, remains among the most widely experienced features of the rights revolution.

The Women's Rights Movement

As the civil rights movement reached its peak, another new and surprising development, the women's rights movement, began to gather force. Its aspirations dated to demands of the nineteenth-century women's movement for an end to their exclusion from the economy and politics, and for greater freedom in matters of sexual privacy. In the late nineteenth century, after losing several key cases in the Supreme Court, the women's rights movement shifted its attention toward gaining a constitutional amendment assuring the right of suffrage. The movement eventually succeeded with the adoption of the Nineteenth Amendment in 1920.

Networks of women's rights supporters lingered in the United States for decades. But the first real steps toward the women's rights movement of the 1960s and 1970s emerged out of President Kennedy's establishment in 1961 of a federal Commission on the Status of Women. The Commission provided the focal point for an emerging network of professional women, and its research and 1963 report, *American Women*, which cataloged the wide range of laws and policies that excluded women from full participation in the economy and public life, served to catalyze a growing outrage among professional, politically active women. In 1963, Betty Friedan published the groundbeaking feminist book *The Feminine Mystique*. Then in 1964, at the height of debate over the Civil Rights Act of 1964, several members of Congress added the term "sex" to the forms of employment discrimination prohibited by Title VII of the act. Some have argued that the proposal was a "poison pill," an attempt by opponents of the landmark antidiscrimination legislation to erode support for the bill, while others have argued that, whatever its origins, the provision passed because of the lobbying and support of women's rights advocates. In any case, the provision's ambiguous origins allowed the first executive director of the Equal Employment Opportunity Commission, the agency charged with enforcing Title VII, to call the prohibition on sex discrimination a "fluke" that deserved no enforcement by the agency.

The EEOC's official intransigence, as political scientist Jo Freeman observed, provoked women's rights organizing. Some officials within the EEOC, favoring the ban on sex discrimination, believed that it might be given life if "some sort of NAACP for women" might emerge to put pressure on the agency to act. Their quiet behind-the-scenes work, in conjunction with organizing efforts by women drawn together by the Commission on the Status of Women, led to the formation in 1966 of the National Organization for Women, still the leading women's rights organization. At about the same time, younger women active in the civil rights and antiwar movement began drawing parallels between civil rights and a yet-to be-clearly articulated women's rights cause. As Freeman observed, "They were faced with the self-evident contradiction of working in a 'freedom movement' but not being very free."[21]

The two currents of the women's rights movement—the professional, politically active women who founded NOW and the younger radicals who formed the campus-based mass movement—soon found that their concerns resonated widely with many women. Indeed, the growing movement deluged Congress and the president with calls for legislation on women's rights. Undoubtedly the members of the Supreme Court were aware of the growing mass-based popularity of the feminist movement.

Similarly, by the late 1960s several sources of support specifically for women's rights litigation were emerging. In contrast to the dominant role played by the NAACP-LDF in civil rights litigation, the organizational support for women's rights litigation has been more diverse, consisting of several key organizations founded between 1965 and the early 1970s. Additionally, the ACLU-supported Women's Rights Project pursued early test-case litigation, in particular the case of *Reed v. Reed* (1971), which challenged an Idaho law that gave automatic preference to men over women as estate executors. In that case, the Supreme Court for the first time struck down a law that discriminated by sex. The ACLU, on the basis of that decision, inferred that the Court might be on the verge of greater sympathy for women's rights claims, and the organization therefore began to dedicate significant resources to women's rights litigation. In particular, the ACLU, with a contribution from John D. Rockefeller III, founded the Reproductive Freedom Project in 1974.

Similarly, funding for women's rights litigation grew significantly in the late 1960s. The most important source was foundation grants. The Ford Foundation was clearly the leader. In 1967, it made a policy commitment to funding reform efforts on behalf of disadvantaged minorities, and a significant proportion of the foundation's grants in this area went toward supporting litigation organizations. Other foundations contributing to women's rights organizations included the Rockefeller Foundation, the Carnegie Foundation, the Rockefeller Brothers Fund, the Field Foundation, the Edna McConnell Clark Foundation, the Kellogg Foundation, and the New York Foundation.

The growing number of lawyers who are women also provided a key foundation of support for women's rights litigation. After 1965, the number of women entering the legal profession began to grow exponentially and, by the mid-1970s, women had become a primary source of the very rapid growth in the number of lawyers. The growing gender diversity of the legal profession significantly contributed to the emergence of women's rights cases in the Supreme Court. Early women's rights lawyers expressed frustration that their male counterparts had little interest in women's rights. To fill the void, women lawyers pushed a number of the early landmark women's rights cases that reached the Supreme Court, among them *Reed v. Reed* and *Roe v. Wade* (1973). For instance, Ruth Bader Ginsburg, appointed to the Supreme Court in 1993, directed the ACLU's Women's Rights Project in the 1970s and, beginning with *Reed*, argued many of the sex-discrimination cases that reached the Court in that decade.

In the context of widely growing support for women's rights in the 1970s, the Supreme Court took up the issue and dramatically transformed American law. In *Reed* (1971), as noted, the Court indicated that it might consider striking down sex discrimination in state laws, and, in *Craig v. Boren* (1976), the Court announced that it would indeed subject sex discrimination in law to "heightened scrutiny." Although the decision disappointed many women's rights advocates who had hoped that the Court would subject sex discrimination to the demanding "strict scrutiny" that applied to race discrimination, the Court's subsequent decisions, with a few notable exceptions, have struck down most forms of explicit sex discrimination. The Court's sex discrimination decisions contributed to the broad and relatively rapid eradication of explicit discrimination on the basis of sex in the nation's laws and policies.

Among the areas of the law in which the Court has been least willing to challenge sex discrimination is military service. In 1979, the Court upheld state laws that gave a preference to military veterans for civil service jobs even though it was clear that such laws aided men more than women, and, in *Rostker v. Goldberg* (1981), the Court upheld Congress's decision to require only men to register for the military draft. Because of the Court's reticence in matters of military service, the 1996 decision in *United States v. Virginia*, striking down the Virginia Military Institute's long-standing prohibition on female enrollment, was especially significant. Although the Court, in an opinion by Justice Ginsburg, the former women's rights lawyer, still declined to endorse strict scrutiny of sex discrimination, the characterization of heightened scrutiny in the opinion came to sound much like a nearly absolute constitutionally based ban on sex discrimination.

The Court has interpreted statutory prohibitions on sex discrimination, particularly those found in the Civil Rights Act of 1964, equally expansively. Beginning in the late 1970s, for instance, women's-rights advocates began arguing that the 1964 act's ban on sex discrimination in employment should be understood as prohibiting sexual harassment at work. The concept of sexual harassment encompasses a range of discriminatory actions, among them both unwanted sexual advances and hostility aimed at driving women from previously male-dominated jobs. Beginning in 1980, the EEOC endorsed the concept of sexual harassment in a policy interpretation that, although significant, lacked formal legal authority. In a series of landmark decisions beginning in 1986, particularly *Meritor Savings Bank v. Vinson* (1986), the Supreme Court subsequently agreed that the Civil Rights Act of 1964's ban on sex discrimination in employment includes a prohibition on sexual harassment.

Additionally, by the mid-1960s the women's rights movement picked up an old women's rights goal and strongly pressed for greater legal rights for freedom of choice in the area of birth control. Advocates of greater availability for birth control methods had suffered criminal prosecution for many decades in the late nineteenth and early twentieth centuries, and some were prosecuted as late as the early 1960s. In 1965 the Supreme Court, after declining to hear to such laws for several decades, decided the landmark case *Griswold v. Connecticut*, striking down, as a violation of the fundamental right of privacy of married couples, a Connecticut law that had prohibited the sale of birth control products and the provision of information about birth control. Under intense pressure to extend the privacy right beyond married couples, the Court did so in *Eisenstadt v. Baird* (1972), guaranteeing access to birth control by unmarried persons as well. In 1973, in the midst of a growing movement that had succeeded in getting a number of states to adopt laws legalizing abortion, the Court decided *Roe v. Wade*, extending the right to privacy to include a fundamental right to choose an abortion during the first two-thirds of the period of pregnancy. *Roe* provoked a firestorm of controversy, ultimately becoming the symbol used to mobilize a broad conservative movement that has greatly affected American politics. In a surprise to many, the Court, in the landmark decision *Planned Parenthood v. Casey* (1992) reaffirmed its commitment to constitutional protection for the right to an abortion.

Even as the conservative Supreme Court of the late twentieth and early twenty-first century has reaffirmed many of the central elements of the rights revolution, it has increasingly taken up cases generated by the growing conservative legal movement. That movement, as political scientist Steven Teles has shown, has emulated the civil rights movement's model of developing organizational and financial support for long-term rights litigation strategies.[22] In recent years, the Court has taken up a number of the conservative movement's key cases, among them challenges to affirmative action in university admissions and challenges to governmental power to take private property (provided compensation is paid) for public purposes. As yet the Court has not provided the conservative legal movement with the resounding support it offered to the civil rights movement in the 1960s.

The Court's Contribution to the Rights Revolution and Its Limits

The Supreme Court undoubtedly contributed directly and indirectly to the rights revolution. For one thing, the Court at one time or another (often after significant delays) favored many of the general goals sought by the era's main social movements and rights-advocacy organizations. With regard to civil rights, the Court supported sweeping changes in the law in such areas as racial segregation in public schools and real estate transactions; federal oversight of state and local policing and criminal trials; freedom of expression and association, particularly related to civil rights organizing; and administrative due process. The Court also endorsed and broadly interpreted congressional civil rights statutes, particularly the Civil Rights Act of 1964 and the Voting Rights Act of 1965. With regard to women's rights, the Court again supported broad legal change by striking down as unconstitutional most forms of sex discrimination in government law and policy, by providing broad interpretations of key provisions of the Civil Rights Act of 1964, and by supporting the women's rights movement's key requests with regard to access to birth control and abortion. In the wake of these movements, the Court's rights jurisprudence spilled over into many other areas of the law, particularly freedom of expression and association and freedom from official establishment of religion.

The Court made equally significant contributions to the rights revolution in a series of less prominent decisions that expanded the remedies available to victims of rights-violations. Many of the Court's key decisions on remedies have worked not only to provide victims of rights-violations with remedies but also to provide mechanisms aimed at generating lasting policy reform of the sources of rights violations. The lasting significance of the Court's decision in *Monroe v. Pape* is that victims of rights violations by local governments may sue in federal court for financial compensation, and subsequent cases made governments, under some circumstances, liable for violations of rights carried out by their employees. Those decisions provided the opportunity both for compensation for victims and incentives for reform by local governments. In similar fashion, in *Brown* the Court endorsed the use of equitable injunctions by federal district courts as a means for requiring institutional reforms in schools. After federal district courts, following the school desegregation model, began using the power of judicial injunctions in the late 1960s to take over and reform state prisons, the Court essentially endorsed the practice in several decisions in the 1970s. Similarly, on the heels of a growing administrative-reform movement pursuing the theory that individual rights within modern bureaucratic organizations are best protected via the adoption of finely tuned organizational policies and rules, the Court endorsed that view in a series of decisions, among them *Tennessee v. Garner* (1985) and *Faragher v. City of Boca Raton (1998).*

The Court's remedial decisions have contributed to a key consequence and expression of the rights revolution, the proliferation of rights-based policies and rules in government settings and the workplace more broadly. Governmental bodies and most major employers, for instance, have adopted employment policies mandating equal employment opportunity in hiring, promotions, and discipline. Although these employment policies are based ultimately on the language of Title VII of the Civil Rights Act of 1964, which prohibits employment discrimination on the basis of race, sex, and other personal characteristics, their more direct impetus was the perceived need to develop some sort of good-faith evidence of compliance in order to fend off possible discrimination lawsuits. Once the courts had endorsed such organizational policies, they spread rapidly throughout the American workplace. The model set by equal opportunity policies is now widely followed in other areas of rights policy. Following the Supreme Court's endorsement of employment policies prohibiting sexual harassment, for instance, virtually all major employers have adopted such policies. Such a policy or rule-based approach is now common in many specialized policy fields too. In policing, for instance, the favored approach to the lingering problem of excessive use of force is the adoption of finely tuned rules banning improper uses of force. In many work settings, additionally, such rule-based approaches are supplemented by formal training and discipline of employees. Undoubtedly the apparently cascading growth of rights policies, rules, training, and discipline contributes to the sense that courts have intervened in many areas of American life.

Although there is little doubt that the rights revolution transformed American law and, with it, many aspects of American society, the transformation has been limited in several important respects, both at particular points in time and in its ultimate development. For one, national security crises have provided the conditions both for sharp restrictions on civil rights and liberties and for significant advances in their protection. The path marked by the courts—toward rights restrictions or greater protection—has varied considerably, in part in relation to the level of support for key rights provided by groups outside the courts.

In the wake of World War I, the country yielded to a "red scare," as the Wilson administration hunted down and deported thousands of politically radical immigrants. In the midst of the crackdown, the Supreme Court handed down a series of landmark decisions upholding the criminal prosecutions and prison sentences of radicals who, among other things, had merely opposed the war or distributed leaflets on city streets. The American Civil Liberties Union was born in the crisis and several leading scholars soon developed a stirring defense of freedom of speech. Justice Oliver Wendell Holmes soon joined the new defenders of civil liberties by writing a strong dissent from a Supreme Court decision (*Abrams v. United States* [1919]) that upheld the prosecution and long federal prison sentence of several men for leafleting on New York City streets. The efforts of Holmes and Justice Louis Brandeis to preserve civil rights and liberties in the red scare climate eventually formed the basis for constitutional protections of civil liberties.

Another occasion of the tension between security and liberty arose during World War II. Prior to U.S. entry into the war, the Court had upheld the expulsion of a Jehovah's Witness child from public school for declining to participate in a mandatory flag salute. But at the height of World War II three years later, in response to widespread vigilante attacks on Jehovah's Witnesses in part for their unwillingness to salute the flag, leading scholars and public groups ranging from the ACLU to the American Legion supported making the flag salute voluntary at the federal level. The Court responded in a new flag salute case by reversing its prior decision, holding that compulsory flag salute laws at either the state or federal level violate freedom of speech. In a ringing decision, Justice Robert Jackson wrote for the Court, "the very purpose of a Bill of Rights was to withdraw certain subjects from the vicissitudes of political controversy, to place them beyond the reach of majorities and officials and to establish them as legal principles to be applied by the courts." He continued, "If there is any fixed star in our constitutional constellation, it is that no official, high or petty, can prescribe what shall be orthodox in politics, nationalism, religion, or other matters of opinion or force citizens to confess by word or act their faith therein."[23] The decision stands as perhaps the clearest judicial statement of the value of judicial protection for civil rights and liberties even in wartime. Yet a year and a half later, over a blistering dissent by three of its justices, the Court in *Korematsu v. United States* (1944) infamously upheld the wartime confinement of Japanese-American citizens in internment camps.

In the early twenty-first-century context, as the "war on terror" and the Iraqi conflict continue, it is clear that civil rights and liberties face new challenges, particularly with governmental efforts to increase secrecy and reduce or eliminate judicial oversight of investigations and detentions. In the wake of the terrorist attacks within the United States on September 11, 2001, the Bush administration claimed broad powers to order the unlimited, unchecked detention of persons alleged to be enemy combatants. Several U.S. citizens were so held, and hundreds of foreigners were held in a U.S. military installation at Guantánamo Bay, Cuba, without the benefit of communication with attorneys and without a chance to challenge the validity of their detention in court. In the spring of 2004, many Americans and much of the world watched in shock as photographs came to light of grotesque abuse by U.S. guards of military prisoners in the Abu Ghraib prison in Iraq. As the scandal escalated prominent public figures in the United States and throughout the world came forward to repudiate the use of torture and to defend basic due process rights even for persons held as enemy combatants during wartime. In the midst of the furor, the Supreme Court issued a pair of landmark rulings in June of 2004, holding that both U.S. citizens and foreigners held as enemy combatants have certain due process rights to contest before a neutral tribunal regarding the validity of their detention. "A state of war," declared Justice Sandra Day O'Connor for the Court in *Hamdi v. Rumsfeld* (2004), "is not a blank check for the president when it comes to the rights of the nation's citizens." She continued, "It is during our most challenging and uncertain moments that our nation's commitment to due process is most severely tested; and it is in those times that we must preserve our commitment at home to the principles for which we fight abroad."[24] In the second decision, dealing with the rights of non-U.S. citizens held as enemy combatants, Justice John Paul Stevens, writing for the Court, quoted a cold war–era Supreme Court decision affirming the right of aliens to challenge the legality of their detention within U.S. jurisdictions: "Executive imprisonment has been considered oppressive and lawless since John, at Runnymede, pledged that no free man should be imprisoned, dispossessed, outlawed, or exiled save by the judgment of his peers or by the law of the land."[25] At the least, the Court's 2004 landmark decisions reaffirm the basic, traditional right to a judicial test, or, for noncitizens, a hearing before some sort of neutral tribunal, of the legality of detention. A host of other civil liberties and civil rights issues implicated in national security measures await court decision in the coming years, and it remains to be seen whether the courts, as they have done in some past wars, will continue to protect individual liberties or, as they have done in other contexts, will facilitate the erosion of individual liberties.

If national security has provided one challenge to judicial support for civil rights and liberties, another challenge has been posed by poverty and related ills.

Civil rights and liberties in the United States are, for the most part, "self-help" promissory notes, in the sense that if an individual's rights have been violated, there will be no enforcement of the right unless the aggrieved individual takes action to make it so. Attempting to invoke or enforce a right commonly requires the assistance of a lawyer, which can be very costly. Naturally, poverty is thus a powerful impediment to invoking or enforcing civil rights and liberties, and it is widely observed that the poor therefore commonly lack access to legal justice. Exercising and protecting one's civil rights and liberties, in other words, too often requires a degree of personal wealth.

As the Supreme Court became increasingly conservative after 1968, it halted several emerging developments in the law, siding with those who wished to keep the new rights from going "too far," particularly with regard to growing demands to lower the financial barriers to the exercise of civil rights and liberties. During the height of the rights revolution, as we have seen, a growing "welfare rights" movement developed and increasingly pressed the Court to create rights protecting the poor from certain disadvantages in public programs—and the Court at first appeared to be heading in that direction. In 1966 the Court struck down poll taxes as an unconstitutional infringement on the right of the poor to vote and, in 1969, it struck down state laws requiring a period of residency before a person could qualify for welfare benefits, on the grounds that such laws placed an unconstitutionally discriminatory burden on the fundamental right to travel. Such cases left open whether the Court would invalidate laws that deprived poor people of rights or privileges that were not constitutionally fundamental. The next year, in *Dandridge v. Williams* (1970), the Court blocked that path, ruling that poverty, unlike race, was not a "suspect classification" and, therefore, that a state law providing smaller increases in welfare benefits with each additional child, and no additional benefits after the fourth, was constitutionally acceptable. The welfare rights movement, with its hopes dashed by the Court, collapsed.

The Court majority has subsequently never wavered from the view that laws that handicap the poor more than others are constitutionally acceptable (unless they hinder the exercise of some fundamental rights). In one of the first and still the most significant such subsequent decisions, *San Antonio Independent School District v. Rodriguez* (1973), the Court narrowly rejected an argument that education is a fundamental constitutional right; therefore, the majority concluded, state policies that finance education primarily on the basis of local property taxes do not unacceptably discriminate on the basis of disparities in income or wealth, even if those disparities produce profoundly troubling differences in the funding and quality of public schools. Similarly, even though the Court has consistently maintained the position that the right of a woman to choose to have an abortion is constitutionally fundamental, a narrow Court majority in *Harris v. McRae* (1980) upheld the federal Hyde Amendment, which bars the use of federal

Medicaid funds for abortions for poor women. The Court has consistently held, however, that some fundamental rights are so important that government must, in effect, subsidize use by the poor. As has been shown, government may not prosecute and convict defendants of serious crimes unless they either can afford their own lawyer or be provided one by the state. Similarly, states may not demand filing fees as a condition for gaining a divorce, or place financial obstacles in the path of those seeking to marry, if they are too poor to meet such expenses.

In the area of racial segregation in public schools, in *Milliken v. Bradley* (1974) the Supreme Court decisively drew a line blocking lower courts from ordering bussing of school children across school district lines. Such cross-boundary bussing remedies were developed by frustrated desegregation advocates attempting to respond to "white flight" into the suburbs. The Court's decision contributed to the rapid expansion of generally white suburbs around old urban core cities in such metropolitan areas as Detroit, Kansas City, St. Louis, and Atlanta, and contributed to the depth of already great disparities in public school financing.

Even as the Court became more conservative, however, it retained a surprisingly lasting commitment to many of the core elements of the rights revolution, even extending them in some key ways. In 1992, in the midst of a prominent campaign to reverse *Roe v. Wade*, as noted, the Court reaffirmed the constitutional right to an abortion. In 2000, in the midst of a similar campaign to reverse *Miranda v. Arizona*, the Court strongly reaffirmed its commitment to that key decision of the criminal procedure revolution. In a number of decisions, particularly the well-known flag-burning cases, the Court continues to lend strong support to a robust right to freedom of expression.

In the end, perhaps the most significant limits to the rights revolution are to be found in pervasive economic disparities in American society. African American family incomes lag significantly behind white family incomes, and these inequalities have actually increased, rather than decreased, in the last several decades.[26] Even more troublingly, the gap in wealth, or total assets, between white and black families is dramatically wider than the income gap: the assets of the median white family are more than *seven times* those of the median black family, and the disparity remains very wide even when comparing families with similar incomes.[27] To some extent such disparities undoubtedly reflect continuing racial discrimination that persists despite the rights revolution. A growing body of very careful research finds persistent racial discrimination in a number of areas of the economy, particularly housing markets, auto sales, and employment.[28] Yet it is also clear that, even in the absence of racial discrimination, inequalities in wealth would cascade down through the generations, perpetuating a troublingly deep economic divide between the races. The persistence of economic inequality and outright discrimination is increasingly reflected in public opinion polls and other indicators of popular attitudes. As political scientist Jennifer Hochschild has observed, while the vast majority of whites believe that the nation has largely done away with racial discrimination, many African Americans disagree and increasingly doubt that the "American dream"—economic prosperity based on hard work—is truly open to them.[29]

If the rights revolution reflected an aspiration by African Americans and women for equal dignity and respect in the democratic polity and the economy, in sum, that aspiration has been only partly met. In the second half of the twentieth century, it swept surprisingly rapidly and thoroughly through the realm of law in court decisions, statutes, ordinances, and administrative regulations. Yet the aspiration remains only partly fulfilled in the life circumstances of many Americans.

Notes

1. Quoted in Samuel Walker, *The Rights Revolution: Rights and Community in Modern America* (New York: Oxford University Press, 1998). This essay benefits from Walker's analysis.
2. Quoted in Jules Lobel, *Success Without Victory: Lost Legal Battles and the Long Road to Justice in America* (New York: New York University Press, 2003), 122.
3. Michael W. McCann, *Rights at Work: Pay Equity Reform and the Politics of Legal Mobilization* (Chicago: University of Chicago Press, 1994).
4. The Margold Report, quoted in Lobel, *Success without Victory*, 119.
5. Gerald L. Rosenberg, *The Hollow Hope: Can Courts Bring about Social Change?* (Chicago: University of Chicago Press, 1991). Michael J. Klarman, *From Jim Crow to Civil Rights: The Supreme Court and the Struggle for Racial Equality* (New York: Oxford University Press, 2004).
6. H.W. Perry, Jr. *Deciding to Decide: Agenda Setting in the United States Supreme Court.* (Cambridge, Mass.: Harvard University Press, 1991), 218.
7. Eric Foner, "Rights and the Constitution in Black Life during the Civil War and Reconstruction," *Journal of American History* 74 (1987), 863–883, at 863.
8. Ellen Carol DuBois, "Outgrowing the Compact of the Fathers: Equal Rights, Woman Suffrage, and the United States Constitution, 1820–1878," *Journal of American History* 74 (1987), 836–862, at 844–847.
9. *Slaughter-House Cases* 83 U.S. 36 (1873).
10. Hendrik Hartog, "The Constitution of Aspiration and 'The Rights That Belong to Us All,'" *Journal of American History* 74 (1995), 1013–1034, at 1014–1015. A classic analysis of the Fourteenth Amendment and the development of an ideology of civil rights.
11. Doug McAdam, *Political Process and the Development of Black Insurgency, 1930–1970* (Chicago: University of Chicago Press, 1982).
12. The discussion of civil rights in the Roosevelt and Truman administrations is indebted to Kevin J. McMahon, *Reconsidering Roosevelt on Race: How the Presidency Paved the Road to Brown* (Chicago: University of Chicago Press, 2004).

13. Mark Tushnet, *The NAACP's Legal Strategy against Segregated Education, 1925–1950* (Chapel Hill: University of North Carolina Press, 1987), 17. See also McAdam, *Political Process*, 83–85.
14. Mary L. Dudziak, *Cold War Civil Rights: Race and the Image of American Democracy* (Princeton, N.J.: Princeton University Press, 2000).
15. McMahon, *Reconsidering Roosevelt on Race*, 188.
16. Quoted in McMahon, *Reconsidering Roosevelt on Race*, 188.
17. With regard to the Civil Rights Act of 1964, the key decisions were *Heart of Atlanta Motel, Inc. v. United States* (379 U.S. 241 [1964]) and *Katzenbach v. McClung* (379 U.S. 294 [1964]); On the Voting Rights Act of 1965, the key decision was *South Carolina v. Katzenbach* 383 U.S. 301 (1965).
18. See Michal R. Belknap, "The Warren Court and Equality," in Sandra Van Burkleo, Kermit L. Hall, and Robert Kaczorowski, eds., *Constitutionalism and American Culture: Writing the New Constitutional History* (Lawrence: University Press of Kansas, 2002).
19. *NAACP v. Alabama, ex rel. Paterson* 357 U.S. 449 (1958), *NAACP v. Alabama,* 360 U.S. 240 (1959), *NAACP v. Gallion* 368 U.S. 16 (1961), *NAACP v. Button* 371 U.S. 415 (1963).
20. Quoted in Belknap, *Constitutionalism and American Culture*, 225.
21. Jo Freeman, *The Politics of Women's Liberation: A Case Study of an Emerging Social Movement and Its Relation to the Policy Process* (New York: McKay, 1975), 57.
22. Steven Teles, *Parallel Paths: The Evolution of the Conservative Legal Movement* (Princeton, N.J.: Princeton University Press), forthcoming.
23. *West Virginia Board of Education vs. Barnette* 319 U.S. 624 (1943).
24. *Hamdi v. Rumsfeld* 124 S. Ct. 2633 (2004).
25. *Rasul v. Bush* 124 S. Ct. 2686 (2004).
26. See, for example, Sheldon Danziger and Peter Gottschalk, *America Unequal* (New York: Russell Sage Foundation, and Cambridge, Mass.: Harvard University Press, 1995).
27. Dalton Conley, *Being Black, Living in the Red: Race, Wealth, and Social Policy in America* (Berkeley: University of California Press, 1999), 1.
28. See, for example, Ian Ayres, *Pervasive Prejudice? Unconventional Evidence of Race and Gender Discrimination* (Chicago: University of Chicago Press, 2001).
29. Jennifer L. Hochschild, *Facing Up to the American Dream* (Princeton, N.J.: Princeton University Press, 1995).

Bibliography

Belknap, Michal R. "The Warren Court and Equality." In *Constitutionalism and American Culture: Writing the New Constitutional History*, edited by Sandra VanBurkleo, Kermit L. Hall, and Robert Kaczorowski. Lawrence: University Press of Kansas, 2002. An excellent summary of the Warren Court's contribution to civil rights.

Davis, Martha F. *Brutal Need: Lawyers and the Welfare Rights Movement, 1960–1973.* New Haven, Conn.: Yale University Press, 1993. An examination of the rise and collapse of the welfare rights movement, a key example of a movement modeled on the civil rights movement, but whose central goals were rejected by the Supreme Court.

Dudziak, Mary. *Cold War Civil Rights: Race and the Image of American Democracy.* Princeton, N.J.: Princeton University Press, 2000. The leading study of the role of the Cold War and international pressure as contributions to U.S. civil rights policy.

Epp, Charles R. *The Rights Revolution: Lawyers, Activists, and Supreme Courts in Comparative Perspective.* Chicago: University of Chicago Press, 1998. A broad comparison of rights revolutions in the United States, Britain, Canada, and India.

McAdam, Doug. *Political Process and the Development of Black Insurgency, 1930–1970.* Chicago: University of Chicago Press, 1982. The leading analysis of the origins and development of the civil rights movement.

McCann, Michael. *Rights at Work: Pay Equity Reform and the Politics of Legal Mobilization.* Chicago: University of Chicago Press, 1994. A key study of the use of rights in generating popular support for a social movement.

McMahon, Kevin J. *Reconsidering Roosevelt on Race: How the Presidency Paved the Road to Brown.* Chicago: University of Chicago Press, 2004. An examination of the politics of civil rights during the Franklin Roosevelt administration.

Patterson, Orlando. *Freedom, Vol. 1: Freedom in the Making of Western Culture.* New York: Basic Books. 1991. A classic analysis of the link between slavery and the concept of freedom in western thought.

Rosenberg, Gerald N. *The Hollow Hope: Can Courts Bring about Social Change?* Chicago: University of Chicago Press, 1991. A leading critique of the view that Supreme Court decisions can enforce policy change against determined resistance.

Teles, Steven. *Parallel Paths: The Evolution of the Conservative Legal Movement.* Princeton, N.J.: Princeton University Press, forthcoming. The first comprehensive analysis of the conservative legal movement.

Tushnet, Mark V. *The NAACP's Legal Strategy against Segregated Education, 1925–1950.* Chapel Hill: University of North Carolina Press, 1987. An important analysis of the National Association for the Advancement of Colored People (NAACP) and its long-term legal strategy to overturn racial segregation.

Walker, Samuel. *The Rights Revolution: Rights and Community in Modern America.* New York: Oxford University Press, 1998. A very readable introduction to the main developments in the American rights revolution, and a lively defense of the key rights against their critics.

14

DISCRIMINATION THROUGH DIRECT DEMOCRACY: THE ROLE OF THE JUDICIARY IN THE PURSUIT OF EQUALITY

Sue Davis

Democracy . . . means voluntary choice, based on an intelligence that is the outcome of free association and communication with others. It means a way of living together in which mutual and free consultation rule instead of force, and in which cooperation instead of brutal competition is the law of life; a social order in which all the forces that make for friendship, beauty, and knowledge are cherished in order that each individual may become what he and he alone, is capable of becoming.

John Dewey

Majoritarianism is a tribute to the failure of democracy: to our inability to create a politics of mutualism that can overcome private interests. It is thus finally the democracy of desperation, an attempt to salvage decision-making from the anarchy of adversary politics.

Benjamin Barber

THIS CHAPTER EXAMINES THE ROLE OF THE JUDICIARY IN promoting equality in a democratic society. The starting point is that the preoccupation with what Alexander M. Bickel termed the countermajoritarian difficulty is misplaced. Indeed, the role that the judiciary has played in checking the power of majority will is fully consistent with the type of representative government that the Framers of the Constitution envisioned; more important for present purposes, judicial review is in accord with the goals of those who maintain that the United States should aspire to be a more democratic society. In order to support this argument I examine the role of judicial review in one particular context: the use of the initiative process as it played out in California and Colorado in two instances in the 1990s.

Introduction: The Myth of the Countermajoritarian Difficulty

It may seem that if the goal is to promote democracy, policies made directly by the voters should merit more judicial deference than those made by legislatures. Voter-made laws, it is commonly assumed, come directly from the people and reflect their will more accurately than legislatures can hope to do. In other words, judicial review of policies made through direct democracy intensifies the countermajoritarian difficulty. I argue, however, that legislation made by the electorate commonly does not reflect anything that can be characterized as the will of the people. Moreover, such laws often reflect prejudice or animus toward a particular group that is disfavored in the political process. Consequently, when called upon to review such policies courts should give them a particularly careful look. In so doing, the judiciary does not obstruct the democratic process, but instead, functions to encourage democratic decision making as well as to promote the goal of equality. Legislative policymaking shares many of the problems of lawmaking by the electorate. There is much room for disagreement concerning which of the two is less democratic and which is more flawed. I do not attempt to resolve such issues here but rather focus solely on the ways in which judicial review of voter-made policy can contribute to, rather than detract from, the goals of establishing a more democratic society.

In *The Least Dangerous Branch: The Supreme Court at the Bar of Politics*, which he published in 1962, Bickel argued that the fundamental problem with judicial review is that it is a countermajoritarian force—a deviant institution in American democracy. There are at least two types of responses to that charge. The first is normative and forms the central concern of this chapter. The other, more empirically based argument warrants brief explanation as it too plays a role in the discussion that follows. A consideration of the meaning of democracy and the purpose of the Constitution readily casts doubt on the credibility of the countermajoritarian difficulty. The argument that when courts invalidate policies made by elected officials they violate fundamental principles of democratic governance loses much of its force once we take into account that decisions made by legislatures can, at best, only hope to approximate the will of the people. Moreover, democracy is not the equivalent of nor is it always consistent with majority rule. Indeed, the specter of an unreasonable or tyrannical majority poses an unceasing threat to democratic society. Democracy, moreover, is not inconsistent with equality. On the contrary, equality is a prerequisite for democracy. As democratic theorists have long maintained, without the equality that makes meaningful participation possible in the decisions that affect peoples' lives, democracy remains an unattainable ideal.

The United States Constitution, moreover, includes structural features, including the separation of powers, checks and balances, and federalism, that limit the power of majorities in the interest of protecting liberty and the rights of individuals. The power bestowed on the judiciary in Article III of the Constitution furthers the same goal of checking the powers of government while the Bill of Rights and subsequent amendments provide additional constraints on the power of government to interfere with individual rights. In short, the Constitution's overall goal is to protect the liberty of the people and the judiciary bears much of the responsibility for furthering that goal. Thus, the aspiration or end of the Constitution is to protect rights against the will of majorities in a way that promotes and protects democracy while judicial review is the mechanism for furthering that end.

Defenders of judicial review have often underlined the distinction between democracy and republicanism to point out that the Framers of the Constitution were determined to insulate government from the will of majorities—which James Madison feared would result in factions acting in a way that would be destructive to the long-term interests of the nation—by providing for government by wise representatives who would filter the passions of the ordinary voter. It is, therefore, easier to square judicial review with a republican form of government than with democracy. While such a distinction is useful in understanding the political ideas of the Founders, my attempt to dispel the myth of the countermajoritarian difficulty takes a different course, relying not on a conception of original intent but rather on the aspirational view of the Constitution as a set of principles that embrace democracy. The type of democracy to which the nation should aspire is one in which all members of the community have a genuine opportunity to participate in a meaningful way in the decisions that affect their lives. Thus, democracy encompasses rights, liberties, and equality, and also political participation, information, and deliberation. Accordingly, guarantees of participation and fairness are needed to ensure that checks on majoritarian preferences are democratic rather than elitist.

For many years jurists and scholars have pointed to the crucial role that the judiciary plays in protecting the rights of individuals from the results of the majoritarian political process. For example, Justice Louis Brandeis wrote in 1927 that judicial review is an important means of protecting against the "occasional tyrannies of governing majorities."[1] In 1940, Justice Hugo Black declared that courts function as "havens of refuge for those who might otherwise suffer because they are helpless, weak, outnumbered, or because they are nonconforming victims of prejudice and public excitement."[2] Justice Robert Jackson pointed out that, "the very purpose of a Bill of Rights was to withdraw certain subjects from the vicissitudes of political controversy, to place them beyond the reach of majorities."[3] Law professor Kenneth Karst noted that, "courts restrain the majority's worst excesses, in the name of the constitutional values that define our national community."[4]

The perspective that such comments reflect coincides with Justice Harlan Fiske Stone's *Carolene Products* Footnote in 1938, which provided the foundation for the Court's adoption of an active role in protecting the rights of individuals rather than the economic rights of business and industry that had earlier been the Court's primary concern. In his famous Footnote 4 Stone noted that the traditional "presumption of constitutionality" of challenged policies should not apply in situations where challenged legislation is within a specific prohibition of the Constitution, where legislation restricts "those political processes which can ordinarily be expected to bring about repeal of undesirable legislation," and where legislation is based on "prejudice against discrete and insular minorities." The *Carolene Products* Footnote not only signaled the Court's new interest in protecting individual rights but also suggested that the justices would be willing to take an active role in reinforcing principles of political equality by invalidating policies that interfered with the democratic process. Thus, judicial review would serve to promote democracy by promoting the value of (at least, political) equality.

A second, more empirical, approach to dispelling the myth of the countermajoritarian difficulty is grounded in the assertion that Robert Dahl made in 1957. He argued that lawmaking majorities have generally had their way; the Court has rarely been successful in blocking the will of such a majority on an important policy issue.[5] More recently, scholars have used Dahl's defense of judicial review to support the claim that the judiciary lacks the capacity to function as a countermajoritarian force. Michael J. Klarman has described the decisions of the Supreme Court as congruent and dependent upon the broad sweep of historical forces. Indeed, by his account the courts lack the capacity to play a heroic countermajoritarian role as protectors of individual liberties. The countermajoritarian difficulty ceases to exist because the judiciary's decisions are not countermajoritarian but rather a product of a variety of factors in the political system. Most frequently the Court takes a national consensus and imposes it on some relatively isolated outliers, and only infrequently does the Court resolve a genuinely divisive issue that tears the nation in half. Even then, roughly half the country supports the result.

Others have defended the role of judicial review against the countermajoritarian charge while at the same time they have disputed the argument that courts lack the capacity to protect individual rights. Mark A. Graber, for example, pointed out that the Court has most often exercised its power to declare both state and national policies unconstitutional when the dominant forces in the elected branches are unable or unwilling to settle some dispute. Elected officials, under such circumstances, "encourage or tacitly support judicial policymaking both as a means of avoiding political responsibility for making tough decisions and as a means of pursuing controversial policy goals that they cannot publicly advance through open legislative and electoral politics."[6] Thus, the conflict is generally not between the Court and the elected branches, he argues, but between different members of the dominant national coalition or between law-making majorities of different institutions. In this view, courts are most powerful when, "the dominant national coalition is unable or unwilling to settle some public dispute." Consequently, the judiciary, far from acting in a countermajoritarian way, supplements the working of the political process by stepping in to resolve conflicts when elected officials do not.

Scholars have also pointed to the constitutional interpretive dialogue between all three branches of government as a means of disputing the counter-majoritarian problem. In this account the premises of the countermajoritarian difficulty are faulty insofar as the judiciary is no less majoritarian than the political branches. Courts do not function in opposition to elected officials but rather as vital participants in the ongoing dialogue concerning the meaning of the Constitution. Courts in, short, are invariably participants in American political life—"a vital functioning part of political discourse, not some bastard child standing aloof from legitimate political dialogue."[7]

In the pages that follow I examine the relationship between majority decision-making and judicial review in the context of the initiative, the mechanism that one-half of the states and numerous municipal governments use to allow lawmaking by the electorate. With this form of policymaking the laws arguably reflect the popular will and are, therefore, more legitimate—because they are the product of a more democratic process—than laws made by their representatives. Consequently, it may seem at first glance that when they are called upon to hear constitutional challenges to such laws courts should be particularly deferential because such laws reflect the closest possible approximation to democratic decision-making. Closer analysis, however, reveals that the judiciary's role is even more crucial in the context of lawmaking by the electorate because that process is marred by organized campaigns that distort and manipulate public opinion to subvert rather than promote principles of democracy. After examining the theoretical argument concerning the role of judicial review to check the results of direct democracy, I turn to an examination of two voter-enacted legal provisions: California's Proposition 187, which would have excluded undocumented immigrants from public services, including health care, social services, and education; and Colorado's Amendment 2, an amendment to the state constitution that prohibited state and local governments from enacting prohibitions on discrimination based on sexual orientation.

The Initiative[8]

Half the states and hundreds of local governments use the initiative process, a form of substitutive direct lawmaking in which the voters bypass the legislative and executive branches to enact laws or amend state constitutions.[9] This form of lawmaking was introduced by the Progressives to take the legislative process away from corrupt politicians who were largely controlled by railroad barons, eastern banks, and industrial monopolists. Used initially to control corporate power, successful initiatives regulated business practices and working conditions. After World War I use of the initiative declined but rose again in the late 1970s when two men launched a campaign to limit property taxes in California. In the early years of the twenty-first century the initiative had become a growing source of legislation and as such, a major force in American politics. Initiative proponents have most recently placed a vast array of issues before the voters including tax reform, education funding, school vouchers, conservation and environmental policy, animal protection, affirmative action, physician-assisted suicide, gun control, campaign finance reform, bilingual education, hunting, gambling, medical use of marijuana, sentencing for criminal offenders, funding for embryonic stem-cell research, tort reform, and the rights of gays and lesbians. The enormous popularity of the initiative is attested to by the fact that in the election of 2004 voters decided 162 ballot measures in thirty-four states. Clearly, the initiative and other forms of direct lawmaking will continue to play a prominent role in the making of public policy.

The initiative process enables the electorate to express its preferences by voting up or down on voter initiated ballot measures and, thus, allows voters to participate directly in making public policy. Thus, the initiative process has been hailed as an instrument of direct democracy—a democratic means of overcoming the shortcomings of representative democracy. The initiative process, however, is riddled with problems. It is questionable whether it accurately reflects majority preferences given the extent to which the process of gathering signatures to place measures on the ballot and the ensuing campaign for their enactment are overwhelmingly financed by and dominated by organized interests that enjoy generous financial support. One commentator noted that, "[I]nitiative measures do not magically become state law as a result of the 'will of the people.'" but rather as a result of the efforts of initiative proponents who, "typically represent particular special interests and are increasingly multimillionaires who seek to influence public policy on their pet issues." Initiative proponents, who are not elected and sometimes are not even residents of the state or locality in which the measure is proposed, are "the driving force behind drafting [the] measures, qualifying them for the ballot, and leading the campaigns to convince the electorate to vote in their favor often spending millions of dollars in the process."[10]

In 2000, journalist, David S. Broder, described the initiative process as a big business in which lawyers and campaign consultants, signature-gathering firms, and other players sell their services to affluent interest groups or millionaires with their own political agendas. These players, Broder noted, "have learned that the initiative is a far more efficient way of achieving their ends than the cumbersome process of supporting candidates for public office and then lobbying them to pass or sign the measure they seek."[11] Initiative campaigns are clearly a far cry from grassroots democracy; indeed, wealthy individuals and special interests have used the initiative to further their own agendas. According to Broder, direct legislation by initiative has come to constitute lawmaking without government and thus threatens the system of representative government.

Broder's arguments are consistent with and lend support to what many others have argued about the initiative process—although it began as an attempt by the Progressives to take political power away from the legislators who were controlled by corporate interests it has now become a tool of well-organized and well-financed special interests that it was designed to combat. While the influence that well-financed initiative proponents exert over the process of lawmaking by the electorate seriously undermines the perception of the initiative as democratic there are other flaws in the process as well. The level of participation, which invariably hovers between 50 and 55 percent of registered voters for presidential elections and falls even lower in midterm elections, also casts major doubt on the notion that initiatives gauge the preferences of the people. Moreover, the percentage of those who vote on ballot measures is even lower because significant numbers of those who vote for candidates at the top of the ballot do not mark their preferences for initiatives and referenda. It has yet to be demonstrated that the full citizenry share the preferences of the subgroup that actually votes on the ballot propositions. Further, it may not even be true that those who do vote on the ballot measures share the preferences of the initiative proponents.

The demographics of such disparities have disturbing implications. Those who typically vote on ballot measures are disproportionately well educated, affluent, and white. Thus, minorities, the poor, and the uneducated are in effect doubly underrepresented in the initiative process because they are less likely to turn out to vote, and if they do, they are less likely to vote on ballot measures. Additionally, these voters are less likely to have the time and other resources that they would need to understand ballot measures. Thus, if they do vote on them, they may not be able to translate their political preferences into votes. Polls have revealed that a very low percentage of voters are confident that they consistently know enough about initiative measures to make an informed decision. This problem, moreover, is not limited to the less educated voters. Ballot measures are often presented in technical terms and are so convoluted that voters might not be able to figure out the policy implications of a "yes" or "no" vote. California's

Proposition 209, which abolished affirmative action, was, for example, titled the California Civil Rights Initiative. If voters need guidance about how to vote, they tend to rely on the information provided by the most vocal groups who are promoting the measures. All of this adds up to confused, manipulated, and deceived voters, what might even be termed the functional disfranchisement of the lower classes. Consequently, it is highly questionable whether the initiatives that are enacted into law are genuine expressions of the will of the majority.

Critics of the state and local governments' heavy use of the initiative emphasize that it typically lacks the requisite deliberative aspect of democratic decision-making, which includes an aggregation of preferences, opportunities for refinement of proposals, informed deliberation, consensus-building, and compromise. With the writing of initiatives there is almost no public debate nor is there opportunity for diverse perspectives to be represented. It is routine for proponents to exclude the measure's opponents from decisions on how to draft the language of a measure. There are no open meeting laws, public notice requirements, hearings to solicit public input, or other guarantees to give the press and public access to the drafting and editing stages of the initiative process. By the time that a measure is ready to be circulated to gather signatures to place it on the ballot it cannot be amended. Voters are simply presented with the option of approving or disapproving a measure. In short, the initiative process is seriously deficient in the elements that are essential to democracy—participation, information, and deliberation.

A sizable number of the initiatives that have been enacted into law since the late 1970s have also been irreconcilable with democracy's mandate for political equality. The initiative process exacerbates the disparate advantage that the financially well endowed enjoy. For example, by limiting property tax increases unless property is sold, California's Proposition 13 favors property owners over others and prior property owners over later ones. Rent control and anti-growth initiatives also favor established residents over newcomers. Even pro-gambling initiatives have regressive effects because lower-income people spend a higher proportion of their income on gambling. Most troubling is the fact that initiatives often reflect racial prejudice and intolerance, which prompted law professor, Derrick Bell, to observe that "the more direct democracy becomes, the more threatening it is." He argued that by enabling voters' racial beliefs to be recorded and tabulated in their pure form the initiative has been a most effective facilitator of the "bias, discrimination, and prejudice which has marred American democracy from its earliest day."[12]

The repeal of California's fair housing law by Proposition 14 in 1963 and similar measures enacted in ten cities provided the context for Bell's critique of direct democracy that he published in 1978. An abundance of ballot measures that followed lend support to his argument. The bias that ballot measures often manifest, moreover, goes far beyond racial prejudice. There have been initiatives declaring English the official language in Arizona, Colorado, and Florida. Voters in Arkansas, Colorado, and Michigan banned funding for poor women seeking abortions. California voters authorized involuntary AIDS testing for sex crime suspects and for assailants of police and emergency workers. In 1994, California voters approved life sentences for those convicted a third time of serious felonies involving rape, burglary, or robbery. In 1996 voters in California approved a constitutional amendment prohibiting affirmative action in public employment, education, and contracting. In Washington and California voters prohibited busing for the purpose of achieving a racial balance in the schools. It was also through the initiative process that California and Arizona abolished bilingual education. In the election of 2004, eleven states used the initiative process to limit marriage to two persons of the opposite sex, thus precluding the possibility of legal recognition of marriages between partners of the same sex.

The initiative process is wanting in the prerequisites of democracy: deliberation, information, participation, equality, majority rule, rights, and liberties. Consequently, in order to promote democracy, the judiciary should take a careful look at laws enacted through ballot measures. Indeed, courts are justified in giving less deference to the products of voter-made law than to policies enacted by legislatures. In cases in which the challenged policies have the effect of disadvantaging members of disfavored groups including immigrants, racial minorities, and gays and lesbians, the judiciary has an even greater responsibility to make sure the laws do not interfere with the principle of equality. In short, in reviewing challenges to laws enacted via initiative, courts are justified in taking an active role in invalidating policies that interfere with equality. In so doing, courts function to reinforce and to expand rather than to erect obstacles to democracy.[13]

In the next two sections I examine two specific uses of the initiative process to support my argument that judicial intervention is justified—indeed, necessary to promote the goal of equality. California's Proposition 187 and Colorado's Amendment 2 provide examples of lawmaking by the electorate that resulted in policies that are inconsistent with principles of equality and that were challenged on constitutional grounds and invalidated by courts.

California's Proposition 187: Immigration Control at the State Level

As the number of people who came to the United States from eastern and southern Europe as well as Asia rose after 1830 so too did the nativist sentiment that justified exclusion on the grounds that people from such distant lands lacked the values and instinct for liberty that distinguished the political culture of the United States. Moreover, popular "scientific" theories of the time held that such people were of inferior racial stock. Thus, they would be unwilling or unable to assimilate into American society. California took a particularly active role in promoting federal legislation to exclude immigrants from China beginning in the

1870s. The state also enacted restrictions aimed at people from China, Japan, and Mexico. For example, California enacted land laws prohibiting immigrants who were not eligible for citizenship from owning property, a statute requiring police officers to be citizens of the United States, and a labor code provision barring employers from employing undocumented aliens if their employment would have an adverse effect on lawful resident workers. Although explicitly racist theories lost their credibility and legal developments rendered legislation targeting particular racial and national groups vulnerable to constitutional challenge, California's largely white electorate continued to perceive immigration, particularly from Mexico, as a serious threat to its political and financial well-being. By the early 1990s the large number of undocumented immigrants who crossed the border from Mexico each year had become the subject of a major political controversy that polarized the residents of the state.[14]

Proposition 187, also known as the "Save Our State" initiative, was submitted to the voters of California on November 8, 1994. It passed with 59 percent of the vote and became law the following day. The measure began with a declaration that the people of California "have suffered and are suffering economic hardship caused by the presence of illegal aliens in this state [and] have suffered and are suffering personal injury and damage caused by the criminal conduct of illegal aliens in this state." It provided for the exclusion of illegal immigrants from all public benefits including health care, social services, and education. The law also required local law enforcement officials to turn suspected illegal immigrants over to the Immigration and Naturalization Service, and required public employees, including teachers and doctors, to report suspected illegal immigrants. It included a clause providing that mothers who attempted to use false documents to keep their children in school would receive mandatory five-year prison sentences.

Five suits challenging the law were quickly filed in U.S. district court. The court issued a temporary injunction on November 11, 1994, and in 1998 issued a decision holding the measure to be in violation of the Supremacy Clause of the Constitution, which provides that federal laws take precedence over those enacted by the states. Proposition 187 was preempted by federal immigration laws.[15] The state appealed the district court's decision to the Court of Appeals for the Ninth Circuit. Governor Pete Wilson, who had made passage of Proposition 187 the focus of his bid for reelection in 1998, lost to his opponent, Gray Davis, who had opposed the measure. Rather than pursue the appeal, the new governor requested mediation to resolve the matter. The mediation concluded with an agreement, signed in July 1999, that no child in the state of California would be deprived of an education or stripped of health care due to his or her place of birth.

According to the district court, Proposition 187 violated the Supremacy Clause of the Constitution insofar as it attempted to regulate immigration—a matter delegated by the Constitution to the federal government and fully covered by federal law. It was also problematic on equal protection grounds though it was not necessary for the court to reach that issue. Had it not been for the Supremacy Clause issue, Proposition 187 would have most likely run afoul of a Supreme Court decision in 1982 invalidating a Texas statute that provided for withholding state funds from local school districts for the education of children who were undocumented and authorized local school districts to deny enrollment to such children.[16] Holding that the statute violated the Equal Protection Clause of the Fourteenth Amendment, a majority of five justices reasoned that the statute imposed a lifetime hardship on a discrete class of children not accountable for their disabling status.[17]

The four dissenters to that decision charged that the Court was engaged in making laws regarding immigration and thereby interfering with the political process. Justice William Brennan's opinion for the majority, however, emphasized principles that would have applied equally to Proposition 187:

> The sheer incapability or lax enforcement of the laws barring entry into this country, coupled with the failure to establish an effective bar to the employment of undocumented aliens, has resulted in the creation of a substantial "shadow population" of illegal migrants—numbering in the millions—within our borders. This situation raises the specter of a permanent caste of undocumented resident aliens, encouraged by some to remain here as a source of cheap labor, but nevertheless denied the benefits that our society makes available to citizens and lawful residents. The existence of such an underclass presents most difficult problems for a Nation that prides itself on adherence to principles of equality under law.[18]

Brennan went on to contend that the status-based denial of basic education that imposed a "deprivation on the social, economic, intellectual, and psychological well-being of the individual, and the obstacle it poses to individual achievement," could not be reconciled with the principles embodied in the equal protection clause.[19]

Was Proposition 187 a democratic expression of the will of the people of California that the courts should have let stand? In the remainder of this section I endeavor to demonstrate that the measure manifested many of the problems that render lawmaking by the electorate inconsistent with principles of democratic decision making. The story of Proposition 187 belies the view that initiatives reflect the will of the people and provides strong support for the argument that judicial intervention is justified when laws made directly by the electorate are challenged. Three activists drafted the measure that was to become Proposition 187 and began to gather signatures to qualify it for the November ballot in 1994. Ron Prince, an accountant from Orange County, is reported to have developed an anti-immigrant animus as a result of a business dispute with a legal immigrant whom Prince alleged was an "illegal." Barbara Coe, one of the authors of Proposition 187, also the president of the California Coalition for Immigration Reform, frequently linked immigrants and violent crime in her public statements. Her campaign literature proclaimed, "We are heartbroken when we learn of yet another brutal murder of an innocent victim, many of them children, at the hands of illegal aliens. . . . And most all, we are outraged by those representatives who allow this activity to continue at the expense of the quality of life for us all and take little action to protect us from the illegal alien perpetrators of violent crime."[20] She also expressed fear of a "takeover" by "pro-illegal activists," and the destruction of the state's financial system as a result of illegal immigration. Undocumented immigrants, she declared, "are endangering, not only our financial system, but they repeatedly illustrate that they hold, not only our laws, . . . but our language, our culture, and our very history in contempt."[21] The third author, Harold Ezell, was Western Regional Commissioner of the Immigration and Naturalization Service during the Reagan administration. During the campaign, Ezell reportedly mentioned that Proposition 187 would be a boon to the people of California who are "tired of watching their state run wild and become a third world country."[22]

California's Republican governor, Pete Wilson, joined the campaign for Proposition 187, and indeed, put passage of the measure at the center of his reelection campaign in 1994. His popularity soared as a result and other elected officials—including Democrats as well as Republicans—began to advocate additional immigration regulations. Proposition 187 consequently became a highly visible issue in the 1994 election. That visibility, however, failed to bring democratic elements of information and deliberation to the campaign.

Supporters promoted Proposition 187 with inflammatory rhetoric as well as misleading and distorting innuendo about California's immigrant population, much of which seemed to be designed to reinforce stereotypes and to evoke resentment and fear of foreigners. For example, Ron Prince remarked to an audience of conservative activists, "you are the posse and SOS [Save Our State] is the rope." Other proponents proclaimed, "Proposition 187 will be the first giant stride in ultimately ending the illegal alien invasion," and that it would drive the encroaching hordes of illegal aliens back to Mexico.[23] A television advertisement in support of the measure showed black-and-white footage of immigrants racing across the Mexican border into California as an announcer ominously intoned: "They keep coming. . . ."[24] Further, in September 1994 an article appeared in the *New York Times* relating the story of an illegal immigrant who was a thief, burglar, and heroin addict: Jorge Luis Garaz Gorena was first deported to Mexico in 1974 but within one week crossed the border illegally to reenter the United States. He was deported five more times over the next fifteen years, but always managed to return. In 1989, Immigration and Naturalization Services lost track of him altogether. He told the *Times* reporter, "After all the time that immigration wasted, I guess they finally just got tired of hassling me. I haven't heard from them for years."[25]

Proponents of Proposition 187 repeatedly made the claim that undocumented immigrants were responsible for California's financial problems and were a drain on the taxpayer. The resulting image was one of hardworking citizens whose tax money went for health care for illegal immigrants and for their children to attend the public schools. Those illegal immigrants, it was implied, crossed the border in order to take advantage of the benefits the state was willing to give them and for which others invariably paid. Thus, Proposition 187 would save large sums of money and go a long way to solve the state's financial woes. One supporting statement, for example, read: "If the citizens and taxpayers of our state wait for the politicians in Washington and Sacramento to stop the incredible flow of ILLEGAL ALIENS, California will be in economic and social bankruptcy." Another proclaimed, "While our own citizens and legal residents go wanting, those who choose to enter our country ILLEGALLY get royal treatment at the expense of the California taxpayer.[26]

The Proposition 187 media director for southern California expressed the same sentiment in a letter to the editor that appeared in the *New York Times*:

> Proposition 187 is . . . a logical step toward saving California from economic ruin. . . . By flooding the state with 2 million illegal aliens to date, and increasing that figure each of the following 10 years, Mexicans in California would number 15 million to 20 million by 2004. During those 10 years about 5 million to 8 million Californians would have emigrated to other states. If these trends continued, a Mexico-controlled California could vote to establish Spanish as the sole language of California, 10 million more English-speaking Californians could flee, and there could be a statewide vote to leave the Union and annex California to Mexico.[27]

The campaign also had the effect of creating confusion about the distinction between legal and illegal immigrants. Polls showed that most voters believed the overwhelming majority of immigrants were illegal even though the undocumented were likely to have comprised no more than 20 percent of the total number of immigrants. According to one commentator, the result was that, "to most people, 'illegal immigrant' was simply a synonym for 'poor immigrant' or 'bad immigrant' or perhaps even 'Mexican immigrant.' "[28]

Clearly, the Proposition 187 campaign did very little to air the issues concerning immigrants from Mexico in a fair and deliberative way. Instead, proponents portrayed Mexican immigrants as criminals, dangerous alien invaders, and opportunists, who preferred to take advantage of the social programs offered by California rather than work to pay their own way. The opponents of the measure charged that its supporters were racist. Additionally, a protest organized by the anti–Proposition 187 campaign in which people from Latin America carried the flags of their countries only served to fuel the perceived threat among white voters of an invasion or takeover by foreigners.

The voting demographics also challenge the perception that passage of Proposition 187 was a reflection of the will of the people of California. Fifty-nine percent of the voters approved the measure. According to exit polls, white voters supported the measure by a margin of 63 to 37 percent while Latinos opposed it by a margin of 77 to 23 percent.[29] In spite of strong opposition from Latinos, the measure passed as a result of the votes cast by whites—a group that comprised 76 percent of the registered electorate but only 60 percent of the total population. In short, the state's Latinos, who make up 26 percent of the population but cast only 10 percent of the votes, were seriously underrepresented.

Jorge Castañeda, one of Mexico's leading intellectuals, highlighted the problem of California's voting demographics when he noted that the minority that actually participates in elections is disproportionately white, middle or upper-middle class, and elderly. He pointed to the Current Population Survey revealing that 55 percent of California's six million Latinos do not have citizenship.[30] Thus, more than three million people—one-tenth of the state's population—are politically disenfranchised. Further, 88 percent of those who vote in California have no children in school while 63 percent of the students in the Los Angeles School District are Latinos, many of whose parents are ineligible to vote.

Clearly, this is a problem for California as a democratic society—a small, privileged minority controls the fate of a largely poor, nonvoting majority and the state is becoming a two-tier society marked by economic inequality and social polarization of enormous proportions. Or, as Castañeda observed, "immigration from Mexico in its undocumented, politically maimed form is directly linked to the 'dedemocratization' of California society."[31]

In 2004, Ron Prince, Barbara Coe, and others continued to pursue voter-initiated measures that would replicate Proposition 187 while Castañeda's recommendation to "redemocratize" California by legalizing immigration and giving foreigners the right to vote in state and local elections continued to reside in the realm of the fantastic.[32] The politics of California continued to be de-democratized by the exclusion of a large proportion of the people residing in the state. Proposition 187 clearly was marred by its lack of deliberation and by distortion and misinformation. Nevertheless, the story of Proposition 187 suggests that it may have made some contribution to the democratic process. California's voters, frustrated by the government's inability to stem the influx of illegal immigrants, enacted a flawed solution to the problem. When the district court invalidated the measure it sparked more efforts by California residents to promote effective restrictive constraints on immigration. Those efforts, in turn, may well have encouraged the federal government to work harder to develop strategies to resolve the problem of illegal immigration. By this account, the judiciary, far from erecting an obstacle to democracy, promoted it by participating in the ongoing national debate regarding immigration policy.

Colorado's Amendment 2: The Voters and the Campaign against Gay and Lesbian Rights

By 1990 Colorado, at both the state and local levels, had begun to enact regulations prohibiting discrimination on the basis of sexual orientation. Denver, Boulder, and Aspen forbade sexual orientation discrimination in employment, housing, education, public accommodations, and health and welfare services. Additionally, an executive order issued by the governor in 1990 prohibited discrimination against all state employees on the basis of sexual orientation. The Colorado Insurance Code in 1992 forbade health insurance providers from determining insurability and premiums based on the sexual orientation of an applicant, a beneficiary, or an insured. Metropolitan State College of Denver prohibited college-sponsored social clubs from discriminating in membership on the basis of sexual orientation and Colorado State University instituted an antidiscrimination policy that included sexual orientation.

In 1992 the voters of Colorado, via a statewide initiative, amended the state's constitution to repeal all state and local policies that prohibited discrimination on the basis of sexual orientation. Further, the amendment prohibited any governmental entity in the state from taking measures in the future to prohibit discrimination based on sexual orientation unless the state constitution was amended to permit such measures. The amendment read:

> No Protected Status Based on Homosexual, Lesbian, or Bisexual Orientation. Neither the State of Colorado, through any of its branches or departments, nor any of its agencies, political subdivisions, municipalities or school districts, shall enact, adopt or enforce any statute, regulation, ordinance or policy whereby homosexual, lesbian or bisexual orientation, conduct, practices or relationships shall constitute or otherwise be the basis of or entitle any person or class of persons to have or claim any minority status, quota preferences, protected status or claim of discrimination. This Section of the Constitution shall be in all respects self-executing.[33]

Amendment 2 was approved by 53.4 percent of those who voted. On the day that the measure was scheduled to take effect, however, a Denver District Court judge issued a temporary injunction to prevent its enforcement on the grounds that it violated the access of gays and lesbians to equal protection of the laws. The Colorado Supreme Court agreed in 1994, by a vote of eight to one. In 1996, by a vote of six to three in the case of *Romer v. Evans*, the United States

Supreme Court invalidated Amendment 2, holding that it disqualified a particular group from seeking protection of the law, and thereby was inconsistent with the U.S. Constitution's guarantee of equal protection in the Fourteenth Amendment. Justice Anthony Kennedy, who wrote the opinion for the majority, noted that Colorado's disqualification of a class of persons from the right to seek protection from the law is "unprecedented in our jurisprudence" and merits careful consideration to determine its constitutionality. Further, he observed, "It is not within our constitutional tradition to enact laws of this sort" that depart from the principles of equal protection and impartiality by limiting access of specific groups to government.

As both the Colorado Supreme Court and the U.S. Supreme Court recognized, substantively, Colorado's Amendment 2 was a particularly egregious attempt to withdraw from one specific group of people all legal protection from discrimination. Justice Kennedy, moreover, explained in his opinion that the amendment had no relation to the achievement of any legitimate state purpose and thus failed even the most lenient standard of review.[34]

Writing for the three dissenters, Justice Antonin Scalia charged that Amendment 2 had been "put directly, to all the citizens of the State," and had been approved by the "most democratic of procedures." In his view the amendment represented "the effort by the majority of citizens to preserve its view of sexual morality statewide." Moreover, he suggested, just as gays and lesbians may use the legal system for "reinforcement of their moral sentiments" their efforts may legitimately be "countered by lawful, democratic countermeasures." Such was the case with Amendment 2, which, he insisted, merely, prohibited "giving . . . favored status *because of their homosexual conduct—that is, it prohibits favored status for homosexuality*." In Scalia's analysis, Amendment 2 was an effort to counter the geographic concentration of gays and lesbians and their disproportionate political power by:

> (1) resolving the controversy at the statewide level, and (2) making the election a single-issue contest for both sides. It put directly, to all the citizens of the State, the question: Should homosexuality be given special protection? They answered no. The Court today asserts that this most democratic of procedures is unconstitutional.[35]

In response to the Supreme Court's ruling, Gary Bauer, president of the Family Research Council, described the judiciary as "an out-of-control" unelected institution and proclaimed that the decision "should send chills down the back of anyone who cares whether the people of this nation any longer have the power of self-rule."[36] In 1999, in response to the Vermont Supreme Court's decision according same-sex couples the benefits of married couples, Bauer stated, "I think what the Vermont Supreme Court did last week was the worst form of terrorism."[37] In stark contrast, an editorial in *The Progressive* praised the decision, noting that, "Fortunately, the Court proved an effective restraint against the tyranny of the majority."[38]

Justices Kennedy and Scalia had understandings of Amendment 2 that were diametrically opposed. Scalia agreed with the measure's proponents that it did no more than deprive gays and lesbians of special rights while Kennedy maintained that it deprived them of legal protection from discrimination. Likewise, Colorado's voters differed over the meaning of Amendment 2 and voted accordingly. The fact of the matter is that a slight majority voted for the measure either out of a belief that special rights were being extended to gays and lesbians and should be withdrawn or on the basis of a conviction that homosexuality is immoral and poses a threat to the values that have made America a great nation or out of confusion as to what exactly Amendment 2 was all about. What does that suggest about Scalia's charge that Amendment 2 had been approved by the most democratic of procedures and the suggestion from Bauer that the Court's invalidation of the measure was undemocratic and illegitimate?

The arguments advanced by a number of legal scholars that have maintained that legislation enacted directly by the voters warrants a careful look when a court reviews it apply with special force to the cases of Amendment 2 as well as California's Proposition 187. First, both Proposition 187 and Amendment 2 singled out a particular group that comprised a minority in terms of voting strength and thereby raise equal protection questions to which the judiciary should be cognizant. Justice Kennedy's suggestion that a provision like Amendment 2, unprecedented and seemingly enacted out of animus toward gays and lesbians, warranted close analysis by the Court applies as well to Proposition 187. Although its proponents claimed that it was motivated by a desire to save the state and the taxpayers' money and to attempt to fill in the void left by the federal government's inability to enforce the immigration laws, it was clearly susceptible to the charge that it was based on animus toward Mexican immigrants. Second, the flaws in the democratic process that marked passage of Proposition 187 were also readily apparent in the campaign for Amendment 2.

The political power of gays and lesbians in urban areas of Colorado, evidenced by the legal protections that were enacted in Denver, Boulder, and Aspen, were deeply disturbing to conservatives who are committed to the view that homosexuality is immoral and is a chosen and changeable behavior. According to that view, those who practice it typically try to recruit others to follow their example. Thus, gays and lesbians pose a particularly insidious threat to marriage, the family, the educational system, and, in general, to traditional lifestyles that include clearly delineated gender roles. At first glance, it may appear that some conservatives in Colorado, determined to stop the spread of immorality and the corruption of homosexuality, began to organize to repeal the antidiscrimination provisions in the law. Indeed, the organized movement for

Amendment 2 presented itself as a grassroots response to the political power of gays and lesbians. *The Denver Post*, for example, reported:

> Well before the election, a group of friends and conservative activists from Colorado Springs–area evangelical churches formed Colorado for Family Values. Their sole issue was stopping what they saw as the immoral creep of homosexual influence on culture and politics. They believed schoolchildren were being recruited into gay lifestyles by overzealous sex education. They were outraged at the wild behavior they saw in gay pride parades. They feared the movement among many liberal cities to protect gays from job and housing discrimination would lead to quotas and watered-down civil rights laws.[39]

In reality, however, the leaders of the campaign for passage of Amendment 2 were far from a local grassroots movement. They received considerable advice and resources from national organizations of the religious right—organizations that began in the mid-1970s and reemerged in the late 1980s when state and local governments enacted measures protecting rights for gays and lesbians. People for the American Way proclaimed that "the Religious Right's anti-gay vendetta is not, as its leaders often claim, a spontaneous outpouring of concern about gay issues. Theirs is a carefully orchestrated political effort, with a unified set of messages and tactics, that is deliberately designed to foster division and intolerance."[40]

Although Colorado for Family Values (CFV), which sponsored Amendment 2, was a local group founded by two Coloradoans, Kevin Tebedo and Tony Marco, and headed by Will Perkins, a car dealer from Colorado Springs, it received major support from the national anti–gay rights campaign conducted by the New Right. There were representatives of five national organizations that were active in that campaign on the advisory board of CFV, including Focus on the Family, Concerned Women for America, and the Eagle Forum. Additionally, although Pat Robertson's Christian Coalition was not officially represented on the board of CFV, it was reported to have had a strong presence in Colorado. There was, in fact, an indirect link between the two organizations. The National Legal Foundation of Chesapeake, Virginia (NLF, a conservative Christian legal organization founded by Pat Robertson and funded by Robertson's Christian Broadcasting Network, but no longer affiliated with Robertson), gave advice to CFV as early as 1991, before the Amendment 2 campaign. The advice was intended to help CFV formulate ballot language that would be politically effective and survive legal challenges. By the end of 1992, the National Legal Foundation had taken over much of the legal work of CFV. A letter from Brian McCormick of NLF advised CFV to stay away from the "no special rights" language in its legal formulations, but to use it as the centerpiece of its public campaign.

Another organization, Focus on the Family, founded by James Dobson in 1977, arrived in Colorado Springs in 1991 to join CFV in the campaign for

Amendment 2, bringing important resources, including 750 employees and an annual budget of nearly $70 million. Focus on the Family also received a $4 million grant from the El Pomar Foundation to buy fifty acres in Colorado Springs.[41] In 1988, Focus on the Family merged with the Family Research Council, headed by Gary Bauer, which distributed a "homosexual packet" that was available through Focus on the Family. That packet included "The Homosexual Agenda: Changing Your Community and Nation," which contained a section on "Starting An Initiative."[42] In 1992 Dobson's organization offered advice to CFV and the use of its employees; its leaders also sat on CFV advisory boards. Additionally, Focus on the Family gave an in-kind donation worth $8,000 to CFV.[43] There were a number of other organizations working for Amendment 2 as well. In 1993 there were fifty-three rightist groups in Colorado Springs—prompting Boulder's city attorney to characterize it as the center of the Christian right in the United States.

The campaign for Amendment 2 was laden with misleading—even outright deceptive—information about gays and lesbians as well as the impact of the measure. The voters heard repeatedly that the measure would do no more than repeal the "special rights" that gays and lesbians had been granted in the urban areas where they enjoyed disproportionate influence over the political process. Those special rights, voters were led to believe, would dilute the protections to which heterosexuals were entitled. The advertisements and flyers in support of Amendment 2 also promoted the view that gays and lesbians posed a threat to the traditional family. James Dobson stated, for example, "I am familiar with the widespread effort to redefine the family. It is motivated by homosexual activists . . . who see the traditional family as a barrier to [their] social engineering."[44] Additionally, just prior to the election, supporters of Amendment 2 distributed 800,000 flyers asserting that "homosexuals commit between one-third and one-half of all recorded child molestations."[45]

Mike Booth, a reporter for the *Denver Post* who covered the Amendment 2 campaign, emphasized the need for fair and accurate information. "That has been sorely lacking from both sides throughout the entire debate, especially from Colorado for Family Values. But both sides have played a role in disseminating information that has hurt the quality of the debate. It has been a very emotional conflict and the need for accurate information is even more important in such a conflict."[46] Informed deliberation was stifled, Booth noted, by opponents of Amendment 2 who referred to CFV as Nazis and Fascists. On the other side, proponents of the measure charged, "They are trying to create a police state where no one can discriminate, where no one can make any choices on anything."[47] Proponents of Amendment 2 frequently relied on the literal interpretations of the Bible to support their position—another tactic that discouraged reasoned debate.

In short, the claim that Amendment 2 reflected the will of the people of Colorado is implausible. The campaign for passage of the measure, supported by national organizations of the religious right and rampant with inaccurate information about both the amendment and the gay and lesbian community, was far from democratic. On the contrary, passage of Amendment 2 stands as a testament to the extent to which voters are vulnerable to manipulation.

The history of Amendment 2 bears a number of similarities to that of Proposition 187. Both measures raised serious equal protection issues insofar as they singled out specific groups that have been disadvantaged—in the case of Proposition 187, excluded—in the political process and have been subjected to discrimination. Moreover, the distortion and confusion that marred the process by which they were enacted into law seriously undermines the claim that they represent anything that can be accurately characterized as the will of the people. Finally, Amendment 2 and its invalidation at the hands of the Supreme Court served to reinforce democracy in a similar way that the controversy and litigation regarding Proposition 187 did.

The campaign for and subsequent passage of Amendment 2 galvanized significant numbers of gays and lesbians throughout Colorado to make their sexual orientation known and to participate more actively in the movement to protect their rights. In 2002 a spokesperson for the organization Human Rights Campaign noted, "The effort to achieve equality for gay people is moving forward on a number of fronts. More and more people feel safe and secure coming out and identifying themselves as gay. That coming out of the closet was from Amendment 2 and all the subsequent organizing. Sometimes a defeat leads to victory."[48] A number of non-gay people were encouraged to join, if only at a minimal level, the fight to protect gay rights by participating in the Boycott Colorado effort during the time it took for the controversy of the constitutional status of Amendment 2 to be resolved. On the other hand, Coloradoans, whether or not they were supporters of the measure, some of whom felt that the boycott was an attack on their state and ultimately would threaten their jobs, were also drawn into the controversy by the boycott. The controversy over Amendment 2, albeit in a different way than one would expect, served to move people to participate.

Judicial intervention, moreover, served to reinforce democratic principles by conveying the message to the states that animus against unpopular groups cannot provide the basis for legal provisions regardless of the process by which those provisions are enacted. Consequently, although drives to eliminate legal protections for gays and lesbians spread to more than a dozen other states after passage of Amendment 2, following its invalidation the number of states protecting gays from discrimination doubled. The number of businesses protecting gay employees from discrimination rose and more employers extended health and other benefits to same-sex domestic partners. Moreover, by 2004 the controversy regarding gay rights had moved beyond issues of anti-discrimination in employment, education, and public accommodations to the legal status of marriage between two people of the same sex.

Still, it is important to take into account that the Supreme Court invalidated Amendment 2 by a vote of six to three and that the dissenters agreed wholeheartedly with the "special rights" analysis that was constructed by the measure's proponents. This suggests a different response to the countermajoritarian difficulty—that is, that the Court invariably functions within the framework of American politics. Thus, while judicial intervention to invalidate measures enacted by the voters is clearly justified and often promotes rather than thwarts democracy, it is far from certain that the courts have the capacity to protect politically disfavored groups from legislation that erects obstacles to equality.

Conclusion

Judicial review of direct legislation can reinforce and expand democratic participation and can promote the equality that is a crucial component of a democratic society in which all members have the opportunity to participate in the decisions that shape their lives. Neither of the ballot measures reflected the will of the people. Instead, both were authored, proposed, promoted, and publicized by special interests that were, in turn, supported by substantial financial resources. Those interests employed tactics that confused and misled the voters and manipulated their fears and prejudices against foreigners in the case of Proposition 187 and against gays and lesbians in the case of Amendment 2.

The judicial intervention that invalidated both measures, far from interfering with the will of the people, actually served to encourage political participation to develop means for resolving problems with immigration in California and to develop strategies for residents of diverse backgrounds, religions, and lifestyles to be more tolerant and to learn to get along in Colorado. Moreover, as courts made clear in both situations, singling out a group for exclusion from benefits or from equal rights cannot be the basis for public policy. Targeting specific groups in the ways that Proposition 187 and Amendment 2 attempted to do is thoroughly inconsistent with democracy and the pursuit of equality. In both cases it was a court that stepped in to reinforce the possibilities of democratic decision-making and to promote the goal of equality.

A final comment: If either Proposition 187 or Amendment 2 had been enacted through the legislative process would courts be justified in invalidating them? I would answer in the affirmative. Although Proposition 187 was clearly preempted by federal regulations on immigration the measure was also questionable on equal protection grounds even though the classification of illegal immigrants does not constitute a suspect class, nor were the rights from which the group was excluded alleged to be fundamental. Still, using the rational basis test a court could have easily found that there was no connection between the regulation and any state interest in limiting the flow of undocumented immigrants and that, therefore, the law was unconstitutional. In the case of Amendment 2,

Justice Kennedy's analysis finding no connection between singling out gays and lesbians for exclusion from protection from the law and any legitimate state interest would have had just as much force if the law had been enacted by the Colorado legislature.

Notes

1. *Whitney v. California*, 274 U.S. 357, 376 (1927).
2. *Chambers v. Florida*, 309 U.S. 227, 241 (1940).
3. *West Virginia State Bd. of Education v. Barnette*, 319 U.S. 624, 638 (1943).
4. Kenneth L. Karst, "Why Equality Matters," *Georgia Law Review* 17 (1983), 245, at 287.
5. Robert Dahl, "Decision-Making in a Democracy: The Supreme Court as a National Policy-Maker," *Journal of Public Law* 6 (1957): 179–295. By lawmaking majority, Dahl meant a majority of those voting in the House and Senate plus the president.
6. Mark A. Graber, "The Nonmajoritarian Difficulty: Legislative Deference to the Judiciary." *Studies in American Political Development* 7 (1993): 35–73, at 36.
7. Barry Friedman, "Dialogue and Judicial Review," *Michigan Law Review* 91 (1993): 577–682, at 581.
8. "During the oral argument in *Reitman v. Mulkey* [1967], then Solicitor General Thurgood Marshall called attention to the fact that California's authorization of discrimination in the private housing market had been enacted by voter initiative. 'Wouldn't you have exactly the same argument,' he was asked, if the provision 'had been enacted by the California legislature?' 'It's the same argument,' Marshall replied, 'I just have more force with this.' 'No,' interjected Justice Black, 'It seems to me you would have less. Because here, it's moving in the direction of letting the people of the State—the voters of the State—establish their policy, which is as near to a democracy as you can get.'" Julian N. Eule, "Judicial Review of Direct Democracy," *Yale Law Journal* 99 (1990): 1503–1590, at 1506.
9. The initiative is the process whereby citizens collect signatures on a petition and place advisory questions, memorials, statutes, or constitutional amendments on the ballot for the citizens to adopt or reject.
10. Glen Staszewski, "Rejecting the Myth of Popular Sovereignty and Applying an Agency Model to Direct Democracy," *Vanderbilt Law Review* 56 (2003): 395–495, at 420–421.
11. David S. Broder, *Democracy Derailed: Initiative Campaigns and the Power of Money* (New York: Harcourt Inc. 2000), 5.
12. Derrick Bell, "The Referendum: Democracy's Barrier to Racial Equality," *Washington Law Review* 54 (1978): 1–29, at 1.
13. There is a very high rate of legal challenge to voter-approved measures. Fifty-four percent of all initiatives that were enacted into law have been challenged in court. In California, that figure rose to nearly two-thirds. Moreover, in more than half of the cases, courts have invalidated part or all of the challenged initiative on the basis that they violated individual rights in violation of the Constitution. Kenneth P.

Miller, "The Role of Courts in the Initiative Process: A Search for Standards." Paper delivered at 1999 annual meeting of the American Political Science Association.

14. It was estimated that 9.8 million people born in Mexico were living in the United States in 2002 and that 5.3 million were undocumented. Jeffrey Passel, "Mexican Immigration to the U.S.: The Latest Estimates," *Migration Information Source*, March 1, 2004. Available at: http://www.migrationinformation.org/USfocus/display.cfm?ID=208.
15. *League of United Latin American Citizens v. Pete Wilson*, 1998 U.S. Dist. Lexis 3372, March 13, 1998. United States District Court for the Central District of California. Article I, Section 8, Clause 4 of the Constitution delegates to Congress the power to make rules regarding immigration and thus precludes the states from making rules admitting or excluding aliens. *Traux v. Raich*, 239 U.S. 33 (1915), at 42. But see, *De Canas v. Bica*, 424 U.S. 251 (1976).
16. *Plyler v. Doe*, 457 U.S. 202 (1982).
17. In *San Antonio School District v. Rodriquez*, 411 U.S. 1 (1973), the justices held that education was not a fundamental right. In *Plyler v. Doe* the Court reasoned that the group, illegal aliens, could not be considered a suspect class because membership in the class was a federal crime, 457 U.S. 202 (1982), at 219. Nevertheless, the Court found that the statute violated the equal protection clause on the grounds that it bore no rational relationship to a legitimate state goal.
18. *Plyler v. Doe*, 457 U.S. 202, at 218–219.
19. Ibid., 222.
20. Handbill, "Barbara Coe for Assembly, 67th State Assembly District," December 1995. As quoted in David M. Reimers, *Unwelcome Strangers: American Identity and the Turn Against Immigration* (New York: Columbia University Press, 1998), 83.
21. Ibid.
22. Ibid.
23. Ron Unz, "California and the End of White America," *Commentary*, November 1999. Available at: http://www.onenation.org/9911/110199.html.
24. As quoted in Kenneth P. Miller, "Constraining Populism: The Real Challenge of Initiative Reform," *Santa Clara Law Review* 41 (2001): 1037–1084.
25. *New York Times*, September 13, 1994. As quoted in Kevin R. Johnson, *Proposition 187: The Nativist Campaign, the Impact on the Latino Community, and the Future*, JSIR Research Report #15, The Julian Samora Research Institute, Michigan State University, East Lansing, Michigan, 1996. Available at: http://www.jsri.msu.edu/RandS/research/irr/rr15.html.
26. As quoted in Miller, "Constraining Populism."
27. As quoted in Kevin R. Johnson, *Proposition 187*.
28. Unz, "California and the End of White America."
29. Jan Adams, "Proposition 187 Lessons," *Z Magazine*, March 1995. Available at: http://www.zmag.org/zmag/articles/mar95adams.htm.
30. Jorge G. Castañeda, "Mexico and California: The Paradox of Tolerance and Dedemocratization," 35.
31. Ibid., 45.

32. California Republican Congressman Representative Frank Riggs proposed a federal law that would allow all states to deny services to illegal immigrants. Although supporters of Proposition 187 failed to collect a sufficient number of signatures for a ballot measure to appear on the November 2004 ballot, they continued to promote a measure for the March 2006 election. That measure, in the form of a state constitutional amendment, would bar the state from issuing illegal immigrants any identification documents, trade licenses or in-state college tuition. It is termed the "Save Our License Initiative."
33. Colorado Constitution, Art. II, 30b.
34. Gays and lesbians do not constitute a suspect class nor was a fundamental right involved. Thus, the majority adhered to the traditional rational basis standard of review. Kennedy noted that, "The primary rationale the State offers for Amendment 2 is respect for other citizens' freedom of association, and in particular the liberties of landlords or employers who have personal or religious objections to homosexuality. Colorado also cites its interest in conserving resources to fight discrimination against other groups. The breadth of the Amendment is so far removed from these particular justifications that we find it impossible to credit them." *Romer v. Evans.*
35. Ibid.
36. Gary Bauer. "Let's Bench Judicial Tyrants." Family Research Council, 1996.
37. "Bauer compares Vermont gay rights decision to terrorism." CNN.com, December 27, 1999.
38. "Get out the champagne—Colorado Amendment 2 struck down by U.S. Supreme Court." *The Progressive,* July 1996.
39. Michael Booth, "When 'Hate' Became Resolve: State's Amendment 2 Led to Gay Protections," DenverPost.com, Sunday, September 29, 2002. Available at: http://www.denverpost.com/Stories/0,1413,36%257E64%257E890479%257E,00.html.
40. Jean Hardisty, "Constructing Homophobia: Historical Background to Colorado's Amendment 2," *The Public Eye*, March 1993. Available at: http://www.dangerouscitizen.com/Articles/1085.aspx.
41. Boulder's city attorney, Joseph de Raismes, reported that the El Pomar Foundation invited CFV to Colorado and gave the organization $4 million to move its headquarters to Colorado Springs. Joseph de Raismes, "Homosexual Rights: Constructive Responses to Colorado's Amendment 2." Conflict Research Consortium. Working Paper 93–27, July 20, 1993 (1). Available at: http://www.colorado.edu/conflict/full_text_search/AllCRCDocs/93-27.htm. One source placed Focus on the Family's employees at 2,200, its annual budget at more than $77 million, and valued its headquarters in Colorado Springs at $27 million. ACLU Washington Religious Freedom. Report on the Religious Right in Washington State by Dan Junas, 1995 Available at: http://www.aclu-wa.org/issues/religious/2.html.
42. Ibid. See also, Don Romesburg, "James Dobson's Darker Side: A Carefully Kept Secret. U.S. News and World Report Cover-Story Fails to Expose It," *GayToday,* Available at: http://gaytoday.badpuppy.com/. For more recent activities of James Dobson and those of Focus on the Family, see Steven V. Roberts, Dorian Friedman,

and Ted Gest, "The Heavy Hitter, *U.S. News & World Report*, April 24, 1995, 34–39; Michael J. Gerson, Major Garrett, and Carolyn Kleiner, "A Righteous Indignation," *U.S. News & World Report*, May 4, 1998, 24–14, at 29.
43. Hardisty, "Constructing Homophobia."
44. Romesburg, "James Dobson's Darker Side."
45. Dale Carpenter, "Victory From Defeat: Ten Years After Amendment 2," October 17, 2002. Available at: http://www.indegayforum.org/authors/carpenter/carpenter30.html
46. Mike Booth, "The Media's Role in the Amendment 2 Controversy," Conflict Research Consortium Working Paper 93–28, July 20, 1993(1). Available at: http://www.colorado.edu/conflict/full_text_search/AllCRCDocs/93–28.htm.
47. Ibid.
48. Michael Booth, "When 'Hate' Became Resolve."

Bibliography

Bickel, Alexander M. *The Least Dangerous Branch: The Supreme Court at the Bar of Politics.* Indianapolis: Bobbs-Merrill, 1962.

Broder, David S. *Democracy Derailed: Initiative Campaigns and the Power of Money.* New York: Harcourt, 2000.

Castañeda, Jorge G. "Mexico and California: The Paradox of Tolerance and Dedemocratization." In *The California-Mexico Connection.* Stanford, Calif.: Stanford University Press, 1993. Pp. 34–47.

Clark, Rebecca L., Jeffrey S. Passel, Wendy Zimmermann, and Michael E. Fix. *The Urban Institute, Fiscal Impacts of Undocumented Aliens: Selected Estimates for Seven States.* Washington, D.C.: Urban Institute Press, 1994.

Cronin, Thomas E. *Direct Democracy: The Politics of Initiative, Referendum and Recall.* Cambridge, Mass.: Harvard University Press, 1989.

Ely, John Hart. *Democracy and Distrust: A Theory of Judicial Review.* Cambridge, Mass.: Harvard University Press, 1980.

Fisher, Louis. *Constitutional Dialogues: Interpretation as Political Process.* Princeton, N.J.: Princeton University Press, 1988.

Klarman, Michael J. *From Jim Crow to Civil Rights: The Supreme Court and the Struggle for Racial Equality.* New York: Oxford University Press, 2004.

Reimers, David M. *Unwelcome Strangers: American Identity and the Turn against Immigration.* New York: Columbia University Press, 1998.

Schrag, Peter. *Paradise Lost: California's Experience, America's Future.* Berkeley: University of California Press, 1999.

Simmons, Charlene Wear. *California's Statewide Initiative Process.* Sacramento: California Research Bureau, 1997.

Court Cases

Carolene Products Company v. U.S., 304 U.S. 144 (1938).

Chambers v. Florida, 309 U.S. 227, 241 (1940).

De Canas v. Bica, 424 U.S. 251 (1976).
League of United Latin American Citizens v. Pete Wilson, 1998 U.S. Dist. Lexis 3372, March 13, 1998.
Plyler v. Doe, 457 U.S. 202 (1982).
Reitman v. Mulkey, 387 U.S. 369 (1967).
Romer v. Evans, 517 U.S. 620 (1996).
San Antonio School District v. Rodriquez, 411 U.S. 1 (1973).
Traux v. Raich, 239 U.S. 33 (1915).
West Virginia State Bd. of Education v. Barnette, 319 U.S. 624, 638 (1943).
Whitney v. California, 274 U.S. 357, 376 (1927).

15

FROM REPUBLIC TO DEMOCRACY: THE JUDICIARY AND THE POLITICAL PROCESS

Mark A. Graber

EARLY NINETEENTH-CENTURY AMERICAN CONSERVATIVES and mid-twentieth-century American liberals aggressively championed judicial power. "[T]he people of America," Gouverneur Morris asserted when condemning Jeffersonian efforts to repeal the Judiciary Act of 1801, "vested in the judges a check intended to be efficient—a check of the first necessity, to prevent an invasion of the Constitution by unconstitutional laws."[1] Justice Hugo Black in *Chambers v. Florida* (1940) declared, "under our constitutional system, courts stand against any winds that blow as havens of refuge for those who might otherwise suffer because they are helpless, weak, outnumbered, or because they are non-conforming victims of prejudice and public excitement." Morris and Black celebrated a strong judiciary for very different reasons. Federalists believed republican courts protected elites from the excesses of democracy. The paradigmatic unconstitutional act requiring judicial intervention was legislation taking property from A and giving it to B.[2] New Dealers believed that democratic courts policed the political process. The paradigmatic unconstitutional act requiring judicial intervention was legislation restricting the speech rights of unpopular minorities.[3]

Judicial attitudes toward democracy and the political process have evolved. From ratification until the New Deal, most justices insisted the United States was a republic. Republican courts protected property from legislative majorities. Charged with checking democratic excesses, the judiciary was the governing institution least prone to expand political freedoms. New Dealers regarded the

United States as a democracy, but disputed the proper role of democratic courts. Some justices maintained courts had a special obligation to protect free speech and related rights. Others maintained that justices in a democracy deferred to elected officials on all matters, unless no reasonable person could justify the practice under constitutional attack. Justices during the Great Society and Reagan Revolution agreed that the United States was a democracy and that justices should police the political process, but disputed whether democracy was more committed to political liberty or political equality. Liberal proponents of political equality claimed campaign finance reforms and self-conscious efforts to increase African American representation promoted constitutional democracy. Conservative proponents of political liberty maintained these measures violated basic democratic norms and constitutional rights.

These different interpretations of democratic politics complicate efforts to survey judicial decisions on political freedoms. Contemporary political theorists debate good democratic practice. Some identify democracy with majority rule. Others insist democracies maximize the persons who influence public policy. Controversies also rage over whether democracy entails substantive liberties, as well as rights to vote and free speech. Some regard democratic freedoms as limited to speech rights, voting rights, and rights against majoritarian prejudices, while others claim that democratic government must safeguard the freedom of conscience. Critics of judicial decisions protecting abortion rights insist that public policies in democracies are made by elected officials. Pro-choice advocates assert judicial protection for abortion rights facilitates democracy because women must control their fertility in order to participate as equals in public life and bans on reproductive choice reflect the gross underrepresentation of women in state legislatures. Several commentators claim rights to basic necessities are necessary for democratic equality. In short, contemporary constitutionalists routinely translate their claims of constitutional wrong into claims of democratic wrong. A survey of judicial practice in cases involving claimed democratic rights, given these rhetorical practices, would devolve into a survey of judicial practice in general.

This survey uses two limiting criteria. First, judicial decisions in cases concerning restrictions on political dissent and voting are emphasized. All contemporary commentators agree on the importance of these liberties, even though the degree of protection is contestable. Second, the practices particular justices have thought democratic are highlighted. Justices for long periods of American history largely ignored rights most contemporary Americans think essential to democracy. What other justices have championed as democratic rights few Americans think deserve that label. Examining the different ways justices have conceptualized democracy and their democratic role may help citizens better appreciate both the complexities of judicial power and the complexities of democracy.

Judicial decisions provide only a small window on the political process. Repressive legal traditions have coincided with more libertarian political traditions. Antebellum free state legislatures did not pass bans on antislavery speech that most state justices would probably have sustained. Libertarian judicial rulings have had limited impacts on speech and voting practices. Journalists refrain from making constitutionally protected criticisms of public figures when they cannot afford to defend a lawsuit or fear losing vital advertisers.[4] Most important, democracies require more than legality to flourish. News as entertainment may be protected by the First Amendment, but few think that contemporary practice is democratically healthy.

Fundamentals

Justices may not correct any practice they think undemocratic. American courts resolve legal disputes by interpreting authoritative legal texts, the highest of which is the Constitution of the United States. Justices are authorized to promote political freedom only when they believe the constitution, legislation, legal precedent or some other source of law warrants judicial intervention. Courts make decisions only when adjudicating lawsuits. Until someone legally complains about an undemocratic process, justices are powerless. Justices are also legally powerless when they lack jurisdiction over cases raising constitutional questions about political processes. As a practical matter, courts are powerless when elected officials are unwilling to comply with judicial rulings protecting speech and voting rights.

The Constitution of the United States establishes numerous practices many commentators think undemocratic. Favorite candidates include equal state voting in the Senate, the electoral college, and a life tenured judiciary.[5] Article I, Section 2 gives persons the right to vote in federal elections only when they "have the Qualifications requisite for Electors of the most numerous Branch of the State Legislature" where they reside. This constitutional provision permits states to curtail voting in federal elections by restricting rights to vote in state elections. Most states when the Constitution was ratified sharply limited the electorate, though suffrage was gradually expanding.[6] The supermajorities required by Article V for amending the constitution are also inconsistent with most democratic norms.[7] Whether these and other constitutional practices are, in fact, adequately democratic is, of course, debatable. Justices, however, are not licensed to participate in these debates. They are bound by clear constitutional commands. Courts may not strike down the Senate or implement a parliamentary system no matter how a judicial majority evaluates the democratic pedigree of those practices.

The Constitution contains several provisions that can be interpreted as supporting democracy. Article IV, Section 4 declares, "[t]he United States shall guarantee to every State in the Union a Republican Form of Government." The First

Amendment declares, "Congress shall make no law . . . abridging the freedom of speech, or of the press; or the right of the people peaceably to assemble, and to petition the Government for a redress of grievances." The post–Civil War Constitution forbids federal and state officials from denying suffrage "on account of race, color, or previous condition of servitude." The Nineteenth Amendment extends this prohibition to "sex." Political freedoms might be derived from the Ninth Amendment, which declares, "[t]he enumeration in the Constitution, of certain rights, shall not be construed to deny or disparage others retained by the people." The provisions in Section 1 of the Fourteenth Amendment declaring, "[n]o State shall make or enforce any law which shall abridge the privileges and immunities of citizens of the United States; nor shall any State deprive any person of life, liberty, or property, without due process of law; nor deny any person within its jurisdiction the equal protection of the laws," provide three potential sources for speech, voting, and other democratic rights.

These constitutional provisions all have drawbacks from a democratic perspective. The Guarantee Clause calls for republican government. Many classical republicans did not think universal suffrage desirable and rejected libertarian understandings of speech rights. The First Amendment limits only Congress. James Madison failed when he proposed a constitutional amendment prohibiting state interference with the freedom of speech.[8] Explicit constitutional bans on race and gender discrimination in voting imply that other discriminations are constitutional. The rights guaranteed by the Ninth Amendment are maddeningly vague. If the Fifteenth Amendment was thought necessary to prevent race discrimination in voting, then the Fourteenth Amendment may best be interpreted as not protecting political rights.

Justices in the United States determine the extent to which these constitutional provisions permit courts to police political processes only when resolving lawsuits. Many constitutional questions about speech and voting rights are not litigated. Victims of possible constitutional wrongs are often unaware of their rights or lack the resources to pursue judicial remedies. Litigation over free speech rights was sporadic at best until such groups as the American Civil Liberties Union established the support structure necessary for sustained constitutional adjudication.[9] Crucial political actors often decide certain democratic questions are inappropriate for judicial oversight. Antebellum Americans debated without judicial assistance whether Congress could constitutionally require states to create single-member districts for congressional elections. Justices did not rule on whether fraudulent voting in Illinois enabled John Kennedy to win the 1960 presidential election.

Jurisdiction provides another legal limit on judicial power to police the political process. Justices may determine the speech and voting rights of Americans only when a constitutional provision or statute gives them power to adjudicate relevant cases. This restriction on judicial power played an important role during the 1860s. During the Civil War and Reconstruction, political dissenters were arrested and held without trial under martial law.[10] Clement Vallandigham was arrested after giving antiwar speeches in Indiana. James McCardle was arrested after attacking Reconstruction policies in the Vicksburg *Times*. The Supreme Court refused to hear both appeals on the ground that no jurisdiction existed. In *Ex parte McCardle* (1869), Republicans in Congress after oral argument had taken place proposed repealing the statute granting the Supreme Court jurisdiction to resolve the case. Refusing to run a race against the national legislature, the justices first delayed reaching a decision on the merits and then denied jurisdiction after Congress passed the repeal bill.[11]

These Reconstruction cases suggest a political limit on judicial capacity to police the democratic process. Justices do not declare unconstitutional laws strongly supported by the national elite. More often than not, justices support restrictions on speech and voting rights because justices agree with elite justifications for those measures. Federalists in Congress and Federalists on the federal bench regarded the Alien and Sedition Acts of 1798 as sound constitutional legislation.[12] On some occasions, justices have thought discretion the better part of valor. *Ex parte Vallandigham* (1864) was probably one such instance. Most commentators believe the judicial retreat on free speech issues during the 1950s was partly a strategic response to legislative threats.[13]

The political environment at other times has been conducive to judicial decisions protecting democratic freedoms. Consider the flag salute cases handed down during the 1940s. The Supreme Court in *Minersville School District v. Gobitis* (1940) sustained local decisions expelling from school children who did not salute the flag. Articles in major law reviews and in such elite opinion outlets as the *New Republic* condemned that judicial ruling. Justice Department officials issued a circular, informing federal attorneys that the administration interpreted federal law as giving all persons a right not to say the Pledge of Allegiance. Robert Jackson and Wiley Rutledge received judicial appointments, in part because they were on record as concerned with protecting civil liberties in wartime.[14] Three years later, in *West Virginia State Board of Education v. Barnette* (1943), the Supreme Court overruled *Gobitis* and held that Americans had a right not to salute the flag.

Courts v. Democracy: 1789–1936

The judiciary was a bystander in the democratic revolutions that took place in the United States from ratification until the New Deal. Suffrage was expanded to all white males, nominally to persons of color, and to women, without any judicial help. Speech was protected, when protected, when American legislators and executives adhered to a libertarian tradition that developed outside the courtroom.[15] Justices often proved more willing to declare unconstitutional legislative efforts to expand the franchise as protect political processes from legislative regulation.

Most justices from 1789 until 1937 did not think the United States was a democracy. No Supreme Court majority opinion written before the New Deal referred to the United States, even casually, as a democracy. The United States, justices routinely declared, was a "republic." A few opinions observed that republics were committed to popular sovereignty and recognized some political freedoms. Justice Samuel Miller described "republican government" as one "where political power is reposed in representatives of the entire body of the people, chosen at short intervals by popular elections." "The very idea of a government, republican in form," Chief Justice Morrison Waite declared, "implies a right on the part of its citizens to meet peaceably for consultation in respect to public affairs and to petition for a redress of grievances." More often, federal justices placed greater emphasis on the republican commitment to economic rights. Justice Joseph Story proclaimed, "the right of the citizens to the free enjoyment of their property legally acquired" was "a great and fundamental principle of a republican government." "Due protection of the right of property," Justice John Harlan agreed, "has been regarded as a vital principle of republican institutions." Justice Stephen Field declared, "a distinguishing feature of our republican institutions" is "the right of every citizen of the United States to follow any lawful calling, business, or profession he may choose."

References to "democracy" in the *U.S. Reports* had negative connotations. "A government . . . which held the lives, the liberty, and the property of its citizens subject at all times to the absolute disposition and unlimited control of even the most democratic depository of power," Justices Stanley Matthews and Samuel Miller stated, "is after all but a despotism." Chief Justice Taft spoke of "the evil genius of democracy." Democracy was not what justices protected, but what justices protected against. A Supreme Court advocate declared, "[a]n oligarchy or a democracy is equally unrepublican: each was equally hateful to the founders of our government, and each is equally subversive of the structure which they erected."[16] The "distinguishing feature" of "a republican form of government," Chief Justice Melville Fuller asserted, is that "while the people are . . . the source of power, their governments . . . have been limited by written constitutions, and they have themselves set bounds to their own power, as against the sudden impulses of mere majorities."

Nineteenth-century justices often expressed elite fears that lower-class Americans lacked the capacities necessary to be good republican citizens. Justices James Kent and Joseph Story led fights against Jacksonian efforts to enfranchise all white males. Universal suffrage, Kent maintained, would allow "the indolent and the profligate, to cast the whole burthens of society upon the industrious and the virtuous."[17] Story regarded property qualifications for voting as the means by which "the property-holding part of the community may be sustained against the inroads of poverty and vice."[18] Similar complaints were voiced when women sought the right to vote. A federal justice in 1873 maintained that such efforts to expand the suffrage resulted in "political profligacy and violence verging upon anarchy." When state legislatures gave women a statutory right to vote in certain elections, several state supreme courts declared such measures violated the state constitution.

Federal justices sharply limited their capacity to police political processes when holding the Guarantee Clause was not judicially enforceable. *Luther v. Borden* (1849) arose in the aftermath of the Dorr Rebellion in Rhode Island. Frustrated by legislative refusals to expand the suffrage, prominent Rhode Islanders drafted a new constitution and declared themselves the new state government. The governor of the established state government responded by declaring martial law. When members of the revolutionary Rhode Island government were subsequently arrested, they claimed that the declaration of martial law was inconsistent with republican government. Given an opportunity to intervene in this political imbroglio, the Supreme Court demurred. Chief Justice Taney's majority opinion held that what constituted republican government was for elected officials to determine. "Under this article of the Constitution," he wrote,

> it rests with Congress to decide what government is the established one in a State. For as the United States guarantee to each State a republican government, Congress must necessarily decide what government is established in the State before it can determine whether it is republican or not. And when the senators and representatives of a State are admitted into the councils of the Union, the authority of the government under which they are appointed, as well as its republican character, is recognized by the proper constitutional authority.

Justice John Harlan was the only member of the Supreme Court in the nineteenth century who challenged this consensus. Race distinctions, his famous dissent in *Plessy v. Ferguson* (1896) declared, are "inconsistent with the guarantee given by the Constitution to each State of a republican form of government, and may be stricken down by . . . the courts."

Disenfranchised Americans would not have fared better had the justices ruled the Guarantee Clause justiciable. Justices before the New Deal did not think American citizens had a constitutional right to vote. A unanimous court in *Minor v. Happersett* (1875) approved state power to deny female suffrage. Chief Justice Waite's opinion insisted that the right to vote was not a privilege and immunity of citizens of the United States. "It is certainly now too late to contend a government is not republican," he wrote, "because women are not made voters." A decade later, the justices unanimously ruled that the government could impose a test oath that banned polygamists from voting.

Justices interpreting the post–Civil War Amendments rarely favored the voting rights of newly freed slaves. Sometimes, judicial majorities narrowly interpreted congressional power to police state politics. Other cases declared defective federal indictments against persons who terrorized black voters. *Williams v. Mississippi* (1898) held that courts would not inquire into the motives underlying voting restrictions in former slave states, even when such measures were publicly championed as means for disenfranchising African Americans. *Giles v. Harris* (1903) ruled that federal courts could not take remedial action when state officials refused to register black voters.

Federal courts more sharply curtailed their capacity to address state restrictions on free speech by holding that the liberties set out in the Bill of Rights limited only federal power. Chief Justice John Marshall's unanimous opinion in *Barron v. Baltimore* (1833) declared, "[t]hese amendments demanded security against the apprehended encroachments of the general government—not against those of the local governments." The first ten amendments, he asserted, were "intended solely as a limitation on the exercise of power by the government of the United States, and [are] not applicable to the legislation of the states." A decade later, the Taney Court explicitly held that the First Amendment did not limit state power. Three decades after that decision, the Supreme Court in the *Slaughter-House Cases* (1873) ruled that free speech and other Bill of Rights liberties were not among the privileges and immunities of United States citizens protected by the Fourteenth Amendment. Basic republican freedoms, Justice Miller's majority opinion declared, remained "left to the State governments for security and protection."

Political dissenters would not have fared much better had nineteenth-century federal courts been willing to require state governments to respect free speech rights. Federal courts during the eighteenth and nineteenth centuries showed little disposition to protect political commentary when federal officials restricted political dissent. Supreme Court justices riding circuit declared that the Alien and Sedition Acts were constitutional. Federalist justices forbade counsel from urging juries to consider the constitutionality of congressional restrictions on speech and practically directed convictions. State justices adopted similarly narrow readings of state constitutional expression rights. Most nineteenth-century justices did reject the crime of seditious libel. As John Peter Zenger's attorney urged in 1735, they regarded truth as a defense to libel and allowed truth to be determined by juries.[19] A few justices insisted that public figures could be libeled only if statements were made in reckless disregard of the truth, but they were ahead of their time. Few state courts had any difficulty convicting persons for blasphemy or subversive advocacy. The main legal protection for free speech until the New Deal was that juries determined whether a speech was true or intended to disturb the peace. This eighteenth-century protection was thought adequate to protect popular criticisms of unpopular colonial governors. Juries provided far less protection for unpopular dissidents criticizing popular figures or policies. Justice Oliver Wendell Holmes, Jr., in 1907 declared that the First Amendment only constitutionalized Blackstone's understanding of the common law, one that prohibited government from preventing speech from being published, but permitted punishment for any reason after publication.

Courts routinely sustained convictions for political dissent during World War I and the Red Scare. Partly inspired by progressive beliefs that government action was necessary to both regulate the economy and secure political loyalty, Congress for the first time since the Alien and Sedition Acts passed laws punishing speech. These measures, the Espionage Act of 1917 and the Sedition Act of 1918, were vigorously enforced. Persons who escaped federal attention, ran afoul of state laws. A major third party movement in the Midwest opposed to the war effort was largely destroyed by criminal prosecutions. The Supreme Court heard and rejected seven appeals from convicted wartime critics, and also sustained federal power to deny mailing privileges for antiwar newspapers.

Justice Holmes in *Schenck v. United States* (1919) offered little protection for political dissent when he declared, the "question in every case is whether the words used in such circumstances and are of such a nature as to create a clear and present danger that they will bring about the substantive evils that Congress has a right to prevent." "Clear and present danger" in 1919 was not a libertarian standard. Charles Schenck was sent to jail, even though the pamphlet he circulated merely asserted that the draft was unconstitutional. "[T]he documents would not have been sent unless it had been intended to have some effect," Holmes asserted, "and we do not see what effect it could be expected to have upon persons subject to the draft except to influence them to obstruct the carrying of it out." Eugene Debs, the leader of the Socialist Party, was sent to jail for publicly supporting those in jail for resisting the draft. His conviction was constitutional, Justice Holmes indicated in *Debs v. United States* (1919), because "the opposition was so expressed that its natural and intended effect would be to obstruct recruiting." The Court demonstrated no more sympathy for obscure political protestors. Jacob Abrams was convicted under the Sedition Act after he urged a general strike protesting American intervention in the Russian Civil War. Although Abrams did not oppose World War One, Justice Clarke declared in *Abrams v. United States* (1919) "the plain purpose of [his] propaganda was to excite, at the supreme crisis of the war, disaffection, sedition, and . . . riots."

The progressive era did witness some harbingers of more favorable judicial attitudes toward democracy. Ignoring *Barron* and the *Slaughter-House Cases*, federal justices at the dawn of the twentieth century assumed that states were constitutionally obligated to protect free speech rights.[20] In 1925, the Supreme Court officially ruled that the Fourteenth Amendment incorporated rights guaranteed by the First Amendment. Every justice in *Gitlow v. New York* (1925) agreed that "freedom of speech and of the press . . . are among the fundamental personal rights and liberties protected by the due process clause from impairment by the States." Henceforth, states would have to establish that their practices were consistent with federal constitutional standards. The turn of the twentieth century witnessed a steady increase in the number of cases in which the justices were asked to protect civil liberties and civil rights. As such newly formed organizations as the National Association for the Advancement of Colored People (NAACP) and the American Civil Liberties Union (ACLU) gained the resources necessary to conduct litigation campaigns, justices were more frequently asked to determine the constitutional status of voting and free speech claims.[21] Prominent intellectuals called on courts to protect expression rights. Ernst Freund of the University of Chicago Law School and Zechariah Chafee of Harvard Law School severely criticized *Schenck* and *Debs* in a series of articles published by the *New Republic*.[22] Learned Hand, already considered a progressive star on the lower federal bench, issued an opinion asserting, "to assimilate agitation, legitimate as such, with direct incitement to violent resistance, is to disregard the tolerance of all methods of political agitation which in normal times is a safeguard of free government." "If one stops short of urging upon others that it is their duty or their interest to resist the law," Hand wrote in *Masses Publishing Co. v. Patten* (1917), "it seems to me one should not be held to have attempted to cause its violation."

These libertarian voices gained valuable Supreme Court allies in 1920 when Justices Oliver Wendell Holmes, Jr., and Louis Brandeis began using the clear and present danger test to protect political dissidents. Much language in Holmes's dissenting opinions simply indicated that obscure political dissidents did not present any threat to public interests. "[N]obody can suppose that the surreptitious publishing of a silly leaflet by an unknown man," his dissent in *Abrams* insisted, "would present any immediate danger that its opinion would hinder the success of the government arms." On this view, the First Amendment protected only speech unlikely to persuade. Yet, Holmes's dissent contained language capable of broader interpretation. "[W]hen men have realized that time has upset many fighting faiths," his dissent in *Abrams v. United States* famously concluded,

> they may come to believe even more than they believe the very foundations of their own conduct that the ultimate good desired is better reached by free trade in ideas—that the best test of truth is the power to the thought to get itself accepted in the competition of the market, and that truth is the only ground upon which their wishes safely can be carried out. That at any rate is the theory of our Constitution.

Partly inspired by Justice Holmes, judicial majorities during the late 1920s and early 1930s provided some protection for free speech. Communists were allowed to hold meetings and raise red flags. Newspapers could be not shut down as a public nuisance. A 5–4 judicial majority reversed the conviction and death sentence of a black Communist organizer who urged the formation of an independent black nation in the Jim Crow South. These decisions did not have substantial impact on society, but they did indicate that the Supreme Court might provide more protection for democratic freedoms than some local legislatures. Some Americans for the first time began to think of courts as allies in fights for political freedoms.

The first decades of the twentieth century witnessed limited judicial protection for the voting rights of African Americans. In *Guinn v. United States* (1915), a unanimous Court declared grandfather clauses unconstitutional. These clauses made exceptions to restrictive voting laws for persons whose ancestors had voted before a particular date, usually the date on which black suffrage was forced upon that state. In *Nixon v. Herndon* (1927), the justices struck down a Texas law prohibiting persons of color from voting in Democratic primaries, a matter of major importance given that the winner of the Democratic primary in the one-party South always won the general election. When Texas amended the statute so that the executive committee of the Democratic party was given the responsibility for determining the qualifications of primary voters, a 5–4 judicial majority declared that provision unconstitutional. By statutorily giving the executive committee the power to determine qualifications, the justices asserted, that committee was made an arm of the state. These decisions were particularly surprising because several years previously, in *Newberry v. United States* (1921), the justices had ruled that political primaries were not subject to federal regulation. When the Texas legislature washed its hands entirely of the primary process, however, the Supreme Court ruled that the Democratic Party was a private organization that could restrict primary voting to white persons.

Justice Louis Brandeis best exemplified the nascent New Deal spirit on the progressive bench. His dissenting opinions were the first to celebrate democracy. Several urged justices not to interfere when legislation promoted greater participation in workplace decision-making. In *Frost v. Corporation Com. of Oklahoma* (1929), Brandeis would have sustained a state law limiting the dollar amount of stock persons could own in certain cooperatives "[i]n order to ensure economic democracy." His concurrence in *Whitney v. California* (1927), originally written as a dissent in another case, specifically justified judicial protection for political dissent as vital to the democratic process. Free speech, Brandeis asserted, was "essential to effective democracy." That opinion refashioned the clear and present danger test into a powerful speech protective standard. Brandeis would permit government to regulate speech only when three conditions were met. The speaker had to incite listeners to illegal conduct and not merely advocate breaking the law, the danger presented by the speech had to be "imminent," and the danger had to be serious. "Among free men," Brandeis insisted, "the deterrents ordinarily to be applied to prevent crime are education and punishment for violations of the law, not abridgement of the rights of free speech and assembly."

This vision of American democracy anticipated judicial developments over the next decades. Brandeis also anticipated New Deal jurisprudence by never penning a defense of voting rights.

Courts and Democracy: 1937–1962

The transition from republic to democracy was abrupt and permanent. The first majority opinion to describe the United States as a democracy was issued on 22 November 1939. *Schneider v. State* declared unconstitutional bans on distributing pamphlets in public places. "Mere legislative preferences or beliefs respecting matters of public convenience may well support regulation directed at other personal activities," Justice Owen Roberts declared, "but be insufficient to justify such as diminishes the exercise of rights so vital to the maintenance of democratic institutions." Five months later, Justice Frank Murphy's majority opinion in a case announcing a constitutional right to picket paraphrased *Schneider* when proclaiming, "[m]ere legislative preference for one rather than another means for combating substantive evils . . . may well prove an inadequate foundation on which to rest regulations which are aimed at or in their operation diminish the effective exercise of rights so necessary to the maintenance of democratic institutions."

References to the United States as "a constitutional democracy," to "democratic institutions," and to "sturdy democratic traditions" after 1939 became staples of Supreme Court majority, concurring, and dissenting opinions. Justices spoke of their "stout confidence in the democratic faith we possess." Major cases routinely provided democratic frames for judicial conclusions. Chief Justice Warren's unanimous opinion in *Brown v. Board of Education* (1954) highlighted "the importance of education to our democratic society." *Miranda v. Arizona* (1966) emphasized the need to ensure "the law enforcement profession is steeped in the democratic tradition."

Judicial opinions from 1939 until 1962 placed particular emphasis on the central role free speech and related rights played in democratic societies. The justices in *Thomas v. Collins* (1945) spoke of "the preferred place given in our scheme to the great, the indispensable democratic freedoms secured by the First Amendment." Freedom of speech "was protected," Justice Robert Jackson's concurring opinion maintained, because the framers "knew of no other way by which free men could conduct representative democracy." Justice Stanley Reed in *Jones v. Opelika* (1942) asserted, "[t]o proscribe the dissemination of doctrines or arguments which do not transgress military or moral limits is to destroy the principal bases of democracy,—knowledge and discussion."

Education and academic freedom complemented expression rights as means for preserving democracy. Justice Frankfurter regarded "the public school" as "at once the symbol of our democracy and the most pervasive means for promoting our common destiny." "No one should underestimate the vital role in a democracy that is played by those who guide and train our youth," he wrote ten years later when opposing legislative efforts to have professors testify under oath about their lectures. In Frankfurter's view, "[t]o impose any strait jacket upon the intellectual leaders in our colleges and universities would imperil the future of our Nation."

New Dealers thought democratic societies provided citizens with a fair, humane criminal process. "A democratic society, in which respect for the dignity of all men is central, naturally guards against the misuse of the law enforcement process," Justice Felix Frankfurter's majority opinion in *McNabb v. United States* (1943) declared when ruling inadmissible in federal courts evidence obtained in violation of the Fifth Amendment. "A sturdy, self-respecting democratic community," he later wrote, "should not put up with lawless police and prosecutors." Supreme Court justices celebrated juries as democratic bodies. Justice Murphy spoke of "the democratic traditions" and "the democratic principles of the jury system." "[T]he proper functioning of the jury system, and, indeed, our democracy itself," he wrote, "requires that the jury be a body truly representative of the community."

Religious freedom and racial equality were the last two pillars of New Deal democracy as articulated by Supreme Court justices. In *Prince v. Massachusetts* (1944), Justice Wiley Rutledge described "religious conviction" as "sacred private interests, basic in a democracy." "Zealous watchfulness against fusion of secular and religious activities by Government itself," the judicial majority in *Illinois ex rel. McCollum v. Board of Education* (1948) reasoned, is "the democratic response of the American community." Supreme Court opinions during and after World War II condemned racism as undemocratic. Justice Hugo Black declared, "racial discrimination . . . is at war with our basic concepts of a democratic society and a representative government." Justice Reed agreed that "exclusion because of race," is "inconsistent with our constitutional democracy."

New Deal justices failed to associate democracy with two other rights. The first, not surprisingly, were property rights. The judicial majority in *Schneiderman v. United States* (1943) ruled that persons who favored the abolition of private property could nevertheless be attached to the principles of constitutional democracy. "Whether the legislature takes for its textbook Adam Smith, Herbert Spencer, Lord Keynes, or some other is no concern of ours," Justice Black declared in *Ferguson v. Skrupa* (1963). The second, more surprising omission, was the right to vote. No majority or concurring opinion issued before 1962 linked suffrage to democracy. Plaintiffs in voting rights cases raised democratic problems only when they alleged race discrimination. "The basis of this action," Justice Frankfurter emphasized when striking down racist voting registration practices, "is inequality of treatment though under color of law, not denial of the right to vote." Only Justice William O. Douglas in several dissents joined by Justice Black asserted that democracies protected the right to vote per se.

This broad judicial consensus that the United States was a democracy committed to free speech, fair law enforcement procedures, and liberal equality did not generate a consensus on the judicial role in a democracy. New Deal justices agreed that democratic courts normally deferred to elected officials. Justice Murphy's unanimous opinion in *Daniel v. Family Sec. Life Ins. Co.* (1949) stated, "a court cannot eliminate measures which do not happen to suit its tastes if it seeks to maintain a democratic system." Justice Black spoke of the "basic conflict in the legal history of America . . . between the people's aspirations for democratic government, and the judiciary's desire for the orderly supervision of public affairs by judges." New Deal justices disputed whether such deference was warranted when elected officials restricted rights associated with democracy. Some justices, most notably Justice Frankfurter, insisted that democratic courts did not declare unconstitutional reasonable restrictions on any right. Other justices, most notably Justice Harlan Fiske Stone, thought aggressive judicial policing of the democratic process a necessary prerequisite for judicial deference to the outcomes of a fair democratic process.

This conflict over the judicial role broke out less than a year after Supreme Court justices began describing the United States as a democracy. The occasion was a lawsuit claiming that public school children had a constitutional right not to salute the flag. Justice Frankfurter's majority opinion insisted that the school board practice met democratic standards. "Except where the transgression of constitutional liberty is too plain for argument," he wrote, "personal freedom is best maintained—so long as the remedial channels of the democratic process remain open and unobstructed—when it is ingrained in a people's habits and not enforced against popular policy by the coercion of adjudicated law." Justice Harlan Fiske Stone disagreed. Justice Frankfurter's view that courts "should refrain from passing upon the legislative judgment 'as long as the remedial channels of the democratic process remain open and unobstructed,'" his dissent maintained, "seems . . . no less than the surrender of the constitutional protection of the liberty of small minorities to the popular will."

Justice Stone had previously outlined the democratic foundations for this more active judicial role in an otherwise obscure opinion abjuring judicial power over economic policy. The issue before the Court in *Carolene Products Co. v. United States* (1938) was whether Congress had constitutional power to ban the shipment of milk "fortified with 'any fat or oil other than milk fat.'" New Deal justices had no difficulty sustaining this measure. "[L]egislation affecting ordinary commercial transactions is not to be pronounced unconstitutional," Justice Stone wrote, "unless in the light of the facts made known or generally assumed it is of such a character as to preclude the assumption that it rests upon some rational basis within the knowledge and experience of the legislators." The accompanying footnote indicated that a "narrower scope for operation of the presumption of constitutionality" might be warranted "when legislation appears on its face to be within a specific prohibition of the Constitution," when government practice "restricts those political processes which can ordinarily be expected to bring about repeal of undesirable legislation," and when "prejudice against discrete and insular minorities . . . tends seriously to curtail the operation of those political processes ordinarily to be relied upon to protect minorities." The judicial role, Stone's *Carolene Products* footnote suggested, was to guarantee the integrity of the democratic process. Democratic justices deferred to legislative judgments in matters involving "commercial transactions" only because courts protected the political freedoms necessary for citizens to identify and repeal bad laws, and struck down laws that unfairly burdened the politically powerless.

This two-tiered standard of judicial review rested on several foundations. The first was relative institutional competence. Many New Dealers believed legislators better able than courts to regulate the economy, but less able to regulate the political process. Elected officials who could be "trusted to recognize dirt or discriminate between dangerous and harmless machinery," Chafee maintained, "cannot be trusted to discriminate between dangerous and harmless ideas."[23] Pragmatism provided a second ground for distinguishing between economic and political rights. Elected officials could best exercise their constitutional prerogative to determine social policy only when various alternatives had been freely debated by the general public. Chafee maintained, "the critical judicial spirit which gives the legislature a wide scope in limiting the privilege of property owners will also tend to allow speakers and writers a wide scope in arguing against those freedoms."[24]

Elite concerns fueled judicial protection for democratic rights. Just as republican elites during the nineteenth century questioned whether average Americans made good republican citizens, so democratic elites during the mid-twentieth century doubted whether average Americans made good democratic citizens. Much social science gave reason for caution; various studies suggested that many citizens had authoritarian personalities, little commitment to democratic freedoms, and little knowledge about politics. These findings led many prominent persons to conclude that elite institutions were necessary to preserve democratic institutions from the anti-democratic spirit of the lower classes.[25]

Justice Stone and his judicial allies won many minor victories during the 1940s and 1950s. Supported by members of the Roosevelt Justice Department concerned with mob attacks on Jehovah's Witnesses, judicial decisions frequently overturned local convictions and laws aimed at members of that sect. Dramatically reversing *Gobitis*, the Supreme Court in 1943 declared that persons had a constitutional right not to salute the flag. "If there is any fixed star in our constitutional constellation," Justice Jackson declared in *Barnette*, "it is that no official, high or petty, can prescribe what shall be orthodox in politics, nationalism, religion, or other matters of opinion or force citizens to confess by word or act their faith therein." Throughout the 1950s, Justices Black and Douglas fought a rearguard action against McCarthyism. Sometimes, with the assistance of Chief Justice Earl Warren, Justice William Brennan, and Justice John Marshall Harlan, their efforts were successful. The Supreme Court in *Pennsylvania v. Nelson* (1956) struck down state laws aimed at the Communist Party on the dubious legal ground that such measures were preempted by federal legislation. Justice Harlan in *Yates v. United States* (1957) overturned the convictions of several minor Communist Party leaders by refusing to interpret federal law as proscribing "advocacy and teaching of forcible overthrow as an abstract principle."

Justice Frankfurter and other proponents of judicial restraint gained the major legal victory of the cold war period when the Supreme Court sustained the convictions of Communist Party officials in *Dennis v. United States* (1951). Chief Justice Fred Vinson declared, "the leaders of the Communist Party in this country were unwilling to work within our framework of democracy, but intended to initiate a violent revolution whenever the propitious occasion appeared." Their commitment to eventual violence justified criminal punishment. "If Government is aware that a group aiming at its overthrow is attempting to indoctrinate its members and to commit them to a course whereby they will strike when the leaders feel the circumstances permit," he wrote, "action by the Government is required." Vinson nominally applied "clear and present danger," but interpreted that phrase as requiring a balancing test. "In each case," his opinion stated, courts "must ask whether the gravity of the 'evil,' discounted by its improbability, justifies such invasion of free speech as is necessary to avoid the danger." Justice Frankfurter agreed that a balancing approach was appropriate, and that elected officials were primarily responsible for applying that balance. Rejecting previous claims that courts should have special solicitude for political freedoms, he opined, "[p]rimary responsibility for adjusting the interests which compete in the situation before us of necessity belongs to the Congress." Frankfurter would "set aside the judgment" of elected officials "only if there is no reasonable basis for" the restriction on speech. "Full responsibility cannot be given to courts" because "[t]hey are not designed to be a good reflex of a democratic society."

Justice Black and Douglas sharply disputed these conclusions. Black's dissent began a two decade assault on balancing tests in First Amendment cases. "I cannot agree," he asserted, "that the First Amendment permits us to sustain laws suppressing freedom of speech and press on the basis of Congress' or our own notions of mere 'reasonableness.'" Douglas maintained, "[t]he First Amendment makes confidence in the common sense of our people and in their maturity the great postulate of our democracy." The American people had proven worth of this trust. "Free speech," Douglas wrote, "has destroyed" Communism "as an effective political party." How "it can be said that there is a clear and present danger that this advocacy will succeed," he concluded, "is a mystery."

Judicial restraint was the dominant New Deal theme in voting rights cases. *Colegrove v. Green* (1946) rejected efforts to have the judiciary cure malapportioned legislative districts. Justice Frankfurter's plurality opinion declared, "[i]t is hostile to a democratic system to involve the judiciary in the politics of the people." He described as "pernicious if such judicial intervention in an essentially political contest be dressed up in the abstract phrases of law." A unanimous Supreme Court in *Breedlove v. Suttles* (1937) ruled that poll taxes did not violate constitutional rights. Justice Douglas spoke for a unanimous court twenty years later when defending the constitutionality of literacy tests. "The States," his opinion maintained, "have long been held to have broad powers to determine the conditions under which the right of suffrage may be exercised, absent of course the discrimination which the Constitution condemns."

New Deal justices supported voting rights only under two conditions. The first was when sustaining national legislation. *United States v. Classic* (1941) held that Congress had broad power to protect the right to vote in state primaries. In these instances, New Deal democratic themes concerning political processes and the judicial role were harmonious. Justices in *Classic* and related cases could expand political freedom by deferring to national elected officials. The second was when plaintiffs alleged "the [race] discrimination which the Constitution condemns." Supported by Roosevelt administration officials, the Supreme Court in *Smith v. Allwright* (1944) declared white-only state primary elections unconstitutional. "The right to participate in the choice of elected officials," Justice Reed asserted, "is not to be nullified by a State through casting its electoral process in a form which permits a private organization to practice racial discrimination in the election."

Democracy v. Democracy: 1962–Present

The judicial commitment to democracy initiated in 1939 continues to this day. Great Society Democrats and Reagan Revolution Republicans on the Supreme Court fight to outdo each other as democratic champions. Judicial opinions commonly refer to the United States as a democracy. Justice John Paul Stevens describes Americans as "a united democratic people," and Justice Steven Breyer speaks of "the Framers' own aspiration to write a document that would 'constitute' a democratic, liberty-protecting form of government." Dissenting opinions routinely accuse the judicial majority of violating democratic norms. Dissents from decisions declaring governmental practices unconstitutional complain, "much [is] lost in the process of democratic decisionmaking, by allowing individual judges in city after city to second-guess such legislative or administrative determinations." Dissents from decisions sustaining government practices complain, "in our democracy [law] enforcement presupposes . . . the effective administration of justice can be achieved with due regard for those civilized standards in the use of the criminal law which are formulated in our Bill of Rights."

Free speech remains central to judicial conceptions of democracy. "Maintenance of the opportunity for free political discussion," Justice Arthur Goldberg declared in *Cox v. Louisiana* (1965), "is a basic tenet of our constitutional democracy." Four decades later, Justice Sandra Day O'Connor wrote, "no robust democracy insulates its citizens from views that they might find novel or even inflammatory." Contemporary judicial opinions frequently emphasize the need for a knowledgeable democratic public. *FBI v. Abramson* (1982) pronounced "an informed citizenry, vital to the functioning of a democratic society." Many justices celebrate popular political engagement. Justice William Brennan spoke of "the enormous significance of citizen participation to the preservation and strength of the democratic ideal." Judicial opinions commonly point to both associative and privacy dimensions of constitutional expression rights. "[T]he constitutional privilege to be secure in associations in legitimate organizations engaged in the exercise of First and Fourteenth Amendment rights," Justice Goldberg declared in *Gibson v. Florida Legislative Investigation Committee* (1963), is "basic to the preservation of our democracy." *Bartnicki v. Vopper* (2001) asserted "[i]n a democratic society privacy of communication is essential if citizens are to think and act creatively and constructively." Government secrecy is constitutionally disfavored. Justice Stevens spoke for all his brethren when he declared, "a democracy cannot function unless the people are permitted to know what their government is up to."

Justices during the 1960s for the first time proclaimed suffrage rights democratically indispensable. Chief Justice Earl Warren in *Reynolds v. Sims* (1964) declared, "[t]he right to vote freely for the candidate of one's choice is of the essence of a democratic society." A year later, Justice Potter Stewart asserted that voting rights were "vital to the maintenance of democratic institutions." "Encouraging citizens to vote is a legitimate, indeed essential, state objective," Justice Anthony Kennedy insisted in *California Democratic Party v. Jones* (2000), and "the constitutional order must be preserved by a strong, participatory democratic process." This right to vote is a right to an equal vote. Justice Black in *Wesberry v. Sanders* (1964) maintained, "[t]o say that a vote is worth more in one district than in another would . . . run counter to our fundamental ideas of democratic government." "One person, one vote," Chief Justice Warren stated, is grounded in "the democratic ideals of equality and majority rule."

American judicial elites, fervently committed to democracy, identified numerous policies as central to a democratic society. Great Society and Reagan Revolution justices wrote about the democratic importance of education, juries, religious freedom and racial equality. In *Plyler v. Doe* (1982), Justice Brennan described "public schools as a most vital civic institution for the preservation of a democratic system of government." Justice Antonin Scalia maintained juries were "the spinal column of American democracy." "[A]ntagonisms that relate to race or to religion," Justice O'Connor declared in *Shaw v. Reno* (1993), are "at war with the democratic ideal." To these traditional democratic icons, various justices added federalism ("a promoter of democracy"), the right to travel ("its importance to decision-making in our democratic society"), collective bargaining ("sanctioned by the philosophy of democratic institutions"), privacy ("functional necessit[y] for "a [democratic] regime"), access to attorneys ("a democratic society needs . . . lawyers who will defend unpopular causes and champion unpopular clients"), referenda ("basic instrument of democratic government"), marriage ("a critical role . . . in our democratic society"), busing ("racial balance in the schools promotes . . . democratic citizenship"), antitrust ("fundamental importance to American democratic capitalism"), anti-delegation ("serious potential threat to liberty and democracy"), an exclusive executive appointment power ("widely distributed appointment power subverts democratic government"), opposition to sovereign immunity ("unsuitable for incorporation into the law of this democratic Nation"), and the census ("mainstay of our democracy"). Democracy in the courtroom and outside presently stands for everything good in the world. Justice Stevens described the United States Open as "America's greatest—and most democratic—golf tournament."

Great Society and Reagan Revolution justices vigorously police the democratic process. When Justice Frankfurter retired in 1962, claims that democratic courts normally deferred when elected officials balanced democratic freedoms largely disappeared from judicial opinions. Many justices pay homage to judicial restraint when speech and voting rights are not at issue. *Warth v. Seldin* (1975) spoke of "the properly limited . . . role of courts in a democratic society." Whether any justice does more than give lip-service to that role is contestable. None are restrained when they believed democratic liberties infringed.

Professor Richard Pildes well summarizes and analyzes "the constitutionalization of democratic politics" in contemporary American politics in his 2004 "Foreword" to the *Harvard Law Review*. "In American constitutional law," Pildes observed,

> political parties now have broader associational autonomy rights than ever before. Constitutional law also now shapes the contours of fair political representation and political equality, as well as the role of group identities in the design of democratic institutions. The financing of all elections, federal and state, and the role of corporations, unions, and parties in elections are now substantially constrained by constitutional law. Supreme Court decisions have transformed the nature of direct democracy. States can no longer structure direct democracy in line with their own visions of participatory democracy. Term limits and other qualifica-

> tions for officeholding imposed on members of Congress by states are unconstitutional; ballot notations informing voters of congressional candidates' positions on specific issues are similarly forbidden. Constitutional law has also altered the longstanding nature of judicial elections. Similarly, issues of voting technology and vote-counting procedures might now be matters of constitutional law. And, of course, constitutional law governs the resolution of disputed presidential and other elections.[26]

This expanded judicial supervision over democratic processes is a global phenomenon, as courts around the world now adjudicate the juxtaposition of numerous issues of social, political, and economic import against democratic ideals.

The increased judicial commitment to policing the democratic process in the United States was first manifested in voting rights cases. Brushing aside Justice Frankfurter's concern that "in a democratic society . . . relief must come through an aroused public conscience," the judicial majority in *Baker v. Carr* (1962) ruled that persons seeking relief from malapportioned legislatures were making justiciable claims. Justice Brennan's majority opinion nominally accepted past judicial precedents holding that "the Guaranty Clause is not a repository of judicially manageable standards." Nevertheless, he concluded, redistricting cases present judicially cognizable Fourteenth Amendment issues. "Judicial standards under the Equal Protection Clause," Brennan wrote, "are well developed and familiar." The next year in *Gray v. Sanders* (1963), the justices announced that "[t]he conception of political equality . . . can mean only one thing—one person, one vote." Applying this standard, *Reynolds v. Sims* (1964) declared, entailed "no less than substantially equal state legislative representation for all citizens." With these words, the Court initiated the reapportionment revolution, one that would significantly change federal and state legislative politics, though not necessarily in ways the justices anticipated. Suburbs were more empowered than inner cities. The main winners proved to be majority party leaders, who proceeded to gerrymander many states in ways that produced legislative majorities far in excess of their popular support.

This judicial commitment to political equality immediately extended to state restrictions on the ballot. Poll taxes were the first to fall. Justice Douglas's majority opinion in *Harper v. Virginia State Board of Elections* (1966) stated that "a State violates the Equal Protection Clause . . . whenever it makes the affluence of the voter or payment of any fee an electoral standard." His conclusion put most voting restrictions in jeopardy. "Where fundamental rights and liberties are asserted under the Equal Protection Clause," Douglas wrote, "classifications which might invade or restrain them must be closely scrutinized and carefully confined." Within three years, judicial majorities made clear that "exacting judicial scrutiny" was required of all "statutes distributing the franchise." "[I]f a challenged state statute grants the right to vote to some bona fide residents of requisite age and citizenship and denies the franchise to others," Chief Justice Warren asserted in *Kramer v. Union Free School District* (1969), "the Court most determine whether the exclusions are necessary to promote a compelling state interest." For all practical purposes, *Harper* and *Kramer* announced a constitutional right to vote under the guise of equal protection. Most adults can be denied the right to vote under these judicial decisions, only if the state elects to make all offices non-elective, a constitutional impossibility in most states and a practical impossibility in all.

The justices proved as supportive to voting rights when reviewing federal legislation that invoked congressional authority under the Civil War Amendments to expand the suffrage. Congress was held to have the authority to determine when a constitutional voting rights violation had occurred and to forbid otherwise constitutional state actions when a reasonable person might think legislation appropriate for preventing future constitutional voting rights violations. *South Carolina v. Katzenbach* (1966) sustained a congressional decision to suspend literary tests in jurisdictions where less then half the voting age population cast ballots during the 1964 national election. That the justices had previously held such restrictions constitutional on their face did not bind the national legislature. Noting legislative findings that such tests were often applied to disenfranchise persons of color, Chief Justice Warren bluntly declared, "Congress may use any rational means to effectuate the constitutional prohibition of racial discrimination in voting." *Katzenbach v. Morgan* (1966) ruled that Congress was constitutionally entitled to enfranchise all persons who had received primary education in Puerto Rico as a means to prevent unconstitutional discrimination against Puerto Ricans. That provision of the Voting Rights Act, Justice Brennan asserted, "may be viewed as a measure to secure . . . nondiscriminatory treatment by government—both in the imposition of voting qualifications and the provision or administration of government services."

New York Times Co. v. Sullivan (1964) inaugurated the reign of heightened judicial protection for free speech. L. B. Sullivan was awarded $500,000 in damages by an Alabama jury after the *New York Times* published an advertisement containing several false statements about his actions during civil rights protests. The decision threatened to bankrupt crucial supporters of Martin Luther King and curtail press coverage of African American protests in the South. A unanimous Supreme Court reversed that state verdict. Justice Brennan's majority opinion detected "a profound national commitment to the principle that debate on public issues should be uninhibited, robust, and wide-open, and . . . may well include vehement, caustic, and sometimes unpleasantly sharp attacks on government and public officials." In order to give First Amendment freedoms the necessary "breathing space," factual errors had to enjoy some constitutional protection. The judicial majority in *Sullivan* prohibited libel suits by public officials unless "the statement was made with 'actual malice'—that is, with knowledge that it was false or reckless disregard of whether it was false or not." "In spite of the probability of excesses and abuses," Justice Brennan declared, free speech was "essential to enlightened opinion and right conduct on the part of the citizens of a democracy."

Five years later, the justices sharply limited government power to punish subversive advocacy. *Brandenburg v. Ohio* (1969) was an appeal by a Ku Klux Klan member who had been convicted under a statute banning criminal syndicalism. The offending expression was, "if our President, our Congress, our Supreme Court, continues to suppress the white Caucasian race, it's possible that there might have to be some revengenance taken." The Supreme Court threw out the guilty verdict. Overruling decisions from the 1920s, the justices endorsed the general standard of free speech protection Brandeis articulated in *Whitney v. California*, minus the explicit requirement that speech cause very serious harm. "[T]he constitutional guarantees of free speech and free press," the per curiam opinion declared, "do not permit a State to forbid or proscribe advocacy of the use of force or of law violation except where such advocacy is directed to inciting or producing imminent lawless action and is likely to incite or produce such action." Justices Black and Douglas went further. They insisted that any variation on clear and present danger "should have no place in the interpretation of the First Amendment."

New York Times Co. v. United States (1971) was the third movement of this libertarian symphony. The justices rejected a Nixon administration effort to obtain an injunction forbidding the *Washington Post* and *New York Times* from publishing classified information about the Vietnam War. The per curiam opinion declared, "any system of prior restraints of expression comes to this Court bearing a heavy burden of presumption against its constitutional validity." The "Government" did "not meet that burden." Individual judicial opinions revealed a badly fractured judiciary. Justices Douglas and Black insisted all prior restraints were unconstitutional. Justice Douglas condemned "secrecy in government" as "fundamentally undemocratic." Justice Black's concurring opinion declared, "[i]n the First Amendment the Founding Fathers gave the free press the protection it must have to fulfill its essential role in our democracy." Justice Brennan suggested "there is a single, extremely narrow class of cases in which the First Amendment's ban on prior judicial restraint may be overridden," namely when papers threatened to publish information analogous to "the sailing dates of transports or the number and location of troops." The Pentagon Papers, in his view, did not meet this exception to normal democratic practice. Justices Potter Stewart, Byron White, and Thurgood Marshall stressed the lack of congressional authorization for the prior restraint. "It would," Justice Marshall wrote, "be utterly inconsistent with the concept of separation of powers for this Court to use its power of contempt to prevent behavior Congress has specifically declined to prohibit." Unlike *New York Times v. Sullivan* and *Brandenburg v. Ohio*, three justices dissented. Justice Harlan criticized the majority for "passing upon the activities of the Executive Branch of the Government in the field of foreign affairs."

Justices appointed by more conservative Republican presidents proved faithful to the *Sullivan/Brandenburg/New York Times* trilogy. Justice O'Connor's plurality opinion in *Virginia v. Black* (2003) cited *Brandenburg* as providing the appropriate test for judging whether persons could be criminally convicted for burning a cross. In *Avis Rent A Car Sys. v. Aguilar* (2000), Justice Clarence Thomas invoked *New York Times Co. v. United States* when objecting to a judicial order enjoining a defendant from using words offensive to his Latino employees. Chief Justice William Rehnquist, Justice Anthony Kennedy, and Justice O'Connor have invoked *Sullivan*'s claim that "debate on public issues should be uninhibited, robust, and wide-open." A unanimous Rehnquist Court repeatedly cited *Sullivan* in *Hustler Magazine v. Falwell* (1988) when overturning a jury verdict awarding Jerry Falwell, a prominent political evangelical, substantial damages from *Hustler Magazine* after that periodical published a clearly labeled parody depicting Falwell talking about committing incest with his mother. Rejecting claims that public figures could recover damages for intentional infliction of emotional damage, Chief Justice Rehnquist declared, "that society may find speech offensive is not a sufficient reason for suppressing it." Tinkering at the margins has taken place, particularly within the constitutional law of libel. Nevertheless, no contemporary Supreme Court Justice has even hinted that the Great Society framework for free speech cases should be substantially modified or abandoned.

Great Society voting rights precedents are also still standing, but on shakier grounds. The more centrist justices on the Rehnquist Court are generally attached to the *Reynolds/Harper/Morgan* trilogy. Both *Harper* and *Reynolds* were cited prominently by the majority opinion in *Bush v. Gore* (2000). One person/one vote remains good constitutional law when congressional districts are apportioned. Substantial deviations have been judicially tolerated when state legislative districts are apportioned. Justice Rehnquist's opinion in *Mahan v. Howell* (1973) held that "the normal functioning of state and local governments" justifies "more flexibility . . . with respect to state legislative reapportionment than in congressional redistricting." With two exceptions, voting restrictions must satisfy strict scrutiny. The first is for elections with a "special limited purpose," such as a vote on water storage proposals. Such restrictions are constitutional if reasonable. The other is for state laws disenfranchising felons. A Burger Court majority ruled that such state bans did not have to satisfy strict scrutiny. Constitutional permission was implied from Section 2 of the Fourteenth Amendment, which reduces state representation in Congress whenever votes were "denied to any of the male inhabitants of such State, being twenty-one years of age, . . . except for participation in rebellion, or other crime." The

Justices vigorously dispute the meaning of federal voting rights acts, but a judicial majority still maintains that Congress has the power under the Fourteenth Amendment to both remedy and prevent constitutional wrongs. Justice Scalia disagrees. He would have the justices significantly modify *Katzenbach v. Morgan*. "Nothing in § five," Justice Scalia insisted in *Tennessee v. Lane* (2004), "allows Congress to go beyond the provisions of the Fourteenth Amendment to proscribe, prevent, or 'remedy' conduct that does not itself violate any provision of the Fourteenth Amendment."

More basic divisions between Great Society liberals and Reagan Revolution conservatives are over what constitutes good democratic practice in free speech and voting rights cases. Justices at the turn of the twenty-first century actively police the political process. They dispute when judicial policing is appropriate. On issues as diverse as patronage, term limits, regulation of political parties, commercial speech, partisan gerrymandering, judicial elections, racial gerrymandering, and the 2000 presidential election, justices do not agree whether the constitutionally challenged practice advances or inhibits democracy. Liberals are activists in cases involving patronage, term limits, and partisan gerrymandering. Conservatives are activists in cases involving regulation of political parties, campaign finance, judicial elections, racial gerrymanders, and the 2000 presidential election. Commercial speech inspires activism in both liberals and conservatives. Theories of constitutional interpretation fail to explain these differences. Originalists ignore history when championing judicial protection for commercial speech and striking down racial gerrymanders intended to increase African American representation in Congress.[27] Critics of originalism engage in lengthy historical exegesis when striking down state laws imposing term limits on national officials. Judicial divisions are roughly between liberals who understand democracy as primarily concerned with political equality and conservatives who understand democracy as primarily concerned with political liberty.

Campaign finance cases illustrate these differences between Great Society liberals and Reagan Revolution conservatives. Both sides to the disputes over whether legislatures may constitutionally regulate contributions and expenditures invoke democratic values. More liberal justices who believe campaign finance laws constitutional are "concern[ed] with the political potentialities of wealth and their untoward consequences for the democratic process." "Leave the perception of impropriety unanswered," Justice David Souter declared in *Nixon v. Shrink Mo. Gov't Pac* (2000), "and the cynical assumption that large donors call the tune could jeopardize the willingness of voters to take part in democratic governance." More conservative justices who believe campaign finance laws unconstitutional declare, "[g]iven the premises of democracy, there is no such thing as too much speech." "[P]rohibit[ing] corporations and labor unions from using money from their general treasury to fund electioneering communications," Justice Kennedy maintained in *McConnell v. Federal Election Commission*

(2003), "silences political speech central to the civic discourse that sustains and informs our democratic processes."

The result is a confusing melange of decisions seemingly designed only to keep law professors and First Amendment lawyers in business. The justices in 1976 ruled that Congress could regulate most campaign contributions "to limit the actuality and appearance of corruption resulting from large individual financial contributions," but not independent expenditures in order to "equaliz[e] the relative ability of individuals and groups to influence the outcome of elections." "[T]he concept that government may restrict the speech of some elements in our society in order to enhance the relative voice of others," the per curiam opinion in *Buckley v. Valeo* (1976) maintained, "is wholly foreign to the First Amendment." Later decisions held that for-profit corporations have a constitutional right to contribute money to referenda campaigns, but not to candidates running for elective office. Most recently in *McConnell*, a badly divided judicial majority ruled most congressional limits on soft money, money raised by political parties for campaigning, are constitutional. Whether these decisions will do more than encourage more creative means for raising and spending campaign funds remains to be seen.

Judicial proponents of political equality and political liberty clash over the constitutionality of racial gerrymanders designed to increase African American representation in Congress. Proponents believe self-conscious efforts to create election districts with African American majorities "provid[e] long-excluded groups the opportunity to participate effectively in the democratic process." Opponents maintain "benign" racial gerrymanders "reinforce racial stereotypes and threaten to undermine our system of representative democracy by signaling to elected officials that they represent a particular racial group rather than their constituency as a whole." In *Miller v. Johnson* (1995), a 5–4 judicial majority declared unconstitutional all gerrymanders where "race was the predominant factor motivating the legislature's decision to place a significant number of voters within or without a particular district." States can, however, self-consciously engage in partisan gerrymanders that create strong Democratic or Republican districts. Given strong Democratic partisanship among most African Americans and continued patterns of residential segregation, the difference between unconstitutional racial gerrymanders and constitutional partisan gerrymanders will often depend on how attorneys for the state legislature describe the legislative redistricting, and on whose attorneys the lower federal courts believe.

Bush v. Gore provides a final illustration of the contemporary judicial approach to policing the political process. Justice Scalia's opinion enjoining the Florida recount during the 2000 presidential election declared, "[c]ount first, and rule upon legality afterwards, is not a recipe for producing election results that have the public acceptance democratic stability requires." "[T]he Florida court's ruling reflects the basic principle, inherent in our Constitution and our democracy," Justice Stevens's dissent replied, "that every legal vote should be counted." All parties wanted courts to police the democratic process. Democrats wanted state justices to force Florida officials to extend deadlines for counting ballots. Republicans wanted federal justices to prevent state justices from overturning state administrative decisions. American justices and citizens simply disputed whether the Supreme Court of Florida or the Supreme Court of the United States was the better democratic police officer.

The Future

Justices have no inherent tendency to promote good democratic practice. For the first two-thirds of American constitutional life, justices protected republican values from more democratic institutions. Proponents of free speech and voting rights more often triumphed in legislative halls than in courtrooms. From the New Deal until the Great Society, justices debated whether democratic courts policed the political process or sustained all reasonable legislative regulations. Political freedoms tended to be protected only when judicial action had some executive support. Contemporary justices actively police politics, but do not agree on what measures best promote democracy. Whether courts better champion democracy than elected officials presently depends on whether such measures as campaign finance reform enhance or debase democracy.

Whether courts will be leaders or laggards during the next democratic revolution cannot be determined. The Supreme Court during the New Deal and Great Society was generally more supportive of political freedoms than most elected officials. Justices during the nineteenth century were far less supportive of political freedoms than most elected officials. Justice Joseph Story during the War of 1812 unsuccessfully urged President James Madison to pass a Sedition Law aimed a stifling wartime dissent.[28] Disputes over democracy further complicate efforts to predict the judicial future. Proponents of the next political revolution will not have their recommendations plainly stamped with nature's democratic seal of approval. Opponents will claim that such measures are democratically perverse. When Lani Guinier maintained that democracy would benefit from a strong dose of proportional representation, critics responded that her proposals were undemocratic and anti-American.[29] No historical reason exists for thinking most justices will be on the right or winning side of this and other disputes over good democratic practice.

Future justices will not perform solos when regulating the political process. Courts do not protect political freedoms that lack resonance in the rest of the political system. Constitutional litigation is politics by other means. Some judicial decisions protecting speech and voting rights help national majorities implement policies opposed by local majorities. Judicial decisions expanding democracy in the post–World War II South were prompted by northern liberals in the Roosevelt administration.[30] Other judicial decisions support some members of the ruling coalition against other members of the ruling coalition. Campaign finance reform has supporters and critics in every national party and branch of the national government.

Future judicial decisions on political freedoms will reflect values held by political elites. Justices during the nineteenth century articulated elite fears that the poor and persons of color could not be good republican citizens. Justices during the twentieth century were moved by elite concerns that lower class Americans lacked democratic virtues. Contemporary decisions in First Amendment cases are consistent with increased libertarian sentiments among American elites. The Supreme Court is rapidly blurring the line between commercial and political speech. Persons are free to use private resources to promote political ideas, but have less access to government or private property. Government may not punish those who burn privately purchased flags, but may forbid protestors from sleeping in a public park when demonstrating against homelessness.

This libertarian turn offers a democratic blessing and curse. Distrust of government and exultation of individual freedom provide powerful grounds for resisting government efforts to impose any orthodoxy. These same values are producing a constitutional environment in which institutions that traditionally had distinctively democratic missions are being transformed into normal business enterprises: Print and broadcast journalism are becoming yoked to profit margins, and college presidents spend much of their time fundraising. These metamorphoses threaten the distinction between political and economic behavior that provided the foundation for twentieth-century judicial protections for speech and voting rights. Why should justices regard General Electric the producer of television shows any differently than General Electric the producer of airplanes? What does academic freedom mean when the purpose of a university is, in the words of one academic bureaucrat, to advance "economic development by developing knowledge-linked activities that enhance technological commercialization, support organizational and community change, and enhance the competencies of workers and professionals."[31] Forthcoming democratic battles against the marketplace will primarily be fought outside the courtroom. The best a democratic judiciary can do is help give citizens the choice between being informed or entertained and students the choice between being educated or credentialed.

Notes

*I am grateful to the members of the Commission for their help, advice, and forbearance.

1. *Annals of Congress*, 7th Cong., 1st Sess. (1802), 38.

2. See John V. Orth, "Taking from A and Giving to B: Substantive Due Process and the Case of the Shifting Paradigm," *Constitutional Commentary* 14 (1997): 337; Mark A. Graber, "Naked Land Transfers and American Constitutional Development," *Vanderbilt Law Review* 53 (2000), 73.
3. See Graber, *Transforming Free Speech*
4. See George W. Pring and Penelope Canan, *SLAPPs: Getting Sued for Speaking Out* (Philadelphia: Temple University Press, 1996); C. Edwin Baker, *Advertising and a Democratic Press* (Princeton, N.J.: Princeton University Press, 1994).
5. See Eskridge and Levinson, eds., *Constitutional Stupidities, Constitutional Tragedies.*
6. See Keyssar, *The Right to Vote*, 8–25.
7. See Stephen M. Griffin, "The Nominee Is . . . Article V," *Constitutional Commentary* 12 (1995), 171.
8. See Veit, Bowling, and Bickford, eds., *Creating the Bill of Rights.*
9. See Epp, *The Rights Revolution.*
10. See Mark E. Neely, Jr., *The Fate of Liberty: Abraham Lincoln and Civil Liberties* (New York: Oxford University Press, 1991).
11. See Stanley I. Kutler, *Judicial Power and Reconstruction Politics* (Chicago: University of Chicago Press, 1968), 100–104.
12. See Curtis, *Free Speech*, 63–68, 88–91
13. Walter F. Murphy, *Congress and the Courts* (Chicago: University of Chicago Press, 1962); Powe, *The Warren Court and American Politics*, 141–156. The seminal studies of strategic behavior by Supreme Court justices are Walter F. Murphy, *Elements of Judicial Strategy* (Chicago: University of Chicago Press, 1964); Epstein and Knight, *The Choices Justices Make.*
14. See Kevin J. McMahon, *Reconsidering Roosevelt on Race: How the Presidency Paved the Road to Brown* (Chicago: University of Chicago Press, 2004), 136–139.
15. See Curtis, *Free Speech*, 12–14.
16. *Pacific States Telephone & Telegraph Co. v. Oregon*, 223 U.S. 118, 123 (1912) (argument of counsel). See Morton J. Horwitz, "The Constitution of Change: Legal Fundamentality Without Fundamentalism, *Harvard Law Review* 107 (1993), 30.
17. James Kent, "Speech at the New York Constitutional Convention, 1821," *Free Government in the Making*, 4th ed. (New York: Oxford University Press, 1985), 369–370.
18. Joseph Story, "Massachusetts Constitutional Convention, 1820," *Free Government in the Making*, 369–370.
19. See *People v. Croswell*, 3 Johns. Cas. 337 (N.Y. Sup. Ct. 1804).
20. See Graber, *Transforming Free Speech*, 34–36.
21. Epp, *Rights Revolution*, 49–51.
22. See Ernst Freund, "The *Debs* Case and Freedom of Speech," *The New Republic* 19 (3 May 1919), 13; Zechariah Chafee, Jr., "Freedom of Speech," *The New Republic* 17 (16 November 1918), 66.
23. Zechariah Chafee, Jr., *The Inquiring Mind* (New York: Harcourt Brace and Company, 1928), 69.
24. Chafee, *Free Speech*, 360–361.
25. See Edward A. Purcell, Jr., *The Crisis of Democratic Theory: Scientific Naturalism and the Problem of Value* (Lexington: University Press of Kentucky, 1973).

26. Richard H. Pildes, "The Constitutionalization of Democratic Politics," *Harvard Law Review* 118 (2004), 31-32, at 28.
27. See Mark A. Graber, "Clarence Thomas and the Perils of Amateur History," *Rehnquist Justice: Understanding the Court Dynamic,* edited by Earl M. Maltz (Lawrence: University Press of Kansas, 2003), 87–90.
28. Donald R. Hickey, *The War of 1812: A Forgotten Conflict* (Urbana: University of Illinois Press, 1989), 70.
29. Clint Bolick, "Clinton's Quota Queens," *Wall Street Journal* (30 April 1993), A12.
30. See Kevin J. McMahon, *Reconsidering Roosevelt on Race.*
31. Ellen W. Schrecker, "Free Speech on Campus: Academic Freedom and the Corporations," *The Boundaries of Freedom of Expression and Order in American Democracy*, edited by Thomas R. Hensely (Kent, Oh.: Kent State University Press, 2001), 239.

Bibliography

Curtis, Michael Kent. *Free Speech, 'The People's Darling Privilege': Struggles for Freedom of Expression in American History*. Durham, N.C.: Duke University Press, 2000.

Epp, Charles E. *The Rights Revolution: Lawyers, Activists, and Supreme Courts in Comparative Perspective*. Chicago: University of Chicago Press, 1998.

Epstein, Lee, and Jack Knight. *The Choices Justices Make.* Washington, D.C.: CQ Press, 1998.

Eskridge, William N., Jr., and Sanford Levinson, eds. *Constitutional Stupidities, Constitutional Tragedies*. New York University Press: New York, 1998.

Graber, Mark A. *Transforming Free Speech: The Ambiguous Legacy of Civil Libertarianism.* Berkeley: University of California Press, 1991.

Keyssar, Alexander. *The Right to Vote: The Contested History of Democracy in the United States*. New York: Basic Books, 2000.

McMahon, Kevin J. *Reconsidering Roosevelt on Race: How the Presidency Paved the Road to Brown*. Chicago: University of Chicago Press, 2004.

Murphy, Walter F. *Elements of Judicial Strategy*. Chicago: University of Chicago Press, 1964.

Powe, Lucas A., Jr., *The Warren Court and American Politics* (Cambridge, Mass.: Harvard University Press, 2000)

Veit, Helen E., Kenneth R. Bowling, and Charlene Bangs Bickford, eds. *Creating the Bill of Rights: The Documentary Record from the First Federal Congress*. Baltimore: Johns Hopkins University Press, 1991.

Court Cases

Abrams v. United States, 250 U.S. 616 (1919).

Avis Rent A Car Sys. v. Aguilar, 529 U.S. 1138 (2000).

Baker v. Carr 369 U.S. 186 (1962).

Barron v. Baltimore, 32 U.S. 243 (1833).

Bartnicki v. Vopper, 532 U.S. 514 (2001).

Brandenburg v. Ohio, 395 U.S. 444 (1969).

Breedlove v. Suttles, 302 U.S. 277 (1937).
Brown v. Board of Education, 347 U.S. 483 (1954).
Buckley v. Valeo, 424 U.S. 1 (1976).
Bush v. Gore, 531 U.S. 98 (2000).
California Democratic Party v. Jones, 530 U.S. 567 (2000).
Carolene Products Co. v. United States, 304 U.S. 144 (1938).
Chambers v. Florida, 309 U.S. 227 (1940).
Colegrove v. Green, 328 U.S. 549 (1946).
Cox v. Louisiana, 379 U.S. 536 (1965).
Daniel v. Family Sec. Life Ins. Co., 336 U.S. 220 (1949).
Debs v. United States, 249 U.S. 211 (1919).
Dennis v. United States, 341 U.S. 494 (1951).
Ex Parte McCardle, 74 U.S. 506 (1869).
Ex Parte Vallandigham, 68 U.S. 243 (1864).
FBI v. Abramson, 456 U.S. 615 (1982).
Ferguson v. Skrupa, 372 U.S. 726 (1963).
Frost v. Corporation Com. of Oklahoma, 278 U.S. 515 (1929).
Gibson v. Florida Legislative Investigation Committee, 372 U.S. 539 (1963).
Giles v. Harris, 189 U.S. 475 (1903).
Gitlow v. New York, 268 U.S. 652 (1925).
Gray v. Sanders, 372 U.S. 368 (1963).
Guinn v. United States, 238 U.S. 347 (1915).
Harper v. Virginia State Board of Elections, 383 U.S. 663 (1966).
Hustler Magazine Inc. v. Falwell, 485 U.S. 46 (1988).
Illinois ex rel. McCollum v. Board of Education, 333 U.S. 203 (1948).
Jones v. Opelika, 316 U.S. 584 (1942).
Katzenbach v. Morgan, 383 U.S. 641 (1966).
Kramer v. Union Free School District, 395 U.S. 621 (1969).
Luther v. Borden, 48 U.S. 1 (1849).
Mahan v. Howell, 410 U.S. 315 (1973).
Masses Publishing Co. v. Patten, 244 F. 535 (S.D.N.Y. 1917).
McConnell v. Federal Election Commission, 540 U.S. 93 (2003).
McNabb v. United States, 318 U.S. 332 (1943).
Miller v. Johnson, 515 U.S. 900 (1995).
Minersville School District v. Gobitis, 310 U.S. 586 (1940).
Minor v. Happersett, 88 U.S. 162 (1875).
Miranda v. Arizona, 384 U.S. 436 (1966).
Newberry v. United States, 256 U.S. 232 (1921).
New York Times Co. v. Sullivan, 376 U.S. 254 (1964).
New York Times Co. v. United States, 403 U.S. 713 (1971).
Nixon v. Herndon, 273 U.S. 536 (1927).
Nixon v. Shrink Mo. Gov't Pac, 528 U.S. 377 (2000).
Pennsylvania v. Nelson, 350 U.S. 497 (1956).
Plessy v. Ferguson, 163 U.S. 537 (1896).

Plyler v. Doe, 457 U.S. 202 (1982).
Prince v. Massachusetts, 321 U.S. 158 (1944).
Reynolds v. Sims, 377 U.S. 533 (1964).
Schenck v. United States, 249 U.S. 47 (1919).
Schneider v. State, 308 U.S. 147 (1939)
Schneiderman v. United States, 320 U.S. 118 (1943).
Shaw v. Reno, 509 U.S. 630 (1993).
Slaughter-House Cases, 83 U.S. 36 (1873).
Smith v. Allwright, 321 U.S. 649 (1944).
South Carolina v. Katzenbach, 383 U.S. 301 (1966).
Tennessee v. Lane, 541 U.S. 509 (2004).
Thomas v. Collins, 323 U.S. 516 (1945).
United States v. Classic, 313 U.S. 299 (1941).
Virginia v. Black, 538 U.S. 343 (2003).
Warth v. Seldin, 422 U.S. 490 (1975).
Wesberry v. Sanders, 376 U.S. 1 (1964).
West Virginia State Board of Education v. Barnette, 319 U.S. 624 (1943).
Whitney v. California, 274 U.S. 357 (1927).
Williams v. Mississippi, 170 U.S. 213 (1898).
Yates v. United States, 354 U.S. 298 (1957).

16

COURTS AND THE DEFINITION OF DEFENDANTS' RIGHTS

David A. Yalof

WHILE THE FREEDOMS OF SPEECH AND PRESS ARE generally hailed as the "preferred freedoms" in our constitutional hierarchy, rights that benefit criminal defendants are often dismissed as privileges that "coddle criminals" and victimize honest citizens. Rights of free expression contribute to the cherished notion of a "marketplace of ideas"; by contrast, defendants' rights are thought to subvert justice by helping factually guilty people to go free. Sadly, politicians in search of votes learn to celebrate the rights of the accused only at their own peril. Meanwhile, legions of officials are sent to office on the strength of well-honed campaign promises that they would never condone letting so-called legal technicalities prevent hardened criminals from being sent to jail.

Of course the hostility now exhibited against the rights of the accused has not always been so prevalent in our nation's history—the Bill of Rights itself stands as a testament to the founding generation's overwhelming devotion to the importance of defendants' rights. In fact, the Constitution reads at times like a "mini-code of criminal procedure," with the Fifth Amendment guarantee of "due process" as its cornerstone. During the initial investigation of a criminal matter, the right of every defendant to be free from unreasonable police searches or seizures is guaranteed by the Fourth Amendment, and the privilege against self-incrimination, encompassing the right to remain silent, is guaranteed by the Fifth Amendment. During the determination of guilt phase, the Sixth Amendment guarantees the right to counsel, to confront and subpoena witnesses and to be informed of the charges against him, the right to a speedy public trial, and the right to a guilt determination by an impartial jury of the defendant's peers. At sentencing, the defendant's right against cruel and unusual punishment and excessive fines comes into play. Finally, if judgment of guilt has been rendered, the right to habeas corpus (which allows prisoners to contest their restraint by authorities) is guaranteed by Article I, Section 9, of the U.S. Constitution, as well as by federal statute.

How does one reconcile vigorous criminal rights protections such as those listed above with a democratic system that embraces rule "of the people, by the people, and for the people"? Certainly the framers of our current system of government never intended the United States to be a democracy in that strict sense. Numerous important features of our government—the two-members-per-state makeup of the Senate, the electoral college mechanism for electing presidents, the two-thirds congressional requirement for overriding vetoes—were inserted into the Constitution precisely to serve as hindrances to simple majority rule.

In truth, democracy refers to more than simply the exercise of brute majority rule. As the writer Raymond Gastil has noted, democracy itself actually draws on two separate heritages.[1] "Tribal democracy" or "village democracy" are terms associated with the universal desire of people to manage their own affairs. The democracy of ancient Athens may well be the most famous example of tribal democracy, but America's own historical origins, which prominently featured voluntary calls for "no taxation without representation" in the British parliament, also connects Americans to this principle. Sometimes contrasting with tribal democracy are notions of a "liberal democracy," which defines itself not simply as a society where the majority rules, but as a political system in which "the basic worth of individuals, their thoughts and their desires" are all affirmed.[2] (The term "liberal" in this context does not link to any specific political doctrine). As Gastil notes, liberal democracies during the past two centuries have abolished political censorship, eliminated slavery, and helped reduce discrimination against women and minorities. Moreover, the international human rights movement is clearly based on the tenets of liberal democracy, rather than tribal democracy.

Unfortunately, democracies have historically tended to be more tribal than liberal, and the rights of the criminally accused rarely flourish in the former form of government. Thus the greatest test of a liberal democracy such as that of the United States may be its willingness to promote and enforce those rights to benefit individuals accused of crimes. There are several reasons for this. First, respect for the rule of law constitutes a central element in any well-functioning liberal democracy. This means not only that criminal laws in particular must be respected and obeyed (as political officials are fond of reminding us), but also that those same officials charged with enforcing criminal laws must similarly defer to the rule of law to curb their own excesses. If officials can arbitrarily and capriciously court the passion of the majorities by imposing extralegal processes or punishments upon the defendant at any given time, there exists no credible rule of law. This explains the constitutional prohibition against the use of ex post facto laws, which would otherwise allow legislatures to criminalize activities and then prosecute previous "offenders." Democratic societies zealously protect the rights of the criminal defendants largely because by doing so, they reaffirm that they remain a society of laws, and not just a society of individuals entrusted with positions of power.

Second, defendants' rights are compatible with a liberal democracy to the extent that they serve the vast majority of individuals in society, including those who may never be brought up on criminal charges. The adage that it is "better to let ten guilty people go free than to let one innocent person go to jail" speaks to the nightmare of an innocent person falsely accused and jailed. To be sure, this nightmare is one that should be disproportionately feared by the less privileged in society. But a democratic nation distinguishes itself from even the most benevolent of monarchies through its willingness to safeguard the liberties of individuals hailing from every economic and social strata. In nondemocratic nations, the actual rights of defendants may vary according to each defendant's political power, monetary wealth, and his or her connections and associations. While access to wealth undoubtedly plays a key role in helping certain defendants gain access to top-flight legal talent in a democracy, even the poorest defendants are at least entitled to the same constitutionally protected rights. Programs such as Legal Aid thus help to actualize democratic values by giving life to these very protections.

Third, true liberal democracies must provide some bulwark against the threat of "tyranny by the majority"; more often than not, the last line of defense comes through the exercise of judicial review, which is defined as the power of judges to invalidate legislative and executive actions that violate some higher law. As many scholars have already noted, judicial review cannot for long hold back an extended wave of popular opinion—eventually some judges will buckle under the weight of public sentiment, or perhaps new judges will be appointed or elected that are more representative of this new public sentiment. Still, judicial review of officials' actions for their adherence to the law remains a sacred trust. In one of the recent "war on terrorism" detainee cases, *Hamdi et al. v. Rumsfeld* (2004), Justice O'Connor wrote that "a state of war is not a blank check for the president."[3] The Court then declared that the detainee could not be held without a "searching review" of the circumstances that warranted his detainment. Judicial protection of the rights of the defendant, especially during wartime, represents one of the great challenges facing any liberal democracy.

Who Defines Defendants' Rights?

Of course rights on paper do not always translate into meaningful protections in practice. The Soviet Union's constitution paid lip service to defendants' rights for more than seventy years—Article 54 of that document provided that "no one may be arrested except by a court decision or on the warrant of a procurator." Yet by all accounts, no branch of government in the Soviet Union ever took these (or most other) rights seriously. Within the United States itself, many of the constitutional rights listed in Amendments Four through Eight applied to federal criminal defendants from the very beginning of the republic, and yet federal criminal trials today have come a long way from those that defendants in federal courts once had to endure. In a democracy, who defines these rights of the accused, interpreting their scope and application to millions of defendants charged with crimes each year? The role that American courts play as adjudicators of disputes over guilt between the accused and the state is by now well-established. The role that judges play in helping to efficiently dispose of cases, whether by encouraging plea bargains, performing bench trials, or through other innovative means, remains controversial, but is equally well grounded in recent tradition. Not so clear is the role judges should play in helping to establish rules defining the rights of criminal defendants in their own courts. Is such rulemaking more properly the province of federal and state legislatures?

Social scientists have long debated both the capacity and legitimacy of courts reaching beyond the immediate resolution of disputes in their courtrooms to bring about larger-scale structural reform of various institutions. Over a quarter of a century ago, Martin Shapiro in his book *Courts: A Comparative and Political Analysis* identified the essential attributes of courts as "(1) an independent judge applying (2) preexisting legal norms after (3) adversary proceedings in order to achieve (4) a dichotomous decision."[4] Naturally, this traditional model provides little discretion for courts to create broad regulatory schemes that define guidelines for the treatment of the criminally accused across the country. Yet the traditional triad consisting of exactly two opposing parties waging a legal battle before a neutral arbiter has proven difficult to maintain in the area of criminal law. Judges are expected to actually administer the criminal law, "that is, to impose the will of the regime on a party being prosecuted by the regime."[5] Most criminal defendants perceive (perhaps correctly) that the court is there as a social controller to enforce the criminal laws, rather than merely as an uninterested third party of a dispute between the prosecution and the defendant. Thus while judicial policymaking may be frowned upon in other contexts, its logic remains more compelling in the area of criminal justice and law enforcement.

To be sure, criminal justice and the courts are inextricably intertwined in this nation's history. Since the beginning of the republic the judiciary has only rarely been excluded from the process of determining defendants' guilt, whether because other institutional actors in the political system conspired to deny the judiciary that role under certain specified circumstances, or because those same powers defined certain events as lying outside the normal parameters of the criminal justice system, and the judiciary proved too timid to stake a more substantive claim in the process. Article I, Section 9, of the Constitution ensures that the privilege of the writ of habeas corpus shall not be suspended "unless when in cases of Rebellion or Invasion the public safety may require it." Even so, President Abraham Lincoln's unilateral suspension of habeas corpus following the arrest of many Copperhead Democrats by military authorities was considered highly questionable, as civilian courts remained open throughout the war. Although Justice Roger Taney, then sitting in his other capacity as a judge on the circuit court, held the action unconstitutional, President Lincoln and the military effectively ignored Taney's ruling and habeas corpus was not fully restored until after the war. In 1866, the Supreme Court ruled that the trial of civilians by presidentially created military courts was unconstitutional, a somewhat belated rejection of Lincoln's action by the Supreme Court itself.

More common have been instances in which American courts conducted pro forma proceedings in which they allowed one-sided prosecutions to proceed with little redress for the accused. Prosecutions under the Alien and Sedition Acts in 1799 and 1800 were not even subject to the Supreme Court's supervision, as it lacked jurisdiction over criminal matters throughout that period. Equally egregious were the pro forma trials of black defendants accused of committing crimes against white defendants in the South at the turn of the twentieth century. Attorneys assigned to defendants by the Courts put up little effort on behalf of blacks accused of committing such interracial crimes. As David Bodenhamer noted in his book *Fair Trial*, in such cases "tainted evidence, irrelevant testimony, outrageous prosecutorial antics and prejudicial jury instructions deprived due process of all substantive meaning."[6] When public passions are most intense, only an active and impartial judiciary stands in the way of a trial process that may be rigged against the accused.

Even if the court's status as a cornerstone of America's system of criminal justice is by now well-accepted, several fundamental questions remain. Are courts meant to be active or passive supervisors of this process? The dispute resolution function of courts inevitably leads to judicial institutions setting policies that govern the process. Yet during the past half century the Warren Court took judicial policy making in the area of criminal justice to new heights, edging out legislatures and executives in the process. What role should courts play in defining the rules that govern this process as a whole?

State Judiciaries and the Plight of Criminal Defendants

Even today, only an extremely small percentage of criminal cases are tried in federal courts; state courts assume the bulk of responsibility for providing criminal justice in the United States. The reason for this unequal allocation is straightforward: far more individuals are accused of violating the criminal laws of state governments than are accused of violating federal criminal laws and statutes. The list of federal crimes today is certainly a diverse one, featuring such offenses as counterfeiting, smuggling, drug trafficking, car-jacking, and even some forms of kidnapping. Additionally, federal law permits convicted state offenders to pursue habeas corpus (a judicial order requesting that a judge examine the legal basis for imprisonment) in federal courts once they have exhausted all state remedies. But for every one criminal case filed in a federal court, nearly three hundred are filed in state courts. And of the largest set of cases that arrive in courts—the routine violations of traffic and parking rules—nearly all are resolved by state or local tribunals.

Although most criminal defendants must contend with prosecutors, judges, and juries in state judicial systems, the rights possessed by criminal defendants, even when they are in state courts, arises out of a combination of state and federal law. This was not always the case. Up until the middle of the twentieth century, state individual rights guarantees (whether found in state constitutions or as interpreted by state courts) were generally enforced in state courts, while federal procedural guarantees (normally found in the first eight amendments to the Constitution) were enforced in federal courts. Because only a handful of provisions of the Bill of Rights at that time were even applicable to state governments, state authorities essentially lived within a constitutional world of their own. And without the federal Constitution interpreted to provide a level of minimum protection for state defendants, the actual rights afforded to the accused under this system varied widely from state to state.

The implications of maintaining a totally decentralized system of defendants' rights for so long were serious. Because due process and procedural fairness for the accused was defined so differently from state to state, markedly different outcomes were routine among similarly situated defendants based solely on the happenstance of where crimes actually occurred. For example, with states free to regulate the procedure of their courts in accordance with their own conceptions of policy and fairness, a handful of state systems denied citizens the right to be free from double jeopardy well into the twentieth century. Other rights were only nominally granted by some states. The right to counsel, for example, meant little if defendants enjoyed no tried-and-true remedy for bringing claims against lawyers who were untrained, incompetent, or lazy. Similarly, the prosecutor's discretion to stack a jury against a defendant varied so widely from state to state (and in some cases from county to county) that in some instances the decision to charge practically merged into an automatic conviction.

The uneven application of defendants' rights as defined by each individual state also created an atmosphere ripe for judicial abuse. Sometimes these abuses were so stark that they garnered widespread interest, such as when African Americans were accused of committing interracial crimes at the turn of the twentieth century. In 1906 the sheriff, prosecutor, and county court judge in Chattanooga, Tennessee, conspired to guarantee the hasty conviction of Ed

Johnson, a black drifter accused of raping a twenty-one-year-old white woman. The so-called irregularities of Johnson's conviction were actually standard practice in local Tennessee courts at the time: black citizens were not called as potential jurors; searches of suspected third parties were conducted without warrants; and a litany of procedural objections at trial were swept aside by a headstrong judge determined to secure a conviction. Johnson's case eventually attracted national attention because its egregiousness led to a U.S. Supreme Court–ordered injunction against Johnson's execution. When an angry mob ignored the Supreme Court's order and lynched Johnson from a bridge near the jail, his case became a noteworthy example of southern-style justice at that time.

An even more famous trial featuring allegations of interracial crimes occurred in Alabama in 1931, when nine black youths were arrested and charged with the rape of two white women. The two attorneys that ultimately agreed to serve on behalf of the accused showed up the day of trial, and thus had no real opportunity to investigate the case. (They were given just thirty minutes to consult with their clients.) In *Powell v. Alabama* (1932), the Supreme Court for the first time held that the Fourteenth Amendment required states to at a minimum provide legal help to poor defendants in capital cases. This legal breakthrough was as notable for what it did not produce; other than being compelled to meet the minimum possible standard for providing counsel to indigent defendants, state courts remained mostly free to set their own terms for defining and implementing procedural fairness for criminal defendants.

The first major blow to state court control over the definition and interpretation of defendants' rights came with the idea that rights provisions in the Bill of Rights might just be applicable to state governments as well if the Fourteenth Amendment—which held that "no state shall deprive" any person of liberty without due process of law—actually "incorporated" (i.e., "encompassed") those rights provisions into its very structure, which applied to state governments. Thus the "incorporation doctrine" was born, at least in theory. But which liberties might be incorporated into the Fourteenth Amendment, and thus made applicable to the states? *Powell v. Alabama* was a highly particularistic decision. The same could not be said for *Palko v. Connecticut* (1937), handed down three years later. Although the Supreme Court refused to apply the right against double jeopardy to state governments in that case, it opened the door to incorporating other Bill of Rights provisions into the due process clause, so long as they adhered to certain unifying principles: Was the absence of the right a "hardship so acute and shocking that our polity will not endure it?" Does it violate those "fundamental principles of liberty and justice which lie at the base of all our civil and political institutions?"[7] By all appearances, the *Palko* formula could have allowed the states to continue to act as laboratories of experimentation in most areas of criminal procedure. Yet in reality, *Palko* set in motion a three-decade effort to apply various rights of criminal defendants to every state court in the nation.

The Court eventually abandoned this amorphous line of inquiry. In its place, the Court began to launch an even more open-ended investigation into whether the procedures were in fact "fundamental." By 1969 the U.S. Supreme Court had incorporated into the Due Process Clause of the Fourteenth Amendment every provision of the Bill of Rights relevant to criminal defendants except the right to a grand jury indictment and the bail provision of the Eighth Amendment. Even *Palko* was overruled in *Benton v. Maryland* (1969), when the Court held that double jeopardy was, after all so fundamental as to be incorporated against the states. Thereafter, courts in all fifty states would be constitutionally required to respect the rights of criminal defendants not to be held twice in jeopardy for their alleged crimes.

As crucial as the incorporation doctrine was in holding state governments to a bare minimum of protections for the accused, the doctrine standing alone could have only a modest impact on defendants' rights. Some states at the time offered the accused more than the federal constitutional minimum, lessening the impact of incorporation nationwide. In truth, the federal constitutional minimum guarantees available to federal defendants in the 1940s and 1950s were limited indeed, especially for those indigent defendants who possessed few resources. The police power of search and interrogation remained far-reaching; no counsel need be provided to the indigent except in capital cases. It would take another judicial revolution altogether for defendants' rights to thrive, with the U.S. Supreme Court forging a path that would compel most states to play a game of catch-up with the national standard.

The Warren Court Revolution in Criminal Justice

When Chief Justice Earl Warren first arrived at the Supreme Court in 1953, there was little to suggest that he would leave as his greatest legacy the broadening and expansion of defendants' rights. First as attorney general of California, and then later as the three-term governor of that state, Warren had established his conservative credentials as a no-nonsense prosecutor and law enforcement officer. Most significantly, he had been a key supporter of the removal and internment of Japanese-Americans from the West Coast during World War II, a black mark for due process in this nation's history. But once Warren occupied the nation's High Court, he helped produce a stream of decisions broadening the reach of the Bill of Rights, including provisions in the Fourth, Fifth, Sixth, Seventh, and Eighth Amendments directly applicable to criminal defendants. With an assist from the incorporation doctrine, the Warren Court's bolstering of the rights of criminal suspects effectively revolutionized the constitutional landscape.

The Warren Court's general attack on the rules of the criminal justice system was essentially launched in 1962, with one of the most controversial decisions of the period. In *Mapp v. Ohio* (1962) a Cleveland woman suspected of harboring a fugitive was victimized by police illegally searching her home and person. The police ultimately found obscene materials in her home, but secured those materials without a warrant. A majority of the Supreme Court went beyond simply voiding Mapp's conviction on the simple grounds that the statute she was convicted under was "unconstitutionally vague"; rather, they held that adherence to the Fourth Amendment "actually require[d]" that illegally seized evidence be excluded at trial. *Mapp* was a groundbreaking decision, and its significance cannot be overstated. Local police and law enforcement thereafter were forced to comply with a federal rule that many of them thought was both wrongheaded and ill-advised. All subsequent Warren Court decisions would have greater bite because of *Mapp* and its implications.

That same year, in *Gideon v. Wainwright* (1962), the Court construed the Sixth Amendment to require that indigents facing felony charges be afforded counsel at government expense to help them prepare for trial. In truth, *Gideon* proved a popular decision with the public, as it equalized the terms of what would otherwise be an unfair fight with the resources of the government. By contrast, other Warren Court precedents restricting the police during the pretrial investigative process would elicit a storm of controversy. In *Massiah v. United States* (1964) and *Escobedo v. Illinois* (1964), the Court tossed out two defendants' confessions that, while admittedly voluntary, occurred in the absence of counsel *after* the two defendants has been indicted. Together, the cases helped to ensure that there would no longer be confessions after indictment without counsel present, an effective ban on such confessions as effective tools of law enforcement.

The Warren Court also was notable for its attempt to "police the police" in innovative new ways. If *Escobedo* and *Massiah* tied the hands of police after indictments were issued, *Miranda v. Arizona* (1966) imposed new rules on the police at even earlier stages of the investigation. In *Miranda* the Court required that the accused be informed of his or her rights prior to questioning, including the right to remain silent and the right to the presence of an attorney. Any circumvention of these warnings would invalidate the confession. Lucas A. Powe, Jr., among others, has remarked on the "legislative quality" of *Miranda*, as it gives disproportionate attention to parts of the opinion that have little to do with constitutional interpretation, and has more to do with offering detailed guidelines to police about how to perform their jobs.

Undaunted, the Warren Court continued to police the police in the wake of *Miranda*. In the twin cases of *United States v. Wade* (1967) and *Gilbert v. California* (1967), the Court ruled that government could not order lineups for suspects without a counsel present; and in *Katz v. United States* (1967), the Court functionally overruled a nearly four-decade-old rule exempting electronic surveillance from the strictures of the Fourth Amendment absent an actual "physical invasion" of the space. *Berger v. New York* (1967) was also significant: Wiretap statutes passed by Congress or the states could not be so broad or lack particularization to such a degree that the purposes of the probable cause requirement (to keep the states out of constitutionally protected areas until they have reason to believe that a specific crime has been or is being committed) would be undermined.

Of course not all Warren Court rulings provided one-sided victories for the accused: *Terry v. Ohio* (1967) upheld a police frisk for dangerous weapons; *McCray v. Illinois* (1967) rejected an attempt by one defendant to force the disclosure of the identity of an informant who had provided probable cause for a search warrant; and *Schmerber v. California* (1966) affirmed that police could take a blood sample from an unwilling person without violating the privilege against self-incrimination. To many, a case like *Terry* represented as dramatic a victory for the police as *Miranda* was a victory for the accused. Regardless of ideological direction, the Warren Court was notable for its willingness to enter deep into this thicket, forcing police departments around the country to rewrite police manuals that had not been altered in decades.

Unfettered state autonomy over the rules of criminal procedure within the courtroom itself also fell by the wayside during the 1960s. Certainly *Gideon* was significant not only for the assistance it provided before trial, but also for how it equalized the competing sides at trial. In *Rideau v. Louisiana* (1963) and *Estes v. Texas* (1965), the Court wrestled with the implications of pretrial publicity on the right to a fair trial. In the former case, the Supreme Court held that showing taped admissions on television before a wide audience (including two of the jurors) had turned the subsequent trial into a "kangaroo court"; by contrast in the latter case, the Court ruled that the presence of cameras in the courtroom per se did not create an unfair trial for the accused.

Perhaps the only critical area of defendants' rights in which the Warren Court was relatively less active was capital punishment. Still, the Warren Court was responsible for various minor breakthroughs that indirectly assisted those sentenced to death. In the 1963 decisions of *Fay v. Noia* and *Townsend v. Sain*, the Court gave new life to the right of habeas corpus (Latin for "present the body"), the traditional procedure by which prisoners challenged the legal basis for their detention. Many of these habeas corpus petitions assisted defendants sitting on death row. The Warren Court also rejected prosecutor attempts to remove jurors simply because of their theoretical opposition to the death penalty in *Witherspoon v. Illinois* (1968). But the more broad-based attacks on the death penalty would not occur until the 1970s, when the Court instituted a moratorium on executions, deeming its applications both arbitrary and capricious in *Furman v. Georgia* (1972). That moratorium proved short-lived; *Gregg v. Georgia* (1976) reintroduced the death penalty as a legitimate means of punishment, on the condition that legislatures create statutory standards to guide sentencing bodies.

The Warren Court's criminal procedure revolution affected the criminal justice systems in all fifty states, as well as the federal system. Crime was a major issue in the United States of the late 1960s, and the Court invested a larger part of its docket (more than 20 percent) to criminal defendants than it did to any other subject matter. Not surprisingly, the Court's sudden new influence in the area of law enforcement would bring it into immediate conflict with the political branches of the federal and state governments, all of whom were less sympathetic to the need for equalizing the playing field for criminal defendants. Some predicted that this revolution would be short-lived: The court had overreached in making unpopular policy, and these rules would thus surely fall victim to hard political realities that favored the interests of victims and law enforcements entities over the accused. As it turns out, the Warren Court's jurisprudential legacy in this context would prove quite resilient, at least in theory. What criminal defendants' rights mean in practice, of course, was a different matter entirely.

Responding to the Warren Court: Defendants' Rights before Congress

Although the political realities of law enforcement politics in the late 1960s compelled a congressional response to Warren Court excesses, most such initiatives barely nipped at the heels of this new criminal justice regime. In 1967 the Omnibus Crime Control and Safe Streets Act was overwhelmingly passed in the House; it came before the Senate the following year. Among the provisions offered in Title II of the legislation were proposals to legislatively repeal both *Miranda* and *Wade*, and a proposal to rip away from the U.S. Supreme Court jurisdiction over confession cases whenever the highest state supreme court had ruled those confessions voluntary. This final threat to jurisdiction was eventually replaced with a provision offering to replace *Miranda* with a "totality of the circumstances" test, by which voluntary confessions would be admissible even if the suspect was unaware of his rights. These efforts to dilute *Miranda* and *Wade* both passed the Senate and became part of the final legislation as enacted. Yet Title II's constitutionality remained an open question then as it does even today—Congress cannot simply overrule decisions of the High Court that interpret the Constitution. After those provisions of Title II had languished from inattention for three decades, the U.S. Court of Appeals for the Fourth Circuit put a new spotlight on this issue in 1999 when it allowed into evidence a voluntary confession from Charles Thomas Dickerson that had been secured without the proper *Miranda* warnings. The Supreme Court in *Dickerson v. United States* (2000) confirmed what had been assumed throughout the years since Title II first became law: *Miranda* remains the precedent, notwithstanding the various attempts of Congress to overrule it.

Title III of the Omnibus Crime Control and Safe Streets Act of 1968 also offered a mixed response to the Warren Court's Fourth Amendment jurisprudence, as manifested in *Katz* and *Berger.* In attempting to lay out easy-to-understand guidelines for electronic wiretapping, Title III provides that evidence of nonconsensual intercepted wire or oral communications may not be used in court except as authorized by the attorney general or the principal prosecuting attorney of the state with a court order, and in adherence to various rules in the act requiring detailed and particularized application. Although the legislation at first appeared to increase the burden on law enforcement even further, wiretapping continued to flourish during the 1970s and beyond "as a wide-open operation" at the federal, state, municipal, and private levels. The executive branch has interpreted the word "intercept" to mean only the oral acquisition of the contents of the phone conversation, excluding from the statute's dictates so-called pen register surveillance that only makes a record of the phone numbers dialed from a given phone and of the times the number was dialed. (The Supreme Court in *Smith v. Maryland* [1979] held that such a pen register does not constitute a "search" under the Fourth Amendment.) Title III's explicit exceptions for warrantless wiretaps in "emergency situations" or when the nation's "domestic security" is threatened have also become the launching pad for infringements on the rights of suspects and of the accused.

Congress may have attacked aspects of the system that favored defendants, but it ducked leveling assaults on the Warren Court precedents themselves. Fearful that judges enjoy too much discretion in the sentencing process, Congress attempted to restrict the range of sentences issued to those convicted of committing federal crimes. Up through the early 1980s, the federal judicial system had utilized a framework of "indeterminate sentencing"—statutes specified the penalties for crimes, but nearly always gave the sentencing judge wide discretion to decide whether the offender should be incarcerated and for how long, as well as whether probation should be imposed instead of either imprisonment or a fine. In 1984 Congress passed the Sentencing Reform Act, which created a United States Sentencing Commission vested with the power to promulgate binding sentencing guidelines that featured a range of determinate sentences for all categories of federal offenses and defendants. Since the late 1980s, that system has been replaced by sentencing guidelines with no options for parole or other less traditional sentencing alternatives. Even a landmark ruling at the beginning of 2005 declaring the guidelines in violation of the Sixth Amendment right to be tried by a jury offered only limited prospects for change—in the wake of the decision, many federal judges indicated that they would continue to adhere strictly to the guidelines in most cases.

Of course where judicial discretion has been directed toward narrowing rather than expanding defendants' rights, Congress has been willing to expand judicial discretion accordingly. Thus in 1984 Congress amended the 1966 Bail Reform Act, which had originally revised bail practices to assure that all persons, regardless of their financial condition, would not needlessly be detained pending their appearance in court. The 1984 amendments addressed the growing problem of crimes committed by persons on release. While the 1966 act focused solely on the need to assure the defendant's reappearance at judicial proceedings, the amendments gave the courts added authority to make release decisions based on the potential danger a person may pose to others if released. By incorporating the safety of the community into bail decisions, Congress in effect transformed the purpose of the original statute.

Another congressional response to the defendants' rights revolution has targeted the interminable number of appeals now available to defendants, especially those on death row. During the 1980s, conservative U.S. senators such as Jesse Helms (R-N.C.) argued frequently for the more bold congressional exercise of Article II, Section 2, Clause 2, which affords the Supreme Court appellate jurisdiction "with such exceptions and under such regulations as the Congress shall make." Frustration among legislators over Supreme Court precedents concerning abortion drove many such proposals, but controversial Warren Court precedents in criminal procedure were also targeted. Could Congress, for example, effectively bar the Supreme Court from hearing *Miranda* cases, or from hearing cases decided by state supreme courts that refuse to apply the exclusionary rule? To date, the legislative effort to restrict appeals has reached fruition only in death penalty cases, where the multiplication of habeas corpus appeals has increased public frustration with the lack of finality in such cases. In 1996 Congress passed the Anti-Terrorism and Effective Death Penalty Act, which featured provisions that curtailed state prisoners' applications for habeas corpus relief beyond the first bite at the apple. Supreme Court review was explicitly denied by the statute in cases where a court of appeals rules on whether to grant or deny such extra appeals. In *Felker v. Turpin* (1996), the Court essentially sidestepped the conflict with Congress: it held that because each prisoner's original habeas appeals must already be filed in the U.S. Supreme Court, there was no reason to conclude that the 1996 law had deprived the Court of its appellate jurisdiction to hear such cases. Such a half-hearted effort by Congress to exercise its Article III power may be indicative of congressional deference to the Court in these and other matters concerning the rights of criminal defendants.

Increased Business for the Federal Courts

Clearly the retirement of Chief Justice Earl Warren in 1969 marked the end of an era; in the decades that followed the tables slowly turned and it was soon state courts, rather than federal courts, that offered the greatest protection to criminal defendants. In a speech delivered at the New York University Law School in 1986, Associate Justice William Brennan actively hailed a fifteen-year trend in which states courts were more frequently finding that that the constitutional minimums set by the U.S. Supreme Court had proved insufficient to satisfy "the more stringent requirements of state Constitutional law."[8] Much of this judicial activity occurred on behalf of criminal defendants in the state courts. Thus, for example, motorists stopped by a police officer could be subject to a full body search consistent with the Fourth and Fifth Amendments, but such intrusions were not justified in California and Hawaii without an additional basis of justification. South Dakota had rejected the so-called inventory search rule, by which police would inventory "everything" in the possession of arrested persons at the stationhouse; that same form of search was authorized under the Fourth Amendment according to *Illinois v. Lafayette* (1983).

With the federal courts increasingly seen as a less friendly venue for defendants, Congress's final tactic in its battle to influence defendants' rights has become particularly significant, sweeping more and more defendants into the federal courts by passing a plethora of federal statutes criminalizing behavior already covered by state laws. Congress has a long history of imposing its power where state governments are already entrenched. Beginning in the 1930s, a spirit of "cooperative federalism" reigned, in which Congress regularly passed regulatory schemes demanding action from the states on a host of different issues, and threatening them with the loss of federal grant money if they did not behave. But the 1970s saw the start of an era in which Congress itself actively passed criminal statutes that would greatly increase the number of defendants coming through the federal judicial system. Drug legislation provides a case in point. Before 1970, federal drug legislation had been sporadic, and mostly linked to the federal government's power to control trade. But when Congress passed the Controlled Substances Act of 1970, it consolidated over fifty federal narcotic, marijuana, and dangerous drug laws into one overarching legislative scheme designed to control the distribution of illicit drugs throughout the United States. The 1980s witnessed the passage of four more major anti-drug bills, including the Anti-Drug Abuse Amendment Act of 1988, which increased the sanctions for crimes related to drug trafficking and set in place many new federal offenses for marijuana possession, cultivation, and trafficking.

Today many more defendants are brought into federal courts where the constitutional minimum of defendants' rights—once considered the gold standard for defendants' rights—now pales in comparison to some of those rights granted to the accused in some state courts across the country. Still, in the battle over defendants' rights in the United States, the Supreme Court, and the legacy left by Chief Justice Earl Warren in particular, continues to hold firm against various entreaties from the legislative branch.

The Warren Court Revolution in Theory and Practice

Unlike the Congress, the president of the United States is blessed with a more direct means of altering the jurisprudence of the Court. Through his power to appoint new justices of the Supreme Court, the chief executive can replace retired justices with like-minded individuals willing to overturn such precedents. Since 1968, every successful presidential candidate has run for office on a platform committed to strengthening the powers of law enforcement. At least two presidents named Supreme Court rulings in this area as chief culprits in this battle. First, Richard Nixon blamed the Warren Court directly for promoting civil unrest, and promised to appoint only conservative "law and order" judges to the bench. Then in 1980, Ronald Reagan strategically targeted several Supreme Court decisions for elimination in his campaign for the presidency, including *Miranda, Mapp,* and *Massiah*. Presidential candidate George H. W. Bush's successful 1988 campaign featured a highly controversial television ad charging his Democratic opponent, Michael Dukakis, with being weak on crime for backing a criminal furlough program as Massachusetts governor. And Bill Clinton became the only two-term Democratic president in nearly half a century in part by establishing his credentials as "tough-on-crime" Democrat—his election campaigns prominently featured calls for more gun control and more police on the streets, and he refused to back away from his past record of support for the death penalty.

Of these modern presidents, Richard Nixon and Ronald Reagan lived up to their campaign promises in at least one respect, naming individuals to the Supreme Court who sported track records of hostility to controversial aspects of the Warren Court criminal procedure revolution. The name of Nixon's first Supreme Court appointment, Warren Burger, originally came to Nixon's attention when the court of appeals judge delivered a 1967 speech at Ripon College charging that criminal courts across the land had been unfairly bogged down with "excessive appeals and gratuitous defense tactics." His final two appointments to the Court were the ideologically conservative assistant attorney general William Rehnquist and the former American Bar Association president Lewis Powell, who had publicly decried the "crisis in law observance" and had openly criticized the Court's *Miranda* decision when he had served on President Lyndon B. Johnson's Commission on Law Enforcement and the Administration of Justice. Even Harry Blackmun, the compromise candidate sandwiched in the middle of these other appointees, had issued several tough rulings in a number of high-profile criminal cases while serving on the U.S. Court of Appeals for the Eighth Circuit.

As president, Ronald Reagan appointed three new Supreme Court justices, and in each instance his administration's vetters worked hard to ensure that the appointees met the president's clearly stated goals for the Court, which included hostility to controversial Warren Court precedents, and a "disposition towards criminal law as a system for determining guilt or innocence."[9] Sandra Day O'Connor's background as a legislator included considerable work on criminal law reforms in Arizona, including her sponsorship of a death penalty bill as well as legislation designed to increase penalties for drug offenders. Administration officials quickly discovered that as an appeals court judge, O'Connor had demonstrated a "healthy disdain for the exclusionary rule," which improved her prospects for a High Court appointment.[10] The decision to promote Associate Justice William Rehnquist to become chief justice in 1986 was made easier by the jurist's nearly unblemished record of conservative criminal procedure rulings. Judge Antonin Scalia's judicial record was similar, sporting not even one opinion in criminal procedure that would be considered "problematic from a conservative point of view."[11] And while Judge Anthony Kennedy actually distressed some Reagan administration officials with his more flexible approach to privacy rights, the same could not be said for his record with respect to criminal defendants' rights, where he "usually favored the prosecution."[12] As a court of appeals judge, Kennedy had occasionally taken care to ensure that all law enforcement activities were at least "reasonable" as a matter of constitutional law, but by all accounts he applied a low constitutional threshold indeed to such considerations.

In sum, everything appeared in place for a sharp reversal of the Warren Court's perceived "excesses" in favor of criminal defendants. The democratic process has produced law-and-order presidents, and those men in turn had appointed law-and-order justices who might theoretically respond to more recent public passions and sentiments. Throughout the late 1970s and 1980s, between four and six of the nine justices sitting on the Supreme Court could have been fairly described as conservative opponents of the Warren Court revolution in criminal procedure. George H. W. Bush's replacement of Thurgood Marshall with the conservative Clarence Thomas in 1991 only tipped this balance further against retaining those controversial 1960s precedents, and returning discretion in law enforcement back to the states.

The "Counterrevolution That Wasn't"

As Vincent Blasi and other students of the Burger Court have been quick to note, this quickly became the "counterrevolution that wasn't" in the area of law enforcement jurisprudence.[13] Although the rules of some of the more controversial decisions were narrowed in significant respects, none were expressly overturned, and many have continued to serve as foundations in the law of criminal procedure. Much credit for this show of deference to past precedents is owed to Justice William Brennan, who as senior associate justice during this period frequently exercised his intermittent power of assignment to forge middle-of-the-road compromises that rescued, and in some cases subtly extended, certain Warren Court precedents in this area of the law. Chief Justice Burger's own missteps in this process have also been documented; by alienating swing voters on the Court, he precluded the possibilities of a focused march against the Warren

Court. Regardless of the reason, the time to act boldly soon passed, and the case decisions that had garnered so much controversy quickly became lasting elements of our civic culture. Meanwhile, even as the opponents of these precedents increased in number on the High Court during the late 1980s, they became less interested in taking on such battles.

Mapp v. Ohio had been the foundation of this revolution in defendants' rights. Chief Justice Burger was a clear opponent of the exclusionary rule, referring to it in *Bivens v. Six Unknown Named Agents* (1971) as "an anomalous and ineffective mechanism with which to regulate law enforcement . . . [based on] an unworkable and irrational concept of law."[14] But time after time he narrowly lost arguments for its elimination. In cases that routinely applied the exclusionary rule, such as *Bivens* and *Coolidge v. New Hampshire* (1971), Burger was unable to obtain the votes needed to secure rearguments on the essential *Mapp* finding that the exclusionary rule was compelled by the Due Process Clause. Burger had to wait nearly a decade and a half for his lone breakthrough on *Mapp*—in *United States v. Leon* (1984), the chief justice secured the votes for an exception to exclusion when a search warrant has been secured and relied upon in good faith. Yet by 1984, even two of the more conservative justices, William Rehnquist and Sandra Day O'Connor, were prepared to resist any attempt by their colleagues to abandon the two-decades-old rule where the potential for abuses are greatest, in instances of warrantless searches. The use of cost-benefit analysis in *Leon* opened the door for the use of good faith exceptions, but essentially closed the door to a hard and fast ban on the exclusionary rule altogether.

Miranda v. Arizona has proven an equally tough nut to crack for even its harshest critics. In *Harris v. New York* (1971), the Court upheld the use of a statement obtained in violation of *Miranda* to impeach testimony at trial. *New York v. Quarles* (1984) upheld a public safety exception to *Miranda*, allowing police to ask questions about guns and secure the area without first "Mirandizing" the suspect. In *Moran v. Burbine* (1986), the Court upheld a voluntary confession secured after *Miranda* warnings were properly executed, even though attempts to provide counsel to the defendant had been stymied by law enforcement officials. Sometimes opponents of *Miranda* even managed to snatch victory from the jaws of defeat. *Rhode Island v. Innis* (1981) should have dealt a significant blow to the controversial doctrine; the Supreme Court held in that case that two policemen talking to each other in the front seat of a police car had not "interrogated" a suspect in the back seat in such a way as to require *Miranda* warnings. Yet the Court was also quick to note that the term "interrogation" does not require formal questions per se; any dialogue that invites a response from the defendant may invoke *Miranda*. Even this victory for the police somehow managed to expand, rather than narrow, the reach of *Miranda* in future cases.

Clearly *Miranda* was diluted by some of these decisions, but the basics of the opinion still hold, and indeed, the holding has become an important part of our national culture. Children exposed to prime time television learn from an early age that every criminal defendant has "the right to remain silent" and "the right to an attorney," including the right to "counsel provided by the state if you cannot afford one." After a decade of fruitless attempts to overturn the decision, even Chief Justice Burger in 1980 declared that he "would neither overrule *Miranda*, disparage it, nor extend it at this late date." As chief justice of the United States, William Rehnquist went a step further in 2000, noting in *Dickerson v. United States* that "*Miranda* has become embedded in routine police practice to the point where the warnings have become part of our national culture."[15] While *Miranda* may have seemed an antidemocratic act of judicial aggressiveness in 1966, by the beginning of the twenty-first century it had been effectively transformed into a cornerstone of the American judicial system, engrained in the American psyche. Indeed, for many *Miranda* has become part and parcel of what a democracy should stand for.

In the area of Fourth Amendment rights against search and seizure, precedents such as *Katz* and *Berger* should have been easy targets for more conservative courts, if only because, as Akhil Reed Amar once wrote, when combined with *Mapp*'s exclusionary rule, the Fourth Amendment becomes "contemptible in the eyes of judges and citizens."[16] Yet once again the Burger Court adhered to the *Katz* framework, allowing a role for some intrusive forms of technology (i.e., airplane flyovers with zoom lens cameras) in law enforcement, but otherwise shutting down police attempts to infringe upon a suspect's "reasonable expectations of privacy." More telling, the extremely conservative Rehnquist Court has issued unanimous decisions in favor of criminal defendants in two recent Fourth Amendment cases. In *Florida v. J. L.* (2000), the Court held that an anonymous tip that a person is carrying a gun is not, without more information, sufficient to justify a police officer's stop and frisk of that person under the Warren Court's *Terry* doctrine. And in *Knowles v. Iowa* (1998) the same Court invalidated a full-fledged "search incident to arrest" in a routine traffic citation case. The Rehnquist Court has more narrowly divided on issues related to technology; still, in *Kyllo v. United States* (2001), the Court by a 5–4 vote ruled against police use of a thermal imaging device that detects sources of heat in nearby buildings without a warrant. If either the Burger or Rehnquist Courts has been seeking to undermine the *Katz* doctrine as an end-around against the exclusionary rule, it's been tough to tell from the stream of cases flowing out of those two courts.

Other Warren Court precedents have not required nearly as much defending, as the goals of Presidents Nixon and Reagan never effectively translated into passions among the current lot of conservative justices to overturn either *Gideon* or *Massiah*. Because the Court in *Gideon* had by its own terms limited the ruling to the felony case at hand, it remained unclear at the time how far that right would be extended. In *Argersinger v. Hamlin* (1972), the Court actually extended the protections of *Gideon* to any defendant facing a term of imprisonment, no matter how minimal. Interestingly, the one area where the Rehnquist Court most transformed defendants' rights on the books concerned the death penalty, where the Warren Court made comparatively fewer inroads. Specifically, the recent Court has tried to streamline the appeals process and eliminate obstacles to the quicker institution of death penalty sentences. Most notably in *Butler v. McKellar* (1990), the Court held that defendants cannot appeal "reasonable good-faith interpretations of existing precedents made by state courts even though they are shown to be contrary to later decisions."[17]

This much is clear: While the Warren Court rewrote much of the public law that governs the criminal justice system, the Burger and Rehnquist Courts in the end became courts of consolidation rather than courts of reversal in this area. Under Chief Justice Rehnquist's leadership, federalism jurisprudence was transformed in favor of greater states' rights, and property rights enjoyed a rebirth. Other areas of criminal law that the Warren Court skirted, such as the death penalty, were also targets of the recent Supreme Court. But in the area of criminal procedure, the imprint of the Warren Court remained very much in evidence at the beginning of the twenty-first century, at least in theory. The Supreme Court continues to maintain its watch over all fifty state criminal justice systems, with forty-year-old precedents still framing the landscape of defendants' rights in this country. Congress, though tinkering at the margins, remains very much ensconced on the sidelines. Still, to get the real story on the state of defendants' rights, one must look below the surface of the Courts themselves. The Warren Court may be responsible for many of the assumptions that overlay defendants' rights today. But what is the practice?

Implementing the Revolution in Defendants' Rights

Appropriately, implementation represents the final piece of the defendants' rights puzzle. All the lip service paid to Warren Court precedents in the jurisprudence of the current Supreme Court does not guarantee that down on the ground such rights will be given meaning and effect for the millions of defendants that work their way through the judicial system. After all, the United States still sports the largest rate of people incarcerated in the world. Clearly the Supreme Court represents only one interpreting population; lower federal courts and state courts also must interpret its decisions. Trial courts in particular play a large role in implementing criminal rights decisions; because only a very small percentage of trial court decisions are successfully appealed, many of these decisions rise and fall at that level. Most of the studies conducted of lower court implementation of the defendants' rights revolution focus on high profile criminal procedure cases such as *Miranda v. Arizona.* In one such study conducted by Donald Songer and Reginald Sheehan in 1989, court of appeals exhibited high levels of compliance with *Miranda*. Yet the same study also found that in the minority of cases where the lower courts did buck the trend against *Miranda*, the vast majority of those noncompliant decisions were never appealed.

Of course the hardest work of implementation takes place on the ground itself. Police, probation officers, and other actors in the criminal justice system must effectively consume many of these decisions and apply them during investigations and while at the station house if the Warren Court–created revolution in defendants' rights is to have the desired effect. The police themselves must be considered most influential in making or breaking criminal rights decisions such as *Miranda*. According to political scientists Bradley Canon and Charles Johnson, police as individuals "did not readily accept the Supreme Court's criminal justice decisions in the 1960's and early 1970's."[18] *Mapp v. Ohio* was especially reviled by law enforcement officers, who saw its most offensive applications at work. *Miranda* in particular was denounced by law enforcement organizations when it was handed down, and there is some evidence that it was adhered to only marginally, with police officers barely taking it seriously, uttering the famous warnings in a manner that could only be interpreted as dismissive. In fact, one study of *Miranda*'s impact in the years following the decision revealed that even after the rights had been read to them, defendants still had no appreciation of what they meant; many still feared being hit or beaten up by the police. In a sense, the Warren Court's revolution was so innovative that the democratic system essentially resolved the tension its innovations caused by putting up with limited compliance at first, as police officers became slowly socialized to this new way of conducting business.

Where does compliance and implementation of these controversial precedents stand today, approximately four decades later? Even in the modern era of law enforcement, police are noted for their ability to deftly maneuver around the Warren Court's edicts. News reports and realistic television dramas such as *NYPD Blue* and *Homicide: Life on the Streets* have communicated to the public what amounts to the modern reality of station-house confessions—some of the most dramatic scenes feature seasoned officers gaining the confidence of suspects by stoking false hopes and claims about the benefits that will accrue with the proper level of "cooperation"; they then are able to secure confessions from suspects who have supposedly "waived" their *Miranda* rights. Of course *Mapp v. Ohio* provides occasional ammunition for defense attorneys, but in a system dominated by the assembly-line system of plea bargaining, the exclusionary rule cannot be litigated enough to make sweeping differences in the criminal justice system. Fourth Amendment search-and-seizure decisions are in some cases so fact-specific and confusing that it is difficult to see how, if at all, police forces can incorporate those rulings into the way they conduct their business.

That said, the Warren Court revolution in criminal defendants' rights clearly affected more than just symbolic change. Police know in some instances that they may be held accountable under the Constitution for such violations, a far cry from before the 1960s when police were accountable strictly to the elected officials above them. Officers can get around *Miranda*, but that action itself only serves to reaffirm *Miranda*'s continuing significance—if its actual scope has been limited by such tactics, that scope serves to reconcile such criminal rights protections—which may be important to a liberal democracy—with a tribal democracy that abhors letting factually guilty people go free despite their own confessions. And of course the obstacles to enforcement and implementation of Warren Court decisions dictating police action are not present to hinder Warren Court decisions that protect criminal rights within the courtroom itself, where most actions are at least on the public record. Thus while decisions like *Miranda* may be diluted somewhat, *Gideon v. Wainright* is automatically consumed and implemented with little question.

Defendants' Rights in the War against Terrorism

The tragic events of September 11, 2001, altered many Americans' perceptions of their place in the global community, and shifted American foreign policy priorities for the foreseeable future. The tragedy also opened their eyes to threats that can emerge from within the nation's borders. Although the hijackers who perpetrated the crimes were almost all Saudi Arabians, they trained at American flight schools, worked with American flight instructors, and boarded the airplanes through security at American airports. President George W. Bush's declared "war on terrorism" featured the doctrine of preemption in foreign policy, which his administration offered to justify a war in Iraq launched in October 2003. Not immediately foreseen was the degree to which new homeland security initiatives might call for new understandings of the rights of the accused. In that sense, the greatest challenge to the modern regime of defendants' rights may be still to come in the years ahead.

From the outset of the administration's highly publicized war on terrorism, America's highly refined criminal justice system featuring a pervasive acceptance of broad rights for the accused has loomed as a daunting obstacle to the otherwise vigorous prosecution of terrorists. In response to the bombing of the federal building in Oklahoma City in 1995, Congress passed legislation directed at reducing the Supreme Court's discretion in reviewing habeas corpus petitions, a move that the High Court gingerly maneuvered around in *Felker v. Turpin*. By contrast, the Bush administration, aided by a Congress standing foursquare in support of the president's anti-terrorism initiatives, has offered a more direct challenge to the defendants' rights framework as applied to suspects in the war against terror.

At the outset, the Bush administration refused to accord detainees the status of full-fledged criminal defendants, which would have entitled them to all the rights, privileges, and immunities discussed above. How then were these detainees classified? As it turned out, the Bush administration was no more interested in giving al Qaeda and Taliban detainees being held at Guantanamo Bay and other military bases the status of Prisoners of War (POWs). More than a half century ago the Geneva Convention Relative to the Treatment of Prisoners of War established guidelines for the treatment of detainees captured in "all cases of declared war or of any other armed conflict" between two or more states "even if the state of war is not recognized by one of them." Captured combatants under the Geneva Convention are entitled to protection against punishment for the mere fact of having participated directly in the hostilities. The Geneva Convention also entitles them to humane treatment and protection, particularly against acts of violence, from insults and from public curiosity. All measures of reprisal against them would be forbidden. Finally, at the conclusion of the hostilities, most POWs have the right to return to their home countries.

Rejecting this framework, the Bush administration sought to rely on the power vested in it by Congress, which originally authorized the president to use "all necessary and appropriate force" against "nations, organizations, or persons" associated with the September 11, 2001, terrorist attacks. Based on that extensive grant of authority, officials cited military manuals in the United States, which refer to some detainees as "unlawful" or "illegal" combatants who are part of or supporting forces hostile to the United States or coalition partners and who are engaged in an armed conflict against the United States. By some estimations, more than six hundred prisoners being held at Guantánamo Bay and other United States military-controlled detention camps had been assigned that label by late 2003. In *Hamdi et al. v. Rumsfeld* (2004), the Court held that detention of individuals falling into that category, for the duration of the particular conflict in which they were captured, is "so fundamental and accepted an incident to war" as to be an exercise of the necessary and appropriate force Congress has authorized the president to use.

Thus the Bush administration essentially succeeded in defining a class of detainees who would never reap the protections normally afforded defendants in the American system of justices. What rights of process, if any, were due such enemy combatants? For the Supreme Court in *Hamdi*, access to the courts was still paramount. The Court agreed that indefinite or perpetual detention was not justified. On one hand a citizen-detainee seeking to challenge his classification as an enemy combatant must receive notice of the factual basis for his classification, and have a fair opportunity to rebut the government's factual assertions before a neutral decision maker. On the other hand, the Court conceded that enemy combatant proceedings might be tailored so as not to burden the chief executive at a time of ongoing military conflict. Thus hearsay evidence—never admitted into evidence in the course of a normal criminal trial—may be accepted as the most reliable available evidence from the government in such a proceeding.

Additionally, the court conceded that the Constitution would not be offended by a presumption in favor of the government's evidence, so long as that presumption remained a rebuttable one and fair opportunity for rebuttal were provided.

In the end, the Bush administration's refusal in its war on terrorism to adhere to the structure of criminal defendants' rights established by the Warren Court and continued by the Burger and Rehnquist Courts met with limited success. The Court's will to maintain a strong civil court presence in cases prosecuted against terrorists bent to a large degree, but it did not break. During the American Civil War, habeas corpus was temporarily suspended without a word of protest from the judiciary until after the hostilities had been completed. During World War II, the Court deferred to the executive branch's internment of Japanese-Americans without any individualized form of judicial review whatsoever. Still, in 2004, a half century of favorable precedents for the accused appears to have built up a reservoir of defendants' rights precedents that could not be drained so quickly. Access to the courts, with an opportunity to disprove the government's case, would be made available even to those defendants accused of wreaking terroristic violence on innocent civilians. The legacy left by the Warren Court included a heightened level of suspicion against official attempts to overthrow this elaborate structure.

Some Final Thoughts

As a countermajoritarian fixture of our democratic system, the Supreme Court is often subject to especially harsh criticism. Chief Justice John Marshall's landmark opinion in *McCulloch v. Maryland* (1819) brought considerable criticism to the chief justice personally, and to the Court as a whole. *Dred Scott v. Sanford* (1857) invited officials to position themselves in defiance of the Court's order, and may have helped contribute to the outbreak of the Civil War. More recently in *Bush v. Gore* (2000), millions of supporters of Al Gore's election campaign were angered by the Court's decision to stop the manual recount of presidential election ballots in three counties of Florida.

Still, outrage at the Court has proven especially persistent whenever it has interceded on behalf of criminal defendants. When the U.S. Supreme Court issued multiple landmark rulings in favor of defendants' rights in the 1960s, it handed the Republicans a popular campaign issue that helped it to win the White House in 1968. Calls for impeachment against Associate Justice William O. Douglas, Earl Warren, and other liberal colleagues were taken seriously by the justices themselves. The civil strife and disorder that marked the close of that decade rendered the Supreme Court a political outlier on law-and-order issues, out of touch with the realities of criminal justice in the United States. Even more significantly, the Supreme Court appeared to be undermining the will of the majority, a strike against tribal democracy to be sure. Of course those same exact facts also offer a strikingly positive view of the court as helping to secure the benefits of a liberal democracy in which civil liberties and political rights are paramount.

State courts, where most of the criminal justice in this country is still conducted, have drawn considerable criticism on this score as well. Frustrations over the acquittals of such high-profile defendants such as O. J. Simpson in California and William Kennedy Smith in Florida gave way to criticisms of the courts for allowing highly paid counsel to manipulate the evidence that had gone before their juries. Cameras in the courtroom and Court TV's round-the-clock coverage have greatly improved the transparency of the process, but at the price of exposing many criminal trials as belabored proceedings that tend to focus on extraneous details rather than homing in on the heart of the criminal activity alleged. The prosecution's failure in 2004 to carry through on rape charges brought against basketball superstar Kobe Bryant epitomized a system that often struggles to translate factual evidence of guilt into actual convictions. Naturally, the defendants' rights regime that dates back to the 1960s contributes to this public perception problem as much as it helps to resolve it.

It may seem surprising to some that the courts, perhaps the institution least well-equipped to create broad regulatory frameworks, have stepped into the breach by assuming the bulk of the responsibility for defining and articulating defendants' right in our democratic system. Even more surprising, the regime of defendants' rights erected in the 1960s has largely held course for the better part of four decades. The more expressly political institutions of our government can hardly be termed satisfied with this arrangement—at various times Congress (and more recently, the executive) have tried to stake their own claim in defining defendants' rights, whether by legislative fiat, ideologically driven High Court appointments, or by other innovative solutions aimed at reducing the type of judicial discretion that has served to expand defendants' rights. Most of these responses from the political branches have had some impact, though it must be considered modest when set against the dominant structure of judicially created defendants' rights erected by the Warren Court during the 1960s. The often slow implementation of these decisions does not betray their importance as symbolic gestures of a liberal democracy's struggle to subsist.

The recent war on terrorism has posed a new challenge for courts in this context: With defendants' rights posing something of an obstacle to prosecutors, the administration's response has been to define suspected terrorists as existing outside the category of defendants altogether. To date, the Supreme Court has moved gingerly in this area, deferring to the broad approach taken by the administration, but still providing safeguards to ensure that access to courts is not threatened. Apparently, even a much more conservative Supreme Court is unwilling to be straitjacketed when it comes to defining the rights of the criminally accused. In that respect, America's brand of criminal justice remains a shiny outlier when compared to that found in most other nations that call themselves "democratic," but which nevertheless fall short of the liberal democratic ideal. Rather than reconciling themselves to democracy, competing interests such as victims' rights have been forced to reconcile themselves with a democracy in which defendants' rights stand front and center, for better or worse.

Notes

1. Raymond D. Gastil, "What Kind of Democracy," *Atlantic Monthly* 265, no 6 (June 1990), 93.
2. Ibid.
3. 124 S.Ct. 2633, 2650 (2004).
4. Shapiro, *Courts: A Comparative and Political Analysis*, 1.
5. Ibid., 27.
6. Bodenhamer, *Fair Trial: Rights of the Accused in American History*, 90.
7. *Palko v. Connecticut*, 302 U.S. 319, 328 (1937).
8. William J. Brennan, "The Bills of Rights and the States: The Revival of State Constitutions as Guardians of Individual Rights," *New York University Law Review* 61 (1986): 535–553, at 548.
9. David A. Yalof, *Pursuit of Justices, Presidential Politics and The Selection of Supreme Court Nominees* (Chicago: University of Chicago Press, 1999), 144.
10. Ibid., 136.
11. Ibid., 146.
12. Ibid., 145.
13. Blasi, *The Burger Court: The Counter-Revolution That Wasn't.*
14. 403 U.S. 388, 420 (1971).
15. 530 U.S. 428, 443 (2000).
16. Amar, *The Constitution and Criminal Procedure*, 30.
17. 494 U.S. 407, 414 (1990).
18. Canon and Johnson, *Judicial Policies*, 83.

Bibliography

Amar, Akhil Reed. *The Constitution and Criminal Procedure: First Principles.* New Haven, Conn.: Yale University Press, 1997.

Blasi, Vincent, ed. *The Burger Court: The Counter-Revolution That Wasn't.* New Haven, Conn.: Yale University Press, 1983.

Bodenhamer, David J. *Fair Trial: Rights of the Accused in American History.* New York: Oxford University Press, 1992.

Breckenridge, Adam Carlyle. *Congress against the Court.* Lincoln: University of Nebraska Press, 1970.

Canon, Bradley C., and Charles A. Johnson. *Judicial Policies: Implementation and Impact,* 2nd ed. Washington D.C.: Congressional Quarterly Press, 1999.

Cole, George F., and Christopher E. Smith. *The American System of Criminal Justice*, 8th ed. Belmont, Calif.: West/Wadsworth, 1998.

Curriden, Mark, and Leroy Phillips, Jr. *Contempt of Court: The Turn-of-the-Century Lynching That Launched 100 Years of Federalism*. New York: Faber and Faber, 1999.

Friedman, Lawrence M. *American Law: An Introduction*. New York: W. W. Norton, 1984.

Goldstein, Abraham S. *The Passive Judiciary: Prosecutorial Discretion and the Guilty Plea.* Baton Rouge: Louisiana State University Press, 1981.

Porter, Mary Cornelia, and G. Alan Tarr, eds. *State Supreme Courts: Policymakers in the Federal System*. Westport, Conn.: Greenwood Press, 1982.

Powe, Lucas A., Jr. *The Warren Court and American Politics.* Cambridge, Mass.: Belknap Press, 2000.

Schwartz, Bernard. *The Ascent of Pragmatism: The Burger Court in Action.* Reading, Mass: Addison-Wesley, 1990.

Shapiro, Martin. *Courts: A Comparative and Political Analysis.* Chicago: University of Chicago Press, 1981.

Court Cases

Argersinger v. Hamlin, 407 U.S. 25 (1972).

Benton v. Maryland, 395 U.S. 784 (1969).

Berger v. New York, 388 U.S. 41 (1967).

Bivens v. Six Unknown Named Agents, 403 U.S 388 (1971).

Bush v. Gore, 531 U.S. 98 (2000).

Butler v. McKellar, 494 U.S. 407 (1990).

Coleman v. Alabama, 399 U.S. 1 (1970).

Coolidge v. New Hampshire, 403 U.S. 443 (1971).

Dickerson v. United States, 530 U.S. 428 (2000).

Dred Scott v. Sanford, 60 U.S. 393 (1857).

Escopedo v. Illinois, 378 U.S. 478 (1964).

Estes v. Texas, 381 U.S. 532 (1965).

Fay v. Noia, 372 U.S. 391 (1963).

Felker v. Turpin, 518 U.S. 651 (1996).

Florida v. J.L., 529 U.S. 266 (2000).

Furman v. Georgia, 408 U.S. 238 (1972).

Gideon v. Wainwright, 372 U.S. 335 (1962).

Gilbert v. California, 388 U.S. 263 (1967).

Gregg v. Georgia, 428 U.S. 153 (1976).

Griffin v. Illinois, 351 U.S. 12 (1965).

Hamdi v. Rumsfeld, 124 S.Ct. 2633 (2004).

Harris v. New York, 401 U.S. 222 (1971).

Illinois v. Lafayette, 462 U.S. 204 (1983).

Katz v. United States, 389 U.S. 347 (1967).

Knowles v. Iowa, 525 U.S. 113 (1998).

Kyllo v. United States, 533 U.S. 27 (2001).

Mapp v. Ohio, 367 U.S. 643 (1962).

Massiah v. United States, 377 U.S. 201 (1964).
McCulloch v. Maryland, 17 U.S. 316 (1819).
McCray v. Illinois, 386 U.S. 300 (1967).
Miranda v. Arizona, 384 U.S. 436 (1966).
Moran v. Burbine, 475 U.S. 412 (1986).
New York v. Quarles, 467 U.S. 649 (1984).
Palko v. Connecticut, 302 U.S. 319 (1937).
Powell v. Alabama, 287 U.S. 45 (1932).
Rhode Island v. Innis, 446 U.S. 291 (1980).
Rideau v. Louisiana, 373 U.S. 423 (1963).
Schmerber v. California, 384 U.S. 757 (1966).
Smith v. Maryland, 442 U.S. 735 (1979).
Terry v. Ohio, 392 U.S. 1 (1967).
Townsend v. Sain, 372 U.S. 293 (1963).
United States v. Leon, 468 U.S. 897(1984).
United States v. Wade, 388 U.S. 218 (1967).
Witherspoon v. Illinois, 391 U.S. 510 (1968).

17

PUBLIC EDUCATION, DEMOCRATIC LIFE, AND THE AMERICAN COURTS

Douglas S. Reed

IN 1922, A PORTLAND LAWYER, AUTHOR, FORMER TELEgraph operator, and one-time labor organizer named George Estes wrote a fable lauding the values of public schooling. In that tale, a farmer living in a small town outside of Portland, Oregon pleads with his grown children to support the local schools. He invokes a mythic image of the one-room school house as the cradle of democracy and praises its role as the great equalizer: "I don't say our public schools are perfect, but if they aren't we ought to all work together and tax ourselves to make 'em as good as they can be made, make 'em the best of all. Then all children would get the best education—the children of the poor as well as the rich. Don't they deserve it? Aren't they entitled to it?"[1] Sentiments that speak to the virtues of common schooling and the need for widespread educational opportunity could not have been better expressed by twenty-first-century liberal educational activists urging the reform of America's public schools. Indeed, Estes dedicated his book to "the Foundation of all Civil and Religious Liberty—The Public Schools of America."

The book begins to look a bit differently, however, when we realize that the foreword is penned by Luther I. Powell, the "King Kleagle" of the Pacific Domain of Ku Klux Klan. The text is sprinkled with cartoons stereotyping Roman Catholic priests and depicting a crusading Ku Klux Klansman on horseback. In reality, the text is a propaganda tract in defense of an anti-Catholic and nativist ballot initiative that required, in effect, all children to attend only public schools. The measure, which passed with nearly 54 percent of the vote in Oregon, would have shuttered all private and parochial schools in Oregon, beginning in 1926. In short, the law made private schools illegal.

The ballot measure eventually led in 1925 to the Supreme Court decision of *Pierce v. Society of Sisters*, a landmark decision that defended a realm of private and autonomous familial control over the raising of one's children and which has been hailed as a cornerstone of educational liberty in the United States. Justice McReynolds, for a unanimous Court, wrote in *Pierce*, "The fundamental theory of liberty upon which all governments in this Union repose excludes any general power of the State to standardize its children by forcing them to accept instruction from public teachers only. The child is not the mere creature of the State; those who nurture him and direct his destiny have the right, coupled with the high duty, to recognize and prepare him for additional obligations."[2] *Pierce* clearly presents us with some odd dynamics: Ku Klux Klan supporters arguing for more equal and better public schools; famously independent Oregon voters, acting either out of anti-Catholic sentiment or flush with enthusiasm for the citizenship-building virtues of common schooling, proclaiming the need for fully "American" schools; a unanimous Supreme Court carving out a right to "educational liberty."

But the central political tension of *Pierce* is one of a democratic electorate seeking to force a particular kind of education on its children and the courts preventing the majority from asserting its will. This tension recurs whenever courts and electoral majorities clash over education in American politics. Courts have a long history of involvement in America's schools and educational governance more broadly. State and federal judges have ruled, variously, on the banning of German language instruction in classrooms, the funding levels and mechanisms of school systems, mandatory segregation of white and African American students, the failure to provide instruction in a language other than English, the provision of financial assistance to Catholic and other religious schools, the ability of schools to suppress the speech of students, to name only a few topics. But the relationship between courts and education is not simply one in which court decrees trump democratic abuses of majority powers. To understand the relationships among courts, democratic majorities and America's schools we must first understand something unique about education as a social and political force: Public education is both a precondition for *and* a contested battlefield of democratic governance. Public education is simultaneously a necessary ingredient to a vibrant democracy and an institution over which interests and political forces fight, sometimes bitterly. We cannot have a democracy without a wide distribution of education and learning; at the same time, control of schools is almost an archetypical form of American democratic practice, particularly in light of the predominantly localist framework of educational governance and administration. To disrupt democratic control of schooling—as courts have done—is, seemingly, to attack the very meaning of democratic self-governance.

Yet courts are caught on the horns of a tricky dilemma: Because democracy requires a widely educated and informed citizenry, courts have sought to ensure equal access to quality schools in defense of democracy, *and* because individuals enjoy, in some fashion, individual rights to education, courts have sought to limit democratic incursions on individual rights to education. American courts have pursued both of these projects simultaneously—seeking to advance and protect democracy by ensuring the distribution and quality of education and seeking to advance and protect individual rights to education by restricting democratic control of public education. As a result, the courts' role in advancing education in a democracy is complex and, at times, contradictory. Often, ensuring that children have access to a quality education (necessary for democratic life) requires disrupting democratic control of education.

Limiting popular control of American schools when that control frustrates the democratic aspirations of public education is thus a recurring tension of judicial regulation of schools, but it is by no means the only one. Courts must also navigate disputes over the appropriate scope of federal and state powers over public education. Indeed, because the constitutional status of education—unlike free speech rights or rights of the accused—is most concrete at the state level and far more vague at the national level, telling the story of courts, democracy, and education requires a full and rich understanding of federalism within the American polity.

Federalism and the Judicial Perception of a Right to Education

Pierce v. Society of Sisters is an important case not only for what it says about educational liberty—the capacity of parents (especially those with resources) to opt out of a state monopoly on education—but also for what it *assumes* about the delivery of public education: that public education is an exclusively state-level social service. In 1925, the federal government's role in education was virtually nonexistent. Since the emergence of the common school movement in the 1840s and the spread of compulsory school attendance in the late nineteenth century, the operation and funding of schools was an exclusively state and local matter. Congress took no more interest in public education—as a matter of national policy-making—than it did in local fire fighting. Not until the launch of *Sputnik* on October 4, 1957, could advocates of a national-level presence in public education secure any significant federal aid to local districts. By successfully arguing that the national security interests of the United States required that the federal government provide targeted assistance to public education, particularly in scientific and technical training, the advocates of an increased federal role in education helped push through Congress the National Defense Education Act (NDEA) in late summer of 1958. But not until the desegregation battles of the 1960s and the enactment of the 1965 Elementary and Secondary Education Act (ESEA), as part of President Lyndon B. Johnson's War on Poverty, did federal aid to education rise to a meaningful level, and it was only through the restrictions that Congress imposed on states and localities receiving these funds that the federal government began indirectly to make educational policy.

The historically limited nature of the federal presence in education stems, in large part, from the fact that any constitutional requirement to provide public education rests with the states, not with the federal government. No education provision exists in the U.S. Constitution, but all fifty states have an education clause, imposing varying levels of obligation on state legislatures. Thus, court interpretations of the right to an education centers on the interplay of state and federal obligations. The judicial perception of the right to an education is seen, as it were, through one of three lenses: (two constitutional, one statutory): First, does the operation of a state educational system violate some other, noneducational federal right (rights of due process, or equal protection of the laws, for example)? Within this context, federal constitutional principles act as minimal guarantees for the state's provision of education. Second, are states complying with the requirements of their own state constitutions? In these cases, state courts evaluate the extent to which state educational systems advance the substantive, positive rights to education variously articulated in the fifty state constitutions. Third, are states in compliance with federal statutes governing the distribution of federal educational aid? In these cases, plaintiffs contend that national statutes impose an obligation on states and local school districts to extend educational opportunities to particular individuals. For example, in *Lau v. Nichols* (1974) plaintiffs successfully contended that the 1964 Civil Rights Act's ban on discrimination in federally funded programs meant that the city of San Francisco must provide instruction in Chinese to some of its students, requiring, in effect, extensive programs of bilingual education in many districts throughout the country.

Given these three judicial perceptions on the right to education, it is important to remember that some of the strongest statements by federal courts concerning a right to an education are repeatedly filtered through the federal prism and limited by the nonexistence of an explicit federal right to education. Although Chief Justice Earl Warren wrote in *Brown v. Board of Education* (1954) that education was perhaps "the most important function of state and local governments" and that "it is doubtful any child may reasonably be expected to succeed in life if he is denied the opportunity of an education,"[3] he was keenly aware that the U.S. Constitution could not direct compel the provision of an education. As a result, he wrote that educational "opportunity, *where the state has undertaken to provide it*, is a right which must be available to all on equal terms."[4] The emphasis added to this quote highlights the state-level obligation of public education. In short, federal courts intervene in public education not because public education is a fundamental national right, but because education is a state obligation that must be delivered under the constraints of federal constitutional principles.

This state-based obligation has given state courts considerable opportunity to advance their own views on a right to public education. Since the early 1970s, plaintiffs challenging the distribution of educational resources within states have forced state supreme courts to interpret substantively the meaning of state education constitutional provisions. This state-level process of defining the right to an education has been anchored by two forces. First, state courts must directly contend with the express language concerning education in state constitutions and, second, they must contend with the political reality that educational policy-making is a central feature of both state budgets and state legislative agendas. Judges are not ignorant of the fact that educational expenditures account, on average, for roughly 35 percent of state budgets nor are they ignorant of the political impact—within the electorate and among legislators—of controversial decisions interpreting educational rights. State courts must navigate these two features of state-level educational policy-making—the substantive rights to education found in state constitutions and the importance of educational politics and finance to the political fortunes of legislators—as they rule on plaintiffs' claims concerning educational rights.

Finally, state and federal courts have both struggled with the statutory interpretation of federal legislation concerning educational policy. The judicial perception (and congressional expansion) of the right to an education in these contexts is often greeted by the states as an unfunded federal mandate, and as those obligations have increased in recent years, some states have threatened to forego federal aid in order to be free of federal strictures. Given state and local budget constraints, however, these threats remain largely rhetorical.

Federal Courts and the Constitutional Boundaries of a Right to Education

The U.S. Constitution is perhaps best seen as a limiting condition on the forms of public education in the United States. The Constitution sets the boundaries for permissible forms of schooling in the United States, and judicial interpretation of those boundaries has frequently prevented democratic majorities from advancing their views of the proper forms of schooling. The most frequent conflicts between democratic majorities and federal courts within the realm of education policy have, of course, been over race and religion, with courts often rejecting locally popular forms of discrimination or influence. But it is also worth noting those occasions when the federal courts have *allowed* state-level majorities to create and maintain school systems that hinder educational opportunity, particularly systems that create economic disparities in education and preserve racially homogenous local control. This section will examine the major federal cases that define the federal boundaries of our systems of schooling, exploring instances in which federal courts have struck down local or state-level school practices and instances in which federal courts have upheld them.

Race and Public Education

As a matter of constitutional law, federal court involvement in public education is typically construed through the law of equal protection. Race, in particular, has defined the trajectory of the federal judicial view of the right to an equal education, but the arc of that trajectory has not always been consistently upward. The arc begins in New Orleans, Louisiana, with Homer Plessy, an "octoroon" in the language of the Court, as he boarded a whites-only railway car in 1892. His appeal to the U.S. Supreme Court of his arrest and conviction under Louisiana's 1890 Jim Crow railway law resulted in the disastrous *Plessy v. Ferguson* decision in 1896. That decision put the Supreme Court's imprimatur upon an interpretation of the Fourteenth Amendment that protected segregationist practices under the doctrine of "separate but equal." The Fourteenth Amendment's promise of "equal protection of the laws" to newly freed slaves withered under the harsh assaults of southern state legislators, who stripped African Americans of both civil and political rights in the 1890s, and the Supreme Court's endorsement of those actions in *Plessy.*

While the doctrine of "separate but equal" promised some small measure of equality, in reality, conditions for African American and mixed race persons in the schools, theaters, boarding houses, restaurants, parks, and public accommodations of the South were grossly inferior. African American schools, in particular, were underfunded and understaffed, with teachers and resources sorely lacking and students taught in ramshackle, tarpaper classrooms, often without books or supplies.

Beginning in the 1930s, the National Association for the Advancement of Colored Persons (NAACP) began to challenge the institution of Jim Crow in the South, first taking aim at the failure of southern states to meet even the most minimal equality protections of *Plessy* and later mounting (through the NAACP's Legal Defense Fund) a wholesale litigation campaign against the doctrine of "separate but equal." That campaign, led by Thurgood Marshall and a small staff of NAACP-LDF lawyers, culminated in the *Brown v. Board of Education* decision in 1954. *Brown*, authored by Chief Justice Earl Warren and backed by a unanimous Supreme Court, rejected the logic of *Plessy v. Ferguson*, claiming that segregation created within the hearts of African American students a "feeling of inferiority" unlikely to be undone.[5] The decision firmly resolved that "separate educational facilities are inherently unequal" and seemed to promise a relatively quick merger of black and white schools across the South.[6]

While the southern response was initially moderate, ardent segregationists soon took up the banner of Old Dixie as they fought to preserve Jim Crow schools. The Supreme Court, in a second *Brown v. Board* decision in 1955, ruled that lower federal courts would oversee the design of remedial desegregation plans and the Court wrote that such plans should be implemented "with all deliberate speed." This moderate phrasing boosted the hopes of those who resisted *Brown* and provided time for state-level resisters to devise further delaying tactics. In Virginia, for example, the state legislature cut off all state funds to local districts that complied with the *Brown* decision and funded scholarships for white students to attend private "segregationist" academies that excluded black students. Virginia's model of "Massive Resistance," along with the tactics of southern politicians such as Alabama's George Wallace and Arkansas's Orval Faubus, who resisted federal court pressures in an effort to curry favor with a southern white majority that favored continued segregation, meant that school desegregation in the Deep South barely crept forward during the first decade after *Brown I*. In the border states, however, some school districts undertook modest desegregation efforts, as did school systems in some larger cities such as Dallas where local business elites could rally support for a more moderate southern response.

Events in Little Rock

During this first decade, the Supreme Court did not provide any meaningful guidance to lower federal courts as to what kind of school desegregation plan was constitutionally acceptable. Indeed, it issued only one other court ruling directly related to desegregation during this time period, *Cooper v. Aaron* (1958), which emerged from the conflict in Little Rock, Arkansas, over the desegregation of Central High. The circumstances of *Cooper* highlight the profound tension the *Brown* decision sparked between federal courts and local and state authorities as they battled over even the most token efforts at integration.

In an effort to halt the court-ordered desegregation of Central High in Little Rock, Arkansas, Governor Orval Faubus on September 2, 1957, mobilized the Arkansas National Guard to "maintain order" at Central High and insisted that public safety required that Little Rock schools "be operated on the same basis as they have been operated in the past." On Wednesday, September 4, nine African American students arrived at Central High to attend school. The Arkansas National Guard refused them entry and a mob of whites heckled and abused the students. After a federal judge ordered Faubus to remove the National Guard, to allow the Little Rock Nine entry to Central High, the students again arrived at Central High and again they were met by boisterous and chanting whites. Although the students made their way into school, the growing and increasingly violent crowds convinced school officials that the situation was too dangerous and they sent the Little Rock Nine home in the early afternoon. The next morning, white crowds again began to gather, and a reluctant President Dwight D. Eisenhower, seeking to avoid further violence, finally intervened, placing the Arkansas National Guard under federal authority (removing them from Faubus's command) and ordering one thousand members of the Kentucky-based 101st

Airborne division to provide protection for the African American students. Under the protection of armed federal troops, the Little Rock Nine gained entry to Central High on September 25, only to be subjected to further threats, taunts, and abuse by white students within the school. The federal troops remained in place throughout the year.

Local and state resistance continued to grow, however, over the school year and the school board, yielding to popular sentiments, sought to reverse the desegregation order. Just prior to start of the next school year, the matter landed before the Supreme Court. Although the Court was enjoying its customary summer holiday, events in Little Rock prompted Chief Justice Earl Warren to call the Justices back to Washington for an extraordinary special session. Immediately upon the conclusion of oral argument, the Court issued a per curiam judgment upholding the desegregation order. Its written opinion, issued two weeks later, was a strongly worded defense of judicial power to define the meaning of the Constitution. The decision insisted that state officials could not resist the ruling of *Brown*, arguing that "no state legislator or executive or judicial officer can war against the Constitution without violating his undertaking to support it."[7]

Rather than providing guidance to federal district courts as they sought to implement desegregation plans, the Supreme Court chose instead to assert its position as "final" arbiter of the meaning of the Constitution. To be sure, the Court did declare that

> State support of segregated schools through any arrangement, management, funds, or property cannot be squared with the Amendment's command that no State shall deny to any person within its jurisdiction the equal protection of the laws. The right of a student not to be segregated on racial grounds in schools so maintained is indeed so fundamental and pervasive that it is embraced in the concept of due process of law.[8]

Yet this resolute and firm restatement of *Brown* could not provide assistance on the concrete steps needed to achieve the promise so eloquently stated. In hindsight, some will debate whether explicit guidance over the mechanisms needed to ensure compliance was more important than a strong assertion of the necessity of compliance itself. What is not debatable, however, is that the violent and physical confrontations in Little Rock between protesters and students—as well as the intense political conflict between Faubus, the state legislature, and the federal executive and judicial branches—revealed the depths of southern opposition to desegregation and the political popularity in the South of that opposition.

From Desegregation to Integration

The problem with the new constitutional vision of racial equality in education that *Brown* promised was that the Supreme Court itself was rather short on the specific steps school districts and states needed to take to realize that vision. Left unanswered for over a decade by the Supreme Court was the simple question of whether *Brown* merely required school districts to *desegregate* (that is, no longer base school pupil assignments on race) or whether districts needed to actively *integrate* their student bodies (achieve racial balance in school populations) in order achieve compliance with *Brown*. During this time of dramatic civil unrest throughout the South—the Greensboro, North Carolina, lunch counter sit-ins, the rise of Martin Luther King Jr.'s Southern Christian Leadership Conference and its repression in Birmingham, Alabama, at the hands of Sheriff Bull Connor and his police dogs, the assaults on a peaceful march in Selma, Alabama, the church bombings in Atlanta that killed four schoolgirls, the murder of three civil rights workers in Philadelphia, Mississippi, by locals determined to intimidate civil rights organizers, to name only a few of the more notorious violent incidents—the Supreme Court issued no rulings on school desegregation. Not until 1968, did the Supreme Court provide some guidance to lower federal courts, which had been grappling with the objective of *Brown* for over fourteen years with little judicial oversight.

In *Green v. County School Board* (1968), the Court confronted an ideal case to test the proposition that *Brown* only required school districts to remove obstacles to African American students who wished to attend formerly all-white schools. New Kent County, Virginia, is a rural area in which the population was composed equally of blacks and whites. Moreover, there existed only two schools, one all white, the other all black. The school district's initial "choice" desegregation plan (which simply allowed black and white students attend either school) produced only modest desegregation, with about 15 percent of the black students attending the formerly all-white school and no whites attending the (still) all-black school. The NAACP-LDF challenged the use of the choice mechanism, claiming it did not meet the mandate of *Brown* to reverse the effects previously mandatory segregation. In his opinion, Associate Justice William Brennan finally articulated an urgent, clear, and concrete test for compliance with *Brown*: "The burden on a school board today is to come forward with a plan that promises realistically to work, and promises realistically to work *now*."[9]

The insistence that simply lifting restrictions on the presence of African American students at white schools did not meet the requirements of *Brown* reshaped the terrain of judicial enforcement of desegregation orders. Under *Green*, school districts had an affirmative duty to remove the stigma associated with clearly inferior and significantly underfunded black schools. The Supreme Court charged southern school districts in *Green* with an "affirmative duty" to create "unitary" school systems "in which racial discrimination would be eliminated root and branch."[10] In short, a "unitary" school district was one in which segregation was simply a memory, not an ongoing fact of schooling. With *Green*'s contribution to the legal struggles over educational equality, the South's school districts now had a clear and explicit goal, albeit an ambitious one.

With the goal of "unitary" status defined, federal judges quickly came to the conclusion that the only technique to accomplish that task was busing. Because residential segregation throughout the United States divided black and white communities, neighborhood schools would still be overwhelmingly racially homogenous. In Charlotte, North Carolina, the school district encompassed the entire Mecklenburg County, including suburban municipalities. An early desegregation plan proposed by Charlotte-Mecklenburg Public School District officials yielded only a modest desegregation: Out of twenty thousand African American students, only 490 attended school with whites under the school district's remedy. The NAACP-LDF challenged the plan in court, arguing that under the logic of *Green* the school district must do more to remedy present segregation. Federal District Court Judge James B. McMillan agreed, approving a desegregation plan that paired black and white neighborhoods across the county and bused students among them.

The matter quickly found its way to the Supreme Court, where newly appointed Chief Justice Warren Burger assigned himself the task of writing the opinion. His decision, backed by a unanimous Supreme Court, strongly endorsed the conclusion of *Green* and put the moral weight of the Supreme Court behind the project of court-ordered busing. Wrote Burger: "In default by the school authorities of their obligation to proffer acceptable remedies, a district court has broad power to fashion a remedy that will assure a unitary school system."[11] Burger concluded that

> All things being equal, with no history of discrimination, it might well be desirable to assign pupils to schools nearest their homes. But all things are not equal in a system that has been deliberately constructed and maintained to enforce racial segregation. The remedy for such segregation may be administratively awkward, inconvenient, and even bizarre in some situations and may impose burdens on some; but all awkwardness and inconvenience cannot be avoided.[12]

The endorsement of busing in Charlotte meant, for all practical purposes, the end of southern delay in the school desegregation battle. Moreover, the combination of *Green* and *Swann* meant that northern districts were on notice as well to remedy any "vestige" of segregation that was the product of official policy, even if the segregation was not required by law. Soon lawsuits in Denver, Boston, Cleveland, and Dayton profoundly blurred the de facto–de jure distinction that northern districts had once thought would isolate them from the rapid desegregation. In the Denver, Colorado, case *Keyes v. School District No. 1* (1973) the Supreme Court ruled that practices designed to preserve segregation in any one part of a school district opened up the entire district to judicially imposed remedial action.[13] By the mid-1970s, the Supreme Court had effectively dismantled the de facto–de jure distinction and federal judges were ordering wide-scale busing programs throughout the country, not just the Deep South.

The Battle of Boston and the End of Busing

No other northern city saw a busing battle as bitter as Boston's. Once the U.S. Supreme Court handed down *Keyes*, it became clear that Boston would soon face court-ordered busing. Under the guise of open enrollment, the Boston School Committee had long practiced race-conscious school assignment of pupils and in June of 1974, Federal District Judge W. Arthur Garrity Jr. found the Boston School Committee to have engaged in segregation in the public schools. He ordered the busing of roughly seventeen thousand Boston students between paired white and black schools, to begin in September 1974. Garrity's decision ignited long-simmering racial and class conflicts throughout the city.

To the opponents of busing, the most audacious busing pair was the linkage of two high schools, South Boston High (in the heart of a white, ethnic working-class, and poor Irish enclave) and Roxbury High, an African American inner-city ghetto. While students from poor households predominated in both schools, neither neighborhood saw the other as an ally. Anti-busing rallies and protests punctuated the summer and fall of 1974 in Boston, with white activists parents leading chants and battling with police, hurling bottles, rocks, and racial slurs at African American students as the school buses rolled into poor white neighborhoods. For their part, African Americans retaliated and clashed frequently with white protesters and students. White school officials in Boston led the charge against Garrity's decision and the busing plan, with Louise Day Hicks, a longtime anti-busing activist and chair of the Boston School Committee, and John Kerrigan, another school committee member, rallying ardent anti-busing foes and urging resistance to the busing plan.

Garrity reacted by asserting greater control over Boston schools. While he declined to order in federal authorities, he threatened to hold school committee members in contempt of court for failing to submit a busing plan for year two of the desegregation effort. Like southern supporters of segregation, white Bostonians opposed to busing saw the intrusion of a federal judge and police into their schools as a personal attack on their neighborhoods and their local self-rule. A leader of the anti-busing movement, Ray Flynn, told a reporter for the *Boston Globe*, "They take our schools, now they take our streets. . . . This is the most degrading thing to South Boston."[14]

In the end, the desegregation of Boston schools (and white leaders' resistance to it) transformed the city, in part by fueling greater flight to the suburbs by whites, including some who opposed desegregation, some who were fearful of lingering violence, and some simply fed up with the long-standing incompetent political leadership of the city's schools. Across the nation, in fact, busing has been linked with increasing white flight, as whites left the central cities of the North and Midwest in record numbers in the 1960s and 1970s. By the late 1970s, in many cities there were few white students remaining to integrate with African American students. This dramatic shift in demographics led to increasing frustration on the part of even good-intentioned school administrators operating under court-mandated busing plans who felt they were fighting demographic forces beyond their control.

The change in the nature of school segregation, from a condition compelled by state law or local practice to a more complex social and economic phenomenon in which real estate markets and metropolitan jurisdictional fragmentation sort households quite effectively by race and class, altered the Supreme Court's views on compliance with desegregation decrees. In *Board of Education of Oklahoma City Public Schools v. Dowell* (1990) the Supreme Court ruled that once a school district had achieved the unitary status called for in *Green* it need not sustain a desegregation plan, even if the cessation of busing yielded renewed segregation. In effect, any segregation that occurred after "unitary" status was not the product of state action, but more amorphous private economic and social decisions concerning household residence. Those segregating influences were beyond the reach of local school districts, ruled Chief Justice William Rehnquist.

With *Dowell*, the period of busing as a major tool of federal judicial educational policy-making came, essentially, to a close. Political support for busing had clearly waned by 1991 and both African American and other activists were pursuing other strategies for educational reform, including school financing lawsuits and other, market-based reforms. The promise of *Brown* has dimmed and the arc of judicial rulings on racial educational opportunity has long passed its zenith, but the tensions and transformations released by the judicial recognition of equal protection rights in education are still flowing through American politics. The students who received better educations and who benefited from judicially imposed racial equality in education are now among our nation's leaders, yet many of the scars of those conflicts still plague race relations today. The tensions between courts and democratic action have perhaps never been so acute in our nation's history nor as productive.

Religion and Public Education

In contrast to the federal decisions on race and education, federal decisions on the permissible role of religion in public education have a far less distinct arc. Indeed, the course of Supreme Court cases interpreting the First Amendment in educational contexts is an erratic zigzag, mapped more predictably by the ideological preferences of Supreme Court justices than any sustained logical coherence to the rulings themselves. Perhaps the only constant in these cases is that large portions of the American public have been far more accommodating of religion in public education than have Supreme Court justices. As a result, the deep level of religiosity in American culture provides the Supreme Court with frequent opportunity to revisit these issues, and as the composition of the High Court changes, new coalitions on the Court emerge to revise or update the constitutional perspective on religion in American schools.

In order to understand the salience of political fights over religion in American schools, we need to understand just how seriously Americans take their religion. On average, 61 percent of Americans attend church once or twice a month and 45 percent attend church every week.[15] Fully 30 percent of Americans consider themselves Evangelical Christians, and in 2003, roughly 41 percent of those polled thought there was "too little expression of religious faith and prayer by political leaders" in the United States.[16] Religion recurs as a political (and judicial) issue in American schools because many Americans deeply value religion and many, if not most, see religion as playing an important role in the upbringing of children. On the other hand, the First Amendment of the U.S. Constitution places unequivocal limits on governmental establishment of religion. The resulting church-state conflicts over religion in public schools (and public support of religious schools) force the courts into the familiar and often politically unpopular position of defending minority rights against majority will.

This is most abundantly clear when we look at the issue of prayer in public schools. Unlike the cases involving state support to private religious schools, the school prayer cases are fundamentally symbolic. Religious enterprises do not contribute prayer books to public schools and the time devoted to prayer during the school day is measured in minutes and moments. The symbolism of the issue, however, taps into deeply held public views about the organization of schools and conduct of students within school. For courts to remove prayer from schools is, for a significant portion of the American electorate, a cause for worry and alarm. The Supreme Court first engaged the issue of school prayer in 1962, when it ruled 6–1 in *Engel v. Vitale* that New York laws requiring or allowing the use of a twenty-two-word nondenominational prayer approved by the State Board of Regents violated the Establishment Clause. In his majority opinion, Justice Hugo Black declared that the short prayer—"Almighty God, we acknowledge our dependence upon Thee, and we beg thy blessings upon us, our parents, our teachers and our country"—amounted to a "state prayer program" and claimed that "government in this county, be it state or federal, is without power to prescribe by law any particular form of prayer which is to be used as an official prayer in carrying on any program of governmentally sponsored religious activity."[17] Whether or not students were coerced into saying the prayer was irrelevant to Black, who contended that the Establishment Clause barred the enactment of any official religious exercise, independent of its coerciveness (or lack thereof).

Public reaction to *Engel* was strong, and partly informed by a perception that the Supreme Court had embarked upon wholesale assault on American traditionalism. Some opponents, particularly those from the South, saw the emergence of a tyrannical court and linked the desegregation cause with the Court's crusade to end prayer in school. Representative George Andrews of Alabama said, "They put the Negroes in the schools and now they've driven God out." Senator Sam Ervin of North Carolina asked "[W]ould we be far wrong in saying that in this decision the Supreme court has held that God is unconstitutional and for that reason the public schools must be segregated against Him?"[18]

Despite the heated opposition, the Supreme Court did not reverse course. A year later, it handed down another ruling striking down school prayer. This consolidated decision emerged from two separate lawsuits out of Maryland and Pennsylvania in which parents objected to the recitation of the Lord's Prayer and compulsory Bible readings at the beginning of the school day.[19] Although the outcome was essentially the same as the *Engel* decision, the Supreme Court was somewhat more divided over whether these policies violated the free exercise rights of students or the Establishment Clause. The opinion of the Court, delivered by Justice Tom Clark, contended that both the free exercise clause and the establishment clause require an official religious neutrality—a neutrality toward religion per se and a neutrality among religious sects.

Despite the Supreme Court's one-two punch in the early 1960s, the American public was not entirely convinced that prayer in school was constitutionally dangerous. Indeed, several studies have shown that a robust majority of Americans favor prayer in schools. In 1974, nearly 68 percent of those polled in the General Social Survey favored reading Bible verses or the Lord's Prayer in school. That figure dropped to around 55 percent in 1985, but in 1984 over 71 percent of those polled in the National Election Survey favored allowing schools to beginning the day school day with prayer.[20] Similarly, numerous studies recount the difficulty of enforcing the school prayer decisions at the local level. Kenneth Dolbeare and Phillip Hammond wrote in 1971 of the extensive failure of localities to restrict school prayer, citing a widespread "banality of non-compliance." Officials in local districts held what they thought were good reasons to not enforce the *Engel* and *Schempp* decisions or, instead, rationalized away the need to ensure that prayer in school did not occur. Similarly, the local power structures of the four small communities that Dolbeare and Hammond studied were virtually unanimous in their support for school prayer and without any institutional or administrative mechanism to ensure compliance, courts were almost powerless to see that their unpopular decisions held sway at the local level. Despite widespread opposition to the Court's rulings, a significant portion of the American public nonetheless endorsed the Court's sharp and clear separation between religion and public schooling, further heightening the democratic debate about the role of religion in schools and in public life more broadly.

As the Warren Court evolved into the Rehnquist Court, the doctrines concerning school prayer evolved as well. Perhaps the most important development of the past decade in the realm of religion and public education has been the emergence of the non-preferentialist doctrine. First surfacing in then–Associate Justice Rehnquist's dissent in *Wallace v. Jafree* in 1985, non-preferentialism argues that the founders did not intend government to be neutral to the idea of religion itself, but that the First Amendment's restrictions on governmental activity merely prevent government from favoring any particular sect of religion. This theory also holds that as long as the government has legitimate secular ends, it may employ nondiscriminatory religious means to accomplish those ends. This reconceptualization of the limitations imposed by the First Amendment expands governmental activity in the religious world in two ways. First, governments may use religious institutions, under this doctrine, to achieve secular purposes. Second, government may, if it sees an interest in doing so, engage in policy making that favors religion over nonreligion, as long as it does not favor any particular religious sect. Non-preferentialism has its critics, however, including the prominent constitutional scholar Leonard Levy, who argues that Rehnquist has fundamentally misunderstood the practices and views of the founders on public assistance to religious institutions.

Despite these criticisms, the development of non-preferentialism has significantly altered the Supreme Court's view of the line between church and state. Perhaps nowhere is this clearer than in the 2002 school voucher case, *Zelman v. Simmons-Harris*.[21] Drawing on earlier cases that linked the doctrine of non-preferentialism to governmental policies on education, this case emerged from state reform in Cleveland schools. Those reforms included a publicly funded voucher scheme that provided limited scholarships to low-income students to attend private schools in Cleveland, including religious schools. Eighty-two percent of the private schools participating in the program were religious schools (predominantly Catholic) and over 96 percent of the more than thirty-seven hundred students participating in the voucher program attended religious schools. Chief Justice Rehnquist, writing for a slim 5–4 majority, concluded that the voucher scheme did not violate the U.S. Constitution:

> [W]here a government aid program is neutral with respect to religion, and provides assistance directly to a broad class of citizens who, in turn, direct government aid to religious schools wholly as a result of their own genuine and independent private choice, the program is not readily subject to challenge under the Establishment Clause. A program that shares these features permits government aid to reach religious institutions only by way of the deliberate choices of numerous individual recipients. The incidental advancement of a religious mission, or the perceived endorsement of a religious message, is reasonably attributable to the individual recipient, not to the government, whose role ends with the disbursement of benefits.[22]

The central elements of the non-preferentialist doctrine are clear here: an individual-level choice to use a governmental benefit at or through a religious institution violates neither the Establishment Clause nor the Free Exercise Clause because the individual, not the state, is choosing to deploy the governmental benefit in a religious context. The state is indifferent to the religious choice exercised by the individual and is indifferent as to whether the individual chooses to use the voucher at a religious or nonreligious school. This formal understanding of the choices students and families make clearly understates the sharp lack of choice many students faced within the Cleveland voucher scheme. Because the voucher covered nearly the full cost of the Catholic school tuition, but not the secular private school tuition, secular schools had little incentive to participate in the program, resulting in fewer nonreligious options for poor students exercising the voucher under in the Cleveland plan. While school vouchers are now constitutionally permissible, local resistance in many areas is still thwarting their expansion, as is the sizable price tag for states and school districts to underwrite the cost of private school tuition.

While the *Zelman* case allows states and school districts to pay for scholarships at religious schools, a 2004 Supreme Court case makes it clear that states and school districts are not *required* to do so. In *Locke v. Davey*, the Supreme Court ruled in a 7–2 opinion, that the state of Washington could exclude "devotional theology" majors from a statewide scholarship program for low- and middle-income students of academic merit. Under the Washington Promise Scholarship program, students who were academically eligible but majored in a religiously devotional course of study were explicitly declared ineligible to receive the state-funded scholarships. The Washington Constitution prevents the state legislature from supporting students who pursue degrees that are "devotional in nature or designed to induce religious faith."[23] Joshua Davey had argued that this ban discriminated against religion. Chief Justice Rehnquist, for the 7–2 majority, wrote that Washington neither infringed on Davey's free exercise rights nor discriminated against him.

With the *Zelman* and *Locke* cases, the Supreme Court has established the poles of public debate concerning public assistance to religious schools. That assistance must be targeted primarily at individuals who must have a genuine ability to choose among religious and non-religious institutions. Beyond those parameters, the doctrine of non-preferentialism creates a significant space for democratic debate about the relationship between religion and schooling. Options exist for cities, school districts, and states to either enable students to enroll (at public expense) in religious schools or to not adopt voucher schemes, but not all options must be exercised. Merely because the Supreme Court has constitutionalized the use of vouchers, it does not necessarily follow that many cities or districts will endorse the notion. Just as the school desegregation cases sparked lengthy vociferous conflict, the role of religion in public education (and the role of public money in religious education) has touched off enormous and ongoing controversy, but the role of the federal courts in these cases has always been to establish the limits and parameters within which cities, districts, and states must design and operate their schools. The federal obligation goes no further.

Localism and Public Education

In order to appreciate the degree to which federal courts have intervened in the racial and religious dimensions of public education, it is fruitful to examine two occasions in which the Supreme Court has *declined* to disrupt state-based educational practices on behalf of a national constitutional value. Two decisions, *San Antonio Independent School District v. Rodriguez* (1973) and *Milliken v. Bradley* (1974) are worth close attention because they highlight the trade-offs the federal judiciary must make as it navigates the complex federal landscape of educational governance.

Rodriguez involved a challenge to the system of financing public education in Texas, a system that relied heavily on local property taxes for school revenues, like most state school financing systems in the United States. Because real estate values vary substantially across districts within a state, a heavy reliance on property taxes produces, without state equalization funds, significant disparities in the per pupil revenues available to districts.

In Texas, at the time of the *Rodriguez* litigation, those disparities were sizeable: Edgewood Independent School District, a poor and predominantly Hispanic district in the central city of San Antonio, generated in the 1967–1968 school year only $26 local dollars per pupil at the highest tax rate in the San Antonio metropolitan area. In contrast, Alamo Heights School District, a neighboring district, generated $333 per pupil in local revenues, at a tax rate two-thirds that of Edgewood's. State funds made up some of the disparity, but when state and local funds were combined Alamo Heights still had over twice the per pupil funds of San Antonio.[24] The *Rodriguez* litigators had hoped that the Supreme Court would view resource equality as an essential component of equal educational opportunity or that the Court would use the language of *Brown* to deem education a fundamental right. Unfortunately for Demetrio Rodriguez and his family, the Supreme Court held in a 5–4 decision that education is not a fundamental right, nor is poverty a suspect classification under the Fourteenth Amendment. The result was that significant resource disparities within American education—both within states and across states—could not be addressed by federal courts.

While the Court strongly asserted the importance of education for society, it relied on a textualist notion of a fundamental right, as well as the existing practices of federalism to justify its refusal to deem education fundamental under the U.S. Constitution. Wrote Justice Powell:

> It is not the province of this Court to create substantive constitutional rights in the name of guaranteeing equal protection of the laws. Thus, the key to discovering whether education is "fundamental" is not to be found in comparisons of the relative societal significance of education as opposed to subsistence or housing. Nor is it to be found by weighing whether education is as important as the right to travel. Rather, the answer lies in assessing whether there is a right to education explicitly or implicitly guaranteed by the Constitution.[25]

After rejecting the view that education was a fundamental right and that poverty was a suspect classification, Powell then contended that Texas's system of taxation and spending was a rational enough basis to defend its system of funding public education from constitutional assault. Moreover, to disrupt Texas's system would be to "intrude in an area in which it has traditionally deferred to state legislatures."[26] Powell added that

> [T]he Justices of this Court lack both the expertise and the familiarity with local problems so necessary to the making of wise decisions with respect to the raising and disposition of public revenues. . . . In such a complex arena in which no perfect alternatives exist, the Court does well not to impose too rigorous a standard of scrutiny lest all local fiscal schemes become subjects of criticism under the Equal Protection Clause.[27]

In *Rodriguez*, the Court's respect for state-level decisions on taxation and educational policy trumped its concern over the inequality in educational resources suffered by the children in districts like Edgewood. The values of federalism, localism, and state fiscal policy—in the absence of an explicit federal right to an equal education—won the day.

The Supreme Court returned to the theme of localism in public education a year later when it handed down the *Milliken v. Bradley* decision. A desegregation case out of Detroit, Michigan, *Milliken* presented Chief Justice Warren Burger with a delicate task. Only three years earlier, Burger had argued in *Swann* that districts must employ strong means to eradicate "all vestiges" of segregation. In Detroit, a federal district judge had found that the city of Detroit had engaged in race-conscious zoning and pupil assignment to in an effort to minimize white flight. As a remedy, the court imposed a metropolitan-wide busing desegregation plan on fifty-three of Detroit's eighty-five suburban school districts. By including the suburban districts, the court hoped to recapture some of the white students who had moved outside the boundaries of the Detroit city school district. Upon appeal, the U.S. Supreme Court struck down the remedy, contending that inter-district remedies could not be used to redress an intra-district constitutional violation. Chief Justice Burger's ruling contended that the remedy overstepped the traditional powers of the federal courts in education by violating the historic practice of local control. Wrote Burger:

> [T]he notion that school district lines may be casually ignored or treated as a mere administrative convenience is contrary to the history of public education in our country. No single tradition in public education is more deeply rooted than local control over the operation of schools; local autonomy has long been thought essential both to the maintenance of community concern and support for public schools and to quality of the educational process.[28]

This "constitutionalization" of the practice of local control in public education relies on a largely imagined democratic practice of school formation. In reality, school districts and school district boundaries are the products of state law, and it would require no enormous stretch of legal imagination to regard state designation of school boundaries as state action reachable under the Fourteenth Amendment. If, under *Keyes*, school districts are to be held accountable throughout the district for racial discrimination in any one part of the district, why should states not be made subject to a desegregation decree, if school district boundaries are constructed in such as way as to encourage or facilitate white flight or continued segregation? Burger's reliance on the historical practice of local control to rescue suburbs from the desegregation order both distorts local control's legal origins and discounts its significant segregative effects.

Taken together *Rodriguez* and *Milliken* show that the Supreme Court has not always pursued greater educational opportunity for school children. Indeed, when values of federalism or the need to protect local control seem paramount, the Supreme Court has shied away from an expansive judicial project of preserving educational opportunity. The difficulty for federal courts lies, at root, in the lack of an explicit right within the Constitution to an education and the need to filter any claims about educational rights through some other explicit guarantee. That difficulty, however, is not present for state courts.

State Courts and the Judicial Interpretation of a Substantive Right to Education

A significant consequence of *Rodriguez* was the relatively rapid turn of litigators to state constitutions to pursue in court legal remedies for unequal spending that federal courts could not redress. Part of a broader legal development, sometimes dubbed the new judicial federalism, this turn to state courts and state constitutions represents a significant development in American constitutionalism. State constitutions play a significantly different role in American law than the U.S. Constitution and are often remarkable instruments. Frequently easy to amend and existing in a legal framework in which states are assumed to have plenary powers, state constitutions often act more as restrictions on state governments than as organic authorizations of power. State education provisions exist in all fifty states, but impose a wide range of responsibilities on state legislatures. While Washington's constitution declares that public education is the "paramount duty of the state"[29] the constitution of Oklahoma merely requires the state legislature to "establish and maintain a system of free public schools wherein all the children of the State may be educated."[30] In Massachusetts, the state legislature labors under a pre-Revolutionary admonition to "cherish learning." More common phrases require states to operate a "thorough and efficient" or "general and uniform" system of public education.

In the wake of *Swann*, *Keyes*, and *Rodriguez*, many civil rights litigators, frustrated by the slow pace of school desegregation and concerned that desegregated schools did not receive sufficient or comparable resources, began a legal campaign of using these state educational provisions, and state-level equality provisions, to challenge in state courts the existing systems of school financing. As the *Rodriguez* case had demonstrated these school funding systems were frequently based primarily on local property taxes and often generated wildly unequal amounts of revenue for school districts. While some states had equalizing formulas to make spending levels roughly comparable, many, if not most, did not.

Thirteen days after *Rodriguez* came down, the New Jersey Supreme Court issued the first ruling declaring a state's system of funding public education as unconstitutional on state grounds. Informed by both the school desegregation struggle and broader claims about educational equality, the New Jersey Supreme Court in the first *Robinson v. Cahill* (1973) decision (there would ultimately be five) interpreted the state's 1875 education clause that required the legislature to provide a "thorough and efficient" education as mandating "equal educational opportunity." To ensure equal educational opportunity, the state must, the Court reasoned, provide a particular level of educational offering. Unfortunately for the Court, that level of education was not self-evident in the New Jersey Constitution. As a result, the New Jersey Supreme Court invented a metric: "The Constitution's guarantee must be understood to embrace that educational opportunity which is needed in the contemporary setting to equip a child for his role as a citizen and as a competitor in the labor market."[31] A "thorough and efficient" education, then, becomes one in which all students, upon graduation, can participate in the democratic process and have some reasonable prospect of finding a job.

This early state constitutional decision on school finance decision exhibits all the tensions that state supreme court decisions on this issue have grappled with for over forty years: How does a court assign meaning to a rather vague clause that is, nonetheless, widely seen as one of the most important functions of state government? Should the court be concerned with the *equality* of the educational system or with the *adequacy* of that system? By what metric do we determine if the educational system is equal? By what metric does a court determine if the educational system is adequate? State supreme courts have issued an enormous range of answers to these questions, ranging from the prosaic to the profound. Whatever the precise formulation, any state supreme court decision that strikes down the existing system of funding public education confronts significant democratic barriers to a wholesale restructuring of public school finance. In short, two options exist: redistribution of existing funds or new revenues. The redistribution of funds from affluent districts to either property-poor or income-poor districts is rarely, if ever, politically popular and often fiercely resisted. As a result, additional taxation is typically required to meet the state supreme court mandate for greater educational adequacy or equity. But new taxes are rarely politically desirable for state legislators. The result is often policy stalemate and institutional gridlock, as Texas saw in the early 1990s when the state legislature battled the state supreme court over the scope of school finance reforms. In a seven year period, the Texas Supreme Court handed down no less than six opinions seeking to influence legislative action.

But not all judicial interventions have produced political chaos. In Kentucky, a decision that struck down the *entire* system of public education—from financing to curriculum to the legal authority of school boards to teacher qualifications—produced a landmark reform within a relatively short time. In addition to its expansive ambitions, the Kentucky *Rose v. Council for Better Education* (1989) decision was remarkable for its explicit invocation of a court case that arguable had no controlling legal authority: *Brown v. Board of Education*. Ruling that the state constitution imposed on the Kentucky legislature a significant constitutional obligation to improve public education, Chief Justice Stephens described *Brown* as the "polestar" of the *Rose* decision. Navigating by the lights of *Brown*, the Kentucky Supreme Court found education to be a fundamental right for all Kentucky school children:

> Each child, *every* child in this Commonwealth must be provided with an equal opportunity to have an adequate education. Equality is the key word here. The children of the poor and the children of the rich, the children who live in the poor districts and the children who live in the rich districts must be given the same opportunity and access to an adequate education.[32]

Thus the federal requirement that states operate schools within the boundaries of the Equal Protection Clause has, in some instances, been reinterpreted by state courts to provide a substantive right to a quality education, a substantive right that, thus far, the federal courts have been unwilling or unable to recognize.

The Judicial Vision of Schooling as a Prerequisite for Democracy

Both federal and state courts have viewed education not simply as an individual right that democratic majorities cannot unfairly restrict or impinge upon, but rather as an essential element of democratic life itself. One strong justification for the expansion of educational opportunities is that without an educated citizenry, particularly in an increasingly complex and interdependent world, democratic self-governance is difficult to sustain. Toward that end, "democratic" or majoritarian decisions to *not* provide education (or to provide an inadequate or insufficient education) are struck down because they undermine the very premise of the democratic project. Among federal decisions, the strongest language can be found in *Plyler v. Doe* (1982), a Texas case in which the state legislature refused to provide state funding to school districts for any pupil that could not document his or her lawful presence in the United States. In his opinion, Justice Brennan highlighted the "importance of education in maintaining our basic institutions, and the lasting impact of its deprivation on the life of the child." He added a few lines, saying that "education has a fundamental role in maintaining the fabric of our society. We cannot ignore the significant social costs borne by our Nation when select groups are denied the means to absorb the values and skills upon which our social order rests."[33]

Similarly, state courts that have ruled on the adequacy of public school financing systems have repeatedly stressed the linkages between schooling and the preservation of democratic institutions and governance. In New Hampshire, the state supreme court relied upon a clause in the New Hampshire state constitution that declared "knowledge and learning" to be "essential to the preservation of a free government" and that "it shall be the duty of the legislators and magistrates, in all future periods of this government, to cherish the interest of literature and the sciences, and all seminaries and public schools."[34] This language, argued Chief Justice David Brock, "expressly recognizes that a free government is dependent for its survival on citizens who are able to participate intelligently in the political, economic, and social functions of our system."[35] As a result, the New Hampshire Supreme Court ordered the state to revamp its system of financing public education, a system that has historically relied almost exclusively on local property taxes. The ensuing political conflict was, in essence, a battle between those who sought to retain the democratic majority's desire for low levels of state spending and those who endorsed the New Hampshire Supreme Court's view that increased educational funding was good not only for students, but for democracy. State-level school funding disputes—just as sharply as racial and religious conflicts—highlight the enduring tension between education as a battleground of democracy and as a prerequisite of democratic politics.

At the federal level, however, the notion that a rich educational offering promotes democratic life is not necessarily the controlling one, however. As Justice

Powell wrote in *Rodriguez*, the federal right to participate in the political process does not necessarily create a corollary right to an education which would enable one to participate better, or even effectively. Because disparities in Texas school funding did not create an absolute deprivation of education, "no charge fairly could be made that the [Texas] system fails to provide each child with an opportunity to acquire the basic minimal skills necessary for the enjoyment of the rights of speech and of full participation in the political process."[36] That is, relative inequality in educational opportunity does not give rise to a federal constitutional claim under this "democratic" theory of participation because the provided (albeit unequal) level of education still enables all citizens to participate in the process. A relative disparity is not an absolute bar to participation, according to Powell.

As is evident in the *Rodriguez* case, the Supreme Court must often weigh competing (and sometimes explicit) constitutional values against a largely implicit constitutional preference for greater educational opportunity. In *Wisconsin v. Yoder* (1972), the Supreme Court ruled that halting education at the eighth grade for religious reasons did not necessarily prevent one from effectively participating in democratic life. This case presented the Supreme Court with a conflict between Wisconsin educational officials and the Amish community in Green County, Wisconsin. The Amish in that area withdrew their children from public schools after eighth grade because they found those schools to be premised on values inimical to the Amish life. These values of competition, ambition, individualism, materialism, and self-promotion clashed with the Amish norms of fellowship, cooperation, collective work, a rejection of worldly possessions, and a rejection of technology. Public schooling beyond the eighth grade, the Amish argued, made it impossible for the community to instill those traits in their children. The state contended that all children needed education to a minimum age of sixteen years in order to fully participate in economic and political life.

Expressing a deep respect for the history and obvious religious conviction of the Amish, Chief Justice Warren Burger concluded that the additional one to two years of schooling would not substantially affect the ability of Amish children to engage the non-Amish world, but they would impose an enormous cost on the Amish community. The Amish, Burger wrote, had in effect substituted their own form of educational attainment, a system of learning that was different from the democratic majority of Wisconsin, but one that was no less valuable to the members of the community.

Conclusion: Democracy and the Judicial Regulation of Schooling

The complex relationships among democracy, judges, and schooling were framed throughout the twentieth century largely through the landmark cases of school desegregation and school prayer. Like contentious politics in other arenas, the judicial politics of schooling were most explosive when they touched on issues of identity and the limits of a democratic majority to regulate the terms of education. New educational policy initiatives in the late twentieth and early twenty-first centuries have changed public education in important ways that make traditional modes of democratic control of schooling increasingly less central to educational practice. Innovations such as charter schools, home schooling, vouchers, and school choice have decentralized educational governance and sought to achieve reform through market-based notions of incentives and competition. At the same time, policy makers and the public's increasing emphasis on standards and accountability have shifted focus away from the inputs to public education and toward the outputs. Recent federal assertions of authority over schools and school districts will in the near future strain and change long-standing norms of local control in public education. States will have to play a much stronger coordinating and centralizing function in educational policy-making in order to meet these federal demands.

All these changes mean that the idea of democratic control—long symbolized in the mind of the American public as the "little red schoolhouse"—will change as well. The question, for judges and for citizens alike, is whether our common experiences of education—and our collective need to transmit common values to our children—will emerge from these changes intact or whether they will be unrecognizably altered. Indeed, our notions of public education could very well be wholly different in fifty years; undoubtedly, the practices of education will be. The changes in public education wrought by the American judiciary over the past fifty years have been enormous and have contributed to the vitality and transformation of the United States; more changes undoubtedly lie ahead. But the constants of citizens, children and the law will undoubtedly provide some measure of continuity, at least to the conflicts if not to their resolution.

Notes

1. Estes, *The Old Cedar School*, 33.
2. *Pierce v. Society of Sisters,* 268 U.S. 510 (1925), 535.
3. *Brown v. Board of Education*, 347 U.S. 483 (1954), 493.
4. Ibid. (emphasis added).
5. Ibid., 494.
6. Ibid., 495.
7. *Cooper v. Aaron,* 358 U.S. 1 (1958), 18.
8. Ibid., 19.
9. *Green v. County School Board,* 391 U.S. 430 (1968) at 439.
10. Ibid., 437–438.
11. *Swann*, 16.

12. Ibid., 28.
13. *Keyes v. School District No. 1,* 413 U.S. 189 (1973)
14. Ronald P. Formisano, *Boston against Busing: Race, Class and Ethnicity in the 1960s and 1970s* (Chapel Hill: University of North Carolina Press, 1991), 77.
15. Pew Research Center for People and The Press, Survey Reports. *Religion and Politics: The Ambivalent Majority*, survey released September 2000 (Washington, D.C., 2000).
16. Pew Forum on Religion and Public Life, *Religion and Politics: Contention and Consensus* (Washington, D.C., 2003), survey released July 23, 2003.
17. *Engel v. Vitale,* 370 U.S. 421 (1962), 430.
18. Robert S. Alley, *School Prayer: The Court, the Congress and the First Amendment* (Buffalo: Prometheus Books), 109–110, citing *New York Times* coverage.
19. *Abington School District v. Schempp and Murray v. Curlett*, 374 U.S. 203 (1963).
20. John C. Green and James L. Guth, "The Missing Link: Political Activists and Support for School Prayer," *Public Opinion Quarterly* 53, no. 1 (1989): 41–57, at 41.
21. *Zelman v. Simmons-Harris,* 536 U.S. 639 (2002)
22. Ibid., 652.
23. *Locke v. Davey,* 124 S. Ct. 1307 (2004), 1310.
24. *San Antonio Independent School District v. Rodriguez*, 411 U.S. 1 (1973), 12–13.
25. *Rodriguez*, 411 U.S. 1 (1973) at 33.
26. Ibid., 40.
27. Ibid., 41.
28. *Milliken v. Bradley,* 418 U.S. 717 (1974), 741–742.
29. Washington Constitution, art. 9, sec. 1.
30. Oklahoma Constitution, art. 13, sec. 1.
31. *Robinson v. Cahill*, 62 N.J. 473 (1973) (*Robinson I*).
32. *Rose v. Council for Better Education,* 790 S.W.2d 186 (1989), 211. Emphasis in original.
33. *Plyler v. Doe,* 457 U.S. 202 (1982), 221.
34. New Hampshire Constitution, Part II, art. 83.
35. *Claremont School District v. Governor,* 138 N.H. 183 (1993), 192.
36. *Rodriguez*, 37.

Bibliography

Alley, Robert S. *School Prayer: The Court, the Congress and the First Amendment.* Buffalo: Prometheus Books, 1994.

Chubb, John E., and Terry M. Moe. *Politics, Markets and America's Schools.* Washington, D.C.: Brookings Institutions, 1990.

Dolbeare, Kenneth M., and Phillip E. Hammond. *The School Prayer Decisions from Court Policy to Local Practice.* Chicago: University of Chicago Press, 1971.

Ely, James W. *The Crisis of Conservative Virginia: The Byrd Organization and the Politics of Massive Resistance.* Knoxville: University of Tennessee Press, 1976.

Estes, George. *The Old Cedar School.* Troutdale, Ore.: publisher, 1922.

Formisano, Ronald P. *Boston against Busing: Race, Class and Ethnicity in the 1960s and 1970s.* Chapel Hill: University of North Carolina Press, 1991.

Hochschild, Jennifer, and Nathan Scovronick. *The American Dream and the Public Schools.* New York, and Oxford, U.K.: Oxford University Press, 2003.

Kluger, Richard. *Simple Justice: The History of* Brown v. Board of Education *and Black America's Struggle for Equality.* New York: Knopf, 1975.

Kozol, Jonathan. *Savage Inequalities: Children in America's Schools.* New York: Crown, 1991.

Orfield, Gary, and Susan E. Eaton. *Dismantling Desegregation.* New York: W. W. Norton, 1996.

Reed, Douglas S. *On Equal Terms: The Constitutional Politics of Educational Opportunity.* Princeton, N.J.: Princeton University Press, 2001.

Rosenberg, Gerald N. *The Hollow Hope: Can Courts Bring about Social Change?* Chicago: University of Chicago Press, 1991.

Tushnet, Mark V. *Making Civil Rights Law: Thurgood Marshall and the Supreme Court, 1936–1961.* New York, and Oxford, U.K.: Oxford University Press, 1994.

Court Cases

Abington School District v. Schempp and Murray v. Curlett, 374 U.S. 203 (1963).

Brown v. Board of Education, 347 U.S. 483 (1954).

Claremont School District v. Governor, 138 N.H. 183 (1993).

Cooper v. Aaron, 358 U.S. 1 (1958).

Engel v. Vitale, 370 U.S. 421 (1962).

Green v. County School Board, 391 U.S. 430 (1968).

Keyes v. School District No. 1, 413 U.S. 189 (1973).

Lau v. Nichols, 414 U.S. 563 (1974).

Locke v. Davey, 124 S. Ct. 1307 (2004).

Milliken v. Bradley, 418 U.S. 717 (1974).

Pierce v. Society of Sisters, 268 U.S. 510 (1925).

Plessy v. Ferguson, 163 U.S. 537 (1896).

Plyler v. Doe, 457 U.S. 202 (1982).

Robinson v. Cahill, 62 N.J. 473 (1973) (*Robinson I*).

Rose v. Council for Better Education, 790 S.W.2d 186 (1989).

San Antonio Independent School District v. Rodriguez, 411 U.S. 1 (1973).

Zelman v. Simmons-Harris, 536 U.S. 639 (2002).

SECTION V

PROPERTY RIGHTS

18

PROPERTY RIGHTS AND DEMOCRACY IN THE AMERICAN CONSTITUTIONAL ORDER

James W. Ely, Jr.

CONSTITUTIONAL DEMOCRACY IN THE UNITED STATES has been characterized by a high regard for the rights of property owners. Indeed, Alexis de Tocqueville, the French commentator on American society, perceptively observed in 1840: "In no other country in the world is the love of property keener or more alert than in the United States, and nowhere else does the majority display less inclination toward doctrines which in any way threaten the way property is owned."[1] Americans have long prized private property and economic opportunity, and the sanctity of property is a notion deeply ingrained in the American mind. Still, the appropriate place of property rights in a democratic society has been contested at various points in our history. Some forms of property, such as slavery, have been abolished outright, and the emergence of the regulatory state in the twentieth century has eroded the traditional dominion of property owners. Today we are witnessing a vigorous debate over the extent to which property as a constitutional right should be protected against majoritarian interference to achieve communal goals.

This chapter explores how the judiciary has promoted democracy through its treatment of property rights. examines the relationship among private property, individual liberty, and democratic government. Part 2 considers the significance of property rights in the establishment of the American constitutional order. Part 3 looks at the judicial role in supporting the rights of property owners between 1789 and 1937. Part 4 describes the marked changes in the constitutional status of property rights as a consequence of the New Deal era. Part 5 analyzes the renewed interest in property rights in recent decades. Part 6 contends that property rights are essential to a democratic society, and that courts should afford a higher level of protection to recognized property interests.

Property, Liberty, and Democracy

A time-honored understanding of democracy is government by majority rule. The parliamentary system of Great Britain, in which an elected legislature exercises power, perhaps best exemplifies this theory of democracy today. However, this was not the model of government enshrined in the United States Constitution. That document confined majoritarianism in a number of ways. The structure of the Constitution, including separation of powers and federalism, temper majority rule. Judicial review of legislation limits the power of electoral majorities. Courts in fact have long exercised immense power in the American polity. The Bill of Rights and its state counterparts, moreover, remove certain fundamental individual liberties altogether from the operation of majority rule. In short, the United States adopted a form of democracy that can be characterized as representative self-government, but with constraints on majority decision-making.

There is a vast literature seeking to reconcile far-ranging judicial review with democracy. Some scholars maintain that courts are attentive to the larger political climate and tend to reflect rather than challenge the will of the majority. Judges, they insist, rarely deviate far from dominant public opinion. In this connection, they note that the Supreme Court has rarely interfered with the broad policy agenda of the political branches of the national government. It has also been argued that judicial decisions, to ultimately be effective, must win popular support, and thus are indirectly tied to the political process. Other observers, however, assert that judicial review is necessarily undemocratic because it impedes the authority of political majorities. Judges, they maintain, tend to come from relatively wealthy and educated backgrounds, and represent elite not popular opinion. Much of this debate turns on how one defines democracy and ascertains public opinion.

Property in a Democratic Society

Similar considerations pertain to an examination of constitutionalized property rights in a democratic society. Clearly a constitutional system that safeguards the rights of property owners may inhibit the will of the majority in some respects, and in that light could be viewed as antidemocratic. Of course, the same could be said of other constitutional provisions to protect individual rights, such as the freedom to express opinions or hold religious views distasteful to majority sentiment. As we have seen, however, American democracy is more aptly described as representative self-government rather than untrammeled majoritarianism. Some limits on majority rule may serve the long-range advantage of all.

Ample historical evidence demonstrates that a regime of private property is a vital prerequisite to the establishment of democratic government. Conversely, a market economy grounded on private property is fundamentally incompatible with an unfree political system. There are several dimensions to the argument that property undergirds democracy. First, stable property rights are a powerful incentive to the creation of wealth and prosperity. Widespread ownership of property in turn gives citizens a material stake in the success of democratic government. As de Tocqueville pointed out, diffusion of property promotes political stability and fosters a climate in which self-government can prosper. To be sure, the existence of private property does not guarantee the triumph of democracy, but its absence renders self-government improbable. Second, the institution of private property serves to preserve the economic independence of individuals that is vital for participation in the decision-making process. People with a secure economic base protected against governmental interference are more likely to feel free to challenge governmental policy. On the other hand, people whose economic livelihood is dependent upon the government will surely be more circumspect. The threat of financial ruin through arbitrary governmental action is a weapon to help maintain political control. This explains why there are so few examples of free societies that do not respect the rights of property owners. Certainly it could be forcefully maintained that without guaranteed property rights the enjoyment of other individual liberties would be empty and largely theoretical. Property was traditionally pictured as a bulwark of liberty because it helped to mark limits on governmental authority over individuals and prevented a concentration of power in the hands of officials. "The right to property," Arthur Lee of Virginia observed in 1775, "is the guardian of every other right, and to deprive a people of this, is in fact to deprive them of their liberty."[2]

Property as a Source of Conflict

Notwithstanding the importance of property in American democracy, the rights accorded property owners have been a recurring source of conflict. Questions have been raised about both the nature and extent of property rights claims. One set of concerns relates to how property should be defined. Property is not defined in the Constitution, and courts have generally looked to state law or custom to decide what interests should be classed as property. To some extent, therefore, the determination of what is property may vary from state to state. At the same time, the Supreme Court has cautioned that states may not by legislative fiat extinguish recognized property interests. The Constitution seemingly contemplates some core meaning for property that states cannot change. If legislators had unlimited power to revamp property law they could destroy all ownership rights and evade the constitutional protection of property. Property intuitively includes physical objects. Historically land was the most valuable type of property. Yet the law increasingly recognized another large category of property composed of intangible items, such as bank accounts, corporate stock, trade secrets, and patents. Indeed, intellectual property is of growing economic importance today. Property currently may be understood as encompassing anything that has exchangeable value. Some types of property have been the subject of sharp controversy. The right to own human beings and alcoholic beverages, for example, generated fierce struggles in U.S. history.

A second set of concerns addresses how far the concept of property ownership extends. Property was early understood to encompass not simply the title to an object but a group of rights inhering in ownership including the ability to maintain exclusive possession, use, transfer, and derive profit. As Justice Stephen J. Field explained in 1877: "All that is beneficial in property arises from its use, and the fruits of that use; and whatever deprives a person of them deprives him of all that is desirable or valuable in the title and possession."[3]

A third area of concern arises from the fact that in a free economy some people inevitably accumulate more property than others. Since the eighteenth century critics have periodically charged that wealth disparities undermine an egalitarian vision of democracy. They worry that wealth confers disproportionate political power, and thus vitiates the goal of equal participation in the political process. Adherents of this view have urged a redistribution of property interests to achieve a sort of rough equality. The modern redistributionist agenda takes the form of calls for minimal economic entitlements guaranteeing basic necessities to all citizens. Such a program, however, tends to entail higher taxation and runs counter to traditional views of the sanctity of property. Moreover, the constitutionalization of property inhibits redistributionist moves by substantially immunizing property from majoritarian government. Thus, the constitutional protection accorded property owners highlights the clash between the libertarian and communitarian ideals of democracy. The prevailing view in American history, however, has closely linked property and liberty, as evidenced by the bedrock status of property rights in our polity.

Property and the Establishment of American Constitutionalism

A strong belief in the need to defend the rights of property owners was a paramount value for the framers of the Constitution. Heirs of the long-standing English constitutional philosophy that regarded the right to property as crucial to political freedom, the framers were concerned to safeguard private property from interference by majoritarian state legislatures. John Adams expressed this view succinctly in 1790: "Property must be secured or liberty cannot exist."[4]

English Constitutional Background

John Locke, the seventeenth-century English political theorist, was especially influential to the framers. Locke insisted that the right to own property, together with the rights to life and liberty, were natural rights that existed before the establishment of political authority. Governments, he asserted, were created by popular consent for the purpose of protecting these natural rights. Lockean ideas helped to weaken claims of absolute monarchy, and to justify representative self-government. Since widespread ownership of land gave most Americans an economic stake in society, the property-conscious views of Locke took deep root in colonial era.

Locke's emphasis on the sanctity of property rights was powerfully reinforced by William Blackstone in his landmark *Commentaries on the Laws of England* (1765–1769). Whereas Locke focused on high constitutional theory, Blackstone sought to summarize the tenets of English common law. Blackstone emphasized both the dominion of property owners and the great importance of private property in English law. He maintained, for instance, that as a matter of common law principle government must provide full compensation when it took private property for public use. Blackstone had an enormous impact on the legal culture of the late colonial era. He was widely seen as furnishing an authoritative account of English law, and the founders drew heavily from Blackstone's conception of the significance of property rights in law.

Revolutionary Era Developments

Reflecting this English legal heritage, the state constitutions of the Revolutionary era included a number of provisions to safeguard the rights of owners. Several state constitutions affirmed that all persons had the inherent right to acquire and possess property. In language derived from the Magna Carta, the constitutions of five states mandated that no person could be deprived of life, liberty, or property "but by the law of the land." Such wording anticipated the Due Process Clause of the Fifth Amendment. Some state constitutions adopted the common-law principle that compensation must be paid when private property was taken for public use. These provisions qualified the exercise of eminent domain power, and were forerunners of the Takings Clause of the Fifth Amendment. A number of state constitutions also banned grants of monopoly, demonstrating a commitment to economic freedom.

The Northwest Ordinance of 1787, which became an important model for drafting the federal constitution, also contained a number of property-related provisions. In addition to a law-of-the-land clause and a takings clause, the Ordinance declared that no law should interfere with private contracts previously made. This was the predecessor of the Contract Clause of the federal Constitution.

Despite these constitutional developments, rhetoric about the sanctity of property rights was not always matched by actual behavior during the upheaval of the Revolutionary era. There was cause to worry about the security of property since the American Revolution generated widespread despoliation of property rights. Many state legislatures enacted bills of attainder declaring named Loyalists to be guilty of treason and confiscating their property without a judicial trial. Several states, most notably Virginia, erected legal barriers to the recovery of private debts owed to British merchants. The widespread seizure of Loyalist property did not bode well for the safety of property rights generally, and the attempted repudiation of British debts threatened commercial credit overseas. Further, in response to the depressed economic conditions that accompanied the break with England, state legislators repeatedly interfered in debtor-creditor relations with a variety of laws calculated to help debtors. Perhaps the most egregious move was the passage of state laws making depreciated paper currency legal tender for the payment of debts. Creditors and merchants pictured these debtor-relief laws as amounting to little more than confiscation of their economic interests. Neither state constitutional guarantees of property rights nor the weak national government under the Articles of Confederation proved able to check these legislative excesses. Consequently, many political leaders became convinced that a more powerful central government was necessary to adequately safeguard the rights of property owners.

Constitutional Convention

It is not by accident, then, that members of the Constitutional Convention repeatedly stressed the importance of property in a free society. Nor is it surprising that a number of provisions in the Constitution pertain to the protection of property interests. The Constitution prohibited both Congress and the states from enacting bills of attainder. It conferred broad taxing power on Congress, but barred the levy of direct taxes unless apportioned among the states according to population. This requirement effectively limited congressional tax authority by making impractical any direct tax that could not be easily apportioned. A group of provisions prohibited the states from abridging property and contractual rights. Foremost among these was the Contract Clause, which barred the states from passing any law "impairing the obligation of Contracts." The Constitution also addressed some specific types of property. Mindful of the growing importance of intellectual property, the framers authorized Congress to award copyrights and patents to authors and inventors. A number of provisions sought to safeguard property in slaves.

Notwithstanding these specific provisions, the framers relied largely on institutional arrangements to protect property owners. The basic constitutional scheme was to secure individual rights, including property, by giving the new national government only limited authority and restricting the exercise of federal government power through an elaborate system of checks and balances. This helps to explain why the Constitution as originally drafted did not include a bill of rights guaranteeing individual liberty.

Bill of Rights

The absence of a bill of rights, however, was one of the major difficulties in winning ratification of the Constitution by the states. Proponents of the Constitution therefore informally agreed to adopt a bill of rights. James Madison took the initiative in drafting the Bill of Rights, drawing largely upon traditional guarantees already recognized in state bills of rights or English common law. Long a defender of property rights, Madison placed important protections for property ownership in the Bill of Rights. The Fifth Amendment contains two key property clauses, providing in part that no person shall be "deprived of life, liberty, or property, without due process of law; nor shall private property be taken for public use, without just compensation." By inserting this language in the same amendment that contains procedural safeguards governing criminal trials, Madison demonstrated his belief in a close tie between property rights and other personal liberties.

Madison further underlined the intimate connection between the rights of property owners and personal freedom in a 1792 essay. He maintained that the concept of property encompassed the right to use one's labor to acquire possessions. Setting forth an indivisible understanding of liberty, Madison characterized a host of noneconomic rights, such as expression of opinions and religious convictions, as forms of property. He insisted: "Government is instituted to protect property of every sort."[5]

The Bill of Rights was originally understood as restraining only the national government. Many states, however, looked to the federal Constitution and Bill of Rights when they subsequently framed their own fundamental laws. State constitutions commonly contained a contract clause, protected persons against deprivation of property without due process, and mandated the payment of just compensation when private property was taken by the state for public use. These developments strengthened the high standing of property and contractual rights in the constitutional culture. Moreover, given the limited application of federal constitutional provisions to the states, the state constitutions constituted an important safeguard for property owners.

Judicial Role in Supporting Property Rights, 1789–1937

From the beginning of the New Republic to the mid-1930s both federal and state courts were vitally concerned to protect property and contractual rights from legislative infringement. In so doing, courts necessarily confined the scope of majority rule regarding the economic rights of individuals. Yet judicial solicitude was congruent with the view that secure property rights were a precondition to a democratic society and encouraged citizen participation in the political process. It was also consistent with the understanding that the Constitution established a federal government of limited powers and left substantial room for private ordering. Moreover, in vindicating property rights courts were implementing widely shared constitutional values. Rather than frustrating majoritarian sentiments, courts were applying accepted norms to situations in which legislators deviated from basic principles.

During the 1790s federal courts made clear their willingness to halt state infringement of the rights of property owners. In *Champion v. Casey* (1792), one of the first exercises of federal judicial review, a federal circuit court struck down a Rhode Island statute granting exemptions from attachment as an unconstitutional impairment of contract. Justice William Paterson, who had been a member of the constitutional convention, declared in *Vanhorn's Lessee v. Dorrance* (1795) that the right of acquiring and possessing property was a natural and inalienable right. Echoing Locke, he added: "The preservation of property . . . is a primary object of the social compact."[6] The pivotal role of private property in emerging American constitutionalism was also emphasized in Justice Samuel Chase's opinion in *Calder v. Bull* (1798). Invoking precepts of natural law, Chase insisted that legislators could not validly enact "a law that takes property from A and gives it to B."[7] This in time became a classic and still cited constitutional maxim that lawmakers cannot simply take property from one person and transfer it to another.

Marshall Court

John Marshall, who served as chief justice from 1801 to 1835, did much to cement the role of the Supreme Court as a defender of the rights of property owners. He felt that strong protection for property both enhanced individual liberties and fostered economic growth. The Court, under Marshall's leadership, embraced a broad reading of the Contract Clause in a line of decisions upholding economic rights against state interference. Marshall interpreted the clause to prevent states from abrogating their own contractual arrangements as well as private undertakings.

At issue in *Fletcher v. Peck* (1810) was the vast 1795 Yazoo land sale by the Georgia legislature to speculators at bargain prices. A subsequent legislature attempted to rescind the grant. Marshall held that the land grand was a contract, and that the repeal act violated the contract clause. He characterized the constitutional restrictions on state legislative power, including the contract clause, as a "bill of rights for the people of each state."[8]

In the landmark case of *Dartmouth College v. Woodward* (1819) Marshall concluded that the grant of a corporate charter amounted to a contract within the scope of the Contract Clause. It followed that a state legislature could not revoke or abridge such a charter. This decision came at a time when investors were increasingly turning to the corporation as a means of promoting economic activity. Marshall's protective attitude toward corporate charters encouraged this trend by creating a legal environment favorable to business corporations. Likewise, the Court under Marshall relied on the Contract Clause to bar the states from revoking grants of tax immunity and from discharging private debts incurred before the enactment of state bankruptcy laws.

The Marshall Court, however, never sought the wholesale displacement of state regulatory power over economic activities. For instance, In *Ogden v. Saunders* (1827) the justices, over a dissent by Marshall, ruled that the Contract Clause applied only to retroactive legislation and hence a state could discharge debts incurred after the passage of bankruptcy laws. The Court also limited the reach of the Contract Clause in *Providence Bank v. Billings* (1830), holding that surrender of a state's taxing authority could not be implied merely from the grant of a corporate charter. This case established the doctrine of strict construction of corporate charters, and anticipated the jurisprudence of Roger B. Taney, Marshall's successor as chief justice.

Under the decision of the Supreme Court in *Barron v. City of Baltimore* (1833) the Bill of Rights restricted only the federal government. The Takings Clause of the Fifth Amendment, therefore, did not figure prominently in the work of the Marshall Court. On occasion, however, Marshall and his colleagues relied on fundamental rights derived from natural law as a basis to block state seizure of private property. The most notable example of this tendency was *Terrett v. Taylor* (1815), in which the Court determined that an attempted confiscation of church land by Virginia was inconsistent with the fundamental principles of free governments and void.

Marshall placed the Supreme Court squarely behind the rights of property owners and his property-conscious jurisprudence had an enduring impact on American constitutionalism for more than a century. The dynamic nature of Marshall's thinking about property bears emphasis. He saw property and contractual rights as keystones to a vibrant market economy and the creation of national wealth. Marshall acted to encourage entrepreneurial freedom and capital formation, not just to uphold existing property entitlements.

For all their concern about the utilitarian dimensions of private property, the justices of the Marshall era never lost sight of the interdependence of economic rights and personal freedom. In *Wilkinson v. Leland* (1829) Justice Joseph Story forcefully articulated this vision: "That government can scarcely be called free, where the rights of property are left solely dependent upon the will of a legislative body, without any restraint. The fundamental maxims of a free government seem to require, that the rights of personal liberty and private property should be held sacred."[9]

Taney Court

Taney, an ardent Jacksonian Democrat, followed Marshall as chief justice in 1836. Under Taney's guidance the Supreme Court largely adhered to the constitutional outlook of the Marshall period, but was more deferential to state authority over economic policy. This inclination was exemplified by the decision in *Charles River Bridge v. Warren Bridge* (1837), in which the justices ruled that corporate charters must be strictly construed and did not convey implied privileges that warranted protection under the Contract Clause. This opinion sustained state legislative authority, and opened the door for new projects and technological advances that might reduce the value of existing franchises.

On the other hand, the Taney Court vigorously enforced the Contract Clause in cases involving debtor-relief laws and grants of tax exemption. In *Bronson v. Kinzie* (1843), for instance, it invalidated two Illinois laws that made mortgage foreclosures more difficult as an abridgment of the obligation of contract. Further, the Court looked skeptically at efforts by local governments to repudiate their bonded obligations. In the famous case of *Gelpcke v. City of Dubuque* (1864) the justices concluded that the validity of an Iowa bond issue could not be impaired by a retroactive interpretation of state law by the Iowa Supreme Court.

State Courts and Due Process

Despite the prominence of the Supreme Court, much of the law governing property and contractual rights before the Civil War was formulated by the state courts. State judges not only expressed concern for the sanctity of property rights but often took the lead in fashioning property-protective doctrines. They did much to elaborate the meaning of the due process guarantee. State courts were the first to grapple with the extent to which due process safeguarded liberty and property interests by imposing substantive as well as procedural limits on the lawmaking process. In several cases state courts struck down as a violation of due process statutes which had the effect of divesting an owner of property for the benefit of another person. Further, state courts employed the due process norm to prevent the uncompensated taking of property by government even in the absence of an express state constitutional provision mandating payment. Thus, the distinguished New York jurist James Kent, in *Gardner v. Village of Newburgh* (1816), equated due process with natural equity, and concluded that owners were entitled to compensation when their property was taken for public use.

In addition to these developments, state courts began to treat due process as mandating the enactment of general laws binding on the entire community rather than special laws that singled out discreet groups for disparate benefits or burdens. This judicial stance reflected a central tenet of Jacksonian democracy—equal rights for all, special privileges for none. It limited the authority of legislatures to enact laws that aided one group of persons at the expense of others, and stamped special or class legislation as illegitimate.

The most significant invocation of the substantive component of due process by a state court in the antebellum era was *Wynehamer v. People* (1856). At issue was a state prohibition statute that outlawed the sale of liquor. The New York Court of Appeals reasoned that the measure constituted a deprivation of property without due process of law with respect to liquor already on hand when the law took effect. It emphasized that the definition of property encompassed the power of sale as well as private enjoyment. This leading case was the first time that a court determined that the due process norm prevented lawmakers from regulating the use of property in such a way as to destroy its value. The *Wynehamer* decision set the stage for courts in the late nineteenth century to enlarge due process protection of property by reviewing general regulatory legislation.

Eminent Domain Law

State courts made other valuable contributions to strengthening the constitutional status of property. A number of state courts joined their federal counterparts in denying the validity of debtor-relief legislation under the Contract Clause. More important, state judges were instrumental in fashioning the contours of eminent domain law. Projects to benefit the general community may necessitate dislocating the property rights of individuals. Eminent domain is the inherent authority of government to take private property for such purposes. It is among the most intrusive of governmental powers because the exercise of eminent domain compels owners of property to transfer their property to the government. The Takings Clause of the Fifth Amendment, and similar provisions in most state constitutions, limit the exercise of eminent domain by requiring that the power be employed for "public use" and that the owners receive "just compensation" for any property taken.

Antebellum state legislatures saw eminent domain as a vehicle to promote economic growth. Particularly anxious to enhance transportation facilities, they widely conferred such authority on private corporations for the purpose of constructing canals and railroads. This action raised the question of what constituted "public use." State courts repeatedly sustained the delegation of eminent domain to canal and railroad companies, reasoning that such private enterprises were carrying out a public purpose by improving transportation. This generous reading of the "public use" requirement helped to weaken it as a restraint on the exercise of eminent domain.

State judges also began to grapple with what governmental actions, short of outright acquisition of title, amounted to a taking of property for which compensation was required. Although the judicial record was mixed, some courts concluded that a physical invasion of land—for example, by flooding caused by a public project—was a taking. State judges increasingly took the view that publicly sponsored interference with the possessory rights of owners was compensable.

The emerging takings jurisprudence, if sometimes shrouded in technical doctrine, required state courts to balance constitutional guarantees of property with the need to accommodate economic and technological changes. At root was the basic question of whether, in a democratic society, the general public or individual property owners should bear the cost of providing social goods. Courts sought to effectuate the underlying constitutional premise that society should not single out a few individuals and compel the sacrifice of their property for public advantage. Judicial decisions affirming the compensation principle strengthened the conditions of self-government by preventing the majority from arbitrarily seizing the property of a minority, and thus chilling participation in the political process. Indeed, the Fifth Amendment Takings Clause is designed to protect the minority against governmental power exercised at the behest of a popular majority.

Nuisance and Police Power

In addition, state courts revamped the law of nuisance to make room for technological innovation. Traditional nuisance doctrine was grounded on the notion that an owner could not utilize his or her property in such a manner as to interfere with the enjoyment of a neighbor's land. This view represented a static understanding of property, and had the potential to retard economic development. To avoid this result, state courts evolved a more flexible nuisance law that weighed the economic and social value of a proposed action against the rights of affected property owners. This meant that utilitarian considerations would bulk large in determining the existence of a nuisance, and often produced an outcome favorable to entrepreneurs. In the leading case of *Lexington and Ohio Railroad v. Applegate* (1839), for instance, the Kentucky Court of Appeals refused to enjoin a railroad from operating on Louisville streets and emphasized that nuisance law must adapt to changing conditions.

In addition to trying to stimulate economic growth, state governments regulated the use of property, under their police power, to safeguard the health, safety, and morals of the public. Such controls limited to some degree the dominion of owners, but state courts upheld a variety of restrictions on the use of property. They readily sustained prohibitions on storage of gunpowder and bans on the construction of wooden buildings in urban areas in order to protect the public from fire. Likewise, state judges upheld some fledgling business regulations. Controls on the export of commodities and the licensing of certain occupations passed muster. Courts also affirmed the validity of statutes requiring railroads to adopt safety features, such as fencing their lines. They afforded lawmakers broad latitude to preserve public morals. These restrictions on use of property and on economic activity were typically directed against specific problems and produced little redistributive effect. Still, the prevalence of police power regulations made clear that owners did not enjoy unfettered power to use their property as they saw fit.

Civil War and Fourteenth Amendment

The Civil War and Reconstruction had important ramifications for the place of property in a democratic society. The Thirteenth Amendment, ratified in

1865, abolished slavery as a form of property. To finance the war, Congress in 1862 enacted the first income tax. The Supreme Court affirmed this levy as applied to professional income, brushing aside the contention that such a tax constituted an unconstitutional direct tax. Following the end of hostilities, however, the income tax became increasingly unpopular and Congress allowed the levy to expire in 1872.

Property rights continued to occupy an important place in constitutional doctrine. Revealingly, the Civil Rights Act of 1866 included the right to make contracts and acquire property as among the liberties guaranteed to freed persons. Moreover, the Fourteenth Amendment, adopted in 1868, stipulated that no state could "deprive any person of life, liberty, or property, without due process of law." This provision greatly enlarged the potential for federal judicial supervision of state legislation abridging the rights of property owners. Thomas M. Cooley, an influential treatise writer, paved the way for a muscular reading of the Due Process Clause. He defined liberty as encompassing the right to make contracts and possess property, and insisted that the due process norm imposed substantive restraints on state legislative power to interfere with economic rights. Cooley also assailed class legislation and the grant of special privileges.

At first, however, the Supreme Court was reluctant to see the Fourteenth Amendment as furnishing a basis for more vigorous federal court review of state laws. At issue in the *Slaughter-House Cases* (1873) was the constitutionality of a state-conferred virtual monopoly over the slaughtering of livestock in New Orleans. Upholding state regulatory authority, the Court majority rejected the argument that the Due Process Clause created a federally protected right to pursue lawful callings. Similarly, the Court sustained state regulatory authority in *Munn v. Illinois* (1877), denying a due process challenge to state laws that regulated the prices charged by railroads and allied industries such as grain elevators. Writing for the Court, Chief Justice Morrison R. Waite ruled that property "affected with a public interest" could be controlled for the common good. Waite further declared that if the legislature abused the rights of owners then "the people must resort to the polls, not to the courts."[10] This comment seemingly indicated that the Due Process Clause afforded little protection against majoritarian decision-making, and that owners of property affected with a public interest must look to the political process not the courts for relief from arbitrary regulation. In a forceful dissenting opinion, Justice Field asserted that the due process norm gave substantive protection to the right of owners to use and receive income from their property. He protested that under the majority opinion "all property and all business in the State are held at the mercy of its legislature."[11] In his view the Fourteenth Amendment guaranteed fundamental property rights against legislative interference, and to that extent limited majority rule.

Emergence of Due Process

By the 1880s state and federal courts were more receptive to arguments that the due process concept protected individual rights, including the use of private property, from unwarranted encroachments by state governments. Judges did not accept legislative exercise of the police power at face value, but rather assessed the reasonableness of controls on economic activity. They began to strike down those laws deemed arbitrary or beyond the legitimate scope of government. State courts played a key role in the evolution of due process principles. For example, in the famous case of *In re Jacobs* (1885) the New York Court of Appeals invalidated an act that outlawed the manufacture of cigars in residential apartments in New York City. Stressing that legislative authority was not unlimited, the court found that the law did not promote public health and amounted to a deprivation of property and liberty without due process.

At the same time that courts were starting to endorse an enlarged understanding of due process, industrialization and the growth of large-scale corporate enterprise increasingly supplanted the older America of farms and rural communities. Business enterprises operated across state lines and created a national market for goods. Employment relations were altered as corporate employees often worked in an impersonal environment and had little bargaining power. Rapid urbanization created a host of housing and health problems. Groups adversely affected by these sweeping changes called for laws to curb predatory corporate behavior and to affirmatively assist the disadvantaged. Some, such as the Populists, were fearful that concentrated wealth in private hands created arbitrary power and undermined political democracy. They advocated redistributive measures, including a graduated income tax.

Judicial Disapproval of Redistributive Policies

As state legislatures responded to these developments by enacting regulatory laws, supporters of property rights sought protection by invoking the Due Process Clause of the Fourteenth Amendment, the Contract Clause, and the Takings Clause. The judicial reaction was divided. Courts usually held that health and safety regulations were valid exercises of state police power. On the other hand, they looked skeptically at laws designed to alter the workings of the market economy or to redistribute wealth patterns.

Judicial determination to limit the redistributive capacity of government was embodied in several lines of Supreme Court decisions. Stepping away from *Munn*, the Court during the 1890s circumscribed state regulation of railroad and utility charges. It ruled that regulated industries were entitled as a matter of due process to a reasonable return on their investment, and that the federal courts could scrutinize the reasonableness of state-imposed rates. The application of the due process norm to state rate making served both to defend investment capital and to prevent states from in effect confiscating railroad property through the imposition of unremunerative rates. The Supreme Court's aversion to redistributive schemes was also apparent in the repeated reliance on the Contract Clause in the late nineteenth century to block attempts by local governments to repudiate their bonded debt. This outcome vindicated the rights of investors in the face of moves to divert public revenue to education and other social needs.

The most dramatic manifestation of the Supreme Court's anti-redistributive principle was *Pollock v. Farmers' Loan & Trust Co.* (1895), which held that the 1894 income tax was a direct tax that had to be apportioned among the states according to population. Although couched in terms of the direct tax clause, the underlying issue in *Pollock* was the legitimacy of using federal taxing power to alter the distribution of wealth. The levy on income was suspect because it breached the widely accepted constitutional norms that rejected class legislation and required equality in the assessment of taxes.

Liberty of Contract

A deep regard for the autonomy of private contracting also informed the process of fashioning constitutional limits on governmental power. As we have seen, the Supreme Court had long employed the Contract Clause to safeguard existing contractual arrangements, both public and private, from retroactive state abridgement. Fueled in part by antislavery ideology, courts gradually took the position that the freedom to make contracts enjoyed constitutional protection. In *Allgeyer v. Louisiana* (1897) the Supreme Court concluded that the right to enter contracts was among those liberties protected by the Due Process Clause of the Fourteenth Amendment. Legislators could seek to justify restrictions on this right by pointing to health and safety considerations, but courts treated liberty of contract as the constitutional baseline. However imperfectly realized in practice, the freedom of contract doctrine was designed to encourage economic opportunity for individuals in a free-market economy.

Strengthened Takings Jurisprudence

The Supreme Court in the late nineteenth century further enhanced the constitutional position of property owners by a more vigorous application of the Takings Clause of the Fifth Amendment. It enlarged the notion of a taking in *Pumpelly v. Green Bay Company* (1871), finding that a physical invasion that impaired the value of land amounted to a taking of property, even though title remained in the owner. It defined just compensation in terms of the market value of appropriated land, and held that the determination of just compensation was a judicial function. In the seminal case of *Chicago, Burlington and Quincy Railroad Company v. Chicago* (1897), moreover, the justices ruled that the payment of just compensation when private property was taken for public use constituted an essential element of due process guaranteed by the Fourteenth Amendment.

Accordingly, the just compensation rule became in effect the first provision of the Bill of Rights to be applied to the states.

Progressive Assault on Constitutionalized Property

The centrality of property rights in the American constitutional order was challenged in the early twentieth century. Anxious to address a number of problems arising from the new industrial order, the Progressive movement urged a more active role for federal and state governments in the regulation of economic activity. Progressives called for the imposition of workplace safety standards, minimum wage laws, abolition of child labor, limits on the hours of work, workers' compensation statutes, and strengthened anti-trust laws. They also successfully pushed for adoption in 1913 of the Sixteenth Amendment, which authorized Congress to tax incomes. This step effectively overturned the *Pollock* decisions and opened the door for a redistributionist use of the taxing power. Directly contradicting the traditional notion of an even-handed tax policy, the Sixteenth Amendment established the legitimacy of taking property from some in the form of taxation for the benefit of others.

Stimulated in part by the Progressive movement, new patterns of legal thought emerged in the early twentieth century. In particular, legal theorists took special aim at the traditional understanding of property and freedom of contract. Believing that constitutional doctrine overstated the importance of property and contractual rights, they assailed the Lockean notion that property was a pre-political natural right. Instead, legal writers argued that property should be reconceptualized as a creation of society that did not entail any fixed set of rights. Property was analyzed in terms of being just a cluster or bundle of abstract legal relationships, an approach that stressed the contingent and changing nature of ownership. This intellectual movement sought to undermine the very idea of property, and thus call into question its high constitutional standing. In an allied move, some prominent scholars asserted that freedom of contract was a myth. Observing that in practice parties often did not have equal bargaining power, they attacked the basic premises of contractual freedom. The full impact of these intellectual tendencies would not be realized until the political and judicial climate was radically altered in the 1930s.

Judicial Reaction to Progressivism

The judicial response to these novel political and intellectual currents was sometimes conflicting. Courts accommodated much of the economic regulation associated with the Progressive movement. They readily sustained state laws banning child labor. They permitted state legislatures wide latitude to enact protective laws for women. In *Muller v. Oregon* (1908), for example, the Supreme Court upheld a state law restricting the working hours for women in factories and laundries, albeit in an opinion that mirrored paternalistic assumptions about the place of women in society. After some initial resistance, both state and federal courts approved workers' compensation laws that mandated payment to employees injured in industrial accidents without regard to fault.

Yet courts remained leery of laws that altered free-market ordering or infringed on economic rights. In the landmark case of *Lochner v. New York* (1905) the Supreme Court struck down a state law limiting the hours of work in bakeries as violative of the freedom of contract guaranteed by the Due Process Clause of the Fourteenth Amendment. This controversial decision rested on the basic premise that individuals could best make decisions regarding their own well-being free of legislative oversight. Dissenting, Justice Oliver Wendell Holmes, Jr., rejected the position that freedom of contract was constitutionally protected. He articulated a philosophy of judicial restraint under which courts should defer to "the right of a majority to embody their opinions in law."[12] The *Lochner* decision remains at the heart of a continuing debate about the role of the judiciary in the American polity. It invites consideration of how far, and under what circumstances, majority rule should prevail over individual claims of right.

In fact, courts invoked the liberty of contract sparingly and upheld most regulatory measures against due process challenge. Nonetheless, the Supreme Court struck down both federal and state laws that banned so-called yellow dog contracts (which made it a condition of employment that workers not join a labor union) as an arbitrary interference with contractual freedom. Similarly, in *Adkins v. Children's Hospital* (1923) the Court overturned a minimum wage law for women and emphasized that freedom of contract in economic matters was the general rule.

Due process review was also utilized to eliminate entry barriers that impeded competing enterprise. At issue in *New State Ice Co. v. Liebmann* (1932) was a state licensing law that had the practical effect of fostering a monopoly in established ice companies by shutting out competitors. Equating the right of free speech with entrepreneurial freedom, the Supreme Court found that the statute unreasonably curtailed the right to engage in a lawful business as guaranteed by the due process norm.

Land Use Controls

As a consequence of urbanization, one person's use of his or her land increasingly affected neighbors. State and local governments therefore started to more vigorously regulate the use of land in the early decades of the twentieth century. Restrictions on the use of privately owned land presented novel issues in balancing the rights of individual owners against community needs. Courts experienced no difficulty in upholding restrictions on the height of buildings as a valid exercise of the police power to reduce the hazard of fire. In 1916 New York City enacted the first comprehensive zoning ordinance, and zoning spread rapidly during the 1920s. With its promise of scientific management of municipal growth, zoning was congenial with the Progressive era fondness for planning and reliance on experts. Motivated in part by elitist assumptions and exclusionary goals, early zoning laws were calculated to preserve upscale neighborhoods and thus maintain property values. One effect of zoning was to classify persons according to income. Given the long-standing stress on the right of individuals to acquire and use property, it is not surprising that some courts were at first hostile to zoning ordinances. Still, in *Village of Euclid v. Ambler Realty Company* (1926) the Supreme Court sustained the constitutionality of a zoning scheme that divided a locality into residential and commercial districts. Analogizing to the common law of nuisance, the Court found that zoning served the public health, safety, and morals. Although such land use controls limited an owner's dominion over his or her own land, they nonetheless helped to stabilize property values within the community. Zoning was therefore highly popular because it was usually consistent with the wishes of most landowners. After *Euclid*, moreover, most courts deferred to the regulation of land use by local governments.

Nonetheless, in other respects the Supreme Court strengthened the constitutional protection afforded owners in the face of proliferating land use controls. In *Buchanan v. Warley* (1917) the justices ruled that a city ordinance requiring racial segregation in residential areas constituted a deprivation of property without due process of law. Declaring that the Constitution safeguarded the essential elements of property, encompassing the rights to acquire and dispose of it, they held that majority sentiment could not override fundamental property rights. The *Buchanan* decision well illustrates the interdependence of property and other personal liberties.

Regulatory Takings

Even more important was the emergence of the doctrine that a regulation of the use of property might be so severe as to constitute a taking of property that required the payment of compensation. During the nineteenth century state courts and leading commentators had grappled with the idea that economic controls might so diminish the usefulness of land as to be tantamount to an outright taking. Justice David J. Brewer advanced this argument in 1891. The Supreme Court recognized the regulatory taking doctrine in the seminal case of *Pennsylvania Coal Co. v. Mahon* (1922). Speaking for the Court, Justice Holmes set forth the key inquiry: "The general rule at least is that, while property may be regulated to a certain extent, if the regulation goes too far it will be recognized as a taking."[13] He determined that a state law that prohibited mining in such a manner as to cause surface structures to collapse was an uncompensated taking of the company's property right to remove coal. For several decades, however, the Court found it hard to differentiate between appropriate restrictions and regulatory takings. Hence, the regulatory takings doctrine was applied infrequently.

It is fair to conclude that until the New Deal era American courts were heavily occupied with explicating the pivotal role of property in the constitutional order. In so doing they were fulfilling the property-centered vision of society held by the founding generation. But the status of property rights would be sharply diminished in the mid-1930s as the result of an economic and political upheaval.

New Deal Constitutionalism

The Great Depression ushered in a period of business failures and massive unemployment. The severe economic downturn stimulated calls for governmental intervention. The election of Franklin D. Roosevelt as president was a turning point in American history. Derived from the legacy of the Progressives, President Roosevelt's New Deal program was premised on the belief that the federal government should actively promote social welfare and manage the national economy. Reflecting this new outlook, Congress and the states enacted a wide variety of measures that increased governmental supervision of business practices and aided the disadvantaged. This outburst of legislation ran directly counter to traditional constitutional doctrine stressing a limited federal government and a high level of respect for the rights of property owners and private market ordering. Impatient with legal constraints, New Dealers quite frankly set out to remake the constitutional order and downplay economic rights. The stage was set for a showdown between the New Dealers and a Supreme Court committed to a conservative legal philosophy.

Supreme Court Confronts the New Deal

State legislative efforts to mitigate the impact of the depression received a sympathetic hearing from the Supreme Court. In *Home Building and Loan Association v. Blaisdell* (1934) the justices upheld a Minnesota law imposing a limited moratorium on the foreclosure of mortgages, brushing aside an argument that the moratorium ran afoul of the Contract Clause. Adopting a balancing approach to the interpretation of the Contract Clause, the justices held that contracts were subject to the reasonable exercise of the state police power. By subordinating the Contract Clause to state regulatory authority, the *Blaisdell* decision hastened the decline of this once-powerful constitutional provision. At the same time, the Court in *Nebbia v. New York* (1934) upheld a legislative scheme setting minimum prices for the retail sale of milk. Marking a shift away from due process review of economic regulations, the *Nebbia* ruling, as a practical matter, enlarged the category of businesses that were subject to price regulation.

Despite this broad reading of state power to revise contract terms and regulate market conditions, the Supreme Court took sharp exception to New Deal congressional legislation. In 1935 and 1936 it voided a series of important New

Deal measures. The principal point of contention was the extent of congressional authority under the Commerce Clause. Adhering to the long-standing distinction between commerce and production, the Supreme Court took the position that Congress did not possess comprehensive power over all business activity. This reasoning doomed New Deal efforts to manage the national economy and bring about social reform. Never before had the Supreme Court invalidated so many acts of Congress in such a short period of time.

New Dealers and liberals grew increasingly upset at what they saw as the Court's obstructionist attitude toward needed economic change. They charged that the Court was frustrating decision making by the majority, and maintained that the justices should defer to the political branches of government. Reelected by an overwhelming margin in 1936, President Franklin D. Roosevelt brought pressure on the justices by proposing a plan to enlarge the size of the Supreme Court. A full account of the bitter struggle between the New Dealers and the Court, as well as the Court packing controversy, is beyond the scope of this chapter. In the end Roosevelt achieved his goal of shifting the Supreme Court's attitude toward economic rights. This episode demonstrated anew that it is difficult for courts in the long run to resist strong currents of public sentiment.

Constitutional Revolution of 1937

Starting in 1937, the Supreme Court began to look favorably on both state and federal economic controls. In *West Coast Hotel v. Parrish* (1937), for example, it upheld a state minimum wage law and stripped freedom of contract of due process protection. It also affirmed a far-reaching power in Congress to regulate virtually all economic activity. In yet another departure, the Court backed away from judicial supervision of utility charges and permitted the states wide latitude in fixing rates.

Known as the constitutional revolution of 1937, this change of direction had a profound impact on the judicial protection of property rights. The Supreme Court now deferred to legislative judgments about economic policy and largely abandoned its historical dedication to the sanctity of private property and contractual arrangements. A central component of New Deal constitutionalism was a judicially created dichotomy between the rights of property owners and other personal liberties. This new outlook was articulated in the famous footnote 4 in *United States v. Carolene Products Co.* (1938), in which the Court indicated that it would afford a higher level of due process scrutiny to a preferred class of personal rights, such as free speech and religious freedom, than for property rights. The rights of owners were put into a subordinate category entitled to only a minimal degree of due process protection. Economic regulations were to be deemed valid, and received only cursory judicial review under a highly deferential "rational basis" test. It is difficult to reconcile the subordination of property rights with either the text of the Constitution and Bill of Rights or with the

Supreme Court's long defense of property rights. Indeed, as we have seen, the framers believed that property and personal liberty were indissolubly linked. However problematic from a historical perspective, the constitutional double standard in *Carolene Products* soon became the new orthodoxy.

For decades after 1937 property rights were of scant interest to most judges or scholars. Deprived of meaningful judicial protection, the security of property interests was largely relegated to the political arena. Federal courts now routinely upheld economic regulations and land use controls. Yet a resort to the polls was not considered to be an adequate guarantee for freedom of speech or religion, or to vindicate the rights of criminal defendants. This raises the question of why property rights were singled out for such disparate treatment. Political pressure arising from the confrontation with the New Deal does not fully explain the Supreme Court's shift. The Court went much further than politically necessary in abandoning property rights. At root the change in the Court's philosophy reflected a liberal legal culture that deemed constitutionalized property to be an impediment to expanded government power and redistributive policies. Property was no longer seen as worthy of much judicial solicitude. The switch also amounted to a rejection of the traditional view that protection of property interests was essential for the maintenance of a free society. Instead of constraining the reach of governmental power as a means of checking excesses by the majority, courts came to rely on expansive free speech as the key to democratic governance.

Debate over New Property

Historically most of the dialogue concerning the constitutional rights of property owners has focused on traditional forms of wealth, such as land and investment capital. Yet, as the welfare state expanded in the wake of the New Deal, federal and state governments became a major source of wealth for individuals. These governmental benefits encompass social security and welfare payments as well as government employment, contracts, and franchises. Historically such benefits were viewed as mere privileges that government could modify or terminate at its pleasure. In the 1960s some commentators proposed that government-conferred entitlements should be treated as a type of "new property" and receive constitutional safeguards comparable to those afforded traditional forms of property. The essence of "new property" was that public benefits should be seen as rights and not just as a matter of government largess. Proponents of this theory, echoing the views of the framers, contend that establishing a more secure basis for public benefits would foster individual liberty, and encourage robust participation in the democratic process without fear of official displeasure. The notion of a "new property," however, was ironic because since the constitutional revolution of 1937 the federal judiciary had demonstrated little interest in the rights of owners. Critics asserted that the idea of "new property" was simply a subterfuge to constitutionalize the welfare state and protect the economic interests of groups allied with political liberals, while declining to take seriously the claims of conventional property owners.

The Supreme Court briefly flirted with the "new property" notion. In *Goldberg v. Kelly* (1970) a divided Court declared that state agencies must adhere to procedural due process norms and give welfare recipients a hearing before terminating their benefits. In the end, however, the justices stopped short of treating governmentally dispensed wealth as constitutionally protected property rights. They regarded government benefit programs as matters of economic policy, preserving wide legislative and administrative authority to manage and even terminate such schemes.

Renewed Concern for Property Rights

Despite decades of judicial and scholarly indifference, the deep respect for the rights of property owners could not be readily banished from the American constitutional order. A changing political and intellectual environment opened the door for a revival of interest in property rights. The judicial activism of the Warren Court era on behalf of the socially disadvantaged and freedom of expression undercut the theory of judicial deference once espoused by Progressive legal thinkers. Moreover, the political hegemony of the New Deal, which had dominated American public life since the 1930s, gradually dissipated. Conservative political gains in the late twentieth and early twenty-first centuries helped to reorient the national policy agenda, stressing lower taxes, deregulation, and free-market ordering. At the same time, scholars associated with the law and economics movement called into question the efficacy of governmental regulation of the economy.

To some extent mirroring this changed political and intellectual climate, federal and state courts have gingerly returned to the defense of property rights. Although the Supreme Court has shown no interest in revitalizing due process review of economic regulations, it has on occasion invoked the Contract Clause to curb state legislative interference with contractual arrangements. Some lower federal and state courts have followed suit. Besides, the Takings Clause of the Fifth Amendment has emerged as the most prominent bulwark of property rights in modern constitutional law. The Supreme Court has strengthened the regulatory takings doctrine in the context of land use controls. In *Lucas v. South Carolina Coastal Council* (1992), for example, the Court found that regulations that deprived an owner of all economically viable use of land amounted to a per se taking of property notwithstanding any public interest justification. Moreover, two years later Chief Justice William H. Rehnquist pointedly observed, "We see no reason why the Takings Clause of the Fifth Amendment, as much a part of the Bill of Rights as the First Amendment or the Fourth Amendment, should be relegated to the status of a poor relation."[14] This comment suggests that property rights are equal in status to other constitutional rights, but the full implications of this insight have not been realized to date.

Indeed, the Supreme Court's recent record concerning property rights has been uneven. The Court, for instance, has made no effort to rein in the free-wheeling exercise of eminent domain to acquire private property for public projects. Thus, in *Hawaii Housing Authority v. Midkiff* (1984) the justices conflated the "public use" language of the Fifth Amendment with public purpose.

In addition to developments at the federal level, it bears emphasis that some state courts have been more solicitous of economic rights than their federal counterparts. Hence, a number of state courts continue to invoke due process or other state constitutional provisions to invalidate laws that unreasonably restrict persons engaging in business activity. Moreover, state courts are more likely to scrutinize closely the "public use" requirement to restrain the government's power to acquire property under eminent domain. In the important case of *County of Wayne v. Hathcock* (2004) the Michigan Supreme Court, overruling an earlier decision, held that eminent domain could not be used to transfer property to a private entity for purposes of economic development. Although both state and federal courts have shown greater regard for the rights of property owners than at any time since the mid-1930s, such rights have not regained the high constitutional standing that they once enjoyed.

Conclusion

The uncertain place of the rights of property owners in modern American constitutionalism reflects conflicting assessments about the continuing vitality of the libertarian tie between property and political freedom. As long as this fundamental issue is unresolved, the judicial role in safeguarding property rights as a component of a democratic society will remain contested. Despite a waxing of interest in the rights of property owners, we have a long way to go before property rights are treated in the same manner as other rights. Although this chapter provides support for the proposition that courts should accord property rights the same protection as other individual liberties, only a sea change in the legal culture about the value of property as a support to democratic governance is likely to bring about this result.

A comparative focus helps to shed light on the importance of private property in a free society. With the collapse of communist regimes throughout the world, new governments have established constitutional guarantees of private property. No doubt this move was motivated in part by a desire to secure the economic benefits of a market economy. But it also underscored the core function of property in making democracy work.

De Tocqueville noted that in the United States "no one makes [an] outcry against property in general." He explained: "Everyone, having some possession to defend, recognizes the right to property in principle." De Tocqueville added that there was no other country "where stronger scorn is expressed for the theory of permanent equality of property."[15] These observations attest to the property-conscious nature of American society and inform the debate over judicial support of property rights as an aspect of democratic self-government. Such comments could suggest that judicial protection was unnecessary because popular opinion and political forces do not threaten the institution of property. After all, courts have done little to uphold the claims of property owners since 1937 and yet society at large still powerfully sustains individual property rights and does not demonstrate sustained interest in redistributive policies. One might well ask if judicial intervention was really necessary. On the other hand, de Tocqueville's judgments could be read to indicate that long-standing judicial efforts to safeguard property rights vindicated a deep popular commitment to private property as an essential element of a free society. In this light, one could maintain that courts operated in accord with public sentiment by defending property rights and contractual freedom for much of our history. Moreover, an individual owner who believes his or her property interest is overreached by government can rarely secure relief in the political arena. The only meaningful source of redress is likely to be the courts. We as a society should heed the admonition of Walter Lippmann, a prominent twentieth-century journalist, who succinctly declared: "Private property was the original source of freedom. It is still its main bulwark."[16]

Notes

*The author wishes to express his appreciation to Mark Brandon and Jon W. Bruce for their helpful comments on an earlier version of this chapter.

1. Alexis de Tocqueville, *Democracy in America*, 2 vols., edited by J. P. Mayer. and translated by George Lawrence (New York: Harper Perennial, 1969), vol. 2, 638–639.
2. Arthur Lee, *An Appeal to the Justice and Interests of the People of Great Britain, in the Present Dispute with America*, 4th ed. (New York, 1775), 14.
3. *Munn v. Illinois*, 94 U.S. 113 (1877), at 141 (Field, J., dissenting).
4. "Discourses on Davila," in *The Works of John Adams*, 10 vols., edited by Charles Francis Adams (Boston: Little, Brown, 1851), Vol. 6, 280.
5. James Madison, "Property" (1792), in *The Papers of James Madison*, 17 vols., edited by Robert A. Rutland and Thomas A. Mason (Charlottesville: University Press of Virginia, 1979), Vol. 14, 266.
6. *Vanhorne's Lessee v. Dorrance*, 2 Dallas 304 (1795), at 310.
7. *Calder v. Bull*, 3 Dallas 386 (1798), at 388 (Chase, J.).
8. *Fletcher v. Peck*, 10 U.S. 87 (1810), at 138 (Marshall, C.J.).

9. *Wilkinson v. Leland*, 27 U.S. 627 (1829), at 657 (Story, J.).
10. *Munn v. Illinois*, 94 U.S. 113 (1877), at 134 (Waite, C.J.).
11. Id., at 140 (Field, J., dissenting).
12. *Lochner v. New York*, 198 U.S. 45 (1905), at 75 (Holmes, J., dissenting).
13. *Pennsylvania Coal Co. v. Mahon*, 260 U.S. 393 (1922), at 415 (Holmes, J.).
14. *Dolan v. City of Tigard*, 512 U.S. 374 (1994), at 392 (Rehnquist, C.J.).
15. Alexis de Tocqueville, *Democracy in America*, Vol. 1, 238.
16. Walter Lippmann, *The Method of Freedom* (New York: Macmillan, 1934), 101.

Bibliography

Alexander, Gregory S. *Commodity and Propriety: Competing Visions of Property in American Legal Thought 1776–1970.* Chicago and London: University of Chicago Press, 1997. A far-ranging but problematic account of American legal thought regarding property in which the author questions the dominance of the Lockean conception of property.

Ely, James W., Jr. *The Chief Justiceship of Melville W. Fuller, 1888–1910.* Columbia: University of South Carolina Press, 1995. A careful and fresh investigation of the jurisprudence of the Fuller Court, emphasizing its commitment to economic liberty and private property.

Ely, James W., Jr. *The Guardian of Every Other Right: A Constitutional History of Property Rights*, 2nd ed. New York and Oxford, U.K.: Oxford University Press, 1998. A balanced study of the key place of private property in the American constitutional system.

Ely, James W., Jr., ed. *Property Rights in American History from the Colonial Era to the Present.* 6 vols. New York and London: Garland Publishing, 1997. An edited collection of leading essays exploring the rights of property owners throughout American history.

Epstein, Richard A. *Takings: Private Property and the Power of Eminent Domain.* Cambridge, Mass., and London: Harvard University Press, 1985. This controversial but influential book urges a generous reading of the takings clause of the Fifth Amendment, and questions the legitimacy of many governmental actions that curtail economic liberty.

Gillman, Howard. *The Constitution Besieged: The Rise and Demise of Lochner Era Police Powers Jurisprudence.* Durham, N.C., and London: Duke University Press, 1993. Thoughtful analysis of nineteenth century constitutional doctrines that limited legislative power.

Horwitz, Morton J. *The Transformation of American Law, 1870–1960.* New York and Oxford: Oxford University Press, 1992. Provides a thoughtful treatment of efforts during the Progressive era to reformulate the traditional conceptions of contract and property.

Hovenkamp, Herbert. *Enterprise and American Law, 1836–1937.* Cambridge, Mass: Harvard University Press, 1991. This ambitious volume charts the interplay between economic theory and the law governing business enterprise.

Kens, Paul. *Judicial Power and Reform Politics: The Anatomy of Lochner v. New York.* Lawrence: University Press of Kansas, 1990. A thoughtful study of a famous case invoking the liberty of contract doctrine.

Nedelsky, Jennifer. *Private Property and the Limits of American Constitutionalism: The Madisonian Framework and Its Legacy*. Chicago and London: University of Chicago Press, 1990. Provocative discussion of how Madison's concern for the protection of private property has shaped the American constitutional tradition.

Paul, Ellen Frankel, and Howard Dickman, eds. *Liberty, Property, and the Foundations of the American Constitution*. Albany: State University of New York Press, 1989.

Phillips, Michael J. *The Lochner Court, Myth and Realty: Substantive Due Process from the 1890s to the 1930s*. Westport, Conn., and London: Praeger, 2001. A fine account of the Supreme Court decisions relying on the due process clause to uphold economic liberty, and arguing that some rulings invalidating economic regulations were justified.

Pipes, Richard. *Property and Freedom*. New York: Alfred A. Knopf, 1999. Stresses that private property has limited governmental power and nurtured democratic institutions.

Scheiber, Harry N., ed. *The State and Freedom of Contract*. Stanford, Calif.: Stanford University Press, 1998. This volume of essays examines freedom of contract, and considers the relationship between economic and political freedom.

Siegan, Bernard H. *Property Rights from Magna Carta to the Fourteenth Amendment*. New Brunswick, N.J., and London: Transaction Publishers, 2001.

Underkuffler, Laura S. *The Idea of Property: Its Meaning and Power*. New York: Oxford University Press, 2003. A helpful study of the notion of property.

Wright, Benjamin Fletcher. *The Contract Clause of the Constitution*. Cambridge, Mass: Harvard University Press, 1938. The classic, if rather dated, history of the contract clause.

Court Cases

Adkins v. Children's Hospital, 261 U.S. 525 (1923).
Allgeyer v. Louisiana, 165 U.S. 578 (1897).
Barron v. City of Baltimore, 32 U.S. 243 (1833).
Bronson v. Kinzie, 42 U.S. 311 (1843).
Buchanan v. Warley, 245 U.S. 60 (1917).
Calder v. Bull, 3 Dallas 386 (1798).
Champion v. Casey, unreported decision, U.S. Circuit Court for Rhode Island (1792).
Charles River Bridge v. Warren Bridge, 36 U.S. 420 (1837).
Chicago, Burlington & Quincy Railroad v. Chicago, 166 U.S. 226 (1897).
County of Wayne v. Hathcock, 471 Mich. 445, 684 N.W. 2d 765 (2004).
Dartmouth College v. Woodward, 17 U.S. 518 (1819).
Fletcher v. Peck, 10 U.S. 87 (1810).
Gardner v. Village of Newburgh, 12 Johns. Ch. 162 (N.Y. 1816).
Gelpcke v. City of Dubuque, 68 U.S. 175 (1864).
Goldberg v. Kelly, 397 U.S. 254 (1970).
Hawaii Housing Authority v. Midkiff, 467 U.S. 229 (1984).
Home Building and Loan Association v. Blaisdell, 290 U.S. 398 (1934).
Jacobs, In re, 98 U.S. 98 (1885).
Lexington and Ohio Railroad v. Applegate, 38 Ky. 289 (1839).

Lochner v. New York, 198 U.S. 45 (1905).
Lucas v. South Carolina Coastal Council, 505 U.S. 1003 (1992).
Muller v. Oregon, 208 U.S. 412 (1908).
Munn v. Illinois, 94 U.S. 113 (1877).
Nebbia v. New York, 291 U.S. 502 (1934).
New State Ice Co. v. Liebmann, 285 U.S. 262 (1932).
Ogden v. Saunders, 25 U.S. 213 (1827).
Pennsylvania Coal Co. v. Mahon, 260 U.S. 393 (1922).
Pollock v. Farmers' Loan & Trust Company, 157 U.S. 429 (1895), 158 U.S. 601 (1895).
Providence Bank v. Billings, 29 U.S. 514 (1830).
Pumpelly v. Green Bay Company, 80 U.S. 166 (1871).
Slaughter-House Cases, 83 U.S. 36 (1873).
Terrett v. Taylor, 13 U.S. 43 (1815).
United States v. Carolene Products Co., 304 U.S. 144 (1938).
Vanhorne's Lessee v. Dorrance, 2 Dallas 304 (1795).
Village of Euclid v. Ambler Realty Company, 272 U.S. 365 (1926).
West Coast Hotel v. Parrish, 300 U.S. 379 (1937).
Wilkinson v. Leland, 27 U.S. 627 (1829).
Wynehamer v. People, 13 N.Y. 378 (1856).

SECTION VI

WHITHER THE JUDICIARY AND AMERICAN DEMOCRACY?

19

THE FUTURE OF THE JUDICIAL BRANCH: COURTS AND DEMOCRACY IN THE TWENTY-FIRST CENTURY

Lawrence Baum

COURTS IN THE UNITED STATES HAVE MUCH IN COMMON with the other branches of government. Yet in some respects they are distinctive institutions: they differ from the legislative and executive branches in what they do and how they do it, and they are partially detached from the mainstream of government and politics. Because they are distinctive, courts and their judges carry out a special function in American democracy, operating as a counterbalance to the other branches and thereby changing the political system.

To a degree, this function is rooted in the state and federal constitutions. But those constitutions left considerable leeway for government to evolve. The roles of the judicial branch in American democracy have developed through two centuries of practice, and they have changed a good deal over time. Today's courts are very different institutions from those envisioned by the framers of the Constitution.

This evolution will continue in the twenty-first century. As we consider the future of the courts, one important issue is how distinctive they will remain. In conjunction with other forces, the challenges posed by pressing national problems will create pressures for courts to align themselves more closely with the other branches and to become more like them. As a result, the roles of the judicial branch in American democracy may change.

This chapter considers the future of courts in the twenty-first century from a broad perspective but gives particular attention to their distinctiveness. The first section discusses the difficulties of predicting the future of the courts and prescribing what the courts should look like. The chapter then addresses three issues that relate to the courts' roles. The first concerns one dimension of court structure, the distinction between generalist and specialized courts. The second concerns the courts as a means of access to government. The third issue concerns the place of courts in politics, specifically control of judges by the public and the other branches of government.

The Hazards of Prediction and Prescription

The judicial branch is diverse. Its institutions range from the Supreme Court, which addresses a few dozen major issues in federal law each year, to municipal courts that process dozens of narrow cases each day. The subjects of court decisions are as different as civil rights, crime, and divorce. Because of this diversity, it is a daunting task even to characterize the courts and their work as they are today. People who offer predictions or prescriptions for the future face a task that is even more difficult, a difficulty suggested by some episodes in recent history.

In the first four decades of the twentieth century, most people viewed the Supreme Court as ideologically conservative.[1] In this view, the primary goal of the Court as a collective group was to protect business enterprises from government regulation through its interpretations of the Constitution. Some commentators went further, arguing that the Court had always been more sympathetic to the economic rights of affluent people and institutions than to the social and political rights of the mass of people. U.S. Attorney General Robert Jackson wrote in 1941, shortly before he joined the Court himself, that "never in its entire history can the Supreme Court be said to have for a single hour been representative of anything except the relatively conservative forces of its day."[2]

But by the time that Jackson wrote, the Court was already changing direction and ending its opposition to government regulation of business. Two decades later there was a more startling development. The Court for the first time devoted the largest part of its work to the civil liberties of individuals on issues such as discrimination and criminal procedure. Since then, the Court's support for those rights has fluctuated a good deal. On the whole, however, the Court has expanded individual rights substantially—on many issues, quite dramatically. One example is the pair of decisions in 2004 (*Hamdi v. Rumsfeld*, *Rasul v. Bush*) that required the federal government to provide some basic procedural rights to suspected terrorists. It is striking that a relatively conservative Supreme Court rejected the arguments of officials in the executive branch that the dangers of terrorism overrode the value of constitutional procedures.

This evolution in the Court's role underlines the difficulty of predicting the future of political institutions such as the courts. The Supreme Court's shift from concern with government regulation of business to concern with individual liberties was perhaps the most important development in the courts during the twentieth century, but it surprised nearly everyone. This failure of prediction reflected the complex forces that shape the Court's policies. It also reflected the tendency to assume that the future will be much like the past.

The difficulty of predicting the future applies to prescriptions for changes in government structures and procedures. Policy makers and others constantly propose changes in the courts, and some of those proposals are adopted. When put into practice, these court reforms often have unexpected effects. Reorganizations of court systems, efforts to eliminate plea bargaining, and changes in the rules for selection of judges produce surprising and unwanted results.

One prominent example is the legislation of 1984 that rewrote the rules for sentencing of criminal defendants in federal court. There had been widespread concern about statutes that left enormous discretion to judges and thus opened the way for arbitrary and discriminatory sentencing. Many judges shared that concern. In response, Congress established a sentencing commission to narrow the range of sentences that judges could impose. But it took only a few years before there was considerable dissatisfaction with the new system. One source of this dissatisfaction was a realization that the discretion the new system took from judges did not disappear but moved to prosecutors.

The surprising results of court reforms have multiple sources. Sometimes the people who advocated changes in the courts failed to understand what they should have known about the likely consequences of their proposals. Often their vision was too limited, in that they reacted to a specific problem with a sense of urgency and failed to think about how their solution would work in the long term. But sometimes the task of anticipating the effects of reforms was simply too difficult.

Another episode—actually, two related episodes—illustrates a different kind of problem in making prescriptions for the courts. As the numbers of cases in the lower federal courts increase, from time to time Congress increases the numbers of judges. As a result, the courts of appeals in some judicial circuits become quite large, and because of their size they may function less effectively. In the past half century, Congress has faced the question of whether two large circuits—the Fifth Circuit in the South and the Ninth Circuit in the West—should be broken into smaller circuits.

Few issues would seem as technical and nonpolitical as this one. Yet proposals to divide the two circuits produced heated ideological debates. Southern conservatives resented the Fifth Circuit's support for civil rights, and western conservatives disliked what they perceived as the liberalism of the Ninth

Circuit on issues such as environmental protection. Both groups anticipated that division would produce more conservative courts in one of the new circuits, and that anticipation spurred their support for division. In response, liberals lined up in opposition. The two sides couched their arguments in terms of judicial efficiency, but they chose sides chiefly on the basis of their ideological views.

This ideological split has been reflected in congressional action on circuit-division proposals. The Fifth Circuit was divided in 1980 only because the old disagreements over civil rights issues had weakened, so that liberals no longer had reason to oppose division. Despite its enormous size—twenty-eight judgeships—the Ninth Circuit remained intact in mid-2005 It may be divided in the near future, but only if conservatives in Congress have sufficient numbers and commitment to defeat liberal supporters of the current structure.

As these episodes make clear, people's prescriptions on any issue concerning the courts depend heavily on their views about public policy. Even the most neutral-sounding proposal for court structures or procedures is likely to affect judicial policies and thus favor some segments of society over others. Aware of this reality, people take sides largely on the basis of who they think would gain and lose if a proposal is adopted.

In watching debates about the courts, then, we need to maintain a degree of skepticism. When people argue for a particular position on grounds that seem neutral, they are often acting on their guesses about what sets of people or types of policy would benefit if their position is adopted. For example, members of Congress sometimes argue fervently for the value of bolstering federalism by keeping certain cases in the state courts or for the value of enhancing uniformity by moving those cases to the federal courts. But most of these members care less about federalism or uniformity than about how the federal and state courts might decide the cases in question. This is true of the current proposals to require that certain class action lawsuits go to federal court. Behind the rhetoric of the two sides lies their shared perception that defendants in these lawsuits, typically businesses, would do better in federal court than in state court.

Thus, thinking about the future of the courts is a complicated matter. Predictions of where the courts are going suffer from inherent difficulties. Prescriptions for the courts are clouded both by problems in predicting the consequences of reforms and by biases that result from people's views about public policy. Keeping these complications in mind, this chapter will not offer confident predictions or prescriptions for the future.

Court Structure: The Drive to Specialize

Inevitably, government organizations change in their structure over time. The presidency has grown enormously, evolving from a tiny office to a massive organization. New types of administrative agencies have been invented. The current legislative bodies of most states look nothing like their predecessors a century ago.

The same is true of the courts. The most obvious trend is growth in the number and size of courts, a trend spurred by the increased volume of judicial business. Less evident, but perhaps more important, is a movement toward greater specialization of courts and judges.

Courts as Generalists

Agencies in the executive branch of government are highly diverse—as different as local police departments, state tax departments, and the federal Department of Labor.[3] But these administrative agencies share the characteristic of specialization. Because each agency deals with only a limited range of policy issues, an agency and its members gain greater expertise and efficiency than they would achieve otherwise. To enhance these benefits, agencies usually contain smaller and more specialized units, and most individual administrators handle only a narrow set of issues.

Administrative specialization brings other characteristics with it. One might be called an organizational mission. When Congress creates a new agency, the members who vote to establish the agency usually expect it to adopt a particular point of view—to represent the interests of farmers or business, to improve education or the environment, to protect civil rights or national security. These missions can wither over time, but they are permanent features of some agencies.

Specialization also links agencies more closely with the political interest groups in their fields. Administrators interact frequently with the groups that care most about their decisions, and an agency can develop an interdependent relationship with certain groups as a result. One example is the relationship between major farm groups and the federal Department of Agriculture.

Missions and clients aside, the people who work in an agency typically approach decisions from the perspective of the field in which they work. Many civilians who serve in the Department of Defense come from the military, and all of the department's personnel are immersed in the issues and problems of defense. This does not mean that they think alike, but they all tend to see defense issues in terms of the needs of the military.

In contrast, the federal district courts and courts of appeals are generalists. While federal courts can hear only certain kinds of cases, those cases still cover a broad range. In a single day of oral arguments, a court of appeals panel might deal with crime, civil rights, personal injuries, and Social Security.

As generalists, these courts lack the characteristics that specialization produces. They have no specific missions, and their judges do not interact constantly with lawyers who represent particular groups. Nor do those judges develop the points of view that result from constant work in one field. Judges may have strong attitudes about criminal law or tax law, but those attitudes are individual rather than institutional.

In these respects, federal courts differ not just from administrative agencies but from other policy makers as well. Like district judges, members of Congress address a very wide range of policy issues. But each member gives far more attention to some issues than to others. One reason is that Congress does most of its work in committees; another is that members concentrate on the issues that most interest them and their constituents. (Those interests are often reflected in their committee assignments.) To a considerable degree, then, legislators are also specialists. Presidents are generalists, but they work primarily with specialists in the bureaucracy and the Executive Office of the President. In the judiciary, more than the other branches, policy makers have a broad perspective rather than a narrow focus.

In some respects, the courts' lack of specialization is a disadvantage. Because they usually lack the expertise of specialists in a field, judges may not fully understand the issues in that field. Commentators sometimes criticize federal judges on the ground that their decisions do not reflect the realities of technology or police work, to take two examples. And judges who constantly shift their attention from one field to another cannot decide cases with the efficiency of an administrator who deals with one set of issues all the time.

These costs are offset by an important benefit, the broader perspective of generalists. Judges find it easier than administrators to comprehend competing positions on issues. Judges are also less likely to develop the parochial points of view that are endemic to administrative agencies and common among legislators.

For these reasons, courts counterbalance the specialization of other policy makers. To take an example, it makes a difference that the final arbiter of police procedure under the Constitution is a court that does not specialize in criminal justice. Lacking a mission of attacking crime, Supreme Court justices can weigh competing goals in a way that criminal justice agencies cannot. In this field, as in others, courts open up the policy making process by fighting against the tendency for government policy to become the province of specialists. In this way courts help to make government decisions more representative of the full range of values and interests in American society.

Specialization in the Courts

Not all judges are generalists. Within courts that hear a broad range of cases, a good deal of specialization occurs in practice. In state trial courts, specific courtrooms and judges often specialize in particular kinds of cases. Divisions devoted to juvenile crime, domestic relations, traffic offenses, or small claims are common. In large courts, the specialization can be quite narrow: within the

Illinois circuit court, some courtrooms in Chicago deal with only specific types of crimes. While judges typically rotate among divisions and courtrooms, at a particular time they have the same narrow focus as administrators.

Many other courts are specialized by law. At the federal level, Congress has established several courts that hear only specific types of cases. Among them are the Tax Court, the Court of Appeals for Veterans Claims, and the Court of International Trade. Many states have separate courts to deal with common issues such as probate and family matters. Across the states there can be found, among others, a Water Court, a Land Court, a Workers' Compensation Court, and an Environmental Court.

Whether judicial specialization is established by law or develops in practice, it reflects an effort to gain the perceived strengths of administrative agencies while retaining the form and name of courts. The efficiency and expertise that are ascribed to specialization can help courts keep up with their caseloads and perhaps improve the quality of decision making. These perceived advantages help to explain why specialized courts have become so common not only in the United States but in other nations as well.

However, specialization can produce the same effects in courts that it does in administrative agencies. A focus on a narrow set of cases and constant interaction with the lawyers who work in an area shape judges' perspectives. Further, decisions to create specialized courts often involve an effort to imbue a court with a mission or point of view. Some of the specialized federal courts were created in part to protect the interests of the federal government, though that goal was seldom proclaimed openly. The mission of juvenile courts was quite explicit: charges against juveniles were to be handled differently from those against adult defendants, with an emphasis on treatment of offenders instead of punishment. When separate environmental courts or environmental units within courts are created, the chief goal has been to secure more effective enforcement of laws relating to the environment. Thus the mission of these courts is quite similar to the original mission of federal and state environmental protection agencies.

Over the past century, there has been a gradual movement toward greater specialization in the judiciary. While many states went through a period of eliminating courts with narrow jurisdiction, that was an exception to the general trend. In terms of actual practice, the court systems of most states are more specialized than they were at the beginning of the twentieth century. If bankruptcy cases are left aside, the great majority of federal cases are still handled by generalist judges, but increasing numbers of fields are left in part or entirely to specialists. Meanwhile, there has been a burgeoning of tribunals in the executive branch that hear appeals from administrators' decisions on issues such as social security. If these tribunals had instead been made courts, the judicial branch would feature even greater specialization.

In both the state and federal systems, there is more specialization at the trial level than at the appellate level. Most trial courts with narrow jurisdiction are reviewed by appellate courts that fit the generalist model. But appellate judges exert only limited control over the courts below them, so specialized trial judges have considerable freedom to shape judicial policy in their fields of activity.

The trend toward court specialization has accelerated in the past decade. Perhaps the most important example is the set of institutions in the states that have been labeled "problem-solving courts." That term is somewhat ambiguous, but it generally refers to courts that deal with certain kinds of criminal cases in a nontraditional way. Rather than focusing on the determination of guilt or innocence, these courts seek to address the underlying problems that lead to criminal behavior. This shift is intended to serve the needs of defendants, victims, and the community. Common examples include domestic violence courts, drug courts, and mental health courts. Juvenile courts as originally conceived also fit this model.

Problem-solving courts have explicit missions. According to one account, "the mission of drug courts is to stop legal and clinical recidivism among nonviolent offenders with substance abuse problems." The same account describes the dominant approach in drug courts as "cooperative, nonadversarial." In line with that approach, the prosecutor, defense attorney, and other personnel "operate as a team when addressing individual case issues."[4] This is a long way from the traditional image of courts as neutral arbiters of cases argued by adversaries.

Departures from the classic image of courts are often controversial, in part because many people oppose endowing courts with missions. Over the years, Congress has rejected proposals for specialized federal courts far more often than it has adopted them, and undoubtedly the same is true of state and local governments. Still, the level of judicial specialization has grown. One reason is that, once established, courts that are specialized by law or practice tend to continue. As a result, there is a kind of ratcheting effect that moves court systems away from the generalist model.

Issues for the Twenty-First Century

The trend toward a more specialized judiciary has received little attention and even less debate. Some legal scholars have discussed judicial specialization as a general phenomenon, but legislators and court administrators focus on specific proposals as they arise. Thus specialization grows not through a grand design but through a series of little choices.

This growth is likely to continue. Indeed, it may accelerate. One reason is that technological change will increase the perception that generalist judges lack the expertise needed to deal with certain kinds of issues. Partly on that ground, patent cases were shifted from the federal courts of appeals to the specialized Court of Appeals for the Federal Circuit in 1982. In the future, policy makers and relevant interest groups may think it desirable to move other kinds of complex issues into specialized courts. A second reason is that, in a world of accelerating change and increasing interdependence, American government and society can be expected to face difficult challenges. The more serious the challenge, the greater will be the interest in enlisting courts as partners of the other branches.

Although they are not part of the judicial branch, the military commissions that President George W. Bush established in 2001 illustrate the impact of this interest. The terrorist attacks earlier that year led to enormous concern about the safety of the United States and its people. As one result, officials in the Bush administration decided that ordinary courts would be inadequate to handle prosecutions of non-U.S. citizens who are charged with terrorist activities. Based on this judgment, they created tribunals that would be devoted solely to prosecutions of accused terrorists and that would operate under rules and procedures quite different from those used in ordinary criminal cases.

It is impossible to predict the new challenges that will arise in this century. To take one example, we do not know the severity of any climate change that takes place. But American government certainly will face significant new strains. The executive and legislative branches are likely to respond by establishing new courts. Those courts will have missions to help solve specific problems rather than to bring a more independent perspective to the issues they decide. Meanwhile, policy makers will continue to create new specialized courts in response to more prosaic problems and demands.

Perhaps this trend is desirable. As discussed earlier, specialization can provide significant advantages. And perhaps some of the problems that government faces are so difficult that we cannot afford to have relatively neutral generalists shaping policy. For these reasons, enhanced court specialization may serve government and society well.

Yet when the courts become more specialized we lose some of the distinctive perspective of generalist judges. As a result, there is a shift in the balance between broad and narrow perspectives on public policy. This shift may be justified by the benefits that accompany it. But those benefits and the costs that may accompany them should be given greater scrutiny. Policy makers and citizens need to face directly a change in American government that has received only limited scrutiny, to consider what kind of court structure best serves the needs of a democratic system in the twenty-first century.

Courts and Access to Government

Whether or not courts have missions, they serve as forums for litigants with missions of their own. In the great majority of cases, those missions are narrow efforts to resolve individual problems or achieve individual gains. People go to court to end their marriages, to win compensation for injuries, to collect debts. In a small but important set of cases, people engage in "political" litigation aimed at changing government policy.

Going to court does not guarantee a favorable result, but it offers a chance to achieve that result. Only those who are able to use the courts can win the victories that courts bestow. For this reason, access to court is a fundamental issue.

In some important respects, Americans enjoy relatively open access to the courts. In sharp contrast with the traditional practice in Japan, states in the United States set standards for their bar examinations that allow most aspiring lawyers to pass and secure licenses to practice law. As a result, the supply of lawyers meets (and perhaps exceeds) the demand for their services. The widely used contingent fee system, in which people pay for a lawyer's services as a proportion of the money they win, reduces the financial barrier to litigation. Access is open in another sense as well: on the whole, judges in the United States are willing to consider arguments that government policies violate legal rules.

Relatively easy access to the courts is an important feature of American democracy. People with specific needs or grievances can use the judicial branch as a means to achieve their ends. For those who seek to shape government policy, the courts provide an additional avenue for their efforts. Thus litigation serves as a major form of political participation in this country. To a considerable degree, the United States has set an example for groups in other countries that use this route to influence government policy.[5]

Open access to the courts facilitates judicial involvement in policy issues. In turn, that involvement accentuates a basic characteristic of American democracy, the dispersion of power that allows people who lose in one government institution to seek redress in another. It also strengthens the Constitution as a constraint on government, because courts that are open to political litigation make it easier to enforce constitutional limits on government action. The protections of the First Amendment, to take one example, gain vigor from the ability of individuals and groups such as the American Civil Liberties Union to litigate against government policies that may infringe freedom of expression.

Use of the courts can benefit any sector of society, but it serves a special function for those who lack meaningful access to the other branches of government. Ordinary people usually have little capacity to influence legislatures or cabinet departments, but the courts are more open to relatively powerless individuals. And groups that have little conventional political power can use the courts to advance their agendas. From one perspective, this was the story of *Brown v. Board of Education* (1954): civil rights advocates who found Congress unsympathetic to their goals in the 1940s and 1950s were able to achieve success in the Supreme Court. In this way the courts fulfill a distinctive function in the relationship between people and government.

Not everyone agrees that easy access to the courts is a good thing. Indeed, most Americans believe there is too much litigation, exacting unacceptable costs from those who must defend themselves in court and from society as a whole. And many people think that the ability to challenge government policies in court detracts from a democratic political system by allowing judges—especially unelected federal judges—to interfere with the resolution of issues by the other branches.

These objections raise fundamental questions about the meaning of democracy. But in reality, participants in public debates on this issue take positions mostly on the basis of narrow interests rather than broad principles. Put simply, everyone wants maximum access to the courts for themselves and the groups they favor and minimum access for those whose goals and interests conflict with their own.

This reality is illustrated by the current conflicts over proposed changes in rules for personal injury cases, changes that go under the label "tort reform." Interest groups that represent manufacturers, insurance companies, and medical doctors are working to secure changes in the law that make it more difficult and less attractive to sue to recover money for personal injuries. For example, they seek to limit the punitive damages that injured parties can win to punish defendants for unreasonable conduct. Lawyers who represent personal injury claimants lead the opposition to these proposals, often with the support of labor unions and consumer groups. Each side argues for its position in terms of the general public interest, but both are motivated by the economic interests of the groups they represent.

Issues involving access to the courts are numerous. This section focuses on two issues that have special relevance to the role of courts in the democratic system. The first is well-known: the relationship between economic resources and effective access to the courts. The second is a less prominent development, the use of contracts to bar people from the courts.

The Economics of Access

What has been said so far about open access to the courts may seem to depart from reality, because people's economic resources certainly affect their capacity to use the courts. In themselves, the fees charged by courts bar some people and cases. More important is the impact of resources on success in litigation. Those who cannot afford lawyers at all are often at a considerable disadvantage, and recognition of this disadvantage keeps many people from using the courts. Further, the quantity and quality of legal services that people obtain reflect what they can spend. The former Enron executives who face criminal prosecution are not in a pleasant situation, but they have a much greater capacity to defend themselves than does the average criminal defendant. For the same reason, there is a very large difference between a small business and Microsoft in the ability to litigate. And because of the correlation between economic status and race in the United States, the economic realities of litigation affect different racial groups differently.

Of course, the courts are not the only place in which economic resources affect what people can accomplish. While people without substantial resources are at a considerable disadvantage in the courts, the disadvantage is not as great as it is elsewhere in government—or, for that matter, in some other sectors of life. Thus, despite inequalities in the ability to litigate, the courts provide an important mode of access to government for ordinary people.

If inequality is no greater in the courts than in other sectors of government and society, one might conclude that it is a reality we should accept rather than a problem to be addressed. Indeed, that is a widely shared view. Yet many other people express concern about this inequality. One reason is that its consequences are relatively easy to identify. Differences among segments of society in the ability to win favorable outcomes in Congress have considerable impact on public policy, but that impact is usually broad and diffuse. In contrast, the advantages of relatively affluent individuals and organizations in bringing and winning cases have very direct effects. Those effects can be troubling, especially when the inability to pay for good legal services dooms a person to prison.

The effects of economic inequality on the ability to use the courts would be eliminated if everyone were given the resources to operate at the level of Microsoft and the Enron executives. In practice, this option is out of the question. For one thing, the financial costs would be enormous. Further, eliminating monetary barriers to litigation would vastly increase the volume of cases, putting considerable strain on the courts. The incentive for people to deal with grievances and disputes in less contentious forums would be reduced. Finally, elimination of monetary barriers to the courts would threaten some interests. Governments and large companies, for instance, benefit from the limited capacities of individuals to bring lawsuits against them.

However, more limited steps have been taken to reduce economic barriers to effective use of the courts. These efforts are aimed chiefly at assisting low-income individuals, those who face the strongest barriers. When judges and other government officials undertake these efforts, one motivation is a concern with simple justice. Another is the hope that effective access to the courts will reduce social discontent and enhance the legitimacy of government.

The biggest steps have come on the criminal side of the law, where individuals are brought to the courts involuntarily and where the stakes for them are often quite large. Over the years, most states accepted the principle that low-income defendants should be supplied with lawyers, but they did not always put this principle into practice. Then, beginning with *Gideon v. Wainwright* in 1963, the Supreme Court reached a series of decisions requiring that indigent defendants in serious cases be given the right to a lawyer's assistance.

State and local governments have given mixed responses to those decisions. They now spend a great deal of money on defense of the indigent. Yet cash-strapped legislators are often reluctant to boost expenditures for criminal defendants, a group whose political power and popularity are decidedly limited. As a result, growth in the numbers of prosecutions has stretched thin the systems to provide lawyers for low-income defendants. In some states, the inadequacy of counsel for defendants in cases involving potential death penalties has become especially evident. This problem was symbolized by the well-publicized case of a Texas defendant who ultimately secured a reversal of his conviction and death sentence after his lawyer slept through large portions of his trial.[6]

Compared with criminal defense, government has been less willing to reduce financial barriers to civil litigation. The Supreme Court has never held that people who are indigent have a right to an attorney in civil cases, even when they are defending against lawsuits. The most important government initiative on the civil side of the law is the federal Legal Services Corporation, which funds local agencies that provide lawyers for indigent people. Legal Services grew out of President Lyndon Johnson's War on Poverty, and support for the program has eroded since then. As a result, its funding has fallen considerably when inflation is taken into account. Congress has also responded to complaints from businesses and governments, often sued by agencies that Legal Services supports, by restricting the kinds of cases that those agencies can handle.

There are also quasi-governmental and private programs to assist low-income people in civil cases. In every state the supreme court or legislature has established a system in which the interest on money that lawyers hold for clients is contributed to groups that provide legal services to the poor. Individual lawyers and law firms also donate time to the poor.

The economic barriers to effective use of the courts can be high even for individuals who are not poor. Few non-wealthy individuals could bring substantial cases to court without some kind of help. However, government has done little to assist middle-income people. Some private mechanisms do assist them along with those in worse economic straits. The most significant is the contingent fee, mentioned earlier. Lawyers in some fields such as personal injury law regularly take promising cases without fees in exchange for a share of any winnings in or out of court. In political litigation aimed at changing government policy, supportive interest groups enable individuals to get to court and make their cases effectively.

Increasingly, individuals represent themselves in court, acting "pro se," rather than using a lawyer. Some are motivated by distrust of lawyers, but the costs of lawyers' services are the primary consideration. In 2003, 44 percent of the litigants who brought cases to the federal courts of appeals were without lawyers, compared with 34 percent in 1993. A survey in Phoenix found that in 88 percent of divorce cases, one or both spouses had no lawyer.[7] As pro se litigants have become more common, judges and others do considerable thinking about how best to serve them. It is not yet clear how disadvantageous it is, on average, to represent oneself. On the whole, however, people clearly are worse off without lawyers. Anecdotes about pro se litigants who represented themselves well are striking, but they represent exceptions to the rule.

In the twenty-first century policy makers will continue to wrestle with the relationship between economic status and access to the courts. In large part, the outcomes will depend on attitudes toward poverty and inequality. The biggest steps to improve access for the poor came in the 1960s, when citizens and government officials were most concerned with poverty. No matter how people think about poverty, the monetary costs of reducing inequality will work against initiatives to improve access for low-income and middle-income people. So will the influence of those whose interests and values favor maintaining limits on access.

A good case can be made that government should do more to reduce inequalities in the courts, at least for criminal and civil defendants. When people find themselves in court involuntarily and the stakes are substantial, there would seem to be a fundamental problem if they cannot defend themselves adequately. Government initiates criminal cases and carries them forward. Government also provides the courts as a service to civil litigants. Those roles give government some responsibility for what happens to people who are asked to defend themselves in court. That responsibility is not fully met if an effective defense is impossible.

Also relevant is the role of the courts as a distinctive means of access to government for ordinary people. Trends in the ability to go to court are uncertain, but the costs of lawyers' services are probably outpacing people's ability to afford them. People can disagree about whether the courts serve a valuable function if they provide a special means of access. But if that function *is* desirable, then resources to maintain it may well be justified even in times of relative scarcity.

Cutting Off Access by Contract

There is a popular and enduring image of Americans as eager to litigate, seizing any opportunities to take their grievances to court. For the most part, that image is false. Like people in other countries, Americans simply live with their grievances or take some action other than a lawsuit far more often than they go to court. As discussed earlier, monetary costs sometimes rule out litigation. But even those who can afford to go to court would prefer to avoid its costs. And there are other powerful deterrents, from the time and effort that litigation entails to the element of interpersonal conflict involved in court contests.

Those who want to act on their grievances can choose from a variety of alternatives to litigation. The most common is simple negotiation between the people involved in a dispute. Some other alternatives are more formal and more public, involving attorneys, neutral parties, or both. In mediation, a mediator works with the two sides to help them settle their dispute. More formal is arbitration, in which an arbitrator hears a dispute and imposes a binding decision on the disputants. Similar though arbitration is to litigation, it can still be preferable to the participants when it offers relative speed in resolving disputes, reduced monetary costs, and greater privacy.

Over the past two decades there has been a movement aimed at increasing the use of alternatives to litigation, under the title of "alternative dispute resolution" or ADR.[8] Participants in this movement promote mediation and arbitration, and they have enjoyed considerable success in this effort. For example, it has always been common for judges to encourage parties to settle their disputes outside of court, but courts increasingly require (sometimes under legislative mandates) that parties undertake mediation or arbitration before going to trial. Companies that provide ADR services, such as the American Arbitration Association and Judicial Arbitration and Mediation Services (JAMS), are prospering.

The popularity of ADR is reflected in the growth of prior agreements that certain kinds of disputes will go to arbitration or another private forum, often with the parties giving up their right to litigate if they are unhappy with the outcome. These agreements most often involve businesses in their relations with other firms, employees, or consumers. On the whole, this development is considered a good thing. It facilitates the resolution of disputes, and it channels potential cases away from overburdened judges and courts.

But these agreements may have negative consequences as well. It is one thing if parties with essentially equal power, such as competing businesses in an industry, agree to take future disputes to arbitration. It is another if one party demands an agreement to arbitrate from someone who has little choice but to accept the terms of that agreement. In this second situation, those who are required to accept arbitration yield their access to court for an alternative that may not serve them well.

This possibility is not speculative. It is now common for businesses to require that prospective employees or consumers give up their right to litigate any grievances they have against the business. Instead, they must take those grievances to an arbitration system that the business specifies under terms that it also specifies. Thus, to take one example, the employment application form for a job at Circuit City Stores in 1995 included a provision under which the applicant agreed "that I will settle any and all previously unasserted claims, disputes or controversies arising out of or relating to my application or candidacy for employment, employment and/or cessation of employment with Circuit City, exclusively by final and binding arbitration before a neutral Arbitrator."[9]

An agreement to arbitrate may be buried in the fine print of broader contracts. Most credit-card customers, for instance, are unaware that they have agreed not to file a lawsuit against the bank that supplies the card. Even when individuals see this provision and understand it, they usually accept it. A job applicant is unlikely to forgo a needed job because of an arbitration requirement.

Someone who wants a credit card may find it difficult to locate a bank that allows its customers to take disputes to court.

There have been complaints that mandatory arbitration systems are biased in favor of the businesses that impose them, chiefly because those businesses specify the rules for arbitration. For instance, arbitration systems are sometimes run by the businesses themselves or by their industries, and independent arbitrators frequently are chosen by the businesses. It is unclear how common and how severe such bias is, but the perception of bias is one concern that has led some consumers and employees to challenge mandatory arbitration in court.

Court decisions on these challenges are mixed, but judges generally uphold clauses that require people to use arbitration. Most important, the Supreme Court has given a broad interpretation to the 1925 federal statute that favors the use of arbitration. As a result, many people are precluded from going to court with claims involving their rights under federal law, even on matters such as racial discrimination. For instance, in 2001 the Supreme Court upheld the Circuit City clause quoted earlier when an employee tried to bring a discrimination case to court.

Unless the Court changes its position or Congress intervenes with new legislation, the use of arbitration agreements to keep workers and consumers out of court can be expected to grow in the twenty-first century. Business leaders recognize the advantages they gain by protecting themselves from lawsuits and, sometimes, by imposing rules that favor their positions. The cumulative result will be a significant change in the legal system.

That change will have its most direct impact on outcomes for specific individuals with grievances against businesses, but there will be broader effects as well. The courts will become less open to ordinary individuals who seek access to government. And the channeling of certain kinds of cases away from the courts will reduce judges' capacity to shape corporate behavior with legal rulings. In effect, some areas of law will be increasingly privatized, leaving government with a smaller role in determining how society deals with issues such as discrimination and consumer rights.

Scholars have given some attention to these consequences, but the use of contracts to limit litigation has not yet become a major public issue. During this century there is likely to be a broader recognition that the legal system has changed through arbitration requirements. At that point judges and other policy makers will have to confront more directly the conflict between the principle that voluntary agreements are enforceable and the principle that people who think their legal rights have been violated should be able to seek redress in the courts.

Courts in Politics: Controlling Judges

In every democracy, the relationship between the courts and the rest of the political system raises difficult issues. Courts carry out important functions that require a degree of autonomy, especially their role in holding the other branches of government to legal rules. But if courts operate without any controls, they may undermine democracy by wresting power to shape policy from the other branches and the public. Thus it is difficult to determine the appropriate balance between autonomy and control.

Debates about this balance are a permanent feature of American politics. Throughout our history, judges have shaped public policy openly and often dramatically. In response, some people in government and politics have asserted that the courts were overstepping their proper roles and should be reined in. Others have defended judges and courts, arguing that their work strengthens the constitutional system and thus that they should be left free to follow their own course.

In the early twenty-first century, these debates are even louder than usual. Legislators and others attack what they see as illegitimate policy making by judges, and they have sought to increase controls over the courts. In response, defenders of the courts decry what they see as threats to judicial independence and try to rally support for maintaining that independence. The outcomes of these debates help to determine the place of courts in the political system.

How Much Control Is Desirable?

The other branches of government and the public have an impressive array of mechanisms to influence what courts do. They largely control court jurisdiction, and they determine judges' salaries and budgets.[10] Chief executives and legislators hold considerable power over the selection and retention of judges, and the general public plays a part in selection and retention that has few if any parallels in the world. If these powers were employed to their fullest, the courts would have little autonomy. But what level of control best serves the needs of our democratic system?

This is a classic example of an issue on which people choose sides according to their evaluations of court policies. An earlier section of this chapter described the Supreme Court's shift from an emphasis on limiting government power over the economy to an emphasis on protecting individual civil liberties. In both eras, people who disapproved of the Court's policies sought to impose greater controls on the Court, while those who approved sought to protect the Court's autonomy.

Reflecting that pattern, today's debate over court autonomy and control follows clear ideological lines. The policies of the Supreme Court and of other federal and state courts are a complex mix of liberal and conservative themes. But it is decisions defining civil liberties broadly—on abortion, links between government and religion, and other issues—that arouse the strongest passions. As a result, conservatives are the primary critics of the courts and liberals their primary defenders.

Leaving aside evaluations of court policies, there are strong arguments in favor of both greater and lesser degrees of political control over the courts. We can begin with the arguments for limited control. The courts must adjudicate cases that have substantial stakes for the litigants, stakes that can run as high as life and death. If judges are subject to political pressure to decide in one way or another, their capacity to reach the best judgment in a case could be impaired.

Further, judges are called upon to determine whether legislative statutes and executive-branch policies are unconstitutional, a role that most people see as fundamental to the political system. Because of this role, judges are guardians of constitutional values such as freedom of speech. Limiting their independence reduces their capacity to support values that are important but that enjoy little support in the other branches or among the general public at a given time.

The arguments for greater control begin with the premise that legislators and chief executives should hold most of the power to make government policy, chiefly because they have a mandate from the electorate. Federal judges certainly lack that mandate, and their life terms reduce their accountability as individuals. Thus it seems proper that the other branches rein in the courts when they disapprove of their policies.

This is especially true if judges frequently engage in judicial activism. Activism is difficult to define, and the term is used rather loosely to attack judges and decisions. According to Supreme Court justice Stephen Breyer, "by judicial activism, what you mean, in part, is a judge who doesn't decide the way I'd like it decided."[11] However, we can use the term to refer to major court-made changes in public policy, especially when judges overrule policies established by the other branches. It can be problematic for a democracy if judges regularly act as activists in this sense, substituting their own conceptions of good public policy for those enacted by legislators.

Thus, the arguments on both sides are compelling. If commentators and policy makers could overcome their ideological biases, they would find it difficult to determine the appropriate balance between autonomy and control for the courts. One implication is that no single degree of control is most consistent with democratic principles. Rather, well-functioning democracies differ considerably in the balance between control and autonomy for their courts.

Autonomy and control could be so far out of balance that the position of the courts is inconsistent with our own form of democratic government. It is not easy to determine when that line has been crossed. However, control seems too great when judges are threatened with severe consequences for ruling one way rather than another. It seems too limited when the courts monopolize policy making on important issues, with the public and the other branches essentially shut out.

Between those two extremes, what we see as the most desirable balance between autonomy and control depends on our judgments about a number of issues, such as the strengths and weaknesses of courts as policy makers in comparison with the other branches. But perhaps the key question is the value of having courts play a distinctive role as protectors of constitutional values, especially limits on government action. The greater the courts' autonomy, all else being equal, the more they will use constitutional provisions to strike down government policies and to deter the other branches of government from stepping outside constitutional limits.

As our history demonstrates, this role is not inherently liberal or conservative. Depending on the issue and on judges' views, either side of the ideological divide may benefit from judicial power to override government policies. Difficult as it is, we need to consider the benefits and drawbacks of autonomous courts independent of which values and interests the courts support in any specific era.

Courts and Their Political Environment Today

The relationships between courts and other political institutions have varied considerably across American history. The state of those relationships in the future will depend on conditions that are difficult to predict. However, history provides some sense of what we can expect as the twenty-first century continues.

In the current era, as noted earlier, there is considerable disagreement about what the balance between autonomy and control looks like. According to some commentators, primarily conservatives, the courts enjoy a high level of autonomy that they have used to achieve considerable power over national policy. But others, primarily liberals, argue that courts and judges are under extraordinary pressure from their political environment, pressure that greatly limits their autonomy.

Those who see the courts as powerful point to their impact on major issues. There is no doubt that courts do make a great deal of difference on some policy issues. Court orders that require desegregation of school districts and reform of prison systems are the classic examples. *Roe v. Wade* (1973) eliminated state prohibitions of abortion, and a series of Supreme Court decisions prohibited religious observances that were common in public schools. Less dramatically, judges shape policy on labor-management relations—to take one of many examples—through their interpretations of statutes.

Yet the structure of government makes it very difficult for any single branch to monopolize policy making, and the courts are no exception. Court rulings on issues such as labor law are simply one element of a process in which the three branches participate, each contributing to the development of law and policy. More often than not, the courts are junior partners in this process, because the basic outlines of policy are set by the other branches and the executive branch actually puts policy into effect.

Even when the courts take seemingly decisive actions, their impact depends heavily on the responses of other policy makers. Congress and state legislatures have limited the impact of *Roe v. Wade* through procedural rules and denials of funding for abortion. In response to the Supreme Court's decisions on school religious observances, school districts often interpret the decisions narrowly or simply defy them. The Court's rulings on school desegregation and voting rights in the South had little impact until Congress and the president stepped in to secure their enforcement. As Douglas Reed shows in his chapter of this book, the effects of court rulings that struck down state systems for funding of education have varied widely across the states, and their impact depends largely on the willingness of legislators to make the changes that courts mandate.

These limits on the power of courts are inherent to our system of government, and they will remain in force in this century. No matter how much autonomy judges enjoy, they will not dominate the making of public policy.

Those who believe that the courts' autonomy is threatened point to several events and trends. Unhappiness with decisions of the New Hampshire Supreme Court helped bring about the impeachment (though not conviction) of its chief justice in 2000. In 1996 President Bill Clinton and congressional Republicans denounced a federal district judge for an opinion in which he criticized the police in New York City, and some members of Congress threatened him with impeachment. Some state judges have been defeated for re-election because of individual decisions or lines of decisions, and officials in the other branches sometimes help to lead the campaigns against judges. A 2003 federal statute and a subsequent directive by Attorney General John Ashcroft were designed to put pressure on federal judges who issued criminal sentences that were more lenient than the range indicated by the federal guidelines at that time. More broadly, criticism and threats of negative action against judges and courts have become more common, and a series of developments led to unusually intense criticism of the federal courts by members of Congress in 2005.

Judges are under the greatest pressure in criminal justice, the field in which the courts' positions contrast most sharply with those of the other branches. Partly because of their role as interpreters of constitutional rights, the policies adopted by judges in the aggregate are more favorable to defendants' rights than those made by legislators, governors, and presidents—though less favorable than is sometimes perceived. Because crime is a serious concern for many Americans, the judges' perceived position is not very popular, and they are criticized a good deal by people who think they are unduly favorable to defendants.

On the whole, however, the other branches and the public use their powers over the courts far less than they might. The number of state judges who are denied new terms because of their votes and opinions in cases is fairly low. Judges have become more vulnerable to challenges by those who dislike their actions on the bench, but the overwhelming majority retain their positions or lose them for reasons unrelated to their decisions.

At the federal level, the mechanism of control that Congress considers most often is limiting court jurisdiction, a step that requires only enactment of a new statute. Over the past half century there has been a long list of proposals to block the Supreme Court or all federal courts from deciding cases on issues such as abortion, school desegregation, and legislative districting. Only a few of these proposals have passed one house of Congress, and so far none have been enacted into law. Even on decisions that aroused broad and deep opposition, such as the Supreme Court's rulings on school prayer, Congress has not acted.

The relatively limited use of mechanisms for control of the courts seems to have several sources. The absence of statutes barring the federal courts from hearing cases in controversial areas provides a good example. Some members of Congress see this kind of statute as illegitimate. They may also be reluctant to make serious incursions on the powers of another branch of government. Finally, the difficulty of enacting controversial legislation gives leverage to congressional opponents of anti-court proposals even when they are outnumbered.

Even occasional use of mechanisms to control courts and the threat they will be employed more often can influence judges. In particular, state judges who watch other judges lose campaigns for re-election may try to avoid decisions that electoral opponents could use against them. Indeed, it appears that some state supreme court justices avoid votes to overturn death sentences in order to protect themselves from electoral defeats. The federal judge in New York City who was denounced by President Clinton and congressional Republicans in 1996 apologized and reversed his decision.

At the same time, much of what judges do suggests that they feel considerable freedom to make what they see as the most appropriate decisions. This is especially true of federal judges, protected by their life terms. The Supreme Court's decisions striking down laws against flag burning and the 2002 decision of a court of appeals against inclusion of "under God" in public school recitations of the Pledge of Allegiance—both very unpopular in the other branches and among the general public—symbolize the considerable independence of federal judges.[12] These decisions also symbolize the courts' distinctive role as protectors of constitutional values. It is difficult to imagine that either Congress or the president would adopt such policies.

Ultimately, it is very difficult to ascertain how much impact the political environment has on judges' decisions. It does seem clear, however, that judges have greater autonomy on some issues than on others. Even if pressures to take pro-prosecution positions in criminal justice have considerable impact, such pressures may be largely absent in other areas of legal policy. It is also true that different judges feel and respond to pressures in different ways; in that sense, even judges on the same court may differ in their independence.

Looking Ahead

The relationship between the courts and their political environment will continue to evolve as this century proceeds. One key question is whether increasing pressures on government to address national and international problems will lead to greater controls on the courts. Will other policy makers and the public conclude that relatively autonomous courts are a luxury we cannot afford?

The answer will depend in part on the kinds of challenges and crises that government faces. The more severe the threat, the stronger will be the feeling that the courts should enlist in efforts to deal with that threat. The Supreme Court received more praise than criticism for its 2004 rulings that the executive branch had unduly limited the rights of suspected terrorists. But if fears of terrorism grow even stronger, rulings of that sort will be considerably less welcome.

If a sense of urgency arises on this or other issues, most judges could be expected to enlist voluntarily in efforts to deal with national problems, even in the absence of pressures and controls from the other branches. Inevitably, judges tend to share any perception of crisis that permeates society as a whole. Far more often than not, the Supreme Court has accepted limitations on personal freedom that the other branches of government imposed during major wars and the cold war with the Soviet Union. Perhaps the most extreme example is the decision in *Korematsu v. United States* (1944) that effectively upheld the mass detention of Japanese-American citizens during World War II. To some extent, such decisions probably reflected the justices' fears of negative reactions if they ruled against the government. But the justices have ratified government actions primarily because they perceived the same threats to national security that other Americans did. Any direct pressures on the Court to fall into line were largely redundant.

The same can be expected in future periods when the nation seems to be in peril. If this century is like the last one, after such a period the courts will return to a more independent role in overseeing government as a sense of national crisis dies down. But if conditions in the country or the world create a long-lasting perception of crisis, judges' reactions will be more difficult to predict. Nor is it clear that policy makers in the other branches will accept autonomous courts that they see as undercutting the government's efforts to deal with serious threats.

There remains the question whether it would benefit the nation for courts to maintain their role as the primary protectors of constitutional values under those conditions. Some people may conclude that the United States cannot afford a judiciary that is free to undercut or negate the policies established by the other branches when important national interests are at stake. Indeed, that has been the view of the George W. Bush administration about judicial oversight of efforts to deal with terrorism. The president and others have argued that in light of the threat to national security, court-imposed constraints on the actions of officials in the executive branch could do severe damage.

Yet if government becomes increasingly powerful in order to deal with serious national challenges, the value of autonomous courts may actually grow.

Important as it is that government be able to act effectively, concentration of power in the executive branch might threaten the values of limited and divided power that are reflected in the Constitution. From this perspective, courts that can act contrary to the other branches are not just affordable but a key to the maintenance of our democratic system. Thus it is not easy to determine what role the courts should play when the country faces difficult circumstances.

Conclusions

Among people who care about the courts, one constant theme is reform. We can be confident that interest in identifying problems in the courts and devising solutions will continue throughout this century. This is entirely appropriate, because there is no reason to be complacent about the current state of the courts. But one lesson of this chapter is the need for humility about reforming the courts. It can be difficult to predict the consequences of a proposed reform and even more difficult to assess whether it is desirable.

The participants in debates about changes in the courts typically have narrow vision. Self-interest motivates some participants, such as those who perceive that they will benefit by opening or closing access to the courts for specific kinds of cases. Others assess the courts through ideological filters, reacting to proposals for change in terms of their predicted effects on the substance of public policy. These biases distort judgments about whether proposals are desirable, and self-conscious efforts to transcend these biases can improve the quality of decisions about the courts.

We should be self-conscious in another respect as well. Major changes in the courts often result from the cumulation of little decisions to deal with specific problems. The judicial system has become more specialized because specific forms of specialization have appealed to decision makers for specific reasons. Similarly, efforts by individual businesses to establish arbitration of grievances by consumers and employees, efforts intended to serve specific goals of those businesses, have the effect of limiting the courts' role in shaping some kinds of policies. There is a need to identify how these cumulations of little decisions may be transforming the courts and to consider whether those transformations are desirable.

This chapter has emphasized that the courts are distinctive institutions in important respects and that their distinctive qualities shape the functioning of the political system. Many of the changes that people propose for the courts have implications for that distinctiveness. In assessing these proposals, in thinking about their potential benefits and costs, we should consider how their adoption might affect the place of the judicial branch in the political system. By doing so, whatever our conclusions may be, we can make it more likely that courts play the roles we want for them in American democracy.

Notes

*I appreciate the extensive and very helpful suggestions from the editors and from the members of the Commission on the Judiciary, especially Paul Carrington, Lynn Mather, Robert Nelson, and Marie Provine.

1. The terms "liberal" and "conservative" have multiple meanings, so definitions should be made explicit. On issues of civil liberties, liberals give more weight to liberty and equality in conflicts with other values than do conservatives. On economic issues, conservatives are more sympathetic to the business community in conflicts with labor and consumers than are liberals.
2. Robert H. Jackson, *The Struggle for Judicial Supremacy: A Study of a Crisis in American Power Politics* (New York: Alfred A. Knopf, 1941), 187.
3. This discussion of courts as generalists is based in part on Shapiro, *The Supreme Court and Administrative Agencies*, chap. 1.
4. Pamela M. Casey and David B. Rottman, "Problem-Solving Courts: Models and Trends," *Justice System Journal* 26 (2005), 44.
5. This development is discussed in Epp, *The Rights Revolution.*
6. The case, *Burdine v. Johnson*, was decided by a federal court of appeals in 2001.
7. The federal court data are from Table 1-2 of "Judicial Facts and Figures," a compilation of data by the Administrative Office of the United States Courts. Available at www.uscourts.gov/judicialfactsfigures/contents.html. The percentage for Phoenix is cited in Elizabeth Amon, "Sue It Yourself," *National Law Review*, 8 July 2002, A10.
8. This discussion of alternative dispute resolution is based in part on Lauren B. Edelman and Mark C. Suchman, "When the 'Haves' Hold Court: Speculations on the Organizational Internalization of Law," in Kritzer and Silbey, *In Litigation,* 290–341.
9. This provision was quoted by the Supreme Court in *Circuit City Stores v. Adams*, 532 U.S. 105 (2001), at 109–110.
10. Under the Constitution, however, the salaries of federal judges cannot be reduced.
11. Janine DeFao, "Judicial Activism on the Docket at Stanford Event," *San Francisco Chronicle*, 24 October 2004.
12. The Supreme Court overturned the court of appeals decision on procedural grounds in *Elk Grove v. Newdow* (2004).

Bibliography

Barrow, Deborah J., and Thomas G. Walker. *A Court Divided: The Fifth Circuit Court of Appeals and the Politics of Judicial Reform.* New Haven, Conn.: Yale University Press, 1988. An excellent illustration of how attitudes toward court policies affect decisions about court structure.

Burbank, Stephen B., and Barry Friedman, eds. *Judicial Independence at the Crossroads: An Interdisciplinary Approach.* Thousand Oaks, Calif.: Sage Publications, 2002. Surveys a range of issues concerning judicial autonomy and external control of courts.

Canon, Bradley C., and Charles A. Johnson. *Judicial Policies: Implementation and Impact.* 2nd ed. Washington, D.C.: CQ Press, 1999. A survey of evidence on what happens to court decisions after they are issued, including the responses of the other branches.

Epp, Charles R. *The Rights Revolution: Lawyers, Activists, and Supreme Courts in Comparative Perspective.* Chicago: University of Chicago Press, 1998. Examines how the courts have provided a means of access for groups seeking the expansion of rights in the United States and other nations.

Heinz, John P., Robert L. Nelson, Rebecca L. Sandefur, and Edward O. Laumann. *Urban Lawyers: The New Social Structure of the Bar.* Chicago: University of Chicago Press, 2005. In a broad analysis of Chicago lawyers, probes differences between the segment of the legal profession that serves businesses and other organizations and the segment that serves ordinary individuals.

Kritzer, Herbert M., and Susan B. Silbey, eds. *In Litigation: Do the Haves Still Come Out Ahead?* Stanford, Calif.: Stanford University Press, 2003. A collection of essays analyzing the relationship between the socioeconomic status of litigants and their success in court.

Nolan, James L., Jr. *Reinventing Justice: The American Drug Court Movement.* Princeton, N.J.: Princeton University Press, 2001. A close examination of the development of one type of problem-solving court.

Rhode, Deborah L. *Access to Justice.* New York: Oxford University Press, 2004. An overview of issues of access to courts, with emphasis on the impact of economic status on access.

Rosenberg, Gerald N. *The Hollow Hope: Can Courts Bring About Social Change?* Chicago: University of Chicago Press, 1991. Presents an argument that courts have limited power to change society even when they actively make policy on major issues.

Ross, William G. *A Muted Fury: Populists, Progressives, and Labor Unions Confront the Courts, 1890–1937.* Princeton, N.J.: Princeton University Press, 1994. Examines efforts at political control of the courts during an era when these efforts came chiefly from political liberals.

Russell, Peter H., and David O'Brien, eds. *Judicial Independence in the Age of Democracy: Critical Perspectives from Around the World.* Charlottesville: University Press of Virginia, 2001. Essays provide an international perspective on the roles and status of courts.

Shapiro, Martin. *The Supreme Court and Administrative Agencies.* New York: The Free Press, 1968. Includes a perceptive discussion of courts as institutions and the impact of specialization.

Unah, Isaac. *The Courts of International Trade: Judicial Specialization, Expertise, and Bureaucratic Policy-Making.* Ann Arbor: University of Michigan Press, 1998. Analyzes the behavior of two specialized federal courts.

Court Cases

Brown v. Board of Education, 347 U.S. 483 (1954).

Burdine v. Johnson, 262 F.3d 336 (5th Cir. 2001).

Circuit City Stores v. Adams, 532 U.S. 105 (2001).

Elk Grove Unified School District v. Newdow, 542 U.S. 1 (2004).
Gideon v. Wainwright, 372 U.S. 335 (1963).
Hamdi v. Rumsfeld, 124 S. Ct. 2633 (2004).
Korematsu v. United States, 323 U.S. 214 (1944).
Rasul v. Bush, 124 S. Ct. 2686 (2004).
Roe v. Wade, 410 U.S. 113 (1973).

INDEX